SHEVIOCK

History
of a
Cornish Coastal Manor
and Parish

Market Cross in Crafthole, Sheviock parish

SHEVIOCK

History of a Cornish Coastal Manor and Parish

Neville Cusworth

Phillimore

Rag pobel Siviek hag Kernow, de, hedhyw hag avorow

For the people of Sheviock and Cornwall, yesterday, today and tomorrow

2009

Published by
PHILLIMORE & CO. LTD
Chichester, West Sussex, England
www.phillimore.co.uk
www.thehistorypress.co.uk

ISBN 978-1-86077-608-3

Printed and Bound by Thomson Litho, East Kilbride

Contents

List of Illustrations

List of Subscribers and Donees

Corinne Abrahams
Ellen Adams and family
Jilly Albenque
Tim and Jane Allen
Prebendary Brian A. Anderson
Bill and Eileen Atkinson
Osman Azis
John Bacon
Sir John Baker, QC
Julia and Glyn Barker
Canon Bryan P. Barnes
Lawrence and Louise Barnes
William Barnes
Margaret Bartlett (née Pengelly)
Mrs M. Bass-Twitchell
Darrell S. Bean
His Hon. Judge Richard Behar
  and Mrs Iwona Behar
Robin and Maddy Behar
Charles Royden Benett
Demelza Grylls Benett
Henry Grylls Benett
Juliet Grylls Benett
  (née Cusworth)
Keith Benson
Tom and Mary Bersey
Margaret Bickford-Smith, QC
  and Stephen Bickford-Smith
Malcolm Biles
Tony Bowditch
Jan Bootland
Iris June Borthwick
  (née Westlake)
Stephen R.R. Bourne
Viscount and Viscountess Boyd
Dr Hugh Bradby
Clive Bradley, CBE
Richard Brewster
Paula Brooks
Fiona Carew Frost Brown
Sue Brown
Wella Brown
Charles and Primrose
  Burnett-Hitchcock
Jean and Laurie Burrell
Robert Bushrod
Mr and Mrs G. Cadwallader
The Cahill family
John Charles Cameron
Geoff and Judy Capps
Sir Richard and Lady Mary
  Carew Pole
Jan Carpenter
James and Anna Carter
Mrs Christine Champion
  (née White)
Anne Chapman
Richard and Sue Charkin
Peter Cheesman
Miss Judith Cocks
Audrey Cole
Gp Capt. R.J. Colver, OBE
Harry and Judy Cridland
Maj.-Gen. (retd) J.C. Crook
Niels and Clare Cross
Ian S. Curtis
Georgia Elise Platts Cusworth
Gregory John Cusworth
Nicholas Neville Grylls
  Cusworth, QC
Rachel Elizabeth Cusworth
Dr Vivien Susan Cusworth
  (née Grylls)
Michèle and Terry Damer
R.S. Damerell
Professor David Daniell
Dartington Hall Trust
Peter and Barbara Davies
Jenepher and Anthony Davis
John Davis
Arthur T. Dawe
James Dawnay
Brigadier Richard W. Dawnay
Ellan Odiorne Derow
Lucy Dickens
Lady Downe
Mrs Hazel Dron
Rosalie and David Dunn
Trystan D.G. Dunn
Sue Dyer
Alison Earle
Colin and Christine Edwards
Dr Anthony and
  Marie-Claude Eisinger
Mr Kay Ellis
Sir Jeremy Elwes
Emmanuel College, Cambridge
Peter R. England
Joy Etherington
Andrea and Warren Evans
David and Susan Evans
Michael A. Evans
Exeter College, Oxford
Stanley Fishwick
John and Yvonne Fisk

Mark Flack
Mrs Sheila Flashman
Derek Fletcher
Anthony and Elizabeth Fortescue
Nicholas Foster
Alison Fox (née Kentisbeer)
Cynthia Gaskell Brown
Henry (Harry) A. Gawan
Dr Ken George
Sir Alexander Graham, GBE
Gordon Graham, MC and
Betty Graham
The Greenwood family
Mabel Grills
Marion and Ray Grinsted
John Richard Glynn Grylls
Honor M. Grylls
Richard G. Grylls
Sally Glynn Grylls
Victoria Candice Grylls
Ken and Gilly Gurr
T.N. Hall
Lorraine Hambly
Peter and Mary Hamilton
F.J. Hancock
Ian Harbottle
Martyn Hardy
Revd and Mrs G. Harper
Michael J. Harris
Peter Harrison
Fiona Harvey
Colin Wills Harvey
Trevor Wills Harvey
Ann Helliwell
John Hill
Mary Hill-Male
Paul and Karalie Hillyer
Lady Mary Holborow
Alan and Laura Holford
Gayle Hollington-Wyatt
Barry Holman
Sir James and Lady Fiona Holman
Christopher C. Hoskin
Millicent Nancy Hoskin
(née Gardener)
Judy Glynn Howard (née Grylls)
Richard Hudson
Mr and Mrs P. Ingall
Ian A.N. Irvine
Susan Irving (née Davey)
Christopher Isaac
Joanne Isaac
John Isaac
Christine Ivamy
Anthony and Barbara Jackson
Professor Ed and Pam Jaggard
Ann Trevenen Jenkin
Tina and Tim Jefferis
Carol and Tony Johnson
Brian Jones
Mike and Chris Jones
William and Margaret Jones
M.B. Jordan
Keble College, Oxford
Diana Kelly
Pauline Kemp (née Davey)
Chris and Gill Kennedy
Joy and John Kentisbeer
Barbara Odiorne Kerr
R.E. and A.M. King
Dr G.M. and Mr J. Kitto
Andrew Knight
Gloria P. Leadbitter
E. Jane Leadbitter
Jonathan and Joanna Leather
Terry Leather
Mrs Hilary Lee
Lt Cdr Edward Lees, RN
H.G.M. Leighton
D. Leighton-Squires
Bob and Jane Leishman
Beth Levinsky
Adrian and Dinah Little
John and Helen Lloyd-Hughes
Andrew and Janet Lockett
Loveday Lowton
Keith Lye
Major T.B. McDowell
Lord Mackay of Clashfern
Jan McKinnon
Lady J. Mansfield
Sir Clive and Lady Martin
David Mashford
Betty Maylam
Louise Meek
Mrs Valerie Milford (née Powell)
Mrs Jean Mills
Mrs Angela Moore
David Moore
Sally Motley (née Rundle)
Elizabeth Nethercott
Mr and Mrs P.M. Nicholas
Kenneth and Guileen
(née Smith) Odiorne
Professor Nicholas Orme
Roy Orford, CBE and
Thelma Orford
Dr Oliver Padel
Mrs Jean Paine
Lord Patten of Barnes and
Lady Lavender Patten
Walter Frederick Paul
The Peard family, Tredis
Sir Brian Pearse
Anthea and Tony Peck
Mr Donald and
Mrs Wendy Pengelly
Peggy Pengelly
Mary Pett
Heather Pidgen (née Hearn)
Catherine Pitman
John and Barbara Platts
Jeremy D. Powne
Mrs Sally Prewer (née White)
Jacqueline Priest
Henry and Constance Pryn
The Pullen Family
The Pullinger family
Melissa Purchall (née Dunn)
Jason Quirk and
Charlotte Wikman
George and Joanna Radford
Derek and Tony Randall
Professor Isabel and Tom Rivers
Peter and Rae Robinson
Brian and June Roseveare
Royal Institution of Cornwall
Gillian Rubin
Jerry Rubin
Sarah Rundle
St Paul's School, Barnes
Malcolm Sanders
Mrs Patricia Savage
Andrew H. Scott

Judy Scott
D.J. Sealey
Brigadier D.G. Sharp, AFC
Mrs Gillian and
Miss Rebecca Shotton
Anna Smales
Joseph Smales
Phyllida and Robin Smeeton
Ingrid Smith
Colin Squires
Claire (née Rundle) and
Mark Stanton
Jennifer and John Stapleton
Nigel and Johanna Stapleton
Michael and Pat Steiner
Stephen J. Stout
Alan and Linda Strowger
Kate and Roo Taylor
A.W. Thomas
Tim Thornton, Bishop of Truro
Professor John Tiley, QC and
Jillinda Tiley
The Torpoint Archives
Brenda Trick
Karen and Geoff Truscott
University of Plymouth
David Vodden
John and Holly Waghorn
Diane and Tony Walters
Mrs D.B. Ward
Joey and John C.C. Warren
Lady Katherine Watney
(née Courtenay)
Philip Waxman
Simon and Isabel Webber
Roy Joseph Westlake
Sir Michael Wheeler-
Booth, KCB
Ian Whittaker
Colin and Renata Whurr
Robert Wiggett
Stephen and Barbara
(née Cusworth) Wilcox
Mark and Cynthia Wilcox
Mrs Susan J. Wilks
Sylvia Hazel Williams
(née Westlake-Williams)
Phillip and Lyn Woods
Canon Humphrey and
Mrs York
Faye Young (née Pidgen)

Foreword

Sir Richard Carew Pole Bt.

Nothing gives me more pleasure than to write the foreword to this quite remarkable book. It is the history of a small coastal parish recounted in the finest and most intimate detail. It is a work of the greatest scholarship and a must for anybody who not only lives in the parish, but also has a love of, or the deepest interest in, Cornish history. It ranges over every aspect of parish life – the church, fishing and agriculture, education, commercial, social and domestic life, war and politics. It presents a vivid picture of a local community through the centuries and how it reacts to outside events. How fortunate it is for us all that the author married a Miss Grylls from one of East Cornwall's oldest families who brought him back to this part of the world – without which this history would never have been written!

Richard Carew Pole

Preface

This book, though relating to a parish of only 2,000-odd acres in extent, covers a time span of nearly four millennia. For the first 3,000 years, what happened on this part of the Rame Peninsula can only be deduced from more general anthropological, linguistic and genetic studies, and from the few local sites of archaeological interest that have so far been excavated. One of these, a bronze-age burial, happens to be on my own fields at Trethill, a fact that first awakened me to the richness of the pre-history and history of the parish of Sheviock. In the tenth century, the charters of the Saxon Abbey of Tavistock are the first to give the name of Sheviock, and in the 11th, Domesday Book is the first document to enumerate the heads of households and to describe the manorial and agricultural arrangements of the parish. These documents and some early charters executed by the Dawneys, few though they are, are enough to enable a coherent account to be given of the earliest periods of Sheviock's history.

The Norman knights to whom William the Conqueror, and his successors, entrusted the safekeeping of the coast along Whitsand Bay were the Dawneys (more properly Dawnays). Their military responsibility eventually extended from Rame Head in the east to Looe Island in the west. These knights were particularly favoured by Edward II, who granted a licence to Sir Nicholas Dawney to found the borough of Crafthole in 1314. The borough was centred on the Dawneys' own manor-house at Blazor overlooking both the bay to the south and the River Lynher to the north. When it was crenellated by Sir John Dawney in 1336, the fortification (as the manor-house had now become) and village must have had very much the appearance of a small *bastide*, or fortified town, similar to those founded by the English kings in the south of France. Sir John Dawney's dovecote, which still stands overlooking Whitsand Bay, is the only part of the ancient manor-house that survives from the 14th century. Two events brought about the destruction of the fortified dwelling. The first was the death, without male issue, of Sir John Dawney in 1346, just before the battle of Crécy. The second was the elevation of Edward Courtenay, lord of the manor of Sheviock, to the earldom of Devon on the death of his grandfather, Earl Hugh, in 1377. Edward departed for his new seat at Tiverton Castle, and his old fortifications at Blazor were dismantled and his dwelling place converted into a farmhouse and later an inn. This 'decapitation' of the lordly dwelling at Crafthole, the centre of the ancient honour of Sheviock, dealt a massive blow to its standing in the world. Thereafter, it became the butt of jokes *de haut en bas* by those who were ignorant of its past.

Sheviock's two fisheries, one by the riverside on the Lynher/Tamar estuary, and the other on the sea, based at Portwrinkle, were first exploited by the monks of Tavistock Abbey. The Dawneys took over the fisheries, and their importance grew steadily as the population of the South West increased, up to the time of the Black Death (1348-9). After a century of stability, the population again began to climb, and the commercial importance of the fishing increased correspondingly. At the time of Domesday (1086), the lot of the 17 bordars or bondmen in the parish can have been little better than that of the four slaves on the demesne farm. The bordars were bound to the soil and were subject to many exactions payable to the lord of the manor or to the church. But the position of the tenantry gradually improved, assisted by a number of infrastructure projects funded by the lords of the manor. Before the development of the modern banking system, they alone had the capital to invest in big projects. The Dawneys invested in the fishing seines and built the first watermill in the parish.

The Courtenay family, which had succeeded to the Dawney estates, suffered disastrously during the Wars of the Roses in the 15th century, and then again during the period of religious turmoil under the Tudors. Their manor of Sheviock was forfeited to the Crown in 1538, and, after a short interlude, was purchased by Thomas Carew in 1558. His descendants have owned it ever since. Thomas's son, Richard, was the author of the famous *Survey of Cornwall*, published in 1602, which is the source of many of the anecdotes included in this book. That learned historian also began the tradition of storing at Antony House records relating to his patrimony. By the kindness of Sir Richard and Lady Mary Carew Pole, for the last few years I have been granted frequent access to these documents. The treasures kept at Antony include a manuscript book written, in about 1628, by Richard Carew the younger. Richard lived in Sheviock for some 19 years, and got to know the local fishermen, farmers and barge-masters. He persuaded his father to co-finance the building of the quay at Portwrinkle. The parishioners had been pressing for this to be built, in order to protect their seine boats and to allow them to land sea-sand to sweeten the acid soil of their fields. Richard's manuscript book shows him to have been a great naturalist. He tamed pheasants, kept bees and propagated thousands of apple trees. From his time up until the Second World War, apple orchards and cider-making played an important part in the agricultural life of Sheviock. Richard's observations on fishing practices on the Tamar estuary in his day are well informed and trenchant. As a conservationist, he was some four hundred years ahead of his time – advocating moratoriums on fishing to preserve stocks.

The Antony records also include leases, accounts and estate maps. Together, these sources illuminate the workings of the manor of Sheviock from its medieval origins until modern times. They preserve the names of many of the principal farmers and manorial officials. They also give the names of the tenements and individual fields on which they worked, many of which names have now fallen out of use. Through the leases we see the way agricultural holdings were created, divided or amalgamated in response to the economic pressures of the day. Often, it is only in these documents that ancient Cornish names are preserved after the 1300s, when English replaced Cornish as the main language used on the Rame Peninsula. The most precious of the estate maps is the beautifully-coloured map executed by Thomas Pride for Reginald Pole Carew in 1775. This map, with its accompanying survey, not only shows the exact locations of the ancient fields and tenements, but also marks the sites of forgotten structures, such as the poor houses west of Crafthole, the quays along the banks of the River Lynher, and the original sites of the manorial mills. Sections from the map are reproduced, with permission, in this book.

After the building of the quay at Portwrinkle in 1612, quite large ships could berth at Portwrinkle. One of the wealthier parishioners, William Hitchins, fitted out a 50-tonne fishing barque, the *Dayestarr.* She was manned by sailors and fishermen from Sheviock. The vessel was capable of sailing with the English fleet to fish for 'Cape fish' – a contemporary term for cod – along the grand banks off Newfoundland. The leases in Antony House, combined with contemporary wills and the records of the court leet of the borough of Crafthole, give an exceptionally full picture of the members of her crew during the reign of Charles I. The chapters of this book dealing with the *Dayestarr*, Portwrinkle and estuarine fishing can thus usefully supplement the more general histories of the fishing industry in the South West.

From the late 1600s until the mid- 1800s, the West Country havens were notoriously the haunt of smugglers. Portwrinkle and Crafthole were deeply implicated in smuggling, which was not regarded as morally wrong. Indeed, Samuel Drew, a member of a landing party of young men from the parish in 1784, went on to enjoy a successful career as a Methodist preacher and writer.

The two Richard Carews had co-financed the building of the original quay at Portwrinkle. Their descendant, Reginald Pole Carew, rebuilt it and also contracted for the building of a big new pilchard cellar and palace in 1792-4. He also encouraged teams of seine fishermen from Mevagissey to relocate to Portwrinkle to restart the local fishing after it had collapsed. Fishing on a large scale finally came to an end during the First World War. It was replaced by fishing for sport and by the tourist industry. In 1911-12, Sir Reginald Pole Carew demolished Thankes House in Antony and recruited investors to re-erect it as the *Whitsand Bay Hotel* in Portwrinkle, also laying out the golf course on the old demesne farm of Blazor.

Documentary evidence shows that Sheviock possessed a parish church at the time that Domesday Book was written, though it is not mentioned in the great survey itself. The church belonged to the Abbey of Tavistock until first the advowson (between 1174 and 1184) and then the tithes (between 1193 and 1279) were stripped from the abbey by the powerful lords of Sheviock. In 1259, the church was dedicated (or re-dedicated) by Bishop Bronescombe – an event whose 750th anniversary will be celebrated in the parish in 2009. Sheviock was one of the most valuable benefices in Cornwall, and only priests with strong connections to the patrons of the living had a chance of being appointed. One of these was John Walle, who had been a chaplain to the Courtenay earls of Devon, patrons of the living. His will, made shortly before his death in 1427, is a rare survival of the testament of a parish priest from the late Middle Ages and, translated from the Latin, is set out in full in this book. The church suffered badly at the time of the Reformation and later at the hands of the Puritans, both structurally and musically. In the late 1700s, serious attempts were made to embellish the services with the musical accompaniment of a small orchestra. The churchwardens' accounts, showing heavy expenditure on music during this period, provide an important corrective to the notion, propagated by the Victorians, that Georgian church music was unrehearsed and of poor quality.

The organs of local government of both the manor of Sheviock and the borough of Crafthole were the courts leet and courts baron, which, in medieval times, met in the great hall of the Dawney lords, and afterwards at the inn built on the site of the ancient manor-house, or (for the manor of Sheviock alone) at Sheviock Barton. Apart from a hiatus during the Civil Wars of the 17th century, these institutions continued to function effectively notwithstanding the changes in ownership of the manor and borough. The records of the court leet of the borough of Crafthole have survived from late Elizabethan times more or less complete until the early 1700s, when the court ceased to function. These records, stored partly in the Antony archives and partly in the National Archives at Kew, allow us to glimpse moments from the daily lives of the fishermen, sailors and other residents of the borough, and of their wives.

For the most modern period, beginning after the First World War, the principal sources used are the memories of those who were alive at the time, and have kindly given their recollections to me, and the records deposited at the Cornwall Record Office at Truro. The names of those who have contributed to the book in this way are set down in the following pages. As the story unfolds, I hope that the reader will agree that it is a story that has been worth the telling.

NEVILLE CUSWORTH

Acknowledgements

I have received a great deal of help in the writing of this book. I must begin by thanking my two principal contributors in the parish of Sheviock. They are Tom Bersey, who has farmed in Sheviock for most of his life, and contributed nearly all of the material dealing with farming in the 1900s, and also contributed freely to many other chapters; and the late Wilfrid Pengelly, a fisherman and coastguard, whose diaries, records and photographs form the core of the chapters relating to the fishing industry, the coastguard and wrecks. I am also most grateful to his son, the late Bert Pengelly, and his daughter-in-law, Peggy, for kindly making all these records available to me. I am also most grateful to Terry Leather, whose vivid recollections and photographs of life as an evacuee during the Second World War enliven many parts of this book; to the late Theodora Colwill, who spent her long lifetime in the parish and contributed much valuable information about life before, during and after the war; to David and Rosalie Dunn for collecting information on the shops and farms in Crafthole; and to Bill Barnes for his useful contributions to the chapter on Highways. I would also like to thank Fred Paul for his recollections, for information on his family, and for the photograph of his parents; Margaret Bartlett, for information on Smuggler's Cottage and the fishermen and coastguards of Portwrinkle and for many historic photographs; John Kentisbeer for his wartime recollections and history of the Sheviock Parish Recreation Club, and his wife, Joy, for supplying photographs, checking the manuscript and providing information on Crafthole; Ian Whittaker, for obtaining information from his father, Hal, on his wartime experiences, for collecting information on the Hill family and the farms at Crafthole and Liscawn, and for photographs; David Mashford for his account of the organ and other musical instruments in use at various times in Sheviock Church; Pauline Kemp for information on members of the Davey family of blacksmiths and agricultural implement makers, resident in the parish from the 1700s, and for her help in obtaining photographs; Mrs Valerie Milford for her recollections of wartime service in Portwrinkle with the Royal Observer Corps; Henry Pryn for information on Sheviock churchtown and for many early photographs. I am also grateful to Peter Hamilton and Bob Leishman, retired farmers, for their valuable input into modern farming methods. I am grateful to Rex and Anne King for letting me see and photograph the Kendall armorial plasterwork in their home, which was once the rectory, and to John Biles for his record of life in the parish in the 1930s and for photographs from that period. I am grateful to Digby Leighton-Squires for making available to me *The History of Trewin House, Sheviock, Cornwall* (2008), written for him by Jean Manco, and for the photograph of Trewin House. I would like to thank my wife's cousin, Richard Grylls, for information on the Grylls/Grills families, and also more widely for help with the Muster and Protestation rolls. I am also grateful to Ellan Odiorne Derow, whose ancestors emigrated from Sheviock to New England in the 17th century, for information on the Odiorne family. I am grateful to Diane Walters for passing on material that she had collected relating to the parish's history and to Peter Nicholas for many helpful suggestions and valuable pieces of information about the parish from the earliest times up to the Civil War. I am grateful to Yvonne Widger of the Dartington Hall Trust Archive for information and photographs relating to the Elmhirsts of Dartington Hall, who at one time owned the Chalet at Portwrinkle. Others who have kindly supplied photographs for this book are Ken Gurr, Elizabeth Nethercott, James and Karen Truscott, and Freda Manning of the Torpoint Archive, to all of whom I am most grateful.

Descendants of the lords of the manor of Sheviock have been most helpful with information about their forebears. I am most grateful to Sir Richard and Lady Mary Carew Pole for their kindness in allowing me such frequent access to their archives and for permission to include photographs of a number of estate maps and of portraits of Carew ancestors. It was particularly kind of Sir Richard to contribute the Foreword to this book. I am grateful to Diana, Viscountess Downe, for her help in relation to the spelling of the Dawnay family name and the photograph of the family heirloom shown in Chapter 5. I am also grateful to Lady Katherine Watney, sister of the earl of Devon, for her help in unravelling the descent of the earldom and the creation and extinction of the marquisate of Exeter.

I also gratefully acknowledge the help that I have received from many academics, who have been generous with their advice and help. I should like to thank Cynthia Gaskell Brown for her help in understanding the pre-history of the Rame Peninsula and Wella Brown for introducing me to the delights of the Cornish language, and teaching me its rudiments. I also thank Dr Ken George for comments relating to Cornish words. I thank also Dr Oliver Padel for his learned and detailed comments and corrections relating to Cornish words and the Cornish language. Any remaining errors are mine alone. I should like to thank Professor Nicholas Orme, Emeritus Professor of History at Exeter University, for his help with the chapters dealing with the church and the school, and for generously allowing me to quote from his many publications. I am also grateful to Professor David Daniell for advice on the section on the Bible in English in Chapter 29, and for permission to quote from his book. I should also like to thank Professor Sir John Baker, Q.C., St Catherine's College, Cambridge, for his help in understanding the proceedings of the court leet of Crafthole in the 17th century; and Jeffrey Hackney, Fellow of Wadham College, Oxford, for his help in understanding Henry Dawney's charters of 1174-1206. I should also like to thank Hon. Professor Ed Jaggard, Edith Cowan University, Perth, Australia, for his help with the lives of the Pole Carews in the 19th century. I am also grateful to Ms Sarah Shawcross of the Wykehamist Society Office for details of the schooling of Sir Richard Carew (1683-1703); to Dr John Maddicott, Librarian and Archivist, Exeter College, Oxford, for information on Sir William Carew (1689-1744) when he was an undergraduate there; and to Dr Chris Fletcher, Head of Western Manuscripts, Bodleian Library, for helping me to access manuscripts relating to Sir William. I am also grateful to John Jones, Dean and Archivist of Balliol College, Oxford, for providing information on Mydhope Wallis when he was an undergraduate at Balliol. I am grateful to Rosamund Reid for giving me sight of her thesis on the work of the architect, George Wightwick, which I have made use of in the section on Trethill House. I am also grateful to the Revd Dr J.E. Platt, formerly of Pembroke College, Oxford, for information on members of the Roberts family, who lived at Trethill and were scholars or fellows of Pembroke. I should also like to thank Anna Tyack of the Royal Cornwall Museum for showing me exhibits from the collection. I also thank Tony Bayfield, Historic Environment Records Officer for Cornwall County Council, for providing me with records of historic and prehistoric sites in the parish. I also thank the staff at the Courtney Library, the Liskeard and Torpoint Public Libraries, the National Archives and the Cornwall Record Office for their invaluable help. I also thank English Heritage for information on buildings in Sheviock. No one can write a history of Sheviock without acknowledging a huge debt to Lt-Col G.A. Kempthorne, whose *History of Sheviock* was privately published in *c.*1934, and to Professor H.P.R. Finberg, whose *History of Tavistock Abbey* (1951) is the definitive account of the monastery that owned the manor of Sheviock for about a hundred years before the arrival of the Normans.

I should also like to express my sincerest thanks to my old friend, the late Matt Thomson of Thomson Litho, East Kilbride, who so kindly agreed to print this book on generous terms, and to Noel Osborne, my fellow Stationer and Past Master of the Worshipful Company of Stationers and Newspaper Makers, for adding this book to the Phillimore list. Finally, I am deeply grateful to my wife, Dr Susan Cusworth (née Grylls), for her continual support and help, for her suggestions and comments on the text and the illustrations, and for her patience over the ten years that it has taken me to write this book.

Neville Cusworth
June 2009

PART I

Early History

1 *Sunrise over the River Lynher. View from the Bronze-Age burial site at Trethill.*

Chapter 1

From the Stone Age to the Roman Invasion

The Stone-Age inhabitants of Britain arrived about 15,000 years ago, after the Ice Age, when Britain was still joined to Europe by a land corridor. Their food was the big game that roamed the open steppes. Their descendants are thought to have survived another period of intense cold about 12,300 years ago. As temperatures rose, big game became scarce and people sustained themselves by hunting deer and other smaller mammals and by fishing and gathering shellfish along the sea-shore. This period, called the Mesolithic, or Middle Stone Age, was marked by many improvements in the technology of tools, which were made by knapping stones and flints. Melting ice separated Britain from the Continent about 8,500 years ago. After this period there was considerable new immigration to the western and southern British Isles from the Iberian Peninsula.

The practice of agriculture did not reach Britain until about 6,500 years ago, although people in the Middle East had begun herding cattle, sheep and goats, and planting corn, 3,500 years earlier. This new era of agriculture is called the Neolithic or New Stone Age. It lasted for some 2,500 years. Neolithic people developed a stone axe on a wooden haft, with which they were able to clear patches of woodland, fashion wooden implements and build more substantial wooden and thatched dwellings. They moved further inland up tidal estuaries and along ridgeways, and developed trading relationships with adjacent groups. For example, they quarried stone axe-heads at Balstone Down, near Callington, and exchanged them for flintstone axes from the chalklands further east. Neolithic people were buried in communal chamber tombs, as at Trethevy Quoit near St Cleer. These tombs are called Megalithic from the huge stones which were used to form them. During both the Neolithic period and its successor, the Bronze Age, which commenced about 4,500 years ago, there were two routes by which new ideas, artefacts and the practice of agriculture reached Britain. One was up the Atlantic coast via Iberia and the other was across the Channel and the North Sea from north-west Europe.[1]

Celtic and Saxon Immigrations

Some scholars believe that the Celts first arrived in western Britain and Ireland during the Neolithic period; but it is only in the Bronze Age that their presence is firmly established. The material culture of the later Bronze-Age Celts included a distinctive beaker pot, the 'Maritime Bell Beaker', which originated in Portugal and has been found in Ireland, Cornwall, Brittany and Iberia. Material records of the Celts, dating from around 600 BC, have been found in Spain and Italy and in Narbonne in southern France.[2]

The traditional, and generally accepted, view is that large numbers of Angles and Saxons first started arriving in a previously Celtic Britain when the Roman armies withdrew in A.D. 410. This idea was first promulgated by the Welsh monk Gildas, who died about A.D. 570.[3] However, one modern scholar, a geneticist by profession, argues that considerable Scandinavian and Germanic immigration from north-west Europe to eastern Britain began much earlier, in Neolithic times, and therefore predates the Roman Conquest by several millennia.[4] A male skeleton from about 2300 BC was excavated at Amesbury in 2003.[5] From the wrist guard that he wore, he has been called the 'Amesbury Archer'. Scientific analysis of the teeth and bones showed that in his youth the man had lived on an alpine diet and that he had been suffering from a severe abscess in his jawbone, which probably caused his death. A recent excavation at Stonehenge indicates that the 'bluestones' from Preseli in Wales were first erected at that time. The conjunction of the two events has led some scientists to conclude that the primary function of Stonehenge was as a place of healing.[6] The Amesbury Archer and other male skeletons buried nearby were interred with a distinctive type of beaker, described as 'All-over-Corded'.[7] These beakers originated in the Netherlands and are found predominantly in northern, eastern and southern England.

2 *A Bronze-Age Beaker similar to the one found at Trethill. (Royal Institution of Cornwall)*

The Early Bronze-Age Burial at Trethill

The culture of the Bronze-Age inhabitants of Britain, whether Celtic or Germanic, was much more individualistic than that of the group-minded Neolithic inhabitants. Prominent males were buried in individual plots with beakers of food to take with them into the next world. One such burial, dating from about 1800 BC, was discovered at Trethill in Sheviock in about A.D. 1880.[8] It is the only one that has so far been discovered on the Rame peninsula. The burial-site overlooks the River Lynher giving a stunning view of the sun rising over the water at dawn. The individual was interred in a stone burial chest, called in Cornish, *kyst veyn*. The chest was described by C. Spence Bate, an amateur archaeologist who saw it shortly after its discovery:

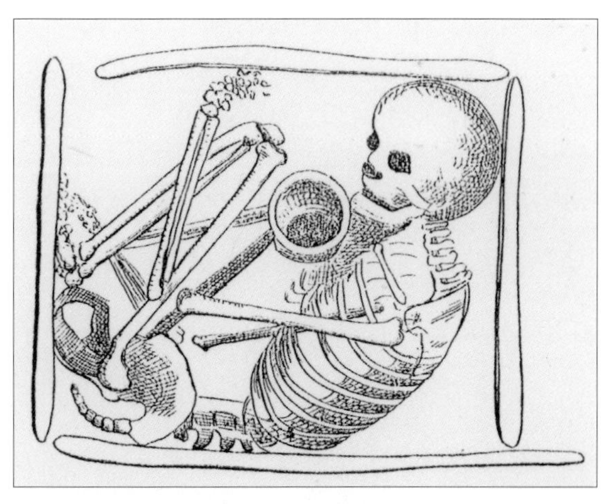

3 *The Kist Veyn discovered at Trethill enclosing a Bronze-Age skeleton and beaker (JRIC 1881).*

> The *kist* [*sic*] was formed by four side stones and a broad cover-stone. The bottom was formed by the soil of the country, but the side and cover stones must have been brought from some distance, inasmuch as they consisted of thick slabs of unwrought slate. … [It was] three feet three inches long, three feet broad, and two feet nine inches deep … It was about three feet beneath the surface of the soil.
>
> [I had] the contents of the *kist* passed through a sieve and carefully examined. I was in this way enabled to obtain several pieces of human bone and some fragments of coarse pottery. … The pieces of pottery were thick and only in small bits, one or two of which placed together enabled me to determine its diameter at the mouth … It was about four inches in diameter, and its surface was marked with lines that were impressed by some twisted cord, probably made of strips of bark, the ends of which overlapped each other …
>
> The skull was situated in the east or south-east, in the corner nearest towards the rising sun, and the knees were doubled up to the chin, the arms being thrown over the legs in a position approximating that in which it exists previous to birth. The food pot has generally been found between the knees and the chin.[9]

The food pot or beaker which is characteristic of such burials has led archaeologists to describe the people who practised this form of interment as the 'beaker people'. The Trethill burial, with its trussed body and shallow mound, and its pot impressed by a twisted cord, is typical of the earliest phase of beaker burials.[10]

During the Bronze Age, mineral deposits were exploited around Caradon. The tin and copper were worked by local smiths and carried along the ridgeways to the Lynher estuary, where they entered a trading network extending to Ireland, Brittany and the eastern Mediterranean. Travelling Irish smiths would exchange Cornish tin and copper for Irish gold. At Pillaton in Linkinhorne parish, the excavation of a chieftain's tomb yielded a magnificent gold cup, now in the British Museum.[11]

The Bronze-Age Burial Mound on Beacon Hill

Interments during the later Bronze Age (after 1000 BC) took the form of cremations. The ashes were then deposited in cemeteries, marked by mounds or barrows. The largest barrows were constructed for the chieftains, who were often buried with

4 *Whitsand Bay and Rame Head taken from the Bronze-Age barrow on Beacon Hill.*

their bronze weapons besides them. Beacon Hill in Sheviock is the site of a number of these barrows, whose presence was remembered in the field names. On Thomas Pride's map of 1775, the fields were called Lower and Higher Burrow and Little and Higher Burrow. The largest barrow was at the top of the hill, where warning beacons were later erected. In 1982, the barrow was excavated by the Cornwall Archaeological Unit (CAU) and the Cornwall Archaeological Society. The finds were recorded by the CAU as follows:

> The barrow had a diameter of about 16m and the main features are a central pit and a ring bank. ... The pit was filled with soil and a range of stone up to 0.7m. Flat stones up to 0.5m lay on top. The ring bank was 10m in diameter by 2.0m wide and 0.5m high. Finds all from disturbed area, include one flake of black flint, [and] two sherds of probably Bronze Age pottery.

A cemetery of ten such barrows was also excavated near Pelynt. Many of the graves contained weapons, including the famous 'Pelynt dagger' of late Mycenaean type, now in the Truro Museum. The weapons were made using stone moulds. During the Bronze Age people lived in settlements of thatched round houses. On good arable land the settlements were open and consisted of no more than a few houses.[12]

The Iron Age

Knowledge of iron working arrived in the South West before 450 BC.[13] Iron smelting, unlike copper smelting, is a two-stage process.[14] The first smelting of the iron ore produces a very impure product. The ore then has to be reheated, hammered out and quenched in water to purify and consolidate it. Iron has a higher melting point than bronze, and furnaces were improved to reach the higher temperatures required. Although iron weapons were weaker than bronze ones, they could be produced more readily and life became more dangerous. To protect themselves from wild animals and aggressive neighbours, people took to living in circular (embanked, hedged or palisaded) enclosures or larger hill-fort settlements. It was during this unsettled period that a family group built an enclosure at *Pendeen* (Cornish for a fortified headland), later called Berry Down, in Sheviock. It was once circular, but only half of it still stands. The bank that survives is 8.0m across at its highest point, 2.5m high and 115m long.[15] There is a similar, more complete construction at Lower Padreda farm (near Perdredda woods) in St Germans, which was formed of two concentric earth banks. There were probably similar constructions on Great Berry Hill and Little Berry Hill in Antony parish. Both the Pendeen and the Padreda structures date from the late fourth or early third century BC. These compounds, called *rounds* in England and *raths* in Ireland, provided defended homesteads for substantial farmers, their kinfolk and dependants. The inhabitants lived in timber round houses erected close inside the boundary walls. These would have been quite large, with neat thatch, and the builders, using iron tools, were capable of a high standard of carpentry.[16] Outside the rounds the settlers grew corn crops and grazed cattle in small fields. They also fished in the River Lynher and the sea. Rounds were constructed all over Cornwall, at an average density of one per square mile. On this basis, there may have been two or three others in Sheviock. Other rounds survive in Maker, and there is also evidence of

5 *Part of the Iron-Age 'round' (walled enclosure) at Berry Down overlooking the River Lynher.*

the existence of rounds in St John and Rame.[17] The only completely excavated round in Cornwall is at Trethurgy, St Austell, which was occupied between the mid-second and sixth centuries A.D. It was excavated in 1973.[18]

Under pressure from other warlike bands, people formed wider kin and tribal groups, acknowledging not only local warrior-chieftains but also kings of tribal confederations. There may have been a royal stronghold at Trerule, a name now incorporated into Trerulefoot. The linguist, J. B. Gover, gives its derivation as *tre* plus Old Welsh *riual* (Old Breton *riwal*), from *rigo-uallos*, meaning 'powerful king'. There may have been another royal seat at Maker, a word derived from the Celtic *magor*, meaning 'ancient ruin'. According to Kempthorne, 'Maker was traditionally a seat of the Cornish chieftains before the [Saxon] conquest.'[19] Liskeard, the *lis*, court, of a chieftain named Kerwyd or Kerret, was also an important royal stronghold.[20] The people living in the rounds of Pendeen, Padreda and elsewhere on the Rame Peninsula probably acknowledged the overlordship of one or other of these kings or princes. There was also a defended Iron-Age enclosure at Rame Head, built to shelter people and their livestock from raiders and to serve as a look-out point.

At the time of the Roman conquest of Britain, the people of the South West consisted of a group of associated tribes called the *Dumnonii*.[21] Trading between the Iron-Age Britons of the South West and the inhabitants of Brittany was continuous between 500 and 56 BC. Tin and argentiferous copper extracted from around Callington were the Dumnonian exports. This trade was conducted through Gallic merchants belonging to a tribe in *Armorica* (modern Brittany) called the *Veneti*. According to Caesar, 'The Veneti are much the most powerful tribe ... They have the largest fleet of ships, in which they traffic with Britain; they excel the other tribes in knowledge and experience of navigation'.[22] The modern port of Vannes in Brittany preserves their name. Their trading post in Britain was Mount Batten at the mouth of the River Plym. But the fleet of the *Veneti* was destroyed by Julius Caesar in 56 BC, bringing this trade to an end. It was in part replaced by trading with the people to the north, the *Durotriges* in what is now Dorset, and the *Dobunni* in Gloucestershire.

The Roman Conquest

Britain was not occupied permanently by the Romans until A.D. 43, during the reign of the Emperor Claudius (A.D. 41-54). The Second Augustan legion and auxiliary troops under the command of Vespasian, the future Emperor, conquered the *Durotriges* in their Dorsetshire hill-forts and then marched to Exeter. Here, in about A.D. 55, in the reign of the Emperor Nero (A.D. 54–68), they built a fort and established their legionary headquarters. With their rear thus secured, the Roman army advanced into Cornwall and, in the first century A.D., built forts at Calstock on the River Tamar; at Nanstallon, on the River Camel; and at Restormel, on the River Fowey.[23] All the forts were near mineral deposits at the heads of navigable rivers. The Romans began to extract tin and silver-lead from Cornwall in about A.D. 60 to 70. The fort at Nanstallon was vacated by A.D. 79, but the one at Restormel appears to have been occupied until the early fourth century. Some of the tin was transported to Exeter and then along the Fosse Way to the Mendips to be used in the manufacture of pewter.

The policy of the Governor, Agricola (A.D. 78-89), was to Romanise the Britons by building towns at strategic points. These then served as centres of administration for the surrounding tribal areas. Thus, Exeter, called by the Romans *Isca Dumnoniorum*, was founded as a self-governing Roman town to be the administrative centre for the *Dumnonii*. Its Council or *Ordo* may have included local tribal chieftains, perhaps including princes from Castle Dore, Lostwithiel, Liskeard, Trerule, and Maker. One of the most important functions of the Council at *Isca* was the assessment and collection of taxes. Subordinate local tax collection points, called *stationes*, were established within the region. The nearest to Sheviock may have been at Mount Batten or Plymouth.[24]

At some time during the Roman occupation, the land west of the Tamar began to acquire a distinct identity within the canton (administrative region) of *Dumnonia*. It became the *pagus* (district) of the *Cornovii*, a sect of the *Dumnonii*. The *Cornovii* are recognisably the ancestors of the Cornish people of today.[25] No Roman towns were established in Cornwall. The way of life of most of the *Dumnonii* outside *Isca* would have been very similar to that of their ancestors in the Iron Age. But instead of rendering labour services to their tribal chieftains, they were now paying taxes to their Roman overlords. They continued to live in small groups in round stone houses, but they acquired better-made black cooking pots and dishes and the occasional coin or trinket.[26]

6 *Two Roman sestertii, probably dating from the reign of the Emperor Hadrian, discovered on Beacon Hill. (Royal Institution of Cornwall)*

Dr William Borlase in his *Antiquities of Cornwall* (1769) states that 'By the late Lady Carew of East Anthony … I was favoured with the sight of several fair Roman coins; but where they were found (though probably in that neighbourhood) I could not learn.'[27] In 1982, two Roman bronze coins were discovered at the site of the Bronze-Age barrow at Trewrickle Farm, suggesting that the Romans kept a look out point or beacon there.[28] According to the late R.D. Penhallurick, the coins are made of *orichalcum* (golden copper). The British Museum believes them to be *sestertii* and most likely dating from the reign of the Emperor Hadrian (A.D. 117-38), though they could date from the reign of the Emperor Trajan (A.D. 98-117).

Under the Romans, improvements were made in the farming equipment and techniques of the *Dumnonii*.[29] The Romans also introduced a better knowledge of building houses and bridges in stone. The Latin words for window, *fenestra*, and bridge, *pons*, entered the Cornish language at this time. One unpretentious Roman-style villa has been unearthed at Magor (*magor*, meaning 'ancient ruin'), near Camborne. But there are no luxurious villas of the kind that have been discovered around Cirencester, Gloucester or Bath, which were built around A.D. 270.

Christianity reached Britain in the second century, and after the reign of the Emperor Constantine (A.D. 306–37), significant numbers of the Romans and Romanised Britons in towns, such as *Isca*, became Christians. A piece of black pottery bearing a Christian symbol, and probably dating from the fourth century was excavated in Exeter in 1945.[30] From the fourth century onwards Christianity had at least a foothold in the South West.[31]

The benefits of the mining to the Cornish were minimal, because all mineral rights were vested in the Emperor. However, the *pax Romana* (Roman peace) did bring some material benefits to the wealthier Dumnonians. Archaeology has revealed in some of the larger Celtic strongholds wine jugs imported from the eastern Mediterranean in the late fourth and fifth centuries. Olive oil, used for lighting and cooking, was also imported.

After the departure of the Romans in A.D. 410, Cornish trade was revived with western Gaul, especially the region around Bordeaux. Pottery jugs from there, dating from the 500s and 600s, show that the trade continued right up to the time of the Saxon advances into the West Country. Cornish tin was exported in return for wine, pottery, and sometimes corn.[32] A Time Team excavation at Lellizzick, near Padstow, in 2007, revealed a trading station occupied from the Bronze Age until well after the departure of the Roman legions. Pottery remains showed that trading with the Mediterranean continued until the sixth century A.D.[33]

Chapter 2

The Celtic Kingdoms, the Saxon and Norman Conquests

Following the withdrawal of the Roman legions in A.D. 410, the Roman *civitas* (canton) of Dumnonia became a native British kingdom, with the princes acknowledging a local royal overlord. For some three centuries thereafter, there was a flourishing Cornish highland society, which, from the sixth century onwards, was largely Christian in character. Though histories of England and Europe often describe these centuries as the Dark Ages, they were remembered as something of a golden age in the bardic songs about the Cornish kings and queens, princes and princesses. The legend of Tristan, Isolda and King Mark has roots in the historical Cornwall of this period. These same centuries also saw a revival of trade between the Mediterranean and south-western Britain. Remains of amphorae from the Mediterranean have been discovered at the royal stronghold of Castle Dore on the River Fowey. Glass and pottery, dating from the fourth to the seventh centuries were also excavated at the high-status, possibly royal, stronghold at Tintagel.[1] They too were imported from southern Spain, France and the Mediterranean. Recent underwater archaeology has confirmed the vibrancy of Mediterranean trade at that time.[2]

One of the earliest recorded kings of Cornwall was Tudwal. His son, *Cunomorus* (Hound of the sea), another name for the legendary King Mark, ruled about A.D. 525-50. His name appears on the pillar called the 'Longstone' at Castle Dore, near Fowey. The inscription on the stone reads '*Drustanus hic iacit Cunomori filius*', meaning 'Drustanus (Tristan) lies here, the son of Cunomorus'. Inscriptions of the '*hic iacit*' type indicate that the person commemorated was Christian. An old Breton manuscript records a meeting between the Christian missionary, St Sampson, and King Mark.[3] Gildas records the name of a later king, *Custennin Corneu*, Constantine of Kernow, who converted to Christianity in his old age (A.D. 589), became a monk at St David's and was made a saint.[4] His son was Erbin. Erbin's son was Gereint. In 600, Gereint led the Cornish at the battle of Catraeth against the Saxons. His sons, Cadwy, or Cado, Iestin (St Just), and Selyf became monks, as did his nephew, Kebi (St Cuby).

7 *The Tristan stone near Fowey, dating from the early 500s. The words* DRUSTANUS HIC IACIT/CUNOMORI FILIUS, *referring to a Celtic king, were carved along the stone.*

In the eighth century, another King Gereint fought against King Ine of Wessex, and may have been killed at the battle of Longborth in Somerset in 710. One of the last of the Cornish kings was *Dumnarth Rex Cerniu* (Dungarth or Dunjarth, King of Kernow), who may have set up the Doniert Stone near Liskeard.[5] According to the *Annales Cambriae* (Welsh Annals), he was drowned in 875, probably in the River Fowey.[6]

The Saxon Invasions of Cornwall

After the Roman legions had departed, the Saxons sought to advance westwards from their settlements in eastern and south-eastern England. The legendary King Arthur was perhaps one of the Celtic war leaders opposing the advance. By the late 600s, the Saxons were pressing close to the River Tamar. The first Saxon intrusion into Cornwall was that of Centwine, King of Wessex. According to the Anglo-Saxon Chronicle, in 682, 'Centwine put the Britons to flight as far as the sea'. This is thought by Professor Payton to refer to north-east Cornwall.[7] Following Centwine's victory, heavy Saxon settlements were placed in the northernmost part of the county above the River Ottery. The Saxon policy was not only to give conquered lands to Saxon lords, but also to put estates in borderland areas under the control of Saxon abbeys. In 705, Ine, King of Wessex (688-725), founded the bishopric and abbey of Sherborne as the religious centre for Wessex west of the ancient Selwood Forest, which lay in the vicinity of the modern town of Frome in Somerset. At about this time, the second King Geraint of Cornwall found it politic to grant to Sherborne Abbey five hides of lands controlling the first crossing point of the River Tamar, at Maker, whose bounds straddled the River Tamar.[8] The part on the western side remained a part of Devon until 1844. King Geraint's act of appeasement was not enough to stem the Saxon advances. In 710, Ine defeated Geraint in battle. This led to the first Saxon settlement between the Tamar and Lynher rivers. The victorious king granted lands between the two rivers to Glastonbury Abbey.[9] Over the next hundred years there were further battles between the Cornish and the Saxons, with the Cornish often in alliance with the Welsh and the Danes. In 722, a combined force of Cornish and Welsh won a victory over the English at a place called Hehil on the Camel Estuary.[10] In 805, King Ine's land grant was confirmed by the new rulers of Cornwall, and the amount of land ceded was increased to 18 hides in Ros (Rame).[11] Saxon monks, farmers and warriors may then have been settled on the peninsula.

In 815, Egbert, King of Wessex, launched a campaign against the Cornish and, according to the *Anglo Saxon Chronicle*, 'raided in Cornwall from east to west'. After his victories, Egbert gave three large estates in mid-Cornwall to the Bishop of Sherborne. These were *Polltun* (Pawton in St Breoke), *Caellwic* (probably Kelly in Egloshayle), and *Lanwithan* (Lawhitton). These places were selected to weaken the Cornish militarily and also to break their independence of spirit.[12] *Lanwithan* then included the stronghold of *Dunheved*, (the present Launceston), the northern gateway to Cornwall, and overlooked the Celtic monastery of St Stephen. *Cellwic* was another military strongpoint and reputedly King Arthur's chief stronghold in Cornwall. The huge *Polltun* estate, situated between Bodmin and Padstow, removed half the territory of the Celtic monks of St Petroc.

In 838, 'a great raiding ship-army' of Danes came to Cornwall to assist the Cornish against the Saxons. Egbert crossed the Tamar again and decisively defeated the combined army at the battle of Hingston Down, near Callington.[13] Danescombe, on the River Tamar, is said to be either the landing place of the Danish army or the place of embarkation and flight of the survivors. The general area of the conflict, at the foot of Kit Hill, can be seen from many high points in Sheviock parish. A consequence of this battle is likely to have been more Saxon settlement on the Rame Peninsula. However, west Devon still contained mixed populations of Saxons and Cornish. In 936, the Saxon King Athelstan expelled the Cornish from Exeter. At the same time he fixed the Tamar as the border between Devon and Cornwall. Cornwall was already thickly settled by Saxons in the north-east and between the Tamar and Lynher rivers. The Rame peninsula was also in Saxon hands, and under Athelstan and his successors became closely integrated into the Saxon coastal defensive system. A Saxon settlement was placed on the Cornish side of Antony Passage to control the crossing point – the name Antony is thought to derive from the Saxon *Anta's tun* (Anta's farm settlement). Sheviock, controlling both another crossing point of the Lynher and also the western end of the Rame peninsula, was probably also settled by a warrior servant or relative of the Saxon king. It was Athelstan who reorganised the six Cornish tribal divisions into hundreds along English lines.[14] It was probably under Athelstan that the parishes on the Rame peninsula took their present shape. The area of the parish of Sheviock appears to have remained unchanged from then until modern times.[15] Although the churches of St Germans and Maker were probably Celtic foundations, Antony church was more likely to have been founded by the Saxons. Except in east Cornwall, the Saxons did not intrude into Cornwall in large numbers. But the result of their military victories was that the lordship of all the great Cornish estates passed into the hands of Saxon magnates or monastic foundations. Domesday Book records that by the time of King Edward (1042-66) all the estates were in Saxon hands. Domesday states that at Maker in Cornwall 'there is 1 hide'; at Rame 'there is 1 hide'; Antony 'paid geld for half a hide'; Sheviock 'paid geld for half a hide'; and Tregantle 'paid geld for 1 virgate of land'.[16] Most of the lands on the Rame peninsula had been awarded to close relatives of the Saxon royal family. In due course, the family ceded them to the church, but the original military purpose for seizing the estates was not forgotten. A charter of King Athelstan, dated 936, removed all impositions from the bishopric of Cornwall except for 'expedition against enemies and sea-watches'.

The Saxon Estates in Sheviock, Rame and Antony

A Saxon monastery had been founded at Exeter before 690. King Edgar founded another at Tavistock in 968. With the foundation of Tavistock Abbey, the written history of Sheviock begins. King Edgar's brother-in-law, Ordulf, Earl of Devon, who was married to Edgar's sister Aelfwynn, supervised the foundation. Aelfwynn gave her estates in Sheviock, Rame and elsewhere to the Abbey to provide an income for it. In 981, the new King, Aethelred, who was the nephew of Ordulf and Aelfwynn, issued a charter confirming the endowment of the estates to the Abbey. Under the charter, the endowment included an obligation to provide armed men in wartime, and to contribute towards the upkeep of fortifications. This obligation was no mere formality, for in the same year Danish raiding parties caused 'great harm ... everywhere along the sea-coast, both in Devon and Cornwall'.[17]

Aelfwynn had also been granted Antony, which she and Ordulf had retained for their own use during their lifetimes. After his death, Ordulf was buried in the grounds of Tavistock Abbey. His bones were later re-interred in the church of St Eustachius, the parish church of Tavistock. A gravestone at the western end of the church marks his final resting-place. In 1066, his descendant, another Ordulf, added Antony to the endowments of the Abbey. He too was buried within the Abbey precincts. The year 1066 was however a fateful year, not only for the people of the South West, but for all the inhabitants of Great Britain, for it was the year of the Norman Conquest and the virtual extinction of the Saxon ruling class. The effects of the battle of Hastings were not felt immediately in the South West. It was not until 1068 that William led his army into the region.[18] King Harold's mother, Gytha, had taken refuge in Exeter. She had been joined there by a large band of Saxon refugees and warriors, turning the town into a centre of resistance. William besieged the city, which surrendered after 18 days. After his victory, William began the construction of Rougemont Castle, the remains of which can still be seen, and marched into Cornwall to obtain the submission of the nobles. He installed as Earl of Cornwall a Breton, Brian, whose native language was virtually the same as Cornish.

8 *Trematon Castle was built by the Normans as their main military stronghold in South-East Cornwall.*

The Dawneys and the 'Honour of Sheviock'

The presence of the Dawneys in Sheviock is first recorded in Domesday Book, completed in 1086.[19] The beginning of the entry for Sheviock reads in translation 'the Church of Tavistock holds Sheviock, and Ermenhald [holds] of it.' The tenant, here called Ermenhald, but called Erbenald in the surviving charters of his descendants, was a Norman knight, the ancestor of the Dawneys. Erbenald, though not one of the great barons of the realm, was a considerable landholder. His holdings were the most extensive of those granted to the ten military tenants of the abbey, being valued at £12 3s. 4d., more than three times the value of the next biggest holding. He was the most important of the abbey's military commanders, with three other knights serving under him. His holdings extended over some 10,000 acres. In return for his military services, he was granted 'the honour of Sheviock', a group of six manors that constituted a single large feudal holding, together with some property in Tavistock. The honour was centred on three manors strategically placed to defend the Rame Peninsula and the western side of the Lynher/Tamar estuary. These were Rame, Antony and Sheviock. The three other manors of the honour, further inland, were Penharget in St Ive, Tolcarne in North Hill, and Trewornan in St Minver.

Erbenald held his land by 'knight's service'. This meant that, in return for the land, he and the other three knights in his retinue were bound to fight for the king for 40 days a year. It was also his duty to watch the coast in case of raids by foreign powers or pirates. It can be inferred that the reason why Erbenald chose Sheviock as the seat

9 *The Dawneys acquired the manor of Pendrim after 1100. It included the borough of East Looe and a castle at the mouth of the River Looe.*

of his honour was because it was the place from which he could best discharge his military obligations. Rame, Antony and Sheviock, extended along most of the length of Whitsand Bay. Tregantel, between Rame and Sheviock, was held by Reginald de Valletort, who also occupied Trematon Castle, the main military stronghold of South-East Cornwall. When, perhaps under Edward II, the Dawneys acquired the manor of Tregantel and Pendrym (Pendrim), they controlled the whole length of Whitsand Bay, except for a strip in St Germans, which belonged to the church.[20] The borough of Looe (East Looe) had been founded on the manor of Pendrym in the 1200s.[21] Sir Nicholas Dawney's tenant on this manor in 1309 was Henry de Bodrugan.[22] The duty of the Dawneys to defend the coastline, whether by land or sea, continued down the ages. In 1338, a year after the commencement of the Hundred Years' War, Sir John Dawney was ordered with two others to array all men between Saltash and Fowey to resist a possible landing by the French.[23]

It seems likely that Erbenald established his dwelling-place, or at least a defensible part of it, at a place called Blazor on the high ground above modern Crafthole. One of only a few surviving medieval references to the dwelling-place of the Dawneys is the entry in the Calendar of Patent Rolls noting that Sir John Dawney had been licensed to crenellate 'his dwelling-place of Shevyok'. In the Calendar for the tenth year of the reign of Edward III (1336) appears the following entry (translated from the Latin original), 'March 19 Westminster. Licence for John Dauney, knight, to crenellate his dwelling-place of Shevyok, co. Cornwall'. Unfortunately, the entry does not specify precisely where that dwelling-place was, and only archaeological excavation could

10 *From their manor-house at Blazor, the Dawney lords had uninterrupted views over the River Lynher towards Trematon Castle.*

now locate it for certain. One of the most likely locations is Sheviock Barton, which is supported by the reference to 'Shevyok', by tradition, and by the fact that it was the principal demesne farm of the manor. The other candidate is the site at the top of the hill at Blazor. This is supported by:

1. Its better strategic location, an important factor so soon after the Norman Conquest. The holding of Blazor stretched from the coast up to the high ground at the top of modern Crafthole. It occupied roughly the area of the modern golf course. The site at the top provides uninterrupted views of both Whitsand Bay and the River Lynher. An observer standing there can survey the entire bay between Looe and Rame Head and, if he wished, could send warning signals to Trematon Castle. The summit provides a good defensive position. It is reached by a hill-side track that climbs steeply up from both the coast to the south and the River Lynher to the north. It also lies astride the main east-west coastal road, so the occupier could interdict the passage of enemies along it.[24] In 1336, Sir John Dawney obtained a licence to crenellate his dwelling-place. It would make perfect sense, militarily, for him to fortify a building on top of Blazor, but it would make no sense for him to crenellate his barton at the bottom of the hill in Sheviock churchtown.

2. Buildings at the top of Blazor were part and parcel of the same legal estate as the dovecote. Certain leases, albeit late ones (from the 1600s onwards), show that the dovecote at Blazor was part of 'Sargent's tenement' and that a 'Great House' (on the site of the modern *Finnygook Inn*) was also part of this same tenement.[25] By law, a dovecote could only be attached to a manor-house or parsonage. Therefore, that great house had manorial status. It is possible that Henry VIII severed the dovecote from Sheviock Barton in 1540 when he separated the borough of Crafthole from what was then his own manor of Sheviock; but there is no evidence for this.

3. The dovecote (built *c.*1336) lay close to the residential buildings which it was later known to serve – the usual relationship for a dovecote to its associated manor-house. The dovecote is placed close to the buildings to which it related in law. No commentator has satisfactorily explained why, if the Dawneys' dwelling-place was at Sheviock Barton, their dovecote was so far away from it. Charles Henderson thought it was to safeguard their wheat from the doves and made a joke about the doves feeding off the peasants' corn. Roger Penhallurick drew attention to the proximity of the sea shore and the molluscs upon which the doves like to feed. But such possible benefits cannot outweigh the huge inconvenience of having a larder so far away from the kitchen if the lords were residing at Sheviock Barton.

4. Both buildings were included in the borough. When the borough of Crafthole was founded in 1314, its boundary was drawn to include both the manorial building at the top of Blazor and the dovecote. With a new foundation, licensed by the king, one would expect it to have a relationship to a castle or manor-house.

11 *The Dawneys' manor-house at Blazor gave them a commanding view over Whitsand Bay.*

The lord's great hall was the focus for all the activities of a borough. It was there that the lord held his courts leet and baron, and it was to that place that the burgesses went to pay their rents and other dues or to seek shelter if attacked. From the 16th century onwards, one sees the hall (then part of the inn) being used for just these purposes, though evidence from earlier centuries is lacking. For all these reasons, I think that the Dawneys built a strong dwelling-place above modern Crafthole when they arrived in the 11th century, and that this was the building crenellated in 1336.

The adjacent fields would have provided excellent grazing for the Dawneys' war-horses. In 1415, when Henry V embarked his army for the Agincourt campaign, each knight was allowed to take with him, at the king's expense, six horses.[26] His man-at-arms was allowed to take another four. Grazing would therefore have been required for many campaign horses as well as those of the lord's wife and family. There may have been up to twenty horses at Blazor, each requiring two acres of pasture.[27] The Dawney lord's best arable fields and his farmhouse were tucked out of harm's way at Sheviock Barton, about three-quarters of a mile inland, and neither his horses nor any pigeons kept at Blazor would have harmed his crops there. Today, the name, Blazor, has largely fallen out of use, except on the lower slopes, where 'Blizor's well' still preserves the old name.[28] Blazor is mentioned in a charter executed at some time between 1174 and 1206. In translation it reads,

> I, Henry Dawney, give absolutely and irrevocably, on behalf of myself and my heirs, to God and St Mary and St Rumon and to Tavistock Abbey, that land at Trewikkel [i.e. Trewrickel] which Erbenaldus and Deintedosa, my ancestors, gave free and clear of all lay or royal services to the monastery at Tavistock. I and my men, that is *Garinus of Blazor* [italics supplied], Reinfrei the Frenchman, Robert the Briton, Edmarus and Osbernus Gogo, having sworn an oath, walked around this same land, namely two acres, together with Hugo Postel, monk of Tavistock and Garinus of Poldreisoc on the day after the feast of St Giles.[30]

This is the first surviving document that records the names of the local inhabitants of Sheviock. It is a group of mixed nationality. There is one Frenchman, Renfrei, perhaps one of the four knights of the honour, or perhaps the Dawneys' steward, and one person described as 'Robertus le Waleis' – Robert the Briton. This person was most likely a Cornishman, and he could have been the bailiff of the manor of Sheviock. There is no certainty as to the nationality of the other members of the group. But some of their names, shorn of their Latin endings, are suggestive of their origins. 'Osbern' sounds Norman-French, 'Garin' is perhaps the same as Warrin or Warren, also Norman-French. Hugo is a French name. Brother Hugo was probably related to Robert Postel, who was Abbot of Tavistock before Abbot Walter (abbot

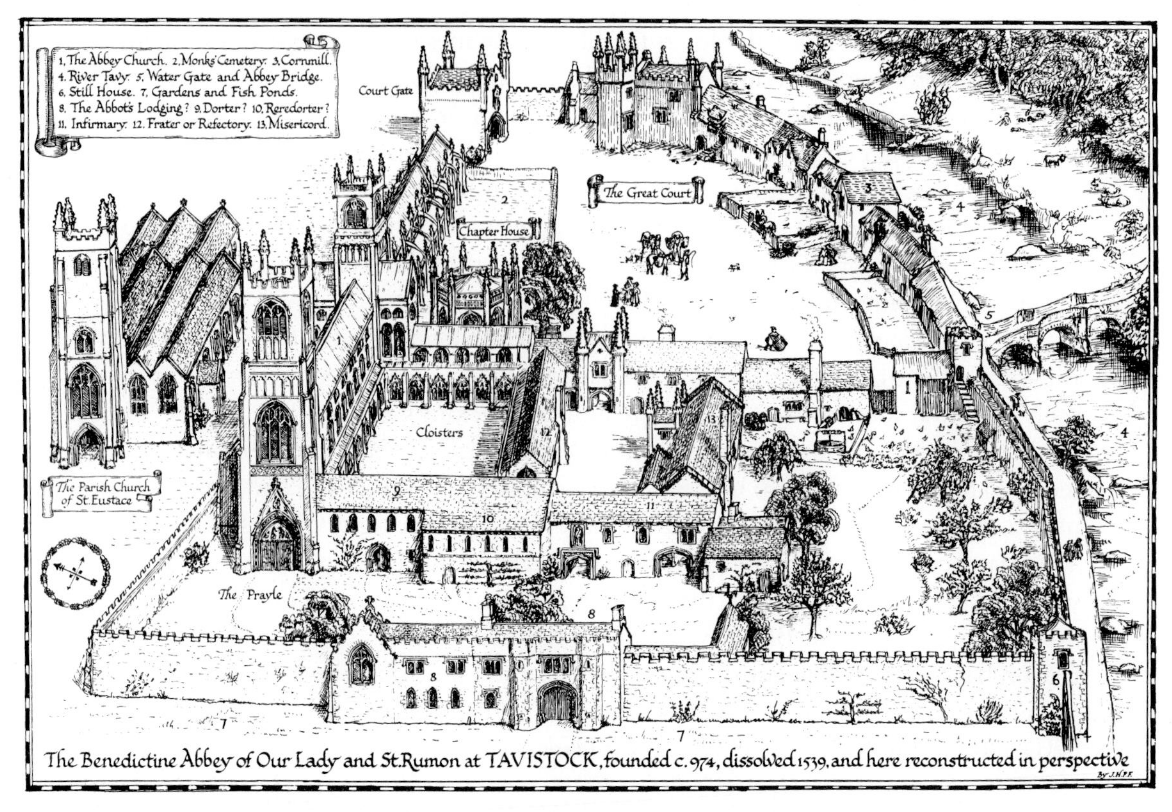

12 *J.N.P. Finberg's Reconstruction of Tavistock Abbey as it might have looked c.1450.*

*c.*1155). He may have been the *salsarius*, the monk responsible for ensuring the regular supply of fish from Trewrickle to the monks at Tavistock. As these eight men paced out the two acres at Trewrickle, those familiar with the land probably led the way, speaking in a mixture of Cornish and French, followed by their superiors, Henry Dawney, Reinfrei the Frenchman and Brother Hugo, conversing in French.

Because there were no maps, and land measurements were not standardised, a perambulation of the kind made by Henry and his party was the only way in which they could be certain of the precise piece of land that was being transferred. The ceremony of 'beating the bounds' is a reminder of this ancient practice. It continued in Sheviock until at least 1613, as is shown by the testimony of the rector at that time, Walter Arundell.[31] It is not clear whether the two acres in question were English or Cornish acres. The historian, H.P.R. Finberg, thought that the gift was expressed in Cornish acres.[32] In 1775, Crowstone Park, by the fishing cove, consisted of just over four English acres, and Monks' Park, lying to the west of it, consisted of just over eight such acres. The land conveyed must have been centred on these fields and is unlikely to have exceeded them in extent. The exact amount of land conveyed is, however, largely immaterial, because the real value of the gift lay in the access it gave to the foreshore and the fishing carried on there. For this purpose, two English acres would have been quite sufficient.

Gogo is a Cornish word meaning a cove or inlet. There is a beach at Portwrinkle called Finnygook, which incorporates this same word plus 'fenny', the English word meaning 'marshy'.[33] Garinus of Blazor and Edmarus and Osbernus 'of the cove' were no doubt chosen to accompany their lord on his perambulation because they lived on or close to the holding being transferred. Edmarus and Osbernus were probably fishermen at what is now Portwrinkle. They were related – most likely father and son – so that the memory of the transaction would be transmitted down two generations. Henry's grant was a confirmation of the earlier grant of his ancestors. The abbot was probably anxious for Henry to confirm the earlier grant because at this time there was some uncertainty as to whether a gift of this kind could last longer than the joint lives of the original parties.[34] The abbot had good reason to be anxious, because Henry later changed his mind and swapped this land for the 15 acres (half a virgate) of land that he owned at Tavistock. As he recorded in another charter,

> I, Henry Dawney and my heirs, have conceded and given the entire fee that we had in the town of Tavistock to the church of the blessed Mary and St Rumon of Tavistock in exchange for the two acres which the abbot and the monastery had in Trewikkel.[35]

13 *Ruins of the entrance to the Abbot's mid-1400s lodgings.*

Henry Dawney's original grant of 1174-1206 continued as follows:

> Furthermore, I similarly give, for the sake of my soul and the souls of my parents, and confirm my deed of grant, to this same monastery of Tavistock, thirty acres of my demesne lands of Sheviock, which my mother, Alaria, previously gave to the aforesaid monastery.

This part of Henry's gift – 30 acres of his demesne lands – was a substantial grant, even if, as seems to be the case, the English acre was the unit of measurement.[36]

Blerrick, Kerslake, Trethill and Liscawn. On the eastern boundary of the parish of Sheviock are the estates of Blerrick, Kerslake, Trethill (also called Nether Sheviock), and Liscawn. An account roll made in 1411 shows Robert Blerok holding Blerrick and Kerslake and Robert Burnard and Roger Whiteford holding tenements at Trethill and Liscawn.[37] A list of the fees of Edward Courtenay, Earl of Devon, was made during his lifetime or just after his death in 1419.[38] It lists 'Blerek Carslak Treuthel et Skawen' among the fees of the earl's manor of Sheviock. The fee (actually half a knight's fee in extent – about 400 acres) was jointly held by Thomas Scraesden (Scregesten) and Robertus Blerek. Robert Blerek and Joanna, his wife, had a daughter, Margarette. She married first Nicholas Tredinnick (Tredinick in St Erney) and then, in 1442, William Mohun. Kerslake appears to have become a separate manor, in fact if not in law, at about this time. Separate court rolls survive for the manor of Kerslake for the years 1564-1640. The manor of Kerslake then consisted of the holdings of Middle Blerrick, Lower Blerrick, Kerslake and Trethill. It included a culver house or dovecote situated in the grounds of the present Trethill House. In 1840, these holdings amounted to 376 English acres.[39]

14 *View of Kerslake valley looking north.*

Tredrossel. On the western side of the parish, Tredrossel, though part of the manor of Sheviock, was leased to Warrin de Herth (Erth), son-in-law of William Dawney the elder. William Dawney the younger was therefore obliged to contract with Warrin in 1286 to allow him, William, to carry water to his mill at Sheviock. The holding of Tredrossel consisted of 187 acres in 1840.

Tredis, Trewin and Sconner. Further west, Tredis, Trewin and Sconner were also carved out of the original manor. An extent of the lands of the late Sir John Dawney was made at Lostwithiel on 30 May 1347. The three holdings of Tredis, Trewin and Sconner are mentioned together as forming half a knight's fee (*c.*400 acres). This half fee is also mentioned in the dower of Sir John's widow, Sibella. It was then in the hands of John Inkpenne.[40] In the list of fees of the earl of Devon *c.*1419, mentioned above, it is stated that Thomas, heir of Thomas Fychet, held half a knight's fee in Trewin and Tredis.[41] All the Courtenay estates were forfeited to the Crown after the attainder of the Marquis of Exeter in 1538, and the Crown appears to have alienated them. A list of the free tenants of the manor of Landrake, dated 1578, states that Tredis 'is a manor and hath in itself both demesne and service'.[42] Trewin, likewise, became attached to the manor of Landrake at that time, and, like Kerslake, possessed its own dovecote or culver house indicating manorial status. Trewin and Tredis were not included in Thomas Pride's map and survey of the manor of Sheviock made in 1775.[43]

In a charter dating from about 1280-90, William Dawney the younger granted 15 acres of his wood called 'Hey(wode)' at Sheviock to the prior and canons of St Germans in return for them giving up their right to take two barges of the said wood.[44] In 1357, Sibella was settled on land called 'Asglake'. A document of 1514 refers to a place called 'Fenton Ogglake' at Sconner, so this may have been part of Sibella's dower lands. The Priory of St Germans came into possession of 'Skonner' at some time during the Middle Ages. The Crown took possession in 1539. After the Crown took possession, Hayewood was parcelled up with Sconner. Queen Elizabeth passed the properties to her favourite, Robert Dudley, Earl of Leicester in April 1574. A month later, the earl sold them to Sir Henry Killigrew, who sold them to Richard Eliot of Port Eliot. In 1617, his son, Sir John (1592-1632), sold to Richard Carew the younger 'all those landes tenements woodes ... and hereditaments called or known by the name or names of Skonner and Haywood ... lying and being as well within as withoute the parishe of Shevioke. All which said premises were sometimes parcel of the late Monastery of St Germans.' The consideration was £50.[45]

Dispositions of the Earl of Devon. After the death of Edward Courtenay, Earl of Devon, in 1419, his son and successor, Hugh, devised (disposed of by deed) Sheviock and other lands to pay his father's debts. Thus, in 1428, the knight's fee in Sheviock, formerly held by the Dawneys, was held half by the earl of Devon and half by the group to whom the lands had been devised. This group included Sir Thomas Arundell, Stephen Trenewith, William Halywell, William Bake (of Bake in St Germans), Robert Clarke, John Scraesden, Richard Smith, William Rossall, John Brempdon, Richard Stacy and William Clarke.[46] Sir Thomas Arundell was married to Margaret, lady of East Antony, daughter of Sir Warrin L'Erchedekne.[47] John Scraesden was no doubt related to Thomas Scraesden, the joint occupier in 1419 of Blerrick, Kerslake, Trethill and Liscawn. Richard Smith was a member of the family of Tregunnick in St Germans and Liscawn in Sheviock.

At various times during the Middle Ages, then, some tenements at the eastern and western extremities of the parish became attached to other manors, and some reputedly became manors in their own right.[48] In 1314, Crafthole became a borough separate from the manor of Sheviock.

15 *William Dawney's charter of 1280-90 granting 15 acres of Hey(wode) to the prior and canons of St Germans.*

Chapter 3

The Cornish Language on the Rame Peninsula

Celtic languages were being spoken in Europe by 1,000 B.C. The archaeologist and historian, Professor Charles Thomas, asserts that 'a hypothetical Common Celtic had emerged by 1,000 B.C. from Indo-European'.[1] A few scholars believe that its origins go back even further into the Neolithic period.[2] The consensus among linguists is that the language came to Britain probably some time in the first millennium B.C. (O.J. Padel). The variant of Celtic preserved in the South West and Wales is called Brythonic. From the first century A.D., Cornish and Welsh Brythonic were beginning to separate.[3] Physical contact by land between Wales and Cornwall was effectively ended after the Saxon victory at Dyrham in A.D. 577. The divergence between the two dialects then increased markedly. In A.D. 511, a Dumnonian chief called Riwalus led a particularly large body of Dumnonians from Dorset, Devon and Cornwall to establish a new colony in *Armorica* (modern Brittany), an area already inhabited by Celtic-speaking people. The Brythonic languages spoken in Cornwall and Brittany were virtually identical until about the time of the Norman Conquest, when they began to diverge. But the Bretons and Cornish could still understand one another so long as Cornish remained a language in daily use – that is until the late 1700s in the far west of the county.

Saxon farmsteads, such as those at *Anta's tun* (modern Antony) and the barton at *Siviek* (modern Sheviock) were established on the Rame peninsula after the Saxon victories of A.D. 710 and 838. These settlements would have caused some native Cornish speakers to pick up English words. But Cornish would still have been the main language in use on the peninsula, as indicated by its long preservation in certain natural features. For example, the little stream in the east of Sheviock parish called *Belerek* (modern Blerrick) (cress-bed), which flowed into Trethill creek retained its ancient name; but it acquired a new one as well, *Kerselac* (modern Kerslake) – Middle English for watercress stream.

The travelling priests from the minster at Lannaled (modern St Germans) who conducted open-air masses for the people of the peninsula until the construction

16 *Kernow a'gas dynergh (literally: Cornwall to you welcome). The welcome board sited at Torpoint.*

of parish churches, were themselves native Cornish speakers. Although they said or sang the masses in Latin, they brought the Christian message and conducted the rites of baptism, marriage and burial in a mixture of Latin and Cornish. During the tenth century, many Cornish officials added Saxon names to their Cornish ones. Thus, for example, the Cornish bishop of Cornwall in 959, *Cemoyre*, was also called *Wulfsige*.[4] Such usage suggests that Anglo-Saxon was being increasingly used in Cornish ecclesiastical affairs, at least until the appointment of the first Norman Bishop of Exeter in 1072.

In the tenth century, the secular administration of Tavistock Abbey's estates on the Rame peninsula would have been conducted in a mixture of Saxon, Cornish and Latin. To oversee their manor of Sheviock, and its important fishery, the Saxon abbot and convent would have installed either a lay official, called a 'sergeant', or a monk to act as their 'reeve'. He may have been based at Sheviock Barton where the monastery's main farming activities were carried on. The sergeant may have been an Englishman who could speak Cornish or vice versa. Cornish tenants on the abbey's estate must have picked up some English in the course of their dealings with the abbey and its officials, but at home they would have continued to speak Cornish. Life on the estate did not change immediately after 1068, because the Saxon abbot of Tavistock, Sihtric, remained in post until his death in 1082.

In the early years after the Norman Conquest, many French words must have been introduced, and there can have been no great incentive to continue to learn Saxon – the language of the ancient enemies of the Cornish. The Saxons were now themselves a conquered people. Most of the local markets were in Cornish-speaking areas. According to Domesday Book, there was a market at Liskeard that belonged to the Count of Mortain, and was worth 4s. to him. There was also a Sunday market at St Germans in 1086, but it was 'reduced to nothing, on account of the Count of Mortain's which is very near to it'. The reference was to the market held at Trematon, near the area settled by the English. It was worth 3s. to the Count. One can assume that farmers attending these markets could still conduct most of their business in Cornish, though with some English needed – especially at Trematon. Gradually, over the centuries, English came more and more into daily use. According to Dr Padel, 'by the year 1200 there must have been English speakers in many parts of east Cornwall, as far as Bodmin.'[5] The first written record of a place name ('Biricome') in English in Sheviock dates from 1286.[6] The Bishop of Exeter, Peter Quinil (1280-91), laid down that every parish priest should teach his parishioners the *Paternoster* (Lord's Prayer) and the *Ave Maria* (Hail Mary) in Latin. He should also teach them the *Credo* (Creed). If Latin was too difficult for them, he should teach it '*saltem in lingua materna*' (at least in their mother tongue). At this time English would have been the mother tongue for most people in Sheviock, though for a few it could still have been Cornish. By about 1300 or a little later, the Cornish language was effectively dead everywhere east of Bodmin.[7]

Increasing Use of English

Three factors in particular favoured an increasing use of English. The first was commerce. Commerce for the farmers meant taking agricultural goods to market and buying other goods there. The main settlements north of the River Lynher – including Callington and Saltash – were largely English-speaking at the time of Domesday Book. Furthermore, in about 1105, King Henry I granted to Tavistock Abbey the right to hold a market in the town of Tavistock *in unaquaque ebdomoda die veneris* – meaning on every Friday.[8] In 1116, the king added the privilege of a three-day fair beginning on the eve of the feast of St Rumon (29 August) and ending on the day after the feast (31 August). Tavistock soon became established as one of the principal markets and fairs in the area. The development of the fishing industry in Sheviock in the 1200s and 1300s also promoted the use of English, because the main markets for the fish were Exeter and Plymouth. So, both farmers and fishermen from Sheviock had an incentive to learn to speak English in order to negotiate successfully, just as today people from all parts of the world learn English for the purposes of international commerce.

The second factor was increased settlement of the Rame peninsula by native English speakers. There were two main drivers of this population shift within the parish of Sheviock. The first was the recruitment of English people to inhabit Crafthole, the new town and borough founded by Sir Nicholas Dawney in 1314. The new town was built at the foot of the old Dawney manor-house at Blazor. However, the new town was not given this name, but rather *Croftilberwe*, a composite of three English words, indicative of the language then in use in the parish. The other driver of population shift was the fact that the family who owned the manor of Sheviock after 1346, the Courtenays, had their principal lands in Devon, a wholly English-speaking area. Their main seat was at Tiverton Castle. Sheviock was no longer, as it had been under the Dawneys, the centre of a Cornish honour. Over the next two centuries many English servants of the Courtenays were rewarded with tenancies in Sheviock, Antony, Rame and other estates in east Cornwall.[9] The Courtenays were also appointing Englishmen as rectors or vicars of their churches in Cornwall. John Walle, appointed rector of Sheviock by Sir Hugh Courtenay in 1415, is just one example. The names of some parishioners of Sheviock who died during the year 1410-11 have been preserved in an account made by John Penhale, the rector's *procurator* (steward).[10] These were John Pethe, Florence, wife of Henry Hendr and John Stawen (Scawen?), Meralda Godhyne, Alice Byllyng and Matilda Symond.[11] The names seem to be a mixture of Cornish and English ones, but it is doubtful whether even those with Cornish names understood or spoke Cornish by this time. A third factor promoting the use of English was intermarriage between English and Cornish people. Intermarriage occurred at all levels of society from the earliest times and must have become increasingly frequent along the banks of the Tamar as the Middle Ages progressed.

English had now been enriched by many Norman-French words, and scholars call it Middle English to distinguish it from Saxon or Early English. The 14th century also saw the English language replacing Norman-French as the language of government and the courts.[12] The English language with all its loan words from Latin and French was also becoming richer and more versatile. English literature of world-class stature was being produced by men such as John Gower (*c.*1330-1408), William Langland (*c.*1330-*c.*1400) and Geoffrey Chaucer (*c.*1342-1400). Ironically, a Cornishman, John Trevisa (*c.*1342-1402), was an important contributor to the renaissance of English, translating Ranulph Higden's *Polychronicon*, a universal history, and parts of Wycliffe's Bible, from Latin into English. He may also have been a contributor to Langland's poem, *Piers Plowman*.[13]

Even where Cornish was still understood in east Cornwall after 1300, it was no longer developing as a living language. This is known because some Cornish place-names that survive in the east preserve the ancient form of certain words – e.g. *cuit* (wood), as in Cutcrew in St Germans (*kuit* plus *kryw*, meaning ford or stepping stones). Cornish speakers west of Bodmin had by this time modified their speech so that the word for wood became *koes*, as in Burncoose near Camborne (*bar an koes*, meaning 'top of the wood').

In the west of the county, the decline of Cornish was accelerated by the progress of the Reformation. The Catholic Church, which used Latin as the universal language for its services, had been generally sympathetic to the preservation of local vernaculars. In 1538, John Veysey, Bishop of Exeter ordered that all or part of the Epistle or Gospel and the *Paternoster*, *Ave Maria*, Creed and Ten Commandments should be taught in Cornish where English was not understood.[14] He also allowed chantry priests to teach children the Seven Works of Mercy in Cornish if they could not understand English. It was also the Catholic Church that had encouraged the writing and performance of the *gwariow* (miracle plays) in Cornish.

But after the Reformation Government policy favoured the use of English rather than Cornish. Henry VIII had had the Bible translated into English in 1539-40 (the Great Bible), and ordered it to be placed in all the churches in England and read aloud. In 1549, Edward VI replaced the Latin Mass with the *Book of Common Prayer*, written by Thomas Cranmer, Archbishop of Canterbury. The new liturgy was wholly in English. This was one of the grievances of the Cornish rebels during the Prayer Book Rebellion that broke out in that year. In their petition to the Government, the rebels declared that 'the Cornyshe men (wherof certen of us understande no Englysh) utterly refuse thys newe Englysh'. The Rebellion was crushed with great ruthlessness. It has been estimated that some 4,000 people were killed in action in Devon and Cornwall and that the Provost Marshal, Anthony Kingston, acting under martial law, executed another 1,000 people in the two counties.[15] His victims included the mayors of Bodmin and St Ives. The Reformation was also harmful in that it cut the Cornish off from the Celtic-speaking Bretons, who still practised the Catholic religion.

Had the Catholic Queen, Mary Tudor (1553-8), reigned for longer, the rising tide of English usage in west Cornwall might have been slowed. She ordered Henry VIII's Great Bible to be removed from the churches. She had the Bishop of London, Edmund Bonner, produce an English book of *Homilies* that was translated into Cornish by John Tregear.[16] But she only reigned for six years and, under Queen Elizabeth, the use of English again advanced. In 1584, the writer and map maker, John Norden, recorded that scarcely one person in Cornwall, except from some very remote district, failed to be able to converse in English with a stranger.[17]

By 1602, Richard Carew was writing,

> The principall love and knowledge of this language, lived in Doctor Kennall the Civilian, and with him lyeth buryed: for the English speach doth still encroche upon it, and hath driven the same into the uttermost skirts of the shire. Most of the Inhabitants can no word of Cornish; but very few are ignorant of the English: and yet some so affect their owne, as to a stranger they will not speake it: for if meeting them by chance, you inquire the way or any such matter, your answere shalbe, *Meea navidna cowza sawzneck*, I can speake no Saxonage.[18]

Carew knew Dr Kennal, who was a Doctor of Civil Law of his own University of Oxford, and a Canon of Christ Church, his own College. John Kennal was made Archdeacon of Oxford in 1561 and was appointed Vice-Chancellor of the University in 1566, the year that Carew went up. He was the holder of three church livings, including St Columb Major in Cornwall, where Cornish was still spoken, and Silverton in Devon.[19] He was made a Canon of the Cathedral at Exeter, where he died in 1591.

Carew's statement that 'Most of the inhabitants can no word of Cornish', was certainly true of his part of Cornwall, the eastern part. But many people west of Bodmin still spoke and understood Cornish. Carew noted also that many Cornish people, even if they couldn't speak the language, still retained smatterings of it. Some of these words and phrases, such as '*Molla tuenda laaz,* ten thousand mischiefs in thy guts', they used as curses and terms of abuse.[20] Others, such as the Cornish versions of the Lord's Prayer, the Apostles' Creed, and the Ten Commandments, which had been used in Cornish (at least in the western parts) 'beyond all remembrance', they retained 'as great a proofe of their devotion'.[21]

PART II

The Manor of Sheviock

17 *Southern part of the manor of Sheviock (from Thomas Pride's map of 1775).*

Chapter 4

The Manor of Sheviock

It may be supposed that the manor of Sheviock originally included all the land in the parish. But by the end of the Middle Ages a number of estates were separated from the manor on both the eastern and western boundaries. These included the manors of Kerslake in the east, and Tredis and Trewin in the west.[1] While some lands within the parish were thus alienated from the manor, a number of holdings in other parishes were added to it. These lands then became part of the manor of Sheviock.[2] The manor belonged to the Dawneys from their arrival shortly after the Norman Conquest until the death of Sir John Dawney in 1346. It then passed to the Courtenay earls of Devon through the marriage of Emmeline Dawney to Sir Edward Courtenay. Their son, Edward, became the Earl of Devon in 1377 and moved to Tiverton Castle. In 1462, on the attainder of the 6th earl, King Edward IV granted the manor to William Neville, Earl of Kent, and after his death in 1463 to Sir Renfry Arundell, the king's servitor. In 1485, after his victory at the Battle of Bosworth, Henry VII created Edward, son of Sir Hugh Courtenay of Boconnoc, Earl of Devon. In the following year, he restored the manor of Sheviock and other properties to him. Henry VIII created Henry Courtenay Marquis of Exeter in 1525. In 1531, some of the marquis's servants were agitating to have him declared heir apparent in the event of the king's death or marriage to a Protestant. He came under suspicion and for a while was banished from the court. In 1538, these old charges were revived and he was attainted and executed for treason. The manor was again forfeited to the Crown. In 1540, Henry VIII transferred the borough of Crafthole (which had been carved out of the manor in 1314) to the Duchy of Cornwall; but he retained the manor of Sheviock in his own hands.[3] In 1541, he included the manor of Sheviock in the dowry of Queen Katherine Howard, but reclaimed it on her execution in 1542. It thus belonged to the Protestant king, Edward VI, at the time of the Prayer Book Rebellion of 1549. In June 1553, the dying king granted the manor to Sir Walter Mildmay, the Puritan Surveyor General of the Court of Augmentations.[4] In 1558, Sir Walter sold the manor to Thomas Carew of Antony. In the wording of the deed of sale, 'Sir Walter

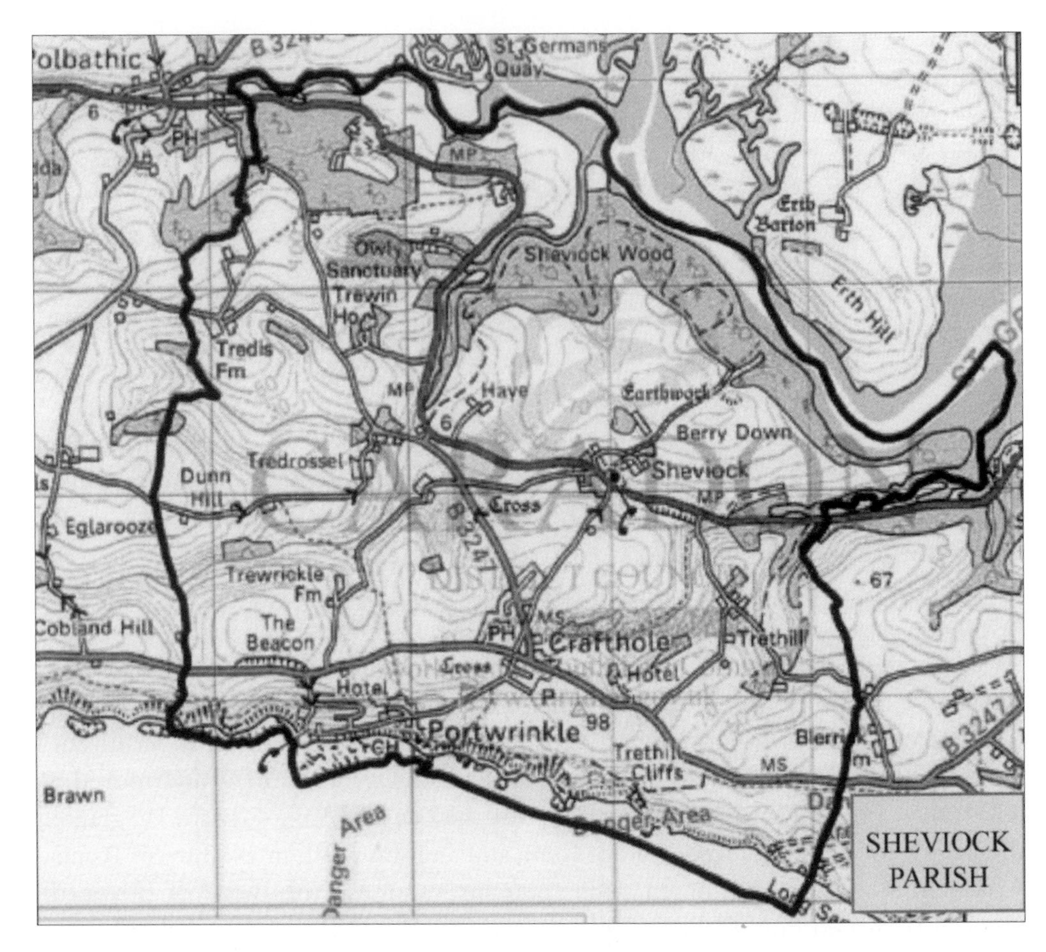

18 *Boundaries of the parish of Sheviock in 2008.*

hath bargained and solde … all that his lordship and mannor of Shevioke … late parcell of the lands and possessions of Henrie late Marquis of Exeter of high treason attainted … [together with] court leates vewe of Frankepledge cattalls waiffs straies free warrenes.' The consideration was 'a thowsande poundes'.[5] The manor has been in the hands of his descendants ever since.

THE MANOR-HOUSE AND DOVECOTE

The Manor-House

The Dawneys built a dwelling in Sheviock when they arrived in the late 11th century. Since publication in 1602 of Richard Carew's *Survey of Cornwall* it has been generally assumed that this dwelling stood on the site of Sheviock Barton.[6] Carew wrote, 'The next parish upon this river, is called Sheviock, sometimes the ancient *Dannyes* inheritance & inhabitance.' A quick reading of this passage might suggest that Sheviock churchtown is the ancient '*Dannyes* inheritance and inhabitance'. But a more careful reading shows that Carew is only stating that the *parish* of Sheviock has that honour. In fact, for the reasons stated in Chapter 2, the Dawneys' manor-house stood at a place called Blazor, on the high ground above Crafthole.[7] It was there that the courts of the manor of Sheviock were held until the ownership of the manor was separated from that of the borough, and it was there that the borough courts of Crafthole were held after the foundation of Crafthole. The modern *Finnygook Inn* stands on the site of the old manor-house. The antecedents of the buildings that are today called Cross House and High Hopes were also included in the borough when it was created in 1314, and therefore also probably stood within the old manorial enclosure. In 1336, Sir John Dawney received licence to 'crenellate his dwelling-place of Shevyok, co. Cornwall'. Thus the manor-house became a fortified stronghold during the Hundred Years War with France. This is the only piece of information that we have about the appearance of the manor-house in the Middle Ages. After the Courtenays had departed for Tiverton, the fortifications were dismantled and the manorial dwellings were converted into farmhouses and in due course an inn. The fields, where once the Dawneys' war-horses had grazed, were given over to agriculture. When the main house on the site became an inn, in the 1600s or earlier, the *borough* courts (but not the manorial courts) continued to be held in the inn.[8]

19 *Horses grazing at Trethill. The Dawneys' warhorses would once have grazed the fields at Blazor.*

20 *The* Finnygook Inn *is built on the site of the ancient Dawney manor-house.*

Most of the Dawney lords would appear to have resided in Sheviock, though they were often away attending to their other estates in Devon or fighting abroad in the king's service. Kempthorne suggested that Sir Nicholas Dawney (*c.*1280-1332), who held the manors of Godlyngton or Godryngton (modern Goodrington), Norton, Cornwode and other estates in Devon, may have resided in that county. Certainly Sir Nicholas received many commissions from the king in connection with Devon.[9] But he was also the founder of the borough of Crafthole, so he must also have spent some time on his manor of Sheviock, supervising the foundation of his new borough. His son, Sir John (*c.*1300-46), who married Sibella Treverbyn sometime before 1325, made his home in Sheviock. It was he who, in 1336, received permission to crenellate his house. After his death on military service in France in 1346, his bones were brought home to be buried in Sheviock. Sir John was the last Dawney lord of the manor. On his death, the lordship passed through his daughter, Emmeline, to his son-in-law, Sir Edward Courtenay, whose son, another Edward, became earl of Devon, and moved to Tiverton.

The Dawneys' Dovecote

Overlooking Whitsand Bay is the famous dovecote built by the Dawneys. Another word for dovecote is 'culverhouse' – *culfre* being an Old English word for a dove or pigeon. The Latin word for a dovecote was *columbarium.* Only lords of manors or the clergy were allowed to keep dovecotes. According to the late ornithologist and historian, Roger Penhallurick, 'Dovecotes were introduced to this country by the Normans, and until the relaxation of laws … the right to keep a *columbarium* was restricted … to manors and ecclesiastical fiefs.'[10] The law was strictly enforced. The vestry of Houghton Conquest, Bedfordshire, for example, instructed the constables

21 *Furze grows abundantly on the high ground above Whitsand Bay. It was an important source of fuel for tenants of the manor.*

to enquire whether any dove houses had been 'Ereckted or mentayned by anny not being lord off the manor or peirson [i.e. parson] of the towne'.[11] This law, combined with the fact that, in all leases surviving from the 1600s and 1700s, the dovecote was legally attached to the 'Great House' at Blazor (modern Crafthole), indicates that the Dawneys built a dwelling there, on the site now occupied by the inn.

The construction date of the culverhouse is not known for certain, but the fact that the Dawneys crenellated their manor-house in 1336, when they would have had many skilled masons on site, makes that date very likely. The Bodrugans' culverhouse at Trethew near Liskeard has been dated to 1309.[12] The Dawneys' dovecote is sited on what would have been at the time mostly rough pasture for grazing horses and sheep, and waste ground. One of the 18th-century field names immediately adjacent to the culverhouse is 'Bramble Park'. The clearance of the brambles to make the park probably occurred after the construction of the culverhouse. Much of the land surrounding the dovecote was covered in furze, important as fuel. Furze continued to be collected for firewood from the rough ground around the culverhouse until the 1950s.[13] The land on the seaward side of the culverhouse was still described as a 'slade', a piece of rough ground, on the 1840 tithe map. An interesting fact relating to the siting of the culverhouse is the observation by Roger Penhallurick that, in addition to feeding on seeds, the birds fed on small *mollusca*, which are of course plentiful along the seashore.

22 *The Dawneys' dovecote was built at their manor-house at Blazor in the early 1300s.*

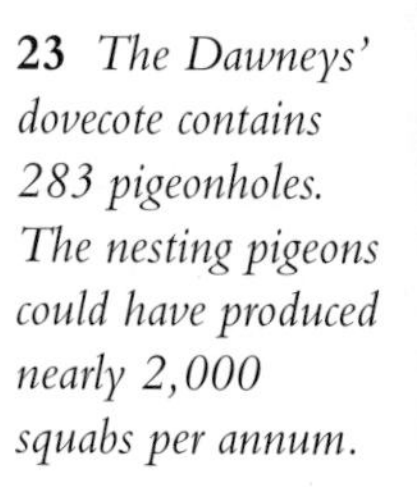

23 *The Dawneys' dovecote contains 283 pigeonholes. The nesting pigeons could have produced nearly 2,000 squabs per annum.*

The species of bird kept in a culverhouse was the feral pigeon or rock dove, *columba livia.*[14] This species has a very short breeding cycle, each pair rearing two 'squabs' (unfledged young) about every six weeks. Thus the lord of the manor's table was well supplied with meat for at least half the year. The Crafthole culverhouse has altogether 283 pigeonholes. The bottom five rows have an average of 20 holes in each row, and the remaining nine rows have on average 22 holes in each. Squabs were taken for eating from May to October. If each hole housed one pair of pigeons, and each pair produced 14 squabs a year, the culverhouse would in theory produce 1,981 squabs per half year or 76 per week.[15] The squabs 'were generally consumed at four weeks, when still succulent'.[16] The rector of Sheviock was entitled to his tithe (ten per cent), amounting to 198 squabs per half year, leaving 1,783 for the Dawney household (68 per week).

24 *Central louvre and nesting holes of the Dawneys' dovecote.*

The Crafthole culverhouse was scheduled as an ancient monument in 1963. In 1973, the Antony estate assumed responsibility for keeping it in repair.[17] It was mostly built using a dry-stone walling technique. The birds entered and left the dovecote through a central louvre in the roof, and also through 14 'throughholes' in the side of the building. Nine of these are on the seaward side of the building and five on the upper or landward side. Originally, a wooden structure called a 'potence' (from the French *potence*, meaning a 'crutch') would have been erected inside. This was 'a ladder attached to horizontal bars which revolve around a central post'.[18] The medieval keeper would ascend the ladder to carry away the squabs for the manorial kitchen. Alighting platforms for the birds were also attached to the central post. The culverhouse would originally have had a stout wooden door to keep out predators and thieves. The recesses for the doorjambs are still clearly visible. The Dawneys' culverhouse continued in use until the 18th century, as shown by a lease made in 1702.[19] The then owners, William Condy of Tavistock, a 'clothier' and his wife, Frances, let the holding, called Sargent's tenement, in which the culverhouse stood, to a yeoman, John Edwards, formerly the 'hind' (farm manager) of the Carew estates. But Condy and his wife specifically reserved to themselves,

> all that one dove house standing and being in one of the feilds ... called by the name of the Culver Parke with full power and lawful liberty to and for him and them his and their servants and workmen ... at all times and seasons to see to the house and [go to and] from the said house with all manner of carryages of timber stone or lime for repairing of the said house and likewise corne and grayne for the nourishment of the said doves and also to put in or fetch away doves or pidgeons at his and their will and pleasure.

When, in 1711, the Condys sold the premises that included the dovecote to Sir William Carew, the building was described as being '*formerly* used as a Dovehouse'.[20] There is no evidence that the medieval building was used as a dovecote after that time, although dovecotes continued to be built. A new one was built at Antony House in 1719-20.[21]

THE DEMESNE FARMS AND BUILDINGS

The demesne farms were the farms directly managed for the lord himself by his hind and his own farm workers. In the Middle Ages, the two main ones appear to have been Blazor (54 acres in 1691) and Sheviock Barton, whose farmland was known as Berry Down and Berry Wells (60 acres). The stewards' accounts of 1709 and 1710 show that Pool had also once been part of the demesne. In addition there was Bailiff's Meadow consisting of five acres in Sheviock churchtown and Gill Ball (five acres), which was the site of the manorial windmill. Later more farmland was carved out of Sheviock Woods to create the holdings of 'the two Hayes' (50 acres each), and Treise's tenement (55 acres). Though probably tenanted from the beginning, they were often farmed together with Sheviock Barton and so are considered here.

Blazor

Blazor was the less important of the two original demesne farms from an agricultural point of view. When Domesday Book said of this manor, 'There are 30 acres of pasture', probably many of them were on or near the cliffs at Blazor. By 1691, when the extent of Blazor was 54 acres, much of the bramble, ferns and furze growing along the cliff tops would have been cleared away. In the medieval period, most of the cleared land at Blazor would have been given over to pasturage for horses and sheep. As mounted knights, the Dawneys would have needed plenty of grazing land.

In 1415, when Henry V embarked his army for the Agincourt campaign, each knight was allowed to take with him, at the king's expense, six horses: his war-horse or 'courser'; a substitute; a lighter saddle-horse or 'palfrey' for riding when he was not in full armour; two 'rouncies' (riding horses) for his servants; and a packhorse for his baggage.[22] If he took more, it was at his own expense. Each esquire was allowed four horses: one war-horse, one palfrey, one rouncy, and one packhorse. When a Dawney lord and his man-at-arms went off to the wars, until the last of them, Sir John Dawney, departed in 1346, he would most likely be taking ten horses with him.[23] He must also have left behind a number of palfreys for his wife and other adult members of his family, and also a few horses to pull carts and ploughs to work the farm. When the lord was in residence, there could easily have been up to twenty horses on the farm, including some mares with foals. Each large war-horse, perhaps consuming the same as a modern Shire horse or Suffolk punch, would need a minimum of two acres of grazing land, and additional feed would be needed in the winter in the shape of corn and hay. A large horse requires two feeds of corn a day, but with less in the summer and hay in the winter.[24] Twenty Dawney horses, if such there were, would therefore have needed most of the 54 acres of the farmland listed in 1691.

Even after the departure of the Dawneys, only a small amount of the land at Blazor was used for arable farming. An account of the tithe of sheaves from Sheviock made in 1410-11 shows that Blazor contributed the second smallest amount of corn out of the nine holdings in the account.[25] By then, Blazor was no longer in demesne, but was tenanted by Roger Campell, whose tithe sheaves fetched £1 3s. 0d. A lease of 1636 refers to the holding as 'the Barton land called Blazor', showing its origin as a demesne farm.

The farm of Blazor extended southwards towards the sea from the east-west highway running through Crafthole. It also straddled Finnygook Lane and is now incorporated into the golf course of the *Whitsand Bay Hotel*. Sometime before 1533, 'John Whydek' was the farmer. In 1533, 'Morice Davy Joan his wife & Richard their son' succeeded Whydek as tenant of Blazor. Henry, Marquis of Exeter, was lord of the manor at this time and his bailiff was Anthony Harry.[26] The marquis was a devout Catholic and Davy's lease was headed 'IHS' (the first three capital letters of the Greek word for Jesus). It was probably during the late 1400s that the tenement was increased in size by clearing away the growths of furze, bracken and brambles that grew along the cliffs. The marquis's two bailiffs probably responsible for this enlargement left their names on the fields called 'Harry's Ball' and 'Kingdon's Park'. By 1636, Blazor was divided into four quarters, three of 13 acres and one of 15 acres. The farmers who worked those quarters lived at the top of the hill in premises that had been built on the site of the old manor-house. Manorial rentals and Thomas Pride's survey and map of the Antony estates made in 1775 contain the names of many of the tenants of the quartered holding.[27]

Quarters 1: 15 Acres; and 2: Thirteen Acres: The south-westerly parts of Blazor consisted of the fields called Skinners Ball, Skinners Ball Meadow (the former Harry's Ball), South Park, West Park, Slade, Bramble Park, Wallis's Hill, Kingdon's Park, and Jury (Jory) Park.[28] The easterly parts consisted of the field known as Barley Park, south of what became (in the 1700s) 'Mrs Mullis's house' in Crafthole, East Park and Little Field.[29] All these fields are marked on Thomas Pride's map of 1775. In 1636, John Stymead, his son, John, and Anthony Stymead surrendered 'all the Barton land called Blazer ... conteyning by estimation fiftene acres of land'. On surrender, the holding was leased to Richard Wallis.[30] The rent for the 15 acres was 11s. 5d. plus two capons (or 2s.). Richard lived and farmed at Sconner, on a beautiful site overlooking the River Lynher. He was also the lessee of a number of valuable properties in Crafthole.

In 1691, quarters 1 and 2 were let to John Nicholls, who became bailiff of the manor in 1697.[31] The rent for the second quarter was the same as for the first one. Nicholls was still renting the two quarters in 1726.[32] His son, Christian, succeeded him as tenant.[33] In 1741, one of the quarters was leased to Peter Kitt (age 29) on the lives of his wife, Mary (age 25) and his one-month-old son, Peter. The rent was the same as it had been in 1653. In 1770, Peter Kitt the younger was the tenant of Blazor and of Hearle's Park.[34] Dinah Kitt, who was also the tenant of the inn at Crafthole, was shown as the occupant of a quarter of Blazor in 1809-10.

Quarter 3: Thirteen Acres: Another quarter included the fields known as Lower and Higher Blazor and a four-acre slade. In 1691, this quarter was let to Richard Wallis's son-in-law, John Edwards, on the lives of himself and his wife, Grace, their son Thomas, and Henry Blake. The rent was 11s. 5d. (i.e. 10s. and some livestock).[35] Edwards became the hind (farm manager) of the Carew estates in Antony and Sheviock in 1706.[36] Edwards was also the tenant of the houses in Crafthole called Sargent's tenement (the modern *Finnygook Inn*) and High House (the former dwelling of Dorothy Arundell), and presumably lived in one of them. Henry Short was renting a part of Blazor in 1726. His rent was 10s. He was also the tenant of a cottage on what is now the car parking space next to the post office.

Quarter 4: Thirteen Acres: Tristram Harry, who died in 1638, and may have lived in what is now called Cross House, was the tenant of the fourth quarter.[37] This quarter stretched from Crafthole down to the sea on either side of Finnygook Lane. Tristram also held the tenancy of nine acres of land called Hearle's Parks.[38] John Harry (born in 1603), Tristram's son, and his wife, Joan (born in 1605), were renting one quarter of Blazor from the Commonwealth authorities in 1653 at a rent of 11s. 4d.[39] Their son,

Tristram, had been born in 1643 and eventually took over the tenancy of the quarter of Blazor and Hearle's Parks previously held by his grandfather.[40] Tristram junior also married a Joan, and they had a daughter called Martha, who married William Chubb, a sailor. In 1691, William Chubb is shown as a co-tenant of Tristram's quarter of Blazor.[41] In 1692, Tristram Harry was appointed reeve and collector of rents for the Carews.[42] He took over the tenancy of Cote in 1694 and left his part of Blazor to be managed by William and Martha Chubb.[43] Martha Chubb was in occupation of two quarters of Blazor in 1766. Her co-tenant was Joan Phillips.[44] Matthew Warren, who was a descendant of Martha Chubb, was the tenant of this quarter in 1775 on the life of Martha, then aged 72. Robert Warren was the tenant of half of Blazor from 1809 to 1821. He was also the tenant of Haye Farm from 1792-1832.[45]

Amalgamation of Blazor Tenements: In 1833-4, Samuel Lyne was farming at Blazor, Cross Park and Hearle's Parks. These holdings together became known as Crafthole Farm. By 1840, when the tithe redemption map was made, Crafthole Farm included 79 acres of Blazor, many more acres having been reclaimed from the growths of bramble, bracken and furze. The tenant then was Samuel's son, William Lyne, who also farmed the Glebe (126 acres).

Blizer's Well: Now boarded up, the well is on the southern side of Finnygook Lane just before the sign for Portwrinkle. It is a variant of 'Blazor's Well'. This was the principal source of fresh water for the inhabitants of Portwrinkle until modern times. Mrs Margaret Bartlett remembers that water from it was piped to 'The Chalet' when she and her husband looked after the property just after the Second World War. When Richard Carew drew up the Agreement for making the quay at Portwrinkle in 1612, he probably had in mind this well when he included the clause 'Lyberty to carry Fresh Water'.[46]

25 *Blizer's Well, on the ancient demesne farm of Blazor, was once the main source of water for the residents of Portwrinkle. It lies on the south side of the lane leading up to Crafthole.*

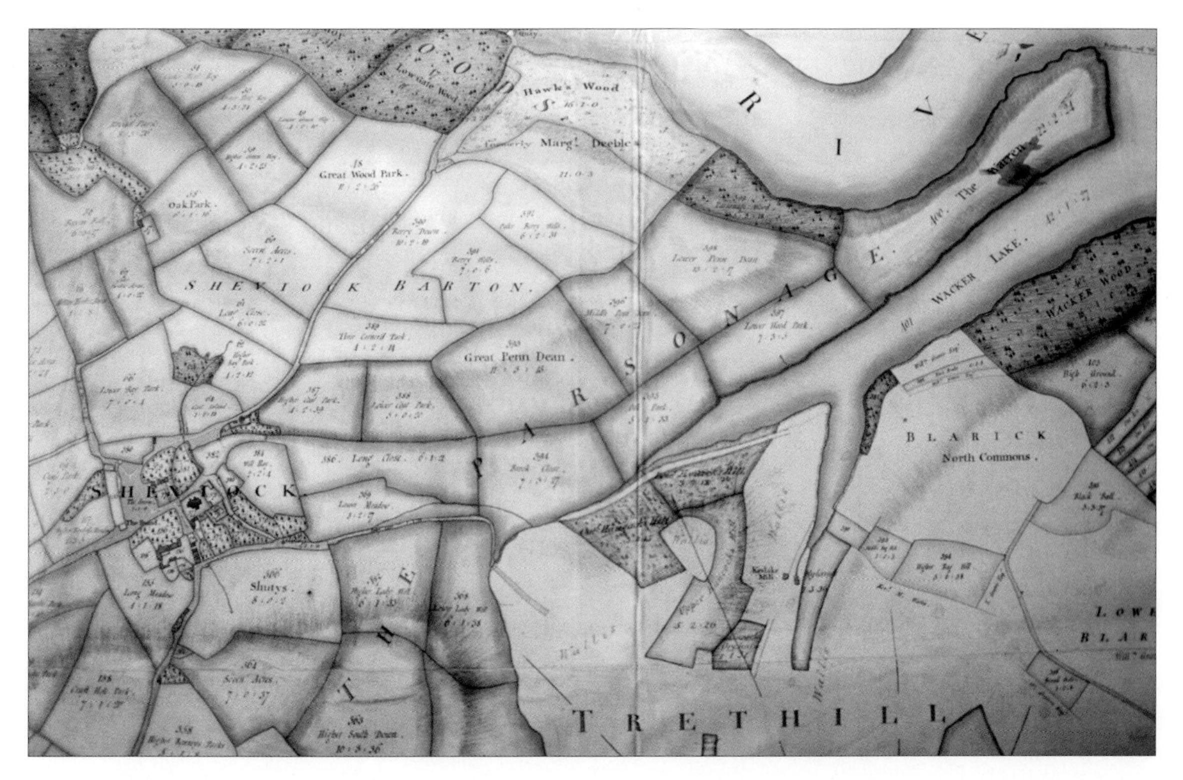

26 *North-eastern part of the manor of Sheviock (from Thomas Pride's map of 1775).*

Sheviock Barton

The word 'barton' comes from the Anglo-Saxon *bere-tun*, meaning enclosure for barley.[47] Over time these large enclosures became particularly associated with manorial establishments, and so the word barton came to mean especially the farm place of a manor. Sheviock Barton has always been the most productive demesne farm of Sheviock manor. When Domesday Book stated that 'In demesne are two ploughs and four slaves', probably all of them were housed at the farm that became known as Sheviock Barton. With the departure of the Courtenays for Tiverton, Sheviock Barton was also let to tenants. It is probable that the farmer there from Michaelmas 1410 to Michaelmas 1411 was one Ralph Icory. An account of the tithe of sheaves in that year shows that Ralph's sheathes fetched 70s., the highest amount in the parish.[48]

From 1540, when Henry VIII separated the manor of Sheviock from the borough of Crafthole, the courts of the manor of Sheviock were probably moved from the old Dawney manor-house at Blazor (modern Crafthole) to Sheviock Barton. When Thomas Carew purchased the manor of Sheviock from Sir Walter Mildmay in 1558, Sheviock Barton was most likely already established as the usual venue for holding the courts of the manor of Sheviock.[49]

27 *Sheviock Barton, once the principal demesne farm of the manor, now provides bed and breakfast accommodation for visitors to Cornwall.*

In the early 1600s, a John and Joan 'Hitchens' were farming at the Barton. John was dead by 1613, when his widow, Joan, took over Cote and Crafthole Parks. Among their children were another Joan, William and Ralph. In 1617, Richard Carew let 'all that Capital Messuage Barton mansion house … together with two Closes of Land called Berry Downe and Berry Wells' to Willyam 'Hichins' (William Hitchens), John's son.[50] The lives named were William, his wife, Agnes, and their son, John. In 1620, the lives of two other children, William and Ursula, were added to John's in place of Agnes, who had presumably died. The holding consisted of 60 acres of land. The rent was £4 and 2 capons (or 2s.) a year, the most expensive holding on the manor.[51] William the elder, who was described in a later lease as a 'merchant', also owned Sheviock's deep-sea fishing vessel, the *Dayestarr*. He died in 1635 and passed the tenancy to his son, John.[52]

John, who was farming at Crafthole Parks as well as Sheviock Barton, died in 1648. A copy of the inventory made in connection with his will is held in the Cornwall Record Office. His lease of the Barton, which was 'determinable on the death of his sister, Ursula Dewstowe' was valued at £120, and his lease of Crafthole Parks was valued at £6. In 1653, at the age of 32, another John 'Hichen' became tenant of Sheviock Barton.[53] Nicholas Smyth, presumably of the Liscawn family, succeeded him. In 1661, Sir John Carew let the Barton, Berry Down and Berry Wells to John Wallis of Sconner and William Hitchins of Sheviock, both described as gentlemen.[54] The consideration was £280. In 1676, Joan Hitchins married the rector of Sheviock, Richard Rolle.

In 1691, Ferdinando Spiller, his wife, Margery, and John Deeble were the tenants of the 60 acres of Berry Wells and Berry Down.[55] The rent was £4 as before. In 1718, Sir William Carew let Sheviock Barton and its fields to Hugh Littleton of St Germans, yeoman.[56] The lives named were Hugh and his sons, Hugh and Thomas. Hugh (the son probably), was paying the church rate (7s. 3d.) for Sheviock Barton in 1748.[57] The occupant of the Barton and Gill Ball in 1770 was also Hugh Littleton, who was paying the old rent.[58] From 1809 to 1832, John Trevan was the farmer. John Liscombe succeeded him in 1833-4, and Trevan moved to Cote and Hawkeswood. He was also farming Vellands Tenement in 1840. From 1858 to 1861, John Sherwill was the occupant of the Barton. In 1871, Nicholas Roseveare junior was the farmer. His father, Nicholas senior, was farming at Tredrossell. J. Matthews was farming at the Barton from 1895 to 1899. Thomas Edgar Bersey was the farmer of about 100 acres at Sheviock Barton from 1921 until 1952. In his day, 71 per cent of the land was used for arable farming, 24 per cent for pasturage, and five per cent for orchards. He was succeeded by his son, Thomas (Tom) Bennett Bersey in 1953. By the end of Tom's tenure in 1991, 80 per cent of this land was arable, 20 per cent was pasture, and there were no orchards at all. In his 1966 lease, a holding called 'Cross' and the former Glebe lands were added to his tenancy, making 231 acres in all.

28 *Berry Down, anciently the principal field of the manor (top) and Great Pendeen, formerly a field of the parson's glebe (bottom of facing slope), seen from the fields at Trethill.*

29 *The last surviving section of the Dawneys' barn. Engraving from Gilbert's* Historical Survey of the County of Cornwall, *vol. 2 (1820).*

The Dawneys' Barn

To preserve the crops during the winter, farmers need weatherproof barns. The earliest-known one in the parish is the Dawneys' legendary barn, probably erected in the early 1300s. The enormous size of the building, which became a subject of village gossip, was most likely connected with the foundation of Crafthole in 1314. That foundation meant that there were many more mouths to feed – perhaps a hundred additional inhabitants – so that a huge granary would have been a necessity. The village gossip about the barn was transmitted orally down the ages until recorded by Carew. He wrote that

> There runneth … a tale amongst the parishioners, how one of these Dannyes ancestours undertook to build the Church and his wife the barne adjoyning, and that casting up their accounts, upon finishing of their workes, the barne was found to cost three halfepence more than the Church: and so it might well fall out for it is a great barne, and a little Church.[59]

The builder, or rather re-builder, of the church may have been the pious Sir Nicholas Dawney, who is known to have gone on two pilgrimages. The style of the re-built church also supports an early 14th-century date. Sir Nicholas's wife was Joan Langdon.[60] The barn said to have been built by her was in continuous use until the 19th century. At his death in 1648, John Hitchens, farming at Sheviock Barton, left 'wheat, barley, pease & oates' valued at £100, nearly as much as the value of his livestock. No doubt most of these crops were stored in the great barn. He also left 'plow stuffe', the implements for tilling the fields, valued at £3. The barn, like most buildings in the parish at the time was thatched with reed, as shown in the engraving of the much reduced building published in 1820 in C.S.Gilbert's *Historical Survey of the County of Cornwall.* According to Gilbert, 'More than half of the Tithe barn, spoken of by Carew, is … taken down;

30 *The Dawneys' barn: the gable end before it fell in 1938.*

31 *The Dawneys' barn: the restored and shortened gable end, 1938.*

but the remaining part shows it to have been of an immense size.'[61] The Revd H.C. Glanville told the story of the eventual demise of the surviving half of the barn in his preface to the Sheviock churchwardens' accounts, written in August 1899:

> The roof of the Dawneys' barn fell in about 1836 or 1837 in the month of November. It was a thatched roof and very heavy with thatch and timber and the men were at work in the barn when it fell in and had only just time to make their escape. It was then the barn of the Barton Farm and was never re-roofed.

The south wall of the barn remained standing until 1938. The story of its collapse and reconstruction is told on a plaque fixed to the wall: 'This remaining wall/ XIV cent. tithe barn/ collapsed Feb. 1938/ erected with same stone. March 1938 J.C.P.' The initials, J.C.P., stand for Sir John Carew Pole. A new and sizeable barn was built at Sheviock Barton in 1837. A stone cross was inset into the outer wall of the barn on a north-facing aperture. In the centre appears the date and on the four arms, beginning at the top and proceeding clockwise, are the initials WP, ICWD, IW and IH. The initials may be those of the men who escaped with their lives when the roof of the old barn collapsed.

32 *The new barn that replaced the Dawneys' barn c.1837.*

Haye Farm (also Hay)

The tenement called Haye was carved out of Sheviock woods sometime before 1600. It was divided into two main parts, each consisting of 50 acres.[62] Amos Odiorne was farming one part of Haye in the early 1600s, and has left his name in the field called 'Addyams'. He married Thomasine Symons in 1611 and died in 1645. In 1653, the holding was let to his widow, aged 70, on the lives of Robert Warren and his mother.[63] The rent was £1 13s. 4d. and two capons, or 2s. Amos and Thomasine had at least two sons, William and Isaiah. In 1654, William (58) and his son, Henry (18), held one part of Haye.[64] Henry was assessed for two hearths in the hearth tax return of 1664. According to the collector, Henry 'returned two short whereof one is a kiln'. This was presumably a limekiln and is the first reference to lime being burned in the parish. The limekiln may have been the one that became attached to the neighbouring Sconner farm in 1696, or another one that has now disappeared. No further mention is made of a limekiln at Haye. Henry was still listed as tenant of the holding of Haye in 1689-90, when he was reeve of the manor.[65] He was no longer tenant in 1691, when Robert Warren was farming half of Haye. From 1694 to 1696, Henry Spiller was the tenant of 'the two Hay Tenements'. He was paid for 'Repairs of Hay-Tenements' in August 1694 and again the following February.[66] In 1703, the tenant of 'the two Hayes Tenements in Sheviock' and of Poole was Robert Harry.[67]

33 *Haye Farmhouse, an 18th-century barn conversion.*

There was originally no farmhouse at Haye. Henry Odiorne may have lived at Higher Clicker.[68] John Littleton, who also leased Gill Ball, was leasing Haye from 1731 until his death in 1735. He lived at Trewin. Though there was no farmhouse at Haye, there was a barn. The barn was thatched and, in January 1732, John Littleton was paid 6s. 8d. 'for 40 sheavs of reed used for thetching the Hay at Sheviock'.[69] A 1767 lease of Blake's wood in Sheviock to John Lyne, who had previously lived at Winnard in St John, describes him as 'now of the Barton of Hay in the parish of Sheviock'.[70] A report prepared for Reginald Pole Carew in 1832 stated that

> Previous to Mr John Lyne's coming into the parish of Sheviocke, the farm of Hay had no house upon it, but had been rented with the Barton of Sheviocke by one of the family of Littleton, it was in fact what is termed an overland tenement. Mr Lyne converted a barn or chall into the present house, on receiving assistance from his landlord.[71]

John Lyne died in June 1771 and was succeeded by his eldest son, John. This John died in 1782 and was succeeded by his brother-in-law, Robert Warren. Warren was also the tenant of part of Blazor from 1809 to 1821. He died in 1832, when the tenancy went to Thomas Every (also spelled Avery). From 1858 to 1861, the tenant was George Haimes, a former gamekeeper.

Livestock on Sheviock Barton and Haye

The inventory of goods of the farmer at Sheviock Barton, John Hitchens, who died in 1648, includes 'oxen, kine [cows for milking], steeres, calves, sheepe, lambes, horses, coltes, hogges, & pullen [poultry]', valued at £102 15s. An account of Sir Coventry Carew's livestock on the Barton and adjoining lands, dated 14 November 1744, shows 14 bullocks, ten 'plow oxen and milch cowes', one bull, four 'fatt oxen', two 'fatt cowes', and four calves.[72] In addition there were six bullocks on the Barton of Haye. On Sheviock Barton, there were 28 pigs. In addition, there were 29 'sheep that are feedinge', and 82 'younge sheep', making 111 in all. There were another 28 sheep belonging to Sir Coventry elsewhere in Sheviock.

Pryor's Wood (and part of Haye)

The Priory of St Germans came into possession of the 15 acres of 'Heywode', part of Sheviock woods, in the 13th century.[73] When Henry VIII dissolved the priory in 1539, he took possession of Hayewood and passed it on to his successors. Queen Elizabeth passed it to her favourite, Robert Dudley, Earl of Leicester in April 1574. A month later he sold 'Skonner and Haywood' to Sir Henry Killigrew. Killigrew in turn sold the properties to John Eliot of Port Eliot. John Eliot sold them to Richard Carew the younger in June 1617 for the sum of £50.[74] Sconner farm and limekiln seem to have been included in the properties conveyed.[75] A survey of the manor of Sheviock made in 1691 shows Philip and Anthony Blake as the tenants of the 15 acres of Pryor's Wood, and what are presumed to be another 15 acres of Haye, for the lives of Henry Blake and Anne (Blake) Dodridge.[76] Philip was Anthony Blake's nephew.

Gill (Gilly) Ball

This tenement of five acres near Sheviock woods was originally created to form the site of a windmill.[77] By 1663, the mill had gone and the field was let to Richard Holman (age 50), a farmer at Trewrickle, at a rental of 3s. 4d.[78] In 1693, John Bloye paid £30 for a 99-year lease of Gill Ball.[79] Phillip Bloye took over the lease, which he surrendered to Sir William Carew in 1713. This was part of the consideration for the grant of a new lease at the same rent to Bloye's son-in-law, John Littleton. Littleton had married Dorothy Bloye.[80] Littleton's 'fine' for the new lease included a golden guinea valued at £1 1s. 6d., payable to Lady Anne Carew, Sir William's new wife.

Littleton was still the tenant in 1726.[81] The field later became part of the farm of Sheviock Barton. 'Gill Ball' is also the name of part of Sheviock woods.

Treise's Tenement

The farmhouse belonging to this tenement is in Sheviock churchtown.[82] It was previously known as 'Blake's tenement'. The Blakes had been farming it since the reign of Queen Elizabeth.[83] Philip Blake (1604-89) was the tenant in 1653 at a rental of £2 0s. 7d.[84] His eldest son, John, was probably living and farming there in the 1660s and 1670s. Another Philip Blake, probably his grandson, was farming there in 1690.[85] The farmhouse still stands and is now known as Orchard Cottage. The farmland covered an area of 55 acres and is marked on Thomas Pride's plan of the manor of Sheviock of 1775, and the accompanying survey.[86] The name 'Treise's' refers to John Treis, steward to Sir John Carew. In 1690, Sir John granted him a lease in Sheviock 'for and in consideration of the good Services which he … hath done and shall doe [for] the said Sir John'.[87] The tenement was the one 'lying and being in Sheviock Church-towne … late in the tenure of Phillip Blake gent deceased & Grace Blake widdow.' In 1698, the trustees of Sir John Carew leased the tenement to John Bloye of Sheviock for a consideration of £380.[88] The rent was as before. The lives named were John Bloye's sons, Nicholas, Phillip and Richard. In 1721, Thomas Ellery was listed as the sole tenant.[89] Philip Palmer took over the tenancy in 1726, at the same rent, and was also tenant of Bailiff's Meadow in Sheviock, for a rent of 11s. 4d.[90] In 1733, Sir William Carew let Treise's tenement to Hugh Littleton, described as a 'yeoman' of Sheviock, for a consideration of £400.[91] The lives named were his sons, Hugh, Thomas and John. In 1746, Sir Coventry Carew issued a new lease to another Hugh Littleton, described as 'of St Germans Gentleman', for a consideration of £68 10s.[92] The tenancy was to commence on the death of the first Hugh's sons. The new lease was on the lives of the lessee and Joan Short, daughter of Henry Short of St Germans, yeoman. She was then aged 24 and shortly afterwards married Hugh Littleton. In 1766, John Carew issued a new lease of Treise's tenement to his steward, James Corinton of East Antony, on the life of Mrs Mary Carew.[93] The new tenancy was to commence on the death of Hugh and Joan Littleton.

Hugh Littleton had moved into Sheviock Barton by 1766.[94] He is listed as farming the 70 acres of Sheviock Barton, Berry Down and Berry Wells in a rental of 1770 and another rental of 1772.[95] Now that the same farmer was farming two adjacent farms, it was possible to let one of the farmhouses as a dwelling with a garden and orchards, but no farmland. The farmland of Treise's tenement, which in any case was not adjacent to the farmhouse, was from then onwards removed from it and incorporated into the farmland of the Barton. Because of the distance of its fields from Treise's farmhouse, a separate barn was built in the middle of Treise's fields.

Bailiff's Meadow

Bailiff's Meadow and Higher Bailiff's Meadow near Sheviock churchtown were usually (until about 1760) let to the bailiffs employed by the lords of Sheviock manor. The occupier of Bailiff's Meadow in 1607, the year of his death, was Ferdinando Spiller, who operated the windmill at Gill Ball and ran one of the inns at Crafthole. His occupancy of this holding and the manorial windmill at Gill Ball suggests that he was bailiff of the manor. The holding then consisted of a cottage and the meadowland. In his will, Ferdinando left the holding to his wife, and after her death to their son, William. The rent for the holding was 10s. and two hens (or 1s. 4d.).[96] His grandson, William, was probably the 'Spiller' mentioned in a rental of 1634 as paying a rent of 10s. to the manor.[97]

In 1663, the holding was let to Phillip Blake, bailiff to 1690, and his cousin, Oliver Grills.[98] Before 1691, the property was let to Richard Bloye. In 1691, it was let to Phillip Bloye and Philip Palmer.[99] In 1693, John Bloye paid £65 10s. for a 99-year lease of the meadow and another £30 for a lease of Gill Ball.[100] Sir William Carew let the holding to Phillip Bloye, in 1712, as from the death of Richard Bloye.[101] The 'fine' included a golden guinea worth £1 1s. 6d, payable to Lady Anne Carew. The lives named were Elizabeth Bloye 'widow' (Richard's wife) and Catherine Spiller 'spinster', who probably married Philip Bloye. The witnesses were Richard Bloye the younger and Samuell Spiller. These leases suggest that Richard and Phillip Bloye were also bailiffs of the manor.[102] In 1726, the meadow alone was let to Philip Palmer, who was bailiff in 1725.[103]

The cottage, 'late Palmers', was let to Walter Waring (Warren) for 2s. At this time, Palmer had moved into Treise's farmhouse.[104] In 1740, Sir William let the meadow to Philip Palmer, as from the death of Catherine Bloye, widow.[105] In 1757, Elizabeth Palmer was lessee of the meadow. The lives named were her own (she was then 26) and those of Thomas Littleton (aged nine) and Philip Palmer, perhaps a nephew (aged four). In about 1760, Elizabeth married Revd Mydhope Wallis, who had inherited the Trethill estate in that year. Wallis was churchwarden of Sheviock in 1762-3 and curate from 1766 until 1774. In the latter year he was again listed as the tenant of a 'house and garden' in Sheviock and Bailiff's Meadow. Elizabeth died before 1780. In that year, Revd Wallis surrendered Elizabeth's old lease of 1757 and Reginald Pole Carew granted him a new one on the lives of Thomas Littleton, Philip Palmer and his own daughter, Ann (age 12).[106] In the 1800s, the meadow, by then divided into two fields, was attached to the inn, the *Carew Arms*.

The Manor Pound

The bailiff and reeve of the manor were responsible for rounding up stray animals and feeding them while they were in their charge. The lord had a right to 'waiffs &

straies' and so owners had to pay a fine to him for their release.[107] While they were in the bailiff's custody, the animals were kept in a square enclosure called the pound. The bailiff, Thomas Harvey, claimed 5s. 'for charge of ye two pigs Brought to ye Mannor pound' in 1692.[108]

The walls of the pound had to be maintained, and in 1692 the reeve, Tristram Harry, paid the mason, Mathew Stanton, 6s. 'for 2 dayes on the mannor pound him selfe his sonn and sarvant as [appears] by his Rect.'[109] In 1726, the mason, William Foard (also Ford), rebuilt the pound at a cost of £3 15s. 9d. for the building and 11s. 4d. for carrying the stones from the quarry.[110] The new pound was located to the west of Sheviock village green on the road from Sheviock to Polbathic (the modern Horsepool Road). It stood to the west of Cote Park House, which was built in 1838 on the site of the village green. The pound is marked on Thomas Pride's map of 1775 and on a plan drawn in 1838 on a lease of Catherine Serpell's house in Sheviock churchtown.[111] In about 1900, the carpenter, George May, built a workshop on top of the pound, taking advantage of the stout walls.[112] Except for one corner, the pound was demolished in 1970 to make way for Henry and Connie Pryn's house, called Marconhest.

Manorial Mills. See Chapter 42, *Mills and Millers.*

34 *The pound at Antony. The similar one in Sheviock stood near the east end of Horsepool Lane.*

Chapter 5

Lords of the Manor

*(Arranged chronologically. Royal and Commonwealth periods of ownership are excluded. Cross-references within this chapter are indicated by **heavy type**)*

The Dawneys (Lords of the Manor, c.1082 to 1346)

The Dawney coat of arms is 'argent, on a bend, cotised, sable, three annulets of the field'. The coat of arms was still visible on Emmeline Dawney's tomb in Sheviock church in the 1700s.[1]

The name Dawney, which is also spelled Dawnay, Daunay, Dauny, and Dauney, is a corruption of D'Aunay (in Latin *de Alneto*). The Viscounts Downe, who are descendants of this family, use the spelling 'Dawnay', which must therefore be presumed to be the correct spelling.[2] There are two places in Normandy called Aunay: Aunay-sur-Odon, south-west of Caen; and Aunay-le-Faucon, on the river Orne near Argentan.[3] The family are thought to have come from one of these two places, and to have arrived in England at the time of the Norman Conquest. According to Lake, 'Sir Payn D'Aunay of D'Auney Castle, in Normandy, came in with the Conqueror'.[4]

Erbenald (or Ermenhald)

Domesday Book (1086) states that 'Eccl[esi]a de Tavesoch ten[et] Savioch. [et] Ermenhald de ea.' This means that the church of Tavistock holds Sheviock, and Ermenhald holds it as a sub-tenant of the church. Erbenald may have been a son of the Sir Payn mentioned in Lake.[5] It is only through a later charter that the descent of the Dawneys from Erbenald is established. A charter executed by one of Erbenald's descendants, **Henry Dawney**, sometime between 1174 and 1206 reads in translation:[6]

> I, Henry Dawney, give absolutely and irrevocably, on behalf of myself and my heirs, to God and St Mary and St Rumon and to Tavistock Abbey, that land at Trewikkel [i.e. Trewrickel] which Erbenaldus and Deintedosa, *my ancestors*, gave free and clear of all lay or royal services to the monastery at Tavistock.

35 *Ring of Richard the Lionheart, presented to Sir William Dawney* c.*1192. This is a modern replica of the original, which is still kept by the family.*

Erbenaldus and Deintedosa were most probably man and wife. In return for his military services, Erbenald was granted 'the honour of Sheviock', a group of manors that constituted a single large feudal holding. It consisted of the six Cornish manors of Sheviock, Rame, Antony, Penharget in St Ive, Tolcarne in North Hill, and Trewornan in St Minver.[7] Erbenald established himself and his family at Sheviock, the seat of his honour.

Herbert Dawney

Son of the above (d.1129/30).[8]

Richard Dawney

Son of the above, held four knights fees under the Abbot of Tavistock in 1166.[9]

Sir William Dawney I

According to Lake,

> Sir Wm D'Aunay was made a general at Acon, now Acre, 4 Richard I, 1192. Having slain a Saracen prince, and afterwards killing a lion, he cut off its paw, and presented it to the king, who in token of approbation took the ring off his finger and presented it to the knight, and ordered that he should bear as his crest a *demi-Saracen with a lion's paw in one hand and a ring in the other*; the family crest to the present day. The ring is still preserved.[10]

Henry Dawney I

Executed a number of charters in relation to his lands in Sheviock between 1174 and 1206.

Henry Dawney II (fl. *c.*1260)

Nicholas de la Pole granted to him all the land of *La Pole et Lanpilot*, for which he was to render 12d. at Michaelmas to Sir Bernard de Bodbran for all service, except Royal service, belonging to land in Sheviock.[11] Henry was probably the lord when Bishop Bronescombe dedicated the altar of Sheviock church in October 1259.

William Dawney II (after 1260-1280)

He held land in Sheviock and St John. It was he who granted Tredrossel from the manor of Sheviock to Warrin de Herth, on the latter's marriage to William's daughter, Elena (see below). In 1278, he presented William de Halton as rector of Sheviock. In 1292, the Abbot of Tavistock carried goods away from the house of his widow, Elizabeth, in pursuit of a claim.[12]

William Dawney III (to *c*.1286)
The son of **William II** and Elizabeth, he died young, leaving his son, **Nicholas**, as a minor. This was to lead to litigation about the advowson of the church of Sheviock. In 1286, he settled a dispute with his brother-in-law, Warrin de Herth, about the lands granted to Warrin on marriage to his sister, and about his own right to use water from those lands to drive his mill at Polscoe.[13]

Sir Nicholas Dawney (*c*.1280-1332)
The son of **William III**, he was said by Lake to be a descendant of **Sir William Dawney I**. He had two sons, **John** and Thomas.[14] He married Joan, daughter of Walter Langdon, and in 1330 presented John de Langdon as rector of Sheviock. In a list of Feudal Aids dated 1303, he is shown as liable for the provision of a man-at-arms on account of his holding in Saviek, another for Tregantel (acquired from the Valletort family), as well as one for the three manors of Trecara (Tolcarne in North Hill), Trelurnal (Trewornan in St Minver) and Cherlenton (Penharget in St Ive). Another knight, John of Rame, also held a knight's fee in Rame under Sheviock. According to the Calendars of Patent Rolls, Nicholas went on a pilgrimage to Jerusalem in 1309, and may have fought against the Moors.[15] In 1312, he was granted a right of free warren over his land – that is a right to hunt with hawk and hounds. In 1313, he went on another pilgrimage, this time to Santiago de Compostela. He and his wife, Joan, were probably the founders of St Nicholas's chapel in West Looe.

In 1314, he founded the borough of Crafthole and Edward II granted him and his heirs the right to hold a weekly market (later two) in Croftilberwe (Crafthole) in his manor of Sheviock, and also an annual fair. In 1317, he was ordered to requisition a ship and crew from Exeter, Sutton, Plymouth, Looe, Fowey or Bridgwater and join Geoffrey de Modesworth in capturing the Scottish pirate, John Dun, and his crew. He was a loyal supporter of Edward II and in 1321 the king's enemies, Queen Isabella and Roger Mortimer, Earl of March, exiled him abroad together with Hugh Despenser the elder.[16] He returned home a year or so later and in 1324 he was put on a Commission of Array for Devon, to recruit soldiers for the king. He held the manors of Godryngton (Goodrington), Norton, Cornwode and other estates in that county. In 1330, he was arrested for his support of the Duke of Kent, the late king's brother, against Isabella. He died in 1332.[17]

Sir John Dawney (1302-46)
The elder son of **Sir Nicholas** and Joan, he married Sibella Treverbyn sometime before 1325, and had a daughter, **Emmeline**. In that year, Edward II confirmed the charter of West Looe and named Sibella (one of the co-heiresses of Odo de Treverbyn) and Sibella's husband, Sir John Dawney, as co-owners of the borough.[18]

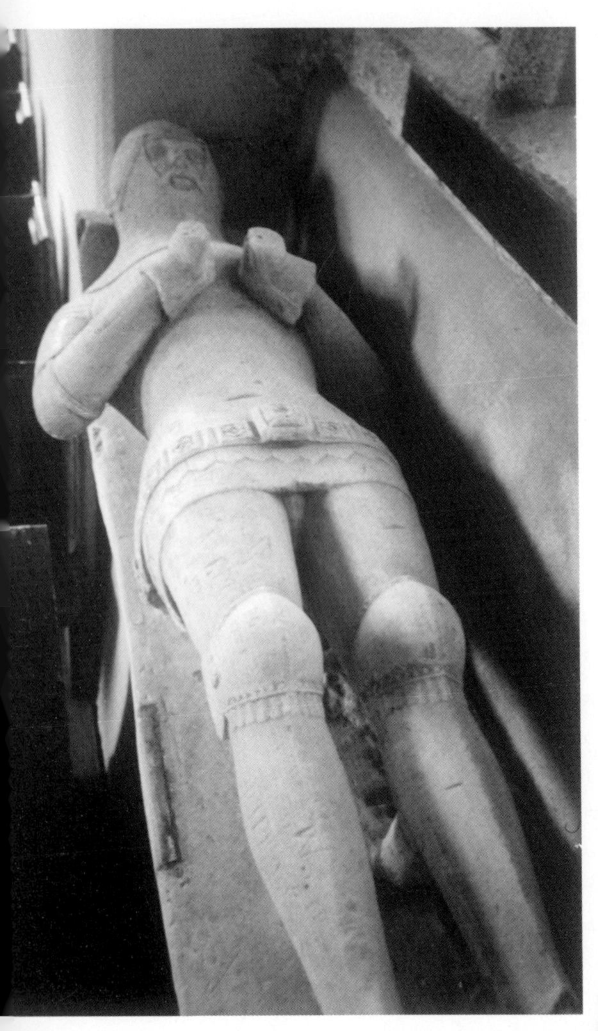

36 *Effigy of Sir John Dawney (1302-46), erected c.1378.*

Through Sibella, Sir John also acquired the manor of Treverbyn, a Domesday manor in the parish of St Austell, and the manor of Porthloo [West Looe] and the borough within it, called Porthpighan, meaning 'the small port or landing place'. He held, besides Sheviock and the borough of Crafthole, the manors of 'Anton', Tregantel (originally a possession of the Valletort family), and Landulph. He had rents in Rame and St Erney and held the advowsons of Sheviock, Landulph and St John.[19] In 1331 and 1332, he went overseas in the service of Edward III. He received licence to crenellate his manor-house in the parish of Sheviock in 1336. Two years later, he was ordered with two others to array all men between Saltash and Fowey to resist a possible landing by the French. He was the last male member of his line to live at Sheviock. In 1341, he was caught in the company of the Abbots of Tavistock and Buckfast and others poaching on Dartmoor.[20] He died on active service in France in Edward III's great expedition of 1346-7. He was in the Prince of Wales's division. The army embarked at Portsmouth and landed in Normandy on 12 July 1346. The English captured Caen on 26 July and then marched eastwards. Sir John

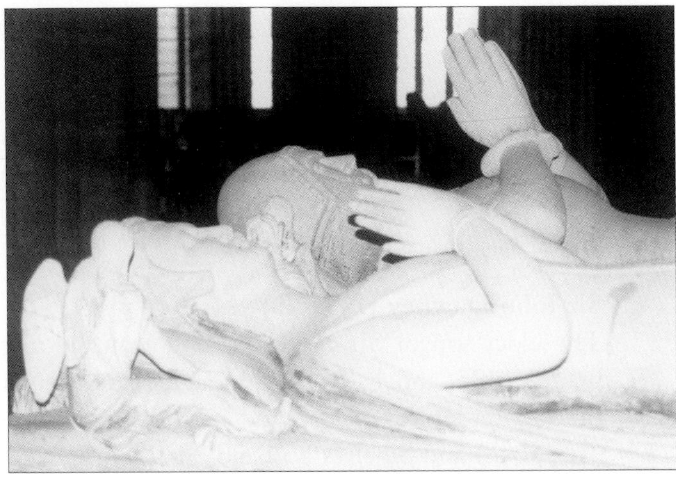

37 *Tomb of Hugh Courtenay (d.1377), Earl of Devon, and his wife, Margaret de Bohun, in Exeter Cathedral. Their third son, Sir Edward, married Emmeline Dawney.*

died 'on the Sunday next before the Feast of St Lawrence' (i.e. on 3 August), probably at Rumesnil where the Prince encamped. Sir John, therefore, did not take part in the battle of Crécy (26 August). Oral tradition, preserved by **Richard Carew** in his *Survey*, is that his body was brought back to Sheviock for burial. The effigy of a knight that lies in the north aisle of the church was probably erected as a memorial to him by his grandson, **Edward Courtenay**, third Earl of Devon. After Sir John's death, Sibella was settled on lands at 'Asglake', perhaps 'Fenton Oglake' at Sconner. She died in 1360 and was buried in the Greyfriars church at Bodmin.

38 *Stained glass windows in Sheviock Church. The window showing the Courtenay coat of arms dates from the 14th century.*

Emmeline Dawney (*c.*1328-70)

The daughter and heiress of **Sir John**, she married **Sir Edward Courtenay**, and thus carried the lordship of Sheviock into the family of the earls of Devon. Her effigy rests on her tomb in Sheviock church next to that of her husband.

THE COURTENAYS (LORDS OF THE MANOR, 1346 TO 1538) [21]

Courtenay is the family name of the earls of Devon. Hugh (died 1340), became the first Courtenay earl of Devon in *c.*1336. The Courtenay coat of arms is 'or, three torteaux gules'. Earl Hugh added a 'label of three points, azure', and this was the coat used by all his direct descendants. It is the coat displayed in a window in Sheviock church.[22] Today, the only visual reminders of the two centuries in which Sheviock belonged to the Courtenays are this piece of stained glass and the effigies of **Sir Edward Courtenay** and his wife, **Emmeline Dawney**, in St Mary's church.

39 *Effigy of Emmeline Courtenay, née Dawney (c.1328-70), erected c.1378.*

Hugh (d.1377), the second Courtenay earl and son of the first, married Margaret de Bohun, who was descended from the Plantagenet kings of England. Their magnificent tomb, featuring the swan badge of Bohun, is in Exeter Cathedral. Their sons were: (1) Sir Hugh (1327-74), who fought at the battle of Crécy in 1346 and was one of the first knights to become a member of the Order of the Garter. (He married Elizabeth de Brian of Tor-Brian. They had one son, Hugh, who died in 1374.) (2) Sir Thomas (d.1340), lord of South Pool, whose effigy, a cenotaph, is in the church there. (3) Sir Edward, who married **Emmeline Dawney** and lived in Sheviock. (Their son, **Edward**, became the third earl.) (4) William (1336-96), who became successively Bishop of Hereford, Bishop of London and Archbishop of Canterbury. As Bishop of London, he presided at a Convocation that met in 1376 to interrogate John Wycliffe. As Archbishop of Canterbury, he suppressed Wycliffite doctrines and procured an Act of Parliament for the imprisonment of heretics. (5) Sir John. (6) Sir Philip, who inherited Powderham Castle and 16 other manors from his mother, and is the ancestor of the present earls of Devon. (7) Sir Piers or Peter (d.1409), who was a noted warrior and fought with the Black Prince in Spain in 1366. He died unmarried and is buried in Exeter Cathedral. (8) Humphrey.

The Courtenay ownership of Sheviock manor and the borough of Crafthole falls into four periods: (1) 1346-1462; (2) 1463-66; (3) 1486-1538; (4) (Crafthole only) 1553-6. After 1538, the ownership of the borough of Crafthole was separated from ownership of the manor of Sheviock, and the borough alone was restored, for a brief period, to the earl of Devon. The Courtenays ceased to reside in the manor of Sheviock after Edward Courtenay succeeded to the earldom in 1377. Courtenay ownership of the manor coincided with two of the most disturbed centuries in English history. The Black Death occurred in 1348-9. The Hundred Years' War, the longest conflict in English history, started in 1337 and continued until the English were expelled from Gascony in 1453. The bloody civil wars, known as the Wars of the Roses, were fought between 1455 and 1485. Finally, the age of the Tudors, 1485-1603, was one of intense religious and political upheaval in which many of the most ancient medieval lineages were ousted from royal favour by those who could give more wholehearted support to the new monarchy and the new Reformed religion.

Unsurprisingly, the Courtenays had had little time to devote to the affairs of the parish during the most intense periods of medieval warfare. However, in the late 1300s, **Edward Courtenay**, the third earl (called 'the blind earl'), son of Emmeline, did adorn the two chapels in the church in which his parents and grandfather were commemorated. By 1485, the Wars of the Roses had caused the complete destruction of this senior line of the family. In 1486, Henry VII ennobled **Edward Courtenay**, the son of Sir Hugh of Ashwater and Boconnoc, and great-grandson of Emmeline Dawney, as the first of a new line of earls. His son, **William**, was the second earl of the new creation. In the early 1500s, his steward was John Kelleway, who is memorialised in the windows of St Neot. Kelleway was also responsible for the earl's manor of Sheviock. At the same time, Anthony Harry was the earl's bailiff there. Ralph Harys (or Harry) of Tiverton was one of the liveried retainers of William's son, **Henry Courtenay**, Marquis of Exeter (executed 1538). Ralph Harys was the glazier of St Neot's church in Cornwall, where he is commemorated in one of the windows, and he could also have been involved in the late medieval glazing of Sheviock's north aisle.

Even when not present themselves, the Courtenays had influence on the parish through the employment they provided. Some of this was hazardous, such as warfare and piracy. Sir Hugh Courtenay of Haccombe, younger son of Emmeline Dawney, and brother of the blind earl, had grown up in the manor house in Sheviock, at Blazor, and would have known many of the inhabitants. His son, Sir Hugh of Boconnoc, owned a carvel, *le Petir Courtenay* of Fowey. In 1461, he was charged with an act of piracy. John Blake was the ship's boatswain and Henry Bray and Walter Colle, clerk, were her victuallers, alongside one of Sir Hugh's sons, also called Hugh. Members of the Blake and Bray families were settled in Sheviock parish and were engaged in the Portwrinkle fishing business for many generations. Members of the Colle or Cole family were also settled in the parish. One of the windows in Sheviock church at one time contained the arms of Cole impaling Kingdon'.[23]

FIRST COURTENAY PERIOD, 1346 TO 1462

Sir Edward Courtenay (d.1372)

The third son of the second earl, he married **Emmeline**, daughter of **Sir John Dawney**, sometime between 1325 and 1350. Emmeline inherited the Dawney estates on the death of her father in 1346, and so brought Sheviock to the Courtenays. Sir Edward was said to be 'of Godlington', also 'Gotherington' in Devon. This is the modern Goodrington, between Paignton and Brixham. The manor was one of many that came to him as a result of his marriage to Emmeline. It seems first to have been acquired by his wife's grandfather, **Sir Nicholas Dawney**. Sir Edward is buried next to Emmeline in Sheviock church. The couple's sons included **Edward**, who succeeded as earl of Devon in 1377, and (Sir) Hugh of Haccombe.[24]

Edward, Earl of Devon (the 'Blind Earl') (*c*.1357-1419)

The eldest son of **Sir Edward Courtenay** and **Emmeline Dawney**, he became Earl of Devon in 1377, on the death of his grandfather. He took possession of his estates in 1378 after a minority of 14 months.[25] He went blind about the year 1400.[26] He married Matilda, daughter of Lord Camoys, and had by her three sons:

(1) Edward (died without issue 1419) went on a pilgrimage to Santiago de Compostela in 1412 and fought with Henry V at the battles of Harfleur and Agincourt (1415). In 1416, he was admiral of the western fleet and sailed to relieve Harfleur. He married Eleanor Mortimer, daughter of the earl of March. (2) **Hugh** succeeded his father as earl. (3) James covenanted to serve Henry VI for a year in France in 1428.

40 *Effigy of Sir Edward Courtenay (d.1372), erected c.1378.*

In 1377, Earl Edward served at sea for three months under John of Gaunt. In 1380, he served with the land forces for three months in France. Three years later, he was at sea again as admiral for the western parts. The following year, he was made Earl Marshal of England and joined in an expedition against the Scots. In 1387, he was one of three commanders of a fleet that defeated a combined French, Flemish and Spanish fleet. The English captured many prisoners and seized 19,000 tuns of wine, which they sold cheaply on their return to England. According to Cleaveland, their success in battle and generosity with the spoils 'begat so high an opinion of their worth in the minds of all men, that they became a subject of praise and admiration'.[27] He was known subsequently as 'the good earl'.

During the 1380s, the earl headed the commissions of the peace in Devon and Cornwall. He was summoned to all the Parliaments of Richard II, Henry IV and (until his death) Henry V, but did not attend in person after 1400. He died at Tiverton and was buried at Ford Abbey. At his death, he possessed three manors in Buckinghamshire;[28] three in Dorset, as well as the advowson of the Priory of Lodres;[29] five manors and two hundreds in Somerset;[30] one borough and one manor in the county of Southampton;[31] 34 manors and hundreds in Devon as well as one honour, two castles, one hamlet and five boroughs in that county.[32] Finally, he possessed 16 manors in Cornwall, inherited from his mother, Emmeline.[33]

Hugh (1389-1422)

The second son of **Edward, the blind earl**, he married Ann (d.1440), daughter of Richard, Lord Talbot, and sister of John, Earl of Shrewsbury. He succeeded his elder brother, Edward, as commander of the English fleet in 1418. He succeeded to the earldom in 1419. He led another expedition to France in 1420. Sir John Arundell of Trerice was in his retinue on that expedition. Although summoned to Parliament in 1420, he was rarely in England. He died very young, leaving an eight-year-old boy, **Thomas**, as his successor. Hugh, his second son, was grandfather to the earl, **Edward**, who was created the first of a new line of earls in 1486.

Thomas (1414-58)

He succeeded his father, **Hugh**, as earl, in 1422. For the first decade of his earldom he was a minor and he took possession of his entire estate only in 1441.[34] He married Margaret Beaufort. They had three sons, **Thomas II**, **Henry** and **John**, all of whom were supporters of the House of Lancaster in the Wars of the Roses (1455-85) and all of whom were executed or killed by the Yorkists. In 1430, he joined Henry VI in the expedition to France during which Henry was crowned King of France in Paris. In 1455, when the Duke of York was made Protector of the Realm, Thomas retired from court and moved back to Devonshire. He died at Abingdon Abbey when en route to rejoin Henry VI on his return to London following the dismissal of the Duke of York as Protector. He gave one portion of the revenues from the rectory of Tiverton towards the foundation, by Henry VI, of King's College, Cambridge.

Thomas II (1432-62)

He succeeded his father as earl in 1458. He was taken prisoner at the battle of Towton, attainted and executed at York in revenge for the previous execution of the Duke of York. On his attainder, the Courtenay lands and titles passed to King Edward IV.

THE YORKIST LORD OF THE MANOR

Neville, William, Earl of Kent (1462-3)

After the execution of **Thomas II**, Edward IV granted Sheviock, Antony and the borough of Crafthole to his uncle, William Neville, but Neville died in the following year. After Neville's death, the estates passed to the Bishop of Exeter and others for 12 years. On the death of Neville, the king also gave Sir Renfrid Arundell (d.1468) of Tremodret (in Roche) a financial interest of £40 in Sheviock and Antony, and the advowson of Antony.

SECOND COURTENAY PERIOD, 1463 TO 1466

Henry Courtenay (executed 1466)

He was the younger brother of **Thomas**. Some of his brother's lands were restored to him. In 1465, he joined the conspiracy of the earl of Warwick against Edward IV. He was attainted for treason at Salisbury and beheaded there in 1466.

John Courtenay (killed 1471)

The youngest of the three brothers, he was restored to the family honours at the restoration of Henry VI in 1470, but he forfeited them upon the return of Edward IV after the latter's victory at the Battle of Barnet, on 14 April 1471. He was killed at the Battle of Tewkesbury on 4 May in the same year.

THIRD COURTENAY PERIOD, 1486 TO 1538

Edward Courtenay (d.1509)

He was the son of Sir Hugh of Ashwater and Boconnoc, and great-grandson of **Emmeline Dawney**.[35] In 1483, he fled to Brittany to join Henry Tudor, Earl of Richmond. In his absence he was attainted and his lands and titles forfeited. He was with Henry Tudor when his army landed at Milford Haven and fought at the battle of Bosworth Field in 1485. The following year, the victorious king, Henry VII, created him Earl of Devon, the first of a new line, and returned his lands to him, including the manor and borough of Porthpighan (West Looe), the manor and advowson of Sheviock, and the borough of Crafthole. With his son, **William**, he helped to defend Exeter against the forces of Perkin Warbeck in 1497. He died in 1509 and was buried at Tiverton. The north aisle of Sheviock church was probably constructed during the reign of Henry VII or Henry VIII – the last 52 years in which the Courtenay earls were lords of Sheviock manor.

William Courtenay (d.1512)

He began his career as a loyal supporter of Henry VII and was made a knight of the Bath at the latter's coronation in 1485. With his father, he helped to hold Exeter for the king against the forces of Perkin Warbeck in 1497. But, by marrying Katherine, younger daughter of King Edward IV, and sister of Henry VII's own wife, Elizabeth of York, he incurred the suspicion of King Henry. In 1502, he was suspected of being involved with Edmund de la Pole, earl of Suffolk, in a conspiracy against the king. The latter escaped to Flanders to the court of his aunt, Margaret, Duchess of Burgundy. William was attainted and imprisoned in the Tower of London for the remaining seven years of Henry's reign. On the accession of Henry VIII, he was released and became a jousting companion of the young king. He was created Earl of Devon in 1511, but died of pleurisy at the king's palace at Greenwich in the following year, before his investiture had been completed. He was nevertheless buried in St Paul's Cathedral with the honours of an earl. He was succeeded by his son, **Henry**.

41 *Henry Courtenay, Marquis of Exeter (c.1496-1538).*

Henry Courtenay (*c.*1496-1538)

He succeeded his father as earl. He married (1) a daughter of John Grey, Viscount Lisle, and (2) Gertrude Blount, mother of **Edward**. As a young man he was a companion of his cousin, Henry VIII. In 1520, he was present at the king's famous meeting with Francis I of France at the field of the Cloth of Gold, where he jousted against the French king. In 1525, he was created Marquis of Exeter. In 1529, he subscribed to the 44 articles against Cardinal Wolsey and, in 1530, was a co-signatory of the letter to Pope Clement VII requesting that he ratify the king's divorce from Queen Katherine.

His second wife, Gertrude, was a reluctant sponsor at the confirmation of Anne Boleyn's daughter, Princess Elizabeth, in 1533. Her real sympathies lay with the former Queen, Katherine of Aragon, and the Princess Mary. She was so vociferous in her opinions that the king warned both her and her husband that 'they must not trip or vary for fear of losing their heads'.[36] In 1536, the marquis was one of the peers who condemned Anne Boleyn to death. In October the same year, the dukes of Norfolk and Suffolk were put in command of an army raised to suppress the Pilgrimage of Grace. Henry Courtenay joined the royal army with a powerful force of his own retainers. But he was undone the following year when another cousin of the king's, Reginald Pole, accepted a cardinal's hat from the Pope and published an intemperate tract condemning the king as a heretic and adulterer. The Pope instructed the cardinal to form a European alliance whose object would be to depose King Henry. Thomas Cromwell warned the king that the cardinal's mother, Lady Salisbury, and another of her sons, Henry Pole, Lord Montague, might unite with Courtenay and other conservatives against him. From then on their days were numbered. In November 1538, Courtenay was sent to the Tower accused of compassing the king's death and plotting to usurp the throne. Old charges, stemming from the actions of his servants in the West Country seven years earlier, were added to the new charges of treason.

According to the historian, Speed, the marquis was accused of saying,

> I like well the proceedings of Cardinal Pole, but I like not the proceedings of this realm; and I trust to see a change of the world: I trust once to have a fair day upon these knaves which rule about the king; I trust to give them a buffet one day.[37]

He was condemned and on 9 December he and Lord Montague were executed.[38] His wife was also imprisoned for a while, but lived on through the reigns of Edward VI and Queen Mary. She died in 1558, the last year of Queen Mary's reign, and as a good Catholic directed in her will that a *Dirige* and a trental of masses should be said or sung for her.[39]

The marquis took some interest in the affairs of Sheviock and his other Cornish manors. His leases in the manor are headed 'IHS'. A portrait of him may be included in the Harys window of St Neot's church, erected in about 1532.[40] The glazier of that church, Ralph Harys, was one of his retainers.

Fourth Courtenay Period, 1553 to 1556 (Borough of Crafthole only)

42 *Edward Courtenay, Earl of Devon (1526-56).*

Edward Courtenay (1526-56)

He was only 12 years old when his father was executed. He was nonetheless imprisoned in the Tower, where he remained throughout the remainder of the reign of Henry VIII and the entire reign of Edward VI, a total of 15 years. On the accession of Queen Mary in 1553, he was released and 'restored in blood'. He was created Earl of Devon, the first of the new line that still continues today.[41] The borough of Crafthole, but not the manor of Sheviock, was restored to him. A borough court was held in the name of Edward Earl of Devon in 1554.[42] When the marriage was agreed between Queen Mary and King Philip of Spain, the Duke of Suffolk, Sir Thomas Wyatt and Sir Peter Carew conspired in an uprising. Courtenay was one of the commanders in the City of London who opposed and defeated Wyatt in 1554. At the subsequent trial of the rebels, it was alleged that their plan was for the earl to marry the Princess Elizabeth. As a result, both he and the Princess were imprisoned in the Tower. However, on the scaffold Wyatt denied that the two of them were involved. In 1555, he was released and travelled to Padua where he died of a fever in 1556. There is a monument to him in St Anthony's church in Padua.

43 *Sir Walter Mildmay (1520-89), financier, Puritan and founder of Emmanuel College, Cambridge.*

THE PURITAN LORD OF THE MANOR

Mildmay, Sir Walter (1553-8)

Sir Walter Mildmay (1520-89) was the fourth and youngest son of Thomas Mildmay of Chelmsford. His father had made a large fortune as the Commissioner for receiving the monastic properties seized from the church by Henry VIII. Walter was educated at Christ's College, Cambridge, where he imbued strongly Calvinist principles. He left before taking his degree to become a student of law at Gray's Inn. He was employed by his father in the Court of Augmentations, set up to administer the confiscated monastic property. When that court was reconstituted in 1547, he was made one of its two surveyors-general. The new arms acquired by Mildmay in 1583 are 'argent, three lions rampant azure'. These arms are the source of those used by his foundation, Emmanuel College, Cambridge.

Mildmay married Mary, sister of Sir Francis Walsingham, in 1546. He was knighted by the young King Edward VI shortly after his accession on 28 January 1547. In September, he helped to prepare an inventory of the late King Henry's wardrobe and was appointed a Commissioner to report upon the Crown revenues. In 1548, he acted on commissions for the sale of former monastic lands and for the maintenance of such grammar schools as had belonged to the dissolved monasteries and chantries. For his services, he received many grants of land in Gloucestershire and Berkshire, some of which he exchanged for manors in Oxfordshire and Northamptonshire. He was granted the manor of Apethorpe, Northamptonshire, in 1552, and there he built his principal residence, Apethorpe Hall. He was elected MP to represent the county in January 1557. When in London, he lived in the parish of St Bartholomew the Great.

In 1550, Mildmay was directed to examine the accounts of the king's mints, and in the following year he superintended the establishment of a new mint at York. In 1552, he was put on a commission to recover the king's debts. Early in 1553, a commission was appointed with orders to collect from the parishes the gold and silver chalices, candlesticks and censers, leaving only one communion cup behind in each parish. Mildmay was the Commissioner in charge of this confiscation, and he was rewarded with the grant of the lordship of a number of manors, including Sheviock.[43] The grant did not include the borough of Crafthole, which remained a Crown property. The confiscation orders relating to church goods were rescinded by Queen Mary on her accession in July 1553. Mildmay lived quietly during the reign of the Catholic monarchs, but his financial acumen was too useful to be totally ignored. On 9 January 1558, he was appointed treasurer of the forces raised for the relief of Calais. But it was too late, for Calais had fallen to the French two days previously. Mildmay sold the manor of Sheviock to Thomas Carew of Antony in 1558.[44]

With the accession of Queen Elizabeth, in November 1558, Mildmay's influence grew. He was made treasurer of her household, and became a member of a committee to re-fill the empty exchequer. In December, he prepared a census of the farms of the royal revenues and rescinded Queen Mary's grants of land, some of which were for the maintenance of convents and monasteries.[45] In 1560, he was made responsible for issuing a new coinage. In 1566, he was appointed Chancellor of the Exchequer. As the brother-in-law of Sir Francis Walsingham, and the friend of William Cecil, Lord Burleigh, he was influential in the Privy Council and in Parliament. He used his influence to shield the Puritans from the attacks of the Bishops, and often urged the Queen to intervene on behalf of the Protestants in the Netherlands. In 1586, he went to Fotheringay to inform Mary, Queen of Scots, of her forthcoming trial, in which he took part as one of the special commissioners.

Mildmay used much of his fortune to support education. He was one of the original governors of Chelmsford School, founded in 1550-1. He gave an annuity of 52s. to Christ's Hospital in 1556. In 1569, he gave an annuity of £20 a year to his old college, Christ's, to be expended on a Greek lectureship, six scholarships and a 'preachership', which was to be filled by a fellow of the college. In 1583, he purchased the site of the dissolved house of the Dominicans or Black Friars in Cambridge, and obtained the Queen's licence to set up a new college. The new foundation, called Emmanuel, was opened in 1588. According to the biographer, Thomas Fuller, when Mildmay came to court after the college was opened, the Queen said to him, 'Sir Walter, I hear you have erected a Puritan foundation', to which Mildmay replied, 'No, madam; far be it from me to countenance anything contrary to your established laws; but I have set an acorn, which when it becomes an oak, God alone knows what will be the fruit thereof.'[46] He died at Hackney on 31 May 1589, and is buried in the church of St Bartholomew the Great in London beside his wife, who had died in 1576. A marble wall-monument commemorates them in the church and there are portraits of them at Emmanuel College. They left two sons and three daughters.

THE CAREWS (LORDS OF THE MANOR, 1558 TO 1771)

Caerau is the plural of the Welsh *caer*, meaning a wall, mound or fortress. '*Caerau*, by helpless foreign tongues pronounced Carew.' [47] The family were early established in Pembrokeshire at a place called Caerau, or the Camps. The arms of Carew are 'Or, three lions passant sable'.

Thomas Carew (1527-64)

He was the son of Sir Wymond Carew (d.1549) and Martha Denny, and great-grandson of Alexander Carew.[48] He married (1) Elizabeth Edgcumbe, daughter of Sir Richard Edgcumbe of Mount Edgcumbe in about 1552 and the couple had four children, Elizabeth, **Richard**, (Sir) Matthew, and (Sir) George. He married (2) Eleanor Strangeways. He was MP for Plymouth in 1554 and 1555. He inherited the manor of East Antony from his father, Sir Wymond.[49] He purchased the manor of Sheviock from **Sir Walter Mildmay** on 17 June 1558.[50]

Richard Carew (1555-1620)

He was the eldest son of **Thomas Carew** and Elizabeth Edgcumbe. His *Survey of Cornwall*, begun in 1586, but not published until 1602, was one of the first accounts of an English county combining contemporary, historical and topographical information. Though written in an agreeably direct and apparently artless style, it was in fact the product of a highly cultivated mind. As a result of his father's early death in 1564, Carew went up to Christ Church, Oxford, when he was only 11 years old. He was a younger contemporary of Sir Philip Sidney, with whom he engaged in a debate in the presence of the earls of Leicester and Warwick. In 1574, he studied law at the Middle Temple. Three years later, he married Juliana Arundell of Trerice. The couple had seven surviving children, (Sir) **Richard**, Gertrude, John, Hobye, Anne, George, and Wymond.

44 *Richard Carew (1555-1620), author of the* Survey of Cornwall.

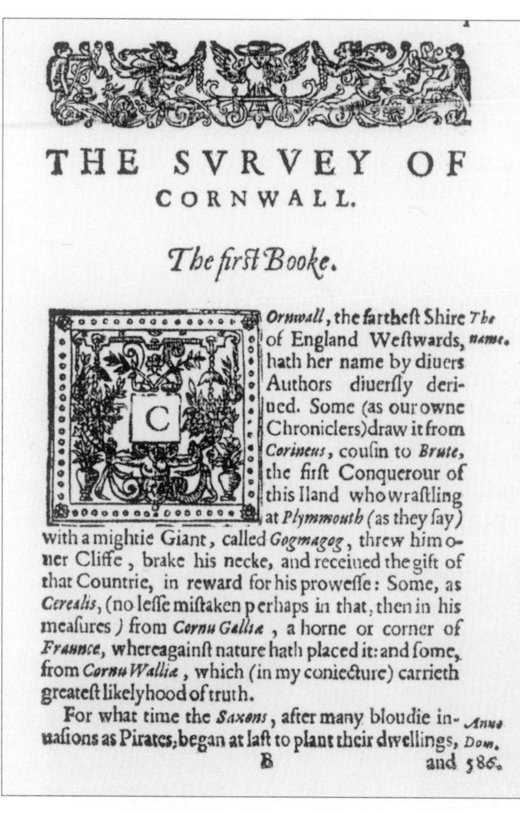

THE SVRVEY OF
CORNWALL.

The first Booke.

COrnwall, the fartheſt Shire of England Weſtwards, hath her name by diuers Authors diuerſly deriued. Some (as our owne Chroniclers) draw it from *Corineus*, couſin to *Brute*, the firſt Conquerour of this Iland who wraſtling at *Plymmouth* (as they ſay) with a mightie Giant, called *Gogmagog*, threw him ouer Cliffe, brake his necke, and receiued the gift of that Countrie, in reward for his proweſſe: Some, as *Cerealis*, (no leſſe miſtaken perhaps in that, then in his meaſures) from *Cornu Galliæ*, a horne or corner of *Fraunce*, whereagainſt nature hath placed it: and ſome, from *Cornu Walliæ*, which (in my coniecture) carrieth greateſt likelyhood of truth.

The name.

For what time the *Saxons*, after many bloudie inuaſions as Pirates, began at laſt to plant their dwellings,

Anno Dom. 586.

B

45 *Facsimile of first page of the* Survey of Cornwall, *published 1602.*

Richard Carew was appointed a JP in 1581, High Sheriff of Cornwall in 1582, MP in 1584 (for Saltash) and 1597 and a deputy lieutenant and militia captain in 1586. At the time of the Armada, he was in charge of 500 men and was responsible for the defence of Cawsand Bay. In his account of the invasion scares of 1588 and 1599, Carew was writing with the authority of an actual participant in the events described. He also wrote from first-hand knowledge on the agriculture and fishing of the county, the two industries upon which life in Antony and Sheviock were principally based. All subsequent accounts of the parish of Sheviock in county histories draw on his descriptions of Crafthole, Portwrinkle and Sheviock and his re-telling of the folk-tales about the Dawneys and their buildings. There is a portrait of him at Antony House. See further F.E Halliday, *Richard Carew of Antony – The Survey of Cornwall* (1953) and *A Cornish Chronicle* (1967). A facsimile edition of the *Survey*, with introductory essays, was published by the Devon and Cornwall Record Society in 2004.

Sir Richard Carew (1580-1643)

The son of **Richard Carew**, he was created a baronet in 1641. He entered Merton College, Oxford, in 1594 and three years later was admitted to the Middle Temple. He went on a diplomatic mission to Poland in 1588-9, also visiting Germany and Sweden, and to France in 1599-1600. In 1601, he married Bridget Chudleigh of Ashton in Devon, with whom he had six children. According to Halliday, he lived in the parish of Sheviock from about 1600 until he inherited Antony in 1620. In 1617, he acquired Sconner from Sir John Eliot and may have lived there before that time as a tenant.[51] He appears to have been the prime mover in the building of the quay at Portwrinkle, which was constructed some eleven months after Bridget's death in April 1611. In 1614, he was elected one of the two MPs for the county of Cornwall and in 1621 was returned for Mitchell. As an MP, he was ahead of his time in that he supported a total prohibition on tobacco imports. In 1622, he married Grace

Rolle, daughter of Robert Rolle of Heanton in Devonshire, with whom he had four more children, all sons. He developed marked Puritanical traits, living frugally and studying the Bible. Like his father, he was an expert naturalist. Instead of shooting pheasants, he tamed them, and he was regarded as 'the most excellent manager of bees in Cornwall'. He was an early advocate of conservation and warned against over fishing. He was a skilled horticulturist, and developed a method of propagating fruit-trees without grafting. He claimed to have planted 20,000, as well as giving thousands away. He gained a reputation for his herbal medicines and dietary advice. He advocated the use of 'warming-stones' for a variety of conditions and his book, *Excellent Helps by a Warming-Stone*, was published in 1640. It consists of case histories or testimonials of those whose conditions were said to have been improved by the use of the stone. Though mildly eccentric, his advice was often very sensible, as the following extract reveals:

> My house being a mile and a quarter from the Church, upon a Christmas day when the Wind blew cold, and there was a hard frost, I caused two of these stones to be heated for me at home, and so carried them to the Church, where putting the one under my feet, and my hands on the other, they kept me so warm in my seat from the beginning of Prayer, during the time of the Service, Sermon, and a long Communion, as I think I could not have been, by a great fire in my house.

He commenced writing his *Memoirs* in 1628.[52] See further F.E. Halliday, *A Cornish Chronicle* (1967).

Sir Alexander Carew (1609-44)

The son of the first baronet, he married Jane Rolle (1605-79), younger sister of his step-mother, Grace. They had eight children including **John**, who succeeded to the baronetcy.[53] Alexander was both a Puritan and a Parliamentarian. He was elected one of the county members for Cornwall in 1640, and voted for the attainder of Charles I's chief minister, the Earl of Strafford in 1641. He attempted to recruit soldiers in Cornwall under Parliament's Militia Ordinance in 1642. After Royalist successes in Cornwall early on in the Civil War he retreated to Plymouth, where he was made Governor of the strategically important St Nicholas (Drake) Island. After Royalist victories in 1643 at Stratton (16 May), Lansdown (5 July) and Bristol (26 July), he entered into a correspondence with Sir John Berkeley, leader of the king's forces besieging Exeter, with the alleged intention of surrendering the island to the king. However, a servant reported him to the Parliamentary authorities and Alexander was taken to London, tried, condemned and executed on 23 December 1644. He refused to admit his fault, declaring on the scaffold, 'All that you can lay to my charge is but intention, and no man knows my intentions better than myself, and they shall die with myself'. Before he died, he led those present in singing the 23rd Psalm, 'The Lord is my shepherd.' There is a fine portrait of this tragic figure at Antony House, reputedly painted on his 21st birthday. See further F.E. Halliday, *A Cornish Chronicle* (1967).

Sir John Carew (1635-92)

The son of **Sir Alexander**, he was ten years old when his father was executed. His body and lands came under the protection of the Duchy and then the Commonwealth until he came of age in 1656. He married first (before 1664) Sarah Hungerford (d.1671), by whom he had two daughters, Jane and Rachel. **Jane** married **Jonathan Rashleigh** of Menabilly and Rachel married Ambrose Manaton. Sir John married, secondly, Elizabeth Norton of Southwick, Hants (d.1679). He married for the last time Mary Morice of Werrington, Devon (d.1698), by whom he had two sons, **Richard** and **William**, and two daughters, Gertrude and Mary. He was MP for Cornwall in 1660 and 1689-90, for Bodmin (1661-79), Lostwithiel (1679-81) and Saltash (1690-92).[54] He was Stannator, Penwith and Kerrier, in 1686 and briefly High Sheriff of Cornwall in 1688.

In Parliament, his position shifted from early support for the Whigs to support for the Tories from 1691. Shortly before his death, he joined with others to build two ships to trade from Cornwall to India independently of the East India Company. In his will, he left £100 to be invested by the corporation of Saltash for the use of the poor. The trustees of his estate were his widow, Lady Mary, her uncle, Nicholas Morice, Hugh Boscawen and Jonathan Rashleigh.

Sir Richard Carew (1683-1703)

Sir John's eldest son, Richard, became the fourth baronet on his father's death. He was first educated locally by the rector of St John, the Revd Robert Eare.[55] The Revd Eare was probably dead before 1710, in which year Mrs Honor Eare, probably his widow, was renting premises in Sheviock (probably in Portwrinkle) for 5s. a year.[56] In 1695, Sir Richard was enrolled at Winchester College, and his mother moved to London, perhaps to be near him. The steward, John Treis, delivered five guineas to 'pars[on] Kendall on Sr Richard's Account going to Winchest'.[57] He may have been in London with his mother when he died.

Sir William Carew (1690-1744)

The younger son of **Sir John**, he succeeded his elder brother, **Richard**, as fifth baronet on the latter's untimely death. He was born on 11 January 1689/90 and, at the age of 12, he was sent to the grammar school at Plymouth, of which John Bedford was then headmaster.[58] In 1704, both Sir William and his liveried manservant, John Pockard, contracted smallpox there. The bill for their doctors, medicines and nurses came to the massive sum of £43, equivalent to almost a year's rents from his manor of Sheviock. In September, Sir William and his servant were well enough to move to Antony 'to take ye Air after ye Small Pox'. Six knives and forks were purchased for their use.[59] After the shock of this near fatal illness, in autumn 1704, Sir William and Pockard moved to Whitchurch near Tavistock where Sir William entered the school of the Revd Christopher Furneaux, a graduate and fellow (1680-8) of Exeter College, Oxford. Although he and Pockard contracted 'the Itch' at Furneaux' school early in 1705, Sir William seems to have been happy there. He gave New Year's gifts to Furneaux, to the usher and to the two school maids. After his recovery he made another gift to Furneaux and his wife, who died in June of that year. While at school Sir William's pocket money was £1 per quarter.

46 *Sir William Carew (1690-1744), painted by Michael Dahl, perhaps at the time of his marriage in 1713.*

In September 1707, Sir William was admitted as a gentleman commoner at Exeter College, Oxford.[60] As such he enjoyed certain privileges, including the right to dine at a separate table in the college hall. For each of the three years that he was there, he was advanced £200 per annum (half in October and half in April). But he seems to have lived above his means and his guardian, his uncle, Nicholas Morice, complained that he 'cannot want money without much ill husbandry and profuseness'.[61] In 1711, he celebrated the completion of his studies by purchasing 'A huntinge whipp, a payer of silver spurrs, a silver snuff box, and a box for the whipp'. He employed a professional huntsman at Antony and kept a pack of hounds. In 1726 and 1727, he was obliged to pay out £4 2s. 6d. to Thomas Gill for 'Damages done to his sheep by a young hound at Mr Bray's & by other dogs'.

Sir William was elected MP for Saltash in 1711. He became one of the two county members for Cornwall in September 1713, when he spent £68 5s. 3d. on election expenses at Lostwithiel. He entertained his supporters at five inns, bought prodigious quantities of ale, and employed as musicians, 'three wayts ... five drummers ... [and] ten men that play'd on Violins'.[62] He supported the Tories and was MP in six Parliaments until his death in 1744.

He took a great interest in the affairs of the parish of Sheviock. In 1711, his steward, Richard Blighe, spent 2s. 9d. at Crafthole and Portwrinkle 'to Encourage the Fishermen'. In the same year, he acquired from William Condy and his son the houses in Crafthole that had once formed part of the ancient manor-house of the Dawneys.[63] The property included the dovecote overlooking Whitsand Bay. In 1712, the 'homage' of the Borough of Crafthole presented him to be their reeve (mayor or principal officer).[64] In the same year, he granted a lease of some fishing cellars in Portwrinkle to a Plymouth merchant for a consideration of 'one guynea of gold & twelve quart bottles of good French clarett'. He was clearly of a sociable disposition.

He was also a Jacobite and was accused of planning an uprising in the West to coincide with the landing of James Stuart in Scotland in 1715. However he came under suspicion and was imprisoned in the Royal Citadel on Plymouth Hoe.[65] The accounts of the steward, John Tom, include a payment of ten guineas 'carryed and deliverd to Sr William at Plym° Fort' on 9 November and another of 20 guineas 'Carryed & Delivered to Sr. William in the Citadel' on 13 November.[66] When he granted a lease of Hearle's Parks to Joan Arundell in 1719, he stipulated that the consideration should include payment of 'one piece of gold commonly called a Jacobus'.[67] The choice of coin, a gold one minted in the reign of James II, undoubtedly had a political significance. Sir William was said to be in touch with Jacobite agents in France in the 1720s and involved with plans for a French landing to restore the Stuarts in 1744.[68]

47 *Gate of the Citadel, Plymouth. Sir William Carew was imprisoned there as a Jacobite in 1715.*

Sir William is noted especially as the builder of Antony House (1719-24), described as 'the finest house of its period in Cornwall'.[69] The architect is unknown, though James Gibbs, who moved in the same Tory circles as Sir William, may have been the designer or have influenced the design. Tonkin describes the baronet as 'a gentleman that in every respect comes up to the merits of the greatest of his ancestors. … [He] hath lately built a stately house here of Pentewan stone; and hath adorned it with gardens etc. suitable to it. From the bowling-green above the house is a beautiful prospect of the river, and of all the country round.'[70]

In January 1713/14, Sir William married Anne, daughter of the Earl of Coventry. Lady Anne presided over a happy and cultivated household. She bore a daughter around 1713 and a son, Coventry, in 1717. In 1726, she was paying a Mr Dore £24 per annum to teach the family to dance, and paying a Mr Spencer the same amount for 'teaching Mis ye Spinnett'.[71] Sir William also engaged Mr Hobbs to teach singing. The family had a 'yaull' or yacht so that they could enjoy a sail on summer days, and in September 1726, the builder, William Foard, was paid 5s. for making 'a Shrimp net for Lady Ann'. When the new house was finished, Lady Anne established an orangery there, and paid 5s. 'for 10 bags of Bark for ye Orange trees'. In March 1727, she ordered '3 hampiers of bottles of water from Bristoll', perhaps one of the earliest examples of the drinking of bottled water. In 1723, Sir William was elected a churchwarden of St Mary's, Sheviock, and his initials (along with those of the other warden, his bailiff, John Harvey) are studded into the south door.

48 *Lady Anne Carew, née Coventry (1696-1734), painting attributed to Michael Dahl. She married Sir William Carew in 1713.*

Sir William's joy in his family and in his house was short-lived – his daughter probably took to her bed in December 1730, when a new nightgown was made for her. She died in March the following year, aged only seventeen. Lady Anne (b.1696), became ill at the end of 1733 and died in January 1733/4, aged thirty-seven. This double blow may have led Sir William to spend more time in Bath and London. By 1738, he had handed over the running of his estates to his son, **Coventry**, who had just turned twenty-one.

49 *A contemporary view of Antony House, built by Sir William Carew in 1719-24.*

Sir William was created a Doctor of Civil Law (DCL) at Oxford on 22 May 1736. On his death on 24 March 1743/4, the Sheviock burial register noted 'The truly honourable Sir William Carew Bart was buried at Anthony [*sic*] at 8 at night'. Although the phrase 'truly honourable' was formulaic (it was also used in recording the death of his son), the evidence left in the church door and in the annals of the borough of Crafthole suggests that this convivial squire was highly regarded in the parish. There are portraits of him and his wife in Antony House.

Sir Coventry Carew (1717-48)

The only son of **Sir William** and Lady Anne, he was named after his grandfather, the Earl of Coventry. He married his cousin, Mary Bampfylde, only daughter of Sir Copplestone Warwick Bampfylde, Bart. Sir Coventry died young and without issue. His widow married Francis Buller, MP for West Looe, in 1749. She died before 1763. In his will, Sir Coventry left money for the foundation of a school in Antony to teach ten poor children to read and write. On his death, the baronetcy passed to the Revd Sir Alexander Carew, vicar of St Wenn, a member of the family settled at Harrobarrow in Calstock. On Sir Alexander's death in 1799, the Carew baronetcy became extinct. Sir Coventry passed his estates in Antony, Sheviock and elsewhere in east Cornwall to **John Carew** (d.1771), second son of John Carew of Camerton in Somerset, and after his death without issue to John's elder brother, Thomas Carew (d.1766) of Crowcombe in Somerset, who however predeceased his brother; and after their deaths to Reginald Pole and then to his sons. See further **Reginald Pole Carew**.

Jane Carew

She was the daughter of **Sir John Carew** (1635-92) by his first wife, Sarah Hungerford. She married Jonathan Rashleigh I of Menabilly (1642-1702). Their daughter, Sarah Rashleigh, married the Revd Carolus Pole of St Breage (d.1730). In the will of **Sir Coventry Carew** (d.1748), Carolus and Sarah's son, Reginald Pole of

Stoke Damerel (1717-69), and his male descendants were named as heirs to Sheviock, Antony and other estates in east Cornwall in the event that the direct male line of the Carews failed. Reginald married Ann Buller of Morval. The couple had three sons, **Reginald Pole Carew** (1753-1835), Charles Morice Pole (1757-1830), who became an admiral and was MP for Plymouth from 1806 to 1818, and the Revd Edward Pole DD (1758-1837), rector of Sheviock (1782-96). They also had two daughters, Anne (b.1752), who married Charles Cocks, first Lord Somers, and Sarah (b.1755).

Jonathan Rashleigh II (1690-1764)

He was described in the will of **Sir Coventry Carew** (d.1748) as 'my worthy kinsman and friend'. By that will, he was granted many Carew estates in west and north Cornwall, some on the death of Sir Coventry; others after the death of Lady Mary Carew (d. before 1763). In the will, he was asked to aid and assist Lady Mary in managing her affairs, and he granted many leases on her behalf in Sheviock and East Antony from 1748 until 1761. In November 1748, the court baron of East Antony was held in his name.[72] William Ellis, formerly steward to Sir Coventry, continued to act as steward for Lady Mary.

John Carew (d.1771)

The second son of John Carew of Camerton in Somerset, he inherited the manors of East Antony and Sheviock and other nearby properties under the will of **Sir Coventry Carew** (d.1748). Subject to the life interest of Sir Coventry's widow, Lady Mary, he was lord of these manors until his death in 1771. John had married Mary Webber and, in the 1760s, granted leases of many properties in the manor of Sheviock to his brother-in-law, Francis Webber.

POLE CAREW (LORDS OF THE MANOR, 1771 TO 1924)

The Rt. Hon Reginald Pole Carew (1753-1835) [73]

He attended University College, Oxford, from 1771 to 1775. Under the terms of the will of **Sir Coventry Carew** (d.1748), he inherited the Carew estates after the death of **John Carew** in 1771. Under that will, he was obliged to add Carew to his name on inheriting the estates. From 1775 to 1780, he travelled widely in Europe, moving through France, Switzerland, Bavaria, Austria, Hungary, Prussia, and the Netherlands. From 1780 to 1782 he visited Denmark, Sweden, Finland, Russia and Poland. In Russia, he met the Empress Catherine the Great and her minister, Potemkin, and reported to the British authorities on the Russian development of new port facilities in the Crimea.

He married, in 1784, Jemima Yorke (1763-1804), only daughter and heiress of John Yorke, fourth son of Lord Hardwicke, the Lord Chancellor. The couple had seven

50 *The Swiss artist, Johann Wyrsch, painted this portrait of Reginald Pole Carew, in Besançon, France, in 1773, when Reginald was on the Grand Tour. Wigs were still fashionable before the French Revolution.*

51 *Reginald Pole Carew (1753-1835), painted* c.*1815.*

children: **Joseph Pole Carew**, Harriet (1790-1877), Agneta (1791-1836), Amabel (1796-1871), John Reginald (1800-4), and three other daughters. Amabel married Francis Glanville of Catchfrench. In 1861, Amabel was living at Sconner House with two of her daughters. Her son, Henry Carew Glanville, was rector of Sheviock (1856-1900). Agneta married Thomas Somers Cocks of Malvern Parva. Their son, John James Thomas Somers Cocks, was rector of Sheviock 1845-55. In 1819, Harriet married John, Earl of St Germans (d.1823). In 1792, Reginald commissioned the landscape designer, Humphry Repton, to produce a Red Book for the gardens, walks and avenues of Antony House.[74] Repton or his son designed the entrance lodge there. In 1808, Pole Carew married (2) Caroline Anne Lyttleton (1774-1833). The couple had two sons, **William Henry** and Gerald (1815-45; rector of Sheviock 1841-5), and five daughters. Their daughter, Juliana (1812-81), married Thomas Robartes of Lanhydrock.

Pole Carew purchased the borough of Crafthole and the manor of West Antony from the Duchy of Cornwall in 1798. In the running of his Cornish estates, he relied heavily on the advice of his uncles, Philip Rashleigh (1720-1811), who acted as his guardian when he was a minor, and Charles Rashleigh (1747-1823), who became his steward. In 1797, he formed and commanded the East Cornwall Gentlemen and Yeomanry Corps. As an important local landowner, he was at the forefront in developing the town of Torpoint, the Torpoint Ferry, the Liskeard turnpike, and the fishing industry at Portwrinkle.

Pole Carew supported the Tory party and was elected MP for Penryn (1782-4), Reigate (1787-90), Lostwithiel (1790-6), Fowey (1796-9 and 1802-12), and Lostwithiel (1812-16). From 1799 to 1802, he was a Commissioner for Auditing the Public Accounts. He was made a Privy Councillor in 1805. Though not by then an MP, he was a bitter opponent of the Parliamentary Reform Act of 1832.

Joseph Pole Carew (1787-1852)
He was the third of eight children of **Reginald Pole Carew** by his first wife, Jemima Yorke. He was briefly imprisoned for debt sometime before 1820. His father cleared his debts and settled money on him, but disinherited him from the Carew estates. These were passed to his brother, **William Henry** (1811-88), on the death of his father on 3 January 1835. He died near Paris where he had been living for some time.

William Henry Pole Carew (1811-88)
He was the son of **Reginald Pole Carew** by his second wife, Caroline Anne Lyttleton. He inherited the Carew estates in 1835 and was elected MP for East Cornwall. He married Frances Ann Buller of Morval. He is said to have planted the avenues of yew running westwards from Antony House.[75] The couple had two sons, **(Sir) Reginald** and Gerald, who married Harriet Buller and, like his uncle, became rector of Sheviock (1900-10).

Sir Reginald Pole Carew, KCB (1849-1924)
The son of **William Henry**, he was a professional soldier, serving in the Coldstream Guards. He was ADC to Lord Lytton, Viceroy of India; and on the staff of General Roberts on his famous march from Kabul to Kandahar in 1880. In 1882, he fought at the battle of Tel-el-Kebir in Egypt. He took part in the Second Burmese War of 1886, bringing back the great bell now in the garden at Antony House. In the South African War, he commanded successively the 9th Brigade, the Guards Brigade and the 11th Division. He retired as a Major-General and was appointed KCB and CVO. He was responsible for dismantling Thankes House in Antony, and having

52 *General Sir Reginald Pole Carew, commander of the 11th Division during the South African War of 1899-1902.*

53 *Antony House cricket team c.1918. Sir Reginald Pole Carew (1849-1924) is seated, centre, next to his wife, Lady Beatrice. Their son, John, is next to her, and their two daughters, Victoria and Mari, sit in front. Major Ellers, in the striped blazer and cap, was the land agent.*

it re-erected as the *Whitsand Bay Hotel* in Portwrinkle (1909-11). In 1901, he married Lady Beatrice Butler for whom the Chalet in Portwrinkle was built. She was the daughter of the third marquis of Ormonde. They had two sons and two daughters. Their eldest son, John Gawen (1902-93), changed his name to **Carew Pole**.

CAREW POLE (LORDS OF THE MANOR, 1924-)

Sir John Gawen Carew Pole, DSO (1902-93)

The eldest son of Lt-Gen. Sir Reginald Pole Carew and the Hon Beatrice Butler (d.1952), he was a regular soldier like his father. He changed his name to Carew Pole on inheriting the Pole baronetcy in 1926. He married (1) (1928) Cynthia Mary

Burns, OBE (d.1977); and (2) (1979) Joan, widow of Lt-Col Anthony Fulford. They had one son, John **Richard** Walter **Carew Pole** (b.1938), and two daughters. After RMC, Sandhurst, he served in the Coldstream Guards (1923-39). He commanded 5th Battalion DCLI, TA (1939-43), and 2nd Battalion Devonshire Regiment (1944). He was a Colonel in the Second Army 1944-45, and served in Normandy, France, Belgium, Holland, and Germany (1944-45). He was mentioned in despatches, and awarded an immediate DSO. He was High Sheriff of Cornwall (1947-8); Lord-Lieutenant (1962-77); chairman Cornwall County Council (1952-63); and Prime Warden, Worshipful Company of Fishmongers (1969-70).

Sir Richard Carew Pole, OBE (Sir John Richard Walter Carew Pole, Bt.) (1938-)

He is the only son of **Sir John Gawen Carew Pole** and Cynthia Mary Burns (d.1977). He married (1) (1966) Hon Victoria Lever (m. dissolved 1974); and (2) (1974) Mary Dawnay. Sir Richard and Lady Mary have two sons, Tremayne John (b.1974) and John Alexander George (b.1975). Sir Richard was High Sheriff of Cornwall in 1979; a governor of Seale Hayne Agricultural College (1979-89); member of Cornwall County Council (1973-93); director Theatre Royal, Plymouth (1985-97); trustee of the Tate Gallery (1993-2003); president Devon and Cornwall Record Society (1999-2000); chairman Combined Universities in Cornwall Steering Committee (2000-3); president RHS (2001-7); and Prime Warden, Worshipful Company of Fishmongers (2006-7).

54 *Deed of sale of the manor of Sheviock. Thomas Carew purchased the manor from Sir Walter Mildmay for 'a thowsande poundes' in 1558.*

CHAPTER 6

Courts and Officials of the Manor

THE MANORIAL COURTS

The post-Conquest records of Tavistock Abbey give some idea of the way that it would have organised its manor of Sheviock before it had to surrender it to the Dawneys in the 11th century.[1] The manor would have come under the jurisdiction of a steward, and below him a *cellarius* (cellarer), who was in overall charge of food supplies. Reporting to the cellarer was a *granarius* (garnerer) responsible for the supply of corn, and a *salsarius* (purveyor of salted fish). These officials lived at the abbey and would have paid only occasional visits to the abbey's manors. However, the *salsarius*, in particular, would have taken a close interest in Sheviock, because it possessed the only sea-fishery belonging to the abbey. On each of its manors, the monastery relied upon a paid official, called the *serviens* or sergeant (equivalent to the bailiff of later centuries), and other nominated bondmen who were obliged to render services without pay in return for their holdings. The most senior of these bondmen was the reeve, who directed the farming operations of the demesne and rendered an annual account to the abbey at Michaelmas (29 September). Occasionally, a monk acted as the reeve, but this practice was prohibited in 1102.[2] As in later centuries, the manorial court, presided over by the steward, was the main instrument of government. The steward would swear in a body of jurors at the court, and they in turn would nominate the other officials of the manor. The manorial courts of the abbot presumably met in the hall of the sergeant's dwelling – perhaps on the site of Sheviock Barton.

The Court Leet under the Normans

The same system of manorial administration broadly continued after the Norman Conquest, except that the immediate lord of the manor, the Norman knight, Ermenhald (or Erbenald) Dawney, was now resident on the manor. He established his dwelling-place and manor-house on high ground near the coast at Blazor and presumably held his courts there.

Early in the Middle Ages, two kinds of court evolved on the manor – one, a court of record, with a minor criminal and a civil jurisdiction, and the other to deal with the customs of the manor. The first of these, called the 'court leet', was responsible for ensuring that every tenant in the community was properly enrolled in what the Saxons had called the 'tithing' and the Normans called the 'frankpledge'.[3] This was a group of people collectively answerable for any breaches of the peace in their area. They were collectively liable to pay any assessments (taxes) or fines imposed on the community. It was very important to the king and to his feudal tenants to ensure that everyone who should be in the frankpledge was properly enrolled and present at meetings of the court. The duty to attend was called 'suit of court' and this obligation became attached to particular tenements. When a meeting of the court leet was summoned, the first act was for 12 freemen of the manor, the 'homage', to be sworn in as a jury. The roll of those owing suit of court was then read out, and the tenants answered to their names. If anyone was absent, the jury pronounced him to be 'in mercy' and he was fined by the court. The duty of checking enrolment and presence was called 'view of frankpledge'. When Thomas Carew bought the manor of Sheviock in 1558, the deed of sale specifically mentioned 'Courte Leates' and 'vewe of Franke pledge' as being included in the property purchased.[4] The jury also made presentments on many other local matters, including the commission of specified crimes ranging from housebreaking to rape, infringements of the bye-laws, and matters relating to wreck of the sea. The court had the power to fine offenders and could order such corporal punishments as whipping or being placed in the stocks. Section 35 of *Magna Carta*, as amended and confirmed by Edward I in 1297, provided that:

> [No] sheriff, or his bailiff, shall keep his turn in the Hundred but twice in the year; and nowhere but in due place and accustomed; that is to say, once after Easter, and again after the Feast of St Michael. And the view of Frankpledge shall be likewise at the Feast of St Michael.

Accordingly, the court leet of Sheviock manor met in October or November and then in April or May. Only a few records of the early courts of Sheviock manor have survived. But there is a record of one held in 1528 in which Robert Smythe of Liscawn was admitted to a tenement in Vellands by Henry Collis, 'overseer'. At another court held on 26 April 1533, the overseer or bailiff, Robert Kingdon granted a lease in Blazor.[5]

At one court every year, the manorial officers were appointed. The court appointed the constables who enforced its orders. Later the constables came under the supervision of the parish vestry and the local magistrates. The village stocks are still preserved in the parish church of Sheviock. In later years, they were used mostly to punish people who were drunk and disorderly, and the usual period of confinement was six hours. In some places, stocks continued to be used for this purpose until the 1800s.[6] The stocks were also used to restrain people who misbehaved in church. The offender would be placed in them until all the churchgoers had left.[7]

In the Middle Ages, manorial courts usually met in the Great Hall or principal chamber of the manor-house. This would have been the Dawneys' manor-house at Blazor from the late 11th century until 1540. In that year, Henry VIII separated the manor of Sheviock from the borough of Crafthole. From 1540, therefore, the courts of the manor were probably moved to Sheviock Barton, while the courts of the borough of Crafthole, which then belonged to the Duchy of Cornwall, would have continued to be held in the Dawneys' old manor-house at Blazor (now the *Finnygook Inn*). When Richard Carew the younger lived in Sheviock, between 1600 and 1620, perhaps at Sconner Farm, the courts of the manor may have been held there. What was important was that the courts should meet on the manor in question and not on some other manor. The actual premises used were of lesser importance. In the 1600s and 1700s, the Duchy courts of the manor of West Antony met at several different premises on the manor, usually farm houses or inns.[8] The later courts of the manor of East Antony were also held at several different tenements on the manor.[9]

A court leet of the manor of Sheviock, held on 13 April 1632, set out the manorial customs in relation to wreck of the sea and the ownership of 'greate fish'.[10] On 8 December 1668, the matter of salvage from a wreck came up again.[11] A 'shipp called *Fellowshipp* late of Plymouth whereof George Cookeworthy was late master' had been driven onshore on 28 November and wrecked near Portwrinkle. The *Fellowshipp* had been carrying a cargo of 'sarges, kersies' and other West Country goods. Sir John Carew had ordered the wreckage and cargo to be salvaged. Some of the salvaged items were presented into court. A sailor and three merchants from Plymouth satisfied the court that they were the original owners of the goods. After paying five shillings into court, they were given title to them.

Towards the end of their existence, courts leet were often combined with the other type of court, the 'court baron', into a single court. By 1725, only one court per annum was being held on Sheviock manor. The steward's accounts, from 1725 to 1729, show that he was presiding at the manorial court for one day in mid-October each year and that his expenses for each visit averaged 9s.[12] The records of the combined court of Sheviock manor have survived from 1763 to 1765, and they show that the court was 'held at Mrs Ann Lord's House in Crafthole'.[13] This was the inn built on the site of the original Dawney manor-house at Blazor. It had been called Sergeant's tenement in 1622, when it belonged to the Duchy of Cornwall. Sir William Carew had purchased the property in 1711, thus bringing it back within the manor of

Sheviock.[14] In 1741, Sir William let Sergeant's tenement to the innholder, William Lord, with reversion to Lord's wife, Ann.[15] In the years 1763 to 1765, the steward of John Carew, James Coryton, held sittings of the combined court of the manor of Sheviock, 'at Mrs Ann Lord's House in Crafthole' – i.e. again at the old inn.[16] 'Special courts' to deal with tenancies were also held there from 1772 to 1807.

The Court Baron

In Norman French, *baron* primarily meant 'man', as in *baron et feme*, meaning man and wife.[17] A manorial lord who had enough free tenants, his *barons*, could hold a 'court baron'. The court was presided over either by the lord in person or, more usually, by his steward.[18] 'Suit of court', the duty to attend, also applied to attendance at the court baron. Only a few records of the court baron of Sheviock have survived, though many have survived from the court baron of the manor of East Antony.[19] By custom dating from the time of Henry III (1216-72), the medieval court baron met every three weeks – hence it was sometimes called the 'three weeks' court'.

The principal duty of the court was to declare and enforce the ancient customs of the manor. Thus, the court baron held before the steward, John Tom, for the manor of East Antony in October 1722, began 'We present all our ancient Customes to be good & laudable & ought to be continued'.[20] The declaration of the customs of the manor was particularly important in the Middle Ages, when much of the agricultural practice was regulated by them. Those customs, as stated and developed by the court, would regulate such matters as the type of grain to be sown in the fields in any particular year, the time for putting the tenants' cattle into the common pastures, the hitching-up of the common ploughs, and the tenants' use of the manorial waste. In Sheviock, the court baron would also have regulated the fisheries and the various dues payable to the lord by the fishermen. It would also have regulated the payment of tolls for the use of the lord's quay by boats from other manors.

The Combined Court

In Sheviock, the courts leet and courts baron were combined in the mid-1700s, and by then they were meeting just once a year.[21] On 29 September 1759, for example, William Ellis, steward of the manor, instructed the reeve, William Bray, to summon all the free and conventionary tenants of the manor of Sheviock at 'the Court Leet & Court Baron of Jonathan Rashleigh Esqr. to be held at the House of Mr Wm Lord in Crafthole … on 15th day of October next ensuing the date hereof by Ten of the Clock in the forenoon, to pay their Rents and Arrears Herr[iots] & Dues, and to perform their Respective Suits & Services'.

Combined courts for Sheviock were held from 1763 to 1765 with James Corinton presiding as steward.[22] At the first of these, held on 19 October, William

Bray was continued reeve and Richard Warren was sworn in as 'hayward'. Six people were taken as tenants and entered on the manorial roll: Samuel Lyne, Charles Pope, the Revd (Mydhope) Wallis, (John) Prinn, Richard Warren and John Walkey.[23] The following year, at the court held on 18 October, Henry Coffin was appointed reeve and Richard Warren was continued as hayward. Mrs Deebel was 'Taken Ten^{t} & sworn'. For the court scheduled for 22 October of the following year, 1765, James Corinton prepared the heading for the court roll, but no entries were made on the record. This may have been due to his sudden illness and death. There is no record of any later courts leet and baron being held for Sheviock manor, except for special courts.

Courts leet and baron were never formally abolished and even today a few still survive, such as that at Ashburton, Devon. At East Antony, a separate court baron survived until at least 1806. The courts baron withered because they were costly to hold, requiring the presence of the steward, and most of the medieval dues were no longer collectable or worth collecting. The courts that survived longest, such as that of East Antony, were close to the manor-house and the office of the steward. At the East Antony court, fines for absence continued to be collected, and increased, to the very end. The decline of the courts leet was due in part to the growth of the jurisdiction of justices of the peace from the 1500s onwards, and in part to the introduction of new forms of local government by statute in the early 1800s.

Special Courts

In the 1700s, a new type of court was devised to record property transactions. This was called simply the *curia specialis* (special court). As with the regular courts it was held before the steward, but the 12 jurors were dispensed with. It sufficed if one or two tenants of the manor were present in addition to the person seeking to register or surrender his lease.[24] In 1788, the Earl of St Germans paid into court an acknowledgement that he had trespassed on the manor of Sheviock in converting a property in Portwrinkle into a bathing shed.[25] The court in question was presumably a special court of this kind.

OFFICIALS OF THE MANOR

The principal officials of the manor were the steward, the bailiff and the hind, who were appointed by the lord. In addition there were various officials nominated by the jury at the manorial court. These nominees were then formally appointed by the lord's steward, who, in the absence of the lord, presided.[26] The officials appointed in the Middle Ages included the reeve, the hayward, and the constables. They also included an ale-taster, a bread-weigher, and a pindar (pound-keeper). Other officials were appointed as the need arose. At East Antony, there was a 'viewer of reparacons'. This seems to have been an unpopular job. In 1627, the viewer, Edward Foskett, was fined 1s. for 'not comming to execute his office'.[27] In 1634, another viewer, William Dweane was again fined 1s. 'for not coming to execute his office this last yeare'.[28] The office of viewer was still being filled in 1806. In the latter year there was also an 'Overseer and Director for clearing the Streets of Torpoint of all the Dung or Manure and all other things that may be deemed a Nuisance therein, and of empounding Pigs & other Cattle that may be found straying or trespassing on any part of this Manor'.

55 *Window in St Neot's church erected by John Kelleway (Callway), early 1500s. The open book is probably a book of hours.*

The Steward

The steward, who was sometimes assisted by a deputy, was responsible for the efficient running of all the manors belonging to the lord, and he usually presided at the manorial courts. The steward to William Courtenay, Earl of Devon, in the later years of the reign of Henry VII and the early years of Henry VIII was John Kelleway of Cullompton.[29] After the earl's death in 1511, Kelleway continued to look after the affairs of his widow, Katherine.[30] She was the younger daughter of King Edward IV, and sister of Henry VII's queen, Elizabeth of York. Sheviock formed part of her dower lands. According to Henry VIII's muster roll of 1522, she received annually £16 'rent and profits of her manor of Shevioke'.[31] The earl and countess of Devon also had land and mining interests in the parish of St Neot, and the same John Kelleway represented his interests there. John himself had land and mining interests in St Neot. Members of his family are shown at prayer in one of the stained glass windows in St Neot's church. There was once a picture of Kelleway himself, but that is now lost.[32] In 1514, John 'Caylwaye' and other commissioners for the Countess, whose offices were at Plympton, sold some of the timber in Sheviock Woods to two Plymouth merchants, Richard Hontyngdon and William Brooking.[33] Kelleway was assessed on £2 of land and £20 of goods in St Neot in 1522.[34] By 1525, the value of his land had increased to £10. He was listed as a tinner in St Neot in 1535. By 1544, the value of his goods had risen to £13.

Kelleway's second wife was Joan, daughter and co-heiress of John Tregarthen, lord of the manor of Goran.[35] She was a formidably strong woman, and bore 14 children to him. Against the odds, he died first, and Joan then married John

Wadham of Branscombe in Devon. She had a further six children by him. One of these, Nicholas, was co-founder, with his wife, Dorothy, of Wadham College, Oxford. Her family erected a monument to Joan and her two husbands in Branscombe church. The well-preserved effigy of Kelleway shows him dressed in his long steward's gown as a liveried retainer of the earl and countess of Devon. The earl's livery was 'crane-coloured' – ashen grey, after the colour of a bird now extinct in England.[36] Above his effigy is his shield, quarterly of four, showing that he was married twice, and that Joan was his second wife.[37] Joan died in 1583.[38]

In 1528, Humfrey Collis Esq., an official described as 'overseer', presented Robert Smythe to a tenement in Vellands at a manorial court held in the name of Henry, Marquis of Exeter. The office of overseer may have been equivalent to that of deputy steward.

The Agreement of 1612 for the building of the quay at Portwrinkle lists one of the duties of the steward. It is stipulated that contributors to the building of the quay who wished to keep their boats in the harbour should enter these boats in the court records 'paying … a penny to the Steward of the said Manor for entering the same'.

The office of steward was demanding and required the holder to be a gentleman who had received a good education. John Treis was steward first to Sir John Carew and then to his widow, Lady Mary, from 1691 to 1697. He was responsible for all the payments into and out of the estate. He sometimes handled large quantities of money, for example, paying to 'Ambros Manaton Esq on my Masters Bond the last payment of his wifes portion … £1000 and quarters interest thereon £15'.[39] At another time, he had to travel to Exeter to exchange all the old coinage for new coinage made at the mint there. At Christmas time, he paid out £10 for the entertainment of the tenants. He had to attend the law courts whenever the estate's interests were involved. For example, he expended 3s. in attending Quarter Sessions at Lostwithiel in October 1693. He needed to be able to read and write in Latin as well as English. When he drew up the bond for

56 *Memorial to John Kelleway (left), steward of the earl of Devon, and to John Wadham, in Branscombe Church, Devon. Kelleway wears the livery gown of the earl of Devon.*

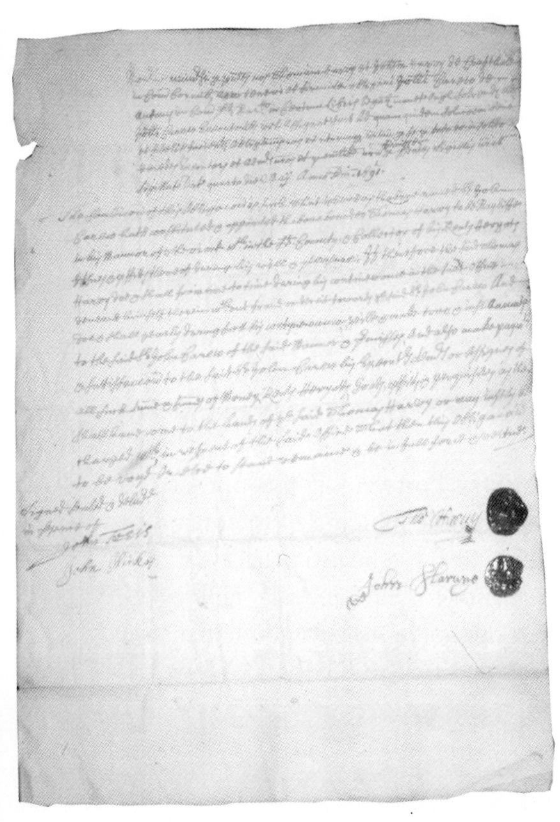

57 *The bond from Thomas and John Harvy to Sir John Carew on Thomas's appointment as bailiff of the manor (1691).*

John Harvey to sign on the latter's appointment as bailiff of the manor in 1691, he wrote the heading in Latin and the text in English. An entry in John Treis's disbursement book tells us where he usually lived and how he died:

> John Treis happen[ed] to be surprized by a sudden death on the 25th day of December 1697: at night in the Chamber at East-Anthony where he usually lodged and kept his Accounts and papers.

Treis's salary was £10 per annum.[40] He was paid another £10 a year for his 'boarding ... and keeping house'. Another of the perquisites attaching to the office of steward was to be given tenancies on the lord's estates. Treis was given a joint tenancy of 'Treises tenement' in Sheviock. He was also given the tithe of sheaves of Insworth (in Maker parish), which he exchanged for a third of the tenement of Carbeile in Antony.[41]

Edward Hoblyn, a London lawyer related to the Carews, was much involved with the estates from 1694 until 1703. At this time the heirs, Sir Richard Carew (1683-1703) and after his death, Sir William, Richard's younger brother, were under the jurisdiction of the Court of Chancery as minors. In 1694, the steward, John Treis, paid Hoblyn £40 'on account of Law Suits'.[42]

Edward Dennys, whose office was in Liskeard, was appointed steward by Sir William's trustees from about 1705 until 29 September 1710. Shortly after Sir William reached his majority (on 11 January 1710), he appointed Richard Blighe as steward. Blighe had previously assisted Dennys as the accountant of the estate. John Tom was steward from 1714 until 1734.[43] In August 1721, Tom charged the estate 6s. 'for 2 days expenses at Bodmin Assizes'. His salary was £30 per annum.[44] Dorothy Tom, who may have been his wife or another close relation, was also employed by Sir William at a salary of £5 per annum. Joseph Andrew, who kept the accounts for Coventry Carew in 1734, became steward in 1735 and continued in post until 1744. He was succeeded by William Ellis, who served Sir Coventry until the latter's death in 1748, and then from time to time served Jonathan Rashleigh until 1761. In the will of Sir Coventry, he was left the sum of £100.

In 1755, the steward was William Corinton (or Coryton). On instructions from Mr Buller, he ordered the reeve, William Bray, to collect money to defray the costs of repairing the quay at Portwrinkle. James Corinton of East Antony, perhaps William's son, was steward for John Carew from 1763 to 1766.[45] In 1765, John Carew granted a reversionary lease of Sconner to Corinton.[46] Corinton appears to have died suddenly, because in 1766 Carew granted a new reversionary lease of Sconner to William Mackworth Praed.[47] William Williams was John Carew's steward from 1767 to 1771. On succeeding to the manors of East Antony and Sheviock in 1771, Reginald Pole Carew appointed Charles Rashleigh as steward. He remained in post until 1792. John Smith, who presided at the court leet of the manor of Drewsteignton in 1794, was probably steward in that year. Reginald's steward from 1796 to 1806 was William Smith.

The Bailiff

The bailiff (Old French for an overseer or supervisor) was the senior salaried employee of the family living on, and usually responsible for just one manor, but sometimes two adjacent ones. With the reeve, the bailiff was responsible for ensuring that all the tenants rendered to the lord the services that they owed to him by virtue of their status or their landholding.[48] Later these services were commuted into rents. The first recorded bailiff of the manor of Sheviock was Anthony Harry, who was bailiff for Henry Courtenay, Marquis of Exeter (1512-38).[49] Robert Kingdon succeeded Harry as bailiff, executing a document installing a new tenant at Blazor in 1533.[50] Later bailiffs included Ferdinando Spiller (probably) in the reign of Queen Elizabeth. A document in the Antony archives shows him witnessing a rental payment and relief due to the Carew manor of East Antony in 1582.[51] Another was John Rawlings (1656-60). Several accounts written by him, and one incident from his life, have survived. Sir Richard Carew recorded his recovery from illness through the use of warming stones, as advocated by Carew in his book, *Excellent Helps by a Warming-Stone* (1652; re-edited 1660):

> being at a friends house, and having drunk some honeyed drink, [Rawlings] was so tortured with pain in his belly and guts, as both himself and those of his house much feared it would have cost him his life, but by the help of the heat of these stones, was made perfectly well again within twenty four hours.

Other bailiffs were Philip Blake (1689-91), Thomas Harvey (1691-93), John Nicholls, who came from St Germans (1697), Thomas Harvey again (1704-10), Phillip Bloy (probably) (1712) and Philip Palmer (1725). The bailiff's salary in 1690 was £4. The 'Bond from Thomas Harvy & John Harvy to Sir John Carew on the Appointment of Thomas Harvy to be bailiff of the manor of Sheviock', dated 4 May 1691, is preserved

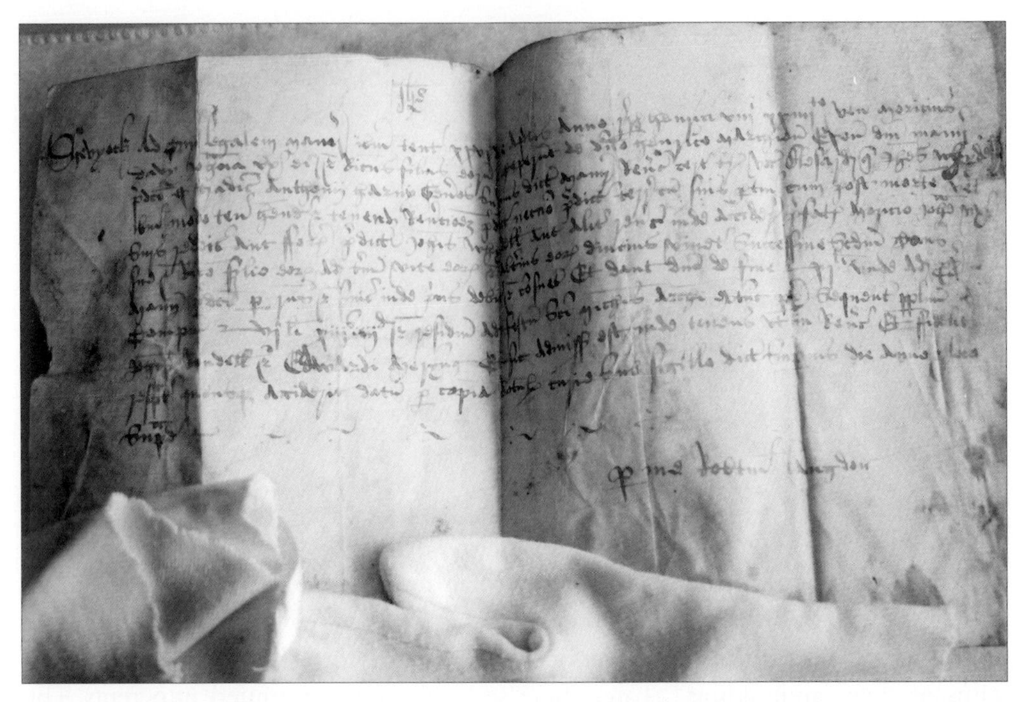

58 *Lease of land in Blazor, dated 1533. The lease, headed with the pre-Reformation monogram 'IHS', was prepared by Robert Kingdon, bailiff of the Marquis of Exeter.*

in the Antony archives. It was signed by the steward, John Treis, and by John Hickes and the two Harvey brothers. From 1704, the bailiff's salary was increased to £5. The bailiff was also the preferred lessee of Bailiff's Meadow in Sheviock.[52]

The Hind

The hind was the farm manager of the demesne lands of the lord's estates. On the Carew estates, the same hind looked after the farms in both Antony and Sheviock. In 1696, the hind was William Guy. He was paid £5 per annum.[53] Around the year 1706, the hind was John Edwards, who later farmed on his own account in Blazor and Crafthole.[54] On 27 July 1726, the hind, Walter Horwell, paid out £11 4s. 2d. to 'the Haymakers & Reapers' at Antony.[55] Two days later, he paid out another £11 19s. 3d. 'for Cutting & Saving the Hay at Sheviock'. Later that year, Horwell was succeeded by William Gill.[56] Gill was paid £10 per annum.[57] The hind to Sir Coventry Carew was John Baulkwill, who was left £10 in the will of Sir Coventry.

The Reeve

The bailiff's assistant, the reeve, had to perform his duties without payment as one of the obligations of his tenancy. Although not paid, one of his rewards was free tenure of the Net Park in Portwrinkle, the land set aside for the fishermen to dry their nets.

On some manors, the office of reeve rotated among the tenants; but in Sheviock the same trusted individuals tended to serve for several years.[58] The reeve had to collect the rents due to the lord of the manor, paying them over to the bailiff or the steward. The 'receiver', probably the same as the reeve, in 1690 was Henry Odyorne, who farmed 50 acres at Haye and may have lived at Higher Clicker. His 'declaration', showing that he had received half a year's rents to Lady Day 1690, is preserved in the Antony archives.[59] In 1692, Tristram Harry as reeve was paying bills and collecting payments on behalf of Sir John Carew. Henry Lavers, who was collecting fishing dues for the lord in 1693, was probably the reeve in that year. Walter Son, who was collecting the same dues in 1694 and 1695, was probably the reeve in those years. John Andrew was reeve for Sir William Carew from 1721 to 1724. His account of Sheviock rents at Michaelmas 1721 is preserved in the archives.[60] The reeve in 1762 and 1763 was William Bray, and in 1764 was Henry Coffin.[61] The steward, James Corinton, gave Coffin a list of the rental arrears to be collected at Michaelmas in that year. The reeve in 1766 was Matthew Phillips.[62] The next recorded reeve was again William Bray.[63] He acted for Reginald Pole Carew in about 1775. His grandfather or great-grandfather, William Bray, weaver, is shown as renting a 'cottage and 60 perches' in Crafthole for 4s. in rentals of 1634 and 1691.[64] The Brays were also involved with the fishing operations at Portwrinkle.

The obligation to perform the office of reeve was specifically included in the leases of certain copyhold tenements, such as the cottage in Portwrinkle now called Smuggler's Cottage. A lease of the premises in 1812 to Thomas Helman required the lessee to 'do and perform the Office of Reeve of and for the said Manor when and as often as thereunto elected or chosen by the Homage or Steward of the said Manor'.[65]

One of the duties of the reeve was to supervise the maintenance of properties on the manor. In 1723, John Andrew as reeve paid 13s. 8d. to the mason, John Holman, for work done on Joan Symon's house. Richard Symons had been the occupant of Southford in Trewrickle before 1657.[66] Andrew's disbursements for materials used in the work included: 4s. 4d. for '400 lasts and carage', 1s. 8d. 'for 1000 & ¼ of last nailes' and 3s. 8d. to 'Mr Jory for 4 bushels of lime and carage'. Next year he paid 6d. to 'Nicolas Hancock for a new twist [hinge] and Nails for Joan Symons Door', 5d. to 'Mr Jory for 2 packs of lime & carage' and 3s. to 'John Holman for work on Joan Symons House … at Portwrinkle'.[67]

The Hayward

The hayward was responsible for ensuring that the hedgerows were kept in good repair, and especially that cattle and sheep did not escape from the common lands onto the enclosed fields. The 'hay' of hayward, comes from the Anglo-Saxon word

59 *Sheviock village stocks are stored in the north porch of St Mary's church.*

'haye' meaning enclosure, and not from 'hay' meaning cut grass. The names of all but one of the haywards of the parish have been lost. The name that has survived is that of the last one, Richard Warren, who was appointed in 1763 and again in 1764.[68]

The Constables

The constables or 'tithingmen' were originally appointed by the court leet of the manor. But with the decline of that court in the 1700s, the appointment came to be made by the parish vestry under the control of the local magistrates. The names of only a few of the parish constables have survived. On 30 March 1633, the Sheviock parish constables, John Blake and Arnott Odiorne, and the churchwardens, presented six parishioners to the justices at the Petty Sessions held at Millbrook 'for selling of ale without lycins'. In 1825, John Trevan, 'constable of Sheviock', witnessed an undertaking by some Looe fishermen not to engage in drift-net fishing within a league and a half (about 4.5 miles) of the shore. The constables would appear to have had jurisdiction over the whole parish including both the manor of Sheviock and the borough of Crafthole.

Chapter 7

Manorial Revenues and Expenditures

No records survive of the medieval court leet of the manor of Sheviock. We therefore have no knowledge of the extent to which the Dawney lords exacted from their bondmen tallages (taxes) such as *chevage* (capitation or poll money), or penalties such as *childwite* (fine for getting the lord's bondswoman with child), that could be claimed and enforced in the court leet of a manor. Other manorial revenues that originated in the Middle Ages and were collected by the court leet were fines for absence on court days, fines for changes of tenancy, and 'reliefs' and 'heriots' payable on the deaths of tenants. Court records show that these survived in Sheviock into the 18th century.

Fines for Default in Homage and Fealty

Failure of a tenant to attend court, whether a court leet or court baron, would result in him being 'amerced' (fined). In the early period, the fines would have been limited to a few pence (3d. in Crafthole). On the Duchy manor of West Antony in 1670, the fine for absence was 6d.[1] On the Carew manor of East Antony in 1739 the fine was 1s.[2] It was later increased, and continued to be enforced there until 1806 or later.

Rents, Reliefs, Heriots, and Harvest Journeys

In 1634, Sir Richard Carew, lord of the manor of Sheviock, was collecting annually from his conventionary (customary) tenants £43 15s. in monetary rents, and also 45 capons, four hens and '1 harvest journey'.[3] The names of conventionary tenants were inscribed on the court roll, and these tenants were given a copy of the entry referring to their tenancy. Hence they were also called 'copyholders'. They were the descendants of the villeins or bondmen of medieval times, and the capons, hens and harvest journey were vestiges of the feudal services that they owed to the lord of the manor. The actual performance of harvest journeys survived into the 1700s. On 31 December 1716, for example, in East Antony, the steward accounted for the receipt of £2 from John Wilcocks in lieu of tithes for Geach's tenement, and noted 'harvest journey performd'. Free tenants paid nominal 'high rents' and sometimes tokens of fealty, such as a 'double rose'.

To collect his rents, the lord sometimes had to resort to distress (seizing goods to the value of the debt). Thus, on 14 December 1697, the steward, John Treis, paid 10s. to 'Nicholls the Baylief two days distraining and attending to distrain Sheviock Mannor Tennants for Arrears of Rent'.[4] He paid out another 10s. in expenses to himself, the bailiff and the reeve for four days' work. A century later, the value of the conventionary rents had hardly changed. Between 1723 and 1728, the Sheviock rents averaged £48. Between 1729 and 1735, they averaged £54. They dropped to £44 between 1736 and 1741, and rose to £51 in 1742. The real market value of the tenancies was reflected not in the rents, but in the fines or premiums payable for obtaining the leases.

On the death of a conventionary tenant, the heir had to pay to the lord a 'heriot' – the best beast or beasts on a holding. The nature and number of beasts payable as heriots varied according to the size of the holding. A 1653 survey notes the monetary equivalent of a heriot for the first time. Thus the heirs of John Harry, who farmed 13 acres in Blazor, would have to pay the lord on his death a 'heriot or 50s'.[5] In 1663, the heirs of Simon Toser, tenant of a house and garden in Portwrinkle, would have to pay 'For Herriot 10s.'.[6] The manorial survey of 1691 tabulated the different monetary equivalents payable as heriots for each holding. They vary from 1s. for Richard Wallis's cellar and palace in Portwrinkle to £5 on the death of Amos Pope who occupied 48 acres at Pool.[7] During Thomas Harvey's second spell of duty as bailiff (1704-10), he had the sad duty of paying 2s. into the manorial account 'for an Heriott [on] the death of my father'.[8]

The usual form of conventionary tenancy by the 1600s was that it was for a term of 99 years provided that certain named individuals were still living. Heriots were payable on the deaths of these named individuals just as on the death of the tenant himself. The bailiff of the manor was responsible for collecting the heriots. Thus the account of Thomas Harvey for 1693 records 'for an heriott on ye death of Rich. Winnicott being a life on ye house of Mary Winnicott in Portwrinkell . . 10s.'.[9] During his second spell of duty as bailiff, Harvey collected £3 2s. as heriot on the death of Richard Dell, who farmed 'Dell's tenement', a 25-acre holding in Trewrickle, as a sub-tenant of John Littleton.[10] Richard Dell was one of the lives named on Littleton's lease. In 1705, Thomas Harvey for the first time accounts for the receipt of certain 'rack rents'. These were leases for a period of years certain.

Receipts from the Mill

Another incident of feudal servile tenure was that the tenant had to grind his corn at the lord's mill, for which the lord received a toll or fee. On Sheviock manor, this obligation continued into the 1600s and 1700s. A lease of Cote, dated 3 December 1674, between Dame Mary Carew and Tristram Harry, yeoman, listed among the obligations 'doing suit to the mill, called Sheviock Mill, with all … corn and grain that shall be spent in and upon the said premises'.[11] This obligation was also imposed on the tenants of Holmans, Blazor, Crowstone Parks, Peakes Park and other copyhold tenements as shown in numerous leases.

Receipts from Sanding Operations

Beginning in the early Middle Ages, farmers collected sand from the beaches during the summer and carried it up to their fields on pack-horses to 'sweeten' their fields. The earliest record in Sheviock dates from 1286, when Warrin de Herth was given leave to fetch sand from 'Trewickel'.[12] After the construction of the quays on the Lynher in the 1200s, and the quay at Portwrinkle in 1612, barges also brought sand into the parish. Again, the farmers distributed the sand by pack-horse. Although sand dug up from the beach was free as a result of the charters of Richard, Earl of Cornwall, in 1250, and Henry III in 1261, the lord was entitled to take a toll from each pack-horse that used the sandways over his land up to the fields. The toll charged on each pack-horse by the Dawney lords of Sheviock is not known. The toll charged by the Stonor lords at Ermington in South Devon was 2d. on each pack-horse in the early 1400s.[13] In 1755, the steward, William Corinton, ordered the reeve, William Bray, to levy a charge of 1s. on each pack-horse.[14] The money raised was to be used to repair the quay at Portwrinkle.

RECEIPTS FROM FISHING ACTIVITIES

Fishing activities gave several opportunities to the lord of the manor to obtain income or benefits in kind. In Sheviock in the 1300s, Sir John Dawney had his own fishing seines. However, there are no records to show what proportion of the catches he kept for his own consumption or use and what proportion he left to the fishermen. In some manors, the lord was entitled to the best fish of every catch – called the 'head' fish.[15] In others, he was entitled to a third of the catch; and in others, to a half of it.[16] It would appear, from evidence given at a post-medieval manorial court, that as well as a percentage of ordinary catches, the lord of Sheviock manor was entitled to all 'great fish', such as tuna. The fishermen also needed to dry their nets. To do so, they hung them from stakes driven into the ground, and they paid the lord for leave to do so on his land. The field called Net Park in Portwrinkle was set aside for this purpose, and charges for using it continued to be levied until modern times, though, as we have seen, the reeve could use it free of charge. The lord was also entitled to a payment from each boat that was dragged onto his foreshore, beyond the reach of the tide.

Sir John Carew (1635-92), left 'A note of my dewes att Wrickle'. It lists his proposed takings from the fishermen:

1 The Twentieth fish of all sortes taken for clensing ye key
2 One share of each [seining] Company for a convenient place to dry the Netts
3 One shilling of every Share [in a fishing seine] from ye p[ar]ishoners & two & six[d] fro[m] strangers
4 All great Fish.[17]

This tariff is based partly on the ancient rights belonging to the lord of the manor ('all great fish') and partly on the provisions of the 1612 agreement for the building of the quay at Portwrinkle, discussed in Chapter 15.

Payment of 'one twentieth' of fish in kind

The payment of 'the Twentieth fish of all sortes' applied to all the fishermen throughout the year. It was payable in addition to the year-end contribution discussed below. All fishermen based in Portwrinkle had to make this payment, even if they were not part of a seining company. These periodic tributes were normally paid in kind rather than commuted into cash. In 1693, fish was sent up to Antony in every month from April to December, and then again in January 1694. The total value of the fish was £3 2s. 1d. In the following year, fish was again sent up to the house each month from May to December. The total value of the fish had dropped to £1 11s. In May 1717, an unnamed fisherman sent 15 mackerel to Sir William Carew at Antony; John Rundell sent 50 pilchards in July, another 100 in August, and (exceptionally) the cash value of another 50 in September. John Holman sent 50 pilchards in August, and another 100 in September. Walter Sonn sent 100 pilchards to Antony in November.[18]

On five separate occasions in April 1722, the bailiff, Thomas Harvey, sent a total of 137 mullets up the house, plus the cash value (6d.) of another five. In that year, only one seine seems to have been able to operate out of the harbour at any one time. The reason for this was that the harbour and quay were in a bad state of repair. 100 pilchards from a seine were sent up to the house in August, and another 100 in September. At this time Philip Palmer, John Harvey and William Bray were going out in single craft and using drift nets to catch the pilchards. In August, Philip Palmer sent up to Antony 100 pilchards from his drifting operations. He caught some more in October and commuted his payment of fish into a cash payment of 4s.[19] Harvey sent 50 pilchards up to the house in November and commuted another payment of fish into 3s. cash. Bray sent 50 pilchards up to Antony in December and commuted another payment into 2s. 6d. John Dyer, who also earned his living as a cooper, sent 100 pilchards to the house in December, and George Bone sent up another 100 in the following January. In January, a total of 53 bass were sent up to the house and another

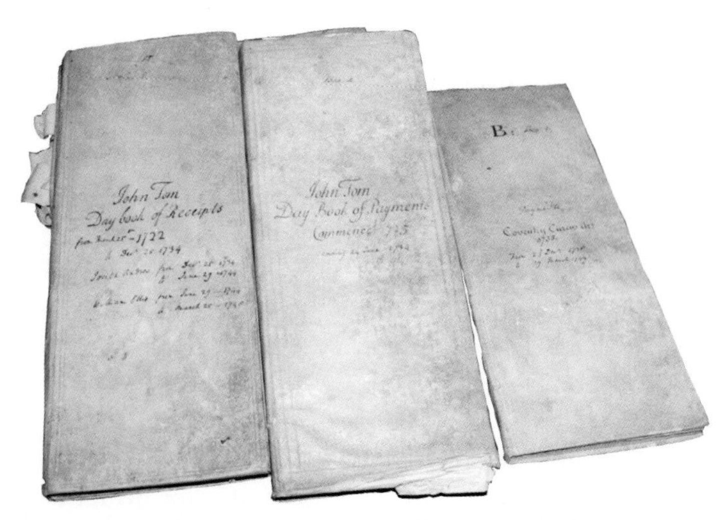

60 *Account books of John Tom, steward to Sir William Carew from 1714 to 1734.*

20 in February. The quay was repaired in February 1723.[20] In March that year, 23 mullets and bass were sent up to Antony. In 1724, three seining companies were again in operation. Philip Palmer and John Harvey each sent 100 pilchards up to Antony in November. In December, William Bray and John Harvey each sent up 100 pilchards. On behalf of Sir William, Coventry Carew in about 1740 also claimed the twentieth part of every catch from strangers visiting Portwrinkle to sell their fish.

Reginald Pole Carew also claimed one twentieth of all sorts of fish from both parishioners and strangers using the port.

Payment for a convenient place to dry the nets

In 1722, the bailiff, Thomas Harvey, claimed on behalf of Sir William Carew one and a half shares for 'the place' (i.e. the use of the net park) in the limited seining operations carried out that year. The rate had gone up from the 'one share' demanded by Sir John Carew. The shares demanded by Sir William paid out 5s. 7½d. at the end of 1722.

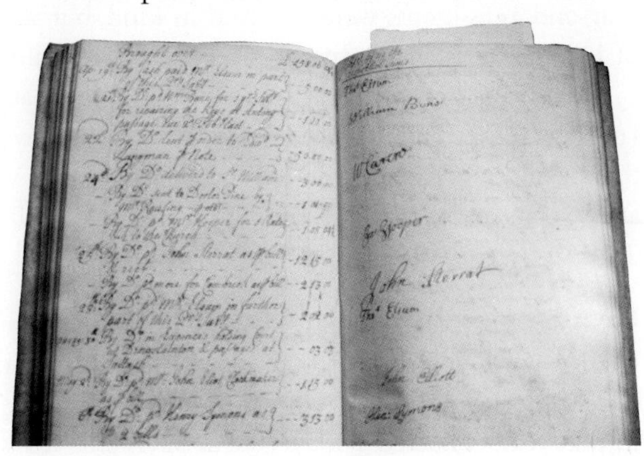

61 *Account book of John Tom, showing signature of Sir William Carew.*

Payment of 1s. per share

The 1612 agreement laid down a scale of charges payable by the users of the quay. Under it, each of the fishing companies paid 1s. per share to the lord per annum, provided they made at least ten shillings profit that year. Under this provision, for the full year 1714, John Prinn's company paid Sir William Carew 9s; Philip Palmer's company paid 7s.; William Bray's and John Rundell's companies each paid 5s.; and Francis Avery's company paid 3s. It will be seen that five seining companies were operating that year, suggesting a total of at least 15 boats using the little harbour. In 1717, Thomas Harvey's company paid 7s. to Sir William; Philip Palmer's company paid 5s.; John Holman's company paid 4s.; and William Braye's company paid 3s.[21] In 1733, when fewer pilchards were caught, but more mullets, Philip Palmer's company paid 6s.; John Dyer's company paid 3s; and Anthony Wallis's and John Harvey's each paid 1s.[22] In 1724, Philip Palmer paid 10s. 'for his Drift Fish' and John Harvey and William Bray each paid 5s. for theirs.

Quay dues

In 1724, five 'strangers' – i.e. fishermen from neighbouring ports – came into Portwrinkle to sell their fish. Each paid 1s. to Sir William for use of the port. In *c*.1740, 'Mr Carew' noted, 'Every Inhabitant of Portwrickle to pay one shilling a year as Acknowledgement & to enter each Boat in Court'. 'Mr Carew' also claimed from 'All strangers who at any time may put in at Portwrickle ... one shilling each time for Quay Dues'.[23] Reginald Pole Carew charged the same amount for 'acknowledgement'.

Payment of fish for profits

Under the 1612 Agreement, for every £1 of annual profit per share that was earned by each seine, the shareholder was obliged to pay the lord of the manor 1,000 fish. These year-end assessments were not paid in kind, but were commuted into cash at the rate of 1s. per 200 pilchards. In February 1715, the bailiff, Thomas Harvey, paid the steward £1 16s. 7½d. 'for fish rec[d] for keyage of the boats at Portwrincle'.[24] The following January, he paid in another £2 14s. 10d. These payments may have been made under this heading. In December 1717, Philip Palmer's year-end contribution was assessed at 600 pilchards; William Bray's was assessed at 450; and John Holman's was assessed at 200. All these payments were commuted into cash.

Payments for storage of fish

Payments were also due to the lord of the manor for storage of fish on the quay (not covered by Sir John Carew's note above). In 1693, Henry Lavers, probably the reeve in that year, collected £3 6s. 10d. as payments for 'store fish' from William Bray, John

Deeble, Walter Son, John Austin, and Symon Sarle. The fish stored were presumably pilchards, because he collected another 5s. 1d. from John Harvey for 'store mackrel'.[25] He paid the money, less expenses, to Sir Richard Carew's steward, John Treis. In 1694, Walter Son paid the steward £2 5s. 'for store fish from the 12th May to the 26th of December 1694, due to the Key'.[26] In the following year, Son collected payments for storing pilchards totalling £2 3s. from Deeble, Bray and Son again and from Richard Austen (probably replacing his father) and Thomas Harvey. He collected another 3s. for the storage of 'molets'. In 1722, only one seining company was in operation and in October it paid 14s. for storage of pilchards.

Payment of 'Protections' by Barge Masters

Under the 1612 agreement, barge masters also made payments, called 'protections', for use of the quay. They stood at 3s. per barge in 1612 and had been increased to 5s. per barge by 1695.[27]

Rents for Fish Cellars and Palaces

The lord also received rents for the cellars erected on or above the foreshore to shelter the boats and their fishing equipment, and the palaces in which to cure the fish.[28]

Receipts from Wreckage and the Lord's Right to Great Fish

A record of the court leet of the manor of Sheviock, held on 13 April 1632, reads as follows:

> The Homage … doe present that Thomas Hunkyn found certen wrecke of the sea, supposed to be Amber grease of Nynety Pownd waight between Keslake Sand way & Blerick Sand Way the XVth day of March last past, wherof th'one halfe is due to the Lord by the custome of the said Mannor. & the other moyty [moiety or half] to the finder, And farther say that a Tunney or any such greate fish coming a shore wth.in the Mannor. one halfe belongeth to the Lord of the said Mannor. And further say by the reporte of Jeoffry Hooper now present and sworne that it hath byn heretofore testified that the Lord of this Mannor. is to have wreck of the sea soe farr in the sea as a man can cast a dart att lowe water.
>
> And John Burt sayes that about 40tie yeares sithence there was a Tunney brought ashore under Keslake grownd and was deliver unto Richard Carewe Esquire nowe deceased by the hands of the said John Burte.'[29]

This presentment was interpreted to mean that wreckage was shared equally between the lord and the finder, but that the whole of a great fish should be given to the lord. Halibut was included amongst the great fish as well as 'tunney' (tuna). The story of the finding of the ambergris (a by-product of the whale) spread rapidly and, like all good fishing stories, was much exaggerated in the re-telling. By the time Dr William Borlase retold it more than a century later in his manuscript for a projected parochial history of Cornwall, the ambergris had grown to be 'about 160lbs weight all in one lump; it seemed like the trunk of a tree broken off from the bottom of it by violence of the waves'.[30]

On the dangerous Cornish coast, wreckage that drifted ashore from shipwrecks was a valuable perquisite of the lordship of Sheviock manor. In 1691, Thomas Harvey collected 17s. for 'wreck timber'. He also charged 2s. for his work in 'carryage & fetching another peece by boat'. Entries in his account for 1693 read: 'for ye feaching home of a pompe with a boat ... 1s' and 'for ye feaching home of a shipes yeards with a boat ... 1s'.[31] On 1 December 1696, the steward, John Treis, spent 2s. 6d. 'at Wrickell saving Wreck'.[32] Thomas Harvey's account for 1704-10 states: 'Received for pte of a ca[b]el and Ancor taken up in Sr William['s] Royalty which was wreak ... £2' and 'received more for wreak ... 2s'.[33] In January 1721/2, the steward paid the reeve, William Bray, £1 1s. 'for salvage of a mast brought by him & others into Portwrinkle'.[34] The Antony accounts show small sums received for wreckage in most years up to 1806.[35] For example, in December 1794, a 'Small stick of Timber' valued at 2s. was taken up by Jane Hooper and Mary Wills at Portwrinkle, and 'a small piece of Deal' valued at 1s. was taken up by James Derry at Liscawne Sandway. In the following February, part of a boat valued at £1 3s. was taken up by Henry Davey, William Shears and others at Liscawn Sandway. Next May, an oar valued at 3s. was taken up by William Gray at Kerslake Sandway. In each case, half the value went to the finders and half to the lord. Another lucky finder was Robert Adams, who in 1794 found a keg of gin washed ashore. He was paid 2s. 4½d. ex gratia 'on account of his Poverty'.

Short of being wrecked, ships could become stranded and the owners could seek permission to land goods from them. This permission was called 'land leave'. In 1691, a Mr Peter of Looe paid the bailiff, Thomas Harvey, £5 to land goods from a stranded ship.

MARKETS AND FAIR

In 1314, Edward II granted to Nicholas Dawney and his heirs the right to hold a weekly market in their manor of 'Shiviok' at 'Croftilberwe' (Crafthole) and a three-day fair in July. The market was to be held on a Wednesday. Later another market was licensed on Friday. The lord took tolls from those who sold goods at the markets. He also received the fines paid for breaches of the assizes of bread and ale by the tenants of the manor. The borough of Crafthole was created at the same time as the market. When, in 1540, Henry VIII separated the ownership of the borough from that of the manor of Sheviock, the right to hold markets and the annual fair adhered to the borough and was lost to the manor.[36]

REVENUES FROM WOODLANDS

The Domesday survey of 1086 showed that some 30 per cent, or about 600 acres, of Sheviock was then woodland. As now, the largest piece of woodland would have been Sheviock woods, followed by Sconner woods, and then the woodland along the banks of Wacker Creek, and the low-lying parts of Kerslake. Over time the timber was felled and 'parks', enclosed fields, were carved out of the woods. The whole of Haye Farm (117 acres) and Treise's tenement (55 acres) were carved out of Sheviock woods. Sconner Farm, though ancient, was enlarged to 83 acres by taking in much of Sconner woods. By 1840/1, when the Tithe Redemption Survey was compiled, the woodland in Sheviock had been reduced to 229 acres.

Sales of timber and coppice wood

The primary value of woodland was as a source of timber or coppice wood. The coppice wood could be sold either for fuel or for turning into charcoal. In the early 1300s, Sir William Dawney granted a close called Prior's Brake in Sheviock woods to the Prior of St Germans to compensate him for giving up his right to take timber from the woods.[37] In 1514, the trustees of Lady Katherine Courtenay sold all the timber in Sheviock woods lying between the Greenawaye and Fenton Ogglake to two merchants of Plymouth for 40 marks (£26 13s. 4d.).[38] From time to time, stands of coppice woods were put up for sale. In the 1600s, when timber or coppice wood was to be sold, a surveyor was hired to carry out a survey of the woodland in question, and a 'cryer' was paid to announce that the survey was to be carried out. In December 1694, the steward, John Treis, paid 12s. for a survey to be carried out, 1s. for a crier to announce it, and another 2s. 2d. for criers to proclaim the forthcoming sale in two towns and four other parishes. A note relating to an 18th-century survey is preserved in the Antony archives. It reads:

> A survey held this 20th of January 1725 at the house of Sibella Warren [probably the former Church House] in Sheviock by John Tom Steward to Sir Wm. Carew Bar^{t} for selling the woods in sd. Parish … viz. Greenaway, containing about 15 acres of about 30 years growth & Gillball wood contg 36 acres or thereabout of the same growth the buyer to be allowed one acre in Greenaway wood for waste and three acres in Gillball wood for waste & to have three years allow'd for felling the first wood & one year more for clearing. The buyer to pay the tithe, and to be allow'd four years for felling & one year more for clearing the lat[t]er.[39]

A note recorded the outcome as follows:

> Contracted & agreed this 20th day of January 1725 with John Tom within mencon'd for Greenaway wood for the sum of [£11 12s. 1d.] per acre according to the proposals & conditions mencon'd in the within Survey. Witness my hand Philip Palmer.[40]

The successful bidders were a syndicate of three: Philip Palmer, John Dyer of Sheviock, cooper, and Oliver Neilder of Antony. They paid a total of £184 5s. over the three years 1727-9. One of the purposes of their bid was to make charcoal. The document of sale records their right to

> Fell, Cut down, Rick, Carry away & Clear [the 15 acres] … and also Liberty to make Coalpits in the said wood & to Dig & take Turf and Moss there for covering the same: And pasture in the said wood for their horses, mares, mules and nags while the coalpacks are filling and their horses lading & not longer or otherwise.[41]

The lord of the manor often required these same woodland products for his own use. Sir William Carew employed Charles Congdon to burn charcoal for him on a regular basis. In September 1727, he paid him £2 3s. for burning 106 packs at 6d. a pack.[42]

In December 1743, Joseph Andrew, acting on behalf of Sir William's son, Coventry Carew, sold to William Copplestone of St Veep (where the Carews owned property), the right to fell coppice wood in Sconner Wood for £7 10s. per acre. In December 1744, Sir Coventry sold half of the coppice wood called Gill Ball wood to Hugh Littleton of St Germans for £7 per acre.[43] In 1745, he agreed to sell about five acres of coppice called Allers near Sconner for £2 5s. 6d. per acre.

Occasionally, the subject of sale was not coppice wood, but timber sawn from mature trees felled on the estate. Thus a note dated 13 July 1767 records that 12 pieces of timber of lengths varying from 14 to 34 feet was sold to Arthur Bartlett at a price of 15s. per foot. The whole bill came to £16 15s. 3¾d. Bartlett was the miller at Wacker, and in 1767 he also took on the lease of Sheviock Mills at Polscoe. Probably he needed the timber to effect repairs at his new mill.

During the early and mid-1900s, larch was grown in abundance in Sheviock woods. When felled, the trees were sent to South Wales and other mining areas for use as pit props. Two full-time woodsmen attended to the work. Today the Forestry Commission manages the woodland on behalf of Antony Estates.

Pannage

During the Middle Ages, a second benefit of woodland was that it provided food for pigs in the form of acorns and beech mast. The right to pasture swine in this way was called 'pannage' and was a source of profit to the lord. The parishioners drove their pigs to a collection point in the parish early in the autumn (perhaps the place called *polbathic*, 'pool for the pigs'). The parish swineherds would then take them up to the lord's woods for their autumn foraging. In 1460, Henry Bodrugan received 8s. '*de pannag' porcorum pastur' in bosco*' (for pannage of pigs foraging in the wood) from his manor of Restronguet, near Truro.[44]

Payments for Hunting (and Fishing Licences)

The third benefit of woodland was as a place for hunting and recreation. In medieval and Tudor times, hunting in the woods would have been for birds, wild boar and deer. There is a Hawks Wood in Sheviock woods, on the eastern side of George's Lane where it meets the River Lynher. The name may derive from its being a favourite breeding ground of hawks, or it may be named after a member of the Hawke family. Another possibility is that it was a piece of woodland set aside for hunting with hawks. In Norman French, these places were called '*places volatiles*'. In 1468 each such place would have fetched 4d. a year.[45] Today the hunting is for game birds in season. A syndicate of local farmers manages the shoot on behalf of Antony Estates.

According to a survey of the Duchy manor of West Antony made in 1608, Ferdinando Spiller, the Sheviock miller and innkeeper, and his daughter, Mary, had, by copy of a court roll dated 23 October 1576, taken a reversion of the rights to fish and hunt water birds in Thankes Bay and Pengelly Bay and half the fishing rights in St Peter's Bay, St John's Bay and Wacker Lake.[46] According to John Norden's survey, Mary was paying a rent of 2s. 8d. for these rights in 1615. The lords of Sheviock manor may have issued similar licences in respect of their stretches of the River Lynher and Trethill Lake.

Manorial Expenditures

The biggest capital expenditures of the manor were for the construction of houses and the building and repair of the quays at Portwrinkle and on the River Lynher as discussed in Part IV of this book. In the 18th century, some manorial lords, including Sir Coventry Carew, began to endow schools for poor children. The endowment of schools is considered in Chapter 38.

Audit Dinners

The tenants settled up the rents and other payments owing to the manor in May and October, when the courts leet were held. It became customary at these times to hold a dinner, called the 'audit dinner'. This may well have been a survival from the 'scotale' of medieval times.[47] Originally all the tenants were required to attend court, swear their fealty and make their payments. The dinners were held after the court meetings. On the manor of Sheviock the dinners survived into the 18th century when they were held at an inn in Crafthole. This was probably the inn that is now called the Finnygook, which was built on the site of the old manor-house of the Dawneys where the scot-ales would once have been held. Although the tenants contributed to the cost, the greater part of the expense was born by the lord of the manor. The accounts of dinners held between 1763 and 1766 have been preserved and are summarised in Chapter 41, *Inns and Innkeepers*.

Feeding the Hungry

The lord of the manor was expected to feed the hungry at all times and to provide special fare for the poor on Christmas Eve. The will of Sir Coventry Carew, who died in 1748, shows how he and his ancestors discharged these responsibilities. He ordered that,

> the person ... who shall have and enjoy [Antony House and its estate] ... shall keep up and continue the ancient and weekly and yearly Customs of me and my Ancestors in the Distribution among the poor every Thursday in the Week by giving each poor person of the [Parish of Antony] one Gallon of Wheaten Meal as far as a Bushell of Wheat[48] will extend and go and ... give among the poor of the several Parishes of Anthony Sheviocke Saint Stephen's next Saltash and Maker on every Christmas Eve yearly eight Hundred Pounds weight of Beef together with five Bushells of Wheat made into Loaves to be also given away and distributed among the said poor according to the ancient Rule and Custom of my Father and his Ancestors.

Chapter 8

Holdings on Sheviock Manor

Most holdings on Sheviock manor were let to tenants.[1] From the late 1600s, these tenancies were recorded in surveys, often accompanied by maps, made for the Carew estates.[2] The best of the maps is Thomas Pride's made in 1775.[3] The process of creating, dividing or amalgamating agricultural holdings has always been a dynamic one, depending on a combination of changes in population, technology and economics. A good example is the land at 'Trewykkell' (Trewrickle). John Penhale's account for 1410-11 suggests that Trewrickle was then a single large holding and that John Sturr was the tenant. His tithes of corn were sold for £3 1s. 4d., the second highest amount in the parish. Only Sheviock Barton yielded a higher sum. But Trewrickle contained much land that was difficult to cultivate. It was probably only in the late 1400s or early 1500s that improvements in technology and techniques allowed the rough areas to be brought under the plough and the land to be sub-divided. The names of the fields in the survey of 1775 identify the problems relating to their cultivation: Chubb's tenement contained 'Stoney Readen' – 'readen' is the Cornish *reden*, meaning bracken.[4] It also included 'Little Slade' and 'Clay Park'.[5] Blight's tenement contained 'Furze Brake', 'Readen', 'Great Slade' and 'Higher Clay Park'. Brown's included 'Marsh', 'Little Readen', 'Higher Burrows', 'Lower Burrows' and 'Slade'. Much of this land therefore would have been impossible to till in the early Middle Ages and for some years after the Black Death of 1348, when labour was very scarce. The problem of invasive bracken has re-emerged with the recent decline in agricultural production.[6]

In the 1500s, landowners began to sub-divide many of the large medieval open fields with walls and hedgerows. The reeve of the manor of Landrake, William Samuell, wrote of Blerrick in 1578 'most of it lyeth in common among [the tenants] undivided and the rest in several closes', showing that the process of sub-division had just begun there.[7] The Revd Walter Arundell (rector 1576-1622) gave a personal account of new enclosures made by him on his glebe land in Sheviock. He listed, '2 Closes called Lady Well divided by mee' and another '2 Closes, divided by mee, called the south downe'.

The division of the land into many small fields was accompanied by the creation of many small separate tenancies.

The process of sub-division started to go into reverse in the 19th century. In 1775, according to Thomas Pride's survey, the manor of Sheviock (which then covered only half the area of the total parish) consisted of 35 tenements covering an area of 1,139 acres. This meant an average of 32.5 acres per tenement. In 1840, there were only 18 tenements on the lands in question, covering some 1,044 acres. The average size had therefore increased to 58 acres. By 1840, many individual holdings had gone, as well as the entire hamlet of Trewrickle, which had consisted of a settlement of five small farms, with all their farmhouses, barns, and outbuildings. There were also three other houses in Trewrickle that did not have their own farmland. The average size of the farms at Trewrickle in 1775 was just 30 acres, but the village was home to some forty to fifty people. The holdings then were Chubb's, Blight's, Peake's, Warren's (also called Brown's or Holman's), and Dell's. Together they covered an area of 185 acres. By 1840, there were just two farms in the settlement, Blight's, consisting of 70 acres, and Samuel Littleton's, consisting of 71 acres. There was one other house and garden. Today there is just one large agricultural holding, Trewrickle Farm, and two houses at Pool.

Individual Holdings on the Manor, excluding Demesne Farms and Trewrickle

Bonne's (Bonneys, Bonnyes, Bunny's) Parks

This holding consisted of 15 acres between Sheviock churchtown and Crafthole and was often farmed with **Liscawn** to which it was adjacent. The name is probably derived from that of the Bonne or Bonney family. In 1669, the parks were described as 'alias Spurryers-parkes', presumably after an earlier occupier.[8] In Henry VIII's muster roll of 1522, William Bonne was assessed for goods worth £8, John Bonne for goods worth £6, and Richard Bonne for goods worth £2. The widow, Joan Bonney, was living in High House up to September 1554.[9] In 1585, Richard Carew granted John Bonne a 99-year lease of a cottage near to Crafthole together with some 60 perches of land.[10] In 1663, Bonne's Parks were let to Thomas Smith of Liscawn for 15s. a year.[11] In 1691, the tenants were Nicholas and Samuel Smith and John Deeble of Liscawn on their own lives.[12] In 1726, the parks were let at the same rent to John Deeble of Liscawn, who was also farming **Vellands** and **Mattick**'s parks.[13] The tenant in 1772 was Mrs Ann Deeble. A Thomas Bone died before 31 January 1715/16, when David 'Dustow' (**Dewstowe**) was buried beside him.

Cote (also Coate)

This holding formerly included seven acres of land. The earliest records show that it was usually let together with **Crafthole Parks**. Often the tenant was one of the principal farmers or tenants on the Carew estates who had retired, or his widow. The earliest recorded tenant was Margery Spiller, the widow of the miller and innkeeper, Ferdinando.[14] Ferdinando had probably also been bailiff of the manor. Margery died before 1613 when Cote and Crafthole Parks were leased to Joane Hitchins, widow of John Hitchins, who had farmed at Sheviock Barton. The lives named on the lease were her own and those of her sons, William and Ralph Hichins. The rent was 12s. 4d. for Cote and 8s. 8d. for Crafthole Parks, as well as one hen (or 8d.) for each holding, payable at Christmas. The tenant was required to do suit to Sheviock manor court and to grind his or her corn at Sheviock Mill.

An entry in the parish registers shows that the cottage was later inhabited by John Arundell (*c.*1630–*c.*1694), second son of the rector, Gregory Arundell. He was paying £1 3s. 6d. in rent between 1656 and 1660. This corresponds more or less with the rent for Cote and Crafthole Parks.[15] 'John Arundell of Coat' was mentioned in the 1691 survey of the manor in connection with (Hodge) **Edwards' Parks**.[16]

In 1694, the steward, John Treis, paid 16s. 6d. to have a survey carried out on 'Coat and Hodgedwards-parks' and he paid a further 1s. 2d. for a crier to announce it. The result was that Dame Mary Carew and her trustees let the holding of Cote to Tristram Harry at the same rent as before on the lives of his wife, Martha, Tristram Stephens (son of William Stephens of Crafthole) and Grace Hamley.[17] John Treis witnessed the lease. In 1726, the cottage was let to Mrs Elizabeth Wallis.[18] In 1770, Cote was let to Thomas Littleton. His brother, Hugh, farmed at Sheviock Barton and Treis's tenement.[19] In 1833-4, Cote and Hawkeswood were let to John Trevan who had previously farmed at Sheviock Barton. From 1858 to 1861, the tenant of Cote was John Langmead. Tom and Mary Bersey, who had previously farmed at Sheviock Barton, became the tenants in 1991.

Crafthole Parks

This tenement of eight acres consisted of three fields near the top of the hill on the north side of the road from Crafthole to Polscoe. It was often let, together with **Cote**. Richard Carew leased the parks to Margery, widow of Ferdinando Spiller, after her husband's death in 1607.[20] In 1613, he leased them to another widow, Joan Hichins (whose husband, John, had farmed at Sheviock Barton) in consideration of the sum of 'one hundred fower score pounds' on the lives of her children. The rent was 8s.8d. and one hen. John Hitchens, who died in 1648, later farmed at Sheviock Barton and Crafthole Parks. In 1663, one Edwards (perhaps John) was farming the parks as a sub-tenant of Gabriel Arundell on the lives of Gabriel's sons, Walter and John, and his daughter, Dorothy.[21] In 1691, the parks were let to Tristram Harry (also the tenant of Cote) on the life of Henry Neilder.[22] In 1721, they were let to John Harvey on the lives of himself and his wife, Amy, their daughter Mary, and

Joan Arundell. The rent was 9s. 4d.[23] He was also renting **Edward's Parks**. In 1760, Jonathan Rashleigh of Menabilly, a trustee of the late Sir Coventry Carew, let the parks to Samuel Lyne of Antony on the lives of Lyne's son, John (age 31) and his grandsons, Samuel (10) and Edward (eight).[24] The consideration was £84 and the rent was 8s. 8d. In 1840, Samuel Lyne, probably a great-grandson, was still farming 22 acres of the merged Crafthole Parks and Edward's tenement. In 1858, the tenant of the 22 acres was John Witton, and from 1859 to 1862 James Jeffrey, who also occupied Poole Farm. See further 'Crafthole Park Farm' in Chapter 13, *Houses, Shops and Farms in Crafthole*.

Cross Parks (also Horse Pool Farm)

This tenement on the north side of the crossroads at 'Stop or Cross' (Stumpy Cross) consisted of two fields, orchards and meadows, containing about eleven acres. The earliest recorded tenant is the 16th-century rector, Walter Arundell. The next tenant may have been Gabriel Arundell, a younger son of Walter, under a lease (now largely illegible) of 1640 on the lives of three of his children, John, Walter and Dorothy.[25] The holding then passed to Alexander Arundell, and to Nicholas Smith, son of Thomas Smith of Liscawn. This information was recorded in the lease of the tenement to Anne Peters dated 25 February 1672. Her rent was 10s. and two hens yearly at Christmas.[26] The tenant had to grind his/her corn at 'the mill called Sheviock mill', do suit of court at the manorial court, and perform customary services. Thomas Dinner succeeded Anne Peters. Then, in 1711, Cross Parks was leased to Griffith Bidlake for 99 years on his own life and that of his daughters. Bidlake's 'fine' for the new lease included a golden guinea valued at £1 1s. 6d., to be given to Lady Anne, Sir William's wife. Bidlake was still the tenant in 1726.[27] In 1748, Hugh Littleton paid the 7d. church rate for the tenement, and was presumably the tenant.[28] In 1751, the holding was let to Thomas Bews (also Bewes) at the same rent. The lease was for 99 years on the lives of his children, William (age 21), Elizabeth (age 14) and Thomas (age nine).[29]

In 1767, in view of advancing age, Thomas Bews the elder passed over all his property, leases, and farming equipment to his son, Thomas.[30] On Cross Parks, he then had two oxen, two cows, two calves, two heifers, two steers, three pigs, one sow and young pigs, 12 ewes and 12 lambs, and two horses.[31] He used the eight acres of his other holding, **Friday's Parks**, to cut hay and grow corn. He was making 20 casks of cider from his orchards in Coombe and Cross Parks.

In 1773, John Carew's widow, Mary, assigned the lease of Cross Parks to Thomas Bews the younger, who was already farming it and was still doing so in 1809-10. William Bews was the tenant in 1820-1. By 1809, the holding had become known as

'Horse Pool Farm', because the farmhouse was in an orchard near the horse pool on the road between Sheviock churchtown and Stop or Cross. In 1833-4, the tenant was Henry March, who also leased the nearby Polscoe Mills. From 1858 until the 1860s, the tenant was the Sheviock innkeeper, John Peter Landry.

Dewstowe's (Harvey's) Tenement

This tenement consisted of a house, stable, garden and two orchards, and eight acres of fields on the east side of the road leading from Crafthole to Sheviock. The fields were called Homer Field, Home Well Park, Well Park and Shut Park (also Shut Post). There was also a small orchard in the Coombes attached to the farm. The tenement lay to the south of **Hearle's Parks**. In 1663, Sir John Carew leased 'all that one messuage & tenement ... late in the tenure of William Dewstow' to John Harvy the elder.[32] The lease was on his own life and that of his son, Thomas. William Dewstowe may have been the son of Dowell Dewstowe, a shipmate of Richard Harle on the *Dayestarr*. The rent was 10s. and one fat capon or 12d. A David 'Dustow' (Dewstowe) was buried beside Thomas Bone on 31 January 1715/16.

In 1737, Sir William Carew leased to Francis Martyn (also Martin) 'all that one Messuage and Tenement ... late in the tenure ... of Thomas Harvey deceased'.[33] The rent was unchanged. Sometime before 1752, the tenement came into the possession of the innkeeper, William Lord.[34] In 1764, Mrs Lord was the tenant.[35] In 1771, John Carew leased it to his brother-in-law, Francis Webber of Exeter.[36] Webber also had the tenancy of a 161-acre holding at Sconner. No doubt sub-tenants actually worked the farms.

Edwards' Parks (also Hodge's Parks)

This tenement of seven acres was situated immediately to the north of Crafthole Parks. John Hodge, one of the farmers after whom the parks were named, was born in 1609. He is first mentioned as a tenant of Sheviock manor in a rental of 1634.[37] A rental of 1653 shows him renting a 21-acre tenement with a farm house in Lower Tregantel in Antony, at a rent of 10s. 10d.[38] His wife, Alice, was then aged 37.

Thomas and John Edwards, probably brothers, lived in Sheviock parish in the late 1600s and early 1700s. Thomas engaged extensively in fishing activities at Portwrinkle and also farmed in a small way. John, who married Grace, daughter of the wealthy Richard Wallis, had three farm tenancies. These were a quarter of Blazor and **Holman**'s and **Peake**'s tenancies. In 1706, John had been the hind (farm manager) of the Carew estates in Antony and Sheviock.[39] The Edwards after whom this holding was named may have been the father of Thomas and John. Neither brother is mentioned in the surviving leases relating to Edwards' Parks.

In 1691, Edwards' Parks was let to John Balsey and John Harvey on the lives of John Arundell of Cote, John Harvey and his wife Amy, and Mary Arundell.[40] The rent was 8s. 8d. In 1726, John Harvey alone leased Edwards' Parks at the 1691 rent.[41] In 1775, Samuel Lyne senior was leasing the parks on the life of his son, William (age 20) and his daughter, Sarah (age 17).[42] From 1809-10 to 1833-4, Samuel Lyne was leasing the parks.

Friday's Parks[43]

This holding consisted of eight acres at the bottom of the road leading from Crafthole to Polscoe, and immediately to the west of **Crafthole** Parks and **Edwards'** Parks. Thomas Fryday was appointed rector of St John in 1519. The most westerly of the four fields comprising the parks was adjacent to the stone cross at the crossroads called 'Stop or Cross' (Stumpy Cross). In 1663, the parks were let to William Hancock and Agupta Moyle, for 8s. 8d.[44] In 1691 (when its extent was given as 12 acres), the tenant is given as 'John Balson (Balsey) by Joan Arundel on the lives of John Arundell junior, Joan and Mary Arundell and Richard Odiorne'.[45] The rent was 8s. 8d. and two hens. Joan Arundell paid the last part of her fine for her lease in 1714.[46]

In 1726, Friday's Parks was let to Henry Short at an annual rental of 10s.[47] The tenant in 1767 was Thomas Bews the elder.[48] Joseph Bickford, the blacksmith, was the tenant in 1809-10. His brother, John, was the miller at Polscoe. In 1833-4, the tenant was Thomas Every or Avery, the farmer at Haye, a demesne farm on the manor of Sheviock (see Chapter 4).

Hearle's (Herle's, Harles, Earles) Parks

Richard Hearle or Harle lived in the borough of Crafthole in the early 1600s. He was a fisherman and a member of the crew of the *Dayestarr* in 1626. He served as portreeve (mayor) of the borough in 1628 and 1634, and was a juror on the court leet of the borough in 1634, 1636-41 and 1644. It is likely that the parks were named after him. His shipmate, Dowell Dewstowe, probably lived on the neighbouring holding, called **Dewstowe's** tenement. In 1634, Richard Hearle leased a holding in Sheviock at a rent of 6s. 8d. The lease was on the lives of his daughters Agnes (born in 1623) and Mary.

The parks were situated on the east side of the road going down from Crafthole to Sheviock. They consisted of three fields containing just over eight acres. Later Cross Park (different from **Cross Parks**, mentioned above), containing two acres, was added to the holding. Cross Park lay on the other side of the road. In 1640, Richard Carew the younger let Hearle's parks to Phillip Wallis of Lanlivery.[49] In 1663, the parks were let to the heirs of Tristram Harry senior, who had died in 1638, on the lives of Agnes Harry (age 40 in 1663), 'Tristram Harry ye third sonn' (age 10) and John Reede (age 40).[50] The rent was 8s. 2d. and two capons or 10s. 2d. The tenant had to do suit and service to the lord's court. The parks are shown on a 1691 survey of the manor as leased to Tristram Harry (born 1643) and Joan Arundell (who probably became his wife), on the lives of himself and Joan, their daughter, Mary, and Robert Harry.[51] The rent was unchanged. In 1719, for a consideration of £105 and 'one piece of gold commonly called a Jacobus' (a coin minted in the reign of James II (1685-88)), Sir William Carew leased the parks to Joan Arundell (born in 1657), widow, on the lives of her daughters, Mary, and Amy, the wife of John Harvy of Sheviock.[52] The rent was now 10s. 2d. and two capons or 2s. In 1726, after Joan's death, the parks were leased to Henry Short of St Germans, at a rent of 12s. 2d.[53] In 1741, Hearle's Parks were leased to Peter Kitt, age 29, on the lives of his wife, Mary (age 25) and his one-month-old son, Peter.[54] Hearle's Parks are marked on Thomas Pride's map of 1775, which shows that Peter Kitt was still in possession. Peter Kitt also leased one quarter of Blazor. The rents were unchanged.

Horse Pool. See **Cross Parks.**

Liscawn.
See Chapter 9, *Outlying Farms and Houses.*

Mattick's (also Maddock's) Parks
This tenement consisted of 12 acres and was adjacent to **Liscawn** to whose tenants it was usually let. The Maddock family have left no other evidence of their presence in the parish.[55] In 1663, Sir John Carew let Mattick's Parks to Nicholas Smith at a rent of 8s. 2d. and one capon.[56] In 1669, Smith surrendered this lease to take out a new lease on a 40-acre holding that included 'Mattickparkes, **Bonnyes**-parkes alias Spurryers-parkes, and the **Vellands**'.[57] The rent was 32s. 8d. and two capons or 2s. The heriot was three best beasts. The rector, Richard Rolle, was one of the witnesses. In 1698, Sir John's trustees let the same enlarged holding to Samuel Smyth on his own life and that of John Deeble, son of John Deeble, mariner.[58] The rent was as before. In 1726, the enlarged holding was let to John Deeble.[59] In 1740, Sir William Carew let the holding to the Revd Samuel Deeble, who became the rector of Sheviock in that year.[60] The lease was on his own life and those of John and Martha Snook, the children of Robert Snook of Antony, shipwright. In 1757, the previous lease was surrendered and Jonathan Rashleigh, as trustee of the will of Sir Coventry Carew, granted a new one to Ann Deeble of Liscawn, widow.[61] The lease was on her own life and on those of her daughters, Ann (age 10) and Martha Smith Deeble (age eight). Mrs Ann Deeble was still the tenant in 1772. In 1811, the executors of Henry Rolt Snook, acting on behalf of John Henry Rolt, a minor, surrendered their leases of

Chubbs, Britton, Finnygook and Roduse, and **Peake's** (half tenement) in return for a new lease of this tenement.[62]

Pool (also Poole)

This holding consisted of nearly 110 acres. The stewards' accounts of 1709 and 1710 show that it was part of the demesne lands of the manor of Sheviock. Its western boundary was formed by the stream (the Drossel) running down to Sheviock Mills (Polscoe). Its northern boundary was the road leading from Crafthole to Polscoe. Its southern boundary was a lane, largely lost, but still traceable at the Trewrickle end, which ran westwards from Crafthole to Trewrickle and then turned north to meet the stream. In about 1250, Nicholas de la Pole let the whole land of 'La Pole et Lanpilot' to Sir Henry de Alneto (Dawney) for a rent of 12d. payable at Michaelmas.[63] In 1410-11, Roger Whiteforde (who was also farming at Trethill and **Liscawn**) was farming at Pool.[64] By then, much of the land was arable. Roger's tithe of corn (ten per cent of the whole) was valued at £1 7s., implying a value of £13 10s. for the whole crop.

In a lease of 1617, part of Pool was let to a member of the Pope family, perhaps Oliver, who was married to Phillipp(a), daughter of Amos Odiorne.[65] A Sophie Pope

62 *The long valley running from Tredis (top) through Tredrossel (centre) and Pool (hidden) to Crafthole.*

is also mentioned. A 1653 survey shows Pool as divided into two holdings.[66] The fields of the one were intermingled with those of the other. The smaller of the two holdings, consisting of 48 acres, was let to Pope (age 45) at a rent of £1 7s. 5d. and two capons. In 1702, Israel Pope was living in the nearby Cross House (called Pope's House on a map of 1825). In 1669, Sir John Carew let part of Pool to John Reed of Sheviock, yeoman, at the same rent.[67] The lives named were John Pope, son of Oliver Pope, late of Sheviock, and Phillipp Blake, son of John Blake of Sheviock. In a 1691 survey, Amos Pope is shown as the tenant at the same rent. The life named was John Pope.

In 1703, a field called 'Mill Park' (three acres) and 'Mill Park Meadow' (two roods), which had been part of Sheviock Mill, were attached to Pool. The tenant of Pool then was Robert Harry, who was also farming 'the two Hayes Tenements in Sheviock'.[68] Later the tenant was Thomas Stephens and the lives were Philip Blake and Thomas Stephens. Stephens is shown as the tenant in a rental of 1726.[69] The same rental shows that the holding was further divided at this time, because Edward Hawke was the tenant of 'part of Poole' (probably twelve acres), and was paying a rent of 9s. In 1750, Jonathan Rashleigh let the holding to William Spriddel (age 24) of Stoke Damerel, shipwright.[70] The rent was £1 7s. 5d. plus two capons (or 2s.) annually. The lives named were his own and those of Thomas Stephens of Rame, fisherman (age 23) and Thomas's sister, Joan (age 24). In 1770, the tenant was Samuel Peter, who was paying £1 9s. 5d.[71] In 1809-10, John Beckford, the miller at the nearby Polscoe, and W. Blatchford shared the 48 acres.

The larger part of Pool and a part of Blazor, consisting of some 60 acres, was let to Richard Arundell (age 38) in 1653 on his own life and that of Elizabeth, his wife, at a rent of £1 11s. 10d. and two capons.[72] In a survey of 1691, this holding in Pool (and a quarter of Blazor) was let to John Dell and Symon Peter (one lease) and to Joan Arundell (the other lease).[73] The rent was £1 1s. 10d. for Pool and 10s. for the part in Blazor. The holding was then let to Tristram Harry junior.[74] The holding was next let to John Palmer, a cooper from St Stephens next Saltash, and then to the executors of Katherine Palmer at the same rent.[75] In 1749, Jonathan Rashleigh let this part of Pool to Zouch Powell, gentleman, of Tywardreath.[76]

In 1754, John Willcocks (also Wilcox) and Arthur Peter were renting separate parts of Pool. In 1770, Samuel Peter was the tenant of this part of Pool (without the portion of Blazor) and was paying £1 1s. 10d.[77] His lease appears to have united the two parts of Pool in the hands of the same tenant for the first time since the 1400s. However, the two parts remained separate entities. Thomas Pride's map of 1775 shows the holding still divided into two.[78] Philip Rashleigh was then the tenant of 51 acres of Pool and Arthur Peter the tenant of the other 57 acres. In 1787, Philip

Rashleigh demised his part of Pool to Arthur Peter for seven years at a rent of £22 10s. per annum.[79] In 1828, Reginald Pole Carew leased the entire holding to John Batten for a term of 14½ years.[80] The rent was massively increased to £125 a year so long as England was at peace, and £156 5s. if England was at war. Batten and John Willcocks (who also rented a quarter of Blazor together) were the occupants until 1834. In 1858, Joseph Tamblingson became the tenant. In 1895, James Jeffery rented the whole of Pool together with **Crafthole Parks** and **Edward's Tenement**. See further 'Crafthole Park Farm' in Chapter 13, *Houses, Shops and Farms in Crafthole.*

Sargent's Tenement

This tenement consisted of a house and nine acres on the heights above Crafthole. The fields were Culver Park, in which the Dawney's culver house stood (4 acres); Crooked Park, going down to the sea (3 acres); and banks and waste by the sea. See further Chapter 13, *Houses, Shops and Farms in Crafthole.*

Sconner Farm and Lime Kiln

Roger Skaner was assessed for goods in Sheviock in 1327. Sconner was called Stonner in 1347 and Resconern in 1410. The latter shows its origin from the Cornish *rid*, which evolved into *res*, meaning a ford, plus a proper name, Conner. In 1410-11, the tenant at 'Resconern, Trewyne and Trenthest' (Sconner, Trewin and Tredis) was John Bake of St Germans.[81] His tithes of corn (ten per cent of the crop) were valued at £2 15s., implying a value of £27 10s. for the whole crop. The Priory of St Germans came into possession of 'Skonner and Haywood' during the Middle Ages. The Crown took possession at the time of the Reformation. Queen Elizabeth passed the properties to her favourite, Robert Dudley, Earl of Leicester in April 1574. A month later, the earl sold them to Sir Henry Killigrew, who sold them to Richard Eliot of Port Eliot. His son, Sir John (1592-1632), led the parliamentary opposition to the government of Charles I and the Duke of Buckingham in 1629. In June 1617, Sir John sold 'Skonner and Haywood' to Richard Carew the younger for £50. Richard may then have been living at Sconner Farm as Sir John's tenant.[82]

One of the attorneys acting for Eliot was Richard Wallis, who later became the tenant of Sconner Farm himself. A survey of the manor of Sheviock in 1653 showed Richard Wallis (age 72) as the tenant of Sconner, on his own life and that of his son, John, then aged forty. The holding then consisted of 88 acres, and the rent was £2 13s. 4d. (plus two capons).[83] In 1653, 'Mr Richard Wallis of Skonner was buryed'.[84] John Wallis succeeded to the tenancy. In his survey of East Hundred (1684), Edward Kneebone included Sconner in his list of 'seats of note'. This was the house attached to Sconner farm, not the villa, which had not then been built. In 1696, the steward, John Treis, made several visits to Sconner to negotiate a new tenancy. The upshot was that Dame Mary Carew and other trustees of her late husband, Sir John, let 'all that Messuage and Tenement & Lime-Kill [*sic*] … called … Skonner' to John Dodridge of Tideford, yeoman. The consideration was the hefty sum of £550, payable in three instalments. The rent was 53s. 4d. plus two capons or 2s. According to a new lease issued to Dodridge in the following year, the premises had been lately 'in the tenure of John Wallis Gentleman deceased'.[85] In 1710, the tenant at the same rent was John Lyne.[86]

Henry Short took on the tenancy in 1724 at the same rent.[87] The premium or fine was £115. [88] He was also renting **Friday's Parks**. The lives named in his lease were Joan and Mary Short. He was still in possession in 1770.[89] In 1765, John Carew let the holding to his steward, James Corinton as from the deaths of Henry Short and Robert Rashleigh, son of Jonathan Rashleigh of Menabilly.[90] Corinton may have died suddenly, because in 1766 Carew let it to William Mackworth Praed as from the same deaths.[91] In 1770, Carew let Sconner and its limekiln to his brother-in-law, Francis Webber, as from the death of Robert Rashleigh.[92] In 1775, Reginald Pole Carew let the properties to Philip Rashleigh of Menabilly as from the death of Henry Short.[93] In 1780, he let them to Francis Webber from the deaths of Robert and John Rashleigh.[94] The tenancy was on the life of Mary, daughter of John Carew. In 1810, the tenant or under-tenant was William Bickford, junior. Richard Bickford succeeded William.

63 *Sconner Farm. The Dawneys granted Sconner to the monks of St Germans in the Middle Ages. Richard Carew the younger purchased it from the Eliots in 1617.*

64 *View north from Sconner Farm. Richard Carew the younger may have lived at Sconner. He became acquainted with many of the bargemen who sailed along the Rivers Tiddy and Lynher, which flow past Sconner.*

In 1823, Reginald Pole Carew came back into possession.[95] In the following year, he let Sconner to Robert Rickard of Sheviock and Jane Harris of Landulph, widow, for 14½ years.[96] The holding had been increased to some 124 acres and the lease contained lengthy good husbandry clauses. There is no mention of the limekiln. The rent had been increased to £70 per annum when England was at peace, and £87 10s. when at war. Next year the holding was reduced in size by 19 acres and the rent was reduced accordingly.[97] Robert was 75 in 1851, and in 1858, William Henry Pole Carew leased the holding to John Rickard for 14 years.[98] Unlike Robert, some thirty years earlier, John Rickard (b.c.1813) was able to read and write. The holding was now some 83 acres in extent. The rent was £73 in peace and £91 5s. in war. H. Glanville was the tenant in 1858 and Francis Glanville in 1859 and 1860. In 1866, Pole Carew let the holding to Thomas Hoskin of Crafthole for 14½ years. The rent was the same as before for the first five and a half years, and then rose to £90 in peace and £112 10s. in war. R. Bennett was the tenant in 1895. In the 1940s and '50s, Harold Waycott was the tenant. He had spent his whole life working the farm with horses. Rather than replacing them by tractors, he decided to give up the farm.

Sconner House

The house was used as a dower-house by Harriet, Lady St Germans (1790-1877), after the death of her husband, John, first Earl of St Germans, who died in 1823. She was a daughter of Reginald Pole Carew of Antony. She had nursed the earl's first wife through her final illness and married the elderly widower in 1819.[99] Pevsner states that the house is 'Regency, stone-built and stuccoed. The design is attributed in part to Repton. Fine pillared entrance hall'.[100] Repton died in 1818, so if he was involved in the design of the house or the landscaping of the grounds, he must have been commissioned during the lifetime of the earl. When the house was built, there was no road separating it from the river, and, according to the late Douglas Pett, the drive to it ran along in front of the house before ascending on the opposite side to that used by the present more direct route. 'This would have followed one of the axioms of Repton's design – namely, that an "approach" should be indirect, opening at a certain point to reveal the whole house to view in a "burst", to be admired by those entering.'[101] For at least 10 years, from 1841 to 1851, according to the census information, the house was inhabited only by the gardener, John Clements, his wife, and their family. Possibly the owners used it as a weekend or holiday residence and were not in residence when the census was taken. In 1861, Amabel Glanville, another daughter of Reginald Pole Carew, was living there with her two daughters and four servants. She was married to Francis Glanville, JP, DL (1797-1881) of Catchfrench. Their second son, Henry, was rector of Sheviock for 45 years (1856-1900). She and three members of her family were still in residence in 1871.

65 *Sconner House, built* c.*1815-20, and used as a dower-house by Harriet, Lady St Germans (1790-1877). This photograph was taken in 1920, when the house was sold at auction.*

Vellands Parks

'Vellands' meant land that had to be 'velled' to keep it productive.[102] The holding, of some 12 acres, lay on the western edge of Liscawn and was usually farmed with it. On the court roll of the manor of Sheviock held in 1528, Robert Smythe was admitted to a tenement in 'Bellond'. In 1663, the tenement was let to Thomas Smith of Liscawn.[103] The rent was 9s. 6d. and one capon. In 1691, the tenants were Samuel Smith and John Deeble on their own lives and that of Nicholas Smith, gentleman. In 1726, it was let to John Deeble at a rent of 10s. 6d.[104] The tenant in 1772 was Mrs Ann Deeble. In 1809-10, John Marks was the tenant of Vellands, **Bonny's** and **Mattick's**. In 1820-1, the tenant was Samuel Lyne, who was also farming at Liscawn. Mr 'Hillman' was probably the next tenant, because in 1833-4 rates were paid on the holding by the executors of the late Mr Hillman. In 1840, John Trevan, who lived at Cote, was the tenant of Vellands. Thomas James was the tenant from 1858 to 1861.

TREWRICKLE AND FORMER HOLDINGS THERE

Trewrickle

John Penhale's account for 1410-11 shows that Trewrickle was then a single large holding and that John Sturr was the tenant.[105] His tithes of corn (ten per cent of the crop) were sold for £3 1s. 4d., the second highest amount in the parish. In 1637,

66 *Trewrickle Farm, now one of the largest in Sheviock.*

Richard Carew the younger let Trewrickle to Richard Hockyn (also Hoskin).[106] The lease was on the lives of Richard's wife, Margery, and his daughters Elizabeth (who married William Peake) and Ursula (who married John Arundell of Cote). The consideration was £220 and the rent was 10s. 4d. The previous lessee had been Ferdinando Bray. Excluded from the lease was the two-acre field 'called Cross-Pke [i.e. Crowstone Park] ... and cellars & pallaces built in the said Close & all howsses under Cliffe'. A note on the back indicates that a new lease was later issued to John Holman. This was the lease of 9 May 1681 granted by Sir John Carew to John Holman of Trewrickle for a consideration of £50.[107] It was on the same terms as before. In 1684, Holman assigned his lease to William Lavers of St Germans, butcher.[108]

In the late 1600s, Trewrickle was subdivided into several tenements. These were **Blight's**, **Chubb's**, **Dell's**, **Peake's**, and **Warren's** (also called Warne's, Brown's and Holman's). Together they covered an area of 185 acres. By 1840, there were just two farms in Trewrickle, Blight's, consisting of 70 acres, and Samuel Littleton's, consisting of 71 acres. There was one other house and garden, called Earle's Piece in 1770, occupied by Edward Elliot Esq. Elliot had been the tenant of certain unnamed holdings in Trewrickle from 1809 to 1834, and Thomas Bewes had been the tenant of other holdings there from 1820 to 1834. From 1858 to 1861, John Cock is recorded as the occupier of 'Trewrickle Farm'. It may be that all the holdings were united into a single farm, as they are today, during his occupation. In 1899, Farmer Jones became the occupier. In 1917, he was succeeded by farmer Higman.

Blight's (also Bligh's)

This tenement consisted of 41 acres (30 in 1653 and 1691). In 1653, it was let to Elizabeth May at a rent of 20s 8d. and two capons.[109] In 1691, it was let to Robert Harry on the life of Elizabeth May.[110] Twenty-one years later it was let to William Mitchell and his assigns on the lives of Ferdinando Wallis, on his own life and that of his son, William. The rent was the same in 1726 when it was let to William Nicholl.[111] The brothers, William and Thomas Bews, were farming the tenement in 1814 when they separated out all their property held in common.[112]

Britton (Brittin; Brittaine)

The holding of Britton was at the western edge of the parish and jutted out into the sea.[113] *Brith* in Cornish means striped or variegated.

The tenement consisted of four acres in 1672 and seven acres in 1775. John Gey, clerk, and one time rector of Sheviock, was the tenant of part of Trewrickle (**Gey's**) and Britton in 1659. In 1663, he sub-let his holdings to Symon Lavers.[114] Two years' later Lavers assigned the lease to William Andrew. Sir John Carew received the surrender of Gey's lease in 1672 and granted a new one to John Pitt of St Germans, husbandman, on the lives of Pitt's son, John, and John and Mary Lavers, children of John Lavers of St Germans.[115] The rent was 2s. 7d. In 1691, the holding was let to Mr Andrew's assignee again on the lives of John Pitt, and John and Mary Lavers.[116] The rent was unchanged. In 1726, it was let to the cooper, John Dyer, at the same rent.[117] Sir William Carew issued a new lease to Dyer in 1741.[118]

Brown's. ***See*** **Warren's**

Chubb's

This tenement consisted of a house and (originally) 14 acres, later increased to 20 acres. In 1653, it was leased to William Chubb, then aged 60, who had been born in the reign of Queen Elizabeth.[119] The rent was 10s. 4d. His son, William, was a mariner (ship's officer) who married Martha, daughter of Tristram and Joan Harry. William junior became a co-tenant of Tristram Harry's quarter of Blazor, which he and Martha managed when the ageing Tristram Harry moved to **Cote** in 1694.[120] William junior surrendered his lease of Chubb's tenement to Nicholas Carkeeke, and, in 1680, Sir John Carew let the 'tenement … commonly called Trewickell … and late in the tenure of Nicholas Carkeeke' to Robert Harry.[121] The lease was on his own life and that of Philip Blake (son of John Blake of Sheviock deceased) and Stephen Holman, son of John Holman of Trewrickle. William Mitchell was the tenant in 1712, when his 'fine' included a guinea that was paid to the new Lady Anne Carew. William Nicholl was renting the holding in 1726 at a rent of 12s. 10d.[122] The holding was again let to William Mitchell in 1734, on the lives of his daughter, Thomasin (age 21) and John Croft (age 26), who became her husband. They had a daughter, Mary Mitchell Croft. In 1763, on the death of Thomasin and John, William Mitchell sold, for £20, the residue of the lease to Nicholas Crews of Fowey, gentleman, and John Croft, presumably son of the former John, a joiner at Plymouth Dock. The orphaned Mary, aged nine, continued to have a life interest in it.[123] The rent was 10s. and two capons at Michaelmas (or 2s.). John was paying 12s. for it in 1770.[124]

In 1759, Jonathan Rashleigh let to William Mitchell the house and garden in Trewrickle that had originally been occupied by Dorothy Chubb and later by Catherine Davy, widow (both deceased).[125] The rent of the house was 4s. and the lives named were William's wife, Mary (age 50) and his children, Elizabeth (age 25) and Richard (age five).

Chubb's tenement was increased to 25 acres. In 1770, John Carew let the tenement to John Snook of Plymouth 'ironmonger' on the lives of his son, Henry Rolt Snook (age 16) and John Brown of Landrake (age 10) from the death of John Croft.[126] In 1802, on the death of Henry Rolt Snook, the trustees of his heir, John Henry Rolt, let it to William Stephens of Sheviock, yeoman.[127] The holding then also included the field called Britton containing about five or six acres. The rent had increased to £23. Stephens surrendered the lease in 1812.

Crowstone Park (also Cross Park also Cliffe Park)

This tenement consisted of a field in Portwrinkle, stretching down to the sea. It is almost certainly the field granted by Erbenald Dawney and his wife, Deintedosa, to the monks of Tavistock Abbey in the 11th century.[128] It is thus the earliest named enclosure in the parish. At that time, its extent was given as two acres. The gift was renewed by Henry Dawney in his charter of 1174 to 1206. However, Henry later changed his mind and took the land back in exchange for some other property that he owned at Taviton in Tavistock. The name Crowstone is a corruption of 'cross stone' and the field was called Cross Park in a lease of 1637. The cross invoked the protection of God and also acted as a landmark for the fishermen. Because of its importance to the fishermen, the park was always excluded from leases of the surrounding agricultural tenement of **Trewrickle**.[129]

Henry Lavers leased the holding in 1691. After 1691, Thomas Edwards and Thomas Ellery leased it jointly until 1726.[130] In that year, the cooper, John Dyer (who paid 9s.), and Thomas Edwards (who paid 3s.) leased it together.[131] By 1775, the area of the park had been increased to four acres and Matthew Phillips was the sole tenant.[132] The holding was let to the Plymouth ironmonger, John Snook, in 1771, as from the death of John Ellery and Joan Edwards. It was described as a 'messuage and tenement with the cellar pallace and close of land called Crawston Park'. The rent was 8s.[133] In 1823, half an acre of land from Crowstone Park was leased to the Commissioners of Customs for the erection of cottages for customs officers.[134]

Dell's (also Gey's or Gay's)

John Gey, clerk, and one time intruded rector of Sheviock, became the tenant of part of Trewrickle and of Britton in 1659. In 1663, he sub-let his holdings to Symon Lavers.[135] Gey is shown as a conventionary tenant of Sheviock manor in John Rawling's account of 1656-60.[136] Sir John Carew received the surrender of Gey's lease in 1667, and granted a new one, excluding 'Brittaine' and a house let to Richard Wills, to 'John Dell of Plymouth merchant'.[137] The new lease was on the lives of Dell and his two sons, Richard and John. The rent was 18s. 1d. In the 1691 survey of the manor, the tenement is still called 'Geys tenement'.[138] The tenant then was John Littleton and the lives named were John and Richard Dell, Dorothy and John Littleton and Thomas Edwards. The rent was unchanged. In 1709, the trustees of Sir John Carew let the tenement to John Littleton for a consideration of £180.[139] Littleton was still renting it in 1726 along with **Warren's** (Brown's). Dell's tenement was said to cover 25 acres in 1691 and 33 acres in 1766. In 1766, the tenement, 'late Dell's', was leased to William

Mackworth Praed.[140] The rent was the same. By 1775, no farmhouse was attached to it and it was being farmed with Warren's.

Finnygook (also Fennygook) and Roduse (also the Roydon or Great Reden)[141]

Finnygook is the name of a five-acre field near the sea at Trewrickle. Roduse is the name of of a six-acre field further inland. In 1738, Sir William Carew let these fields to Arthur Peters of Sheviock (age 46).[142] The rent was only 6s. 6d, but the consideration was £127 6s. The lives named were his own and those of his wife, Sarah (age 54) and Joan Chubb, daughter of William Chubb of Sheviock (age 27). Joan became Joan Phillips. These fields had previously been occupied by Ann Wallis, and before her by Robert Harry. Samuel Peters was in occupation in 1764.[143] In 1766, John Carew let the fields to his steward, James Corinton, as from the death of Joan Phillips.[144] In 1770, the tenant was John Snook, who was also the tenant of **Holman's**.[145] In 1802, the trustees of John Henry Rolt, a minor, sub-let the fields and three other fields, to Thomas Holman for 14 years.[146] It was a condition of the lease that the tenant 'Shall and will take and provide for all such parish apprentices as shall or may be bound on the said premises'.

Gey's. *See* Dell's above.

Holman's (also Hollman)

This was one of the largest tenements in Trewrickle, consisting of some 45 acres. It included the fields called Monks' Park (8 acres), West Park (6 acres), Higher North Down (4 acres), Lower North Down (3 acres), and **Great Readen** (5 acres). It was adjacent to **Warne's**. A survey of the manor of Sheviock made in 1653 shows that it was then let to Richard Holman (age 40) on his own life and that of his son, John (age 20). The rent was £1 5s. 10d. and two capons (or 2s.). In 1691, it was let to John Holman on his own life and that of John Holman of Tresmeer. The house and garden that went with it were let to Blanch Chubb on the lives of Dorothy and Blanch Chubb; and later they were let to John Holman on the lives of Katherine and Catherine Holman. The rent for the house was 4s. From 1710 to at least 1726, John Edwards was renting one third of Holman's tenement at a rent of 9s. 3½d. A John Holman continued to farm the other two thirds at a rent of 18s. 6d.[147] In 1761, after the death of Holman, Jonathan Rashleigh let the whole tenement to John Snook of Plymouth, shipwright, who was also the tenant of **Finnygook and Roduse**, at the original 1653 rent.[148] He was still the tenant in 1770, paying the same £1 7s. 10d.[149]

A Mr 'Hillman' was tenant of part of Trewrickle in 1820-1. He was probably the 'Thomas Helman' who rented Smuggler's cottage in 1795 and Net Park from 1809 to 1833.[150] He was dead by 1834.

Peake's (also called Parke's) See **Warne's.**

Southford

Richard Symons was the occupant of this tenement in Trewrickle before 1657. In that year, Sir John Carew let to Richard Wills, husbandman, a plot of ground in Southford containing twenty yards of land.[151] The consideration was that Wills had promised to erect and build a dwelling house on the plot. The rent was 6s. In 1726, the house was let to Elizabeth Earle at a rent of 6s.[152] In 1770, the tenant at the same rent was Martha Roach.[153]

Warne's (also Warren's; also Brown's; also Peake's)

The earliest Warne or Warren recorded in Sheviock was Thomas Warne, one of the guarantors for the building of the quay at Portwrinkle in 1612.[154] He was an investor in one of the three fishing syndicates in the parish. The next recorded Warrens were Ezekiel and Robert. Ezekiel was a sailor on Sheviock's 50-ton fishing vessel, the *Dayestarr*, in 1626. Robert, who may not have been related to Ezekiel, was shown as a 'clerk' (person in holy orders) inhabiting a house with three hearths 'and one other in a bakehouse' in the 1664 Hearth Tax return.

Warne's tenement contained some 48 acres, including a house, and stretched between Trewrickle and Tredrossel.[155] Sometime before 1653, it was divided into three parts. Two parts each fetched a rent of 18s. and two capons (or 4d.). The third part fetched a rent of 10s. 4d. In 1653, one of the larger portions was let to Richard Holman on his own life (then age 40), that of Elizabeth Eustice (age 20), and that of Robert Holman, son of Digory Holman of Laneast. In 1691, this part was let to John Littleton on the lives of Robert Harry and John Harry, and later the lives of John Littleton and his sons, John and Philip. In 1716, Sir William Carew let to John Littleton 'Warne's Tenement ... formerly in the tenure of George Brown and late in the tenure of Robert Harry dec'd'. The consideration was £220, and the rent was 18s. 4d. The lease was on his own life and the lives of his sons, John and Philip.[156] In 1770, the tenant of the 'moiety of Warren's tenement called Brown's' was Samuel Littleton. The rent was 18s. and 2 capons.[157]

The second of the larger portions was let to one Elizabeth (age 60) in 1653. The consideration was £220 and the rent was 18s. 4d. In 1691, this part was let to Robert Harry on the life of William Peake. This part included the three fields, Bake's (or Beak's) Park, Truscott's Park, and West Meadow between Trewrickle and Tredrossel. William Peake was a co-lessee of the tenement with Robert Hancock.[158] The next lessee (before 1708) was Robert Harry. Harry sold his interests to Tristram Harry and John Pope, and they in turn sold theirs to John Neilder of St Stephens by Saltash, John Edwards of Sheviock and Elizabeth Wallis, widow. In 1716, these three sub-let the holding to John Littleton.[159] With this lease, Littleton was farming both halves of Warren's. In 1726, William Nicholl, John Edwards and John Littleton rented Peake's half tenement in equal thirds. Each paid a rent of 6s. 5½d.[160] One of these thirds must have fallen in by 1729, when Sir William Carew let a second third to John Littleton.[161] In 1771, John Carew let to John Snook of Plymouth 'Ironmonger' a 'Third Part … of Peaks half tenement (to wit) North Down, Munks Down [i.e Monks' Park], and one Meadow containing three quarters of a acre … now or late in the possession of William Mitchell.'[162]

In 1691, the smaller part of the tenement was let to William Lavers, a butcher of St Germans, on the life of Elizabeth Hocken.[163] The rent of this part was 10s. 4d. and two capons. This part was let to Edward Eliot in 1722 on his own life and those of John Holman (age 36) and Arthur Peter (age 30).[164] John Carew let this part of the holding to his steward, James Corinton in 1766.[165] At that time Arthur Elliott was farming the land. Corinton's lease was to commence as from the death of Charles Rashleigh, a son of the late Jonathan Rashleigh. But the lease never took effect. Instead on 12 December in the same year the tenement 'commonly called by the name of Trewrickle' was leased to William Mackworth Praed.[166] The rent was unchanged. The tenant after Edward Elliott was Philip Rashleigh. In 1772, Zouche Powell was farming the land on the life of Charles Rashleigh.

67 *Pool House in the 1930s. The tenement of Pool was occupied at various times by members of the Pope, Arundell and Peter families.*

Chapter 9

Outlying Farms and Houses

Tredrossel, Trewin, Kerslake, Poole, and Sconner were described by C.S.Gilbert in 1820 as 'villages in this parish'.[1] Trethill, Tredis (divided into Higher and Lower) and Blerrick (which was divided into three parts) could also have been described as villages. This was because all these places were remote from the main centres of population and because, in the 1600s and 1700s, cottages for smallholders and agricultural workers clustered around the main dwellings. Many of these cottages were demolished in the mid- or late 1800s, though their remains can still be seen, for example at Trethill. With the recent conversion of many disused barns into homes, we are now seeing the re-emergence of the small remote 'villages', such as those at Kerslake, Tredis, Tredrossel and, most recently, Trethill.

Blerrick (also Blarrick)

Blerrick and **Kerslake** were respectively Cornish and Saxon words for the same thing, namely a place or stream where watercress was growing. Kempthorne suggested that the Dawneys held the right of presentation (the advowson) of the rectory of Sheviock by virtue of their occupation of Blerrick.[2] In fact, their right came about as part of the arrangement by which, in one charter, Henry Dawney renewed his mother's grant of lands in Sheviock to Tavistock Abbey, and, in another, promised Abbot Baldwin to cease claiming the right of presentation to Antony. In return, the Abbot recognised Henry's right to present to the rectories of Sheviock and St John. However, it is quite possible that the advowson was later sold for a period when the owners of Sheviock manor (or the heirs after a death) needed cash; and it is also possible that Kerslake manor, which included Middle and Lower Blerrick, was sold or pledged at the same time. Higher Blerrick is not in Sheviock, but in the former Duchy manor of West Antony.[3] In the 1500s, parts were attached to the manors of Landrake and Penpoll.

Higher Blerrick

In 1578, Sir George Carew and Sir Andrew Corbett held two acres Cornish in Blerrick by knight's service of the manor of Penpoll. Their tenants were Walter Code Esq.,

William Noble, Richard Prinne, and John Sargent.[4] Wimond Serell, John Champion and John Sargent held a further 1¼ acres Cornish in Blerrick by knight's service of the manor of Landrake. The whole of Blerrick then contained 200 English acres.

The modern Blerrick Farm is on the site of Higher Blerrick. Edward Kneebone, writing in 1684, writes, 'Blarrick, in it the House of Corrall, gent, West Antony, an ancient Barton, long since divided into 4 dwellings.' In 1613, the tenant of two holdings in Higher Blerrick was Thomas Harry of Antony and his wife, Elizabeth. They let one holding, consisting of six acres, to a weaver, Emanuell Gaiche (also Gayche) for a consideration of £100.[5] They let another to John Gaiche. In 1629, John Gaiche married Joan and left his holding in trust to her if she survived him, and then to his son Daniell, who had just married.[6] The trustees were Alexander Hancock, a tenant of the adjacent **Kerslake** manor, and Thomas Reepe, son of the weaver, William Reepe of Sheviock.[7] Robert Honney, the Crafthole scrivener, acted as one of the attorneys. In 1649, Daniell Gaiche let his holding to John Hodge for a consideration of £80.[8] In the following year, John Hodge and his mother, Joan, sub-let this same holding, which consisted of a house and a garden plot containing 20 yards of land, to a sailor, Benjamin Kerswell of Antony, for a consideration of £11.[9] The rent was 2s. a year. Eleven years later John Hodge sub-let a holding consisting of 30 yards of land to Emanuell Gaiche of Antony, weaver, for a consideration of £7.[10] The rent was 2s. The lives named on the lease of 1661 were Emanuell's children, Stephen, Temperance and Mary. Emanuell's occupation of weaver, and the name he chose for his daughter, suggests that the family were Puritans.

The tenant of the third holding in the early 1600s was Thomas Sargent, no doubt a descendant of the John Sargent who was a tenant in 1578. He died before 1630 and left his interest to his daughter, Joane, who married first one Hodge (perhaps John) and then George Seccombe. When, in 1630, Joane's son, John Hodge, married Thomasine Jacob of Antony, this holding was left in trust to provide first maintenance for Joane and then a widow's portion for Thomasine in the event of John's death.[11] John and Thomasine Hodge had a daughter, Susan. When Susan married Robert Wilshman in 1658, the marriage portion of £75 was secured by his holding in Higher Blerrick.[12]

In 1613, Walter Pryn of Harberton, Devon, and his son, Robert, no doubt descendants of the Richard Prinne who was a tenant in 1578, were the tenants of the largest part of Higher Blerrick. They let a house and some twenty acres of land to Henry Sargent of Sheviock. At the time Mary Wood was living in the house. Three years later, Henry made an arrangement with Mary Wood and let the same property to his son, William Sargent, on a 99-year lease for a rent of 20s.[13] The lives named on the lease were William, and Elizabeth Prynn, daughter of Thomas Prynn of Antony, deceased. The lease to Henry Sargent excluded a field called Well Park, which was in the tenure of John Warne. A field called Well Park lay between Middle Blerrick and Kerslake, so the house let to Henry Sargent may have been the property later known as Middle Blerrick (see **Kerslake** below). William Sargent was also the tenant of Sargent's tenement in Crafthole, which included the modern *Finnygook Inn*.

At a vestry meeting held on 18 April 1788, William Graves was given leave to build a pew for the occupiers of Blerrick by the wall in the north aisle of Sheviock church.[14] Most of Graves's land was in West Antony. David Cock was farming Higher Blerrick in about 1792.[15] John Stroud, previously at Kerslake, was farming there in 1809-10. The farmer ten years later, and still in 1833-4, was Mr Hawking (also Hawkings) who also farmed at Trethill. In 1858, Thomas Matthews was the tenant, and the Matthews family are still farming there.

Lower Blerrick

Philip Blake (1604-89), gentleman, who lived at Lower Blerrick, was a free tenant of the manor of Kerslake as shown in the manorial roll, which survives *inter alia* for the years 1636 and 1640.[16] This manor included lands in Middle Blerrick, Lower Blerrick and Kerslake. Philip Blake's younger son, Anthony, lived with him at Lower Blerrick. The house was a large one, with five hearths.[17] In a survey of the manor of Sheviock of 1691, Ferdinando Wallis and Anthony Blake (Philip's son) were shown as jointly holding half an acre of land 'Cornish' in Lower Blerrick and Trethill, for which they were paying a 'high rent' of 1s.[18] Lower Blerrick farm is now in the parish of Antony.

Kerslake

The Manor of Kerslake

Blerrick and Kerslake were respectively Cornish and Saxon words for the same thing, namely a place or stream where watercress was growing. This is the stream that is fed from the high ground between Blerrick and Trethill. There is a field called Well Park above the modern dwelling called 'Kerslake Mill'. The stream flows through the grounds of Kerslake Mill and emerges as a shoot of water near the road below the house. Kerslake Mill was not a mill in the Middle Ages. It was then the site of Kerslake manor. The manor-house probably became ruinous in the 18th century. A map made in 1742 and amended and annotated in 1829 describes the building on the site as merely a 'mowhay' (an enclosure for ricks). After leaving the grounds of the modern Kerslake Mill, the stream fills two ponds and continues along the bottom of the valley to feed the original Kerslake Mill at some distance down the valley. This mill was situated in boggy ground and later came to be called 'Bog Mill' or 'Bag Mill'. The stream finally joins a creek of the Lynher, called Trethill Lake. At this point, a tidal mill, called Denabole, was constructed in the 19th century, but was in use for only a few years.[19]

Robert Blerok was holding the tenements of Blerrick and Kerslake in 1411. His tithes of corn (ten per cent of the whole) were valued at £2 3s. 6d., implying a value of £21 15s. for the whole crop. In the same year, Robert Burnard and Roger Whiteford were holding tenements at Trethill and Liscawn, and their tithes were valued at 33s., implying a value of £16 10s. for the whole crop.[20] A list of the fees of Edward Courtenay, Earl of Devon, was made during his lifetime or just after his death in 1419.[21] It includes these four tenements among the fees of the earl's manor of Sheviock. Sometime afterwards these estates were effectively, if not legally, separated from the manor of Sheviock, and separate court rolls survive for the manor of Kerslake for the years 1565-1640.[22] The manor or reputed manor of Kerslake seems therefore to have been created sometime between 1419 and 1565. It then consisted of the holdings of Middle Blerrick, Lower Blerrick and Kerslake itself. It included a culver house or dovecote situated in the grounds of the present Trethill House.[23]

68 *Moiety of the manor of Kerslake from Thomas Pride's Map of 1775.*

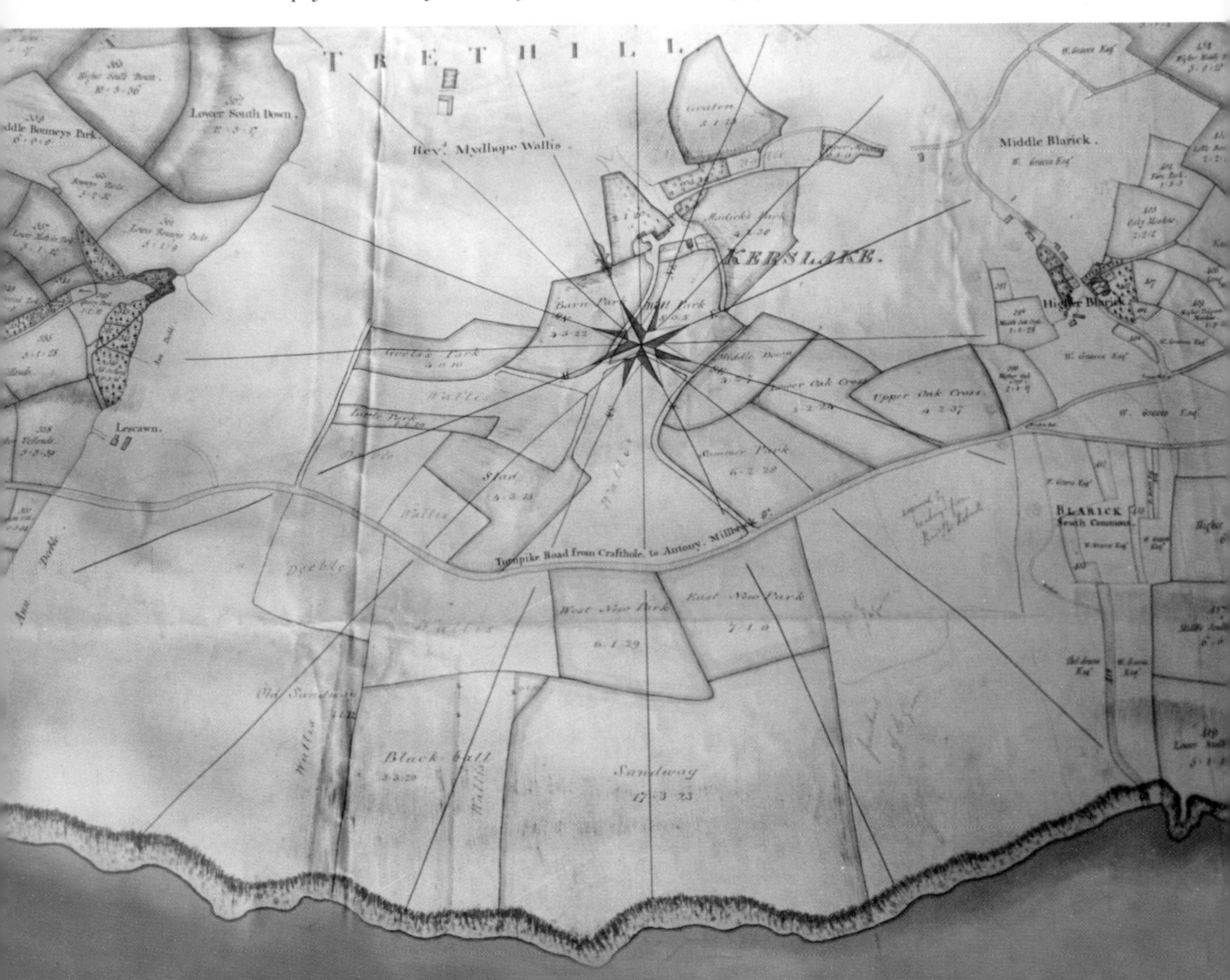

One of the entries on the court rolls states that 12d. was also due to Mr Carew of Antony for his manor of Sheviock, showing that a tiny portion of the estate lay in that manor. This was still the situation in 1691 when a survey of the manor of Sheviock stated that 'Francis Hoblyn Esq holdeth there [i.e. in Kerslake] one half Acre of lands Cornish & pays yearly 1s'.

Lords of the Manor

Stephen Medhop (Mydhope) of St Martins by Looe was named as the lord of Kerslake manor on the rolls of 1607 and 1608. In 1640, the lord was John 'Medhoppe', gentleman, brother and next heir of the late Revd Thomas Medhoppe of Cambridge, son and heir of the late Stephen Medhop.[24] By 1685, ownership of the manor of Kerslake had passed from the Mydhopes to the Hoblyn family. In that year, Francis Hoblyn of the Inner Temple let 'the moiety or halfendeall of the mannor or reputed mannor of Kerslake ... alias Kerstlake Blericke and Trethill' to Sir John Carew.[25] In 1742, the lord was John Hoblyn, who probably continued to let the land to the Carew family.[26] The lord in 1750 was Miss Damaris Hoblyn of Croan. The manor was then entailed, and she executed an indenture to break the entail and convert the property into an estate in fee simple. On 27 November 1751, as part of her marriage settlement, she conveyed the manor to her husband, Francis Kirkham. Forty years later, Damaris Kirkham of Croan 'widow' sold 'all that the manor or Lordship of Kerslake' to Reginald Pole Carew for £2,260.[27] The land conveyed included the 88 acres already let to the Carews and shaded in brown on Thomas Pride's map of 1775.[28] This was only the central and southern part of the manor of Kerslake. The eastern part, consisting of Middle and Lower Blerrick, and of about the same extent, appears to have been in the occupation of the Blake family. In 1855, William Henry Pole Carew sold to the Revd Samuel Wallis Roberts of **Trethill**, 88 acres (probably those coloured brown on Pride's map) for the sum of £2,182 15s.[29] The land conveyed included Well Park, Hancock's Hill, Grills, and Higher and Lower Cross Parks as well as Blackaball and Sandway along the coast.

Apart from a small area of Trethill, the estates of Trethill and Liscawn were alienated from the manor of Kerslake at an early but unknown date. These estates reputedly constituted a separate manor. In a lease granted by George Uppeton of 'Poslege' (Puslinch near Newton Ferrers) in Devon, Trethill was described as being in the manor of 'Nether Sheviock'. Uppeton died before 1618. From the 1500s, Liscawn belonged to the Smith family, and may have been attached to their manor of Tregunnick in St Germans. From the late 1600s, Trethill belonged to the Wallis family. Few early deeds relating to these holdings have survived.

Tenants

The court roll of the manor of Kerslake contains the rents paid for various years between 1565 and 1640.[30] The free tenants are listed as Philip Blake (1636, 1640), Coles (undated), John Harry (1608, 1609), Pope (1608, 1609), William Sargent (1608, 1609, 1636, 1640), John Smyth (or Smith) (1565, 1608, 1609), and Thomas Smyth (1636 and 1640). The Smiths farmed at Liscawn in Sheviock and Hendra in St Germans. One Streke is also listed as a free tenant on an undated roll.

The conventionary (copyhold) tenants are listed as Hancock (1565), Alexander Hancock (1607, 1608, 1609), Harry (1565), John Naunter (1607, 1608, 1609), John Pope (1607, 1608, 1609), John Sargent (1565), and Robert Sergeant (1575). In 1607, Alexander Hancock held a tenement for three lives and was paying £4 and two capons per annum. The rent indicates that this was the largest holding, consisting of some 88 acres. He was therefore leasing the moiety of the manor owned by the Medhops and the Hoblyns, and some of the fields in that moiety are named after him.[31] John Naunter held a tenement for three lives and was paying £1 6s. 8d. and two capons per annum, implying a holding of about 26 acres. John Pope held a tenement for 21 years and was paying 8s. and one capon per annum, implying a holding of eight acres.

Sometime after 1622, Hancock's tenement was let to Gregory Arundell, who was rector of Sheviock until he was deprived of his living by the Puritans. He died in 1654.[32] After his death, the holding passed to his son, Richard, and after that to Richard's daughter, Edith. In 1640, John Mydhope granted a 21-year lease of the manor of Kerslake at a nominal rent to his sister, Ann Osgoode of St Ewe, and to his brother-in-law, John Hickes of Trevethick. Edward Kneebone (1684) described 'Keslake' as 'the seat of Gennis extinct'. The reference was probably to 'John Gennys Merchant' to whom the holding was next let (acccording to a much later lease of 1744).[33] The next two tenants were Ferdinando Wallis (1694-1738) of Trethill and then his sister, Anne.[34] In 1750, 1754 and 1755, Anne Wallis was renting the property from Damaris Hoblyn for £4 13s., showing that it was the same tenement of 88 acres that had been leased by Alexander Hancock in 1607. The rights under Anne Wallis's lease passed to John Wallis the younger of Callington (and formerly of Camelford). In 1760, Francis Kirkham of Croan let the holding to the Revd Mydhope Wallis, who became curate of Sheviock in 1766.[35] The lease was on his own life and that of Elizabeth Palmer, spinster (age 30), who was to become his wife. The new lease took effect on the death of John Wallis the younger. John Stroud was the tenant of this part of Kerslake in 1792.[36] William Martin was the tenant from 1809 until the 1820s. In July 1810, 16,000 slates were delivered for the roofing of the barn. In 1833, the tenant was Mr Batten or Buttons, and seven years later he was succeeded by J. W. Angeer. The Revd Samuel Wallis Roberts of Trethill took over the tenancy in 1858.

Lantic

Lantic (*nant* + *diminutive*) in Cornish means 'Little Valley' (Padel). The old farmhouse, which is now ruinous, stands in St Germans parish, just on its border with Sheviock parish. John Lavers, who had been a fisherman on the *Dayestarr* in 1626, was described as being 'of Lantick' in the Sheviock parish register which recorded his death by drowning in 1650. The two fields, Higher and Lower Lantick, are in Sheviock parish and are shown as part of Dell's (Gey's) tenement (33 acres) in Thomas Pride's Map and Survey of 1775.[37]

Liscawn

This tenement can be traced back to the reign of Edward I, when William Dawney conveyed to Nicholas Scawen and Lady Matilda, his wife, 'half an acre in Lanscawyn'.[38] Half a Cornish acre was at least seven and a half English acres and perhaps as much as twenty-five. According to Kempthorne, this William was the father of Nicholas Dawney (*c.*1285-1333), the founder of Crafthole. Robert Burnard and Roger Whiteforde were farming at 'Truthill and Launstawen' in 1410-11.[39] Liscawn was the property of the Smiths for many generations. Richard Smyth held land in Sheviock in 1428.[40] Thomas Smyth was living at Liscawn before 1461.[41] He was succeeded by his son and grandson, both called John. In 1488, John Smythe granted lands in 'Lanscawen' to Alexander Carew and others. In 1716, the parish register states that 'Mr Samuel Smith was buried, being a gentleman'. He was the last male of his line.

The property passed to his sister, Martha, who was married to John Deeble. Their son, the Revd Samuel Deeble, rector of Sheviock 1740-50, inherited Liscawn and lived there. On his death, the property passed to his daughter, Martha. She let it to William Dunrich from *c.*1768, then to John Pollard in 1809-10, and then to Samuel Lyne. After

69 *Lanscawen (the valley of the elder trees) with Vellands (top right).*

Martha's death, *c.*1812, her second husband, Mr White, sold it to Messrs Flood and Lott, bankers of Honiton. They sold it to Erasmus Roberts (1754-1816) of Trevol in Antony, and he left it to his nephew, John Coryton Roberts (1784-1864).[42] The estate then consisted of some 70 acres. It passed to his son, Erasmus Coryton Roberts (1832-after 1885). In 1858, Wightwick Roberts, one of the three brothers living at Trethill, was the occupier, and he may have leased or purchased it from Erasmus. The estate then passed to John Dobree Anderson Roberts (Colonel Roberts, d.1945). Simon Hill was farming Liscawn as a tenant from 1881. His son, John, had taken over by 1889. John's eldest daughter, Mollie, married H. Arnold Hoskin, and Arnold and his son, John, were farming at Liscawn before the Second World War. They had a herd of prize-winning white pigs. Arnold's son, John, was still farming there *c.*1945-50. From 1925 to 1968, the property belonged to Ince Estates. In the 1950s, the farmhouse was converted into a private club. The tenant, W.H. Williams, opened a restaurant there in 1963 and took in overnight guests. The property is today the *Liscawn Inn*.[43] Below the house is a small reservoir, formerly known as Dawney Pool.[44]

Polscoe (also Polscove). See Chapter 42, *Mills and Millers.*

Sconner. See 'Sconner' and 'Sconner Villa' in Chapter 8, *Holdings on Sheviock Manor.*

Tredis (also Treadis)

In 1460, Nichola, late wife of Robert Reynolds, conveyed to Peter Hebert lands in 'Tredhyst' in Sheviock.[45] In the list of fees of the manor of 'Shevyok' of Edward Courtenay, earl of Devon *c.*1419, it is stated that Thomas, heir of Thomas Fychet, held half a knight's fee in 'Trenthest' (Tredis) and Trewynna (Trewin).[46] This is said to be the inheritance of his mother, Ricarda, daughter of John Inkpenne.[47] On the attainder of the Marquis of Exeter in 1538, Tredis was forfeited to the Crown. It was said to have been given to Anne of Cleves by Henry VIII as part of his divorce settlement in 1540.

A list of the free tenants of the manor of Landrake, dated 1578, and by then belonging to the Eliot family, states that Tredis 'is a manor and hath in itself both demesne and service'.[48] In the list, the extent is given as 150 English acres. The same list states that John Moyle holds half an acre Cornish (between 7.5 and 25 English acres) there by knight's service, suit of court (presumably to the manor of Landrake) and a rent of 2s. Probably in the reign of Queen Elizabeth, Tredis was divided into Lower Tredis (also called just 'Tredis') to the east and Higher (or Upper) Tredis, to the west.

Lower Tredis: When Tredis was divided, Lower Tredis was purchased by the family of Peter or Peters. John Peters was one of the guarantors for the building of the quay at Portwrinkle in 1612.[49] He was born about 1576. He left £40 to his grandson, Arthur, who was living in his father's house at Lower Tredis in the early 1600s. Arthur died at sea in 1651 and left a bequest to his sisters, Anne and Tabitha.[50] Another John Peter was owner of Lower Tredis in 1754. He was succeeded by Samuel Peter in about 1792.[51] The Revd Edward Pole, DD, who was rector of Sheviock from 1782 to 1796, purchased Lower Tredis from the Peter family. In the 1840/41 Tithe Redemption Survey, Lower Tredis was said to contain just over 105 acres.

A stretch of the Liskeard turnpike road, created in 1760, ran from Crafthole to Polbathic via Tredis, where there was a turnpike gate. When the Revd Edward Pole built Tredis House (on the opposite side of the road to the farmhouses at Higher Tredis and Tredis) he apparently incorporated the toll-house in his new residence. From his new house he was able to see the spire of Sheviock church in the distance. The Revd Pole was the younger brother of the Rt. Hon. Reginald Pole Carew of Antony. He died in 1837. His son, Reginald, was rector of Sheviock from 1825 to 1839. In 1831, he received permission from the Bishop of Exeter, on account of illness, not to live in the rectory at Sheviock churchtown. He asked instead to be allowed to continue to live 'in the house of my father situated in the said parish, and about a mile distant from the church'.[52] Arthur Bewes was the tenant farmer of Lower Tredis in 1809. In 1861, a Miss Pole was in occupation of 'Tredis Farm' (i.e., Lower Tredis Farm). In 1872, Mrs Anna-Maria Pole was the owner.[53] In 1889, Henry Pole and Jane Pole were responsible with other members of the Primrose league for erecting a small obelisk in the grounds of Tredis Farm. F. Payne was the tenant of part of Tredis in 1899.

70 *Lower Tredis House, the home of the Pole family from the late 1700s to the early 1900s.*

Tredis Barn, once a part of Tredis Farm, was converted into a house and art gallery (Morley Contemporary Art) by Lawrence and Louise Barnes in 2006.

71 *The obelisk at Tredis erected by Henry and Jane Pole and other members of the Primrose League in 1889.*

Higher Tredis: In his description of East Hundred (1684), Edward Kneebone included what was probably the dwelling at Higher Tredis in his list of 'seats of note' in Sheviock, then occupied by the Hawkyns (also Hawkins) family. In 1754, Mrs Deeble was the owner of Higher Tredis and William Bickford was the tenant. John Avery was the occupier *c.*1792.[54] In 1810, Thomas Littleton purchased Higher Tredis for his second son, the Revd Hugh, who had been curate of Sheviock since 1802.[55] The Revd Hugh died in 1830, leaving Higher Tredis, then tenanted, to his son John, who also inherited Trewin from his uncle John in 1849. In the 1840/41 Tithe Redemption Survey, Higher Tredis was said to contain just over 96 acres. The Littleton family remained the owners of Higher Tredis until the 1870s, sometimes farming it themselves, and sometimes letting it to a tenant. Today, David and Cindy Rice have an egg farm at Higher Tredis.

Tredrossel (also Drozell, Drossel, Tredrusel and Treadruzel)

The meaning of Tredrossel, which was spelled Tredrusel in 1286, has now been lost. The stream, called 'Drossel', which rises near Lantic Farm and flows down to Polscoe Mill may have taken its name from the farm. The stream forms a small part of the border between the parishes of Sheviock and St Germans.

72 *1286 agreement between William Dawney the Younger and Warrin de Herth for a watercourse through Tredrossel.*

William Dawney the elder granted the tenement of Tredrossel to Warrin de Herth (Erth) on the latter's marriage to his daughter, Elena. The grant included one acre Cornish (i.e. *c.*15-50 English acres) to be held by knight's service, and another two acres Cornish to be held in socage.[56] A dispute between Warrin and his brother-in-law, William Dawney the younger, concerning this grant and water from the Drossel to drive the manorial mill at Polscoe was settled in 1286. For his part, William confirmed to Warrin all the properties covered by his father's grant 'land, meadows etc. and pasture for 6 oxen in his own keeping in manor of Sheviock'. He also granted him a right of way to carry wood from the wood of 'Labiricome' to his land of Tredrossel.[57] He also granted him a right of way to get sand from Trewrickle (i.e. from the beach at what is now Portwrinkle). For these rights, Warrin would pay him 19s. a year and render suit of court twice a year. At the same time Warrin agreed to allow William to draw a reasonable head of water from his land at Tredrossel and lead it to his mill at Sheviock, where it would join the stream flowing from Trewrickle.[58] The price for the water supply was 12d. per annum. This same sum was still being paid in 1725, when the lord of the manor acknowledged its receipt for the watercourse 'through my Barton of Tredrussel'. In the 16th-century list of fees belonging to Edward Courtenay, Margaret, daughter and heir of John de Ert (Erth) is listed as holding land in Tredrossel.[59] Tredrossel remained part of the manor of Sheviock throughout the Middle Ages. Simon Odiorne was tenant in 1410-11.[60] His tithes of corn were worth £2 5s., implying a value of £22 10s. for the whole crop.

73 *Walter Hoskin purchased Tredrossel in the 1920s, some ten years before this picture was taken.*

William Bond, listed as a free tenant of the manor of Landrake in 1578, is said to be the occupier of Tredrossel, which must by then have been alienated from the manor of Sheviock. William Rundle was the tenant in 1636.[61] In his description of East Hundred (1684), Edward Kneebone described the estate as 'Drussell, a large village, the lands of James Bond Esq.' In 1725, the owner was J. Keast. In 1770, the owners were the heirs of John Neels. The farm of Tredrossel belonged to the Littletons of Trewin in the 1700s and 1800s. Thomas Littleton was farming it in 1810 and was succeeded by his son, John, who was still there in 1834. The tenant from 1858 to 1861 was Nicholas Roseveare. In 1840, Tredrossel consisted of 187 acres. Walter Hoskin purchased Tredrossel in the 1920s.[62] Tredrossel was the largest cider-making farm in the parish. It had eight apple orchards in 1841 and was the last one to produce cider, only discontinuing production in the 1960s.[63] Clifford Hoskin succeeded to the farm, which he ran with his wife, Millicent, until his retirement in 1969.

Trethill. See also **Kerslake** above.

Robert Burnard and Roger Whiteforde were farming at 'Truthill and Launstawen' in 1410-11. Their tithes of corn (ten per cent of the whole crop) were worth £1 13s., implying a value of £16 10s. for the whole crop, the sixth largest out of the nine principal holdings in the parish.

Trethill House and estate

The estate at Trethill is referred to as 'Mr Upton's lande' in the glebe terrier prepared by the Revd Walter Arundell in 1602. In his submission, he referred to '2 closes called Lady Well divided by mee, and conteyning as I suppose 9A [acres] banded by East with [bounded on the east side by] Mr Uptons lande'. This was George Upton of Puslinch, near Newton Ferrers in Devon. According to a survey of West Antony made in 1608, George Upton was also the tenant of a house and fields in St Johns.[64] He died before 1618. In a lease granted by him, Trethill was said to be in the manor of 'Nether Sheviock', but this was probably an invented manor. The William 'Uppeton' who granted a reversionary lease of a dwelling and tenement in Trethill to Philip Blake on 1 February 1624, was his son.[65] William Upton also appears to have let the lands in St John's to Blake.[66] On 26 February 1684, Anthony Blake, gentleman, and Mrs Elizabeth Bagely, widow, let Trethill and fields in Trethill to Mr Jonah Lavington, surgeon and Mr Richard Cotton, merchant for one year. On 19 January 1693, Anthony Blake and Elizabeth, his wife (the previous Mrs Bagely) conveyed some land at Trethill to Henry Wallis, who had just married Elizabeth Hodge of St Germans. The price was

74 *Trethill House was designed by George Wightwick for the Revd Samuel Wallis Roberts and built in 1840-1.*

75 *Captain Samuel Wallis of Trethill greeting the Queen of Otaheite (Tahiti) in 1767.*

£605 7s. 6d. Henry Wallis then built at Trethill the 'convenient mansion' described by Maclean in his History of Trigg Minor. [67]

On 17 January 1706, five years after Henry Wallis's early death, his widow purchased from James Gibbs, MD another tenement in Trethill, formerly Sargent's tenement, for £90. Part of this tenement lay to the south of Upton's land. It is referred to in the glebe terrier submitted by the Revd Walter Arundell to the diocese of Exeter in 1602.[68] William Sargent was the tenant of this land, then part of Kerslake manor, in 1640. Henry and Elizabeth's son, Ferdinando Wallis, who was High Sheriff of Cornwall in 1736, succeeded to the estate. When he died two years later, it passed to his sister, Ann (d.1760) and then to her cousin, the Revd Mydhope Wallis.

In 1791, the estate became the property of Captain Samuel Wallis, RN, the circumnavigator, who discovered many islands in the South Seas, including Tahiti. His tenant *c.*1792 was John Sobey.[69] On Captain Wallis's death in 1795, the estate passed to his cousins, Ann and Elizabeth Wallis. Ann Wallis became the wife of the Revd Bryan Roberts (d.1808), and thus brought half the Trethill estate into the hands of the Roberts family. Elizabeth Wallis, who inherited the other half, married the Rev. John Bennet. In 1797, the Revd Bryan Roberts let the old Wallis house, then called Trethill Barton, and its land, to a farmer, Nathaniel Hawkings. It was during this long agricultural tenancy that the house began to decay. C.S. Gilbert, in 1820, described Trethill as 'a genteel house, now in a state of decay, and a very beautiful estate'.[70] The accounts in the Chancery case brought by the children of the Revd John Bennet against their uncles show that in 1812 Hawkings was paying a yearly rental of £240 6s.

On the death of Ann Roberts (née Wallis) in 1836, her eldest son, the Revd Samuel Wallis Roberts (1793-1863) inherited the estate. He was a gentleman scholar, a Founder's Kin Fellow of Pembroke College Oxford at the time he inherited. Because of his inheritance, he was forced to vacate his Fellowship, which he did in 1839. He then set about building a new villa for himself and his two brothers and sister on the estate, which at that time consisted of some 150 acres. For his new house, he chose a design that can be described as 'non-Palladian Italian', and commissioned the Plymouth-based architect, George Wightwick, to design it.[71]

Wightwick had been an assistant to the famous neo-classical architect, Sir John Soane, in London. In about 1830, he settled in Plymouth and entered into the architectural practice of John Foulston, whom he succeeded as principal. By 1839, Wightwick was the leading architect of his day in the Plymouth area. He was also a distant cousin of the Revd Samuel Roberts, whose youngest brother was actually christened Wightwick. The house commissioned by Roberts cost exactly £1,800 to build. The account is preserved in the CRO and the designs are preserved in the RIBA in London. Building commenced in 1840 and the house and its matching stable block were completed in 1841. The old house was pulled down and the stone re-used in the new building work.

In 1855, W.H. Pole Carew sold to Samuel the moiety of Kerslake manor that Reginald Pole Carew had bought in 1791.[72] On Samuel's death in 1863, the estate passed to his brother, John. On John's death in 1881, it passed to his sister Anne, who bequeathed it to her cousin, J. D. A. Roberts in 1883. He died in 1945 and in 1948 his daughter, Winifred, sold the estate to Ince Estates.[73] Fred and Pat Rundle, who were farming the land, purchased it and divided the house into three flats. They later sold the house but retained most of the farmland. The house was re-configured as a single dwelling and bought first by Ted and Phylis Aldred, then by James and Susan Schnadhorst, who ran it as a refuge and Christian community, then by Charles and Primrose Burnett-Hitchcock. Neville and Susan Cusworth purchased the house in 1995 and the adjacent fields and woodland in 1996.

Trewin

'Ric.de Trewinna' was one of the witnesses to a quitclaim given by William de Alneto (Dawney) to Roger Pole at the Feast of Pentecost in 1267.[74] Trewin or *Trewinna* probably means 'the white house'.[75] 'Regnald de Trewynna' was a witness to an indenture relating to William Dawney's mill at Polscoe in 1286. An extent of the lands of Sir John Dawney was made at Lostwithiel on 30 May 1347, following Sir John's death in France during the Crécy campaign. The three holdings of Tredis, Trewin and Sconner are mentioned together as forming half a knight's fee (about 400 acres). This half fee is also mentioned in the dower of Sir John's widow, Sibella. It was then in the hands of John Inkpenne.[76] In 1410-11, the tenant of 'Trewyne' (and of Sconner and Tredis) was John Bake of St Germans.[77] In the list of fees of the earl of Devon *c*.1419, it is stated that Thomas, heir of Thomas Fychet, held half a knight's fee in Trewin and Tredis.[78]

By 1578, Trewin had become attached to the manor of Landrake. Like Kerslake, it possessed its own dovecote or culver house indicating manorial status. In a list of free tenants of the manor in 1578, the occupiers of 'Trewinna' were shown as Ralfe and Oliver Wallis.[79] John Dodridge was the tenant *c*.1635, according to a deposition he gave in the case of *Rolle* v *Blake*.[80] He deposed that 'he formerly was an Inhabitant within the said Parish of Shiviock by the space of five and thirty yeares and lived in a tenement there called Terwin [Trewin]'. He was presumably a tenant of the Wallis family. In the Hearth Tax roll of 1664, a Richard Wallis is shown as inhabiting a house with four hearths. The farm land of Trewin amounted to 141 acres in 1841.

Although English Heritage concludes, on stylistic grounds, that the oldest part of the house dates from about 1725, Kempthorne states that it was built in 1750.[81] This is more plausible, since it accords with the new ownership of the Littleton family about that time. Gilbert, writing in 1820, said of Trewin, 'The house is modern, the grounds are finely wooded, and washed by the waters of the River Lynher'.[82]

76 *The central part of Trewin House was built for John Littleton* c.*1750.*

Hugh Littleton (1682-1761) was settled in Lanjore, St Germans. He may also have acquired a lease of Trewin, because a Hugh Littleton paid a church rate (5s. 4d.) for it in 1748.[83] The lessee could, however, have been one of his less prosperous cousins already living in Sheviock. Trewin was described as 'being parcel of the manor of Sheviock' in a lease of 1753 between Jonathan Rashleigh (acting for the widow of Sir Coventry Carew) and William Michell.[84] John Littleton (d.1764), son of Hugh of Lanjore, was the first of the Littletons to live at Trewin. When he married Jane Boger in 1758, he settled an annuity of £40 per annum on her, payable out of his 'Capital Messuage Barton Farm and Lands commonly called ... Trewin', so he must by then have been the owner. After the death of Sir Coventry Carew in 1748, the Carew estates in Sheviock were administered by trustees until Reginald Pole Carew inherited them in 1771. These trustees may have sold Trewin to the Littleton family in order to raise capital to pay bequests and defray legal expenses.

John Littelton died without issue in 1764, leaving Trewin to his nephew, Thomas (1747-1815). Thomas married Theophila, daughter of John Roberts of Trevol, Antony. John Littleton, their son, lived at Trewin from 1815 until his death in 1849. John's nephew, also called John, inherited the estate and lived there until his death in 1869. He built the new wing on the south side of the house, which has his initials and the date, 1851, inscribed on a datestone at the back. He was succeeded by his son, John (1859-1910), who planted the magnificent avenue of copper beeches in 1905. The head gardener at the time was a member of the Pengelly family of Portwrinkle.[85] John's son, also called John (1886-1953), inherited the estate and built the billiard room at the rear of the house in 1911. He moved to South Africa and let the house to tenants for much of the time. From 1932 until 1944, the tenant was John Crace, who lived there with his wife and three daughters. He was the great-grandson of John Gregory Crace, founder of the firm of John Gregory Crace & Son, interior decorators and furniture manufacturers (1768-1919). Among the executed works of the firm was a grand coffered ceiling for Longleat House.

In September 1945, Trewin was purchased by Kimberley Foster, CBE, who lived there until his death in 1979. His wife, Gertrude, and sons, Nicholas and John, continued to live there until Gertrude's death in 2007. Most of the land was sold in 1983. The estate was then purchased by D. and A. Leighton-Squires, the current owners. Trewin has its own quay on a creek of the River Lynher. Reginald Pole Carew undertook to rebuild the quay in 1832.[86]

Chapter 10

Sheviock Churchtown

Sheviock churchtown grew up around the church and the principal demesne farm of the manor of Sheviock.[1] This farm, Sheviock Barton, was situated at the centre of the most productive fields of the manor. The fields radiate from the farm towards Sheviock woods to the north; Berry Down and Berry Wells to the east; Crafthole Parks to the south; Poole to the south-west; Haye and Sconner to the west. With the farm placed in this central position, the teams working the fields had roughly equivalent distances to travel to reach them from the barton at all points of the compass. The village was close enough to the River Lynher to take advantage of the waterborne access to Saltash, Tavistock and Plymouth, but also sufficiently hidden and remote to avoid easy attack by enemies.

Church House; the Little Brew House

Before the introduction of church rates in Queen Elizabeth's reign, churches raised much of their money through church ales that were held originally in the church and churchyard, and later in 'Church House'.[2] This was the name given to the building that was used for holding the ales and for the official business of the parish – such as meetings of the vestry. Church houses were typically erected between the late 1400s and the mid-1500s. In earlier times, church business had taken place in the nave of the church or in the churchyard. But with the introduction of pews at the end of the Middle Ages, there was no longer a large open space in the middle of the nave.[3] Sheviock's Church House stood to the south-east of the churchyard and just outside its walls. It was probably built in the early 1500s, and a 'little Brew House' stood next door to it. By about 1600, church ales were being attacked by the Puritans. Carew defended the holding of the ales, but recognised that they were unpopular with many of his contemporaries.[4] According to a statement made by Walter Warren in 1764, a 'Little Brew House' belonging to Church House stood on the east side of Church House. It stood between Church House and 'the Little House where Wm Smith now Lives'.[5] It was probably knocked down by Joseph Clinnick when he rebuilt Church House as an inn.

77 *Sheviock churchtown c.1938. Apart from the church, the village is dominated by Sheviock Barton (left) and the old rectory (centre) with their barns and outbuildings. The Victorian rectory (right) has been moved away from its farm buildings.*

With the introduction of the church rates as the main means of raising money, the church house could be said, in part at least, to have become redundant. Sheviock's church house had ceased to be used for regular parish business sometime before 1691. In that year, it was let to Judith Prin (or Pryn), a shopkeeper, whose shop was nearby.[6] The rent was 2s. 4d. to the lord of the manor and another 3s. 8d. to the church. In 1706, it was leased at a rent of 6s. per annum to Henry Austen on the lives of himself, his wife, Anny, and their daughter, Anne. It was described as 'old, ruinous and decayed'. The tenant owed 'suit of court and mill'.[7] In 1726, Church House was leased to Walter Warren, again for 6s.[8] Walter Warren was a tailor. Auctions of manorial woodlands between 1730 and 1740 were held at 'Sibella Warren's house', which is probably this same house (see also 'Warren's Cottage', below). In 1764, the house was leased to Mrs Deborah Bartlett, a widow then aged 60, at the same rent. In 1779, Matthew Bartlett, Deborah's son and heir, was the tenant. He was one of the village blacksmiths. In the same year, he sub-let it to Joseph Clinnick (1735-1802).[9] In 1786, Clinnick was granted a new lease on condition that he should rebuild the premises. He did so and ran the new building as an inn, the *Carew Arms*.[10]

The first post office in Sheviock parish was probably the one established *c.*1850 at the *Carew Arms*. In 1861, John Peter Landry was postmaster and his brother, Richard, was sub-postmaster. Richard was postmaster from about 1871 until his death in 1881.

Daniel Sargent's Inn

It is recorded in the law case of *Rolle* v *Blake* that two commissioners, Thomas Dandy and Hannibal Gryles, examined a witness, Nicholas Sargent, at the inn of Daniell Sargent on 25 April 1674.[11] In 1639, Daniell, who had previously been a sailor, took a sub-lease of premises in Sheviock churchtown from the farmer, Richard Chubb. Chubb himself was the tenant of Richard Carew the younger. The premises leased were 'the whole dwelling house ... or cottage' and 'the whole herbe garden lyeng on the North side of the said dwelling house' together with part of a 'plot of ground [with] stone floors or town place which hath been lately used by ... Gabriell of Sheviock ... husbandman for a Reeke [rick] place.' He also leased the 'Courtlage belonging unto the said Cottage on the South side of the same'. But part of the rick place and a strip of land nine feet in breadth and running along the entire frontage of the house 'known by the name of the Church of Shevoc house [i.e. Church House]' was reserved out of the sub-lease by Richard Chubb. From this description it would appear that the inn stood to the east of the old Church House.

The rent of the head lease was 5s., which was to be paid by the sub-tenant, who also paid an additional 4d. to Chubb. The lease was on the lives of Richard Chubb, Margaret his daughter, and Agnes Hawkes (or Hawke) of Sheviock. Agnes was probably Richard's married daughter. Margaret may have become Daniell Sargent's wife. The witnesses to the lease were William Odyorne, William Sargent (probably

78 *The former* Carew Arms *inn, converted into two cottages, in the early 1900s. There was so little traffic that children could play on the dirt road in front of the cottages.*

related to Daniell) and the Crafthole scrivener, Robert Honney. In a manorial survey made in 1691, Daniell Sargent's house and garden is shown as being in the occupation of Edward Hawke, at a rental of 6s. 8d. Hawke also had a lease of Clicker.[12]

Clicker (also High or Higher Clicker)

The word Clicker comes from a Cornish word related to the Welsh *clegyr*, meaning a 'cliff' or 'steep place', which accurately describes the site of this house. In 1726, 'Higher Clicker House' was let to Edward Hawke, a tailor, for 2s.[13] Hawke was also the tenant of Sargent's house in Sheviock churchtown (rent 6s. 8d.) and part of Poole (9s.). In 1742, Sir William Carew let to George Warren, yeoman, a 'dwelling house garden and little meadow commonly called by the name of High Clicker … and part of a certain tenement … formerly in the possession of one Odihorne.'[14] The latter tenement was Haye (see Chapter 4, *The Manor of Sheviock*). Higher Clicker is described as a 'messuage [house] garden and orchard' in Thomas Pride's map and survey of 1775. Its area was given as one rood. By then the occupant was Richard Warren on the lives of George Warren (age 51), Gregory Warren (age 56), and Richard Warren (age 48). By the early 1900s, the cottages had gone, and the land was used for allotments. The carpenter, George May (1866-1931), acquired the plot and built a wooden bungalow there, later occupied by his son, Walter. It burned down and was replaced by the present one in about 1974.[15]

Cote Cottage [16]

Cote today consists of a cottage and garden. The cottage is said to be mid-late 1600s.[17] The holding formerly included seven acres of land. The earliest records show that it was usually let together with Crafthole Parks. Often the tenant was one of the principal farmers on the Carew estates, who had retired, or his widow. The earliest recorded tenant was Margery, the widow of Ferdinando Spiller, a farmer, miller and innkeeper.[18] Ferdinando had probably also been bailiff of the manor. Margery died before 1613 when Cote and Crafthole Parks were leased to Joane Hitchins, widow of

79 *Cote Cottage, built in the 1600s, the home of Tom and Mary Bersey, who for many years farmed at Sheviock Barton.*

John Hitchins, who had farmed at Sheviock Barton. An entry in the parish registers shows that the cottage was later inhabited by John Arundell (*c.*1630–*c.*1694), second son of the rector, Gregory Arundell. The tradition of letting Cote to the retired farmer of Sheviock Barton continues to this day. The current tenants are Tom and Mary Bersey, who farmed at Sheviock Barton from 1953 to 1991.

George's House (and George's Lane)

In 1648, Henry Rolle and other trustees of the late Sir Richard Carew, let a plot of ground in Sheviock woods containing about three land yards to 'George Winnacott of Sheviock husbandman'.[19] The consideration for the lease was that George should '(by Godes Assistance) Erect and build a convenient house and cellar' on the land. We can be sure, therefore, that George's Lane is named after this George Winnacott. The cellar was probably used to store fishing gear. The lease was on the lives of George Jeffery, son of the cordwainer (shoemaker) Peter Jeffery of Sheviock, and Silvester and Thomas Blake of Plymouth. The rent was 2s. Richard Holman witnessed the lease.

The account of John Rawlings, bailiff of the manor, made between 1656 and 1660, shows that George Winnacott also shared a tenement in Portwrinkle with Joane Lavers. According to one undated account of Rawlings, George owed £1 13s. 4d. and Joane owed £3 on property in Portwrinkle.[20] An account of 1656 noted that together they owed rent of £2 17s. 1d. and were to be distrained.[21] George was probably a son of John Winnacott, who had been a sailor on the *Dayestarr* in 1626. Another son was probably the John Winnacott, also described as a husbandman, who leased ten land yards in Crowstone Park (big enough for a fishing cellar) for 10s. in 1649.[22]

Orchard Cottage (Treise's Tenement)

English Heritage dates this building to the mid-1600s, with alterations of late 1600s or early 1700s. Its plan is described as a '3-room and through passage plan, with lower end to right, formerly at lower ground level, heated by rear lateral stack.' In the hall there is a cloam (clay) oven with clay door and handle. The lower end fireplace has the oven recess remaining. The antiquity of the building has caused it to be wrongly identified in the past with the Revd Walter Arundell's almshouses and with the 17th-century inn. But it is in fact the house belonging to what was once a farm of the manor of Sheviock.[23] The true identity of the building and the farmland belonging to it are established by Thomas Pride's Plan of the Manor of Sheviock of 1775, and the accompanying Survey. In these, the tenement is described as 'Tresis's Tenement'.[24] The name refers to John Treis, steward of the Carew estates from 1692 to 1697.[25]

Before Treis became tenant, at least three generations of the Blake family were the occupiers. In 1602, the Revd Walter Arundell described part of his glebe as 'a little orchard plott joyning with the Towne place, b[ou]nded in the weast side with Blakes

80 *Orchard Cottage was the farmhouse of Treise's tenement in the late 1600s.*

mowhay and apple garden'. This Blake was probably the father of Philip Blake (1604-89), who was the tenant of Treise's tenement in 1653.[26] In 1690, another Philip Blake, grandson of the first, was the tenant.[27] In that year he married Mary Knight, which probably accounts for the change of tenancy in the following year.[28]

In 1691, John Treis became joint tenant with Philip Bloy and Thomas Ellery. Treis was known to lodge at East Antony, where he had his office, so the actual farmers and inhabitants were probably Bloy and Ellery. The tenancy was for three lives, and those designated in 1691 were John Treis, Philip Bloy and Richard Bloy. Richard Bloy was probably bailiff of Sheviock manor in 1690, and Philip was probably bailiff in 1712, as both were tenants of Bailiff's Meadow in those years. The value of Treis's tenement was put at £30 and the rent was given as £2 0s. 7d. (as in 1653). On death or alienation, a heriot of a 'best beast' or 40s. was payable. In 1721, Thomas Ellery was listed as the sole conventionary tenant of 'Treses tenement'.[29] In 1725, Philip Palmer was appointed bailiff of the manor, became tenant of Bailiff's Meadow, and in 1726 took over the tenancy of Treis's tenement.[30]

Hugh Littleton was the next tenant of 'Treises tenement'.[31] The dates of his leases are 25 June 1733, 4 August 1746 and 12 December 1766. By this time the value of the farm had increased to £50. Hugh also farmed the 70 acres of Sheviock Barton, Berry Down and Berry Wells.[32] Now that the same farmer was farming two adjacent farms, it was possible to lease one of the farmhouses as a dwelling with a garden and orchards, but no farmland. The farmhouse was later converted into two cottages. These were acquired by Bill and Margaret Jones in 1980 and converted back into a single dwelling, called Orchard Cottage.

81 *Barn Cottage, built on the site of the Dawney's ancient barn in 1838.*

The farmland of Treise's tenement, which in any case was not adjacent to the farmhouse, but was separated from it by one of the fields of Sheviock Barton, was from then onwards removed from it and incorporated into the farmland of the Barton. Because of the distance of its fields from Treise's farmhouse, a separate barn had been built in the middle of Treise's fields, at some distance from the farmhouse.

Other Cottages

Barn Cottage (Landrey's Cottage)

In 1838, the trustees of William Henry Pole Carew let to John Landrey of Sheviock, innkeeper, a dwelling house, stable and garden containing about 13 perches of land.[33] The lives named were Edward Landrey (age 27), and John's grandchildren, Ann Clinnick Landrey (age six) and Henry Landrey (age five). They were the children of John's son, Joseph, and his wife, Jane. The cottage was built at the northern end of the site of the ancient barn of Sheviock Barton, and hence its modern name, Barn Cottage. The roof of the Dawneys' barn had collapsed in about 1837. Instead of rebuilding the barn to its former dimensions, it was decided to build the cottage at the northern end of the old barn.[34]

Clicker Cottages

These cottages stood opposite Higher Clicker. They are still remembered by some people in the village.

Cote Park House (Catherine Serpell's Cottage)

In 1838, William Henry Pole Carew and others granted to Catherine Serpell of Crafthole, widow, aged 57, a lease of a piece of ground in Sheviock churchtown containing about 10 perches.[35] The ground in question had been part of the old village green, which had been destroyed to make way for the new turnpike road. The consideration for the lease was that she should erect a substantial dwelling-house on the land. This is the house that stands at the junction of the A374 and Horsepool Road. It is now called Cote Park House. The rent was 10s. The lease was on the lives of her son, Thomas (age 25), daughter, Esther (age 31), and grandson, Francis Haimes (age two). Francis's father, George, was a gamekeeper, and later became the farmer at Haye. In 1841, Catherine Serpell was still living in Crafthole, and described herself as an innkeeper.

Faith Sargent's Cottage
In 1657, Sir John Carew leased to Faith Sargent, spinster of Sheviock, a 'dwelling house & garden in Sheviocke Churchtown'.[36] She signed the lease with her mark. The rent was 1s. 4d.

Martin's Houses and Shop
In 1841, the trustees of Thomas Somers Cocks and Francis Glanville the younger, and William Henry Pole Carew, let 'Two dwelling houses Shop and premises ... in Sheviock ... containing ... about Thirty Six Perches of Land' to Thomas Martin, a licensed victualler of Devonport.[37] He was already occupying the houses. The lease was on the lives of his children, Mary (age 15) and John (age 12) and Thomas Rowe, a victualler of Torpoint (age 35). The rent was £1 16s. The property is the first house to the west of the church on the north side of the A374.

Palmer's Cottage
In 1671, Sir John Carew let to Phillipp Palmer 'sone of Amos Palmer of the parish of Sheviock Husbandman', 'all that Cottage House & Plott of ground for an herb garden ... and adioyning to a dwelling-Hows heretofore in the tenure of Nicholas Byland deceased & now in the tenure of Abraham Palmer.'[38] The lease was to commence on the death of Amos's wife, Grace (née Kellow). The lives named were his own and that of Jane Bloy (or Bloye), daughter of Philip Bloy of Sheviock. She probably married Philip and became Jane Palmer. Philip Palmer, probably their son, became bailiff of the manor in 1725. The rent was 2s. plus one capon or 12d.

Tollhouse Cottage
See Chapter 40, *Markets, Highways and Turnpikes.*

Warren's Cottage
In 1723, Sir William Carew let to Walter Warren 'of the parish of Sheviocke ... Tailer' the 'cottage (now fallen down) with a garden plot thereunto adjoyning in Sheviocke ... adjoyning to the house where John Warren now dwells, late in the tenure of Jane

Palmer'.[39] The rent was 2s. The lives named were Walter, his brother, Robert, and Christian, daughter of John Nichols of St Germans, 'Tailer'.

Rectories

The Glebe House

This was the rector's house from the 1500s until the building of the Victorian rectory between 1842 and 1844. In 1602, the rector, Walter Arundell, described the house in a glebe terrier simply as, 'a hale [hall] a kitchen a buttery. Chambers over them'. The house was probably thatched at this time. In a note to the church authorities dated 1613, Arundell stated, 'I have bestowed £200 upon the repair of the glebe houses etc.'[40]

In a terrier of 1680, the Revd Nicolas Kendall described the rectory, rebuilt by himself, as,

> One dwelling-house tiled, in which is one kichin paved with slatt, one larder flourd, one room called the sinke, paved with slatt, one hall floured, one dayry floured, one buttery paved with slatt, one entry paved, five chambers of a floor, & one cock-loft, one chamber plaistered & one little chamber, one study.[41]

82 *The Glebe House, formerly the rectory of Sheviock. In the background is Glebe Barn, one of the rector's barns converted into a dwelling-house.*

83 *The coat of arms of the Revd Nicolas Kendall (rector 1680-1739) above the fire-place in The Glebe House.*

The new features of the house are that tiles have replaced the thatch on the roof; the kitchen, scullery (the 'sinke') and the buttery have been paved with slate; the hall and dairy have been floored (perhaps with cobbles); there is a new entry, paved with slate; there is a new cock-loft, probably under the roof-tiles; and there are a number of new rooms. These include the large chamber in which the Kendall coat-of-arms is depicted in a plaster overmantel above the fireplace. Below the shield is the carved Kendall motto, *virtus depressa resurgit.*[42] The plaster ceiling of the same room is decorated with Tudor roses.[43] Kendall's other additions are a small chamber and a study. According to English Heritage, the house was probably again remodelled in the mid-1700s, and a rear service wing was added in 1892.

In 1831, the rector, the Revd Reginald Pole, received permission from the Bishop of Exeter, on account of illness, not to live in the old rectory; but instead to continue to live 'in the house of my father situated in the said parish, and about a mile distant from the church'.[44] The house in question was Tredis.[45] He installed his curate, the Revd James Crowley, in the Glebe House at a stipend of £100. This was the last time it was used as the parsonage house. In 1837, the Revd Pole let it to the tenant farmer of the Glebe Farm, and at the same time he obtained permission for his new curate, the Revd Samuel Wallis Roberts, who was still a fellow of Pembroke College, Oxford, to live in rented accommodation in Antony parish. In 1840, the Revd Roberts built his own house, Trethill House, in Sheviock parish. The Church Commissioners sold the old parsonage house with the glebe in 1923.

The Outbuildings

In 1602, Walter Arundell described his outbuildings as, 'By south the hall a Courte, a wheat barne, a Brewhouse, over dry planching a floor to make malt. By north the hale, a stable, a stall and a Barne for oteis [oats]. Implements none.' Like his house, Arundell's two barns and his brew-house were almost certainly thatched. In 1680, Nicolas Kendall described his outbuildings as, 'two barnes, whereof one tiled and the other thetcht, one brewhouse tiled, one little stable, and chamber over the same tiled, one other stable & one oxen-house, both thetcht, four hoggshouses'. The new features of the outbuildings were that the wheat barn and the brew-house were tiled; there was a new tiled stable with a room above it; and there were new pig-sties.

The Old (Victorian) Rectory

The imposing Victorian rectory was built for the Revd Gerald Pole Carew between 1842 and 1844. Unfortunately there is no record of the architect. The receipts for the building costs of £1,728 4s. 9d. are preserved in the Devon Record Office. Payments were made in seven instalments between 1 June 1842 and 12 January 1844. In addition, £38 15s. was paid to John Collins 'for the chimney pieces supplied by me for the Parsonage House Sheviock'. These have since been removed. The Governors of Queen Anne's Bounty paid £1,096 14s. 9d. of the total and the Revd Gerald Pole Carew paid £670 5s. Pole Carew did not live to enjoy his new rectory for long, because he died in 1845 aged only twenty-nine.

The Modern Rectory
The modern rectory was built in 1970.

The Glebe Land

The church at Sheviock possessed a large glebe, consisting, in the 1600s, of nearly 100 acres of farmland adjacent to the rectory. *The Cornwall Register* (1847) gives the extent of the glebe as 102 acres, making it the sixth largest in Cornwall.[46] The glebe land, named from the Latin *gleba* (soil), passed to each successive incumbent to farm as he thought best. In the Middle Ages, in return for his glebe, the rector paid a rent to Tavistock Abbey. The rector's *procurator* (steward), John Penhale, was paying an annuity of 3s. to the Abbey of Tavistock in 1410-11, and the same amount was still being paid in the reign of Henry VIII.[47] In most parishes at this time, the parson's glebe was only a virgate (30 acres) or less, putting him on the same economic level as the peasant farmer.

From time to time, the archdeacon of the diocese required the incumbent to make a return of the land in his occupation. This return was called a 'terrier', from the medieval Latin *liber terrarius* (book of lands). No medieval terriers have survived for Sheviock, but there is a 'computus' (account) roll covering the period from Michaelmas 1410 to Michaelmas 1411. It was made by the steward, John Penhale, who was looking after the glebe and the rector's tithe income in the absence of the rector, Richard Donscombe. The glebe land extended eastwards from the rectory along the north bank of Wacker creek and southwards from it on the western side of Ladywell Lane. Penhale wrote:

> He accounts for 20s received for 3 closes called Sheviock, Lampark, and Medepark, let to William Gyst and John Penven, and for 5s. 9d. for 2 closes called Byrydoune and Wilpark, viz., for one-quarter of the year and no more because they are let to Simon and Richard Odyhorn and others to cultivate the said parcels of land … and for 24s. received for 1 close called Southdowne let to John Penhale, and for 6s. 8d. for 1 close called Cowenpark from John Penhale and John Campell, and for 5s. 6d. for a close called Woodeparke let to Roger Whiteforde with wood pasture, and for 12d. received for a tithe of the demesne field called Medenepark let to John Arundell, and for 2s. 8d. for 1 close called Loggenpark … and for 3s. 4d. received for the herbage of the great garden let to John Penhale. Nothing for the pasture in Pyrihay, Southay, Oxhay, because it is depastured by one horse of the rector's.[48]

The earliest surviving terrier was made by the Revd Walter Arundell in 1602. He made another in 1613, but that has been partially destroyed. The Revd Nicholas Kendall completed another in 1680.[49] The 1680 terrier described the glebe lands as follows:

> two courtes, two orchards, three herb-gardens, conteining by estimation, one acre or thereabout; one close called the Well-Hay, cont. one acre & quarter; another called the Long-Close, cont. four acres; the great Penend, cont. ten acres; the Middle and Lower Penend cont. ten acres; the Wood, cont. eighteen acres; the Wood-Parke, cont. five acres; the East-Parke, cont. four acres; the Broom-Close, cont. five acres; the Meadow, cont. two acres; one Close called the Seaven Acres, cont. five acres; the Higher Ladywell, cont. four acres; the Lower Ladywell, cont. four acres; the Higher South-Down, cont. eight acres; the Lower South-Down, cont. four acres; & the New Meadow, cont. three acres & halfe & bounded as followeth; viz., with the lande of Sir John Carew Baron, on the West, North & East & Southeast; & on some parte of the North, with the lande of James Bond Esq.; of William Gibbs clarke & Philipp Blake gent. on the Southeast, and with an arme of the sea on the Northeast & Southeast.

Between 1680 and 1840, the main change to the glebe was that more of the woodland had been turned into pasture or arable land, leaving only five English acres of woodland. The Church Commissioners sold the glebe land to Antony Estates in 1923.

Glebe Barn

The barn belonging to the Glebe farm was converted into a dwelling in modern times.

84 *The Old Rectory was built for the Revd Gerald Pole Carew between 1842 and 1844.*

PART III

Crafthole

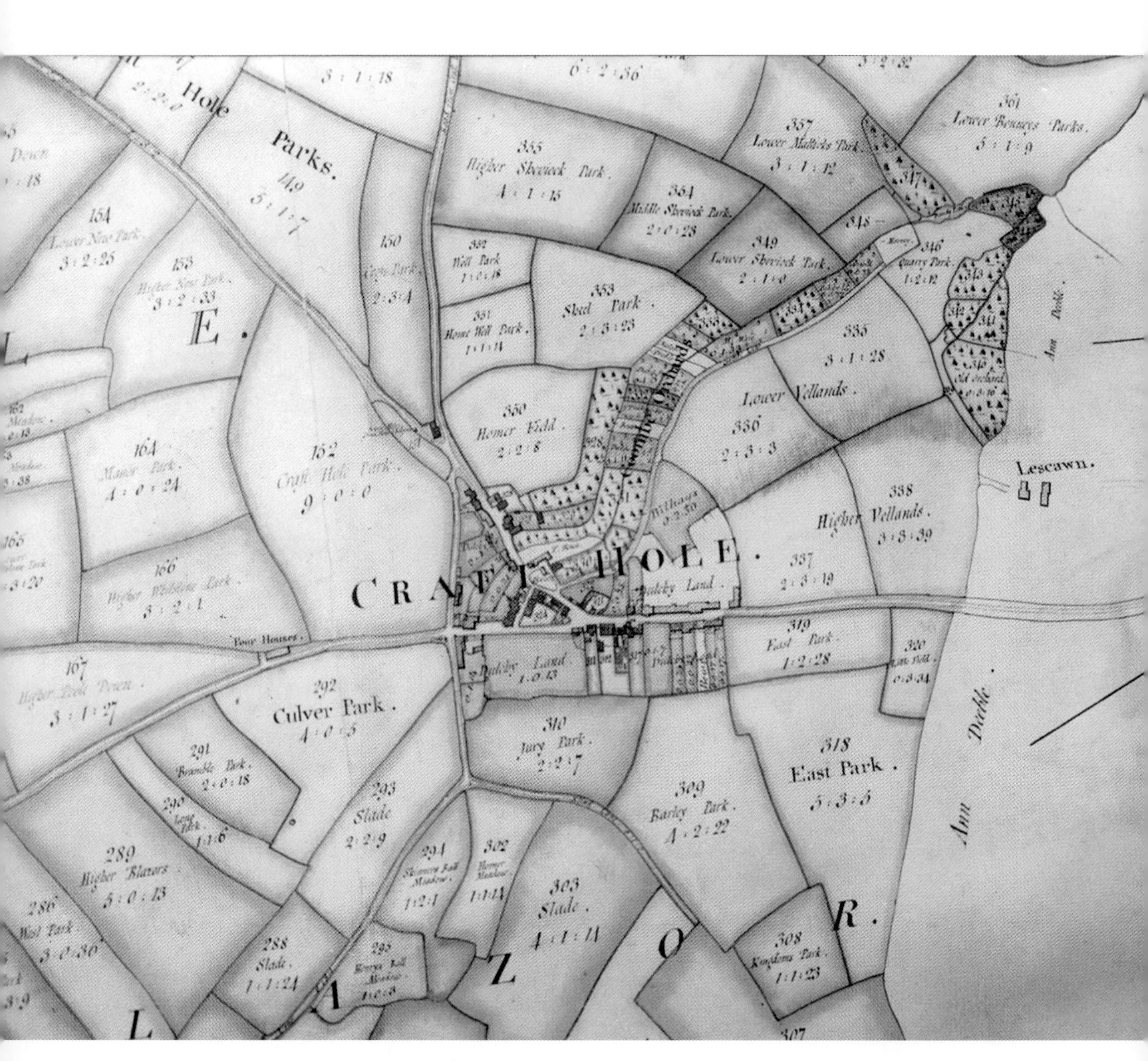

85 *Thomas Pride's plan of Crafthole made in 1775. The darker-toned houses belonged to Reginald Pole Carew; the lighter ones to the Duchy of Cornwall. The plan shows that 'poor houses' once stood west of the village.*

CHAPTER 11

The Borough of Crafthole

The name, Crafthole, consists of two elements, 'croft' and 'hill' or 'hole'. The meaning of 'croft' in Middle English, the language in use in Sheviock when Crafthole was founded, was 'enclosed arable plot'.[1] It may refer to the small plots of land into which the new borough was divided when it was first created in 1314. When the borough was founded, the name is given as 'Croftilberwe'. In 1441, it was referred to as 'Croftole Burgh'. In the surviving court rolls of the 1500s and 1600s, the name of the borough is given as 'Crofthole'. Richard Carew, who wrote his *Survey of Cornwall* in the late 1500s, was one of the first to describe the village as 'Crafthole'. The first court roll to use an 'a' in the name dates from 1712.[2]

The derivation of the second element is unclear, but the weight of authority favours 'hill' rather than 'hole'. Carew suggested 'hill' because of its high site. This view is shared by the Cornish language scholar, O.J. Padel, who writes: 'the place is situated on a hill, so *hyll* is greatly preferable, despite the numerical weight of spellings with 'o.'[4] The reason for the change to 'hole' could be simply a matter of euphony. In a way, though, 'hole', meaning a 'hollow place', does also fit the topography, and perhaps this was why the inhabitants were comfortable with the change. There are two places called Hole in the adjacent parish of Antony. The nearer of these was 'Brockhole', or badger hole, lying between the River Lynher and Scraesdon.[5] Though elevated, the village of Crafthole is centred on a depression in the ground between three higher places, south, east and west, and a steep dip to the north, called the Coombes. The Coombes were also part of the borough, and although in later centuries were largely given over to orchards and garden plots, they may have contained more dwellings in the 14th century.[6]

Crafthole: A Medieval New Town

Sir Nicholas Dawney obtained a licence from King Edward II to found a new borough at Crafthole in 1314. The establishment of new towns in England was most intense in the period between 1066 and 1230, when 124 new towns (72 per

86 *The coat-of-arms of East Looe incorporates the arms of Bodrugan.*

cent of all medieval new towns) were founded. In the next 60 years, a further 24 (14 per cent) were founded. Between 1291 and 1330, when Crafthole was founded, a further 12 (7 per cent) were started.[7] So, the foundation of Crafthole came right at the end of the great movement to endow new towns. It also came just before the scourge of the Black Death (1348-9) virtually put an end to new foundations until modern times. Devon and Cornwall had a very high percentage of the English new towns, with Cornwall having some 30 planted towns between 1141, when Launceston was founded, and 1327, when Penzance received its charter. The earl of Cornwall was the founder of most of the Cornish new towns. In only a few cases was the founder a lesser magnate, such as Sir Nicholas Dawney. Hugh and Odo de Treverbyn are mentioned in connection with the foundation of Porthpyghan (West Looe) as a borough between 1237 and 1243; Walter de Ralegh founded the borough of Michell in St Enodor in 1239; and Henry and Odo de Bodrugan were responsible for the endowment of East Looe between 1284 and 1320.[8]

The inspiration for the foundation of Crafthole probably came from the successful foundation of West Looe by the Treverbyn family. Sir Nicholas Dawney was on intimate terms with the Treverbyns. Sir Nicholas's son, John, was to marry Hugh de Treverbyn's daughter, Sybella, a few years after the foundation of Crafthole. In a deed dated 11 July 1336, the Bishop of Exeter stated that Sir John's ancestors had erected the chapel dedicated to St Nicholas at West Looe. These ancestors were most likely Sir Nicholas and his wife, Joan Langdon. The dedication to St Nicholas was appropriate, as he was the saint who was believed to protect fishermen.

The Charter of the Borough

When a new borough was licensed, a formal charter was prepared setting out the rights and privileges of its inhabitants. It is to this charter that James I's surveyor was referring when he wrote, 'This is reputed a borough town (a poore one), the charter thereof I could not see'. Many charters were based on the models of earlier charters. Because of the close relationship that existed between the Dawneys and the Treverbyns, it is likely that the charter of Crafthole was based on that of West Looe, granted in *c.*1243.[9] In 1325, King Edward II confirmed the charter of West Looe in these words:[10]

For Roger Prideaux and Elizabeth his wife, and others.

The King, to whom etc. greeting. We have inspected the Charter which Richard heretofore Earl of Poictou and Cornwall made to Odo de Treverbyn, in these words:–

> To all to whom this present writing shall come, Richard Earl of Poictou and Cornwall greeting, Know ye, that I have granted, and by this my Charter have confirmed, for me and my heirs, to Sir Odo de Treverbyn and his heirs, that his Borough of Porbuan [Porthpyghan or West Looe] shall be a free Borough, and that the Burgesses of the same Borough shall be free and quit of all customs, and they may buy and sell all merchandizes in markets and fairs, and in all places throughout the whole County of Cornwall. Also I have granted to the same Odo and his heirs, that if any one shall reside for a year and a day in the same Borough without just claim [being made to return him], he shall, according to the law of other free Burgesses, be quit of all neifty [the manorial services due from *nativi* (bondmen)] and slavery. Also I have granted to the said Odo and his heirs, for me and my heirs, that they shall have in the same Borough a market on Wednesday in every week, and a fair once in the year, to continue for three days, to wit, on the eve, on the day, and on the morrow of Saint Michael; so that the aforesaid Odo and his heirs shall receive and have all issues and all advantages pertaining to the said fair; saving everywhere all pleas which pertain to the Crown of the Lord the King. Wherefore we will that the same Odo and his heirs shall entirely and peaceably hold the aforesaid liberties for ever. And that their Grant shall be preserved, ratified, and unshaken, I have testified this present writing by the affixing of my seal, these being witnesses: Hugh de Saint Philiberto, Ralph de Sulling, Robert Fitzwilliam, Walter Fitzwilliam, and Richard de Kilvard, Auger de Tregorioz, and many others.

Now we, the Grants and Confirmation aforesaid ratifying and confirming the same, for us and our heirs, as much as in us lieth, do grant and confirm to Roger Prideaux and Elizabeth his wife, the cousin and one of the heirs of the aforesaid Odo, and to John Danny [Dawney] and Sibilla [Sybella née Treverbyn] his wife, the cousin and other heir of the same Odo, and to the heirs of the same Elizabeth and Sibilla, as the Charter aforesaid reasonably testifieth, and as the same Roger, Elizabeth, John, and Sibilla, and the ancestors of the same Elizabeth and Sibilla, the liberties aforesaid, from the time of the Grants and Confirmation aforesaid, have hitherto reasonably used and enjoyed.

In witness whereof etc. Witness the King, at Porchester, the 22^{d}. day of September.'

The Privileges of the Charter

The privilege of Crafthole to hold a market was identical to that of West Looe, even to the day of the week on which it was to be held. The grant of an annual fair for three days was also similar, except that at Crafthole it was to be held around the feast of St James rather than the feast of St Michael. The right of settlers to claim the status of freemen after residence for a year and a day was probably also the same. The provision concerning freedom to attend other markets and fairs without paying tolls was probably also similar, except that this freedom may have applied throughout England (apart from London) from the start, and not been confined to Cornwall.

When Hugh de Treverbyn enlarged the 'libertyes and antient customs' of the burgesses of Porthpyghan in the early 1300s, the new privileges were to be the same as those of Helston and Launceston.[11] The privileges of Helston, granted by King John in 1201, were firstly the right to have a merchant guild. But there is no evidence for the existence of a merchant guild in Crafthole. The second privilege enjoyed by the burgesses of Helston was freedom throughout the realm (not just in Cornwall) from *theloneum*, *pontagium*, *passagium*, *stallagium*, and *lestagium*.[12] These imposts may be translated as: general tolls; tolls for crossing bridges; tolls for passing through a district; tolls for erecting market stalls; and tolls levied in markets for licence to remove goods. An alternative meaning for *lestagium* is tolls paid on landing goods at a port. The burgesses were also freed from an impost called *sollagium*. An English translation is 'soilage'. This was a payment by way of ground rent for the use of the soil – conceivably it might be claimed when a tradesman unshipped his goods from horseback and laid them on the ground.[13]

The actual charter of Crafthole was granted by Edward II, and he, of course, had the power to grant all these exemptions from toll throughout England, not just in Cornwall. The exemptions granted did not, however, apply in the City of London. The third privilege of Helston's burgesses was the right to present or defend in their

87 *The charter of West Looe may have been the model for the lost charter of Crafthole. St Nicholas's Chapel (centre) was probably erected by Sir Nicholas Dawney and his wife, Joan.*

own borough courts all pleas relating to goods or tenures arising from or in their borough, except pleas of the Crown.[14] Crafthole also had this privilege, as shown by the holding of courts baron and courts leet in the borough from the 1500s to the 1700s. In Launceston, the mayor and burgesses claimed the assize of bread and ale within the town.[15] This meant that they kept the fines payable for breaches of the assize. In Crafthole, the lord of the manor kept the fines.

Markets: In 1314, Edward II granted to Sir Nicholas Dawney and his heirs the right to hold one market a week in their manor of 'Shiviok' at 'Croftilberwe'. This was to be held each Wednesday. Later, another was licensed on Friday.[16] Fridays, Saturdays and many Wednesdays were 'fish days' according to the rules of the Catholic church, so Crafthole's market days were appropriate for a parish with a thriving fishing industry.

The Fair at the Feast of St James: The king also granted Sir Nicholas the right to hold an annual fair lasting three days, on the vigil (eve), feast and morrow (following day) of St James (25 July). St James was believed to be buried at Compostela in Spain. That town was re-named 'Santiago' (St James) de Compostela in his honour. It was the second most meritorious place (after Jerusalem) for a pilgrim to visit. In 1313, just a year before he founded his new borough of Crafthole, Sir Nicholas Dawney had himself travelled as a pilgrim to the shrine of St James at Compostela.

The Site of the New Borough

The new town of Crafthole was sited below the lord's manor-house at Blazor at the top of the hill. The fields of one of the demesne farms, called Blazor, lay to the south, south-east and south-west of the manor-house. This was the less productive of the two demesne farms of the manor, and was probably used mainly for pasturing the many horses belonging to the knightly family of the Dawneys.[17] There may already have been one or two cottages on the site before the establishment of the new town, and the 'Garinus of Blazor' mentioned in Henry Dawney's charter of 1174-1206 may have lived in one.[18] From their elevated manor-house overlooking Whitsand Bay to the south and the River Lynher to the north, the Dawneys were in a good position to protect their settlement. This protection would have been an important consideration for the first settlers, and it was further increased when Sir John Dawney was licensed to crenellate his dwelling-place in 1336. This crenellation may have involved the construction of a separate keep or watchtower and a battlemented perimeter wall, but no traces of any fortifications remain.

Several kinds of visitors would have come to the new borough. First of all, people having business with the lord of the manor – and it will be remembered that the parish was the seat of the 'honour of Sheviock', which consisted of several manors. Secondly, merchants dealing in fish would come to buy their stock from the fishermen of the parish. The new borough was also on the main east-west thoroughfare, so the settlers would benefit from the trade of merchants, pilgrims and others passing through.

Although there is no written evidence, the inhabitants may have had the right to cut the furze that grew so abundantly on the cliff tops. It was used as fuel. Another cheap source of fuel was bracken, called in Cornish *reden*. 'Readen', alone or in compounds, is the name of several fields to the west of the borough. The right to cut bracken was included as a benefit of burgage tenure in a number of surviving English and Welsh charters. Celia Fiennes in her tour of 1698 noted that bracken (fern) was being used as fuel by the inhabitants of Penzance: 'Little or no Fewell – turff and Furse and Ferne.'

88 *The medieval town well in Well Lane. The pump probably dates from the 1800s.*

89 *The new pump on the main road was probably constructed c.1900.*

The Town Well

The town well was situated a little way down Well Lane leading to the Coombes. Water was simply scooped out by bucket. The old well is still clearly visible, though now protected by a wooden door. It was important to keep the water pure and it was not permitted to clean produce at the well. In October 1616, the fisherman, Samuel Maister, was presented at the court leet of the borough for washing '*halevia anglic.* pilchardes *iuxta fontem Burgi*' (for washing '*halevia*, pilchards in English, at the borough well') and for allowing the 'roppes *piscini*' (fishing nets) to fall into the water.[19] At the same court, the innkeeper, William Sargent, was fined because '*aquabat spadones*' ('he watered plants') and presumably allowed dirty water to flow back into the well. Probably in the 1800s, a new bore-hole was dug at the side of the main road, near the top of Well Lane. This was completed with a pump and a big circular pump handle. It continued in use until mains water was brought to Crafthole at the beginning of the Second World War.

The Plan of the New Town

Although there may already have been peasant cottages in Crafthole before 1314, it is clear from its regularity that an entirely new ground plan was prepared for the borough. The plan was a simple one. The building plots were measured out along both sides of the main road through the borough, up to the point where the road forks. Each house was set in a rectangular plot of ground that could be used to grow herbs and vegetables. The standard size of plot was 22 perches. In addition, the land in the steep-sided Coombes was carved into similar-sized plots. These plots were an integral part of the borough and could be leased by the burgesses or their tenants to cultivate as orchards or vegetable gardens, or to keep an animal or two. At least one cottage was erected in the Coombes in the 1500s, and there may have been cottages there in the 1300s and 1400s.

The houses/shops built on the plots along the main road had their narrow sides and shop windows facing the street. The market place consisted of the space between the two rows of houses/shops. On market days, the owners would place or let down a trade counter in front of their shops. The ground between the two rows at the centre of Crafthole is fairly flat, so that carts and stalls stationed there would not slide downhill. The space between the two rows was very narrow because of the limited amount of level ground. As a result, when horses stopped outside these buildings and left their piles of dung, they created an unacceptable nuisance, and a number of presentments were to follow at the court leet for causing such nuisances.[20]

90 *Plan of Crafthole from the 1840 Tithe Map. Apart from the two cottages to the west of West Lane, the plan is the same as it was in 1775.*

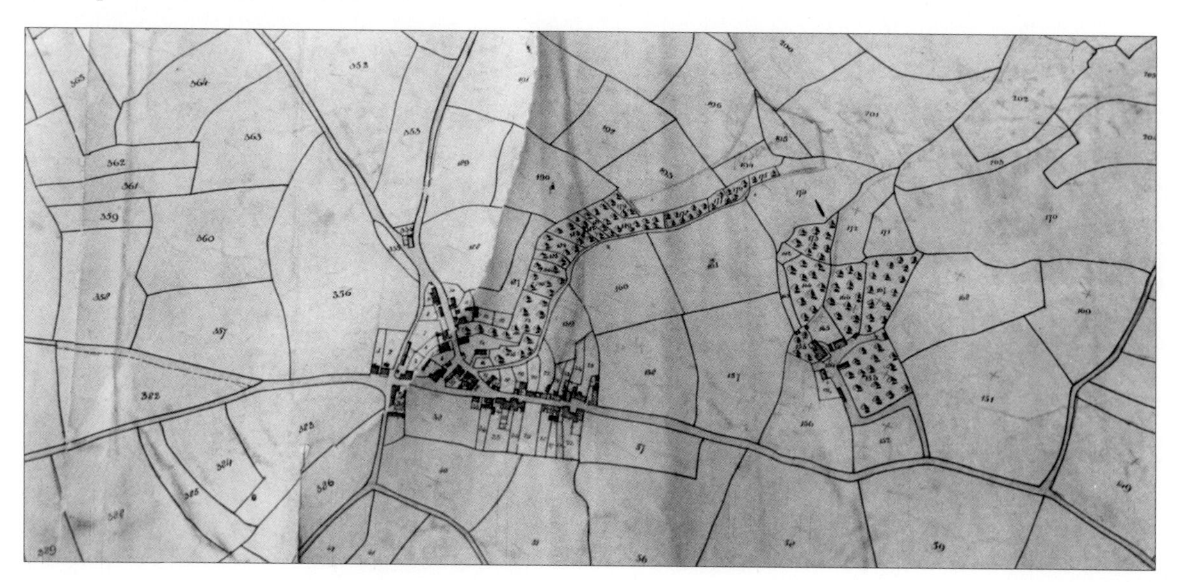

The cottages built in Crafthole were small, with little plots of land behind them. In other words, the cottages were designed not for farmers to live in, but for those who plied a trade.[21] One gable of an old house in Crafthole, called Cosy Cot, stands opposite today's post office. It was probably built in the 1600s or early 1700s. Though now incorporated into a modern house, old photographs of Cosy Cot give some idea of what the original dwellings were like. The original cottages would have been thatched.

The legal limits of the new town were very precisely drawn. These limits can be clearly seen in Thomas Pride's map of 1775.[22] They included Sir Nicholas's own manor-house and the field in which his dovecote or culver-house stood. The western boundary of his manor-house (now called West Lane) met the southern boundary of the borough (defining the southern edge of the Crafthole cottage gardens) at right angles. When the manor-house was divided up into three farmhouses (or two farmhouses and an inn) after the departure of the Courtenays for Tiverton, these houses were legally part of the borough. By 1600, the houses were identifiable as High House, Cross House and Sargent's tenement (the modern *Finnygook Inn*). Many of the tenants of these houses are shown as jurors of the borough in 17th-century court rolls.[23]

It was standard practice when developing a new town to let 'burgages' as empty building plots. It was then up to the tenant to erect one or more houses or cottages upon his burgage plot.[24] Usually the lord of the manor granted a rent-free period of between seven and ten years to the tenant to help him with the building costs, and in

91 *Crafthole photographed in 1963, showing the new developments south of the village.*

some places he donated the building materials.[25] The properties built on the burgage plots were legally separate entities from the plots themselves. Thus, when, in the early 1700s, Sir William Carew bought some of the houses/shops within the borough from their previous owners, he, or his lessees, still had to pay ground rents to the Duchy of Cornwall for the plots. Thomas Pride's survey of 1775 shows that George Westcote, who had inherited the tenancy of Sargent's tenement (the village inn), and Jane Harvey (widow of the bailiff, John Harvey) paid rents to Sir William's descendant, Reginald Pole Carew, for their properties; but also paid 'quit rents' of 9d. each to the Duchy of Cornwall for the burgage plots. Likewise, Simon Wayte, whose house and orchard were situated at the point where Well Lane joined the main road through Crafthole, paid rent to the Carews and a quit rent of 1s. 6d. to the Duchy for two burgage plots. John Taw, the butcher, who occupied a house at the point where the road from Polscoe meets the main coast road, paid 4s. 6d. to the Duchy as well as his rent to the Carews. Charles Blight occupied the tollhouse on the south side of the main highway. He paid 10s. to the Duchy as well as his rent to the Carews.[26]

92 *Cosy Cot before the modern rebuilding. The construction of the chimney and the walls made of cob suggest that it was built in the 1600s or even earlier. It would originally have been thatched.*

A Parliamentary Survey of 1649 lists some two dozen burgage plots.[27] An examination of Thomas Pride's map of 1775 and the Tithe Redemption map of 1841 shows about the same number of plots. There were ten on each side of the main road and it is likely that these were the original ones measured out by Sir Nicholas's surveyors with their surveying ropes in the 1300s. After the departure of the Courtenays, the

93 *Women in Crafthole baked their bread in cloam (clay) ovens until the introduction of cast iron ranges in the nineteenth century. This one is at Cosy Cot.*

94 *Crafthole c.1930. The charabanc was probably hired for an outing. The thatched cottages on the left of the picture and High House in the distance have gone since the photograph was taken.*

site of their fortified manor-house was used to erect the three large houses mentioned above and a few farm buildings and cottages.

Assuming an average of four to five people per dwelling house, the original borough of 20 houses must have been planned for about 80 to 100 people. To feed the newcomers, Sir Nicholas had to increase the amount of corn grown in the parish, and probably carved new fields out of Sheviock woods and Sconner woods for this purpose. To grind the additional corn, he may have had a new windmill built on a five-acre field, called 'Gill Ball' taken out of Sheviock woods. By the late 1500s, there were many more dwelling houses in Crafthole than building plots, and many of those houses were themselves in multiple occupation. In many new boroughs, with extensive privileges granted to new residents, the standard rent for a burgage plot was 1s. But Crafthole offered only modest privileges to the new inhabitants, so that the ground rent was fixed at 9d., and remained at this level so long as the borough continued to exist.[28]

A Borough with an English Name

The new borough was called *Croftilberwe* (Croft-hill-borough) – a name composed of three English words, indicative of the language then in use in the parish. English-speaking vendors were already in the 13th century buying fish from the parish of Sheviock and carrying it into Devon. A law case from that time has given us a not very savoury picture of two of these vendors. Roger Chapman of 'Shevyek' and his brother Henry killed John Walecu (perhaps Wallis) in his house in Sheviock. This house, according to Dr James Whetter, was probably a tavern.[29] A 'chapman' is an itinerant vendor. So here we have an instance of two brothers, perhaps Englishmen, judging by their name, resident in Sheviock, and falling out with a native parishioner and murdering him. Sir Nicholas perhaps counted on the establishment of a new borough, with its portreeve (mayor) and law court, as a measure to curb lawlessness as well as being profitable to himself. After the laying out of the building plots of Crafthole in the sheltered spot below the manor-house, the chapmen would have had a convenient place to lodge when meeting the Sheviock fishermen. The new borough was nearly equidistant between the two fishing places – one on the seashore and the other on the River Lynher.

The First Inhabitants

Sir Nicholas may have deliberately encouraged native English speakers to take up residence. He already had tenants in fishing areas, such as Landulph and Antony on the Cornish side of the Tamar. He also had tenants possessing other skills in inland areas of Devon, such as Cornwood and Norton, which were English-speaking. Some craftsmen and traders from the principal towns of Devon, such as Tavistock, Plympton and Plymouth, may also have been attracted. His connection with the Treverbyns and the borough of *Porthpyghan* (West Looe) could have led to some immigration from that Cornish-speaking fishing port; but Sir Nicholas probably did not encourage migration from there in case it harmed the interests of his friends, the Treverbyns. The names of some parishioners of Sheviock (not necessarily residents of Crafthole) who had died during the year 1410-11 have been preserved in an account made by John Penhale, the rector's *procurator* (steward). They suggest a mixed population of native Cornish and English people.[30]

Harold Fox has drawn attention to the fact that, around 1300, there were far fewer people along the 320 miles of the Cornish coastline than there were along the 197 miles of Devon's.[31] Whereas Devon had 250 taxpayers per mile of coast, Cornwall had only 107. Therefore, starting a new borough next to their existing fishery at Portwrinkle, would have been attractive both to the Dawneys, to better exploit their fishery, and to the fisherfolk from the more crowded fishing villages of

Devon. The earliest surviving records of the borough of Crafthole, from the late 1500s and early 1600s, show that fishermen and sailors formed the biggest single group of inhabitants.[32] Elsewhere, records survive of the occupations of the first inhabitants of a number of medieval English new towns.[33] These included ale-brewers, bakers, blacksmiths, butchers, carpenters, cooks, masons, shoemakers, tailors, and weavers. All these craftsmen and tradesmen were to be found in Crafthole in later centuries, and many were probably there from the beginning.[34]

Ownership of the Borough

From the foundation of the borough until 1346, the Dawneys owned both the borough and the manor of Sheviock. In 1346, with the death of Sir John Dawney, the ownership of both borough and manor passed in marriage to the Courtenays, earls of Devon. In 1462, on the attainder of the sixth earl, King Edward IV passed both properties to William Neville, Earl of Kent, and after his death in 1463 to Sir Renfry Arundell, the king's servitor. In 1486, Henry VII restored both properties to Edward Courtenay, son of Sir Hugh Courtenay of Boconnoc, and created him Earl of Devon. He was Emmeline Dawney's great-grandson. In 1538, his grandson, Henry, Marquis of Exeter, was executed for treason and the properties were once again forfeited to the Crown.

In 1540, King Henry VIII transferred the borough to the Duchy of Cornwall, but retained the manor of Sheviock in his own hands.[35] The rights granted by Edward II to hold markets then passed to the Duchy as owner of the borough. Up to this time, it is likely that the separate courts for the borough of Crafthole and the manor of Sheviock had been held in the same part of the old manor-house. By the early 1500s, this had been replaced by, or converted into, three substantial houses. The largest of these, called Sargent's tenement, had become an inn by 1620. It was called 'the Great House' in 1825 and is now the *Finnygook Inn*. After 1540, the courts for the manor of Sheviock were probably removed to Sheviock Barton. In 1553, Queen Mary restored the borough of Crafthole to Edward Courtenay, Earl of Devon.[36] A court leet of the borough was held in the name of Edward, Earl of Devon in September 1554.[37] In 1556, the earl came under suspicion and moved abroad. On his death without issue, the borough reverted to the Crown.

From the execution of Charles I in 1649, until 1660, the borough belonged to the Commonwealth. The Commonwealth authorities had some difficulty in collecting their rents. A note on the Parliamentary Survey of 1649 reads: 'The rent [of the borough] being per annum £1 11s 8½d hath not been paid by the said tenants for these last two years.'[38] The borough was restored to the Duchy at the Restoration. Sir William Carew purchased Sargent's tenement in 1711.[39] He thus brought the old manor-house back within the manor of Sheviock for the first time since 1540.[40] In

1741, he let this property to the innholder William Lord, with reversion to his wife Ann.[41] When the steward of the Carew estates resumed the sittings of the combined court leet and court baron of the manor of Sheviock in the years 1763 to 1765, he was able to hold them 'at Mrs Ann Lord's House in Crafthole', as it was once again within the manor of Sheviock.[42] In 1798, the Hon Reginald Pole Carew purchased the entire borough from the Duchy for a mere £260, indicating that the profits from the borough were then minimal. Reginald had completed the process started by Sir John Carew in 1691 of bringing the borough of Crafthole and the manor of Sheviock back within the same ownership after an interval of 258 years.[43]

The Sixteenth Century

Richard Carew described Crafthole as it was in the 16th century, when it belonged to the Crown. But he was as much concerned with raising a smile as with describing the borough accurately, and the information he gives is sketchy. He wrote:

> In this parish standeth Crafthole, which by the high site, might more fitly be termed Open hill, a poore village but a much frequented thorow-fare, somewhat infamous, not upon any present desert, but through an inveterate byword, *viz*. That it is peopled with 12 dwellings, and 13 cuckolds: for as the dwellings are more [than] doubled, so (I hope) the cuckolds are lesse [than] singled. Howsoever, many wayfarers make themselves glee, by putting the Inhabitants in minde of this priviledge; who againe, especially the women (like the Campellians in the North, and the London Bargers) forslow not to baigne them (unless they plead their heels the faster) with a worse perfume, [than] Jugurth found fault with in the dungeon, where the Romannes buried him alive, to attend his languishing and miserable death.

As we have seen, there were never as few as 12 dwellings, except when the first ones were still being built. The information that 'the dwellings are more than doubled' refers to the fact that many single burgage plots contained several dwellings on them, and many of the existing dwellings had been subdivided for multiple occupation. The 'Campellians in the North' must be a jocular reference to the Scots. London 'Bargers' (bargees) had an infamous reputation for foul language.[44] 'Jugurth' (Jugurtha) was a Numidian prince who defied the Romans in the early second century BC.[45]

The Feudal Incidents of Tenure in the Borough

In a number of respects, the holding of a tenancy in the borough was similar to other kinds of manorial tenure. As on ordinary manors, there was a duty of suit of court, and those who did not attend were liable to pay a fine (3d. for freeholders and copyholders; 2d. for mere residents until the reign of King James, when it went up to 3d.). There was a duty to fill the office of portreeve, and when the reeve swore his oath of office a fine was payable (2d.). As on other manors, whenever the status of a tenant changed in some way, a payment was due to the lord. These payments included fines on alienation of property, fines payable on succession to a holding, and the heriot, payable by customary tenants (copyholders) on death. These incidents of tenure, feudal in origin, were sources of profit to the lord. According to a valuation of the borough made during the Commonwealth period, a free tenant of the borough paid on every death a 'relief' which was double the rent.[46] He paid the same amount if, as he was entitled to do, he alienated the property. A copyholder paid a 'heriot' of double the rent upon the death of every life named in his lease and he paid the same amount on surrender of his lease. Unlike the freeholder, he was not allowed to alienate the property, but had to return it to the lord if he wanted to leave. In the period 1628 to 1640, the lowest amount received by the Duchy in fees and fines at any one court was 1s. 2d. and the highest was 5s. 3d. The average was 2s. 3d.

The Seventeenth Century

The importance of Crafthole in the 17th century derived mainly from its participation in the flourishing fishing industry of the Rame peninsula, thanks to the little ports at Portwrinkle and on the Lynher. 'It lieth very near the sea, and the people live mostly by fishing' reported a Crown Surveyor to James I.[47] It was also important as a collecting centre for wool used in the Devon cloth trade. Several weavers lived in or near the borough.[48] As a result of Crown ownership, men of quality filled its offices. Investment in the borough was facilitated by its system of landholding by 'burgage tenure' – that is, by paying a certain monetary rent, rather than rendering labour services to the lord. Freehold burgages could, with relative ease, be bought and sold and subdivided into multiple units. This meant that anyone with sufficient capital could invest in property in the borough and benefit from the rental income of the tenancies. Up to the time of the Civil War, Crafthole had a commercial importance that it did not regain until the late 1700s. In fact, it became decidedly overcrowded. There were very many sub-divisions of property. The Parliamentary Survey of 1649 showed that John Harvey owned '3 parts of 4 parts of one messuage or cottage house, curtilege garden and orchard'. He also owned three parts of another one and Henry Spiller held '3 cottages and a quarter part of a fourth part of a house in one burgage'.[49]

Chapter 12

Courts and Officials of the Borough

Edward II's grant of borough status to Crafthole meant that its burgesses were freed from the labour services attached to agricultural tenancies. They were also freed from many tolls normally payable on journeys to other market places in Cornwall or the rest of England. They were spared too from having to travel to Launceston or some other Cornish town to attend the sheriff's 'tourn' (court) to resolve commercial disputes or answer for a range of criminal offences. Instead these matters could be dealt with in the borough's own courts. Surviving records prove the existence of two types of court at Crafthole: firstly the *curia legalis* or court leet (law court), which dealt with criminal offences as well as the collection of fees and fines, and secondly the court baron, which dealt with the customary law of the borough. It is likely that a special merchants' court also sat during the annual fair and on market days. These courts were known as courts of 'piepowder', from the French *pieds poudrés*, referring to the dusty feet of the itinerant merchants who used them.

The Court Leet

The court leet was a court of record, presided over by the lord's steward. The full title of the court was *curia legalis cum visu franciplegii domini* – court of law with view of frankpledge of the lord. Sometimes the title is given in full on the record, as in the court held on 12 October 1635, sometimes it is shortened simply to *curia legalis.* The court leet was a public jurisdiction obtained by royal grant. The Statute for View of Frankpledge of 1325 gave the courts jurisdiction over offences against the Assize of Bread and Ale; and various statutes against using false measures, balances and weights.[1] The courts also had jurisdiction over specified crimes ranging from housebreaking to rape.

It was a contempt of court to refuse to give evidence.[2] Tristram Harry was fined two shillings *pro contemptu* for refusing to give evidence when ordered to do so by the steward at a court held in Crafthole in April 1608. It was also an offence to be disrespectful to the steward. In 1593, Simon Peter was given the heavy fine of

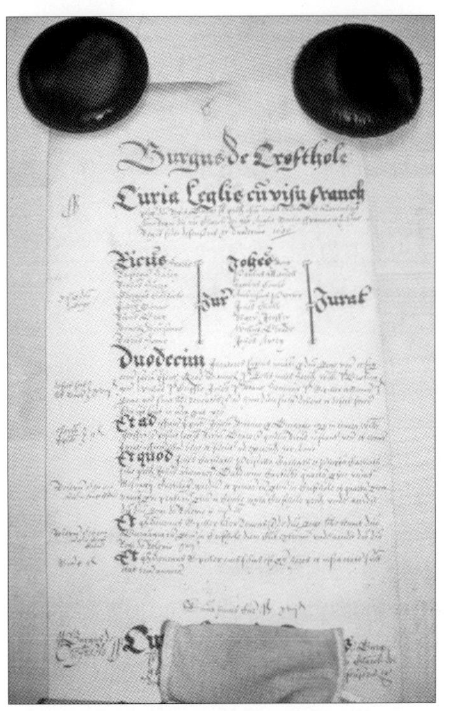

95 *The roll of 9 November 1636 of the curia legalis (court leet) of the borough of Crafthole is written in a fine court hand. It records* inter alia *that Henry Spiller senior has died and been succeeded by his son, Henry, as a free tenant of the borough.*

10s. for making a rude gesture at him. Toby Langdon, who came from a gentry family, but had an unruly disposition, was fined a shilling for making another contemptuous gesture in 1613.[3]

A scrivener (writer of court hand) recorded the proceedings of the court in Latin. From 1607 to 1640 the scrivener was most probably Robert Honney or Hunney, who is described as 'scrivener' in a lease of 1707.[4] He lived in the borough and served as juror on many occasions after 1607. He also served several times as portreeve. The roll of those owing 'suit of court' was read out, and the tenants answered to their names. Absentees without lawful excuse were fined. The jury or 'homage' was then sworn in. Their 'presentments', once accepted and pronounced by the steward, constituted the judgments of the court. Every male resident within the borough over 12 who had dwelt there for a year and a day had to take part in the proceedings. Thus in April 1592, the jury presented that Richard Bunnye (Bone), Oliver Elliotte (Eliot) and Robert Cloke had all attained that age in the previous year and ought to have been present in court. The following August they were each fined 2d. for absence.

In accordance with s.35 of *Magna Carta*, as amended and confirmed by Edward I in 1297, the court leet of Crafthole, with its view of Frankpledge, met mostly in October or November.[5] It then usually sat again in April or May. However, meetings also took place in Crafthole in June (1596), July (1594), August (1592 and 1597), and September (1596). Most absentee landlords would find attendance burdensome, so they were content to pay the fine (3d.) for non-attendance.

Because the court leet administered not the lord's will, but the king's justice, the lord could himself be 'presented' in his own court. Thus, in 1607, the jury presented that the village pound was in need of repair and that the portreeve should have it repaired as soon as possible. As King James was the lord of the borough at the time, he was in effect being presented. In the following year, the jury presented John Naunter, who lived at the nearby High House, for breaking the pound, and he was fined 1s. In 1623, the jury presented that the borough had no pound at all.[6] At the 1730 court, the jurors presented 'the want of a pair of stocks', 'the want of a cucking stool', 'the want of a pound' (again) and 'the want of a pair of scales to weigh bread'.[7] The cucking stool (from the Old English word *cucken*, meaning to look) was a chair on which scolds or fraudulent traders were tied to be exposed to the jeers of the bystanders. At this date it was the duty of the Duchy of Cornwall to provide these items, so the lord, the Duke of Cornwall, was in effect being presented.

The Court Baron

In Norman French *baron* primarily meant 'man', as in *baron et feme*, meaning man and wife.[8] A manorial lord who had enough free tenants, his *barons*, could hold a 'court baron'. The court baron had jurisdiction in pleas of land and in personal actions involving suits for less than 40s. In theory it was distinct from the 'customary court' of the manor, whose purpose was to record the transfer of copyhold land. In practice, a single court administered both jurisdictions.[9] The court was usually presided over by the lord's steward, but the lord could also sit in person.[10] All the tenants of the borough, whether freeholders or copyholders, were required to attend, as were other residents.

By custom dating from the time of Henry III (1216-72), the court baron normally met every three weeks – hence it was sometimes called the 'three weeks' court'. The principal business of the court was to declare and enforce the ancient customs of the manor or borough. Thus, in one of the last sittings of the court of the borough of Crafthole, held in 1712, the jurors stated that it was their intention to present '*omnes antiqu[a]s consuetudines Burgi predicti ut antiquo usitat[as] fuerint*' (all the ancient customs of the aforesaid borough as they used to be kept in the old days).[11] The declaration of manorial customs was particularly important in the Middle Ages, when much of village life and work was regulated by custom. The court had power to make bye-laws enforcing the customs of the borough and also regulating social behaviour.

Every year, and normally at its Michaelmas sitting, the court would appoint the officials of the borough. Regrettably no records of the court baron have survived from the medieval, Tudor or Stuart periods, when the court would have been at its most active. But records have survived from 1712 and 1713, by which time the court had become fused with the court leet. In 1712, the jurors presented the popular Sir William Carew to be reeve; William Avant to be ale-taster (*gustator cervitiae*) and Peter Jane to be clerk of the market. In that year the borough could muster only seven jurors. From the old Sheviock families were Anthony Blake, Tristram Harry, Thomas Holman, John Stephens, Thomas Waite (also Wayte), and Peter Jane.[12] Edward Pirrey was a newcomer.

In 1713, the borough could raise only six jurors. These were Anthony Blake, Thomas Waite, John Jenkin, Peter Jane, Tristram Harvey and Henry Jorey (Jory). They presented Samuel Rolle *armiger* as portreeve (mayor). In a rental of 1714, Samuel

Rolle 'esquire' is shown as renting what had been 'Dodridge his house and garden' in Crafthole for £1 9d. a year. Samuel was the son of Sir Samuel Rolle and Anne, daughter of Richard Carew the younger.[13]

The Court of Piepowder

There is no surviving evidence of the borough's court of piepowder. But such a court was incident as a matter of common right to every fair, whether or not it was mentioned in the charter granting the fair.[14] In a law case of 1508, it was also accepted that a court of piepowder was incident to every market. The purpose of the court was to adjudicate on mercantile disputes that arose during the fair or on market day. The whole case was heard and judgment given on the same day or, if a jury was called, overnight. The judges would have been a panel of merchants, perhaps presided over by the manorial steward. In Crafthole, the court did not survive the medieval period.

To resolve commercial disputes on the manor of Sheviock between the fishermen of Portwrinkle (which was not within the borough) and between them and visiting merchants, Richard Carew set up his own seigneurial mechanisms in 1605 and 1611.[15]

The Venue for the Courts

A full meeting of the courts, involving about 20 jurors and officials, as well as all the adult males of the borough, would have required a suite of rooms, including one large meeting room. In a medieval borough, all the profits arising from it, whether from the tolls of the markets and fairs, or the rents of the burgesses, or the fines imposed on defaulters, belonged to the lord who owned it. The courts were therefore usually held in the hall or the great room belonging to that lord. The courts of boroughs protected by castles were usually held in the castle. John Leland makes it clear that this was still the case in Boscastle in the early 1500s, even though the castle was by then in a ruinous state. He wrote, 'The Lord Botreaux was lord of this town … and had a manor place, a thing as far as I could (ascertain) of smaul reputation, as it is now, far unworthy the name of a

96 *Interior of the* Finnygook Inn. *The borough courts were held in the hall of the Dawneys' manor-house when it was at Blazor, and after the departure of the Courtenays, in the principal room of the inn.*

castel. The people ther caulle it the Courte.'[16] Similarly, the Duke of Cornwall's courts for the manor and borough of Liskeard were held within the precincts of the castle until they were discontinued in 1845.[17] Where the lord resided in a manor-house, the rooms of that dwelling-place would be used. The rooms used for meetings of the courts of the manor of Coldridge, Devon, were described in a case of 1647. They were 'a fair large roome' for the hearing of cases, a withdrawing room for the jury, a room for the accommodation of prisoners, a kitchen, a dining room and other offices.[18] The manor-house of the Grylls family at Lanreath acquired the name Court Barton from its use as the venue for the manorial courts. The borough courts of Crafthole would have been held in the great room of the Dawneys' manor-house at Blazor, situated on the high ground above the new town. The modern *Finnygook Inn* now stands on the site of the old manor-house. When, in 1825, Lord Clinton conveyed the remainder of a long lease of that property to Reginald Pole Carew, it was described as,

> All that messuage tenement or dwelling house called *the Great House* [italics supplied] with the Barn Stable Yard Garden Orchard and appurtenances ... and now or late in the possession of Dinah Kitt as the lessee ... containing by measurement one rood and thirty seven perches.[19]

When the premises became an inn, in the 1600s, or earlier, it is likely that the borough courts continued to be held in the principal rooms of the inn.[20] It is known that they were held there in the 1700s. Special courts were held there from 1772 to 1780 (George Westcott, innkeeper); in 1781 and from 1785 to 1796 (William Crocker, innkeeper); 1797-1800 (John Binney, innkeeper), 1801-1803 (Elizabeth Binney, innkeeper); 1804-1807 (Andrew Kitt, innkeeper and Elizabeth); and 1807 (William Bews and Elizabeth). Elizabeth Binney (b.1769) may have re-married Andrew Kitt as her second husband and William Bews as her third husband, or simply been their business partner.

The Judge

The judge of the court was the lord's steward. The first name that has been preserved is that of John Kelleway.[21] He was steward to William Courtenay, Earl of Devon, in the later years of the reign of Henry VII and the early years of Henry VIII. After the earl's death in 1511, Kelleway acted for his widowed countess, Katherine, younger daughter of the late king, Edward IV, and sister of Henry VII's queen, Elizabeth of York. In 1514, John 'Caylwaye' and other commissioners for the countess, who were then based at Plympton, sold some of the timber in Sheviock Woods to two Plymouth merchants, Richard Hontyngdon and William Brooking.[22]

In 1540, Henry VIII transferred the borough to the Duchy of Cornwall, so that the steward to Edward, Prince of Wales and Duke of Cornwall, later Edward VI, became steward of the court. Usually, a deputy steward of the Crown or the Duchy presided at the courts in Crafthole. The borough passed to Queen Mary on her accession in 1553. The Queen restored the borough to Edward Courtenay, who was created Earl of Devon.[23] A borough court was held in his name in 1554.[24] In 1556, the earl came under suspicion and moved abroad. On his death without issue, the borough reverted to the Crown. The stewards appointed as judges during the periods of Royal ownership were usually considerable men in the county.

Upon her accession in 1558, Queen Elizabeth became lord of the manor and borough of Crafthole. The name of only one Elizabethan judge has been preserved. From 1591 to 1594, Thomas Parkins acted as steward for the Queen's borough of Crafthole, and presumably for her other Cornish manors.[25] He was assisted by Robert Paddon. James I's steward and judge was Richard Billing. His deputy was Nicholas Rawe. The names of the judges from 1628 up to the time of the Civil War are preserved in the Antony archives. From 1628 until 1644, Christopher Oughe served as 'deputat.', or deputy seneschal (steward), and (until 1634) Elizei Hele served as 'cap.', or collector (from the Latin *capio*, a 'taking'). From 1635 until 1639, the collector was William Corinton or Coryton.

Oughe lived at St Ive and was a cousin of Jonathan Rashleigh of Menabilly. He witnessed Richard Carew the younger's lease of land in Blazor to Richard Wallis in 1636.[26] He also featured as one of the case studies in Carew's book, *Excellent Helps by a Warming-Stone* (1640), because of a condition apparently caused by his duties:

> Another [patient] having by long sitting up and writing by night gotten a great cold and pain in the Elbow and flesh of his left Arm; which both continued and increased with much numbness and deadness feared the utter decay of that hand and Arm, applying this Warming-stone unto his sad grief, is now by the blessing of God so well recovered thereof that he feels the same no more then if he had never had any infirmity therein.

Stewards were usually rewarded with tenancies on manorial lands – i.e. Crown or Duchy lands when the lord of the manor was the King or the Duke of Cornwall. The heirs of Christopher Oughe were still listed as freeholders on the Duchy manor of West Antony in 1664.[27] William Coryton of Newton was MP for Grampound in 1640 and then for Launceston (for a short while) in 1641. He was also Vice-Warden of the Stanneries, from which post he was temporarily dismissed for maladministration in 1641.

From the execution of Charles I in 1649 until 1660, the borough belonged to the Commonwealth. The borough was restored to the Duchy at the Restoration. In 1712, the deputy steward of the combined court was Antony Nicoll. In 1730, the deputy was Edward Bickford.[28]

The Twelve Jurors of the Borough

The steward or his assistant summoned a dozen or more of the more substantial residents of the borough to serve as jurymen, called 'the homage'. The functions of the jury were both inquisitorial and judicial.[29] It was their duty to check that all those who were obliged to be present in court were in fact there, and to 'present' to the court the names of absentees, who would then be fined. Once accepted by the steward, the presentments became the findings of the court. The jury also had a duty to present persons who had committed offences. They could do this from their own knowledge, or on the basis of reports made by the borough officers. In their presentments, the jury both declared the defendants guilty and set out the penalties to be imposed – usually small 'amercements' (fines). Although physical punishments could also be imposed, such as being placed on the 'cucking' stool or in the stocks, there are no instances of such penalties being imposed in the surviving records.

The jurors were responsible for electing the portreeve. The other officers of the borough – the ale-taster, the bread-weigher, the pound-keeper, and the clerk of the market – if such were to be appointed, were elected at the court baron. Records from the merged court of 1712 show the appointment of an ale-taster and a clerk of the market in addition to the portreeve. The records from 1730 show the appointment of an ale-taster and bread-weigher as well as the portreeve.

The jurors were responsible for notifying the court of all changes of ownership or deaths in the borough. On all such changes, a fine or 'relief', and in the case of death of a copyholder, a 'heriot', was payable into the court. The names of the jurors in surviving rolls of 1576, 1590 to 1644, 1663, 1712, 1713 and 1730 are set out in Appendix 2.

The Office of Portreeve

All tenants, whether free or customary, were bound to execute the office of portreeve if elected by the jurors to do so. This election usually took place at the Michaelmas court. The portreeve (in Latin *praepositus*) was the principal officer of the borough. His principal duty was to collect the rents, fines and heriots due to the lord of the borough. He was also responsible for law and order within the borough. It was he who enforced the assize of bread and ale and suppressed nuisances. The parish constables were not officers of the borough, but they could exercise jurisdiction within it. From the 1500s onwards, they brought offenders (such as those who sold ale without a licence) to the nearest justices of the peace and not to the borough courts.[30]

The Hue and Cry: One of the duties of the portreeve was to call for a 'hue and cry' when someone was seen in the act of committing a crime. When the call was given, all the able-bodied men of the borough were obliged to arm themselves and give chase.[31] On 1 September 1620, the portreeve, Toby Langdon, observing such an act, called for '*le huy and Crye*', but one of the residents, Nicholas Rith, refused to join in. He was fined 6d. at the November court leet for his *malum exemplum* (bad example).

In a valuation of the borough made in the Commonwealth period, the portreeve is described as 'portreeve major', i.e. mayor. The jurors usually elected the wealthiest burgesses to perform the office, but allowed them to field deputies. The deputies agreed, for a fee, to carry out the official duties. In this way what was in theory an unpaid office often became welcome paid employment for a few selected individuals.

Portreeves in the reign of Queen Elizabeth

Those elected portreeve in the last years of Queen Elizabeth's reign included Thomas Moresyde (Moreshed) (1592), Thomas Smythe of Liscawne (1593), Tristram Harry (1595), and William Brookinge, merchant (1596), all of whom got John Chubbe to deputise for them. In 1596, Tristram Harry was again elected and served the office himself. John Sonne was elected and served in 1599. When Thomas Smythe was again elected in 1600 he got the innkeeper, William Sargent, to serve for him.

Jacobean Portreeves

Those elected portreeve in Jacobean times were Richard Harry (1604), John Hunnckyn, described as a gentleman (1605), Alnet Harry (1606), John Skynnerd (April 1608), and William Spiller (October 1608), all of whom put in Laurence Odihorne as their deputy. In 1607, John Sonne was elected as portreeve, but he refused to serve and was fined 3s. 4d. for setting a bad example. Tristram Harry served the office himself in 1609. John Naunter was elected in 1610, but he got Laurence Odihorne to act for him. William Rundell was elected and served the office in 1611. In 1612, John Smith of Liscawne was elected, but got the scrivener, Robert Honney to serve. The following year the rector, Walter Arundell, who owned property in the borough, was elected, and also got Honney to serve. In 1614 John Criffell was elected and served, and in 1615 John Moreshed was elected and served. John Skynnerd was elected again in 1616, but got Robert Honney to serve. Alnet Harry was elected again in 1617 and got John Mitchell to serve. In 1618, John Smith of Liscawne was again elected and got Dowell Dewstowe to serve. When Smith was elected for the third time the following year, he got Toby Langdon to serve. Thomas Sonne was elected and served in 1620. In the following year the rector, Walter Arundell, was again elected and got John Curle to serve. In 1622, Tristram Harry was elected and served. In 1623, John Skynnerd was again elected and he got Toby Langdon to serve. In 1624, the jurors elected two people, Thomas Pommery and Elizabeth Crosse, as portreeve, and they got Richard Harrell to serve for them. In the 21 years of the reign, only six portreeves served their own terms of office. Laurence Odihorne, at the beginning of the reign, was the most frequent deputy, serving on six separate occasions.[32] Arnott Odiorne, perhaps a son or nephew, served as the parish constable in 1633.

Portreeves in the Reign of Charles I

William Jeoffrey was elected and served as portreeve in November 1625. Richard Wallis was elected in 1626 but got Toby Langdon to serve. Henry Spiller was elected in 1627 and got Richard Harrell to serve. Women who were widows of burgesses could be called upon to serve as well as men and Elizabeth Spiller was elected in 1628. She chose Richard Harrell to serve for her. Richard Beare served on behalf of George Carkeeke in 1629. In 1630, Edward Moreshed was elected and served. Joseph Hunkyn was elected in 1631 but got Richard Beare to serve. In 1632, Tristram Harry was elected and served the office. The following year Richard Wallis was elected but got Richard Beare to serve. John Sonne was elected in 1634 but got Richard Harrell to serve. Sir Samuel Rolle was elected in 1635 but got Richard Beare to serve, as did John Dweane in 1636. In 1637, the rector, Gregory Arundell, who owned property in the borough, was elected but appointed Toby Langdon to serve. The record for Michaelmas 1638 is missing. In 1639, Robert Creffell (or Criffle), the son of William Creffell, gentleman of St Germans, appointed Robert Honney as his deputy.[33] Members of the Honney family were also resident in St Germans. In 1640, Thomas Smith of Liscawn was elected and appointed Richard Mitchell to serve. The records for 1641 and 1642 are missing. In the 15 years of Charles's reign for which records survive before the Civil War, only three of the portreeves who were elected served the office. All the others put in deputies, of whom Richard Beare appeared most frequently, serving on five separate occasions.

Portreeves during the Civil War

The records survive for only two years after the outbreak of the Civil War. In 1643, Sir Samuel Rolle was elected portreeve and got Richard Beare to serve. In 1646, John Sonne was elected and served the office.

Portreeves in the reign of Queen Anne and George II

The names of portreeves during the reigns of Charles II, James II, and William and Mary have been lost. In the reign of Queen Anne, in 1712, in one of the most singular elections, the homage, consisting of Anthony Blake, Tristram Harry, Thomas Holman, Thomas Waite, John Stephens, Peter Jane and Edward Pirrey, elected Sir William Carew as portreeve.[34] He owned property in the borough, and so was eligible. No doubt he, too, put in a deputy, but the records for this have not survived. In 1713, they elected Samuel Rolle, son or grandson of Sir Samuel, to be portreeve. No records of election survive for the reign of George I. In 1729, in the reign of George II, the homage elected Edward Dodridge, and in 1730 they elected John Lampen, a gentleman.[35] He was the last recorded holder of the office.

The Parish Constables

According to C.S. Gilbert, writing in 1820, the portreeve was supported by constables.[36] These were most likely the constables of Sheviock parish exercising their jurisdiction within the borough of Crafthole as well as elsewhere in the parish. None of the surviving records of the court leet mentions a constable.

Presentments at the Court Leet

Fines for Non-Attendance

Burgesses had to swear fealty to the lord of the borough on admission to their burgage and to attend the borough courts.[37] Wealthy absentee owners of property in the borough in the early years of James I's reign included William Brooking, who paid fines of 3d. for non-attendance in 1604 and 1606, Richard Avery, who paid fines in 1604-1607, Henry King, who paid fines in 1604, 1606 and 1608, and John Dweane, who paid fines in 1607 and 1608. In the reign of Charles I they included William Creffell of St Germans, who paid fines for non-attendance from 1628 to 1639, when he died; Joseph Hunkyn, gentleman, who paid fines in 1629, from 1631 to 1635, and in 1637, 1638 and 1640; Francis Bickdon, who paid fines in 1630, 1633 and 1635; John Dweane, who paid fines in 1636 and 1637; Simon Rowe, shipowner of Antony and Stonehouse, who paid fines from 1631 to 1636, and in 1638 and 1641.[38] (Rowe also paid a fine in 1663, after the Restoration.) The most prominent investor in the borough was Sir Samuel Rolle, MP for Callington, who had a long lease of 'the Great House', the modern *Finnygook Inn*. He was a major investor in the cloth industry. He paid fines for non-attendance from 1635 to 1644. Sir Richard Carew, great-great-grandson of the historian, and lord of Sheviock manor from 1692 to 1703, acquired land in the borough, which then belonged to the Duchy of Cornwall. In 1693, his bailiff, Thomas Harvey, had to pay his 3d. fine for 'suit of cort at ye Borough Court of Crafthole'.[39]

Other frequent absentees in the reign of Charles I included Richard Wallis (fined from 1628 to 1630); Roger Skynnard or Skynnerd (fined in 1628-1630, 1632 and 1634); Edward Moreshedd (fined in 1632, 1635, 1636 and 1643); George Carkeeke (fined in 1635 and 1636); Baldwin Carkeeke (fined in 1637 and 1638); and Thomas Smith, gentleman, of Liscawn (fined in 1641). This was a bit hard on George Carkeeke, who was a ship's officer, as he was often away at sea. Along with their property, the heirs of former burgesses inherited the liability to attend court, and likewise had to pay fines for non-attendance. Thus, the heirs of William Brooking, gentleman, paid fines in most years from 1619 to 1644.[40] The heirs of John Dweane paid for non-attendance in 1639 and 1640; and the heirs of William Creffell paid fines from 1640 to 1644.

People who lived in the borough, but did not own burgages, were also obliged to attend court. The records show very few absences of local men in this category. Emanuel Bowhay (another sailor) was fined in 1638 and 1643; Walter Peake (also a sailor) was fined in 1640; and Roger Jeoffrey was fined in 1644. Other residents fined for non-attendance were Toby Langdon, fined in 1633 and 1640; William Jooles (or Jewell) and George Jenkyn, both fined in 1639; and John Avery, fined in 1640.[41] Toby Langdon was a gentleman in reduced circumstances who served for others as portreeve in 1619, 1623, 1626, and 1637. He was presented to the justices at the petty sessions at Millbrook in 1633 for 'selling of ale without lycins' and was often presented at the court for abusive and unruly behaviour.

Unruly or Abusive Conduct

Fines were payable for minor cases of disorderly conduct. In the last few years of Queen Elizabeth's reign (1591 to 1603) there were just two presentments for law and order offences. In 1593, Simon Peter was fined 10s. for making a rude gesture within the court, and in 1594, William Holleford and William Peter were fined 3s. each for starting a fight in which Holleford drew William Peter's blood.

The 23-year reign of James I (1603-25) was the most unruly of those for which records survive. There were some 22 presentments for law and order offences. In 1606, Richard Harell was fined 2s. for attacking John Harry junior and drawing his blood. At the same court, Alexander Hancock was fined 3s. 4d. for attacking Richard Sargent and drawing his blood. In 1607, the jury found Thomas Harson guilty of attacking Thomas Avery and shedding his blood. At the same court, they found Richard Harell guilty of assaulting Martin[a], the wife of William Rundell, and he was fined 6d. In 1610, William Coller and his wife, Alice, insulted the portreeve, Laurence Odihorne and his son, Alexander, and shed Laurence's blood. At the May court, Coller was fined 6d. At the October court that year, Maria, the wife of Walter Lugger was fined 6d. for insulting Robbin Newell and drawing his blood, and Oliver Peter was fined the same amount for insulting Robin Couch and drawing his blood. In April 1614, Johanna, the wife of Richard Harell, was fined 4d. for physically assaulting John Tealder. At the same court, Agnes Jeffery was presented for insulting Richard Battyn. Both women were given a second fine of 2d. at the court held in May 1615. Agnes's feud with Battyn evidently continued: she was fined another 2d. in the court held in April 1616, for assaulting him, and another 2d. at the court held in May 1617. At the end of April 1616, the excitable Toby Langdon attacked Robert Honney and drew blood by hitting him on the head with a stone. He was given the rather derisory fine of 2d, perhaps because the jury thought that he had been provoked by Honney in the shouting match for which each of them was fined 2d. But when the next year he again insulted Honney, he was given the more substantial fine of 1s. 6d. and he was fined another 1s. for a further insult offered to Honney. In 1618, Richard Sargent was fined 3s. 4d. for assaulting John Earle and drawing his blood. William and John Chubb were each fined 6d. in 1619 for attacking John Bone and drawing his blood. In November 1620, Digory Downing was fined 6d. for setting on Richard Sargent and wounding him. Toby Langdon was fined again (6d.) in October 1621 for attacking John Bone. In April 1622, Nicholas Rith, who had refused to turn out for the hue and cry in 1620, was fined 1s. for abusing John Earle. In October 1623, Toby Langdon was again fined 6d. – this time for attacking Richard Sargent. Women could sometimes be as unruly as the men. In October 1623, William Rundell's wife, Martha, was fined 1s. for attacking Rabidigia Tanckyn and wounding her with a key.

The portreeve was himself frequently in trouble for failing to fine miscreants. In 1606, Laurence Odihorne should have fined John Odihorne and others for failing to be sworn in as jurors at the assizes. In 1609, Jane, the wife of Oliver Peter, insulted the portreeve, Tristram Harry, when he was attempting to enforce the court fines. He should have fined her, but he put himself at the mercy of the court by failing to do so. In May 1610, Laurence Odihorne was again in trouble, firstly for not fining John Smith, gentleman, who had failed to do homage for his free tenancy; secondly for not fining William Coller and his wife, Alice, when they abused him and his son and wounded him; and thirdly for not fining Thomas Palmer, who had damaged the borough's cattle pound by throwing things at it. There are many other examples.

During the first 19 years of the reign of Charles I, from 1625 to 1644 (though the records of 1642 are missing), there were only four presentments for law and order offences. In 1626, Toby Langdon was fined 1s. for assaulting John Bone and drawing blood. In 1629, Digory Downing was fined 4d. for assault and battery on Maria Prideaux and for verbally abusing her. The reeve was instructed to ensure that in future Downing should treat her with '*amicitia, bona et catella*' (friendship, goodness and tenderness). In 1639, Maria, wife of John Sonne, and her daughter, Elizabeth, were fined 4d. for assaulting Ralph Holman when he was repairing the king's highway. Finally, in 1641, Agnes Beard was fined a shilling for insulting the reeve, Robert Mitchell, and carrying off a loaf of bread intended to be weighed.

Unauthorised Works and Public Nuisances

The jurors were no respecter of persons when it came to making presentments. Elizabethan Acts of 1598 and 1601 had provided for the compulsory levying of rates for poor relief and for the purchase of materials to set the poor to work. But there was no provision for houses within which this work could be done. In 1618, the rector, Walter Arundell, apparently at his own expense, erected a house (*domus*) or workhouse (*officina*) as suitable premises for this purpose. Unfortunately, he used the walls of the village pound as the base for his new workhouse, so that there was no pound in the borough for holding stray beasts. At the court leet held in April of that year, the jurors presented him for his unauthorised actions.[42] There is, however, no record of a penalty being imposed. The site of Arundell's house and workhouse is probably that marked as 'Poorhouses' on Thomas Pride's map of 1775.[43] It lies on the road to Downderry to the west of the present market cross. In May 1623, the jurors were still complaining of the lack of a pound. It was also one of the complaints in the last recorded court leet held in September 1730.[44]

The residents of the borough needed a good supply of clean water for many purposes. The authorities were quick to pounce on anyone polluting the well. In October 1616, the fisherman, Samuel Maister, was presented at the court for washing pilchards in the well.[45] At the same court, the innkeeper, William Sargent, was fined for watering plants in the well. It was tempting for some of the residents to divert the natural watercourse towards their own land. In October 1618, Thomas Buller was fined 6d. for digging up the street (probably Well Lane) to divert the stream of water. Richard Mitchell confessed to a similar offence at the court held in April the following year. These two may have possessed gardens or orchards lower down Well Lane, in the middle of which the well was situated.

In October 1618, the innkeeper, William Sargent, placed himself at the mercy of the court for allowing a substance, perhaps train-oil, to sully the clean surface of the king's highway.[46] In 1632, Richard Mitchell was fined a shilling for making a pile of muck (*lutum*) in front of the shop (*ostentum*) of the cooper or innkeeper, William Jeoffrey, to the harm of both Jeoffrey and the other inhabitants of the borough. The muck in question was probably horse dung, as Mitchell was a farrier (shoer of horses) by trade. In 1635, Richard Beare was fined 2d. for making a heap of muck within the borough to the great harm of the king (whose highway it was) and of travellers.

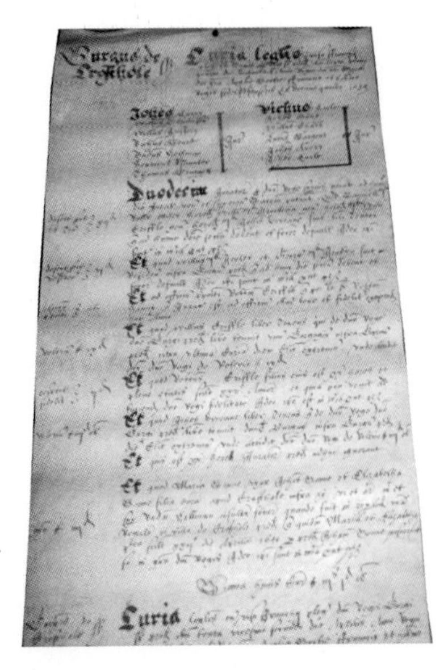

97 *The court roll of 14 December 1639 records that Maria and Elizabeth Sonne assaulted Ralph Hollman when he was repairing the king's highway in the town of Crafthole.*

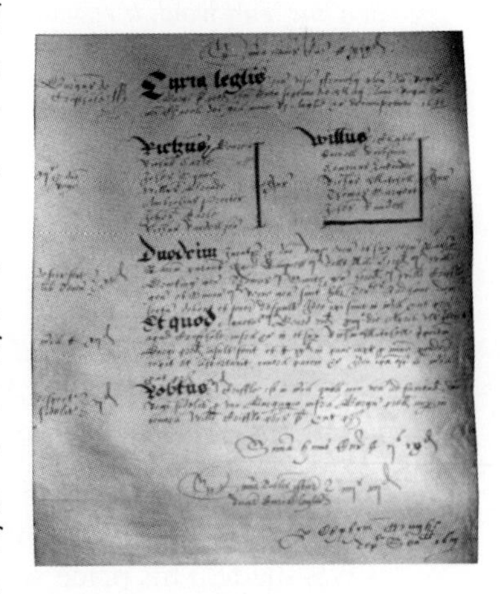

98 *The court roll of 7 May 1641 records that Agnes Beard insulted Richard Mitchell and snatched away her loaf of bread before it could be weighed.*

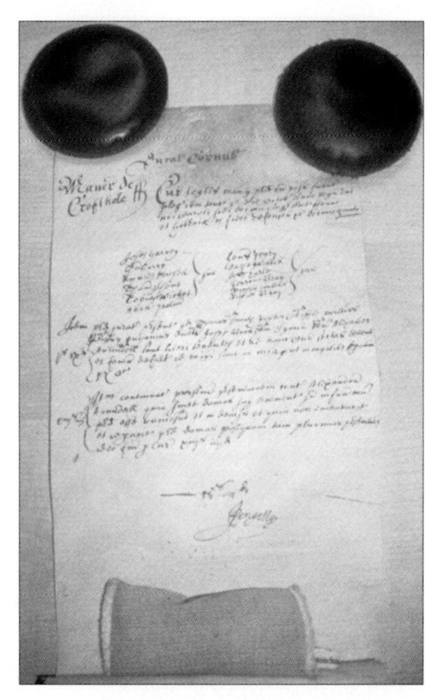

99 *The court roll of 2 October 1663 is the first that survives after the Restoration. Though still written in Latin, it is no longer written by a scrivener in a fine court hand. It records the fine imposed on Alexander Arundell for allowing High House to fall into disrepair.*

Weights and Measures Offences

The women did most of the bread-making and therefore were the most likely to infringe the ancient weights and measures statute, known as the Assize of Bread and Ale (*Assisa Panis et Cervisiae*). The Assize was originally issued by Henry III in 1266. In relation to bread, the Assize laid down a scale of required weights for loaves sold at the standard prices of a farthing, a half-penny or a 1d. The required weights fluctuated according to the price of corn in any particular year.

In May 1625, Elias Burne, farmer, and skipper or mate of the fishing barque, *Dayestarr*, had to pay a fine of 6d. on behalf of his wife, Fanny, who had sold bread that had not been weighed. At the May court in the following year, Thomasina Bake, Jeremiah Williams and Elizabeth Germans were all presented for the same offence. In 1632, Johanna Pollard was fined, probably 1s., for refusing to allow the reeve, Richard Beare, to weigh the bread she was selling. In 1635, two sailors' wives, Agnes Beard and Elizabeth Rooby, together with Maria Marmelle, were fined 1s. each for refusing to allow the reeve, Richard Hearle, to weigh their loaves. Their husbands, Peter Beard and John Rooby, were crew members of the *Dayestarr.* Agnes was fined another shilling in 1641 for insulting the reeve when he came to weigh her loaves. For the first three minor offences of selling under-weight loaves, the baker would by fined; but for a fourth offence would be subject to 'the judgment of the pillory'. In Crafthole, this punishment probably involved being tied to the cucking-stool or being placed in the stocks and so being publicly humiliated. Therefore, the women preferred to be fined for refusing to let the portreeve weigh their loaves, rather than risk a string of convictions leading to the cucking-stool.

The Assize of Ale regulated the quality of the beverage and the price of a given quantity. Again, the permitted price depended on the price of the grain from which it was made. This price was also fixed annually by the magistrates. All alcoholic drinks had to be sold in measured vessels. When someone had ale to sell, he or she erected a pole outside the premises with a bush attached to it. This let the ale taster or 'conner' know that there was a new brew there to be tasted. At the court leet held in Crafthole in November 1620, William Sargent was fined 4d. for selling wine in an un-measured quantity.[47] In 1636, Johanna, wife of the fisherman Dowell Dewstowe, was fined 1s. for selling alcoholic drink, probably ale, in an unmeasured quantity.

Recovery of Debt

In the extant records there is just one instance of a complainant coming to the court to recover an unpaid debt.[48] It comes from the court roll of 28 April 1618, and reads as follows:

> Christiane Odihorne, widow, complains against Thomas Briggett in a plea of debt: which Thomas Briggett was *attached* by the petticoat, waistcoat and partlet [a kind of collar worn over a woman's dress] by John Mitchell, deputy portreeve of the aforesaid borough, to answer the said Christiane Odihorne in her aforesaid plea; and because Thomas Briggett at this day has not appeared, therefore the aforesaid goods are to be forfeited to the lord prince and are to be appraised by Richard Mitchell and Dowell Dewstowe.[49]
>
> goods forfeited 13s. 4d

Briggett had married a widow, Joan Odyarne, in 1612 or 1613. He was a sailor on the *Dayestarr* in 1626. Dowell Dewstowe was a fisherman on the same vessel. Some forty years after this incident, the bailiff of the manor of Sheviock, John Rawlings, listed Thomas Briggett, either the sailor or his son, in his accounts (1656-60) as owing 14s. for property he then rented in Portwrinkle.[50]

The Institutions of the Borough after the Restoration

The period of the Civil War and the Commonwealth dealt the institutions of the borough; its courts and its officials a blow from which they never fully recovered. The difference between the pre- and post-war status of the borough is clearly seen by comparing a pre-war court leet roll – say that of 1636 – with the roll of 1663, the first after the Restoration. The latter, though still written in Latin, has not been recorded on parchment, nor has a professional scrivener done the writing. There is a sense that in the new post-Commonwealth age, and in spite of the restored monarchy, it was no longer acceptable to pay to the Duchy the medieval fines and reliefs on changes of tenure or 'heriots' on copyholder deaths. By 1712, the roll spelled out that the system of paying fines on alienation of property '*finis est*' – is over. The market too withered in the face of stronger competition from neighbouring centres. But the institution of the court limped on for a few more years. In 1663, the jurors, who were mostly still from the old families, presented Alexander Arundell, who lived in High House, for allowing his house to become ruinous and in decay. He was fined the considerable sum of 13s. 4d. as there had been many previous presentations. Alexander was then aged 64 and his house, a thatched dwelling in the highest position in the parish, was frequently battered by high winds. In 1682, the names of Tristram and Robert

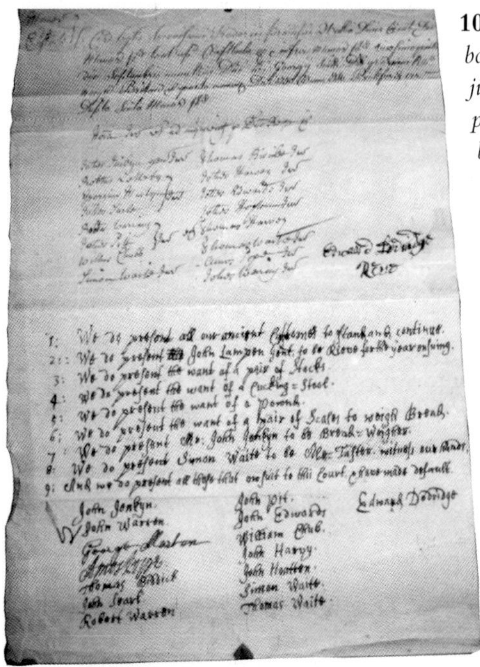
1: We do present all our ancient Customes to stand and continue.
2: We do present John Lampen Gent, to be Rieve for the year ensuing.
3: We do present the want of a pair of Stocks.
4: We do present the want of a Cucking-Stool.
5: We do present the want of a Pound.
6: We do present the want of a pair of Scales to weigh Bread.
7: We do present Mr: John Jenkyn to be Bread-Weigher.
8: We do present Simon Waite to be Ale-Taster.
9: And we do present all these that ow suit to this Court, & have made default.

John Jenkyn. John Warren. John Pitt. John Edwards. William Chubb. John Harvy. John Heatton. Simon Waite. Thomas Waite. Robert Warren. Edward Dodridge

100 *Only the heading of the roll of the combined court of the borough held on 24 September 1730 is written in Latin. The jurors complained of the lack of a pair of stocks, a cucking stool, a pound, and scales to weigh bread. They nonetheless appointed a bread-weigher and an ale-taster.*

Harry and Martha Harry from the old Sheviock families were entered on the admission roll of the borough. All the rest were newcomers.[51]

The Last Courts

In 1711, Sir William Carew purchased 'Condey's Lands in Crafthole', including the inn built on the site of the old Dawney manor-house.[52] It was then known as Sargent's tenement, from the name of a previous innkeeper, William Sargent. The last full courts of the borough (the combined courts leet and baron) were held at the old inn in 1729 and 1730.[53] In 1730, the jurors summoned were John St Aubyn, gentleman, Robert Letheby, George Martyn, John Sarle, Robert Warring (Warren), John Pitt, William Chubb, Simon Waite, Thomas Bidlake, John Harvey, John Edwards, John Heyton (Heatton), Thomas Harvey, Thomas Waite, Amos Pope, and John Warring (Warren). The jurors made a final attempt to revive the old customs and institutions of the borough. They made nine presentments as follows:

1. We do present all our ancient Customes to stand and continue.
2. We do present John Lampen Gent, to be Rieve (*sic*) for the year ensuing.[54]
3. We do present the want of a pair of Stocks.
4. We do present the want of a cucking-stool.
5. We do present the want of a pound.
6. We do present the want of a pair of scales to weigh Bread.
7. We do present Mr. John Jenkyn to be Bread-Weigher.
8. We do present Simon Waite to be Ale-Taster.
9. We do present all these that ow (*sic*) suit to this Court, & have made default.'

All those summoned to appear on the jury signed the roll (or had the portreeve sign for them), except John St Aubyn, Robert Letheby and Thomas Harvey. The roll was also signed by the outgoing reeve, Edward Dodridge. Reginald Pole Carew purchased the entire borough from the Duchy in 1798. By then, borough courts were no longer being held.

Special Courts

With the lapsing of the full courts, a new mechanism had to be found for registering copyhold transactions. Accordingly, in Crafthole, as on other manors, the steward resorted to holding a *curia specialis* (special court) without the 12 jurors required for a full court. It sufficed if one or two tenants of the manor were present, in addition to the person seeking to register his copyhold lease. A special court of this kind was held at Crafhole in the name of HRH Frederick, Prince of Wales, Duke of Cornwall, and lord of the manor of Crafthole, on 16 December 1730, before Edward Bickford, deputy steward, and two tenants. At that court, Martha, widow of Tristram Harry, surrendered her lease of Willhays cottage, garden and orchard, on condition that a new lease was granted to Amos Pope and his children.[55] George and Thomas Westcott, nephews of the innkeeper William Lord, came to another special court held in Crafthole before the deputy steward, John Kimber, and two tenants, on 26 December 1755. They took delivery of a reversion of the same property.[56]

Another special court was held at Crafhole on 1 April 1796, before Mark Bath, deputy steward, in the presence of Peter Kitt and Richard Keast, two tenants of the manor. As Peter Kitt was landlord of the inn that is now the *Finnygook*, the court was almost certainly held there. At the court, Anthony Pike was admitted tenant of the two dwelling houses, two gardens, two small orchards, and two little meadows, containing about three acres, that had formerly been occupied by Mary Bawden (née Mary Warren). The rent for each of the two houses was still the same 9d. set as the burgage rent when Crafthole was founded in 1314. The rent for the orchard and meadows had however been increased to 9s. 4d. The fine for admission was £121 17s. The tenancy was for the lives of Anthony's children, William, Anthony, and Sally.

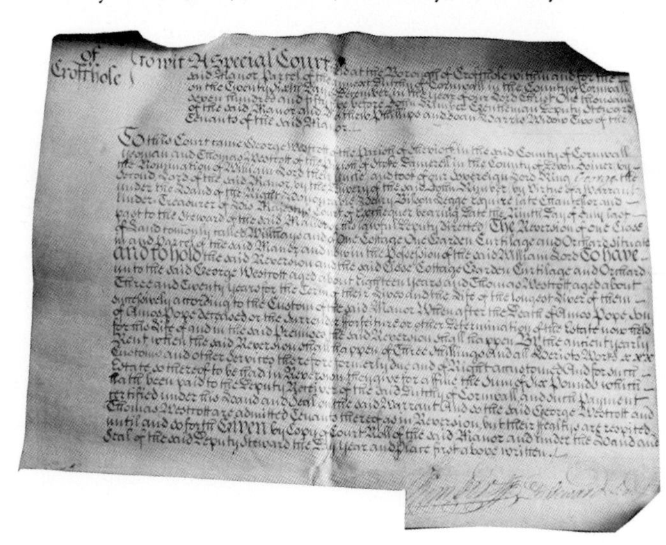

101 *After the demise of the courts leet in the early 1700s, property transactions took place at 'special courts' held without juries. This one of 1755 recorded George and Thomas Westcott's tenancy of Willhay.*

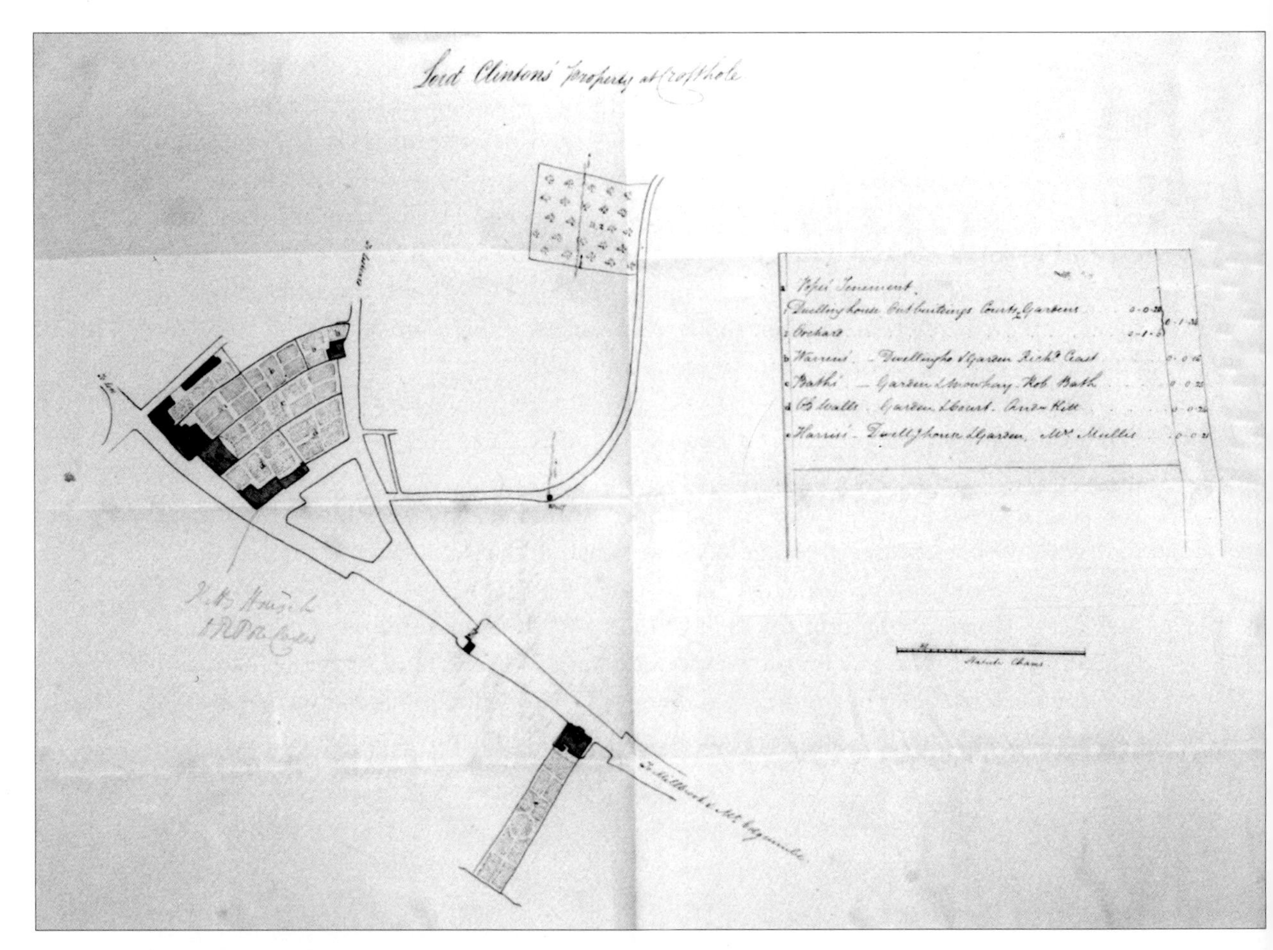

102 *This sketch map shows the properties transferred by Lord Clinton to Reginald Pole Carew in 1825. It also shows the toll-gate in the centre of Crafthole.*

Chapter 13

Houses, Shops and Farms in Crafthole

The land that was included in the borough of Crafthole lay in four main sections. The first was the land that had been the site of the lord's fortified manor-house in the 14th century and which by the 1600s consisted of three large houses and the medieval dovecote on the fields at Blazor. But most of the dwellings in the borough lay in the second section, which ran along both sides of the main east-west road through the village. A third section consisted of a few houses running northwards along the road to Polscoe. The last section was the land known as the Coombes. This was mostly given over to orchard plots, but also contained one or two cottages. It was reached by the steep path known as Well Lane.

The custom of the borough allowed for the subdivision of houses into several separate dwellings, and also for the partition of the orchard plots and gardens into multiple tenancies. Furthermore, additional houses could be squeezed onto the burgage plots. Newly-created tenancies that were not freeholds were entered on the borough roll. The new tenants were said to hold their properties 'by copy of court roll' followed by the date, and were thus called 'copyholders', as distinct from the freeholders.

A few individual property holdings in the borough can be identified in the reign of James I (1603-25). Simon Rowe, a gentleman shipowner of Antony and Stonehouse, was entered on the 1612 roll as copyholder of one tenement in one burgage (rent 9d.). Robert Criffle ('Creefield'), gentleman, was entered on the same roll as copyholder of a cottage in one burgage (rent 9d.). Edward Moreshead, a sailor on the *Dayestarr*, was entered as copyholder of a cottage in one burgage (rent 9d.). Philip Sonne was entered as copyholder of one tenement in two burgages (rent 1s. 6d.). Alnet Harrie was entered as copyholder of one cottage and two burgages (rent 1s. 6d.). He was also entered as the copyholder of a third part of two further burgages (rent 6d.).

A Parliamentary Survey made in 1649 lists the property holdings of eight freeholders and seven copyholders in the borough.[1] The freeholders owned 13 burgages and the copyholders another eight, making a total of 21 burgages. On these 21 burgage plots, there were some 33 dwellings. The freeholders included some substantial merchants involved in the cloth and fishing industries. Of the freeholders, Jonathan Chapman held two houses with one orchard and meadow (rent 1s. 6d.). John Harvey, a newcomer to the borough, held three parts of four parts of one cottage, curtilege, garden and orchard, and also three parts of another cottage, curtilege, garden and meadow in 'Combe' and Crafthole (rent 9d.). The heirs of the merchant William Brooking held the other quarters of the two properties.[2] Richard Wallis, gentleman, held seven dwellings in five burgages (rent 4s. 1½d.).

In 1635, John Skinner, gentleman, a free tenant of the borough, had transferred to Sir Samuel Rolle three burgages as well as other property (relief 2s. 6d.). In 1649, Sir Samuel Rolle held six cottages in one burgage (rent 2s. 6d.). He also held one other house there (rent 1s.). Thomas Smith, gentleman, whose principal dwelling was at Liscawn, held three cottages in two burgages (rent 1s. 6d.). Henry Spiller held three cottages and a quarter of another house in one burgage (rent 9d.). William Jeffery junior held a quarter of a cottage and two burgages in free socage (rent 1s. 6d.).

HOUSES AND FARMS

The Old Dawney Manor-House (Sargent's Tenement)

Either in the reign of Queen Elizabeth (1558-1603) or King James I (1603-25) John Smith of Tregunnick had acquired the head-lease of five valuable burgages in Crafthole from the monarch. The properties, which centred on the Dawneys' old manor-house at Blazor, were held in free tenure. In 1622, Smith sold this head-lease to Richard Wallis of Sconner for £104.[3] In a Parliamentary rental of 1649, Richard Wallis's properties were described as 'seven dwellings in five burgages'. In his will, executed in 1654, Richard bequeathed the head-lease to his eldest son, John. John surrendered this lease to a Tavistock clothier, William Condy, and his wife Frances. As a result of this transaction, the properties were later referred to as 'Condey's lands'.

The most substantial of the properties was the Dawneys' old manor-house, which contained some nine acres of land, and included the historic 14th-century dovecote. At the time of Wallis's purchase, William Sargent, an innkeeper, was the sitting sub-tenant of this property. Because the old manor-house, its fields, and the dovecote had been in the occupation of Sargent, they were often referred to in later leases as 'Sargent's tenement'. The rent was £1 6s. 8d, the highest in the borough.[4] William was the son of Henry Sargent, a conventionary (copyhold) tenant of the borough in 1592.[5] Henry may have been the previous landlord of the inn, but there is no proof of this. William was certainly an innkeeper. At the court leet of Crafthole held in November 1620, he was fined 4d. for selling wine of an un-measured quantity. According to rentals of 1608, 1609, 1636 and 1640, William was also a free tenant of the manor of

Kerslake in Sheviock parish.[6] He also occupied property in Higher Blerrick. Probably he cultivated orchards on both those tenements to produce cider to sell at his inn.

In 1650, Richard Wallis sub-let 'Sargent's tenement', to his son, Richard II, and his wife, Isott (daughter of Willyam Sparkman of St Germans), for life; and after their deaths to their daughters, Grace and Mary.[7] This lease then devolved to Grace and Mary. Grace married John Edwards and Mary married a Mr Cole. When, in 1654, the Condeys became the head-lessees, they renewed the sub-lease of the inn to Edwards except for Culver Park, and the dovecote standing therein, which they retained for their own use throughout the Commonwealth period.

Mary Wallis sold her interest to Edwards. John and Grace Edwards were occupying the property in 1702 and were probably still running it as an inn. Edwards was also a farmer, leasing a quarter of Blazor. In 1702, Sargent's tenement was valued at £10, and still commanded a rent of £1 6s. 8d. John Edwards became the hind (farm manager) of the Carew estates in Antony and Sheviock in 1706.[8] The Condeys let two other houses and gardens to John Edwards on his own life and that of his son, Thomas. These probably stood to the west of the inn.[9] The combined rent of the two houses was 10s.

Sir William Carew purchased the head-lease of the five burgages from William Condy and his son in 1711.[10] Sir William was paying 'high Rent to the King's Manor of Crafthole' in respect of Condey's lands in March 1715.[11] In 1718, Sir William let Sargent's tenement, except for the dovecote, to John Edwards junior, grandson (through his mother, Grace) of Richard Wallis of Sconner, on the surrender of Edwards' earlier lease.[12] John Edwards was still renting 'Sargent's House' at the same rent from Sir William in 1726. John Edwards died in 1735. In 1741, Sir William let Sargent's tenement to another 'innholder', William Lord (born *c.*1704), at the same rent. The tenant also had to pay 4s. 6d. to the Prince of Wales as owner of the borough.[13] The fine or premium for the lease, paid over seven years, amounted to £151 6s. 9d., including interest.[14] The lease was on the lives of William Lord, his wife, Ann (born *c.*1706), and their nephew, Thomas Westcott, son of the shipwright Richard Westcott of Topsham.[15]

From 1763 to 1766, when Ann Lord was running the inn, the manorial courts of the manor of Sheviock were held there.[16] In 1766, John Carew let the tenement, which was 'now or late in the tenure of Mrs Anne Lord' to James Corinton.[17] The lease was to take effect on the deaths of Mrs Lord and Thomas Westcott. In 1775, George Wescote became the occupier of Sargent's tenement for the life of Ann Lord (aged 68) and Thomas Westcote (aged 47) as shown on Thomas Pride's map and survey.[18]

Sargent's tenement appears to have become the subject of a long lease (200 years) owned by Samuel Rolle (1632-*c.*1720), son of Sir Samuel Rolle, MP for Callington. The Rolle estate passed to Lord Clinton.[19] Reginald Pole Carew purchased the residue of the lease of this and other Crafthole properties from Lord Clinton in 1825, for the sum of £250.[20] In the conveyance, the property is described as

> All that messuage tenement or dwelling house called the Great House with the barn Stable Yard Garden Orchard and appurtenances ... and now or late in the possession of Dinah Kitt as the lessee ... containing by measurement one rood and 37 perches.'

The description, 'the Great House', is consistent with the view that the property was built on the site of the old manor-house. The plan of the house is shown on the 1825 map of the property, where it is described as 'Kitt's House', because it had been let to Dinah Kitt, perhaps the daughter of the former innkeeper, Andrew Kitt. In 1804, Andrew Kitt rented two gardens west of Kitt's House, heretofore in the possession of William Lord afterwards of Thomas Westcott, for 10s.[21] The lease was on his own life (age 35), and the lives of his wife, Elizabeth (35) and Mary Ann Beckford (eight). See further 'Inns at Crafthole' in Chapter 41, *Inns and Innkeepers*.

Cross House and Farm

This house was built on what was probably the western end of the medieval dwelling house of the Dawneys. The present house certainly includes some early features, including a spiral stone staircase leading to the upper floor. A piece of timber bearing an early date was revealed after bomb damage in the Second World War, but no one alive today remembers the date. Cross House appears to have been one of the dwellings that formed part of 'Condey's lands'. The house may have been occupied by members of the Harry family in the 1500s and 1600s. It was close to the Harry family's farming tenements in Blazor.[22]

103 *Cross House was built at the western end of the old manorial enclosure. It was a farmhouse until 1952.*

In 1702, a house and garden, perhaps this one, was let by the Condeys to Richard Pope on the lives of Esdar, Patience and Joanne Pope for 12s.[23] In 1726, Israel Pope was leasing a house and garden, probably the same one, for 12s., from Sir William Carew. He also leased a little orchard from him. The house called Cross House today is called 'Pope's House' on a map of 1825.[24] In the late 1700s, Matthew Warren lived in what is now Cross House and farmed 29 acres of Blazor.[25] In 1833-4, Samuel Lyne was farming at Blazor, Cross Park and Hearle's Parks.

The acreage of Cross Farm was increased in the 19th century, but reduced again to just 34 acres after the building of the golf course in 1905. It then included some fields lying along the road to Polscoe. The farmer at the time was probably Harold Hoskin, for there is a story preserved in the family that 'the old man was very upset to lose [the acres at Blazor] because they were his best fields'.[26] His daughter, Jessie, married Harold Bersey, and the couple took on the tenement as an arable and dairy farm.[27] On one occasion, Harold ploughed through a nest of wasps or bees, which attacked him and his horse. He stopped to unhitch the horse and ran off. The angry insects chased him all the way back to Cross House, getting inside his clothing and stinging him as he went.[28] The farmhouse continued to be lit by oil lamps until the death of Jessie at the end of 1962.[29] The barns belonging to the farm lay adjacent to the house in West Lane. In 1952, Tom Bersey, the farmer at Sheviock Barton, took over the farming of the land that was formerly part of Cross Farm.

High House

The house derived its name from the fact that it was built on the highest point of land in the borough of Crafthole. The present house, built on the ruins of the earlier dwelling destroyed in 1940, is called High Hopes. It is possible that High House was once part of the manorial enclosure crenellated by Sir John Dawney in 1336. It later became a farmhouse.

The first known tenant of the farmhouse on the site was Joan Bonney, widow, who was the tenant in the reign of Philip and Mary (1553-8), up to September 1555.[30] She was succeeded by Philip Naunter. John Naunter held the tenancy in the last years of the reign of Queen Elizabeth (d.1603). Dorothy Arundell, wife of the former rector, Walter, and their sons, George and Alexander, succeeded Naunter as tenants. They were entered in the roll of 7 August 1612 as copyholders of High House and three little gardens with two closes of land containing about an acre of land (rent 9s. 4d. and a capon, later consolidated as 10s.).[31] Dorothy moved there with her sons, George, Emanuel and Alexander after the death of her husband in 1622. In 1649, Dorothy was dead, but George (aged 66) and Alexander (aged 50) were still living there. Alexander continued to live in the house after the Restoration. High House may have been the one described in the schedule of Condeys' lands in 1654 as an 'old and ruined house and garden'. In 1663, Alexander Arundell was 'presented' by the jurors of the borough court for allowing his house to become ruinous and in decay. He was fined 13s. 4d. 'after many presentations'.

Jane Peters, widow, came into possession in the early 1700s. In about 1750, William Chubb was the occupier of High House. In 1755, he passed the tenancy to his daughter, Joan Harris, widow (age 47), and then to his grandchildren, Robert Warren (age 28), husbandman, and Mary Warren (age 15) (later Mary Bawden).[32] From this disposition the property became one of the three included in 'Warren's tenement'.[33] In 1796, Anthony Pike took over the tenancy from the Prince of Wales on the lives of his sons, William and Anthony junior and his daughter, Sally.[34] The rents were unchanged. Pike had to pay a fine of £121 17s. for entry onto the court roll. The house survived until 1940, when it was blown up by a German mine.[35] At the time, it was occupied by the butcher, Albert Bersey.

The Blacksmiths' Cottages and Shops

In 1698, William Condy and his wife let a 'cottage dwelling house and herb garden' in Crafthole to Thomas Waite, 'blacksmith'.[36] It stood on the south side of the main road, with the house of Henry Richards on the east, and the 'shopp heretofore of

104 *This postcard from the 1930s shows, on the right, what was probably the second Methodist chapel. Next to it, the low roof of the old blacksmith's shop projects forward towards the road.*

one John Earle Blacksmyth' on the west. The rent was 8s. Waite was able to read and write. The lives named on the lease were his own and those of his children, Simon and Joan. In 1710, the Condys granted Waite a new lease of the 'Cottage house, and the Smiths-Shopp and Garden' commonly called 'Roaches Tenement'.[37] The rent was 8s. By 1726, Thomas Wayte had died and 'widow Wayte' was still leasing her old house and garden for 8s. In 1764, the occupier was John Searle.[38] Simon Waite succeeded to his father's business.

In 1705, the Condys let another cottage in Crafthole to Waite on his own life and the lives of his children, Simon and Joan.[39] It had been in the possession of Mary Sargeant. The rent was 6s. per annum. This lease was also renewed in 1710. Joan became Mrs Bewes and died in 1745.

In 1745, Sir Coventry Carew let Mary Sargent's former premises to John Williams of Crafthole, blacksmith (age 35). The rent was 6s. The life of Joan Bewes was added.[40] The lease is endorsed 'Expired & new lease granted to Taw in 1774'. The 1774 lease to the butcher, John Taw, gives the location of the premises, describing it as the 'dwelling house garden and premises situate at Crafthole being the corner house between the Saint Germans and Looe [Downderry] Roads'.[41] The house stood on what is now the eastern corner of the garden of Lynher Villa.

In 1791, Reginald Pole Carew let a cottage and garden that stood near the corner of West Lane and the road to St Germans to Joseph Bickford (b.1761) of St Germans, blacksmith.[42] It is probably the house marked 'Warrens' on the 1825 map of Lord Clinton's property, for it had once been occupied by William Warren. The rent was 8s.

In 1815-16, the blacksmith, Robert Bath, did work for the church. He occupied a garden and mowhay east of Cross House in Crafthole.[43] In 1829, he rented a 'dwelling house with garden ... situate on west of turnpike road leading from Millbrook to Liskeard formerly in occupation of Gregory Warren since of Richard Keast.'[44] The rent was £1 10s. A map of Crafthole made in 1825 shows a small house and garden called 'Warrens', then belonging to Lord Clinton, on the road to Polscoe.[45]

The business premises of the blacksmiths, Henry Davey (1746-1825), his son, Henry (1775-1851), his grandson, John (1814-76), and John Henry Davey (1846-1923), were on the north side of the main road through Crafthole, at the eastern end. The smithy continued in operation until 1909. The modern dwellings on the site are called 'The Anvil' and 'Forge Cottage'.

See also 'Lynher Villa' below and 'Blacksmiths' in Chapter 39, *Trades and Crafts*.

Lynher Villa

This property is thought by the present owner, Joy Kentisbeer, to have been built *c.*1856. It first appears in the 1871 census, when John Davey (1814-76), and his wife,

105 *Lynher Villa was built* c.*1856. In 1871, the blacksmith, John Davey (1814-76), and his wife, Elizabeth, were living there, with one servant girl, Eliza Opie. These may be the people shown in front of the house.*

Elizabeth, were living there, with one servant girl, Eliza Opie. These are probably the three people shown in the photograph reproduced in this book. Davey had achieved success first as a blacksmith and then as an agricultural implement maker.[46] In 1881, the house was occupied by Richard Pawley, a naval pensioner from Wales, with his wife and family. In the early 1930s, Lt.-Col. Kempthorne, author of *A History of the Parish of Sheviock* (*c.*1934) lived in the villa. During the Second World War, the house was occupied by Mrs Wilson and her daughter, Lina, a nurse.[47]

Bryant Hayes

In 1555, Henry Spiller, his wife Elizabeth, and son Ferdinando, took a lease of a copyhold cottage called Bryant Hayes in Crafthole.[48] Ferdinando, who died in 1607, operated the windmill at Gill Ball near Sheviock Woods and also ran Bryant Hayes as an inn.[49] The copyholders recognised during the Commonwealth period were Elizabeth (born in 1586), wife of William Spiller (deceased), and their sons Henry (deceased) and George (born in 1608). Their rights had been entered on the court roll of 26 October 1607. In 1649, Elizabeth and George still lived in Bryant Hayes, which had half an acre of land attached to it (rent 9d.).[50] The modern house on the site, owned by David and Rosalie Dunn, is called Tirada.

In 1691, Sir John Carew purchased 'Spiller's holdings' in the borough. These are listed as a 'house and garden' tenanted by John Balsey (rent 4s.), a 'house and garden' tenanted by Emanuel Carkeeke (rent 4s.), one quarter of a 'house and garden' (rent 7s.), and one quarter of an orchard (rent 3s. 5d.). This was the 'upper and lower' orchard that had formerly been part of Bryant Hayes and that later belonged to the cooper and innkeeper, William Jeffrey senior (dead before 1649). There was also a 'house and garden', described as 'in hand and decayed', but for which the rental would have been £1 if the property had been sound and tenanted (perhaps Bryant Hayes), and an orchard, tenanted by Richard Pope (rent 2s.).

In about 1750, William Chubb was the occupier of 'Bryanthaies'. In 1755, he passed the tenancy to his daughter, Joan Harris, widow (age 47), and then to his grandchildren, Robert Warren (age 28), husbandman, and Mary Warren (age 15) (later Mary Bawden).[51] From this disposition the property became one of the three included in 'Warren's tenement'.[52] In 1796, Anthony Pike took over the tenancy of all three properties from the Prince of Wales on the lives of his sons and daughter.[53] The rents were unchanged. Pike had to pay a fine of £121 17s. for entry onto the court roll.

Walter Sonne's Cottage

In 1570, Walter Sonne, his wife, Joan, and their son, Thomas, became copyholders of a tenement in Crafthole, and Walter built a new cottage there.[54] The cottage was later occupied by Joan Odiorne under a copyhold dating from 1612 (rent 9d.). It may be the one shown on the map of Lord Clinton's property, described as 'Warrens'.[55] In about 1750, William Chubb was the occupier of this cottage. In 1755, he passed the tenancy to his daughter, Joan Harris, widow (age 47), and then to his grandchildren, Robert Warren (age 28), husbandman, and Mary Warren (age 15) (later Mary Bawden).[56] From this disposition the property became one of the three included in 'Warren's tenement'.[57]

Gill Haye (Wilhay) and Welshes Haye

Gill Haye and Welshes Haye were adjacent and the two tenements were usually let as one. The first surviving record dates from 1580 when Thomas and Margaret Harry and their son, Tristram, took a lease of 'Willhaies', a little meadow containing half an acre.[58] The officials executing the lease were John Kyndon (Kingdon), Leonard Lower, armiger (entitled to a coat of arms), and John Gill, gent. Gill may have given his name to the tenement. In 1592, Tristram's lease was transferred to John Harry.[59] John (born 1576) and Margaret Harry were entered on the court roll of 1612 as copyholders of Wilhays, with one little garden and orchard adjoining it (rent 1s. 6d.). Wilhays is located about half way along Well Lane on the south side. In the court roll of the borough for October 1640, this little garden and orchard was called 'Grylles walles' otherwise 'Gillhays','Welshes' or 'Welshayes'. 'Grylles walles' may refer to the fact that a cottage had formerly been built there. Certainly there was a cottage there when the tenement passed to a later Tristram Harry and then to his widow, Martha. In 1730, she surrendered 'the cottage and garden and curtilege called Willhays' and the orchard to the Prince of Wales, then lord of the manor of Crafthole, on condition that he granted a new lease to Amos Pope and his children, Amos and Mary.[60]

In the mid-1700s, the tenant was the innkeeper, William Lord, who was also the tenant of Sargent's tenement. He sub-let the property back to Amos Pope, junior, who was a tailor at Plymouth Dock. In 1755, William Lord, gave the reversion of his lease of Wilhays to his nephews, George and Thomas Westcott.[61] George became the innkeeper in Sheviock (1772-80) and Thomas was a joiner at Plymouth Dock. Amos Pope, aged 76, was still in occupation of Wilhays in 1798. George Westcott was dead by then, but Thomas still held the reversion. The rent had doubled to 3s. Westcott also held a cottage, garden and orchard in Crafthole, and two orchards in the Coombes of just over one acre in extent. He was aged 66 in 1798, but had been reported in Spry's Survey and Valuation of 1792 as being 'very feeble'.

In 1803, the tenant of Wilhays was the cordwainer (leather worker or shoemaker), Peter Kitt. The lease was on the lives of his sons, Andrew and William, and his daughter, Ann. He agreed to build 'a good dwellinghouse' on Wilhays within two years.[62] In 1840, Thomas Serpell was the tenant.

The Scrivener's House; Mrs Mullis's House

A dwelling house, garden and meadow, formerly occupied by the scrivener, Robert Honney, were described in a lease of 1707 as lying 'between the lands and tenements of Richard Carew of Antony on the east and south sides, the lands of ... John Morshed on the west side and the king's highway on the north, containing 16 yards of ground'.[63] Robert Honney, who would have required a sizeable room in which to conduct his business, was active as a scrivener from 1613 to 1636. The house stood on the south side of the road leading from Tregantel to Crafthole. The description places it at the eastern end of the main street.

A widow, Elizabeth Mullis, arranged for a room in her house to become the first Methodist meeting room in the parish in 1795.[64] Her house may have been the one formerly occupied by the scrivener, Robert Honney.

William Bray's House

Members of the Bray family were involved with the fishing operations at Portwrinkle and were also weavers. Several members of the family were elected to serve the office of reeve of the manor of Sheviock. A William Bray is shown as renting a 'cottage and 60 perches' in Crafthole for 4s. in a rental of 1634.[65] Emanuel Bray, possibly William's brother, was the father of a Richard Bray (b. *c.*1630). In 1657, this Richard married Joan, daughter of the weaver William Reepe. A William Bray, perhaps their son, is shown as renting a 'cottage and 60 perches' in Crafthole for 4s. in a rental of 1691.[66] He was renting the property on the lives of Joan Bray (his sister, who became Joan Prin), William Bray junior (IV), Patience Bray and Margaret Kneebone.

William Bray IV was born in 1688. He had presumably taken over his father's old tenancy in Crafthole. In 1711, Sir William Carew let to William Bray of Crafthole, weaver, a 'House Garden and a Little Meadow containing … about twenty yardes [i.e. 60 perches] of land'.[67] The rent was 4s. These were most likely the same premises as those originally leased to William Bray in 1634. The site was at the north end of West Lane, with the meadow on the west of the lane and the cottage on the east. William Bray was reeve of the manor in about 1775.[68] In 1722, one of the two William Brays was also renting a cellar and palace in Portwrinkle at 9s. a year for his fishing operations.

The next tenant of the cottage and meadow in Crafthole was Elizabeth Earl, widow of John Earl of Southford in Trewrickle. In 1762, she is shown as renting 'Late Wm Bray's House Garden Meadow in Crafthole yearly rent 4s.'[69] 'Late' must mean here 'formerly' – William was then 74 and he may have gone to live with a relative.[70] If Thomas Pride is correct, Elizabeth must have been his sub-tenant. William Bray's house in Crafthole stood on the site of what is now 'The Cottage', next to Crafthole House (formerly Crafthole Farm). His small meadow lay on the other side of West Lane on the site of the present Sydenham House and the new house next to it. The house and meadow are shown on Thomas Pride's map in the Antony archives.[71]

Cosy Cot

Only the chimney stack and cloam oven survive of the ancient dwelling that once stood on this site. The original cottage may have been built in the 1600s or even earlier. The walls were made of cob and the roof would originally have been thatched. The names of the earliest tenants have not survived, but in the 1900s it became the home of the Andrews family, whose descendants still live there.

The Toll House

See Chapter 40, *Markets, Highways and Turnpikes.*

Crafthole House and Farm

In *c.*1860, Thomas Hoskin (or Hosking) (1830-1908) built Crafthole House (once called Reservoir View). He and his wife, Jane, were farming the 79 acres of Blazor previously farmed by William Lyne.[72] They called this holding Crafthole Farm. Hoskin also had a 14½-year lease of Sconner Farm (83 acres), which commenced on 29 September 1866.[73] Hoskin was also a master mason, employing five men. A

106 *This photograph, taken in the 1930s, shows John Hoskin standing in front of Crafthole House. The house was built c.1860 by Thomas Hoskin, his great-grandfather, who also built the shop at the far end.*

piece of slate or stone, displaying lettering and used as a sample for his tombstone business, is still preserved by the family. Hoskin built his own farmhouse in the centre of Crafthole, on the road leading to Sheviock and Polscoe.[74] He also built the cottage next door. He and his wife also ran a grocer's shop (see 'Shops in Crafthole' below), that sold many dairy products produced on the farm. His son, Harold (b.1857) and his wife, Elizabeth (née Brooks) (1859-1905) succeeded Thomas.[75] Harold and his son, Arnold, took out a new tenancy of the farm in 1921. The acreage had been altered and reduced as a result of the building of the golf course in 1905. In 1940, the farm consisted of some 70 acres: about 20 acres around Cross Park and Higher Well Field; some 25 acres at Higher Sheviock Park, Maddock's Park, Higher Clicker, Higher 'Bonus' (Bonne's) Park, and Lower Well Field; some 27 acres at 'Villeins' (Velland's), Lower Sheviock Park, Furze Park, and Middle and Lower Bonus Park; as well as a few remaining acres of farmland on Blazor (Jory's or Tory's Park). [76] Arnold married Mollie Hill of Liscawn and, on the retirement of his father-in-law in the 1930s, he also took on the farm at Liscawn.[77] The herd of prize-winning white pigs that they had bred at Liscawn was moved to their mowhay situated between Polscoe Road and Sheviock Road. The boar that serviced them was kept by Tom Bersey at Sheviock Barton. On one occasion, before Tom could take the boar up to Crafthole when the pigs were in season, it escaped, ran up Sheviock Road and serviced the sows without help from the farmers.

107 *The medieval Market Cross at Crafthole from a photograph taken in the 1920s. Behind it stands the post office run by Florence Eliot.*

Ian Whittaker's father, Hal, who married Arnold and Mollie's daughter, Lois, and lived at the farm, remembered helping to pick up sheaves of oats and wheat and loading them on to the chassis of an old Wolsey car on which a wooden platform had been constructed. He also helped with layering the hedge at the bottom of the orchard, where it bordered Well Lane, and assisted with picking the apples in the autumn. Ian, then aged about five, remembers Arnold harvesting his corn after the war, using a tractor to pull a cutter/binder:

> Mollie would take a tea meal out to the field for the men. When we were down [from London], my mother would help with this. I can remember going to the field, sitting on a cloth among the stubble, watching the arms of the machine slowly circling as it was pulled along.

There were two barns attached to the farm on the opposite (eastern) side of the road: South Barn and Middle Barn. Middle Barn was also the dairy. When Arnold retired from farming in the 1950s, Crafthole Farm was joined with Crafthole Park Farm.

Crafthole Park Farm (Sydenham House)

In 1775, Samuel Lyne, who lived and farmed at Liscawn, was farming Edward's Parks (11 acres) and Crafthole Parks (11 acres). Samuel Lyne the younger was farming the same 22 acres from 1809. In the 1950s, the farmers were Steven Grills (married to Rita) and his son Eric. They lived at Sydenham House. Their fields included Crafthole

108 *Steven and Rita Grills ran Crafthole Park Farm from Sydenham House in the 1950s. The barns belonging to the farm, on the eastern side of the road, have now been converted into dwellings.*

109 *Wilfred Lee standing outside the shop that was attached to the* New Inn *in the 1940s.*

Park and part of Pool. On the retirement of Arnold Hoskin from Crafthole Farm (see above), the farmland of Crafthole Farm was joined with that of Crafthole Park Farm. The barns belonging to Crafthole Park Farm were on the opposite (eastern) side of the road from Sydenham House. Now converted into dwellings, they are called Willow Tree, Old Barn and Caer. On the retirement of Grills in the 1960s, his fields were added to those of Sheviock Barton, then being farmed by Tom Bersey. See further 'Crafthole Parks' and 'Pool' in Chapter 8, *Holdings on Sheviock Manor.*

SHOPS IN CRAFTHOLE

Hoskin's Shop: In *c.*1850-60, the farmer and mason, Thomas Hoskin (or Hosking) (1830-1908) built Crafthole House in the centre of Crafthole, on the road branching from the top road to Sheviock and Polscoe.[78] He and his wife, Jane (1833-1927), also ran a grocer's shop at the southern end of the house. Jane continued to run it after her husband's death. A photograph of the shop, with the young John Hoskin, Thomas's great-grandson, standing nearby, was taken in the 1930s. The shop ceased trading before 1939.[79]

Thomas was eventually succeeded in the shop by his grandson, (Harry) Arnold Hoskin (1886-1969) and his wife, Mollie (Mary, née Hill, 1891-1983). The shop sold clotted and separated cream, 'scald' milk, sweets and groceries, including tea.[80] In the 1930s, a notice on the outside advertised Lyons tea. Mollie made the cream from the family's own herd of cows. John Biles remembered the shop at that time:

> We used to have the option of clotted or separated [cream], the latter being cheaper, having a "nutty" taste, and containing a higher level of milk solids. The residue ... left over from the clotted process became "scald" milk. I can hear now the whine of Mollie Hoskin's hand-operated separator, with its long spouts, one delivering the cream, and the other the liquid.

110 *The first recorded house on the site of the post office was built in 1679. Charles Bligh, a farmer, took a lease on the property in 1744. He and his wife, Ann, became the first turnpike-gate keepers in 1760.*

At the north end of Crafthole House, Thomas Hoskin also built 'The Cottage', originally for his mother-in-law, Philippa Heath (d.1891). It was purchased by Arnold Hoskin in 1927, but was let to Eddy Callaghan and his wife, Frances (Doll), until 1948, when Hal Whittaker and his wife Lois (née Hoskin) moved in.

The Sweet Shop: Between 1910 and 1920, a small wooden hut was erected in the front garden of Myrtle Cottage (the modern Tirada) for the sale of sweets.

The Shop at the New Inn: During the Second World War, William and Hylda Hearn ran a small shop attached to the *New Inn* (now the *Finnygook Inn*).[81] The shop sold meals as well as groceries.

The Shop in the Old Toll-house: Wilfred and Hilary Lee opened a shop at the old turnpike-keeper's cottage in the 1950s, replacing the shop at the *New Inn*, and added the post office to it in the 1960s (see below). This ceased trading as a shop in 2008, but re-opened as a community shop in 2009. The post office continues to function.

Post Offices in Crafthole

The 'telephone' notice outside their shop suggests that Thomas and Jane Hoskin kept a post office in Crafthole in the early 1900s. The first postmistress remembered before the Second World War was Miss Florence Eliot, whose house, Cross Cottage, and post office stood west of West Lane (next to the corner house). The next was Mrs Rita Grills (widow) at Keyham Cottage, two houses to the east of the present post office. From *c.*1939 until the 1960s, Mrs Dolly (Adele) Channings ran the post office from her home at Marlborough House.[82] When Dolly retired, Hilary Lee added the post office to her shop at the old toll-house. Her daughter, Heather (Mrs David Pidgen) helped in the shop with Patsy Channings. The current postmistress is Mrs Ellen Adams.

Modern Developments

Small housing developments were built on the edges of Crafthole in the 1970s and 1980s. These were, in order, Burns View, Cross Park, Carew Close, Kimberley Foster Close and Sheviock Lane (1984).

PART IV

The River Lynher, Portwrinkle and the Fishing Industry

111 *Portwrinkle Harbour at low tide.*

Chapter 14

The Quay at the Riverside and Fishing in the Lynher and Tamar Rivers

Sheviock has two shorelines that can be used as landing places, one on the sheltered northern riverside of the peninsula, and the other, *Porthwrikkel* (the landing place at the cove – now called Portwrinkle), on the southern (seaward) side. The northern landing place was on the River Lynher.[1] The quay, or quays (for there may have been more than one), on the River Lynher were the only ones at which large vessels could be loaded and unloaded until the quay was built at Portwrinkle in 1612.

The Saxon monks of Tavistock, in the tenth century, were the first to organise and equip a fishery in Sheviock, in order to guarantee themselves a constant supply of fish.[2] Tavistock Abbey was therefore the first place to which fish was regularly exported from the parish. It is likely that, in order to transport their fish, the monks were the first builders of a quay on the Lynher. Domesday Book, written on the orders of William the Conqueror in 1086, makes no explicit mention of fishing in Sheviock, or anywhere else in the county. However, as has been suggested in relation to other parishes, the existence of a fishery may be implied both by the large number of *bordarii* (cottagers) – 17 – and by the high valuation of the parish (60 shillings).[3] This was the annual value of the parish accruing to the Abbey of Tavistock.

The Quay on the Lynher

The existence of a quay on the Lynher may be inferred from a charter dating from about 1280-90, when William Dawney the elder granted 15 acres of his wood called 'Hey(wode)' at Sheviock to the prior and canons of St Germans in return for them giving up their right to take two *barges* of the said wood.[4] If the prior and canons had been removing timber by barge, it is likely that there was a quay for the barges to come alongside. A quay on the Lynher was used to transport timber right up until modern times. In 1761, when some wood merchants purchased 35 acres of coppice wood in Gill Ball wood in Sheviock, they were allowed 'one Guinea towards making up and reparing the keys or Quays of and belonging to the said premises [of Gill Ball wood] for loading Barges or Boats.'[5] Thomas Pride's map of 1775 shows several quays and

112 *Thomas Pride's map of 1775 shows several quays along the banks of the River Lynher. It also depicts the field called Gill Ball, where a windmill once stood. The miller sold bread and ale to the bargemen.*

landing places along the riverside of Sheviock woods which could have been used to carry away timber. A quay would also have been used for transporting building stone. According to Polsue, stone from Caen was used in rebuilding the church of St Mary's in the early 1300s.[6] The use of a riverside quay for estuarine fishing on the Lynher and Tamar rivers may also be inferred from a document of 1337, called the Caption of Seisin.[7] This document refers *inter alia* to the fishing seines of Sir John Dawney (1302-1346). It states that they are exempt from paying tolls 'for passing through Tamar water'. There was also a landing-place for a ferry that crossed the river on the main route to Tavistock. A cottage for the ferryman and quay superintendent may have stood near the ferry crossing from the earliest times, though none is recorded until the 1600s. A house built by the monks of Tavistock for the same purpose was known to have existed at Morwelham Quay in 1230.

Port Roy

A section of Sheviock woods bears the name, Port Roy, and is so marked on Thomas Pride's map of 1775. However, it is not known what this name means, how old it is, or whether it has anything to do with the quays. It is not immediately adjacent to the site of the quay that stood at the end of George's Lane. The piece of woodland called Port Roy lay further west. The name, Port Roy, was also used as a field name on a holding called Treise's tenement.[8]

George's Quay

The permanent quay on the Lynher came to be called 'George's Quay', after George Winnacott. In 1648, Henry Rolle and other trustees of the late Sir Richard Carew let a plot of ground in Sheviock woods containing about three land yards to 'George Winnacott of Sheviock husbandman'.[9] The consideration for the lease was that George should '(by Godes Assistance) Erect and build a convenient house and cellar' on the land. The cellar was probably built to store fishing gear. George's Lane and George's Quay were both named after this George Winnacott. George and his brother, John, were also engaged in fishing at Portwrinkle. George's lease was on the lives of George Jeffery, son of the cordwainer (leatherworker or shoemaker) Peter Jeffery of Sheviock, and Silvester and Thomas Blake of Plymouth. The rent was 2s. Richard Holman witnessed the lease.

George's Quay was used by Portwrinkle fishermen right up to modern times when the weather was too rough to attempt to enter the harbour at Portwrinkle. When a gale blew up, the fishermen would sail or row all the way round Rame Head into Plymouth Sound, up the Tamar and then westward along the Lynher until they came to the quay. There the boat was moored to the riverbank while the crew walked

113 *The River Lynher at George's Quay. Low tide has revealed the footings of the old quay.*

home to Portwrinkle via George's Lane and Sheviock churchtown, carrying with them all the portable gear from the boat. When the weather improved, the reverse procedure took place.[10] The 17th-century fishing barque, the *Dayestarr*, may also have berthed at George's Quay when the weather was too rough to attempt the harbour. Her owner was William Hitchens, who died in 1635.[11] A 'Wm Hutchins deceased', who may have been a descendant, is shown in a manorial survey of 1691 as having rented the 'key in ye wood' for 2s.[12] However, the younger Hitchens seems to have been operating a sailing barge rather than a deep-sea fishing vessel. In May 1692, the steward, John Treis, wrote in his account book, 'Recd of Wm Hichens 2/3 of ye Barge Share for one year ended Michs. 91 & then shee became uselesse . . £2 2s 8d.'

A steward's record of the mid-1700s shows one of the quays being used to transport wood from Sheviock to Antony. On Monday, 27 April 1747, four of Sir Coventry Carew's estate workers were busy felling trees in Sheviock woods. A month later, on 25 and 26 May, two of them were engaged in carrying the wood to the waterside. The next day four of the men sailed in the barge carrying the wood from Sheviock to Antony. On 29 and 30 May, they carried the wood up from the quay at Antony, probably to the yard adjacent to Antony House, where they made a wood rick. The work of felling, carrying, loading, unloading and ricking the wood continued through early June, when finally the ricks were thatched to keep the wood dry.[13]

The volume of business at the quays increased steadily until the early 1900s. Timber and woodland products were frequently moved from Sheviock woods by barge. A regular ferry service from St Germans Quay via George's Quay to Devonport Market commenced in the 1800s. Farmers took agricultural produce to the market and returned with other goods or cash. The ferries were originally powered by sail, but in 1855 paddle steamers were introduced, operated by Messrs Gilbert and Wilcocks from Saltash. These were later replaced by diesel-powered boats. The last of these was run by Harry Dayman in the 1930s.[14]

The Windmill near the Quays

A windmill once stood on the high ground above Sheviock woods. It provided victuals for the bargemen and fishermen who used the quays. See further Chapter 42, *Mills and Millers*.

The Supply of Fish to South-West Devon

The *per capita* consumption of fish in Devon in the Middle Ages is reckoned to have been higher than that in England as a whole.[15] Partly this was because a large number of people, especially the tinners living around the fringes of Dartmoor, had little or no access to agricultural land.[16] Fish would therefore have been a very important source of protein for them. Partly it was because Devon had a particularly high number –

26 per cent – of people living in towns and therefore dependent on the importation of foodstuffs. The most important of these towns was Exeter, which also acted as a hub for the receipt and redistribution of fish to other centres.[17] Fish was transported to Exeter both by ship and by packhorse. South-west Devon was also the seat of a number of powerful land-owning families with large households. The foremost of these was the Courtenay family, with its principal seat at Tiverton. They had other seats at South Pool, close to Kingsbridge, and Powderham on the River Exe. The Courtenays were lords of Sheviock from 1346 until the mid-1500s. Such households were large consumers of fish, especially in the period from Christmas to Easter. The 18th-century historian, Ezra Cleaveland, tells a story that clearly illustrates this point:[18]

> In [1307] there arose a great contention between [Lord Courtenay] and the mayor and commonalty of the City of Exeter; the occasion this: the Lord Hugh Courtenay on a certain market-day sent his caterer to buy fish, at which time there were only three pots of fish in the market; the bishop's caterer likewise came, and both of them thinking the whole to be too little for either of them, they strove about the fish: the mayor on his part minding the good of the city, and that others also might have the benefit of the market, did decide this controversy, and delivered one pot of fish to the Lord Courtenay's caterer, another of them to the bishop's, and a third he reserved for the market: the Lord Courtenay being advertised thereof, thought himself wronged by the mayor, in not having all the fish, and shortly after coming to the city, he sent to the mayor to come to him (it seems the mayor was a retainer to him), the mayor well-knowing the Lord Courtenay's displeasure towards him, and the reason of it, called his brethren together to the guild-hall, and acquainted them with it, and told them, that he was then going to him, and desired them to go with him, and to assist him if there were occasion.
>
> He then went to the Lord Courtenay's house, and was had into his lodging-chamber, and the door was shut upon him; and then the Lord Courtenay began to chide the mayor for what he had done; and when none of his answers would satisfy him, the mayor took off an outer garment which he then wore, being the Lord's livery, and delivered it to him, whereat the Lord flew into a great passion; and the citizens being at the door, and fearing the mayor would come to some hurt, knocked at the door, and then demanded their mayor, which being, after sundry requests, denied them, they attempted to break open the door; which the Lord Courtenay perceiving, and doubting what might ensue, desired the mayor to pacify the people, which was soon done, and so they all quietly departed.[19]

It was perhaps the pressure of demand from Exeter and its surrounding area that caused Henry Dawney around 1200 to take back the two acres of land at *Porthwrykkel* that his ancestors had gifted to Tavistock Abbey. It was this same demand, as illustrated in Cleaveland's story, that encouraged Henry Dawney's successors, Sir Nicholas and Sir John, in the early 1300s to develop their fisheries on the River Lynher and *Porthwrykkel* so intensively.

Sir John Dawney's Seines

Much of the fishing in the estuaries around the Rame Peninsula in the Middle Ages was seine fishing. A seine net is a long net with buoyancy aids on one side and weights on the other so that it drops vertically into the water. Fishing with a seine net involves three or four boats. The net is drawn out from one boat by another one and then formed into a circle to enclose the fish. The first surviving reference to seining in the Tamar estuary is in the account of Roger de Ingepenne (Inkpenne), dating from 1287-8. Roger was steward and sheriff of Cornwall and in his return for the honour and manor of Trematon he accounted for '5s from the seines this year'.[20] Each seine paid 1s. for the right to fish in Tamar Water, and there were never more than five or six at a time. The Dawneys also had their own seignorial fishery. This is known because of the mention of the seines of Sir John Dawney in the Caption of Seisin of 1337. In this document it is stated that Sir John's seines were exempted from paying custom for crossing through Tamar Water.[21] It is not known how many seines Sir John had at this time, but with the foundation of the village of Crafthole by his father in 1314, the fisheries must have grown considerably since they were started by the monks of Tavistock Abbey in the tenth century. Sir Nicholas Dawney received licence to establish his new borough of *Croftilberwe* (Crafthole) in 1314. Together with the licence for the new borough came permission to hold a market. The original grant mentions only one day a week, Wednesday.[22] But the historian, Sir William Dugdale (1605-85), says there were two, Wednesday and Friday.[23] Friday is of course the traditional fish day in Catholic countries, so the Friday market was perhaps frequented particularly for fish. Chapmen (travelling vendors) bought their fish in Crafthole and carried it on pack-horses to sell in Tavistock, Exeter and other centres of population.

Effect of the Black Death on the Fisheries

The Black Death, which arrived in the West Country in 1348, brought the Duchy fishery of Trematon to a temporary halt. According to an official, 'Lynher Water [was] abandoned to the hands of the lord in the time of the pestilence and [is] not yet leased for lack of tenants'.[24] The Sheviock seines may also have been badly affected, but, as the next record shows, they were not discontinued for long. In 1349-50, the Havener of the Duchy of Cornwall accounted for '2s. 3d. received from the tithing of Schevyek for the price of 1 boat with all its equipment in which John Hurneway, Walter Damerell and others were drowned, appraised before the coroner.'[25] Sir John Dawney had died in 1346, and the new lord of the manor was his son-in-law, Sir Edward Courtenay. However it was not he who made the purchase, but men from the 'tithing of Schevyek'. So, just a year after the onslaught of the Black Death, the men of Sheviock were seizing the opportunity to acquire a second-hand fishing boat that had been involved in a tragic accident. Two hundred years later, seiners were still fishing in the River Tamar, as evidenced by Carew's description of their operations below Mount Edgcumbe in the late 1500s:

> A little below the house, in the Summer evenings, Sayne-boats come and draw with their nets for fish; whither the gentry of the house walking downe, take the pleasure of the sight, & sometimes at all adventures, buy the profit of the draughts.[26]

Fishing in the Tamar from seine boats continued up to the 18th century.

The Oyster Fishery on the Lynher

There is a reference to the catching of oysters in the River Lynher in a document of 1297-8. There is another mention in the Caption of Seisin of 1337, which reads 'Among the obligations tenants [of the borough of Trematon] owe to the lord is an annual toll of 1½d. at Michaelmas for oysters ... They are also required to sell 1 gallon of shelled oysters to the constable of the castle for 1d, as well as 100 in their shell for ½d.'[27] Carew distinguished between the species caught in the Lynher and those caught in the Tamar, writing,

> The Oysters dredged in this *Lyner*, finde a welcomer acceptance, where the taste, & not appetite, is Cater for the stomack, th[a]n those of the adioyning *Tamer*, which groweth (as I coniecture) because *Lyners* lesser streame leaveth them to bee seasoned, with a more kindely and better relished saltnes.

Oysters continued to be dredged from the Lynher and the Tamar until the 18th century. In February 1712/13, Sir William Carew's steward, Richard Blighe, paid £1 19s. to Sir William's boatman, John Harris, 'for dredging Oysters 26 times at 1s. 6d. the time'.[28] The following December he paid him another 12s. 6d. 'for dredging oysters'.

114 *The confluence of the Rivers Tiddy and Lynher (under the viaduct) opposite Sconner. Oysters dredged from the Lynher were said to taste better than those caught in the Tamar.*

115 *The harbour at Portwrinkle is still used by fishermen who set out crab and lobster pots from mid-winter to June.*

Chapter 15

The Landing Place and Quay at Portwrinkle

The people who inhabited the Rame Peninsula between 6,500 BC and 3,500 BC were skilled fishermen.[1] The later immigrants who arrived from the continent of Europe in about 1,800 BC, and ushered in the Bronze Age, had learned how to preserve foodstuffs in salt, and were probably the first to cure fish along the Cornish coast. During the Iron Age, beginning in about 450 BC,

> primitive nets and long lines, probably baited with limpets, appear to have been in use … and were probably set both from the shore and from small skin-covered vessels. These practices are assumed to have continued throughout the Romano-British and early medieval periods.[2]

Remains from fish eaten during the 400s and 500s A.D. have been found at Gwithian in western Cornwall.

The Southern Coastline

Sheviock's southern coastline is some three miles long. Steep cliffs form much of it, but at low tide there are sandy beaches at Finnygook, Particle and Blackyball.[3] Further to the east, the long stretch of sand, called Long Sands, begins. Steep paths formerly led up from the sands to the fields at Liscawn and Kerslake. They were called Sandways or Sandaways.[4] The sandy beach at Finnygook is the site of the main landing place of the parish. It is the only place of shelter between Looe and Cawsand. It came to be called in Cornish *Porthwrikkel*, the modern Portwrinkle. For much of its history there was no village there. The boats of the fishermen, most of whom lived at Trewrickle or, later, Crafthole, further inland, were simply hauled up onto the shore after a voyage. Simple shelters for the boats and fishing gear, called 'cellars', came to be constructed on or above the foreshore. In the late 1500s or early 1600s, some of these cellars were converted into dwellings, and new dwellings were built, creating the fishing village of Portwrinkle.[5]

The Anglo-Saxon and Medieval Fisheries

After the conquest of Cornwall by the Saxons, Aelfwynn, sister of the Saxon King Edgar, gifted the parish of Sheviock to Tavistock Abbey, sometime between 968 and 981. This gift must have been especially welcome to the monks. Under the strict Benedictine rule monks were forbidden to eat meat, so a good supply of fish was extremely important to them. It is likely therefore that the Saxon monks of Tavistock organised and equipped a fishery at Sheviock in the tenth century. By the time of the Norman Conquest of the South West of England in 1068, the monks had been supplied with fish from Sheviock for about a hundred years. With the grant of the land of Sheviock to the Norman knight, Ermenhald (Erbenald), sometime between 1068 and 1082, this supply was threatened. The Saxon monk who was Abbot of Tavistock at the time of the Conquest, Sihtric, remained in post until his death in 1082. He must have been a forceful individual, courageous and eloquent enough to make a successful protest to the new lord of Sheviock, about the evil consequences to the monks of losing their fishery. As a result of Sihtric's representations, Ermenhald and his wife, Deintedosa, gave to the Abbey the two acres of land at 'Trewikkel' from which their fishing operations were carried out. For about a century afterwards the gift held good, and when, sometime between 1174 and 1206, Henry Dawney renewed the grant, it looked as if the land would continue to belong to the Abbey for the next century.[6] However, with a rapidly rising population and an increasing demand for fish, perhaps leading to friction between the monks and the local fishermen, Henry changed his mind, and exchanged those two valuable acres for 15 acres of land that he owned at Taviton, near Tavistock.

The land at 'Trewikkel' that was the subject of the gift would today be said to be at Portwrinkle, but the name Trewikkel was then applied to all the land extending from the medieval village of Trewrickle right down to the foreshore. This is proved by a charter of 1286 granting a right of way to Warrin de Erth to 'get *sand* from Trewikkel'. The two acres granted to the Abbey can almost certainly be identified with the field called Crowstone (Cross-stone) Park marked on Thomas Pride's map of 1775. A cross once stood in this field to serve both as a place of prayer and as an easily recognisable navigation mark. Such coastal crosses were commonly erected at fishing places in the Middle Ages.[7] The monks' enclosure lay west of the lane running north from modern Portwrinkle. This lane may originally have formed the boundary between the fishing cellars and palaces of the monks to the west and those of the men of Sheviock to the east. To the west of Crowstone Park lay another field, called in the 18th century 'Monks' Park', perhaps a reference to the association with Tavistock Abbey that stretched back to Anglo-Saxon times.[8]

Orders concerning Fishing at Portwrinkle

During the medieval period, the regulation of the fishing would have been through the manorial courts of the Dawney lords of the manor, but no records of these courts have survived. By the early 1600s, Portwrinkle had become a commercially important fishing centre. The jurisdiction of the manorial courts still survived, but additional regulations were needed to keep order among the fishermen and to resolve disputes between them and the merchants who bought their fish. Accordingly, in 1605, Richard Carew prepared 17 orders to regulate the fishing activities, as follows:[9]

Orders established at Portwrinkle by Richard Carew & assented unto by the Owners of Sellars & Sainers of Pilchard there the 13th August 1605

Taking

1. The Owners shall imploy ye parishions before straungers allowing them for their shares as they shall deserve.
2. They shall not crosse one another in their working upon payne to forfeit xxs to ye Lord of ye Mannor for each time.
3. They shall serve the Cuntry before the merchants at ye same price yt ye merchant will give.
4. Next to ye Cuntry they shall serve the merchants at Portwrinkle wth ye one half of yre [their] Fish at least, if they will take so much.

Selling

5. The said merchants shall give notice to ye Hewers before hand wt [what] quantity they will take.
6. They shall pay 2s. lesse in a Last th[a]n ye best price at Causam [Cawsand] for yt time.
7. Off [of] ye Fish wch is carryed to other places they shall sell the one halfe at least at ye towne [i.e. Portwrinkle], where, if they be not well used I will, either procure them remedy or sett them at liberty.

Saving

8. The Savers of Pilchards shall not wilfully suffer the filth to runn through the way nor into ye sey upon payn. Ye owner of the sellar to forfeit for each offence vis viiid.

Recconing

9. If ye Masters of ye Boats or any other can be proved to have made a false recconing they shall loose y re place there for eie: & forfeit double ye summe soe imbeaselled.
10. In all indifferent matters ye greatest respect shalbe had to ye ten[a]nts whose ground bordereth upon ye port, next to ye ten[a]nts of ye mannor in yt parish, thirdly to ye parishioners not ten[a]nts, 4thly to my ten[a]nts of other places, & lastly to meer strangers.

Moaring

11. Noe man shall crosse his boate in ye way of drawing up, upon payne to forfeit Xs.

12. Such as have brought in new Boats this yere shalbe at ye charge of enlarging ye place or make a new place.
13. All those offences & all other contrversies about these affaires shalbe weekly ordered at Portwrickle on ye Satturdaye during ye seaning time by persons indifferently chosen or ye greater parte of y^m not being parties – namely ye parson of ye parish [the Revd Walter Arundell], John Warne, Thomas Symon, Lavers Bligh & Olliver Wallis.

Judging

14. If they cannot decide it or y^f they be parties then y^e same to be adiudged by my self or myne eldest sone.
15. If any disobey these ordinaunces they shall loose all benefitt of y^e place hereafter.
16. Each Boate of y^e parish shall pay $1^{s.}$ a yere, & each straunger not of y^e parish xviii^d a yere but this shall not warrant y^m any right hereafter w^{th}out my yerely leave.

Paying

17. Item each Company shall pay me a share, and if a single share amount to 40^s: they shall beside pay me a half a Last [i.e. 5,000] of Fish, if to five markes [i.e. £3 6s. 8d] a whole Last [i.e. 10,000].

Remember the poore'

116 *The 'way of drawing up' at Portwrinkle. In 1605, Richard Carew's orders provided that 'Noe man shall crosse his boate in ye way of drawing up.'*

The Building of the Quay at Portwrinkle

In 1612, Richard Carew and his son Richard (who became the first baronet) entered into an agreement with the parishioners of Sheviock to build a quay at Portwrinkle. Once the quay was built it was possible to bring barges and deep-sea fishing vessels into the little harbour. A 50-tonne vessel called the *Dayestarr* was based at Sheviock in 1626.[10] Edward Kneebone, a local man who wrote a survey of the Hundred of East in 1684, described 'Wrinkle-cleve' (i.e. Portwrinkle) as 'a large fisher towne, having an excellent key or mould, standing the rage of the South Sea, sufficient to secure all their boats, and good large barks [barques] upon occasion'.[11] The use of the plural is interesting. Sir James Bagg's survey is probably conclusive that Sheviock itself only had one ship in 1626. His instructions were that the local constables should register for each port not only 'those [ships and barques] that are there at present' but also 'those that are abroad'.[12] However, there was no reason why other barques should not put in occasionally, and there were also several barges belonging to the parish of Sheviock.

In an unpublished autobiographical fragment, Richard Carew the younger explained how the quay came to be built:

> not longe after the death of my wife [11 April 1611] I was entreated by the bargemen of my parish to build them a key, and advised by my friendes the rather to doe it, that mine imploymente therein, might make mee somewhat the les remember her losse; which woorke I was not unwillinge to doe, beecaus I saw it likely to prove a benefit to my neighbours, and I hoped thereby the better to inable my selfe to doe good, to my country, in a larger measure, if it pleased God to give mee opportunity, for the makinge of which I was to use many woorkmens labors.[13]

There are two documents at Antony House concerning the agreement. The first looks like a preparatory draft.[14] The second is a fair copy of the actual agreement.[15] The agreement stipulated that the total cost of the quay was not to exceed £300. The guarantors on the part of the parish were firstly four local gentlemen. The first named was Richard Wallys (1581-1654) who may have been a lawyer, as he acted as 'attorney' for Sir John Eliot, when Sir John sold Sconner to Richard Carew the younger in 1617. Wallis later farmed at Sconner himself and became the tenant of property in Crafthole and Blazor. The other three were John Peter (also Peters) who farmed at Tredis, Philip Wallis who farmed at Hearle's Parks, and Alexander Hancock who farmed at Kerslake.[16] For the farmers, the value of the quay was that it would enable the masters of sailing barges to bring sand closer to their fields near the south coast than they could do by using the existing quay on the River Lynher. The sand could then be loaded onto horses or donkeys to carry onto their fields for the improvement of the soil.

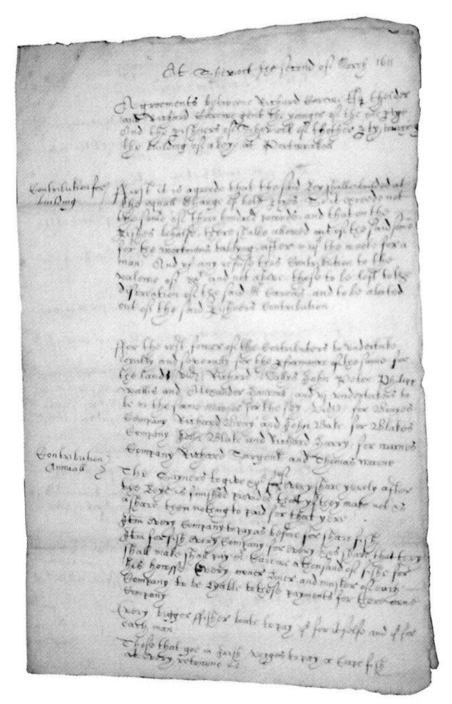

117 *The 1612 Agreement for the building of the harbour at Portwrinkle.*

The second group of guarantors were the 'undertakers' (financial backers) of three fishing syndicates, namely Richard Bray and John Bake (for 'Braye's' Company), John Blake and Richard Harry (for Blake's Company), and Richard Sargent and Thomas Warne (for Warne's Company).[17] These companies operated seine boats for coastal fishing. Under the Agreement, they were to pay to the lord of the manor dues of one shilling a year. The other seiners of the parish were to pay one shilling per share of each seine, provided the seine yielded a profit of at least 10s. per share at the year-end. Visiting seine boats were to pay nothing if they unloaded pilchards at the quay. The Carews were receiving small payments each year for sale of 'key-fish at Portwrickle' until sometime after 1734.[18] In 1723 and 1728, more than £9 was received. But in 1734 the amount had dwindled to 5s.

The agreement also made provision for 'bigger fisher boate[s]' able to 'goe in Irish voyges'. Although such boats could have lain alongside the quay on the River Lynher before 1612, no owners of barques are named in the agreement, so probably there were none prior to 1612. Each bigger fisher boat was to pay annually 2s. 'for itself' and 2s. 'for eache man' (i.e. for each member of the crew). The term 'Irish voyges' may have been a euphemism for voyages to fish off the coast of Newfoundland. According to the agreement each vessel making one of these voyages was to pay 'a Cape fish at every retourne'. A Cape fish was almost certainly a dried cod. Cod were now being caught in large numbers off the Avalon peninsula in Newfoundland. The southern points of the Peninsula are called Cape St Mary, Cape Pine and Cape Race. Further south in New England lies Cape Cod.

The 1612 agreement also provided that the 'barge[s] of the parish' bringing sand for the farmers were to pay three shillings per annum.[19] As a result of an accident on the river, the character of one of the Sheviock barge owners has been preserved.[20] According to F. E. Halliday, this was William Chark, a neighbour of Richard Carew the younger.[21] The younger Carew lived in Sheviock parish, probably at Sconner Farm, from the time of his marriage in 1601 until the death of his father, Richard the elder, in 1620. The sail of one of Chark's barges had been stolen, so Chark went to a 'calker' (astrologer or fortune-teller) to find out what had become of it and in due course he recovered his sail. Carew thoroughly disapproved of the practice of consulting astrologers, so he told Chark that, although he had recovered the sail, 'within a twelvemonth hee shold finde, hee shold neither gaine nor save by it.' Carew continued,

> and within 2 – or – 3 moneths after, havinge solde some sande in the country for ten shillinges, and castinge [casting a spell for] the winde and tide to serve well for his other barge, that wente with the saile which had been stolen from him, to bee likely at the same time to bringe him an angell [22] more, as hee was in hope thereof returninge homewards singinge, one of his acquaintance met him on the water, and asked him if hee hearde any newes, he told him noe, then replyes the other, your barge is lost, when he asked how, hee said Mr Porter's barge and his were turninge upon the tide, and neither of them wold give way unto the other, for his barge was stemmed, and sunke in the river, and hee lost barge, maste, saile, and all, except the men which it pleased God to preserve.

The name, though not the characters, of another family of bargemen has been preserved. Four generations of the Grills family of Sheviock plied the trades of mariners or bargmen.[23] The first on record is Philip Grills, mariner, who was born in Sheviock in 1690, married Dorcas Prin in 1725 and died at sea two years later. His son, Philip, orphaned when only a year old, became a bargeman. He married in 1759 and their son, Philip, born in 1766, followed in his father's footsteps. He married Elizabeth Geach, and their son, another Philip, was born in 1793. He too became a bargeman and died in 1871 when the era of the sailing barges on the Lynher and Tamar rivers was drawing to a close. Another member of the family, William Grills, leased a house in Wilcove in Antony in 1722.[24] In 1732, he was one of three barge masters paying a rent of £2 4s. for use of the sand quay at Wilcove.[25]

118 *This photograph of the harbour in the early 1900s was made into a postcard for visitors. It shows the eastern arm of the quay in a dilapidated state. The figure on the donkey is Theophilus Pengelly.*

The Agreement for Building the Quay

The Agreement for building the first quay at Portwrinkle reads as follows:

At Sheviock the second of March 1611[26]

Agreements betweene Richard Carewe esq^{re} the elder and Richard Carewe gent the younger of the one partye and the parishners of Sheviock of the other party touchinge the building of a Keye at Port Wrickell.

CONTRIBUTION FOR BUILDING

First it is Agreede that the said Key shalbe builded at the equall Charge of both partyes, so it exceede not the some [sum] of three hundred pownds and that on the parishes behalfe there shalbe allowed out of the said some [sum] for the workmens tabling, after iij^{s} the weeke for a man: and yf any refuse this contribution to the valewe of xx^{li} and not above, those to be left to the discreation of the saide Mr Carews, and to be abated out of the said parishners contribution.

For the rest fower of the contributors to undertake joyntly and severally for the performance of the same for the land (vid[elicet]) Richard Wallys John Peter: Philipp Wallis, and Alexander Hancock, and by undertakers to be in the same manner for the sey [sea] (vid) for Brayes Company Richard Bray and John Bake, and for Blakes Company John Blake and Richard Harry, for Warnes Company Richard Sargent and Thomas Warne

CONTRIBUTION ANNUALL

The Sayners to give xii^{d} of everye share yerely after the Keye is finished provided that yf they make not x^{s} a share then nothing to be paid for that yere[27]

Item everye Company to pay as before for shares fish[28]

Item for fish everye Company for every xx^{s} share that they shall make shall pay Mr Carew a thousand of fishe for his howsse, Every owner, huer, and master of each Company to be lyable to these payments for there owne Company

Everye bigger Fisher boate to pay ij^{s} for it selfe and ii^{s} for eache man:

Those who goe in Irish voyges to pay a Cape Fish at every retourne

Everye Barge of the parish that belongeth to the said Key to pay yerely iij^{s}

RETRIBUTION

No owner to bee admitted but such as dwell in the parish

Such straunge boats as bring any thing to the Contributers shall pay as they doe at other places.

The Sayne boats that Come with Pilchards to pay nothing.

Item the Contributers to have the preferment at the Key before straungers.

Each of the Contributers to have this priveleage for iij lives

COVENANNTE

Item Lyberty to carry Fresh Water [29]

Item The sonnes of the saide Carewe to be as free as inhabytants[30]

Covenante for Sayners

They to serve Wrickell Merchannts for xij^{d} a last [10,000 fish] within Causon [Cawsand] middle price.[31]

Item pitts to bee made for keping the trayne water in convenyent places by the owners of sellers [cellars] ether above Clefe or under Clefe uppon payne of vj^{s} viij^{d} every one that shall make defalt herein, and the said vj^{s} viij^{d} to be levyed by waye of distresse[32]

The parishners to be imployed before strangers

The Contributers to joyne with noe strangers for being owners

Item if the key happen to be in decay after it is builded the Lord shall repayre it againe or otherwise not to have the said xii^{d} for a share untill it be repayred.

Item every one of the Contributers that shall have any boates there shall yerely enter the same in Courte paying only a penny to the Steward of the said Mannor for entring of the same'[33]

The quay built under this agreement proved a great boon to the fishermen of Portwrinkle, but it also led to disputes between the owners of the fishing syndicates and the individual fishermen of the parish. Richard Carew's orders of 1605 had provided that owners should employ the parishioners before strangers, a provision repeated in the 1612 agreement about the building of the quay. The 1612 agreement also provided that the contributors to the building of the quay should 'joyne with noe strangers for being owners'. However, the owners seem to have circumvented these rules from time to time, and this preyed on the conscience of the elder Carew. In his will of 1619/20 he made a provision that:

> Whereas I have erected a kay at Portwreckel with a promise that the Contributors of the parish should enjoy certaine privileges there according to the articles of agreement betweene us my will is that if anie owner of the manner of Sheviok doe infringe anie of the said agreements the said parishioners performing what on their partes is to bee don, then the more parte of myne Overseers [the executors of his will] surviving shall out of my woods in Sheviak make satisfaction to the parties soe wronged after there [their] discretion.[34]

Gregory Arundell's Articles for the Conduct of the Portwrinkle Fishermen

After the construction of the quay, the system of dispute resolution laid down by Richard Carew in 1605 seems to have remained in place. Under this system, a panel of respected local people headed by the rector was supposed to assemble on Saturdays in the seining season to adjudicate on any breaches of the rules and to resolve any disputes between individuals. But Walter Arundell, the rector who had been in post when the rules were drawn up in 1605, died in 1622 and was replaced by his son, Gregory. Gregory lacked his father's charitable disposition and understanding of human conduct. He was, to say the least of it, heavy-handed and sanctimonious. As owner, like his father, of the tithe of fish, he must also have had an interest in many of the matters in dispute. The rules that he drew up for the men of Portwrinkle begin with a preamble:[35]

> First whether it will not bee better for the sayners to content themselves with Gods blessings that of his bounty hee shall bee pleased to give them according to his word and will, then [than] by greedy striving for more to make them loose all presently, and answer for their wickedness before his Seate of Judgment, where no Secrets can be hid That for mine own part I had rather loose all which I have of them th[a]n to see Christians deal so wickedly with one another.
>
> That if they will performe their promises in dealing truly and justly; and Assist mee faithfully in punishing every offender, then I shall ever bee ready to doe them all the good I can. And that they must blame none but themselves if by a contrary course they inforce mee to oppose them for the tyme to come; and seeke my Remedy by due course of Law for all the wrongs they have heretofore done mee. I desire therefore speedily to know whether they will consent to these following Orders according to their owne agreement with mee or no; that I may follow that course which will be fittest for mee; and that I take it with much distaste, that when I appointed them a tyme twise, to meet me at the key, they neglected mee, so much, as that they would not vouchsafe to come to talke with mee, that the busness might bee righted according to reason; which will make men very carefull henceforward to Suffer my Patience no longer to bee thus abused.

He then sets out his ten 'Articles to be observed by the Portwrikell men':

1. I would have them name every person upon whom they thinke fitt to bestow fish in Charitie; and to expresse their reason for every severall person, and to assigne the quantity which every one shall have and to appoint divers persons of Trust, who shall openly deliver it accordingly, in a sober and quiet manner, which if they shall not duely attend, they shall have no more.

2. That every man bee content with his just due out of the whole; and that none presume like greedy Dogs to catch what they can, by snatching, biting, or tearing out of any Nette, or Boate.

3. That every Master of a Boate undertake for every one of his Company, to have these Orders duly kept; which if any breake, they shall bee presently turned out, if they doe not forthwith make it openly knowne that every offender may bee duly and speedily punished.

4. That all the fish which is sold bee bargained for openly; and so delivered quietly in the view of every one; and that there be no forestalling; and that they bring a Note from the Merchant, of the quantity they have delivered them; and of the price at which they were sould; and hee or they that makes the best Markett, be reasonably rewarded for his honesty and care; with commendation before all the rest to encourage others to doe the like, that honesty and painfullnesse be duly considered, and that persons of such quality be mostly imployed.

5. That whosoever shall discover any false and secret deceiving, bee liberally dealt withall, for manifesting the truth; and that there bee allowance given for secret spies, to keepe them in order; and that there bee no riotous spending when they goe to market; but that they behave themselves civilly and so returne

6. That both seller and buyer of Fish taken by falsehood or force, bee both shamed and punished[36]

7. That those that come to fetch fishe to carry into the Country, bee openly served by persons appointed for the same purpose above Cliffe, and not at the Key, according as they come, and stay in order; that whosoever will do otherwise, let his name be taken, and that hee bee sufferd to have no more.

8. That all the recconings be openly duely and soberly made; and that at the latter end of the yeare, if there bee any thing left in the stocke that it bee presently divided or bestowed on such, as have best deserved it, by their honest and carefull service, or discovery of other deceipts.

9. That if any take extraordinary paines at any time, that they bee not their owne Carvers, but that others take their turnes by course, or that they bee considered in some other faire open and orderly way.

10. That in the beginning of every yeare, every one whom this concernes put his hand hereunto in token of his consent; and that any that are admitted after the beginning doe the Like when they are received; and that the same course bee continued every yeare

Greg Arundell Rector of Sheviock

These articles, requiring the fishermen to spy upon one another (article 5), compare most unfavourably with the sensible and mutually advantageous orders issued by Richard Carew in 1605. It is small wonder that the fishermen refused to meet him at the quay and that during the Commonwealth period (*c.*1650) it was the author of the articles, Gregory Arundell, who was himself 'presently turned out' of his living. He was replaced by the Puritan divine, John Gey. To be fair to Arundell, he was not himself grasping, and failed to collect in kind all the tithes to which he was legally entitled.[37]

Repairs to the Quay

The quay at Portwrinkle seems always to have had two arms: a long one to the south, slightly curved in shape, and a short one to the north. The southern arm, in particular, faced the full force of the south-westerly gales and was damaged by storms on many occasions. Under the terms of the 1612 agreement, it was the lord's responsibility to keep the quay in good repair. In 1692, Matthew Stanton, a stonemason, gave a receipt to Thomas Harvey, the bailiff of Sheviock manor, for 3s. 8d. 'being in full for three dayes work for my selfe and my sarvent, on ye key at port wrinkle.'[38] In 1715, Thomas

Stanton, together with his son, Thomas junior, and John Stanton and Thomas Bray spent a total of 10½ days erecting a new bollard at the quay. Further remedial work was carried out on in February 1723. Seven men worked a total of 397½ days on carrying out repairs.[39] The total cost was £23 11s. 3d.[40] The steward gave the masons another 6d. 'for drink'.[41] In July 1731, the mason, William Foard, and his four men were paid £4 3s. 11d. for 68½ days' work on the quay.[42] The steward spent another 18s. on 'Beer to the fishermen helping about the stones'.[43] The stones used in the repair came from Plymouth, and Stephen Edwards was paid £1 for 'fetching and carrying to Plym° 12 Butts'. Francis Avery spent four days, at 1s. a day, 'splicing the Ropes & sling^{g} the Butts'. In 1755, on instructions from Mr Buller, William Corinton, the steward, ordered the reeve, William Bray, to collect money to defray the costs of repairing the quay at Portwrinkle. He was to charge 1s. for each horse using the sandways to spread sand on the fields. In spite of this, the condition of the quay so deteriorated as to make it virtually unusable.

In 1792, Reginald Pole Carew agreed to repair the curved southern arm (called the counter-quay) and to rebuild the north arm, with a quay adjoining, with 'stone, lime and other materials'. The contract for doing the work was given to Thomas Stedman of Plymouth Dock. Pole Carew also agreed to 'cleanse the bason of the said quay or pier … from all sand mud stones and rubble' and (in response to the objections of the fishermen from Mevagissey who were being asked to man the new seines) to spend 'the sum of thirty pounds in cutting down or blowing up and clearing the rock or rocks situate at the entrance of the said quay or pier'.[44] This agreement to repair and rebuild the harbour coincided with the grant of a lease to build a new and substantial pilchard cellar and palace at Portwrinkle.[45]

The work of cleansing the basin took 16 weeks, and up to 20 men with shovels were employed on the work.[46] The men were tinners, who were paid an average of 2s. 6d. per day, plus some travelling expenses. The bailiff of the manor also spent 12s. on 'Liquer for Tinners when Breaking the Rocks', and on another occasion Reginald Pole Carew ordered 15s. to be spent on 'Liquer for Fishermen and Tinners'. The total cost of the building work was more than £180 and the cost of the cleansing operation was more than £134. The local mason, Philip Goard, was also paid 8s. 5½d. for 'Fixing the Guide post and for Repairs of the New Quay', and the local smith was paid £1 14s. 'for Iron work for the Guide post & for Moarings to the New Quay'. Portwrinkle now had a functioning harbour again. It was used for harbouring seine fishing boats and for mooring sand-barges until the early 20th century and is still in use for small fishing craft.

There is a record of severe storm damage to the new harbour on 2 February 1822, requiring major repairs and the south-east pier was washed down in 1824.[47]

Minor repairs were carried out in 1849, when 2s. was paid 'to John Andrew's donkey to carrying stone'. In addition to the periodic need to carry out repairs to the quay, rocks and stones hurled onto the harbour bed had to be removed in most years. The bill for removing them came to £1 or more nine times between 1849 and 1912.

By 1932, the quay was again in urgent need of repair, and Leonard and Dorothy Elmhirst, who had acquired the Chalet on Portwrinkle beach in 1928, took an interest in the matter. Leonard instructed his solicitor, Sydney Bowden, and an engineer to produce an estimate for repairing the quay.[48] His idea was that the repair would be a co-operative effort between the landlord, the relevant Government ministry, and the 'Portwrinklers', who were reported by Bowden to be 'eager and willing to help'. Nothing came of his scheme, however, and in 1938 he wrote to a Commander Collard, RN, at the Fisheries Office in Plymouth, asking 'what chance there is of giving assistance towards the repair of the harbour at Crafthole'.[49] The answer was that there was no chance. But in spite of these setbacks, the quay is still there, and today is owned and periodically repaired by Caradon District Council. In 1984, the Council appointed W.B. Pengelly and J. Isaac as Joint Honorary Harbour Masters.[50]

119 *Lobster pots waiting to be put out at Portwrinkle c.2006.*

120 *A barque like the* Dayestarr *fishing off Newfoundland. The fishermen fished with lines and hooks from the barrel-like projections along the sides of the vessel. (Detail from Herman Moll's map of North America* c.*1715 in the Atlas Royal: BL Maps 148.e.1. (11).)*

Chapter 16

The Dayestarr *and her Crew*

In the reign of Henry VIII (1509-47), ships from the South West began to fish for cod off Newfoundland. The corporation of Plymouth agreed, in 1543, to pay an extra 8d. to the watchman at Rame Head for lighting beacons 'by night when the Newfoundland men came in'.[1] In the 17th century, the leading shipping centre on the Rame peninsula was Millbrook, with 17 ships (1,050 tonnes), followed by Antony, with five ships (300 tonnes) and Sheviock, with just one ship, the *Dayestarr* (50 tonnes).[2] Nearby, Saltash had six ships (400 tonnes). Together these four ports had 29 ships (1,800 tonnes). They were all on or near the estuary of the River Tamar and had close connections with each other and with Plymouth. The leading ports of the South West at the time were Dartmouth and Torbay, with 92 ships (5,590 tonnes), followed at some distance by Plymouth and Stonehouse, with 65 ships (3,620 tonnes). These figures were contained in a survey carried out in about 1626 by Sir James Bagg (Vice-Admiral of South Cornwall, 1622-41; and of South Devon, 1628-37).[3] Bagg's survey also recorded William Hitchens the elder as the owner of the *Dayestarr*.[4] William's father, John, who had died before 1613, had farmed at Sheviock Barton, the principal manor farm of Sheviock.

The interconnections between the ship owners and crews of the various ports on the River Tamar were many and varied. Hitchens himself was not only connected with Sheviock Barton, but also had property in Saltash, where the Carews also had substantial interests. Richard Carew, the historian, sat as MP for the town in the late 1500s. Simon Rowe, who was the owner of the 65-tonne *Prescilla* and the 55-tonne *Joane*, both of Antony, was also the co-owner, with William and John Rowe, of the 80-tonne *Truelove* of East Stonehouse. He also owned a property in Crafthole in the parish of Sheviock, and was a juror there in 1629. William Rowe owned five ships in addition to the *Truelove* of East Stonehouse: one in Stonehouse (the *William and Margarett*), one in Plymouth (the *Retorne*) and three in Millbrook (the *Tryall*, the *Concord* and the *Amytie*). Manides Govet, a 'sailor servant' on the *Dayestarr*, may have been related to Henry Govett, a sailor from Antony; and Edward Moreshed, a 'sailor servant' of Millbrook, was probably related to the Edward Moreshedd who lived in Crafthole and was a sailor on the *Dayestarr.* Millbrook with its six shipwrights was the ship repair centre for the entire Rame peninsula (and also the place where the court of petty sessions for the peninsula was held). The will of William Harry of Sheviock, 'mariner' (ship's officer), also shows these interconnections. He died in 1626, the year of the survey, tragically young. At the time of his death his wife, Priscilla, was pregnant.[5] Among the possessions he left were 'his sea instruments and bookes', which were valued at £3. A note made at the end of his will summarised the most recent of his shipping activities:

> I delivered untoe Thomas Dawe of Milbrooke xvi hundred of fish in the shipp called the *Abraham* of Millbrooke bound for Ireland beesides one thousand more I sold to Pasco Lavory Master of the same shipp.

Thomas Dawe was listed in Bagg's survey as a sailor of Millbrook and Maker. The 'xvi hundred of fish' were valued in the inventory attached to Harry's will at £4. The *Abraham* was a two-deck vessel with a burden (holding capacity) of 80 tonnes. Though normally unarmed, she was capable of carrying six guns. Her owner was John Evans.[6] Pascho Lavory was master at the age of thirty-two.[7] In October 1627, at Plymouth, Bagg requisitioned the *Abraham* to take part in the ill-fated expedition in support of the French Huguenots at the Isle de Ré.[8]

Newfoundland cod fishing was highly profitable, but it was also very demanding of manpower. The voyage to Newfoundland and back would last for at least four months. Ship owners had to scour the villages and towns near the coast for sailors and fishermen. William Hitchens sought his crew for the *Dayestarr* from the parish of Sheviock. Most of the men lived either on the manor of Sheviock or in the borough of Crafthole, then a part of the Duchy of Cornwall. A survey of the mariners and ships of South Devon, made on the orders of the Duke of Buckingham in 1619, gives a good idea of the types of journey that could have been undertaken by the *Dayestarr.* This survey noted that the port of Topsham possessed 22 ships varying in size between 10 and 120 tonnes.[9] There were 12 ships of comparable size to the *Dayestarr.* Six of these were then on voyages to Newfoundland. These were the *Mynion* (60 tonnes), the *Dyamonde* (50 tonnes), the *Providence* (60 tonnes), the *Delight* (50 tonnes), the *Hopewell* (40 tonnes), and the *Michaell* (45 tonnes). The other ships were at San Lucar (two ships) (probably Sanlucar de Barrameda, west of Cadiz), San Sebastian (either San Sebastian de la Gomera in the Canary Islands or Donostia-San Sebastian, on the Bay of Biscay), and Madeira. One ship was still in Topsham. William Rowe's ship, the *Retorne* of Plymouth (120 tonnes), 'came from Newfoundland' according to a letter from Sir James Bagg to Sir John Coke on 28 August 1627.

Cod Fishing off Newfoundland

Between 1615 and 1640, approximately 200-300 ships left England each year to fish for cod off Newfoundland.[10] The western fishery merchants were known collectively as the 'Western Adventurers'. Their ships left England in April, arriving off Newfoundland about a month later. Upon arrival, the crew prepared 'fishing rooms' on shore and built or refurbished the small boats that would accompany (or be carried by) the mother ship to the fishing grounds. After five or six weeks of preparation, the crewmen sailed out to the fishing grounds. The objective of the West Country fishermen was to catch comparatively small cod, averaging 10-12 lbs. They fetched about 1½d. each on the wholesale market. The seven fishermen on the 50-tonne *Dayestarr* would be expected to catch about 100,000 fish (50 tons) on each trip. The catch would also yield about six tons of train oil. The owners would have paid out some £250 to fit out the vessel and could expect revenue of about £1,500 and profit of about £1,250. One third of this (£417) was divided amongst the master and crew, and two thirds (£833) was shared between the owner and the victuallers.[11]

The fishermen fished with lines weighted with lead, which were dropped from the mother ship or from 'dorys', small rowing boats manned by single fishermen. These were built by crew members in Newfoundland and left on shore to be collected at the beginning of each new season.[12] When the fishing was over, the crew unloaded the fish from the mother vessel onto the Newfoundland shore, where the landing stage was erected and the 'fishing rooms' were prepared. These were used for dressing (cleaning and trimming) the cod and pressing out the cod liver oil and the train oil. The cod were then dried and cured (lightly salted) on spruce branches spread out on the beaches.[13]

If, as seems likely, the *Dayestarr* made voyages to Newfoundland, as a protection against piracy she would have sailed in the company of vessels from the other connected ports along the Tamar Estuary. The familiarity of the English crews with the north-east coast of the American continent was in due course to lead to emigration there. Members of the ship-owning Hitchens and Rowe families settled in the United States. In the 1950s, a Colonel Hitchens of the U.S. Army called at Sheviock Barton and declared that it was the home of his ancestors. When the Old State House in Boston was re-built after a fire in 1747, it was a John Rowe who urged that a wooden cod should be carved to hang in it.[14] There are places called Torbay in both Newfoundland and Nova Scotia. The Western Adventurers exported much of the cod caught on the Grand Banks. Carew says that in his day most of the casks of pickled or dried fish were exported to France, Spain and Italy.[15] As we have seen, they were also exported to Ireland. In these Catholic countries, cured cod (called *bacalao* in Spanish) and pilchards were in high demand for consumption on 'fish' days.

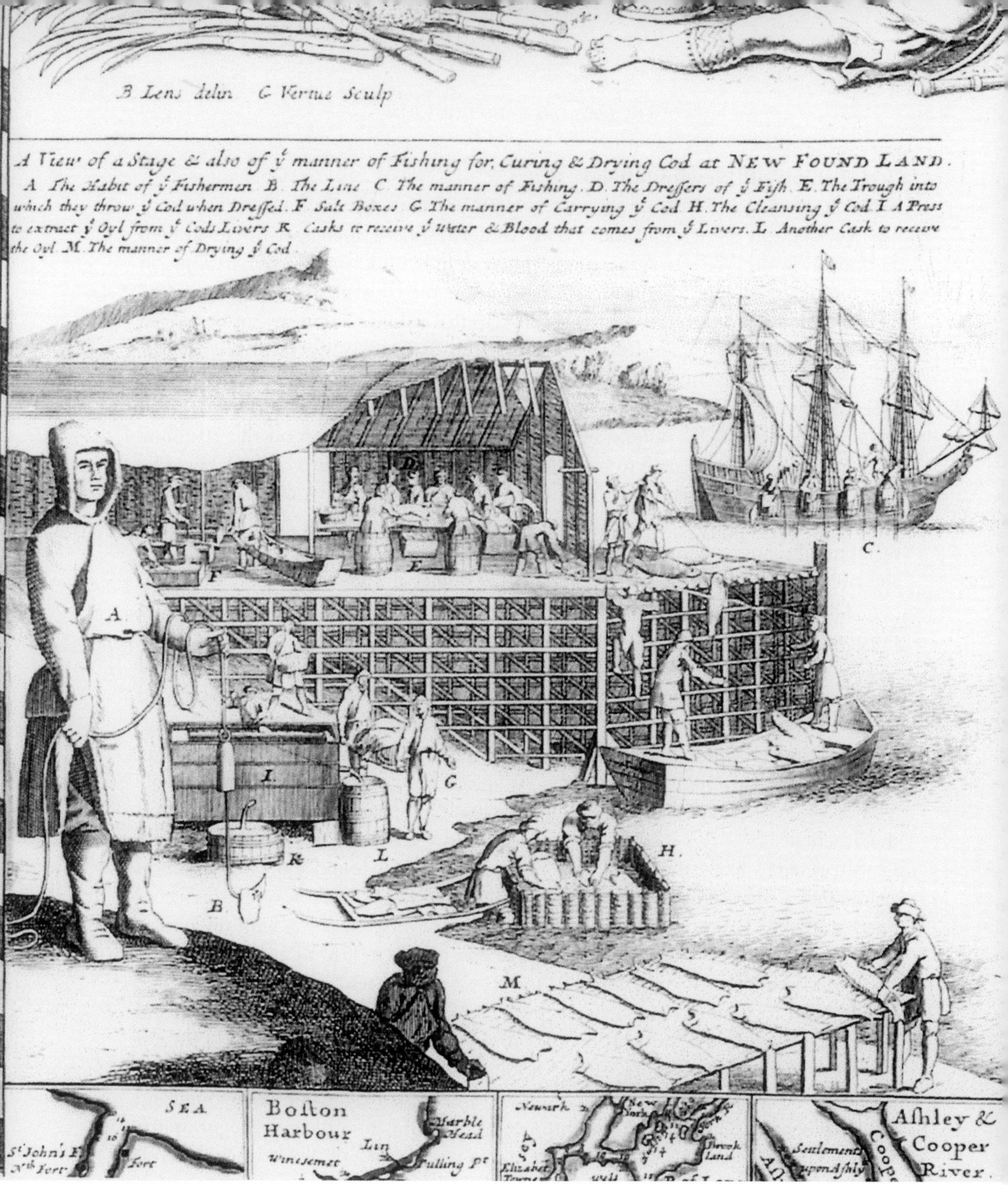

B Lens delin G Vertue Sculp

A View of a Stage & also of ye manner of Fishing for, Curing & Drying Cod at NEW FOUND LAND.
A The Habit of ye Fishermen B The Line C The manner of Fishing. D The Dressers of ye Fish. E The Trough into which they throw ye Cod when Dressed. F Salt Boxes G The manner of Carrying ye Cod H. The Cleansing ye Cod. I A Press to extract ye Oyl from ye Cods Livers K Casks to receive ye Water & Blood that comes from ye Livers. L Another Cask to receive the Oyl. M. The manner of Drying ye Cod

121 *'A view of a Stage and also of ye manner of Fishing for, Curing and Drying Cod at New Found Land'. (Cartouche from Herman Moll's map of North America c.1715 in the Atlas Royal: BL Maps 148.e.1. (11).)*

The Crew of the *Dayestarr*

The *Dayestarr* was listed as having a crew of 35, apparently all Sheviock men, plus six 'sailor servants', probably boys, making 41 in all. She was distinctly overcrowded, and many of the men would have had to sleep on deck. The fact that she was so crowded, with seven professional fishermen on board, makes it almost certain that in 1626 the *Dayestarr* was manned for the Newfoundland fishing grounds. In 1665, the king was to issue Letters Patent restricting the number of men on a 50-tonne vessel to thirty.[16] The parish constables who recorded the names for Sir James Bagg's survey listed them under four headings: fishermen, mariners, sailors and sailor-servants.[17]

Fishermen: The fishermen were John Batt sen., Dowell Dewstowe, Richard Harle, William Hellyar (Helliar), John and Richard Lavers, and John Lythibie.[18] Dowell Dewstowe, William Hellyar and John Lythibie were old friends, having together witnessed the will of the young sailor, John Blighe of Sheviock, as far back as 1607. Blighe's mother, Elizabeth, became Elizabeth Hellyar. Dowell Dewstowe, Richard Harle and William Hellyar all lived, or owned property, in the borough of Crafthole, and served on the jury of the court leet that was held there twice a year. William Hellyar and Dewstowe served on the jury from 1628 to 1638 and again in 1640. Dowell Dewstowe, who was described as a 'husbandman' in an inventory of 1633, may have farmed the tenement later called 'Dewstowe's', consisting of a house, stable, garden, two orchards and eight acres of fields, on the east side of the road leading from Crafthole to Sheviock churchtown. The tenement lay to the south of Hearle's Parks, perhaps named after an ancestor of Dowell's shipmate, Richard Harle.[19] Dowell's wife was called Johanna. In 1635, Richard Carew the younger granted a building lease to William Dewestowe of Crafthole, 'fisherman', to erect a fishing cellar and palace in Portwrinkle.[20] William, who certainly occupied the tenement called Dewstowe's, described above, may have been Dowell and Johanna's son.

Richard Harle, who was a juror in 1630-2, 1634, 1636-41 and 1641 must have been ashore in April/May and October/November of those years, when the courts were held. Three fields on the road from Crafthole to Sheviock churchtown were known as Harle's Parks. They may have taken their name from the Richard Harle who had been a juror of the court leet of Crafthole in the reign of Queen Elizabeth.[21] They contained just over eight acres of land. Harle served as 'portreeve' (mayor or executive officer) of the borough in 1628 and 1634. William Hellyar was on the jury in 1629, 1630 and 1632. John Lythibie was the tenant of a 'dwelling house courtlage & garden' in Portwrinkle and he was still alive in 1646.[22] He also appears to have owned a fishing 'cellar' there, as he was renting premises for just one shilling, the usual rent for a cellar, in 1634.[23] He was married to Alice and had a son, William.

The fisherman, John Lavers, appears to have come to a tragic end. 'John Lavers of Lantick', which is in St Germans parish, but on the western boundary of Sheviock parish, was drowned on 20 June 1650 along with 'John Rooby'. They were both buried in Sheviock parish.[24] It seems likely that the two men had been shipmates on the *Dayestarr* in 1626: one of the sailors on the ship was named as 'John Ruby'.

Members of the Lavers family had an extensive involvement with fishing in Portwrinkle. Henry Lavers, fisherman, and John and Richard Lavers were all tenants of the manor of Sheviock, living in 'Wrikle' (i.e. Trewrickle), whose harbour-side came to be called Portwrinkle. Henry Lavers leased a dwelling house, courtelage and garden in Portwrinkle in 1649 on the lives of himself and his wife and daughter, both called Sibella.[25] In 1656, the Commonwealth authorities noted that Richard Lavers owed rent of £6 4s. and was to be distrained.[26] The account of John Rawlings, bailiff of the manor, made between 1656 and 1660, shows that Richard Lavers then owed only 1s. 4d.[27] John Lavers the younger shared a tenement with George Winnacott (Winnicot), after whom the quay on the River Lynher was later named. According to the account of 1656, they owed rent of £2 17s. 1d. and were also to be distrained. In 1663, the collector of rents for Portwrinkle prepared a list of properties and their rents. On the back of this he wrote: 'Ann Lavers claimes a house & garden in Wrickle for her life & Thamesine Hitching Sinoby Hoskins but hath pd no rent nor never had any lease for it.'[28] Thamesine and Sinoby may have been related respectively to the shipowner, William Hitchens, and to the mariner, Robert Hoskins.

Mariners: The 'mariners' were the ship's officers, able to read and write, use nautical instruments and read charts. There were three of them: Elias Burne (Barne), George Carkeeke (also Carkett or Carkeet), and Robert Hoskins. One of these was presumably the master of the ship, but which one is not known. Elias Burne and George Carkeeke both lived in Crafthole and both died in the same year, 1633. Burne, or his father, was a juror of the borough court in various years from 1606 to 1630.[29] Burne's wife was called Fanny. She got into trouble in May 1625 for selling bread that had not been weighed.[30] Carkeeke was married to Margery and in July 1625 the couple had a son, Emanuel. Carkeeke served on the jury of the court in 1628, 1631 and 1632.

Neither Burne nor Carkeeke had great wealth. Carkeeke's estate was valued at £13 13s. 6d. The most valuable item by far was his 'wood' valued at £8, followed by 'keeves tubs barrels and other wooden vessels' valued at £1 6s. 6d. No doubt most of these vessels were used for carrying or preserving fish. He also had 'sea implements' valued at 15s. George Carkeeke paid for Richard Beare to act as portreeve instead of him in 1629, so he may have been at sea at that time. The total value of Burne's estate was £11 15s. 10d. Most of the value came from his household goods, including bedding worth £2 12s. and pans and cauldrons worth £2 10s. The only items certainly or probably relating to the sea were '2 coffers' worth 3s.; 'his sea instruments', worth only 3s. 4d.; and 'other implements of ye saye not particularly named', worth just 1s. 4d. One of the two men who took the inventory of Burne's estate in 1633 was Dowell Dewstowe. He was described as a 'husbandman' not a fisherman, indicating either that fishing was a secondary activity for him or that he had given up the sea by then.

Sailor Servants: There were six boys, called 'sailor servants': John Batt jun., Manides Govet, John Harte, Robert Hill, Amos Peter (also Peters), and John Sergeant. Amos Peter lived in Crafthole and served as a juror on the borough court in 1629.[31] John Peters had farmed at Tredis in the latter part of the reign of Queen Elizabeth. The boys' job in Newfoundland would have been to 'dress' (clean and trim) the cod.

Sailors: There were 25 sailors. These were John Burne, Peter Beard (Berd), Emanuel Bowhay (Bohey), Thomas Briggett (Briget), William Broade (Broad), William Giles, Edward Hawke, Francis Hoskin, David Lythiby, Oliver Maister (Maisters), Edward Moreshedd (Mooresheed), Henry and John Naunter (Nauter), Walter Peake, Thomas Peperel, Oliver Peter, John Ruby, William Sergeant, Thomas Tenny, Coranish Tradinham, John and Richard Truscott, Stephen Vinton, Ezekiel Warren, and John Winnicot (Wicot).[32]

Nine of the sailors lived in the borough of Crafthole and served as jurors on the borough court in the period 1628 to 1644. The jurors were Peter Beard, Emanuel Bowhay, Thomas Briggett, William Broade, Edward Moreshedd, Henry Naunter, Walter Peake, Oliver Peter, and John Ruby. Attendance at the courts was compulsory, and fines were imposed on absentees. Edward Moreshedd, who owned a burgage in Crafthole, was fined for non-attendance in 1632, 1635, 1636 and 1643.[33] According to a Parliamentary Survey, he (or his son) was still living in his cottage in Crafthole in 1649. Thomas Briggett was a poor man with a history of debt. In 1618, he borrowed 13s. 4d. from the widow, Christiane Odihorne, to whom he was related. He was unable to repay it and Christiane went to the borough court to recover it.[34] Some forty years later, the bailiff of the manor of Sheviock, John Rawlings, listed Briggett, probably the sailor or his son, in his accounts (1656-60) as owing 14s. for property he then rented in Portwrinkle. In 1691, Briggett's house and 'palace' in Portwrinkle was noted in a survey as being 'fallen down'.[35] The rent had been 2s.

John and Henry Naunter were the sons of John Naunter.[36] In the last years of the reign of Queen Elizabeth and the first years of that of James I, John senior was the tenant of High House in the borough of Crafthole and three little gardens with two closes of land containing about an acre of land. The rent of the property was 9s. 4d. and a capon, later consolidated as 10s.[37] At the court leet of the borough held on 7 August 1612, John surrendered his copyhold lease of High House and its acre of land to the Duchy. Dorothy Arundell, wife of the former rector, Walter Arundell then took out a new lease on the property. From 1607 to 1609, John Naunter senior was a conventionary tenant of the manor of Kerslake, on the eastern boundary of Sheviock, for three lives.[38] His rent was £1 6s. 8d. and two capons a year, suggesting a holding of upwards of twenty acres. In 1634, John junior was renting a property in the manor of Sheviock for 13s. a year.[39] He died in 1648. In his will, made orally before witnesses, he left goods to the value of £34 1s. 6d.[40] His most valuable asset was his 'sea craft' worth £8. His bed and bedclothes were worth £5 10s. His clothes and cash were worth £3. He had the use of two houses. He left 'the hall house' to John Hawke, together with 'two chambers the one over the new house and another over the entry'. He also left Hawke his 'bedd in the house furnished as now hitt is', some other furniture and 'the fish house without the back doore'. Edward Hawke had been one of Naunter's shipmates on the *Dayestarr.* John Hawke may have been Edward's son.

So far as his own family was concerned, Naunter gave to his grown up daughter, Thomazin, 'the little chamber above the hall with the little orchard', and he gave to Thomazin's daughter, Mary, two shillings. He had another daughter, Joane, and a son, George, who also received two shillings each. Presumably they were infants.[41] The residue of his estate went to his wife, Elizabeth. One of the witnesses to the will was Philip Blake, son of the John Blake who had been a member of the consortium that had built the quay at Portwrinkle in 1612.

The sailor, Emanuel Bowhay, and his shipmate, Walter Peake, both lived in the borough of Crafthole, although they did not own burgages. As residents they were also obliged to attend court. Emanuel Bowhay, was fined for non-attendance in 1638 and 1643 and his shipmate, Walter Peake, was fined in 1640. There was formerly a tenement in Trewrickle called 'Peake's tenement'.

Thomas Peperel was married to Thomasyn. In 1625, the couple had a daughter, Margery. They probably had a son as well. In 1707, David Pepperell [*sic*], a hellier (mason), leased a house, garden and meadow in Crafthole.

William Giles may have lived in Sheviock or the neighbouring parish of St Germans. A William Giles bore witness to a nuncupative (oral) will made aboard ship by the young Arthur Peters of Tredis who died on a voyage out of Plymouth at the end of 1654.

John Ruby, as we have seen, was drowned with the fisherman, John Lavers, on 20 June 1650. His body was not washed ashore for some time, and he was finally buried on 9 July. The sailor, William Sargent, could have been the son of the innkeeper at Crafthole, William Sargent, who was the tenant of 'Sargent's tenement'.[42]

Richard Truscott of Sheviock died unmarried in 1655.[43] In his nuncupative will he described himself as a husbandman. He left £4 to his cousin, Joane Harry, and another £4 to Joane, the daughter of his cousin, Thomas Harry. The rest of his goods he left to his cousin Thomas Harry, who was the executor of his estate.

Stephen Vinton was probably a tenant of the manor of Sheviock. A survey of 1691 shows a house and garden in Portwrinkle leased to Robert Vinton, perhaps Stephen's son, on the life of 'Eliz. Lavers (now Vinton) wid.' The rent was 15s. A Bridget Vinton was paying a rent of 5s. for a house in the manor in 1721.

Ezekiel Warren's home may have been the tenement in Sheviock manor known as 'Warrens'. It stretched between the hamlets of Trewrickle and Tredrossel, about half a mile to the north-west of Trewrickle, and contained 48 acres of land including a house. Sometime before 1653, the holding was divided into two. In 1691, one half was let to Robert Harry on the life of William Peake.[44]

John Winnicot [Winnicott] may have been the father of John and George. John junior, described as a husbandman, rented ten land yards (big enough for a fishing cellar) in Crowstone Park in Portwrinkle in 1649.[45] He is shown in John Rawling's account (1656-60) as owing rent of £1 10s.[46] In 1648, George Winnicott built a house and fishing cellar at the quay on the River Lynher, later known as George's Quay.[47]

The dwelling places of Thomas Tenny and Coranish Tradinham are not known.

Wives of Crew Members in the Borough of Crafthole

Between 1628 and 1644, there were eight presentations for minor law and order offences in Crafthole – any major ones being by then reserved for the petty sessions at Millbrook. Half of these involved the wives of crew members of the *Dayestarr*. In 1635, two of the sailors' wives, Agnes Beard and Elizabeth Rooby, together with another woman, were fined a shilling each for refusing to allow the reeve, Richard Harle (also a fisherman on the *Dayestarr* in 1626), to weigh their loaves. In 1636, Johanna, wife of the fisherman Dowell Dewstowe, was fined a shilling for selling apples that had not been weighed. In 1641, Agnes Beard was in trouble again. She was fined a shilling for insulting the reeve, Robert Mitchell, and carrying off a loaf of bread intended to be weighed.

Property of Crew Members

A number of property transactions in the borough of Crafthole involved crew members. In 1628, Richard Crosse transferred to Gilbert Mitchell the former tenancy of the fisherman, Richard Harle (relief 4d.). Gilbert Mitchell then transferred the holding to Simon Rowe, the ship owner of Antony and Stonehouse (relief 4d.). Simon Rowe already held property in the borough. In 1612, he had been entered on the roll as copyholder of one tenement and one burgage (rent 9d.). In 1636, Francis Bickton transferred to George Carkeeke, probably the son of the mariner, a quarter part of a cottage, curtilege and orchard in Crafthole and a quarter part of a small meadow in

Coombe, a part of the borough (relief 9d.). The sailor, Edward Moreshedd, had been entered on the same roll as copyholder of a cottage in one burgage (rent 9d.).

The Building and Fate of the Dayestarr

It is not known where the *Dayestarr* was built. It may have been in Dartmouth, which had 60 shipwrights at that time.[48] However, in the early 1600s many Cornish vessels were built in Holland.[49] The expense of building the ship was no doubt recouped by the profit to be made from the Atlantic cod fishing. Her fate is unknown. But she was not shipwrecked, because her crew of 1626 all returned safely to Sheviock, some to be lost to the sea later. Some sixty years afterwards, Edward Kneebone, a local man who wrote a survey of the Hundred of East in 1684, described 'Wrinkle-cleve' (i.e. Portwrinkle) as 'a large fisher towne, having an excellent key or mould, standing the rage of the South Sea, sufficient to secure all their boats, and good large barks [barques] upon occasion'.[50] But there are no further records of individual ships of the size of the *Dayestarr* giving Sheviock as her home port. Most likely, the danger of navigating through the rock-strewn passage into the little harbour deterred other ship-owners from repeating Hitchens' daring initiative.

122 *The 1840 plan of Portwrinkle shows the Coastguard cottages erected in 1823 (top left) and the E-shaped fishing cellars erected in 1792 (bottom centre).*

Chapter 17

The Fishing Industry at Portwrinkle

Eighteen species of fish or crustaceans are recorded as having been caught along the south Devon coast between 1086 and 1550.[1] The same species were caught off the south-east Cornish coast. These were bass, cockles, cod, conger, hake, herring, ling, mackerel, mullett, mussels, oysters, pilchards, plaice, porpoise, prawns, salmon, skate and whiting. The most important commercial catches up to the mid-1300s were herring and hake.[2] Pilchards, a mature form of sardine, which originate in subtropical waters and swim north to spawn at the entrance to the Channel in the spring, are first mentioned in 1341, when some were imported at Exeter. Their first appearance in the accounts of the Duchy Havener is in the 1360s, when foreign merchants were buying them straight from the fishing boats and paying a fine to the Duchy for 'forestalling' the market. By the late 1300s, pilchards had replaced hake as the most important commercial fish for Cornwall.[3] By then, improvements in the curing process enabled a much higher proportion to be preserved.

Sir Richard Carew, son of the historian, was a keen conservationist and, in his manuscript book of 1628-30, he tells of the over-fishing of herrings in the Tamar:

> For if the fishes of the sea, which god makes so abundantly to encrease, and multiply, bee soe soone consumed in all well inhabited countryes, by the greedy, and disorderly takinge of them; as when they com into harboroughs [harbours] to breed, as within a shorte space there bee very few, if any lefte, of great multitudes which have usually in former times commen into those places; to shed their spaun ... Within these ten or twelve yeeres, wee have had this performed in this river. For heringes comming in hither and yeeldinge reasonable store to the first finders, were within one yeare so spoiled, by the rude multitude of takers, that wee have hearde no newes of them since. Which reason dissuaded mee from adventuringe to beestow chardge in nettes to take them, when this fish came first and was taken fast by my lande, and the nettes dried thereon.[4]

Sir Richard also witnessed the opposite effect, when abstinence from fishing led to an increase in the number of pilchards and hake coming into the river:

123 *This 1795 watercolour by John Swete shows nets drying on Sidmouth Beach, Devon. The Net Park in Portwrinkle was used for the same purpose.*

> surely god out of his greate wisdome, as hee hath ordained the seventh day for his service, makes our own forbearinge to take our fish on that day, beneficiall unto our selves, as wee may perceive by these last yeeres past, when by reason of the dearth of salte, our neighbors forbare the takinge of pilchardes, it broughte after it, greater store of them, and such plenty of hakes, as the like had not been in 40 yeeres beefore.[5]

Salmon also came up the rivers to spawn, and still do. Sir Richard had a conversation with a salmon fisherman in which he was informed that fishermen had for some time been marking the fish on their journey back to sea after spawning, so that they could discover whether the same fish returned in subsequent seasons. He wrote:

> some salmon takers when they founde them over spente by their breedinge, in the river, [were accustomed] to marke them, that they might know them to bee the same, when they tooke them again, which they had let goe beefore, a thing which (they say) they ordinarily doe, and soe sendinge them leane to the sea, at their returne from thence, receive the same again fatt.

In 1648, a local writer, Edward Kneebone, complained that whereas previously the sea around Cornwall had abounded in 'ling, hake, herring, codds, pilchards, and many other sorts', fishing had suddenly ceased to be profitable.[6] But if there was a dearth at that time, it did not last for long. Pilchards and other species continued to be profitably fished in south-east Cornwall, apart from a few barren years, until the mid-1800s. According to the Revd Daniel Lysons, there was still 'a considerable pilchard-fishery' at Portwrinkle in 1814.[7] On 16 December 1713, the steward of the Carew estates at Antony paid £1 to a Thomas Wicket 'for one Hundred of Buckhorne & Forty pounds of Ling'.[8]

124 *Drawing by E.W. Cooke, 1848, showing fishing cellars on the foreshore. Early cellars at Portwrinkle would have looked much the same.*

Curing and Exporting the Fish

The earliest reference to curing and exporting fish from Cornwall is a document of 1202, which granted to certain merchants from Bayonne the pre-emption of all hake and conger *cured* in Cornish ports. The simplest method of curing fish, widely practised in the Middle Ages, was drying them in the sun.[9] But later, various methods of curing in smoke or in salt were introduced, and Bayonne was the most important source of the salt used in the curing process. By the 1400s, fish were the most important Cornish export after tin.[10] According to the historian, Richard Carew, the pilchards

> are saved three maner of wayes: by fuming, pressing, or pickelling.[11] For every of which, they are first salted and piled up row by row in square heapes on the ground in some [cellar], which they terme Bulking, where they so remaine for some ten daies, until the superfluous moysture of the bloud and salt be [soaked] from them: which accomplished, they rip the bulk, and save the residue of the salt for another like service.[12]

The preservative method chosen depended on the destination of the fish. If they were destined for the nearest French ports, the fish could be pickled in brine. But, in the words of Carew:

> Those that serve for the hotter Countries of Spaine and Italie, they used at first to fume, by hanging them upon long sticks one by one, in a house built for the nonce, and there drying them with the smoake of a soft and continuall fire, from whence they purchased the name of *Fumados*:[13] but now, though the terme still remaine, that trade is given over.[14]

125 *Eastern wall of the Portwrinkle fishing cellars erected in 1792-4.*

The salt for preserving the fish was either produced locally in salt pans or imported from Bayonne or one of the other salt-making centres along the western coast of France. These extended from Guérande in Brittany to Bayonne near the Pyrenees in the far South West. However, from 1364 onwards, Bourgneuf Bay came to dominate the European salt-making trade.[15] The Bay lies below the estuary of the River Loire between Brittany and Poitou. The extensive salines there, which made use of a process of evaporation by the sun, were highly productive. This 'Bay salt' was the salt principally used in the later Cornish curing industry.[16]

When fish were cured by salting and pressing, oil, salt and water leaked out. To catch the leakage, a channel was set into the floor of the curing cellar or palace and this drained into a 'train-pit'. When the quay was built at Portwrinkle in 1612, the seiners were obliged to covenant that they would make pits 'for keeping the trayn water in convenient places'. Defaulters were to be fined 6s. 8d.[17] The oil in the train-pit was skimmed off, clarified and sold for various uses, such as lighting, soap-making, waterproofing boats and tanning leather.[18]

126 *The courtyard of the fishing cellars erected in 1792-4. The lower storey was left open for the curing of fish.*

When Wilkie Collins, the novelist, described the curing process at a pilchard cellar in St Ives in 1850, it had hardly changed at all from Carew's day, except that the period in which the pilchards lay 'in bulk' had been extended from ten days to 'five or six weeks'.[19] The work of curing the fish was done by women. The old salt, which had been used in the curing process, together with any bruised or damaged pilchards, was also used as manure.[20]

Packing for Export

After the pilchards had lain for sufficient time in bulk, they were taken out, washed clean in saltwater and packed for export in hogsheads.[21] These were straight-sided casks, bound with withies. Those that were to contain pickled fish were made leak-proof, but those that were to contain salted and dried fish were deliberately made leaky. Richard Carew described how the fish were preserved for the export trade in his day:

> Then those which are to bee ventred for Fraunce, they pack in staunch hogsheads, so to keepe them in their pickle … and [those destined for Spain and Italy] after they have bene ripped out of the bulk, [raised] upon sticks, and washed, they pack them orderly in hogsheads made purposely leake, which afterward they presse with great waights, to the end the traine may soke from them into a vessell placed in the ground to receyve it.[22]

On the left of the courtyard of the 18th-century fish-cellars at Portwrinkle stood the salt-house.[23] Long beams were slotted into its outer wall.[24] Large pressing stones or 'bullies' were hung onto the ends of the beams. These weighed about one hundredweight and had an iron hook leaded into them. One or two were preserved in the cellar by the late Bert Pengelly. The pressing process continued for about a week, the casks being headed up three times with extra fish as their contents settled.

The Export Merchants

In the 1500s and 1600s, most of the casks were exported to the Catholic countries of France, Spain, Italy and Ireland, which observed 'fish' days in accordance with the Church's teaching. In the early 1600s, much of the export business was in the hands of Dutch merchants. One Antony Wiet, who was shown as living in Sheviock in 1641, may have been connected with this trade. But English merchants were not far behind. One of the Plymouth merchants who exported pilchards to France was Richard Trevill, who exported them to La Rochelle and Bordeaux. In 1635, his name appears in the records of the court leet of East Antony, because he failed to attend the court.[25] The Trevills acquired Rame Barton, and many members of the family are buried at Rame, including Richard, who left £5 4s. to be distributed annually to the poor.[26] Thomas Hitchens (or Hutchens), the son of William Hitchens of Sheviock 'merchant', was another who was engaged in the fish export trade.[27] His ancestor, another William Hitchens, owned Sheviock's fishing barque, the *Dayestarr*, in 1626.[28] Plymouth exported 16,924 hogsheads of pilchards in 1632 and 8,520 in 1634.[29]

Before the Civil War, a hogshead of pilchards fetched about £1 on the export market. After the War, prices rose substantially, and reached £4 a hogshead in the 1670s.[30] Dr Whetter has traced the export of pilchards by Cornish merchants to Venice, Leghorn and Naples back to 1648.[31] In the late 1700s, the Napoleonic wars prevented exports to most of the continent. But a new market was found for the fish in the West Indies, where pilchards were used to feed the Negroes on the plantations. Because of the great

127 *The loft of the Portwrinkle fishing cellars was used for the storage of nets and for the housing of seasonal workers.*

heat there, the fish had to be cured twice before packing. When exports to Europe started again in 1815, the main market was again Italy, and especially Naples.[32] Other ports where the fish was landed were Ancona, Civita Vecchia, Genoa, Leghorn, Trieste and Venice.[33]

Local Consumption

In Cornwall, pilchards were eaten fresh by poor people 'chopped up with raw onion and salt, diluted with cold water, eaten with the fingers, and accompanied with barley or oaten cakes'.[34] They were also salted or smoked to be eaten during the winter months, 'each cottage, on average, laying by about 1,000 fish'.[35] The inventory of the goods of Mary Hitchens of Sheviock, widow, who died in 1640, includes 'a fishe howse & pallace' valued at £6; and the will of the fisherman, John Naunter of Sheviock, who died in 1648, refers to his 'fish house without (i.e. outside) the back doore'.[36] In May 1719, Mary (Molly) Wicket, one of the kitchen maids at Antony, laid out 5s. 'for oatmeal & fish', probably to feed the estate workers.[37] In 1800, William Jenkin, steward of Anna Maria Hunt of Lanhydrock, wrote that 'there are a great number of families in this neighbourhood who never provide themselves with any other kind of food but barley bread, potatoes and salt pilchards from one week to another'.[38]

The Portwrinkle Fishermen or 'Wricklemen'

The Huers and Seiners

Pilchard fishing was one of the main activities of the Portwrinkle fishermen from the mid-1300s until the 1840s. To spot the shoals of pilchards, 'huers' (callers or signalmen) were positioned along the cliff-tops. The custumals (records of manorial customs) of Stokenham manor on Start Bay in Devon provide evidence from the early 1300s of the use of huers to spot the fish and to alert the fishermen to its presence.[39] Richard Carew described the operations of the seiners and huers in the late 1500s:

> To each (seine) there commonly belong three or foure boates, carrying about sixe men apeece: with which, when the season of the year and weather serveth, they lie hovering upon the coast, and are directed in their worke by a Balker, or Huer, who standeth on the Cliffe side, and from thence, best discerneth the quantitie and course of the

> Pilcherd:[40] according whereunto, he cundeth (as they call it) the Master of each boat (who hath his eye still fixed upon him) by crying with a lowd voice, whistling through his fingers, and wheazing [certain] diversified and significant signes, with a bush, which hee holdeth in his hand.[41] At his appointment they cast out their Net, draw it to either hand, as the Schoell lyeth, or fareth, beate with their Oares to keep in the Fish, and at last, either close and tucke it up in the Sea, or draw the same on land, with more certaine profit, if the ground bee not rough of rockes. After one companie have thus shot their Net, another beginneth behind them, and so a third, as opportunitie serveth. Being so taken, some, the Countrie people, who attend with their horses and paniers at the Cliffes side, in great numbers, doe buy and carrie home, the larger remainder is by the Marchant [merchant] greedily and speedily seized upon.[42]

In 1612, when the quay was built at Portwrinkle there were three principal seines in operation: Braye's Company, consisting of Richard Bray, John Bake and other shareholders; Blake's Company, consisting of John Blake, Richard Harry and others; and Warne's Company, consisting of Thomas Warne, Richard Sargent and others.[43] They were small co-operative ventures, with members of the syndicates leasing the necessary storage cellars and curing palaces.

Fishermen are always at the mercy of the elements, and the Sheviock parish registers sadly record the deaths of many of them. John Lavers of Lantic was drowned on 20 June 1650 along with John Rooby (Ruby).[44] It seems likely that the two men had been shipmates on the *Dayestarr* in 1626. In July 1651, Nicholas Williams of St Germans and his son, Robert, were drowned at Wrickle Cliff and buried in Sheviock. John Prin, John Bone, and Richard Rundle and his son, Nicholas, were all drowned on 16 June 1718. In February 1729, Henry Lavers and Luke Tawe lost their lives at sea. Their bodies were not recovered for some time, and they were buried at the beginning of March. At the beginning of October 1749, John Bickle, Walter Avant and John Stear were all 'unhappily drowned', perhaps victims of the wreck of the *Two Friends*.[45]

By the late 1700s, the harbour had become dilapidated, and the small co-operative seines had ceased to function. What was needed was the injection of new capital to rebuild and clear the harbour, to build a large cellar and palace, and to fit out the seines in a proper way. In 1792, Reginald Pole Carew agreed to put up the capital to restore the quay at Portwrinkle and clean out the sand from the harbour basin if other undertakers would rebuild the cellars and equip the fishing seines. He therefore sought tenders from contractors for the building of the cellars and the fitting out of the seines. One would-be consortium consisted of two Cawsand fishermen, two innkeepers from Dock (Devonport), a tobacconist, a cooper from Liskeard, two farmers from St Germans, and Thomas Bewes of Trewrickle. Bewes was the only local man, and he was already the tenant of fishing premises in Portwrinkle. However, this group suffered from a lack of capital. The second would-be contractor was Jon Binns of Looe, whose offer to build cellars, a salt house, and a new pier, seemed too good to be true. In September 1792, Pole Carew contracted with Thomas Lockyer, a Plymouth sailmaker, and Edward Cock, a gentleman of Mevagissey. These two also had a wealthy silent partner, Thomas Daniel of Truro, who took up six of the 16 shares in the undertaking. They agreed not only to build a substantial cellar and salt house, but also

> within the space of one year ...[to] fit out one pilchard sean [seine] from Portwrinkle ... with proper boats nets and other materials and a sufficient number of men thereon according to the custom used and observed on the pilchard fishery at Mevagissey.[46]

Cock's plan was to recruit seiners from Mevagissey to do the fishing. However, these fishermen made objections

> against the Rock which lies at the Entrance of the Quay as they must frequently go in and out at Night fishing [and] they are in great danger of loosing [*sic*] thaire lives and Craft.[47]

Pole Carew took note of these objections and contracted with Thomas Steedman of Plymouth Dock, the builder of the new quay, to create an entrance passage 30-foot wide by blowing up the rocks barring the passage way.[48]

The contractors were also required to 'cure and save all the fish to be caught by them with such sean [seine]'. They were to pay their landlord a royalty of 1s. for each hogshead of pilchards cured and another 1s. for each hogshead of train oil produced from the curing process. If other seines started to operate, these royalties would be reduced to 9d. The seiners were given licence to dry their nets in the Net Park. For this privilege, a royalty of 5s. would be payable for every 100 hogsheads of pilchards caught and cured.

When a shoal of pilchards was taken at sea, it was first mainly enclosed by a large seine net stretched between two boats; then a smaller boat with another net, called a 'stop' net, stopped up the escape route from the enclosure. The boats would usually go out in a team of three boats. The team consisted of a principal boat, some 33ft long, which carried the seine net and had six oarsmen and a helmsman; and a follower (or 'volyer' in local speech), some 22ft long, which carried the smaller stop net, mooring ropes and grapnels, and had four oarsmen.[49] Finally there was a tender called a 'larker', 'lurker' or 'lurcher'. This little boat, about 15-18 ft long, carried the master seiner (unless the huer on shore carried out this function), and another fisherman. Its object was to help drive the fish into the enclosure, and then to carry the fish ashore if they were caught at some distance from the land.[50]

Increasing Use of Drift Nets

After the Restoration of 1660, seining companies had begun to complain about single boats using drift nets to catch pilchards before they could swim close to the shore. In

1662, they persuaded Parliament to make it illegal to use drift nets from 1 June until 30 November (the pilchard fishing season) within a league and a half of the shores of Devon and Cornwall. In Portwrinkle, by 1722 the quay had become so dilapidated that it was impossible for the seining companies to use their boats. Instead, Philip Palmer, John Harvey and William Bray went out in single craft with drift nets to catch the pilchards in spite of the prohibition. In 1723, after the repair of the quay, the use of drift nets gradually declined at Portwrinkle.

In 1792-4, Reginald Pole Carew had invested a lot of capital in repairing and rebuilding the quay and cleansing the harbour basin at Portwrinkle. Thomas Lockyer, Edward Cock and Thomas Daniel had also spent a considerable amount of money in building large new pilchard cellars and equipping and manning the new fishing seine from Mevagissey. In spite of this investment, they found it hard to make a profit. Thus, when they found five fishermen from Looe using drift nets within the prohibited zone during the pilchard season, they determined to make an example of them. Quoting the 1662 Act, they forced the five fishermen to make a public apology and 'promise never to repeat the like offence'.[51]

According to the 1841 census, William Pengelly, described as a fisherman (aged 55) and his wife, Elizabeth, were living in Trewrickle. John Pengelly, 35, described as an agricultural labourer, was living nearby in Portwrinkle. Another fisherman, John Andrew, aged 70, was also living in Portwrinkle. A second John Andrew, aged 40, described as an agricultural labourer, also lived there. Probably the Pengellys and the Andrews listed in the census return were fathers and sons, and made their livings combining fishing with potato growing. The only other resident of Portwrinkle described as a fisherman was Anthony Davey, aged sixty-five.

Account Books of the Later Portwrinkle Seines

Account books of the Portwrinkle seines from 1846 to 1917 are kept in the Cornwall Record Office in Truro, and one other is the property of the Pengelly family of Portwrinkle.[52] They begin when pilchard fishing was nearly over in Whitsand Bay and was being replaced by mackerel fishing. In 1846, for example, one of the seines caught mackerel worth £103 1s. 8d, but pilchards worth only £12 18s. 0d. In the following year, takings from mackerel amounted to £129 13s. 9d. and there were no proceeds from pilchards at all. But exceptionally, in 1869, along with the mackerel, an 'exceedingly large shoal' of pilchards was caught.

The Poor Man's Endeavour *and the* Union

In 1846, one of the fishing seines was called the *Poor Man's Endeavour* (also the name of the boat). In 1861, the gross receipts of the seine amounted to £41 16s. ½d. The captain's poundage was £2 1s. 0d. leaving net receipts of £39 15s. ½d. The expenses

128 *The fishing seine called the* Poor Man's Endeavour *operated in c.1840-80. In this photo, Joseph Pengelly (seated right) is paying the men their shares during the season. The tall man on the left is Joseph's brother, Theophilus. The third man from the right (standing) is George Andrew.*

of the season amounted to £15 12s. 6d., leaving a profit of £24 2s. 6 ½d. to be divided among the shareholders.

In 1849, a new mackerel seine called the *Union* was formed to work in concert with the *Endeavour*, although sometimes it worked alone. The members of the new seine were Mr and Mrs Eastcott (4 shares), John P. Landrey (2 shares) and his brother, Richard (1 share), who ran the *Carew Arms* inn at Sheviock, and one share each for Joseph Landrey (a butcher in Crafthole), Mathew Earle, John Westlake, James Clements, and John Giddy, Samuel Southern and John Andrew junior (all described as agricultural labourers, living in Crafthole). The Landreys were also the principal shareholders in the *Endeavour* seine. The Clements family also had shares in both, as did the Westlake family.

From 1857 to 1861, the *Union* seine suffered a series of losses and the treasurer wrote in the account book, 'A Better year Next I Hope By the Blessings of God'. His prayers were answered. In 1863, the seine's receipts amounted to £45 0s. 4d. and its disbursements totalled £37 4s. 8d., so that a profit of £7 15s. 8d. was recorded. The expenses included £15 15s. for a new boat; £8 18s. for a new seine net; £2 for sails and spars; £1 for cellar rent; 7s. 6d. for quay dues; 12s. for bark; and 2s. 6d. for coal. The bark and coal were used for an operation called 'barking the seine'. This meant purifying the seine net by immersing it in a hot bath containing oak bark.

In 1869, new regulations required numbers to be painted on each boat and its sails, and this was duly done.

New Boats and Seines

When new boats were acquired, the postman was paid to paint the names on the boats. He was paid 1s. in 1870, 2s. in 1873, 2s. 6d. in 1876, 6s. in 1877, and 4s. in 1880. At this time the usual pay for a day's work by a labourer was 2s. A new boat, the *Daring*, was introduced in 1875; another, the *Fox*, in 1876; and another, the *Stag*, in 1881. Each was a separate seine or syndicate, and they operated sometimes in concert and sometimes independently until 1905. The principal shareholder in the *Daring* was Joseph Landrey (9 shares). Others were John Pengelly, John Andrews, Joseph and James Westlake, and William Clements. Shareholders in the *Fox* were Theophilus and Joseph Pengelly (2 shares each) and single shares to John Pengelly senior, John junior, John and Henry Andrews, Charles Dawe, Richard Giddy, William Letten, George Stribling, Joseph Channings (landlord of the inn at Crafthole), William Westlake and William Haimes. Shareholders in the *Stag* were Joseph Landrey (11 shares), and one each to John Andrews, James and William Westlake, John Sargeant, and Harry Hoskin. In 1905, all three seines became part of a new enterprise, the Mackerel Seine Company.

In the late 1800s, syndicate losses in several years exceeded gains. For example, in 1881 one seine lost £25 8s. 5d.; and in 1884 another lost £22 2s. 10d. There were also losses in 1886 and 1887; but a profit was recorded by one seine in 1888 giving it an average profit for the 3 years of 1s. 10½d. per share. In 1890, each shareholder in one seine received £1 10s. 3d. after payment of poor rates and income tax. In 1898, one of the seines paid out 11s. 6d. per share.

The Last Years of the Seine Boats

As part of the new Mackerel Seine Company, the same boats were still working up to the First World War. In 1905, the total receipts of the company were £21 0s. 10d, but no dividend was paid, though a credit balance of £12 10s. 2d. was carried forward to 1906. In 1906, residual expenses took care of the previous credit balance. 1907 was a better year and a dividend of 12s. per share was paid; in 1908, the dividend went down to 8s. 2d. per share; in 1909, it went down further to 4s. 2d. In the latter year, an amount of 15s. 6d. was expensed on 'getting seine up the cliffe after shooting at shoal of Bass and getting seine home'. No dividends were paid from 1910 to 1916.

129 *A mackerel-fishing boat at Portwrinkle in October 1909. Tourism was then beginning to overtake fishing in commercial importance and this scene was printed onto a postcard.*

In 1914, the Government paid the company £18 'for troops billeted in cellars for 2 months'. In 1916, the *Daring* was sold for £5 to Mr J Pryn of Looe. In 1917, Messrs John Pearse of Plymouth auctioned off all the remaining boats, seines and other gear for a total of £64 12s. 0d. A final dividend of £1 4s. 2d. per share was paid out. After the First World War, the seines as such no longer functioned. The big shoals of fish were caught further off shore by steam trawlers and drifters operating out of Plymouth, Looe and Newlyn. Such vessels could fish all the year round. The era of the seine collectives, with boats powered by sail and oar, was over.

130 *A mackerel-fishing boat in the 1920s. The tall man leaning on the net is Theophilus Pengelly. The picture may have been posed for a souvenir postcard.*

The Fishing Families

Although the old seine collectives had been wound up, the Andrews, Dawe and Pengelly families continued to fish on their own account. In 1951, Mrs Andrews, then 79, told Crispin Gill of the *Evening Herald* that in the old days in the mackerel

131 *Theophilus Pengelly carrying his fishing box up the hill from Portwrinkle harbour. It is marked with his own distinctive sign.*

season, fishermen would come into the hamlet from 'all over the place' and sleep in the net loft of the old pilchard cellar. She could remember Betsy Dawe, an old woman, living at the top of the steps on the outside of the cellars. They had a 'huer', whose shout would alert the men to a shoal coming in.[53] According to Mrs Andrews 'You could hear Charlie Dawe holler right down to Downderry'.[54]

Each family had its own fleet of fishing boats. The Pengelly boats were the *Fearnot*, a 17-foot crabber; the *Ripple*, a 20-foot general purpose fishing boat; the *Onward*, like the *Ripple*, but faster; the *Pearl*, an 18 foot crabber, and one of the first to be fitted with an engine (in 1921); the *Sweetbriar*, a 15-foot boat for seine netting. They also owned the *Edna*, a 13-foot rowing boat used as a tender and for inshore fishing from Wacker Quay on the River Lynher. In 1950, they had another small craft built for them, the *Lendor.*[55] The Andrews family had three boats, the *Elsie*, a 22-foot boat for netting pilchards; the *Annie*, of 18-foot; and the *Vixen*, a small rowing/sailing boat. The Dawe family originally had four boats, the *Lady Beatrice*, named after Lady Beatrice Pole Carew (the original owner of the Chalet at Portwrinkle), the *Myrtle*, the *Hermit*, and the *Rover*.

Competition

The greatest competition to the Wricklemen came from the fishermen of Looe. According to the late Bert Pengelly, one of the most remunerative catches was whiting; and when the Wrickle boats were anchored and the whiting were biting well, the Portwrinkle fishermen would not haul in their lines until the Looe boats had gone by, so not disclosing their catch. Instead they would have their tea – saffron cake and non-alcoholic cold drinks. It wasn't until the advent of the thermos flask that they could drink hot tea.

Fishing during the Second World War

The Second World War gave a new, though temporary, impetus to on-shore fishing with lines put out from the beaches between Portwrinkle and Kerslake Sandaway. Fishing from boats, including inshore trawlers, still took place in Whitsand Bay during the war years. But for a long period after the evacuation of Dunkirk in May/June 1940, boats were not allowed to fish at night. There were also fewer boats fishing during daylight hours, because many of the regular trawlers had been requisitioned

133 *Wilfrid Pengelly beginning the construction of a lobster pot in March 1966. He is using withies grown at Trewrickle.*

132 *A willow plot at Trewrickle. From the earliest times, willows have been cultivated for their supple branches (called withies), used to make baskets, lobster pots etc.*

134 *Wilfrid Pengelly with a completed lobster pot.*

for minesweeping and other naval duties. As a result, the bay was teeming with fish at this time. A seven-year-old evacuee from south London, Terry Leather, who was then living at the *New Inn*, Crafthole, recorded his experiences of fishing during the war:

> We usually had three lines, and having baited them [with sand eels] it was time to put them out to sea.[56] … There is a crop of rocks which form part of the bay which the locals called Blackyball Point. When the tide goes out these rocks are left high and dry … The tide usually took about one and a half hours to flow on to Blackyball Point. After about an hour, Uncle Wilf would pick up the lines in turn, as he could feel when a fish was hooked.[57] Then he would say to me, 'There's one on this line, Tel'. It was not long before I could tell when a fish was on the line myself. I can still remember the thrill of catching my first bass – I was so excited. It was a wonderful sight to see a beautiful silver bass thrashing about coming through the surf.

We would also go night fishing … Due to the war and the blackout we were not allowed to use lanterns, so we used shielded torches instead. Usually we would pick a spring tide and a clear night, with a full moon. When the moon was out, it lit up the beach like day. We were never alone on the beach fishing at night, as it was popular with the locals. Sometimes we would put the lines out early evening, then go down to the beach at first light to take the fish off. These lines, called 'boulters', were anchored into the beach with large stones

In my later years, Uncle Wilf would let me go fishing with my best friend, Chuffy, and other boys from the village …[58] On one occasion, my friends and I had been down to Blackyball Beach baiting night lines, and putting them out later after we finished school. We would then go back down early morning to check for fish. We did this for two nights running and we hadn't caught much at all. On the third night, my friends decided to give it up for a while. Me, being very keen, decided to give it one more try.

We had a little dog called Lucky. That afternoon after school I went off with Lucky down to the beach. It was a spring tide, so the lines were out a long way. I decided I would move one line very close to Blackyball Point. The next morning, I called Lucky and off we went to the beach to check the lines. The two lines that were out a long way failed to produce once again. … When I located the third line, I couldn't believe my eyes. There was a fish on every hook and this line had 15 hooks on it. One of the fish was a 22lb conger eel … I now had the task of getting [the fish] up the cliff and home … When I arrived home, Auntie Hylda and Uncle Bill had just woken up to the sound of me coming in. Auntie Hylda called out, 'Is that you, Tel?'[59] I was so excited that I ran upstairs and in my excitement said, 'Look what I've caught!' and tipped all the fish out onto the bedroom floor. 'Oh, my, what a catch!', said Auntie Hylda, 'but not on my bedroom floor!' The news of my catch caused quite a stir in the village. The local fishermen were out in force next day, with the result that many more good fish were caught.

135 *Terry Leather on the cliffs above Blackyball beach. Terry was evacuated from London during the Blitz of 1940, and lived with the Hearn family at the* New Inn, *Crafthole, where he was taught to fish.*

136 *Bert Pengelly (top left) and his son, Don, at the tiller of their fishing boat,* Onward, *in 1984.*

On the Beach at Lantic

In the summer time, all the family would go up to Lantic Farm and go down on Uncle Herb's beach.[60] On a spring tide, rocks that you could not get at on a normal tide were now exposed. Uncle Wilf knew just where to look for the large eating crabs. … We used to go out with just our swim suits on and wearing canvas shoes, so that we could climb over the rocks. Uncle Wilf used a long steel rod shaped into a hook at one end. This enabled him to get right into the rock crevices where the crabs would get. We used to catch some wonderful crabs. We also used to go catching prawns in the large rock pools under the seaweed, using a large net with a long handle. We used to work the net through the weed, and every so often empty the net of prawns.

137 *Don Pengelly standing beside the* Onward *in Portwrinkle harbour in 1984.*

Post-war Fishing

In January 1950, out in their boats the *Pearl* and the *Sweetbriar*, and also having the use of William Dawe's boat, the *Iris*, the Pengellys took a catch of four tons of bass off Freathy and landed them on the beach there. They took one and a half tons of the catch and the seine net back to Portwrinkle by small boats; but before the remainder could be collected later that same day, the weather deteriorated. The remaining two and a half tons had to be carried up the cliff path, and the sharp fins of the bass scraped the men's backs raw. In February 1952, the family caught 29 cwt of bass off Kerslake Sands, but there was no market for them, so they were sold locally for a mere eight pence a pound. In April 1952, the Pengellys took a catch of five tons of bass. After the fish were caught a storm blew up and over four tons had to be taken up the cliff. Nearly a ton was sold, door to door, around Millbrook. Even in its hey-day, commercial fishing was a seasonal business, and so as a sideline the fishing families of Portwrinkle cultivated potatoes.[61]

Today, there is little fishing from Portwrinkle. Just one boat goes out regularly. In summer, some 230 to 240 crab pots are laid out and collected. Until 1998, many of the crab pots were still made by hand from withies cut from the willow plantation between Trewrickle Farm and Pool Farm Cottage. In winter, a Portwrinkle boat bases itself in Looe for the purpose of flat fish netting. However, commercial fishing in Whitsand Bay has given way to fishing for sport, and the Bay is reckoned to have some of the best bass-fishing beaches in the country.

138 *Good-sized crabs, like these caught by Peter Lobb of Crafthole, can still be found in the sea near Portwrinkle.*

139 *Smuggler's Cottage had been built for Thomas Helman in 1795. This photograph, taken c.1890, shows (L to R) Joseph, Mary, Walter and Theophilus Pengelly. Mary with her water jugs is ready for a trip to Blizer's well.*

Chapter 18

The Village of Portwrinkle

Until the development of Crafthole in the 14th century, the biggest concentration of fishermen, whether full-time or part-time, was at the village of Trewrickle, not far from the seashore. Two acres of land near the seashore, to the south of Trewrickle village, had long been used by the seiners of the Abbey of Tavistock. Henry Dawney confirmed the grant of this land to the Abbey between 1174 and 1206, but then took it back again in exchange for some land that he owned in Tavistock. Today the willow trees growing in a small plot at Trewrickle are the only reminder of the fishing and farming families who once lived there. The willows are still cropped annually to provide withies for various uses.

The Construction of 'Cellars' and 'Palaces' at Portwrinkle

In the early medieval period the villages of coastal parishes were often sited at some distance from the seashore, both to shelter the houses and cottages from the wind and to be out of sight of marauders. Some of the inhabitants of these villages gained a part of their livelihood from the land and another part from taking fish and other products from the sea.[1] Hence they have been called 'fishing farmers'. For their fishing operations they needed places near the shore to store their boats, oars, sails, nets, fish, salt, barrels, anchors, etc., and also places in which to cure the fish. The solution adopted was to erect 'cellars' (store houses) and 'palaces' (curing houses) near to the seashore. These cellars and palaces were the earliest structures erected on the foreshore at Portwrinkle. Families throughout the parish, not just those living in Trewrickle or Crafthole, leased ground from the lord of the manor to build such structures. The Dawneys were probably issuing such leases from the earliest times. Indeed the reference to 'Sir John Dawney's seines' in 1337 and the boat purchased by men of the 'tithing of Schevyekk' in 1349 strongly suggest that this was so. Edmarus and Osbernus Gogo, mentioned in Henry Dawney's charter issued between 1174 and 1206, may also have had cellars of this kind. The first tenant mentioned by name in a surviving lease is William Bray. He was the occupant of 'one cellar and palaice' in 1605.[2]

The dimensions of the cellars are known from records of Sheviock manor in the 17th century. In Portwrinkle, the 'cellar and howsse' built by Edward Blighe, 'husbandman' (farmer) in 1635 was 'in length thirtie two feete' and in breadth 'with the walles eighteen feete'.[3] The cellar let to Emanuel Gaich in Portwrinkle in 1663 measured 19 feet in one direction.[4] The rent was 2s. That let to Walter Crapp sometime before 1675 measured 30 feet.[5] The rent was likewise 2s. Such cellars would have been suitable for storing boats between eighteen and thirty feet long, as used by seiners right up to modern times.

A 'palaice' was a covered building with an open side and curtilege (courtyard), in which the curing process was carried out. In 1605, Richard Carew granted a 99-year lease to 'Olyver Wallys' of Sheviock to build a cellar and palace.[6] Oliver Wallis's new premises were bounded on the east and north sides by the lands and tenements of William Bray, on the west by the common way leading from Trewrickle to Portwrinkle and on the south side by Bray's cellar and palace.[7] Oliver, who lived at Trewin, paid a rent of 5s. plus a capon, or one shilling in lieu thereof. The lives named in his lease were those of his son, Oliver, and his grandsons, William and Ferdinando. These three were still the tenants in 1634.[8] In 1635, Edward Blighe, was renting a palace next to his cellar that was 45 feet long and 18 feet broad.[9]

By the 1630s, habitable cottages were also being erected amongst the cellars and palaces. In 1633, Richard Carew the younger granted a lease to Richard Lavers for the 'dwellinge house late erected att Portwinkle with a pallace & garden adioyning'.[10] The rent was 16s. Rentals survive for 1634, which indicate that at least 16 premises (houses, cellars and palaces) were being rented in Portwrinkle. Oliver Wallis the younger was renting his father's former premises. William Odihorne was leasing premises on the lives of his brother, John, and his sister, Emblyn, for 6s. 8d.[11] William Harry leased what may have been a house and cellar for 6s. 8d. (life of Elizabeth, his sister). John Naunter, a fisherman, and his sons, John and Henry, were also renting premises for 6s. 8d.[12] John died in 1648 and in his will referred to his 'fish house without (i.e. outside) the back doore'. Dorothy, the widow of the rector, Walter Arundell, and her sons, Gabriel and Emanuel, were renting premises, probably in Portwrinkle, for 5s. John Chub, his brother, James, and his sister, Love, were renting another property at the same rent, as was Lawrence Bligh, on the lives of Joane his wife and Joane, his daughter. Emanuel Gaich was also renting premises for 5s. Richard Bray was paying 3s. 4d. for a property. Three tenants were paying 2s. a year, probably for cellars. These were William Bray, John Rundell (by the lives of Richaund, his wife, and Henry, their son), and William Rundell (by the lives of Davy and Oliver, his sons). Finally, four tenants were paying just 1s. a year, no doubt also for cellars. These were Richard Bake (two premises), Margery Warne (by the lives of Thomas, her son, and Mary, her daughter), Rundell and John Letheby (by the lives of Alice, his wife, and William, their son).[13] In 1635, Richard Carew granted William Dewestow of Crafthole, 'fisherman', a lease to build a cellar and palace on land that had formerly been leased to Lawrence Bligh's widow, Joan.[14] This stood next to the cellar and palace rented by William Odihorne.[15] The rent was 5s.

In 1646, William Rundell, who was described as a 'mariner' (ship's officer) took a reversionary lease from the executors of the late Sir Richard Carew of the dwelling house, curtilage and garden then in the tenure of the fisherman, John Letheby. The rent was 10s. The lives named were William Rundell and his wife, Thomasin. In 1656, George Winnacott, after whom George's Lane in Sheviock churchtown is named, and John Lavers were renting premises in Portwrinkle and had got into arrears.[16]

The first rental after the Restoration, dating from 1663, lists mostly houses or cottages, with only one unattached cellar. Quite possibly the Parliamentary authorities had been unable to collect rent for the cellars. According to the rental, Oliver Wallis junior held the old tenancy, which was now described as a 'house and palace'. He held it by the lives of his son, Peter, and Katherine Hooper of Saltash. The rent remained the same, except that the capon had been replaced by an extra 1s. on the rent. Rents at this time were fixed at a rate of 1s. per yard of the front of the house. Thus Simon Tozer held a tenancy of a house and garden in Portwrinkle with a frontage of ten yards and paid a rent of 10s. He held his lease by the lives of Joane, his wife, and their sons, Edward and Simon. David Reed held a tenancy of a 'dwelling house garden and courtlage or pallas yard for the saving pilchards and other fish', with a nine-yard frontage.[17] It stood in the Net Park on the east side of Symon Lavers' premises and he paid 9s. a year. Thomas Austen rented a house and palace with a 16-yard frontage and paid a rent of 16s. He held by the lives of his wife, Mary, and their son, John. Emanuel Gaich rented the cellar referred to above by the lives of his son, John Stephen, and his daughters, Agnes and Mary. William Richards rented a house and garden with a six-yard frontage by the lives of his wife, Susanna, and their daughter, Ruth, for 6s. a year. On the back of the rental the collector has written 'Ann Lavers claimes a house & garden in Wrickle for her life & Thamesine Hitching Sinoby Hoskins but hath pd no rent nor never had any lease for it'.[18] Altogether, therefore, the premises for which rents were being paid in Portwrinkle in 1663 were: three 'houses and palaces', two houses and gardens, one cellar, and the dwelling of Ann Lavers, making just seven premises in all.

The Large Cellars at the Quay

One group of cellars erected before the Restoration was the 'fower cellars and two pallaces therunto adjoyning & appertayning & being under the cliffe & within the key at Portwrickle ... and which late were in the tenure or occupation of Thomas

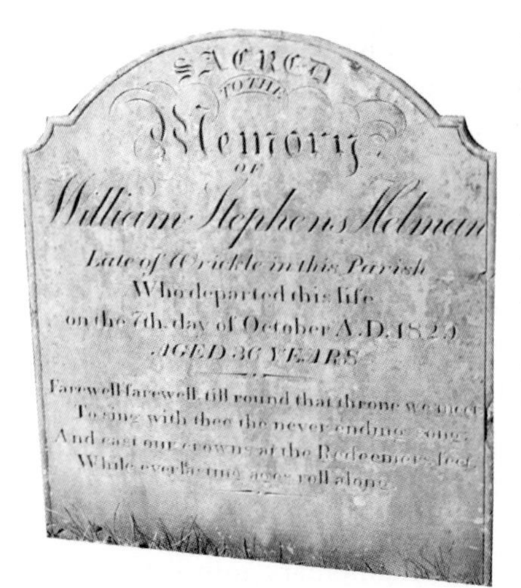

140 *William Stephens Helman 'late of 'Wrickle' died in 1829, aged only 36.*

Smith gent ... and Nicholas Carkeek.' In 1673, these premises, large enough to house the boats and equipment of an entire seine, were leased to Nicholas Smith, Thomas's son, at a rent of 11s.[19] The Smiths were gentleman farmers at Liscawn. Nicholas Carkeek was also a farmer in the parish. The George Carkeek who had been a ship's officer on the *Dayestarr*, was probably his father or grandfather. In 1691, Benjamin Dunning, a Plymouth merchant, was renting these same four cellars and two palaces at a rental of 11s. by the lives of himself, his wife, Elizabeth, and two others. In 1712, Sir William Carew, recently down from Oxford, granted a new lease to Dunning at the same rent of the 'four ... cellars & two pallaces ... under the cliffe and within the key at Portwrinkle'.[20] But they were now described as 'decayed'. The condition of the lease was that they should be rebuilt within one year. The consideration for the grant was 'one guynea of gold & twelve quart bottles of good French clarett'.

A Large Fishing Village

By 1691, Portwrinkle could reasonably be described as a large fishing village. A rental of that year shows that Richard Wallis had taken over Oliver Wallis's old tenancy, again described as a 'cellar and palace' at 6s. a year.[21] This stood between the sea and the house that became known later as Captain Browne's house. Robert Harry had taken over William Harry's 'cellar and palace' at 6s. 8d. Elizabeth Jane, widow of the parish clerk, and Thomas Harvey jointly rented another cellar and palace for 2s. Henry Lavers rented another with a house attached by the life of John Lavers junior and John Holman junior, at a rent of 8s. John Harvey was renting a cellar and palace for 1s. a year by the life of his son, Thomas. In addition, there were a number of 'houses and palaces' in the village. The three most expensive were let at 16s. each. Bridget Lavers occupied one with gardens attached.[22] She also rented two cellars and linhays for 7s. each. Mary Austen, widow of Thomas, continued to rent his former house and palace for 16s. Jone Rundell, widow, and William Chubb rented the third at the same rent. These two also rented another one for 10s. Thomas Sone rented a house and palace for 15s. Emanuel Carkeet (or Carkeek), rented 'houses & pallace', by the lives of himself and Jane Carkeet, for 11s. 8d. Oliver Wallis junior rented another house and palace, called Slyn's House, for 10s. John Dyer (a cooper) and Robert Warren each rented a house and palace for 9s. Another house and palace was normally let for 6s., but was then without a tenant.

141 *Smuggler's Cottage in Portwrinkle c.2006. The slate roof replaced the previous thatch in the 1930s.*

'Captain Browne' had taken over a large fish cellar in Portwrinkle, 'late Jane's', in 1689, at a rent of 6s. He may once have been the master of a sailing barque. He was paying £1 for 'houses and courtlege' in 1691. There were a number of other houses and cottages. Robert Vinton rented a house and garden (by the life of Elizabeth, his wife, née Lavers) for 15s.; Robert Harry and Katherine Odyhorn paid 10s. for ten yards of premises (by the life of John Odyhorne) as did Mary Winnacott. Silvester Blake had a house for which he was paying only 2s. a year. Symon Lavers rented a house and cellar for 1s. 4d, a tenancy that was later taken over by William Lavers junior. A note in Richard Blighe's survey book of 1699 stated that William Lavers was to 'repayr his Houses at Portwrinkle or be prosecuted'.[23] In 1710, the cottage that is now called 'Smuggler's Cottage' was let to the sailor, Richard Grills. By 1727, it was inhabited by 'widow Grills', who was in arrears with her rent.

Most, if not all, of the houses and cottages in Portwrinkle were thatched. A manorial account shows that the thatcher, John Clinnick, was paid 1s. for repairing the house of Ann Winnacott (perhaps Mary's daughter) in 1726. He used 12 sheaves of reed and 300 spars on the job. The fact that the buildings were thatched and were exposed to the south-westerly gales, meant that many of them had a short life. The cellar and palace of 'Dewstone' (presumably a descendant of Dowell Dewstowe a fisherman on the *Dayestarr*), which had been rented for 5s. a year, was marked 'washed down' in the 1691 survey. In the same survey, Simon Tozer's house, which, with its garden, had been worth 10s. a year, was marked 'down'. In the survey book of 1699, a note states that Simon Tozer is to repair his house and pay his rent.[24] Similarly, in the 1691 survey, William Bray's house, worth 9s., was marked 'in decay', though it was later repaired. Susan Richard's house was also marked 'in decay', and Walter Crapp's 30-feet of building, rented by the lives of Stephen, Agnes and Mary Geach (Gaich), was marked first 'in decay' and then 'down'.[25] Emanuel Carkeet's second house and palace, which he had rented for 2s. a year, was marked 'fallen down'. However, the house was repaired and re-let to Thomas Brigget, but was again marked 'washed down'. The cellar and palace belonging to the Crafthole scrivener, Robert Honney, which had been worth 6s. 8d., was also marked 'washed down'. Walter Peter's cellar and palace, which had been worth 2s., was marked 'in decay'. Edward Truscott's house and palace, which had also been rented for 2s., was marked 'in decay' and then 'washed down'. By the end of the 1600s, then, more than 30 buildings connected with the fishing industry stood in Portwrinkle, and another ten or so were in decay or had been washed away.

Sir William Carew's Renovations

Sir William Carew undertook numerous minor repairs of the quay at Portwrinkle as well as a major reconstruction in 1723. He also encouraged a wholesale rebuilding of the village of Portwrinkle. In 1712, as well as leasing to Benjamin Dunning the cellars and palaces within the quay mentioned above, he leased to him the cellar and palace formerly in the possession of Richard Lavers.[26] In the following year, Sir William leased to Gabriel Randell, a 'sarge [serge] maker' from Liskeard 'all that one dwelling house cellar and courtledge … formerly in the possession of George Browne deceased'.[27] This was the same Captain Browne who had rented a large cellar in 1689. It was a condition that Randall, Francis Fox (a mercer from St Germans) or John Edwards, the former hind of the Carew estates in Sheviock and Antony, should repair the premises.

142 *The sea front at Portwrinkle, c.1900. Smuggler's Cottage, on the right, was then thatched. The old pilchard cellars, built in 1792-4, are at the extreme left.*

The rent was 20s. At the same time, he leased to those three men two decayed cellars and palaces situated between the sea and the late George Browne's dwelling house and cellars.[28] Richard Wallis (in 1691) and William Lavers, both deceased, had previously occupied the premises. The rent was 6s. 4d. In the same year he leased a dwelling house and garden in Portwrinkle to John Edwards for 2s.[29] In 1715, he leased a house and palace to the cooper, John Dyer, for 9s.[30] These premises had formerly been leased to David Reed and Hugh Hooper, deceased. By 1770, this house was described as 'down'.[31] In 1715, he also leased to Stephen Edwards of Maker, 'baulker' the 'house and pallace with a courtledge adjoyning to the Crowstone Park in Portwrinkle late in occupation of William Odyorne deceased'.[32] The rent was 10s. In the same year he leased to John Harvey a cellar and palace then in the tenure of Thomas Harvey, and previously in the tenure of Marjory Warren [Margery Warne].[33] The rent was 1s. In 1718, he leased to Thomas Ellery and Thomas Edwards of Cawsand a 'cellar and palace now fallen into decay' and the four-acre field called Crowstone Park. The rent was 8s. In 1722, he leased a house and palace in Portwrinkle to the same Thomas Edwards at a rent of 10s. plus two capons.[34] The consideration was 'one broad piece of gold commonly called a Jacobus'. In 1726, he leased two dwelling houses, a cellar and palace to Mary and Martha, the daughters of Walter Sone (also Sun), 'mariner' (ship's officer), who was the current tenant.[35] These premises had originally been let to Emanuel Carkeek, whose daughter, Jane, was Walter's wife. The rent was 11s. 8d. The houses stood to the east of the house formerly occupied by Richard Lavers. Mary Sone was still living in this house, with its attached cellar and palace in 1770.[36]

By 1726, there were eight houses, 12 palaces and 11 cellars in Portwrinkle.[37] Thomas Ellery had taken over Captain Browne's house and palace and also Oliver Wallis's old cellar and palace. Thomas Edwards had taken over Benjamin Dunning's cellars and palaces within the quay and another house and cellar (late Skinner's). John Rundle (Rundell) had succeeded his mother, Jone, in her house and palace. John Dyer and Robert Warren still occupied their same houses. Walter Sone and his family were living in the old house and palace of his father-in-law, Emanuel Carkeeke. William Chubb had moved into Slyn's house, previously occupied by Oliver Wallis junior. Martha Roach was living there in 1764.[38] Stephen Edwards now occupied Robert Harry and Katherine Odiorne's old cellar and palace. William Bray continued to occupy his old cellar and palace, now repaired. Thomas Harvey, the reeve and collector of rents for the manor, who had been named as a 'life' in his father John's 1691 tenancy, now rented a cellar and palace in his own name for 2s. In 1730, Sir William Carew let to Oliver Neilder, yeoman, and John and Hugh Littleton, a 'house, cellar and palace (now in decay and ruinous) with a garden'.[39] Henry Lavers had rented these premises in 1691 and Edward Bligh had been the tenant before him. The rent was 8s., as before. In 1736, Sir William let the house now known as 'Smuggler's Cottage' to John Prynn.[40] Mary Horwell (also Harrell), who sold beer to men working on the quay in 1731, may have kept a tavern in Portwrinkle. She was renting a house there for 8s. 8d. in 1770.[41]

Sir William Carew died in 1744 and after his death the number of dwellings in Portwrinkle contracted sharply. In 1764, John Edwards' house (perhaps Dyer's old house, as the rental was 9s.), was described as 'burnt down'.[42] In 1770, Benjamin Dunning's decayed cellars and palaces were said to be 'down'. So, too, were Stephen Edwards' cellar and palace, Thomas Edwards' house and cellar (late Skinner's), Thomas Harvey's cellar and palace, and John Harvey's cellar and palace.[43] Thomas Pride's Survey and Map of 1775 describe only about half a dozen buildings.[44] These included what appear to be two or three 'cellars and palaces'. William Bray was shown as the tenant of a field behind the houses, called the Net Park, 'by order of his office being Reeve of the Manor'.[45] In addition, there were four houses arranged side by side along the road running northwards from the shore. These were rented respectively by John Rundell (probably a descendant of the Rundell listed in the 1634 rental); Thomas Ellery and Thomas Edwards of Cawsand; Robert Warren; and Oliver Neilder. In 1764, Rundle's house was occupied by Harvey and another tenant (rent 16s.), and Thomas Edwards' house was occupied by Joan Edwards (rent 11s.).[46] Thomas Edwards' house was converted into a 'bathing shed' by Lord Eliot in the summer of 1788.[47]

Reginald Pole Carew's New Leases

In 1783, Reginald Pole Carew let to William Reskilling, fisherman, a 'decayed dwelling house with the backlet and garden therunto belonging' for 10s. a year.[48] The condition was that Reskilling should build a 'substantial and convenient dwelling house' there within two years. He also let a 'house, courtlage and garden' built on a nine-yard plot in Crowstone Park to a fisherman called Henry Coffin, for 9s. a year.[49] This stood on the north-west side of the large cellar and palace newly erected in 1792-4 (see below). By 1788, what had been Captain Browne's house was described as a 'decayed dwelling house cellar and courtlage ... formerly in possession of one George Brown deceased ... and commonly called Brown's Walk'.[50] In that year, the ground was let to Paschoe Spuddle, mariner, for only 7s. on condition that he should build a good substantial dwelling house there within three years. The site was next to the house that been in the possession of William Lavers, deceased.

The New Fish Cellars: When, in 1792, Reginald Pole Carew agreed to restore the quay and harbour at Portwrinkle, he also agreed to lease to Thomas Lockyer of Plymouth, sailmaker, and Edward Cock of Mevagissey, gentleman, 'such piece or parcel of waste land or ground ... on the clift at Portwrickle as [they] shall think necessary and convenient for the purpose of erecting ... cellars and other buildings'. For their part, Lockyer and Cock agreed to build 'one or more good and sufficient cellar or cellars ... proper and convenient in every respect for the curing and saving of pilchards'. They agreed to spend £200 on the buildings. Having as a silent partner Thomas Daniel of Truro, they were well placed to do so. The lease was for 99 years. The building stone was to be supplied by Pole Carew 'from the ruins of such old buildings situate at Portwrinkle ... as have fallen into hand'. He also agreed to allow Lockyer and Cock to open quarries on his land to extract any further building stone that they might need.[51] This is the pilchard cellar whose shell can still be seen at Portwrinkle. The land it was built on had formerly been in the occupation of Philip Palmer (the western part), William Chubb (the eastern part) and Thomas Bewes (the southern part).

The new cellar was built on a north-south axis, with wings at each end enclosing a courtyard. The lower of the two storeys on the long side was open to the west where it faced the courtyard. The floor of this side, covered with sea-rounded pebbles, was where the fish were cured. The new building was completed by 1794, and in August of that year a consortium of merchants and tradesmen, including Lockyer and Cock, was formed to take on the lease of the premises. They were tenants in common with a perpetual right of renewal. The annual rent was £2 17s. With the harbour now functioning again, seine boats and crews fishing regularly, and new enlarged cellars erected for curing the pilchards, a new period of relative prosperity began. In 1804,

143 *Thatched cottages at Portwrinkle c.1900. A cottage like this was converted into a 'bathing machine' by Lord Eliot in 1788, the first indication of the coming tourist industry.*

144 *These cottages at Portwrinkle were marked on Thomas Pride's map of 1775. The white buildings were the home of the Dawe family in the 1900s.*

200 hogsheads of pilchards were caught, the best catch ever recorded at Portwrinkle.[52] In 1813, the lease of the cellars was sold to a widow, Mrs Kitt, the innkeeper at Crafthole.[53]

In 1820, a new consortium of Plymouth merchants took over the lease of the fish cellars built by Lockyer and Cock.[54] They described themselves as 'Proprietors of the Portwrinkle Fishery'. One of the lives named on the new lease was that of Edmund Lockyer, Thomas's son. He was now 36 years old and a captain in the East India service. In 1834, this lease was assigned and the whole business was sold at auction at the Exchange, Woolster Street, Plymouth, to another consortium of merchants. The sale included three seine nets, two seine boats, a follower (in local parlance 'volyer'), two 'lurchers', a small boat, 36 oars, 36 grapplings, 25 warps and grappling ropes, a stop or tuck seine, an old seine, 10 'mawns' (large two-handled baskets), 10 'flaskets' (long shallow baskets), buoys, and press poles (for pressing down the lids on the casks of fish). It also included old and new salt for curing the fish, and the copper vat used for a process known as 'barking' the seine nets.[55] Isaac Nicholls of Plymouth, a member of the new consortium, was the occupier in 1840. In 1845, the cellars changed hands again.[56]

By this time, the upper enclosed storey of the Lockyer and Cock fish cellars was being used to house the families of migrant workers. They came to help with the fishery in the season. This began in July, reached its peak in August, September, and October, and tailed off towards the end of the year. The fireplace openings along the upper wall could still be seen in 2000. This storey was also used as a net loft. Along the northern side of the fish cellar were the facilities for 'barking' the seine nets. At the end of a fishing season the seine nets with their constant exposure to seawater and fish would require curing or purifying. This was accomplished by lowering the nets down from the upper storey into a copper vat of boiling water below, to which the oak bark was added. The tannin in the oak acted as a purifying agent. If properly looked after in this way, a seine net would last for 60 to 70 years.

145 *Ellen Pengelly outside her grocer's shop in Portwrinkle. Note the advertisement in the window for 'teas'.*

Smuggler's Cottage stands on the sea front to the east of the cellars.[57] Beneath the floor of the cottage are two cavities, big enough to store kegs of contraband liquor. The initials 'TH' and the date '1795' are carved above the front door.[58] The initials probably stand for Thomas Helman. In 1812, Reginald Pole Carew let to Thomas Helman (b.1747) of Sheviock, yeoman, 'a Messuage Tenement or Dwelling House and Garden' in 'the Village of Wrickle' at a rent of 5s. a year. The 1812 lease may have replaced an earlier one to Helman. The tenant, Helman, was probably the same person as Thomas 'Hillman', who was the tenant of Net Park in 1809-33 and of part of Trewrickle in 1820-1. He was dead by 1834. According to the 1812 lease, the previous tenants had been successively Richard Grills (lease of 1710), John Bowhay, and John Prynn (lease of 1736). The 1812 lease was on the lives of Helman (age 65), his wife Elizabeth (49), and William Stephens Helman (19), their son. After the last life, it was re-let to the fisherman, William Pengelly (b.1781). The Pengellys acquired the freehold in about 1949.

The map and survey made for the purposes of tithe apportionment in 1840 shows the five houses in the village occupied respectively by William Pengelly (Smuggler's Cottage), John Andrews junior and John Burrows, Hester Littleton, John Pengelly and Thomasin Beaver, and William Blatchford. It also shows Coastguard Cottages, then just 20 years old.[59]

The Grocer's Shop. Nelly (Mary Ellen), wife of Theophilus Pengelly, kept a grocer's shop in Portwrinkle, at the house called Penlea, from *c.*1925 to 1948.[60]

146 *Watercolour (mid-1700s) showing contraband goods (probably brandy and tea) being landed at Whitsand Bay.*

CHAPTER 19

Smuggling, Coastguard and Wrecks

SMUGGLING

Many of the residents of the parish of Sheviock were involved in the smuggling business in the late 1700s and early 1800s. A traveller to Cornwall in 1799, George Lipscomb, wrote, 'Smuggling seems to constitute a regular trade, among the lower orders of people, on this coast – and some hundreds gain their livelihood by it.'[1] An account of an attempt to land smuggled goods at Portwrinkle in December 1784 was later told by one of the participants, Samuel Drew, to his son. Samuel was 19 at the time of the incident. In 1830, his son included the story in a biography of his father.[2] By then, Samuel had become a celebrated Methodist preacher and the author of several books.[3]

> Smuggling, at the time of Mr Drew's apprenticeship, was more common in Cornwall than it is at the present day. Very few esteemed it a breach of moral duty and to engage in it was not considered dishonourable. The ingenuity frequently displayed in baffling pursuit and evading detection, gained the applause of the public, who regarded the officers of the revenue as enemies of the common good. This was an occupation quite congenial with Samuel's adventurous spirit.
>
> Notice was given throughout Crafthole, one evening about the month of December 1784, that a vessel laden with contraband goods was on the coast, and would be ready that night to discharge her cargo. Such services were liberally compensated, in consideration of the risk and personal exposure; and this was no trifling inducement to a youth who had to maintain himself upon eight shillings a week.
>
> At night Samuel Drew, with the rest of the male population made towards the port [Portwrinkle]. One party remained on the rocks to make signals and dispose of the goods when landed; the other, of which he was one, manned the boats. The night was intensely dark; and but little progress had been made in discharging the vessel's cargo, when the wind rose, with a heavy sea. To prevent their vessel from being driven on the rocks, the seamen found it necessary to stand off from the port, and thus increased the hazard of the boatmen. Unfavourable as these circumstances were, all seemed resolved to persevere and several trips were made between the vessel and the shore.

The wind continuing to increase, one of the men belonging to the boat in which Samuel sat had his hat blown off, and in striving to recover it, upset the boat, and three of the men were immediately drowned. Samuel and two or three others clung to the boat for a considerable time: but finding that it was drifting from the port, they were obliged to abandon it and sustain themselves by swimming. They were now about two miles from the shore, and the darkness prevented them from ascertaining its direction. Samuel had given himself up as lost, when he laid hold of a mass of floating seaweed, which afforded him a temporary support. At length he approached some rocks near the shore, upon which he and two of the men, the only survivors of the seven, succeeded in getting; but they were so benumbed with cold, and so much exhausted with their exertion in swimming, that it was with the utmost difficulty they could maintain their position against the force of the sea which sometimes broke over them.

147 *Samuel Drew in the early 1800s. He was apprenticed to a shoemaker in Crafthole and nearly drowned while helping to land contraband spirits at Portwrinkle in 1784.*

Their perilous situation was not unperceived by their comrades; yet their calls for help were, if heard, for a long time disregarded. When the vessel had delivered her cargo and put to sea, a boat was despatched to take them off; and now finding in what condition Samuel and his wretched companions were, after having been three hours in the water, and half of the time swimming about, the others endeavoured to compensate by a show of kindness for their previous inhumanity.

Life being nearly extinct, the sufferers were carried to a neighbouring farmhouse and the inmates compelled by threats to admit them. A fire was kindled on the hearth, and fresh faggots piled on it, while the half drowned men, who were placed in a recess of the chimney, unable to relieve themselves, were compelled to endure the excessive heat which their ignorant companions thought necessary to restore animation.

One of the party, supposing that fire within would be not less efficacious than fire without, and believing brandy to be a universal remedy, brought a keg of it from the cargo landed, and with the characteristic recklessness of a sailor and a smuggler, knocking in the head with a hatchet, presented them with a bowlful.

'Whether we drank it,' observed Mr Drew, on relating this most perilous adventure, 'I do not know. Certainly not to the extent recommended or I should not now be alive to tell the tale. My first sensation was that of extreme cold. Although half roasted, it was a long while before I felt the fire, though its effects are still visible on my legs, which were burnt in several places. The wounds continued open more than two years, and the marks I shall carry to my grave. After leaving the farmhouse, I had to walk about two miles through deep snow to my lodgings. When I think of the complicated perils of that night, I am astonished that I ever survived them.'

Another method adopted by the smugglers was for a ship, usually from the Channel Islands or France, to approach the English shore and drop overboard small kegs (called 'tubs') of contraband spirits. On-shore smugglers would then row out to the spot marked by buoys and 'creep up' (pull up) the tubs with a small grappling iron.

In 1823, a coastguard station was established at Portwrinkle to prevent contraband tubs being landed or crept up, and immediately saw action. A letter dated 22 September 1823, from the lieutenant in charge of the Looe station refers to the Portwrinkle gig:

> The tubs thrown overboard by the boats chased by the Looe and Portwrinkle gigs on the morning of the 7th were about 24 in number. The smugglers have since swept up and landed 6. A smuggling party is now assembled in the neighbourhood of Crafthole, and also at a place called Hay [*sic*] Farm for the purpose of being ready to attempt the landing of the goods now under water.[4]

The tenant of Haye Farm, from 1792 to 1832, and of part of the coastal tenement of Blazor, from 1809 to 1821, was Robert Warren, who also rented premises at Portwrinkle.[5] He and his family had been running an inn at Bryant Hayes in Crafthole until 1775.[6]

On 8 October, the Looe customs officer, again assisted by his colleague from Portwrinkle, reported on another attempted landing:

> The C.O. [customs officer] Port Wrinkle assisted me in creeping for the tubs, and, as the moon rose, so as the mark buoy could be seen, we crept up the smugglers' creep line, and continued to creep till 12.20 am. We recommenced creeping at 10 next morning, and at about 2 pm succeeded in creeping up 58 tubs.[7]

In 1831, the *Cornubian* of 10 June reported a violent confrontation between officers of the 'Preventive Service' and the inhabitants of Sheviock:

> *Affray with Smugglers*
> On Tuesday morning, Mr Foot, of the Preventive Station at Cawsand, lodged in the Customs Warehouse at this port 46 kegs of brandy and geneva [gin], which were captured in the presence of a party of smugglers at ½ past 11 o'clock on the previous night at Sheviock.[8] The force of the smugglers was apparently about 30, but in consequence of the hour this could not be exactly ascertained, nor their persons identified. Mr Foot and four men called on them to surrender the kegs, and alternately employed persuasion and threats to prevail on them to do so, but the smugglers set them at defiance, and challenged Mr Foot and his men, and swore vengeance on them if they made any attempt at capture. They were armed with bludgeons, and on Mr Foot's proceeding to seize the kegs they made a sharp resistance. Mr Foot, his son, and his three men (a fifth being left in charge of the boat) then fired several times on them, and it is possible from the number of shots that several smugglers must have been wounded: one, Mr Foot apprehends, must have been killed, as it appeared to him that the ball entered his mouth, and he dropped. They were heard to say 'Come let us take up the poor fellow,' and after that moved off. One man, named Sampson Trevan, is taken, and after an examination before the Magistrates on Tuesday, was remanded to a future day. He is now in custody on Board the *Arrow*, tender to the *Harpy* cutter.[9] It is not known whether the party was composed of persons belonging to the neighbourhood or from more distant parts. Some appeared to be seafaring men.'

The smuggler, Sampson Trevan, may be the same person as the 'Sampson Trevan, agricultural labourer' living in Crafthole at the time of the 1841 census. If so, he would have been in his mid-20s when arrested for the smuggling offence. He might have been a great-grandson of Sampson Trevan, Sheviock farmer, who married Frances Lord in about 1765.[10] The Lords were then the innkeepers of the inn at Crafthole (the modern *Finnygook Inn*). John Trevan (b.1776), was the farmer at Sheviock Barton from 1809 to 1832. In 1825, he was appointed constable of Sheviock. In 1831, when the smuggling incident took place, Dinah Kitt was the landlord of the inn at Crafthole.

In 1833, another smuggling attempt took place. A revenue officer reported that '21 tubs are taken by the Cawsand crew in the galley, *John*, of Cawsand; the remainder are still sunk off the Eddystone. They are part of a 'crop' belonging to John A ... of Downderry, "who was seen near Crafthole, lying by a hedge, drunk".'[11]

These accounts make it clear that a large number of young men from the parish were members of the landing parties, and that the locals farmers were giving them assistance.

THE COASTGUARD

The Coastguard Service[12]

The Office of Customs and Excise established the Coastguard Service in 1822. Its original purpose was to prevent smuggling. In 1831, the Service was placed partly under the control of the Admiralty, and it became wholly their responsibility in 1856. By this time smuggling had been brought more or less under control and the duties of the coastguard were widened to encompass the protection of the shores of the United Kingdom and lifesaving. The men recruited were usually former Royal Navy personnel who could be called up again on the outbreak of war. In 1823, a coastguard station was established at Portwrinkle and the terrace of six houses still called Coastguard Cottages was completed. The station officer lived in the westernmost cottage, in front of which stood a watch house and a flagpole. In 1868, a boathouse, which housed two coastguard cutters, was built above the pilchard cellars. The coastguards patrolled seven miles of coast, from Freathy Shute in the east to the River Seaton in the west. During the First World War, the coastguards were reinforced by Sea Scouts, but in the Second World War, assistance was provided by elderly local men. The coastguard boats were sold in 1924.

The Service operated a policy of appointing coastguards who were not local, and the names of many of the men living there show how effectively this policy was implemented. Lt John Sergeant RN was the chief officer from 1835 to 1845. During his time the station officer (SO) was Alexander Hamilton from Scotland.[13] The four RN seamen reporting to him came from Ireland. These were Edward Kennedy, John

148 *Coastguards were first stationed at Portwrinkle in 1823. This posed picture from c.1902 shows two of them supposedly on lookout duty.*

Murphy, Richard Perry, and James Waterson. In 1851, the SO was Lt. Peter Inskip RN; the chief boatman, John Holton, came from Polperro.[14] The boatman, William Litton, came from Brixham. All the other boatmen, John Reardon, Michael Flynn and Francis Beatty, came from Ireland.

In 1923, HM Coastguard became a civilian force and control was transferred from the Admiralty to the Board of Trade. Its primary role was changed to lifesaving rather than anti-smuggling. In 1926, the number of regular coastguards at Portwrinkle was reduced to two, the former coastguard cottages were vacated and two new semi-detached ones were built for them on the cliff road, with a flagpole in front of them.[15] It flew the red and gold Board of Trade flag with a crown in the centre on days when exercises were held. A new watch house was built on the cliff edge below the old pilchard cellars.[16] In 1932, the two regulars were re-assigned elsewhere and Portwrinkle became an Auxiliary Coastguard station

149 *This picture of the Portwrinkle coastguards may have been taken on 9 August 1902, the coronation day of King Edward VII. The chief boatman appointed in 1900, Henry Stimpson, and his wife, Mary, had two daughters, Victoria and Priscilla. The coastguard, John Horn, appointed in 1899, and his wife, Louisa, had four children, Harold, Henry, Flossy and Louisa.*

150 *The coastguard cottages at Portwrinkle in 2008.*

under a 'volunteer-in-charge'. Wilfrid Pengelly, a local fisherman and potato grower, was appointed the first volunteer-in-charge. He retired in 1961. Auxiliary stations were responsible for maintaining watches when thick and rough weather persisted or when persons were known to be 'standing into danger'. However, during the Second World War, a watch was maintained continuously day and night. The boundaries of the Portwrinkle station now extended from Cawsand (Plymouth breakwater) in the east to Polperro in the west, and they were linked to the regular stations at Rame Head and Looe by telephone. After 1932, the Portwrinkle station was manned by the volunteer-in-charge and two other auxiliaries. In the same year, a Coast Life Saving Corps of volunteers was formed to assist the regular coastguards in lifesaving. At Portwrinkle, some 20 members of this Corps formed the rescue rocket crew who used breeches buoys and other equipment to rescue those in danger along the coast.

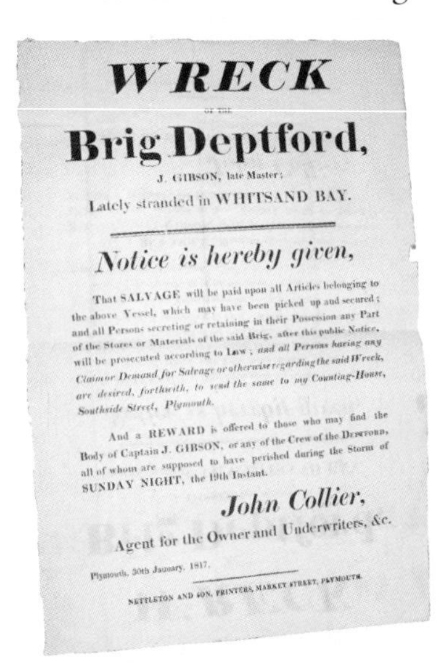

WRECK

OF THE

Brig Deptford,

J. GIBSON, late Master;

Lately stranded in WHITSAND BAY.

Notice is hereby given,

That SALVAGE will be paid upon all Articles belonging to the above Vessel, which may have been picked up and secured; and all Persons secreting or retaining in their Possession any Part of the Stores or Materials of the said Brig, after this public Notice, will be prosecuted according to Law; *and all Persons having any Claim or Demand for Salvage or otherwise regarding the said Wreck, are desired, forthwith, to send the same to my Counting-House, Southside Street, Plymouth.*

And a REWARD is offered to those who may find the Body of Captain J. GIBSON, or any of the Crew of the DEPTFORD, all of whom are supposed to have perished during the Storm of SUNDAY NIGHT, the 19th Instant.

John Collier,

Agent for the Owner and Underwriters, &c.

Plymouth, 30th January, 1817.

NETTLETON AND SON, PRINTERS, MARKET STREET, PLYMOUTH.

151 *Posters were circulated in coastal villages to encourage people to hand in wreck goods to the authorities. This one relates to the* Deptford, *wrecked in 1817.*

LIFESAVING AND WRECKS

Lifesaving

In 1849, life-saving apparatus was installed at Portwrinkle. This included rocket-propelled lines and breeches buoys. Originally, the apparatus was housed in a small building in Donkey Lane at the eastern end of the coastguard cottages and was wheeled to where it was needed on a hand cart. In 1868, the boathouse was built above the pilchard cellars. The cliff-rescue wagon, which was by then pulled by horses, was also housed there and the life-saving apparatus was moved there from its old site.[17] In *c.*1920, the horses were replaced by a lorry, and in 1931 all the lifesaving apparatus was moved to a new building in Crafthole (demolished in 1965).

The regular full-time coastguards had been assisted by volunteers and auxiliaries since 1901. When assistance was required by a vessel in distress, the volunteers were assembled as a 'rocket party'. At one time there were 21 of these civilian volunteer members of the Coast Life-Saving Corps at Portwrinkle. They were called out in an emergency by the firing of a maroon. They practised their rescue operations regularly. Mrs Theodora Colwill recalled,

> Every now and then the rescue team would have to go out on the cliffs at Trethill for practice. Many village folk would follow the large wagon loaded with the men and equipment. ...There was great excitement when the rocket was shot out to sea and a man was rescued by the breeches buoy. When the maroon was fired at Portwrinkle and the signal went up to say there was a real emergency, everyone in the parish was on the alert.

Between 1872 and 1960, the Portwrinkle coastguard rendered assistance to 24 vessels and one aircraft.[18] The coastguard post at Portwrinkle was closed in December 1984.

Wrecks before 1900

In the days of sail, many ships were wrecked in Whitsand Bay, but records are scant.[19] Occasionally the churchwardens' accounts record the burials of drowned people whose bodies were washed up on the parish shores. Often the reeve or bailiff accounted to the lord of the manor for timber or ropes salvaged from wrecks. In 1749, a vessel

152 *This unnamed ship was wrecked in Whitsand Bay in the late 19th century.*

called the *Two Friends* was wrecked below Crafthole. Mr Ellis, who was probably the steward of the Carew estates, William Ellis, witnessed

> a vast number of people some with axes others with hatchets, horses and short crooks breaking to pieces and carrying away everything. Elizabeth Hurrell of Wrinkle in the night heard guns to fire and people crying out.[20]

The Wreck of the *Chancellor*

The SS *Chancellor* was a steam trawler. She set off from Plymouth on Monday, 15 January 1934 intending to fish for a few days around the Eddystone lighthouse.[21] Two days later a south-westerly gale blew up and thick fog set in. The skipper decided to head for home. After sailing for a couple of hours the trawler ran onto rocks east of Portwrinkle. The ship became wedged in a rocky outcrop and so stayed upright. The captain ordered the crew to assemble on deck, and to let off flares and burn bedding and clothes to attract attention. The Plymouth lifeboat arrived on the scene, but the sea was too rough to bring the lifeboat close enough to the *Chancellor* to get the men off. Fortunately, Wilfrid Pengelly at the Portwrinkle coastguard station had seen the fire on the foredeck. The life-saving teams from Portwrinkle and Rame Head rushed to the coast near the wreck and rigged up a breeches-buoy from the shore to the ship. They rescued the whole crew in less than an hour. The Board of Trade awarded their Silver Shield to the volunteers at the two coastguard stations for the most efficient coastal rescue of 1934. This was the first time this shield had been awarded for a Cornish rescue. To celebrate the event, a grand dinner was held at the village hall in Crafthole (now Coombe Barn Cottage), with a barrel of cider supplied by Leonard and Dorothy Elmhirst from their estate at Dartington. The *Chancellor* was washed ashore at high water spring tides at the bottom of Wiggle cliff (Treninnow Beach), four miles east of Portwrinkle. The wreck was wedged against a high rock on her port side. Parts of the wreck could still be seen in the year 2000.

153 *Wilfrid and Annie Pengelly with their daughter, Margaret, beside the wreck of the* Chancellor *in 1934. The coastguards from Portwrinkle and Rame rescued every member of the crew.*

154 *Members of the volunteer life-saving team practising with a breeches buoy in the 1930s.*

Crash-Landing of a Wellington Bomber

On 24 July 1942, a Royal Canadian Air Force squadron, based at RAF Partington in Yorkshire, took part in a daylight raid on the German battleships *Gneisenau* and *Prinz Eugen* at Brest. One of the Wellington bombers that took part in the raid was *Wimpy V for Victor*, whose crew consisted of one Englishman, two Scotsmen, one Australian, and two Canadians. Fighter opposition on this raid was particularly heavy, and Sergeants Craig, McNeil, Leonard, Bain, Hughes and Higgins in *Wimpy V for Victor* were engaged by four Me109s. They were pursued across the Channel until just south of the Eddystone lighthouse. Higgins, the rear gunner, and Hughes, the front gunner, each shot down one of the German planes. But many bullets from the Messerschmitts also hit the Wellington and its crew. Higgins was wounded in his legs and thighs as his turret was put out of action. McNeil, the co-pilot, was wounded by cannon shot in his foot. It was five days before his 20th birthday. The fabric of the plane caught fire, and Bain, the wireless operator, struggled with, and finally extinguished, the flames. The plane was losing height steadily, and at four p.m. the pilot, Craig, was forced to crash-land his aircraft in the sea near the shore west of Tregantle Fort.

155 *Wilfrid Pengelly at the coastguard hut overlooking Portwrinkle beach. The shield awarded for rescuing the crew of the* Chancellor *can be seen through the window.*

156 *Life-saving volunteers from Portwrinkle on the wagon used to carry their rocket and life-saving equipment. The wagon was used to rescue the crew of the* Chancellor *in 1934.*

Margaret Pengelly and her uncle, Theophilus, had been watching the stricken aircraft. Theophilus called his brother, Wilfrid, the coastguard volunteer, and the two of them dashed to the harbour and boarded their boat. Thus, as the crew were scrambling into their dinghy, the motor boat was putting out from Portwrinkle to pick them up. To hasten progress, one of the brothers steered and the other assisted the engine by rowing. They soon reached the bomber's crew and took them safely on board. Back at Portwrinkle, the two wounded airmen were taken to hospital and the villagers gave the other four hot food and dry clothes. Later the aircrew were commended in despatches and the Pengelly brothers were given an award by the RNLI. The evacuee from London, Terry Leather, remembers the same incident:

> I remember going off down to the beach … to see the plane. We could only see it from a certain distance as the police and security men were guarding it, due to the fact that there was so much live ammunition on and around the plane … I picked up some empty shell cases as a souvenir. In the coming days the plane was dismantled piece by piece and taken away.

157 *A company of the volunteer Life-Saving Corps practising rocket drill in 1952. L to R: Edward May, Wilfrid Pengelly, Bert Pengelly, Alec Davey.*

On 28 May 1969, the co-pilot, Hugh S McNeil, with his wife, made a return visit to Portwrinkle.[22] They were taken back to the place where the aircraft had ditched 27 years earlier.

The Wreck of the MV *Kodima*[23]

The most recent wreck at the time of writing was that of the MV *Kodima*, a Maltese-registered cargo ship. On 1 February 2002, she was on passage from Norrkoping, Sweden, to Libya. She was carrying timber planks, some of which were stored in her holds and some on deck. As she was proceeding down the English Channel, she was struck by gales, beginning at Force 8 but gusting up to Violent Storm 11, with waves between 19ft and 27ft high. At about 1900 hrs, her deck cargo shifted to port, causing a list of 15 degrees. By 0450 the following morning the list had increased to 40 degrees. When the ship was some 28 miles from Falmouth, her engines and generators failed. The captain called for assistance and he and the crew of 15 were winched to safety by helicopters from RNAS Culdrose. The winds and currents blew the stricken vessel towards Whitsand Bay, where she grounded off Tregantle Beach. About 70 per cent of the cargo was lost overboard and much of the timber planking was washed up on the beach at Tregantle. People from Sheviock and further afield removed much of the timber to erect garden sheds and fences. Salvage tugs refloated the *Kodima* on 16 February and towed her to Falmouth where she was sold.

158 *MV* Kodima *was abandoned after being struck by gales en route from Sweden to Libya in 2002. She and her cargo of timber drifted onto the shore at Tregantle.*

PART V

Agriculture

159 *Sheviock Barton (far left top) nestling among the capacious cornfields of the manor.*

Chapter 20

Early History of Agriculture

The first people to practise agriculture in Britain were Neolithic people who arrived about 4500 BC. These people had knowledge of the raising and management of cattle and sheep, and of the cultivation of grain. The immigrants brought with them a new tool, the stone axe, mounted on a wooden haft. With this primitive implement they were able to clear small patches of woodland or scrub to plant their grain and graze their animals. New immigrants from Spain introduced the craft of copper smelting to the South West sometime after 2500 BC. One such immigrant was buried at Trethill.[1] By 1500 BC, the impact of the coppersmiths had had such a profound effect on people's way of life that archaeologists designate the period as the 'Bronze Age'.

In agriculture, revolutionary new tools were developed, such as the 'palstave', a digging implement with a bronze head, rather like a mattock. A hoard of eight heads for these tools was found hidden under a boulder near Bovey Tracey. The pointed spade, a tool still used in Devon and Cornwall, also made its first appearance during this period. At this time also, farmers began to harness oxen to the plough. The fields were small, so two oxen would have been quite sufficient. The plough then was a light wooden object, made from a bent bough, with the tip hardened by charring over a fire. The happy accident of a storm blowing sand over a late Bronze-Age farm at Gwithian, west of Camborne, has shown the actual furrows left by a plough of this type, indicating that the farmer ploughed the land from top to bottom and then from side to side. Where the plough could not reach, he used a pointed spade, whose marks were also still visible to the archaeologists. The Bronze-Age farmers on arable lands lived in round thatched houses, arranged in little groups of two to four. These were placed at the edges of the tiny fields, each field only about a quarter to half an acre in extent. The fields were roughly square in shape, to suit their criss-cross ploughing method. Sometimes they would have used 'breast ploughs' in their small fields. These were simply but arduously worked by manually pushing or pulling a horizontal bar at the end of the plough shaft.[2]

Iron-Age Farmers

During the Iron Age, which commenced in the South West in about 450 BC, agricultural tools became more freely available to farmers. The method of fashioning iron tools with a hammer and an anvil was simpler than the earlier method of using stone moulds to cast bronze tools. The basic shapes of the tools were similar to those in use during the Bronze Age. There is a piece of high ground in Sheviock whose adjacent fields are called *Pendeen* or *Pendyne* (Cornish for fortified headland) and Berry Down. This is the site of an Iron-Age 'round', whose Celtic inhabitants farmed these hills from about 450 BC.[3] It is estimated that there were some 700 of these rounds throughout Cornwall.[4] Although they look like hill-forts – and local children in Sheviock used to call the Sheviock round 'the Roman fort' – they are not fortresses, but enclosed farms or homesteads. They may have been occupied by just one extended family, or perhaps two or three. They continued in use until well into the fifth century A.D. The farmers undertook both arable cultivation, in small square fields, and raised cattle – typically, the Celtic short-horns. Coinage was hardly used, and a person's wealth was reckoned according to the number of cattle he owned.

Farmers after the Roman Invasion

The Romans arrived in the South West about A.D. 55, bringing with them many new farming techniques. They fitted the wooden plough with an iron share (cutting edge) and later with a coulter (a cutting blade in front of the share), though they had no mouldboard to turn the soil over.[5] They also developed a long-handled tool that was a combination of an axe and a mattock – probably the ancestor of the medieval 'beat-axe'.[6] They also edged wooden spades with iron.[7] The Romans gave land intended for cereals two or three ploughings each year. They also understood the value of manuring the ground, an operation that they carried out after the second ploughing. Roman farms usually included a compost pit. This would have contained animal dung, together with leaves, weeds and household waste. The Romans also introduced the scythe, thus enabling meadows to be cut and the grass used to sustain cattle through the winter. Celtic farmers and peasants settled near Roman farms would have learned some of the Roman farming practices. Some of the Latin words relating to agriculture, such as *falx*, which became the Cornish *falgh* (scythe), *furca* (fork), *castanea* (sweet chestnut), *fagus* (beech), *fructus* (fruit), *columba* (dove), *piscis* (fish), and *porcellus* (pig) entered the Cornish language.[8]

Celtic Farms after the Roman Departure

Between A.D. 450 and 650, the farmers abandoned the rounds, which were usually situated on the highest ground about 300 feet above sea level, in favour of open settlements somewhat lower down the hillsides – but still usually one or two hundred feet up. As Finberg has observed, 'as a highland people, the Britons of the south-west avoided heavy soils and thickly wooded valleys; they preferred the open ground and light soil of the foothills.'[9]

Farms beginning with 'Tre(f)-: The Cornish prefix *tre(f)-* signifies an agricultural settlement or farm. Tredis, Tredrossel, Trethill, Trewin and Trewrickle are examples of such settlements in Sheviock. Tredis was spelled *Treuthehast* in 1342. The meaning of the second element is unclear. Tredrossel, spelled *Tredrusel* in 1286, is situated near a stream called *Drossel.*[10] The stream, which may have taken its name from the ancient farmstead, is shown on Thomas Pride's map of Antony estate done in 1775.[11] Trethill, spelled *Treyuthell* in 1393, combines *tre(f)-* with a personal name.[12] Trewin, spelled *Trewinna* in 1267, probably means 'the white house' (Gover). Trewrickle, spelled *Trewykkel* in the late 12th century, appears to incorporate an anglicised form of the Cornish word *gwigell*, a diminutive of *gwig* or *gwic* (also *gook*) meaning 'a cove' or inlet (Gover).

Other Places with Cornish Names[13]*:* Places with Cornish names often indicate prominent natural features, sufficiently remarkable to the Celtic inhabitants for the name to stick. Examples of such places are Sheviock itself, from the Cornish *siviek* meaning 'strawberry place'; and Liscawn, probably from *nant* meaning 'a valley' and *skawenn* meaning 'elder tree'. Liscawn was spelled *Lanscawyn* in 1360 (Gover). *Polscoe* or *Polscove* may be another compound of *pol* plus *skawenn*, meaning 'pool or stream of the elder trees'.[14] But the fact that barges came that far up the creek to deliver limestone and sea-sand, may indicate that the second element of the word derived from *skath*, meaning a large boat or barge. Blerrick, spelled *Bleroc* in 1202 and *Blerak* in 1286, derives from the Cornish *belerek* meaning 'a bed of cress'. The name Sconner was spelled *Rosconner* in 1280 and *Resconern* in 1410. The first element probably derives from *rid* (which evolved into *res*), meaning 'a ford'. The second element derives from *Conner* or *Cuno-morus*, a personal name.[15]

Agriculture under the Saxons

King Aethelred's charter of A.D. 981 shows that Sheviock had been a possession of Aelfwynn, the Saxon noblewoman who was sister of the previous King Edgar (959-75). Her husband, Ordulf, had been chiefly responsible for the foundation of Tavistock Abbey, and Aelfwynn added Sheviock to the original endowment. It was probably in the late tenth century that the centre of Sheviock churchtown assumed broadly the shape that we know today.[16] The monks would have placed someone on their manor to look after their economic interests. Usually a layman, called a 'sergeant', was put in charge of a monastic manor, but sometimes a monk was installed as 'reeve'.[17] His responsibility might have been to pay to the abbey a fixed 'farm' of so many days' supplies each year of commodities such as fish, wool and corn. The person in charge would have constructed a barn to store the corn before it could be sent to the abbey. The monastic farm buildings probably stood where Sheviock Barton stands today.

Celtic farmers probably continued to farm the original *tre-* farmsteads, with their small square fields. But they would have been required to pay tribute or render labour services to the new Saxon overlord, first Aelfwynn, then the abbey, represented locally by its sergeant or reeve. The Cornish farmers would have witnessed the arable land coming under the Saxon plough with its innovative mould-board, which created the distinctive ridge and furrow patterns, and they would soon have copied it. This innovation led to the introduction of long open fields, which could be tilled more efficiently by eight-ox plough teams. The new powerful plough-teams were also able to tackle the lower, boggier slopes.

Agriculture at the Time of Domesday Book

The first written account of the agriculture of Sheviock is the entry in Domesday Book of A.D. 1086. One of the features of this document is that it not only describes

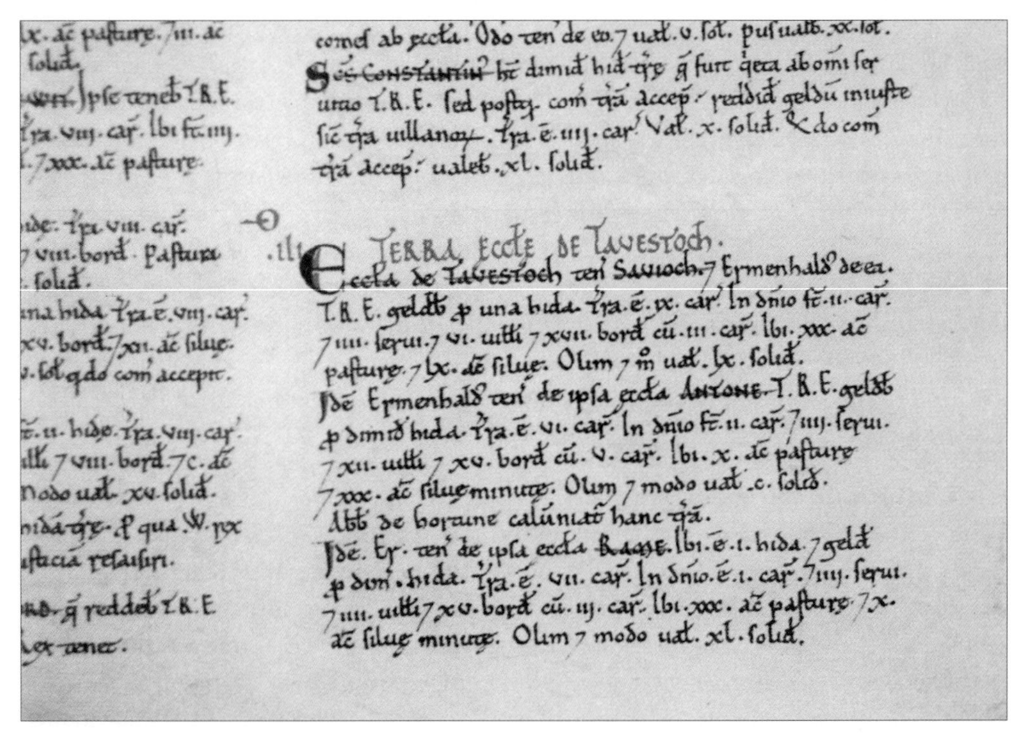
TERRA ECCLE DE TAVESTOCH.

160 *The entry for Sheviock in Domesday Book. The heading* TERRA ECCL[ESIA]E DE TAVESTOCH *means The land of the church of Tavistock.*

the situation as it was only 20 years after the Norman Conquest, but also looks back to late Anglo-Saxon times. The entry for Sheviock in the official (Exchequer) version reads in translation,[18]

> The Church of Tavistock holds Sheviock, and Ermenhald [holds] of it. In the time of King Edward it paid geld for one hide.[19] There is land for nine ploughs. In demesne are two ploughs and four slaves; and [there are] six villans and 17 bordars with three ploughs. There are 30 acres of pasture and 60 acres of woodland. Formerly, as now, worth 60s.

The tenant, Ermenhald (called Erbenald in later documents), was a Norman knight (the ancestor of the Dawneys). The 'geld' mentioned in Domesday was the tax originally levied to pay off the marauding Danes, and hence called the 'Danegeld'. It was usually levied at the rate of 2s. a hide, but at the time of Domesday, the rate was 6s. The high rate of tax was probably connected with King William's need to fight off another threatened invasion from Denmark.[20] At this time, a hide was of uncertain size but was often as large as a whole parish, much of the land being uncultivated. Later, the hide came to mean 120 arable acres, the average amount of land that an eight-ox team could plough in the course of the eight months in which ploughing took place (October to May). Geld was not payable on land that was the 'demesne' (home farm) of the lord of the manor, but only on land that was farmed by his tenants. As one of the purposes of Domesday Book was to record how much tax was collectable from England, the compilers of the official version of the book decided to exclude untaxed land. They therefore omitted the fact that Ermenhald kept one virgate (about 30 acres) in demesne. However, this information is preserved in an earlier version of the book, called the Exon. Domesday.[21]

As Domesday Book says that there is 'land for nine ploughs' (which may include the demesne) , it is implied that there are in total 1,080 arable acres (9 x 120), about half the total extent of the parish. According to the Tithe Redemption Survey of 1840/41, the parish extended over 2,122 acres, of which 1,692 were arable.[22] The 1,080 arable acres of A.D. 1086, worked by five ploughs, is 64 per cent of the arable acres mentioned in the 1840 Survey.[23] Domesday Book also gives the woodland as 60 acres and the pasture as 30 acres. These must be Cornish acres, of uncertain extent; but a multiple of 12 English to one Cornish acre would give 720 English acres of woodland and 360 acres of pasture. Adding the arable acres gives a total of 2,160 acres, very close to the known extent of the parish in 1840. Using this rough method of calculation, the total picture of land use at the time of Domesday seems plausible enough: about half the land was brought under the plough at some stage, about a third was woodland or covered in furze, and about 17 per cent was pasture. We also know from the Exon. Domesday that Ermenhald's livestock consisted of three head of cattle (*animalia*), 53 sheep and 12 goats, in addition to an assumed number of 16 oxen needed to pull his two ploughs – a very modest total for a knight with so much land. The milk from the cows was probably reserved for Ermenhald's own family.

According to Domesday Book, the six *villani* and the bordars had three ploughs between them. Omitting the bordars, it would appear that one plough was shared between two *villani*. Together, the six *villani* with their three ploughs had an ability to plough 300-360 acres. Within the parish as a whole, there were farm implements and oxen capable of ploughing 500-600 of the total 1,080 arable acres. The reason for the disparity between the number of acres that could be ploughed with the farming equipment available and the total number of ploughed acres, was the amount of waste land and the system of infield and outfield cultivation. The infield, or part of the land nearest the farmstead, was always well manured and subject to intensive tillage. The outfield was the area of furze, scrubland or bog usually furthest from the farm and most difficult to till. 'Part of this was broken up at long intervals, cropped for two or three years in succession and then abandoned to the furze and rough grasses, after which the process would be repeated on another division.'[24] As the Middle Ages progressed, more outfields came into regular cultivation, and some fields would be permanently enclosed with 'hedgebanks'; such fields then became known as 'parks'.

The six villans enumerated in Domesday Book may very plausibly be identified with the occupiers of the ancient Cornish farms on the high ground at Tredis, Trewin, Tredrossel, Trewrickle, and Trethill. Another may have farmed at Sconner or Blerrick. The typical villan tenement consisted of a virgate (30 acres) of land – the same amount that Ermenhald was reported to have in demesne. The 37 acres of the current Trethill estate is about the size of one of these ancient villan tenements. It is bounded by two natural boundaries: the stream flowing from Kerslake to Trethill Lake, and the boundary formed by a creek of the River Lynher (parallel to the A374), and two man-made boundaries: Ladywell Lane and part of Trethill Lane. The typical villan owed his lord a combination of money rents, labour services and renders in kind.[25] In 1086, money rents of villan tenements might amount to 4s. to 6s. per virgate, with the tenant also required to perform occasional ploughing or carrying services for his lord, and reaping for him in harvest time. Sometimes, he paid a lower rent, but was required to work on the demesne farm for two or three days a week.

A 'bordar' typically owned a small area of land (less than five acres) and worked for four or more days a week on the lord's demesne or perhaps, in the case of Sheviock, in his fishery. He may also have had to pay a rent of a shilling or two and deliver certain renders in kind (probably fish, hens, eggs or pigs). He lived in a cottage with a small garden. We can imagine some of the 17 bordars mentioned in Domesday Book, living in cottages in Sheviock churchtown. One may well have been installed at this time in what is now Cote Cottage. Others, engaged in fishing, probably lived near the coast at Trewrickle – the predecessors of Edmarus and Osbernus Gogo, mentioned in Henry Dawney's charter of 1174-1206.[26] In Cornwall as a whole, the bordars constituted 45 per cent of the total population; but in Sheviock, they constituted 63 per cent of the total. The high number of bordars may be due to the fishing activities being carried on in the parish. The four slaves or serfs (*servi* in Latin) worked exclusively on the lord's demesne, doing his ploughing, and living in his barton. The average price of a slave was 20s. (eight times the value of an ox). By the early 12th century, the *servi* had merged with the bordars as the lowest peasant class.

Because the villans and bordars would be expected themselves to have families (the standard multiplier is four or five), we can assume a total parish population of between 100 and 125 people in A.D. 1086. This was well above the county average. The total population of Cornwall at that time is thought to have been about 27,000.[27]

The Domesday statistics show that Sheviock and the other east Cornwall manors had both the highest populations per square mile (perhaps due to Anglo-Saxon settlement and fishing) and the highest ratio of ploughteams to the square

161 *Sheep and cut corn on the fields at Trewin, seen from Haye Farm.*

mile in Cornwall. Antony indeed had an excess of ox-teams over ploughlands. The value of the manor of Sheviock is given as 60 shillings, the same as in 1066. This was the annual value accruing to the Abbey of Tavistock. There were five ploughs, so the average worth per plough was 12s. This was more than double the Cornish average of 5s. 6d. The excess of value may have been due in part to the presence of the valuable fishery, which had already been exploited by the monks of Tavistock Abbey for about a century. The fishing may also explain why Sheviock had retained its value since the time of King Edward, when most tenanted Cornish manors had dropped in value.

Chapter 21

Field Names in Sheviock

Field names give valuable information about the early history of a parish. The names of the Sheviock fields were recorded on Thomas Pride's Map made for the Carew estates in 1775 and on the great map and inventory of the parish made in 1840 and 1841 for the purposes of the Tithe Redemption Act.[1] The vast majority of the field names in the parish are English, with only a few being certainly Cornish, with one or two others containing some Cornish elements.

Cornish Field Names

Britton: The origin of this name is unclear. *Brith* in Cornish means striped or variegated, but it is hard to see what in the topography could be so described.

Canna: At Haye farm there is a field called Canna Park. On Thomas Pride's map of 1775, the field is called Conner Park. This may refer to the Conner of *Res-Conner* – i.e. Sconner. But Canna is a common English field name, consisting of the word 'can', probably in the sense of 'container, hollow' (Padel).

Clicker: The field called Higher Clicker, which is on land to the east of Sheviock Barton, comes from a Cornish word, *kleger*, related to the Welsh *clegyr*, meaning a 'cliff' or 'steep place'.

Fennygook: The field name 'Fennygook', as in 'Fennygook Knowle', a little patch of pasture and furze, comes from fenny (marshy) and *gook*, meaning inlet, ultimately from Cornish *gogo* (cave) (Padel). There is also a five-acre field called 'Great Fennygook'. Both the fields are in Trewrickle and are marked on the 1840/41 Tithe Map. The 'Venegooke Close in Sheviock' left by Robert Hancock of Hendra in St Germans to his fifth son, Nicholas in 1663, no doubt referred to one or both of these same fields.

Readen or *Roaden*: A number of fields near Trewrickle farm incorporate the word 'readen' (sometimes spelt 'roaden' or 'roadon'). For example, Stoney Readen in Chubb's tenement, Readen in Blight's, Further Readen in Dell's and Little Readen in Brown's or Warren's.[2] 'Readen' here probably derives from the Cornish word *reden*, meaning fern or bracken. In the Middle Ages bracken was important as fuel. It is very invasive, and makes farming difficult.

Roduse: This is the name of a field in Trewrickle. The meaning is obscure, but as it is near the fields that incorporate the word *reden* (meaning fern or bracken), it may have an associated meaning.

Venton: There is a field at Sconner farm called 'Venton Over' (Fenton 'Ogglake' in a sale of timber dated 1514 and Venton Auger on Thomas Pride's map of 1775). The word *venton* may derive from the Cornish word *fenten*, meaning a spring. But the English *fen-ton* ('marsh farm' or 'marshy enclosure') is extremely common in Cornwall and Devon (Padel), and this meaning would also fit the topography.

ENGLISH FIELD NAMES

Trees and Bushes

The English field names tell us about many species of trees and bushes that abounded in the parish.

Ash: There was an Ash Park in Higher Tredis. Ash was 'used for the shafts of waggons and parts of the undercarriage, for the helves of many kinds of tools and implements, for ladder poles, crates, [and] gate hurdles' because of its resilience; and 'for the curved handles of scythes' because it responded well to steaming.[3] Old ash also made the best firewood. There is still a fine ancient ash hedge at Lantic farm (now part of Trewrickle Farm). On Thomas Pride's map of 1775, the road that runs east from Sheviock churchtown is called Ashy Lane.

Bramble: The ubiquitous bramble was commemorated in Bramble Park in Crafthole and Bramble Slade at Sconner Farm.

Broom: There was a Broom Park at Higher Tredis, a Broom Close at the Glebe and a Broom Ball at Sheviock Barton. The term was formerly used for any coarse shrub, such as gorse, heather, or holly, as well as broom (*cytisus scoparius*) itself, that could be used for sweeping.[4] In Sheviock, gorse or furze is the most common of these plants.

Elder: There were elder plots in Sconner, Sheviock Barton and Trewin. Though the Cornish name for the plant, *skawenn*, does not survive as a field name, it has survived as part of the holding called Liscawn.

Furze: The popular name for gorse (*ulex europaeus*), is very common in the parish, especially along the cliff-tops. There were Furze Parks at Crafthole (Vellands Tenement), Haye, Pool and Sconner. There was also a Furze Hill at Higher Tredis. It was the most important source of fuel for the early inhabitants of Sheviock.

Oak: There was an Oak Park in Sheviock Barton, and Sheviock woods are still noted for their oak stands. In the Middle Ages, oak was used to build ships, houses and mills. Later it was used to make props for the mines.

Willow: It was cultivated by fishermen to make lobster pots and crab pots, and by the farming community to make hurdles, to bind barrels and to make baskets. There were willow plots at Higher Tredis, on the rector's glebe, and in Crafthole (Vellands Tenement). There were willow gardens at Tredrossel and Crafthole (Landreys' Holding). There was also a willow plantation at the bottom of Ladywell Lane. There was a Higher Willow Park at Sconner, and an Orchard Willow Plot at Trewrickle. The Trewrickle plot is still used by the Portwrinkle fishermen for harvesting withies, which are cut in February.[5]

Crops

Cultivated crops are occasionally incorporated into field names, such as Rye Lands at Kerslake and Rylands Brake at Trethill. Rye lands generally meant arable land not suitable for growing wheat, but which would support crops of rye. There was also a Barley Park at Crafthole.

Birds

Birds too have left their mark in the field names.

Doves: At Trewin there was a field called Culver Park, and at Trethill there was another called Culver Meadow. Overlooking Whitsand Bay is the famous culverhouse built by the Dawneys. *Culfre* is the old English word for a dove or pigeon, so a culverhouse means a dovecote. The presence of culverhouses at Trewin and Trethill (on Kerslake Manor) therefore shows them to have been built on medieval manors. The culverhouse at Trethill survived until fairly recently, and was still marked on the Ordnance Survey map of 1906. It stood near the south-eastern tip of the grounds of Trethill House, close to Kerslake stream.

Ducks: There were Ducks' Pond Orchards at Trewin and Trethill.

Hawks: There was a Hawks Wood in Sheviock woods, on the eastern side of George's Lane where it meets the River Lynher. The name may derive from its being a favourite breeding ground for hawks; but another possibility is that it was a wood set aside for hunting with hawks. There was a Hawks Park at Higher Tredis. On Thomas Pride's map of 1775, there are Lower and Higher Hawkes' Parks at Poole Farm. These fields were situated between Sheviock and Polscoe Mills. The place is still a favourite hunting ground for hawks. They often rest on the telegraph poles beside the A374.

Edward Hawke was a sailor on the *Dayestarr* in 1626 and another Edward Hawke was a tailor living at Higher Clicker a century later, so the places mentioned above may be associated with this family rather than the bird.

Animals

Cattle: There was a Bull's Meadow and a Calves Meadow at Tredrossel.

Lambs: Lambs were very precious to the farmers, who often kept them in special enclosures, where they could be closely watched. There was a Lamb Park at Trewin; and there were Great and Little Lamb Parks at Liscawn. There was also a Lamb Park at Haye.

Pigs: There was a Pig's House Orchard at Liscawn.

Names derived from Topography and Farming Practice

Ball: Several fields are called 'ball', as in Skinner's Ball in Crafthole and Broom Ball in Sheviock Barton, Harry's Ball above 'the Chalet' in Portwrinkle and Blackyball in Kerslake. The 'ball' element simply refers to the rounded shapes of the fields in question.

Brake: A 'brake' refers to rough land where bracken and 'brake weed', a small weed of poor soils, grow. It might be broken to grow a crop, and hence came to mean land fit to be broken.[6] There were brakes at Tredrossel and Tredis. Prior's Brake next to Haye Farm was granted by William Dawney, lord of Sheviock, to the Prior of St Germans in 1260 in exchange for the latter's right to take wood from Sheviock woods.[7] In this case, therefore, the brake was probably used for coppicing.

Chall or *Ox-chall*: There was a Chall Orchard at Poole in 1775 and a Chall Park at Sconner in 1840. 'Chall' or 'Ox-chall' are old West Country words for a barn or stall. The orchard and park recorded in 1840 were located near one of the barns of the related farmhouse.

Gratna and *Gratton*: There were gratnas at Higher Tredis and Sconner. These names probably derive from 'gratton', which means cultivated, ploughed land.[8] There was also a gratton at Kerslake. In 1840, this consisted of five acres of arable land.

Homer and *Yonder*: Fields that are nearer the farm than some other reference point were called 'homer', and those that were further away are called 'yonder'. Thus at Sconner there was a 'Homer Lea Park' and a 'Yonder Lea Park'. At Trethill, the meadow beyond Kerslake stream was called 'Yonder Meadow'.

Hony Bush: This was the name of a field at Higher Tredis. This may refer to the production of honey from hives or a nest of wild bees in the field.[9]

Meadow: On the 1840 Tithe Map, 28 acres of land in Sheviock were described as meadows. These were present in every farm in the parish. At Trewin and Trethill the meadows were sometimes described as 'lawns', because, from the 1700s, they constituted part of the landscaping of the house and park. Meadowland was used for the production of hay, which was used to sustain cattle through the winter. It was also the best land for rearing sheep. Hence it was the most valuable type of land. According to Robin Stanes, a well-watered meadow, closed off from stock from October, and re-opened to sheep from February to April, could carry up to twenty ewes and their lambs per acre.[10] These were the early fat lambs, or Easter lambs. To water the meadows, the farmers sometimes dug 'gutters' in them. The meadows then became known as 'gutter meadows'. Sometimes the meadows doubled up as orchards. After April, the meadows could be watered again and laid up for hay.

Park: The most common description of all for the fields was 'park', a Middle English term for a piece of ground of anything between one and 40 acres, enclosed by a hedge. Parks were often taken out of adjacent woodlands (often indicated by such names as 'wood park' and 'wood field') or areas of previously uncultivated lands, indicated by such names as 'furze park', 'broom park' or 'bramble park'.

Slade: A number of fields were termed 'slades'. John Field describes a slade as 'a shallow valley, a piece of greensward in a long depression in the fields, too marshy to cultivate'.[11] Robin Stanes describes it simply as a flattish valley field.[12] There were slades in Crafthole, Kerslake, Sconner, Higher Tredis, Trethill and Trewrickle.

Shooteys and *Shute*: These terms may describe a water shoot or a sloping field. On Thomas Pride's map of 1775 there is a field named Shutys. In the 1840 Tithe Map, the field is named Shooteys. In the 1922 lease between Sir Reginald Pole Carew and Thomas Bersey this same field is called Shooters. It contains seven acres of pastureland and extends along the A374 with its western end abutting the road leading from Sheviock to Crafthole. It slopes steeply down towards Wacker Creek.

Tun: The Cornish *tre(f)*- meaning a farming settlement was rendered in English as 'tun' or town. Some of the field names charmingly describe their situation relative to the 'tun'. Many are called 'bove town' (above the farmhouse). There were Bove Towns at Sconner, Tredis, Tredrossel, Trethill, Trewin and Trewrickle; and there was a Bove Way at Liscawn. There was an 'Under Town' at Higher Tredis.

Twinaway: This is a corruption of 'between the ways', i.e. a field lying between two roads. There was a Twinaway in Trethill.

Vellands: This holding lies between Crafthole and Liscawn. The most likely derivation is from the English 'vell' or 'fell', the greensward that was dug up and burned to provide nutrients for the soil. In July 1729, on the Carew estates at Antony, the steward paid the women 'for burning the vell'.[13] Thus Vellands meant land that had to be velled to keep it productive.[14] The high site would also make it suitable for a windmill.

However, on linguistic grounds, Oliver Padel thinks that derivation from the Cornish *an velin*, meaning 'the mill', is unlikely here.[15]

Personal Names

Sometimes a former occupant, the first farmer to make a clearing or park, or a former owner or benefactor was commemorated in the field name.

Friday's Parks: This eight-acre holding near Stumpy Cross may derive its singular name from the family of Vridie (1286), Fridia (1327) or Fredea (1428). Roger Fridia lived in St John in 1327 and Thomas Fredea lived in the hundred of East in 1428.[16] Thomas Fryday was appointed rector of St John in 1519. The hamlet of Freathy in the parish of St John may have taken its name from the same family. Alternatively, but less likely, the family may have taken its name from the place.

Gill Ball and *Gill Haye*: Gill Ball (near Sheviock woods) and Gill Haye (in the Coombes in Crafthole) may take their name from an Elizabethan official called John Gill.[17]

Hancock's Hill: This hill is in Kerslake. Alexander Hancock was a tenant of Kerslake Manor in the early 1600s; William Hancock settled lands in Sheviock on Henry Wallis in 1692 in anticipation of the latter's marriage to Elizabeth Hodge and subsequent move to Trethill.

A number of other families and individuals have also given their names to fields and tenements in Sheviock. There was a Grills Park in Kerslake. There was an Addyham (Odiorne) in Haye. Situated near Crafthole were Jory's Park, Skinner's Ball, Skinner's Slade, Kingdon's Park, Harry's Down and Harry's Ball. Blackaball is possibly a corruption of 'Blake's Ball', since the Blake family farmed at nearby Blerrick in the mid-1600s. At Trewrickle were Petty's or Pitty's (1775), Petty's Meadow, Simon's Meadow and Chubb's Park. At Tredrossel were Harris Down, Rundle's Down and England's Down. Tredrossel also boasted Truscott's Hill, Painter's Hill, and Toke's Park. Trethill had David's Park, Barrett's Park, Giddy's Meadow and Blake Plantation.[18] There was a Maddock's Park (Mattick's in 1775) and a Maddock's Orchard at Kerslake. There was also a Maddock's Park in Crafthole (Vellands Tenement).

Common Land

According to the 1841 Agreement for the Commutation of Tithes in Sheviock, there were then 42 acres of common land. Much of this was near the cliff face, south of Liscawn. But at Pool and Tredrossel there were fields called 'Maina Park'. According to Gover, the derivation of Maina is from the Old English *gemaene*, meaning 'common', so these may also once have been common fields. There were also fields farmed in common at Kerslake and Blerrick.

Chapter 22

Livestock

The Domesday record shows that sheep were the predominant species in Cornwall in 1086, constituting 80 per cent of the whole. They were followed in order by cattle, goats, swine and horses. We know from the Exon. Domesday that at Sheviock, Ermenhald's flock of 53 sheep also formed the biggest element of his livestock, followed by 16 oxen (the assumed number for the two ploughs), 12 goats and just three head of dairy cattle. As a knight, Ermenhald would also have kept many horses on his land.

Oxen and Horses: An ox is the 'castrated male of the bovine species of ruminants' (OED). Oxen, which require less nourishment than a horse to perform effectively, were used for all kinds of draught purposes. In 1796, William Marshall records that six growing steers or four aged oxen were the usual plough teams in the South West.[1] In the late 1100s, the padded horse collar had been introduced into the South West. This enabled horses to pull carts or ploughs without their windpipes becoming blocked by the harness. Gradually more and more horses were introduced onto the farms. In the 1200s, a heavier and better-made horseshoe was invented.[2] Whereas oxen ploughed more slowly than a man's normal walking speed, horses ploughed more quickly. But on the other hand, while oxen could survive on just straw, horses needed hay and corn in winter. Sometimes two oxen were worked with two lead horses. By the 1200s, surpluses of barley and oats enabled farmers to keep more horses, and sometimes two horses were worked alone to pull the plough. At this time the usual task of the oxen or horses was to plough about three-quarters of an acre per day.

An ox team required both a driver to drive the oxen forward and a ploughman to steer the plough. The ploughman would carry a ploughstaff, a long stick with a small iron spade at one end, used to clear the coulter and mouldboard from time to time. The driver was usually a boy armed with a goad, a long stick with a pointed iron prod at one end. The goad had been introduced into Britain by the Romans.[3] A horse-drawn plough, by contrast, could be managed by a single ploughman, who managed the horses with whip-reins. The plough itself was wheel-less until sometime in the 12th century. Oxen continued to be used for ploughing until the late 1800s. In 1815, Thomas Littleton of Trewin bequeathed to his younger son, Thomas 'two working oxen' along with other livestock.[4] One attractive feature of the two-man ox team was the system of chants used by the team to guide the oxen. Marshall heard them in Devon and east Cornwall in the late 1700s, and wrote, 'the plough boy chants the counter tenor with unabated ardour through the day, the plowman throwing in, at intervals, his hoarser notes'.[5] The last recorded ox team in the district was at Blerrick farm in the 1890s.[6]

Cattle: An inventory of the goods of William Harry, mariner, of Sheviock, who died in 1626, includes 'ii keene [i.e. kine or cattle] and one hefer' [a heifer is a young cow that has not had a calf and does not yet produce milk]. These three animals, which would be kept to produce milk, butter and cheese, were valued at £8. The animals in question must have been considerably superior in breed to the single cow that was recorded in the inventory of goods of John Naunter of Sheviock, mariner, who died in 1627. This poor specimen was valued at only £1 10s. The 'three keene & fower other bullocks' of Tristram Harry, who died in 1638, were valued at £15 6s. 8d. In the 1600s, the milk output from a cow was some 600 gallons per year, compared with about 1,000 gallons from a cow today.[7]

In the 1700s, Marshall described the native cattle of Cornwall and west Devonshire as somewhat similar to Herefordshires, but 'in Cornwall the breed gets coarser; with somewhat larger and more upright horns'. In 1811, G.B Worgan described them as 'very small, black, short-nosed, coarse-boned.'[8] In the first year, the calves were kept within enclosures, but in the next were sent to graze on common lands or on hill pastures. Heifers were brought into milk at two and a half to four years old; and steers (oxen) were broken into the yoke at similar ages. The steers were then worked until they were anything up to twelve years old. The Cornish lands were thought by Marshall to be better adapted for bringing cattle forward (because of the early grass-growing season) than for finishing them for market. This is still the case today.[9]

During the Middle Ages, hides from cattle were the third most important Cornish export after tin and fish. Cornwall was the chief exporter of hides in southern England. The peak years of hide exports were the 1280s. A cattle disease, called murrain, afflicted herds in 1319-21 and the trade never regained its former importance.[10]

Sheep: In the century following Domesday Book, the number of sheep on the bigger estates increased ten times.[11] At the time of Domesday Book, sheep were kept as much for their milk as for their wool and meat. The ewes' milk was made into cheese, a practice that has been revived in Sheviock in the recent past.[12] By the 1200s, wool was by far the most important product from sheep. England became the biggest wool-producing country in Europe. But before the practice of enclosure became widespread in the later Middle Ages, and particularly in the 1500s, the sheep that grazed upon the waste and open grounds of Devon and Cornwall were rather poor specimens. At Tavistock Abbey, the monks sheared only two pounds of wool per sheep, compared with between seven and 15 pounds per head from a modern breed.[13] Until the 1300s, the raw wool was exported to be made up into cloth in the Low Countries and in France; but after that time it was made up into cloth before being shipped abroad.[14]

In the Middle Ages, the wool from Sheviock and other parts of south-east Cornwall was sent to fulling or, in local parlance, 'tucking' mills for manufacture into a coarse type of cloth. Many of these mills were situated in and around Tavistock.[15] The lengths of cloth, called 'straits', were white, grey or russet in colour and rough and hairy in texture. But at the end of the Middle Ages, a new manufacture of finely spun and woven cloths called 'kerseys' was made from the Cornish wool. By the 1600s, the wool in east Cornwall was being spun into yarn locally and then sent up to Exeter to be made into the cloths.

162 *The South Devon cross is a popular breed in South-East Cornwall. This one was auctioned at Liskeard Market in 2008.*

Carew observed that making enclosures, and sanding and manuring the fields, had hugely improved the diet, and therefore the quality, of Cornish sheep. When, in earlier times, they had grazed on the open, untreated lands, they 'had generally little bodies, and course [coarse] fleeces, so as their wooll bare no better name, th[an] of Cornish hayre'. But, he went on, 'since the grounds began to receive enclosure and dressing for tillage, the nature of the soyle hath altered to a better graine, and yeeldeth nourishment in greater abundance, and goodnesse, to the beastes that pasture thereupon.' As a result, he claimed,

> Cornishe sheepe come but little behind the Easterne flockes, for bignes of mould, fineness of Wooll, often breeding, speedie fatting, and price of sale, and in my conceyte equall, if not exceede them in sweetnesse of taste, and freedome from rottennesse and such other contagions. As for their number, while everie dweller hath some, though none keepe many, it may summe the totall to a jolly rate.[16]

163 *Many farmers alternate sheep and cattle grazing to ensure optimal cropping of the grass. These sheep are grazing at 'Ladywell', a field at Trethill above 'Our Lady's Well'. The well is situated on the former glebe land of the church of the Blessed Mary at Sheviock.*

Edward Kneebone, who was also a local man, and wrote 80 years after Carew, was equally positive, writing:

> Sheep, of the finest woole of these parts, called Cornish hairre, are in great plenty ... On the south, such as breed their owne have as large and as fine woole as most knowne in England ... Woole, as the naturall growth of the sheep, is plentifull; for the greatest wrought up to yarne in this country, and sold in open markets to the Devonshire buyers, who send it as farre as Exon [Exeter], and otherwheres, to be wrought into white kersyes and searges.[17]

In 1695, John Treis, the steward of the Carew estates, paid 18s. for 'four yards Kersy for great Coat', probably for the footman, John Pearse.[18] In 1697, he paid 1s. 4d. for 'dying and pressing four yards sarge for his suit'.[19]

An inventory of the goods of one of Carew's tenants, William Harry, mariner, who died in 1626, includes ten sheep, valued at 50s., and wool, valued at 20s. An inventory of the goods of Tristram Harry, another tenant, who died in 1638, values 'all sheepe and lambes' at 50s., implying another small flock of ten. Anthony Blake, a gentleman farmer active after the Restoration, farmed 43 acres at Middle and Lower Blerrick and Kerslake on which he kept more than 20 ewes with their lambs. Their fleeces and lambs were worth some £15 per annum.[20]

During the 1600s, the principal owners of property in the borough of Crafthole, as tenants of the Duchy, were Sir Samuel Rolle, MP for Callington, and William Condy (or Cundy). Both were active in the cloth industry. Sir Samuel Rolle was buying up wool from the farmers of Sheviock and other parts of east Cornwall and then sending it to Callington to be spun into yarn. The yarn was sent from there to Exeter where it was used to manufacture serges. William Condy and his wife, Frances, were themselves clothiers of Tavistock. They were related to the Wallises of Sconner and Crafthole. The Condys not only owned properties in the borough of Crafthole, but also rented part of the holding of Blazor, a good property for sheep grazing. According to a rental of the manor of Sheviock of 1691, 'Will. Cundy gen holdeth there [i.e. in Blazor] in socage & pays yearly 7s'.[21] So Rolle and Condy were practising what in modern business parlance is called 'vertical integration' – owning as much as possible of the supply chain from raw material to end customer.

In the 1700s, Marshall noted that the time of putting the rams to the ewes, and therefore also the lambing season, was early compared with most other districts. Another striking feature that he observed was that the wool remained unwashed before it was sheared. The term for such wool was 'wool in the yolk' because of the yellow yolk-like matter that adhered to it.

Goats: In 1086, goats were important to the rural economy as a source of milk. As we have seen, Ermenhald had a flock of twelve. But by 1200, due to the increase in cattle and sheep production, their numbers had substantially declined.

Swine: At the time of Domesday Book, the domestic pig was very similar in appearance to the wild boar – that is to say, dark in colour, with a hairy body and long legs. Indeed, it is thought that in some areas pigs may have been kept as only partly domesticated animals.[22] Pigs were fed in autumn on beechmast, chestnuts and acorns in the woods, where they were tended by swineherds. Sheviock woods have always been famous for their oak-trees.[23] The Cornish words *polbathic* and *polpathic* mean the 'pool for the boars'. Two places in the parish bear this name, both near woods and water. They may have been the places to which the parishioners drove their pigs early in the autumn for collection by the swineherd who would take them up to the lord's woods for their autumn foraging. Over time, selective breeding improved the species of pig for human consumption, and by the 1600s herding swine in the woods was no longer practised. Instead nearly every Cornish family kept a pig or two. The inventory of William Harry of Sheviock, mariner, who died in 1626, includes 'his piggs', which were valued at 50s. Tristram Harry, husbandman, who died in 1638, had fewer pigs, since 15s. was thought to be the value of 'all the hoggs'. In 1680, the rector, Nicolas Kendall, possessed four 'hoggshouses'.

Marshall noted with horror that in Cornwall the pigs were shut up in narrow, close hutches – without separate open enclosures – to fatten them up until they were slaughtered. Tom Bersey attests to the fact that this practice continued right up until the 1950s. Many of these pigsties can still be seen in Sheviock and other parts of south-east Cornwall. But they have now been given over to other uses, such as storage sheds. The swine were fattened with potatoes, barley or oats ground, or barley boiled.

Rabbits: The Normans introduced rabbits into England. The first known mention of them is in a charter of Bishop Bartholomew of Exeter (1161-84).[24] The Normans farmed them for their meat and their fur. The warren in Sheviock was located at Warren Point, stretching across the eastern tip of the rector's glebe. By placing the warren on a headland it was relatively easy to catch the rabbits with dogs and nets. The fact that the warren was surrounded by water on all sides except the western one also helped to contain (but did not prevent) the unwanted spread of the rabbits.[25] Carew wrote dismissively of rabbits (then called 'conies'): 'Of conies, there are here and there some few little warrens, scantly worth the remembring'. But in fact a warren continued in operation at Antony until the 1700s. In November 1713, Richard Blighe, the accountant to Sir William Carew paid £1 15s. to John Sawdy 'for Netts for the Warren & Twaine [twine] & Cord made by old Hob'.[26]

As they multiplied, rabbits became a serious pest. Tom Bersey remembers the hunts which the farmers organised. They set up long lengths of netting, with copious loose folds at the bottom, at one end of a field and then marched towards them from the other end. As they marched, they banged implements and whistled to drive the rabbits into the nets. Once ensnared the rabbits were quickly dispatched. A wartime evacuee, Terry Leather, also recalled hunting rabbits with dogs during the 1940s:

> In those days, the farms were overrun with rabbits, which did a lot of damage to the crops. Although they were trapped and caught on a regular basis, it was still an uphill task to keep them under control. As boys, we were always out rabbiting in our spare time. …
>
> On the farm [at Lantic] we had a very good dog, a lurcher called Prince. He was very fast and not many rabbits got away from him. Ken, Chuffy [Terence Bean] and me kept ferrets, which were used to clear out large rabbit warrens (sometimes referred to as a set) with every hole netted.[27] On most occasions the ferrets had to be coped.[28] This prevented them from attacking and eating a rabbit.

The advent of myxomatosis in the 1950s finally brought the excessive rabbit population under control.

164 *Free range chickens and pigs at Glebe Farm c.1945. Arthur Holman, the farmer, stands on the right next to the blacksmith, Tom Ough.*

165 *Labourers unloading material, perhaps lime or sand, from a barge onto a cart. Cartouche from an 18th-century map of West Antony.*

Chapter 23

The Soil and Crops

Certainly from Roman times, and perhaps earlier, farmers were aware that the productivity of the soil could be enhanced by the application of manure. In the Middle Ages, other soil enhancers also came into use. In Cornwall, the soil was enriched by applying 'beat ashes' and sea-sand as well as dung. Sea-weed and fish manure were also added as improving agents. Lime first came into use in the 1600s.

Dung: The dung which came from the cattle and sheep on the farms was the most readily procured manure. Sheep could be fed on pasture during the day and folded on arable at night, thereby manuring it. This saved the trouble of handling the dung, a very labour intensive operation.[1] On the Carew estates at Antony, in the first six months of 1747, the heaviest month for dunging was May, when 48 days of labour was spent on it (18.2 per cent of total labour).[2] Except in February and March, when ploughing and sowing took precedence, dunging was a constant and significant activity every month, with one man more or less permanently engaged upon it. W. H. Pole Carew's lease of Sconner Farm to Thomas Hoskin, which commenced in 1866, required Hoskin to apply 50 tons of good farm yard dung per acre in the third year after he had taken two successive corn crops. The practice still continues today. In the 1700s, farmers in some places were purchasing 'Plymouth dung' – that is, the scrapings of the streets of Plymouth, which was transported to the places where it was needed by barge and packhorse.

Beat-burning: 'Beat-burning' was a method of preparing the ground for corn crops. According to Finberg, it can be traced as far back as 1246 on the Tavistock Abbey estates.[3] The process involved lifting the grasses and weeds (called the spine) from a piece of waste ground with a mattock or a plough fitted with a velling share, or an implement called a 'beat-axe'. The beat-axe was a long-handled implement that originally had an axe on one side, to cut through any thick roots, and a flat blade on the other like a mattock.[4] After being pulled up, the spine was allowed to dry. When dry it was harrowed. The dry pieces of turf and spine, then called 'beat' were raked into heaps or 'beat-burrows'. A handful of straw was pushed into each heap and then set alight. After the fire had consumed the heaps, the remaining ashes were spread over the field, sometimes mixed with sea-sand. Carew described the operation as follows:

> For first, about May, they cut up all the grasse of that ground, which must newly be broken, into Turfes, which they call Beating. These Turfes they raise up somewhat in the midst, that the wind and Sunne may the sooner drie them ... After they have beene th[o]roughly dried, the Husbandman pileth them in little heapes, and so burneth them to ashes.[5]

An inventory of the goods of Ferdinando Spiller of Sheviock, who died in 1607, includes 'betaxes' as well as drills and shovels. An inventory of the goods of Richard Harvey of Sheviock, who died in 1645, includes 'one little beataxe 2 reape hookes and some old boardes' together valued at 1s. 4d.

Beat-burning was very labour intensive. It was, therefore, practised less in seaside parishes like Sheviock, where sea-sand, sea-weed and fish manure were easily obtainable alternatives, than in inland parishes. On the Carew estates beat burning was carried out intermittently, and it was usually the women who did the back-breaking work. In July 1729, the steward paid £2 1s. 1d. to 'the women for burning the vell'.[6] The following July the hind (farm manager) paid labourers £9 10s. 4d. 'for making hay & burning Vell'. Next month he paid them 11s. 'for burning 11 acres of Vell & Beat'. When Marshall wrote his *Rural Economy of the West of England* in 1796, the practice of beat burning still formed 'a principal wheel in the present machine or system of the Devonshire husbandry'. It continued in use there until the 1900s.[7]

Sea-sand: Cornish land is very acid because of the high rainfall. For many crops, such as wheat or barley, it therefore needs to be 'sweetened'. One such sweetening agent is sea-sand. In about 1250, Richard, Earl of Cornwall and King of the Romans, issued a charter permitting all the inhabitants of Cornwall to take sea-sand without payment for the purpose of increasing the fertility of their lands.[8] Henry III confirmed the grant in 1261.[9] The sand, particularly if formed from pulverised shells and corals, plus some seaweed, is rich in calcium carbonate. The earliest mention of its use in Sheviock is in 1286, when Warrin de Herth (brother-in-law of William Dawney the younger) received licence from William to get sand from Trewrickle (i.e. Portwrinkle) to use on his barton of Tredrossel.[10]

The farmers were well aware of the variable quality of the sand used to dress the fields. As Carew wrote in 1602,

> This sand is of divers kindes, colours, and goodnesse: the kinds, some bigger, some lesser; some hard, some easie. The colours are answereable to the next Cliffes. The goodnesse increaseth as it is taken farther out of the Sea.[11]

Sand was dredged up in different parts of Plymouth Sound and carried along the coast and up the estuary in barges. In the 1300s, the earls and dukes of Cornwall began to tax the barges carrying the sand. From 1302 to 1316, there were usually 16 barges in the estuary paying this levy. According to the Caption of Seisin 1337, 'there is … a certain custom of 12d. per year from every barge carrying sand'.[12] Because of the military services provided by the Dawney lords of Sheviock and their tenants to the lord of Trematon Castle, their barges were exempt from the custom. Sometimes, sea sand and beat ashes were combined. Carew in the early 1600s described the manner of their application:

> An ordinarie Horse will carrie two sackes of Sand, and of such the borderers on the Sea, doe bestow, 60 at least, in everie Acre, but most Husbands [i.e. farmers] double that number … A little before plowing time, they scatter abroad those Beat-boroughs [heaps of ashes], & small Sand heapes upon the ground, which afterwards, by the Ploughes turning downe, give heate to the roote of the Corne.[13]

An inventory of the goods of Tristram Harry of Sheviock, taken after his death in 1638, includes 'sand buts with the saddles', valued at 5s. The names 'Sanders Lane' in Portwrinkle and 'Carslake [Kerslake] Sandaway' show the routes which Sheviock farmers took from the beach. The quay at Portwrinkle (after its construction in 1612), the landing stages on the creeks at Trewin and Trethill, and the medieval quay (later George's Quay) on the River Lynher were also used to unload sea-sand brought in from Plymouth Sound. On the Antony estates, in the first half of 1747, May was the only month in which sanding was carried out.[14] One to three men devoted some 36 days to sanding the fields in that month. On many of those days, dung was spread at the same time.

Lime: The use of lime as a sweetening agent was known in Devon in the 1600s.[15] The first reference to it in Sheviock is in the hearth tax return of 1664. Henry Odiorne was assessed for two hearths. According to the collector, Henry 'returned two short whereof one is a kiln'. Henry was tenant of the agricultural holding of Haye in 1689-90, so it seems likely that the kiln was a lime kiln.[16] The practice of lime dressing greatly increased in the 1700s. In 1753, Trehawke of Liskeard wrote to Dr William Borlase, 'Our Manure or Dressing is of late years somewht alter'd in many parts of the County and that to advantage by the use of Lyme but still sand may be reckoned the chief manure.'[17]

18th-century lime kilns still stand at Polbathic and Sconner, on a creek of the river Lynher. The slaked (burnt) lime was obtained by burning a variegated stone or marble extracted from quarries at Cattedown, near Plymouth. This was carried up the estuaries by barge. Lime kilns were built at the heads of the creeks. In the 1800s, the kilns were usually built in pairs, so that while one was burning, the other was cooling,

166 *The limekiln at Polbathic at the home of Jean Mills. The opening for the fire is clearly visible. Alternate layers of lime and culm (anthracite) were thrown into the kiln from above.*

thus allowing the farmers to remove the lime. The walls of lime kilns were extremely thick – wide enough on the top for horses or donkeys to pass round them and deliver the stones which they had carried up from the barges. On the top of the kilns the stones were broken up and thrown into the kilns with shovels. The fuel for burning the lime was chiefly or wholly Welsh culm (anthracite).

Seaweed: Also called 'ore' or 'ore weed' seaweed has also been used as a fertiliser in Sheviock from time immemorial. As Carew explains:

> Orewood … is a weed either growing upon the rockes under high water marke, or broken from the bottome of the sea by rough weather, and cast upon the next shore by the wind and flood. The first sort is reaped yeerely, and thereby bettereth in quantity and qualitie: the other must be taken when the first tyde bringeth it, or else the next change of winde will carry it away. His use serveth for barly land.[18]

Ore weed was still being used to fertilise potato fields between the two World Wars.[19] Cornish calcified seaweed is still sold today as a fertiliser to lift PH levels and to increase soil fertility. It is also recommended as a fertiliser and inhibitor of rot for apple trees.

Fish manure: During the centuries that the pilchard and mackerel fishing industry flourished in Portwrinkle, the old salt that had been used in the curing process and rotten fish were also used to improve the fertility of the land.

Good Husbandry Clauses: In the 1700s, lawyers drawing up agricultural leases began to introduce so-called 'good-husbandry clauses'. For example, a lease of Trethill Barton and farm made in 1797 between the proprietor, the Revd Bryan Roberts, rector of Drewsteignton, and Nathaniel Hawkings of Antony, yeoman, provided as follows:

> (the tenant) shall and will bring into and upon every acre … fifty bushells of well burnt stone lime or 100 sacks of good salt sea sand … and after such dressing shall not take out more than three crops of corn or grain and one of clover … one only of which said crops of corn or grain (but not the last) shall be of wheat.

In 1802, a similar clause was included in a lease of Chubb's tenement in Trewrickle. The clause provided that the tenant should bring onto the land 'one hundred and sixty seames or horse loads of saltwater sand or good stable and stall dung or ten hogsheads of good well burnt lime' which he was to 'spread about according to good husbandry'.[20] Furthermore, he was not to take more than three crops of corn or grain after such dressing. Also, he was to sow with the last crop of corn 'in every acre ten pounds of good clover seed and one part of good ever seed'.

The Crops

Sowing: Although seed drills were invented by Jethro Tull in the 1700s, sowing continued to be done by hand on many small farms until well into the 20th century. The seed was scattered from an apron, or from a 'zillup' (seedlip), a wooden basket hung around the neck, or from a seed 'fiddle', operated by moving a bow across a whirligig under the seed bag.[21] The most intensive month for ploughing and sowing on the Antony estates in the first half of 1747 was March.[22] In that month, two men and two boys with their ox teams spent a total of 37 days ploughing and three men spent a total of 55 days engaged mainly in sowing. The two activities together took up 37 per cent of the total labour available in the month.

167 *The farmer, Eric Grills of Crafthole Park Farm, with horse and cart in the 1950s.*

Harrowing: An inventory of the goods of Tristram Harry of Sheviock, who died in 1638, includes harrows. The soil was harrowed to break it down prior to sowing. Before the introduction of the seed drill, it was also harrowed after seeding in order to cover the seed and protect it from birds. Under their unyielding wooden yokes, oxen hated the operation of harrowing, because of the jerking of the heavy implement behind them.

Crop succession: Two or three course rotation of crops was practised at least as early as the 14th century. This might be wheat, rye or oats and then grass. Carew in his *Survey* says that even after applying all the fertilisers then in common use 'the Tiller can commonly take but two crops of Wheate, and two of Oates, and then is driven to give [the land] at least seven or eight yeares leyre [pasture] and to make his breach elsewhere'.[23] Because oats were the last crop in the succession, they came to be known as the 'farewell crop'.

Root Crops: The growing of root crops, such as turnips, had originated in Holland. Turnips were planted soon after beat-burning at midsummer. The farmers then hoed the fields to get rid of the weeds. By November they could let their cattle and sheep into the fields to feed off the turnips. This not only saved the labour of digging up the turnips, but fertilised the fields at the same time. The growing of turnips became a regular part of the rotational system.

Potatoes had become an important crop in Cornwall by the 1690s.[24] The potatoes were used for human consumption and for fattening pigs.

Oats: Oats are the crop best suited to a damp climate. On the Tavistock Abbey estates, three distinct types were grown: *avena nuda* or *minuta* (pill-corn), where the husks do not adhere to the grain, but leave it bare; *avena grossa (et nigra)* (large or black oats); and *avena mixta*, a mixture of the two. Pill-corn, which continued to be grown in Cornwall until the 1800s, served for rearing calves and foals and its meal was also used for making porridge.[25] Large oats were introduced in about 1330. They were used to feed poultry and to fatten pigs. On the Tavistock Abbey estates, they were also malted to provide ale for harvesters from 1460 onwards. The residues sieved from the large oats were called 'tail oats'. They were used for horse fodder or for making porridge in Lent.[26] On the Antony demesne farms, oats constituted nearly 30 per cent of the crops grown in 1747.[27]

Rye: Rye would flourish on the poorer soils, and rye bread was the common food of poor people in the early Middle Ages. On the Tavistock Abbey estates, it was not until 1460 that wheaten bread as well as rye came to be served to harvesters. On the Antony demesne farms, no rye was grown in 1747.

Barley: Although known in Cornwall since the Bronze Age, barley was apparently not grown successfully on the Tavistock Abbey estates during the Middle Ages. Whereas rye and oats can withstand some acidity, barley and wheat need lime or sand to sweeten the soil. However, by the 1500s, barley had come into general use, as noted by Carew, who wrote:

> Barley is growne into great use of late yeeres, so as now they till a larger quantitie in one Hundred, then [than] was in the whole Shire before: and of this, in the deare seasons past, the poore found happie benefit, for they were principally relieved, and the labourers also fed, by the bread made thereof; whereas otherwise, the scarcity of Wheate fel out so great, that these must have made many hungrie meales, and those out-right have starved ... This increase of Barley tillage hath also amended the Cornish drinke by converting that graine into Mault, which (to the il relishing of strangers) in former times they made onely of Oates.[28]

An inventory of the goods of Richard Harvey of Sheviock, who died in 1645, includes 'one ackir & quarter of barly & 3 score rakes of wheate' valued at £4 10s. On the Antony demesne farms in 1747, barley constituted nearly 30 per cent of the crops grown.[29] One of the farm labourers was given the task of grinding some of the barley into malt, usually on one day a month, except in May when three days were devoted to it.

Wheat: Carew distinguished two sorts of wheat grown in his time. The first, called 'French', was bearded, and needed the best soil. It cost the most effort but yielded the best results. The second was called 'notwheat', because it was unbearded. It was easier to grow but gave more modest yields. The inventory of William Harry of Sheviock, mariner, who died in 1626, included 'his corne' [i.e. wheat or barley], valued at £14, and 'corne threshed' valued at £3. The corn was his most valuable property, worth some 20 per cent of his whole estate. The inventory of Tristram Harry of Sheviock, who died in 1638, included 'wheate and barly in the barne and mowhaye', valued at £15 and 'corne in the grounds with other corne threshed and in park', valued at £10. His corn was likewise the most valuable part of his estate, worth fully a third of his entire estate. On the Antony demesne farms in 1747, more wheat was grown than any other crop. It constituted more than 40 per cent of the crops grown.[30]

Harvesting

Reaping and Binding: The method of harvesting in east Cornwall had certain characteristics that derived from the fact that the produce was carried from the fields on horseback, rather than on carts. According to Marshall:

> Every article of corn is bound; even the rakings of barley and oats that have been mown! But this, in the horseback husbandry, was perfectly right. Sheaves, or bundles of any sort, are not only much fitter for loading between crooks, but are much handier to be pitched, or rather to be flung, from ground to floor, to the top of the rick or mow ... than loose corn.[31]

168 *The Pengelly family making hay at Pool Field (between Crafthole and Pool Farm) in the 1940s. Left to right, Lawrence, Bert, Margaret, Wilfrid, Jack Stephens, Joe (in bowler), unknown, Lester (standing on rick), Bill Hancock, Mrs Cole.*

The corn was reaped either with a 'yowing hook' (a hewing or hand-reaping hook) or a scythe until the advent of cutting machines. Mowing 'engines' were invented in the 1600s. The steward of the Carew estates, John Treis, paid 4s. 6d. for '2 Blocks for ye Mow Engin' on 12 August 1693.[32] Where scythes were used, four men with scythes were able to reap an acre a day. Women or boys followed the harvesters, binding the sheaves and setting them up into 'shocks' – stacklets of seven to ten sheaves. Where ten were gathered, nine sheaves were formed into a square, with three sheaves on each side, and the tenth placed across the top. When the last sheaf had been cut, the harvester would shout out the 'harvest holla'.

Arish mows: The shocks were often left to stand in the fields for a few days before they were considered dry enough to be made into ricks. If the weather was bad, or the labour not immediately available to carry the wheat into the farmyard, the shocks were gathered up and formed into 'arrish mows' or stacklets in the fields.[33] Dr William Borlase described an arish mow as:

> a regular, solid cone, about twelve feet high, the beards all turned inwards, and the butt end of the sheaf only exposed to the weather; the whole cone is finished by an inverted sheaf of reed, or corn, and tied to the upper rows.[34]

The purpose of the arrish mows was to preserve the corn, which might be wheat, oats or barley, from the wind and the rain until it was ready for removal to the rickyard at the farm. There is a record of an arrish mow being set up in the fields at Trethill in about 1882. It was a stack of barley and was being put up on a very high and windswept site overlooking the River Lynher. To support it with a wooden prop, the farmer, Mr Hill, ordered a hole to be dug, some three feet deep. In digging the hole, the men unearthed a prehistoric burial chamber.[35]

Shocking and Stacking: The harvesting of grain was one of the most labour-intensive of all agricultural activities. In the 1800s, the earlier 'mowing engine' was improved with the addition of a 'cutter bar' or finger bar using a reciprocating blade. The scythe and sickle were now entirely replaced as a means of cutting corn crops and hay. Another development was the 'self deliverer', which consisted of rotating rakes which deposited the cut corn in small piles ready to be bound. The binding still had to be done by hand until the invention of the 'self binder' by William Deering of America in about 1880. This machine cut the corn and neatly bound and delivered the sheaves tied with string ready to be shocked. Even after the introduction of cutting and binding machines, the process of shocking and stacking remained unaltered until the introduction of the combine harvester in the 1950s. At harvest time, the farmers would effectively pool their labour. In the words of Tom Bersey:

169 *The Pengellys' haymaking picnic at Pool Field in the 1940s. Left to right, rear: Bill Hancock, Jack Stephens, Maggie, Joe (in bowler), Mrs Cole, Lester (seated with mug), Lawrence (with dog). Seated, centre: Wilfrid and Margaret; seated, right (wearing cap) Bert.*

170 *'Arishmows' (field stacklets approximately 12 feet high) were used to dry corn in the 1700s, as seen in this detail from a drawing of Enys House by W. Borlase:* Antiquities *(1769), p. 88.*

> farmers were always ready and willing to help one another at harvest time by lending men and horses – without payment. The womenfolk provided large quantities of food – often washed down with cider that had been made on the farm. The cider was a great attraction to the labourers.[36]

An evacuee, Terry Leather, recalls the process during the 1940s:

> Our job was to pick up [the sheaves] and stand them in groups of six, called a shuck (or shock). They had to be dried out ready for stacking into a rick. If in the meantime we had rain, then they all had to be turned by hand to dry out again ... When the rick was made, it was constantly checked for heat combustion by inserting long steel rods into it. If, when checked, the rods were too hot, the rick was pulled apart in order to cool it down ... Many ricks were destroyed by fire due to internal combustion, before any fire engine could get to them. The same methods were used in making hay.

Carrying: Marshall describes the very labour-intensive operation of carrying the harvest produce from the fields to the farmyard on horseback before carts came into general use.

> In carrying sheaf corn on horseback, the sheaves are packed in between the crooks, head to tail, with the butts outward, and carried up even; piling the load considerably above the horse's back ... A string of horses being thus laden, a boy travels them soberly to the barn or rickyard; where they are unloaded ... The whole string unloaded, the boy mounts, and, standing upright between the crooks, trots or perhaps gallops his horses back to the field; frequently, to the no small dismay, or perhaps injury, of peaceful travellers. A somewhat uncivilised practice.[37]

To carry the harvest to the rickyard, the string of horses first gave way to carts – two-wheeled vehicles in the 1700s. Later on, the carts gave way to wagons – four-wheeled vehicles with 'lades' (high ladder-like supports) back and front. The load was tied down with two ropes. Each rope was pulled tight by a 'tumblejack' or windlass attached to the back of the wagon.

Crying the Neck: When the last sheaf from the bottom of the wagon was about to be pitched onto the rick, the wagoner would shout 'I have'n, I have'n'. The men building the rick would reply 'What have'ee?' 'The neck, the neck', answered the wagoner as he pitched the last sheaf of the harvest onto the rick. In some parishes, the last sheaf was taken into the farmhouse and hung under the roof until the next harvest. The practice of crying the neck is still carried on in some parts of the West Country, where corn is cut with a binder to save the straw for thatching.

Stacking in Mowhays or Rickyards: If not erecting arish mows, Cornish farmers would carry the corn straight from the field to the farmyard and stack it in mowhays (groups of ricks), to allow it to dry.[38] To prevent the rats and mice from getting into them, the ricks were built on layers of faggots or on staddle stones supporting a wooden platform. A number of these staddle stones have been found in Sheviock.

Threshing: The next operation was to separate the grain from the straw. This was done on the threshing floor in the centre of the barn. The grain ready for threshing was stored at either end of the building. Threshing was generally done by means of a flail until the advent of threshing machines in the early 1800s. Threshing was the most labour-intensive activity of all on the farm, and it continued throughout the year. In the mid-1700s, the hind of the Antony demesne farms permanently employed ten men (plus or minus one) to work on the two demesne farms at Antony (Horson and Gimpson) for six days a week. The steward's records show that, in the first six months of 1747, those men were occupied in threshing in every single month.[39] On average, 25 per cent of their total labour each month was devoted to threshing. In the two peak months of January and February, the total number of days spent threshing were respectively 71 (41 per cent of the total labour available) and 88 (37 per cent).

In Cornwall and west Devon, the threshing of wheat and rye was often done by beating it by hand across a cask so as to preserve the straw from damage. The unbruised straw could then be used for thatching or for litter. Most houses and barns in Sheviock were thatched until the 19th century. On the Carew estates in Antony, in the first six months of 1747, the heaviest month for making reed was May, when 18 days labour was spent upon it.[40]

Winnowing: The final operation was to separate the pure corn from the chaff (the husks) by the action of the wind. The farmers would have the sacks of corn transported from the barn into some windswept field where the farm laborers or the womenfolk or boys would carry out the winnowing operation, tossing the corn in the wind on old sacks and catching the edible part on sheets spread out on the ground. The inventory of goods of Tristram Harry of Sheviock, who died in 1638, includes 'sacks shoes and winnowing sheets', valued at 6s. 8d., and shows that this was how winnowing was carried out on his farm. Perhaps his wife, Jane, was in charge of the operation. The practice disgusted William Marshall, who described 'the mistress of the farm perhaps being exposed in the severest weather to the cutting winds of winter in this slavish and truly barbarous employment'.[41]

In 1747, winnowing on the Antony demesne farms was done by the male farm laborers, and it was done in the barn. It was carried out intermittently for at least half the year. The process began on two days at the end of January (five men threshing and winnowing barley), continued through three days of February (three men threshing

171 *The roundhouse at Sheviock Barton erected c.1837. Horses would rotate a beam to activate machinery for threshing and other agricultural purposes.*

and winnowing oats; two men winnowing wheat and barley; two men threshing and winnowing wheat), two days in March (four men threshing and winnowing oats, and taking in and winnowing corn), two days in April (one man winnowing; three men bringing the corn into the barn from the mow and winnowing it), three days in May (five men bringing in and winnowing the corn; two men winnowing; one man winnowing), and two days in June (two men winnowing on one day; one man on the next).[42] Fifty years later, the machine fan was invented and it gradually replaced winnowing by hand.

Many back-breaking jobs apart from winnowing were done by women. In April 1731, the hind of the Carew estates paid £5 19s. to women for 'Harrowing, leasing [releasing] stones etc.'[43] In March the following year, he paid another £5 3s. 2d. to the 'women gathering stones & picking turneps'. Whereas men were generally paid 1s. a day for agricultural work at this time, the women workers were paid only 4d.

The Advent of the Threshing Machine: In the 1780s, Andrew and George Meikle of Scotland invented an efficient threshing machine that could be powered by horses, water or steam. C.S. Gilbert wrote in 1817 that 'thrashing machines, on the improved construction invented by Baker of Exeter have become very general, and few large farms are without them. All of them, except a small number wrought by water, and one by steam, are worked by horses.'[44] There still survives at Sheviock Barton the wheelhouse or roundhouse within which this 'horsepower' was contained. It is built onto the side of the barn. The horses inside (usually two) turned a big wooden beam. This was connected by means of a series of large cast iron cogs to a shaft that turned, as required, a chaff cutter, a reed comber, a threshing machine or a winnowing machine. All of these were manufactured by William Brenton Ltd of Polbathic.[45]

Over time, more and more threshers came to be worked by steam. Permanent steam engines were built inside their own specially constructed engine houses on the bigger farms to drive threshing machines through a system of belts and pulleys. The stone chimney of one such steam engine is still preserved at Higher Trethill Barton.[46] The large engine at Trethill also powered a saw in an adjacent saw-pit. Later still, threshing machines were hauled from farm to farm by steam traction engines working on a contract basis. These machines were in use during the Second World War, and the evacuee, Terry Leather, remembers the excitement of the arrival of the threshing machine:

> The threshing machine … would visit all the farms in turn. This machine was towed to the field and parked by the side of the rick that was to be threshed. It was driven by long leather belts, which were connected to a large steam engine. I can still remember the steam engine puffing away with its long belts flapping, and the shuffling of the threshing machine. The sheaves of corn were fed in to the top of the machine, which

> separated the corn from the chaff. The corn was fed into large hessian sacks to be stored. We always had the dog on the site, as there were so many rats to be caught ... There were [also] lots of rabbits in the corn. At the end of the day ... Prince, the dog, had caught between 30 and 40 rabbits. When there were large catches of rabbits like that, Uncle Herb would take them to Liskeard market to be sold. When we were working out in the field in the summer, lunch was brought out to us. Auntie Flo would bring us out hot Cornish pasties and bottles of cold tea.[47]

The last such contractor in Sheviock was Harold Dawe, who lived at No 2 Kowloon in the churchtown. His threshing machine was in use up to about 1960, when it was abandoned on Berry Down. In addition to the driver of the machine, a thresher required ten people to feed it and carry out the other ancillary operations. When the threshing machine was on the farm, neighbours would come to help. As remembered by Tom and Mary Bersey, the farmer's wife, at lunchtime, would prepare a 'threshing dinner' for all the helpers. The advent of the combine harvester in the 1950s removed the need for the travelling threshing machine and its small army of helpers.

172 *The chimney at Trethill erected c.1841. An engine attached to it would have worked threshing and winnowing machinery and also a circular saw.*

Haymaking: In the early spring, the stock was kept out of the meadows and pastures so that the grass would grow long and lush. In June and July, the farmer began cutting the hay. He did this in the middle of the day, because the dew made it too wet in the morning and evening. Before mechanisation, the hay was cut close to the ground with a scythe. Often, a line of men would work together to scythe the field quickly. Each man cut a 'swathe' of about ten feet – five feet on either side of him. After cutting, the hay was 'tedded' – tossed in the air to dry. If hay is stacked or baled wet, the sap within it can heat up and catch fire.

Chapter 24

Fruit and Orchards

The earliest piece of evidence relating to the wild fruits of Sheviock is the name 'Sheviock' itself, for in Cornish *siviek* means 'strawberry place'. The earliest Celtic inhabitants would have carefully noted a place where delicious wild fruits could be gathered, and marked its whereabouts by attaching the name of the fruit to the place. Richard Carew, in 1602, wrote about the wild fruits such as 'Whurts [i.e. whortleberries or bilberries], Strawberies and Raspies [i.e. raspberries]' which grew in the district.[1] There was no need for him to mention blackberries, which were too common to merit attention. To this day, the villagers of Sheviock know where to go to gather the wild strawberries. One of the best places is said to be the old road between Polscoe and Sheviock churchtown, the original 'strawberry place' from which the parish gets its name. Terry Leather, a London evacuee, remembers picking wild strawberries with Mrs Hearn of the *New Inn* in the 1940s. The area is still good for the cultivation of strawberries. Cote in Sheviock churchtown used to have a strawberry field up until the 1930s. Sconner too had noted strawberry gardens. In 1942, a one-roomed hut at 'Sconner strawberry gardens' was occupied by Jack Nettle, then over 70 years old.

Orchards and Cider

In Domesday survey of 1086, there is no mention of orchards in Cornwall, only of woodlands. One of the earliest accounts relating to apple orchards in Cornwall is a set of accounts from Penlyn in 1297, which mentions the expenditure of 1d. for oil 'bought for the cider press'.[2] The first mention of an orchard in south-east Cornwall is an apple orchard belonging to the Bishop of Exeter. This was at his manor of Cuddenbeke in St Germans. In a document of 1327, it is noted that one dole of cider produced there was sold for 10s.[3] At Woodbury in Devon, a farmer named Thomas Huntbear was paying tithes on apples and pears between 1423 and 1435.[4] After the destruction of the monasteries in 1536 and 1539, references to orchard planting become increasingly frequent. The archivist, Christine Edwards, has transcribed a letter written sometime after Michaelmas 1584 by Anthony Corne to Edward Arundell concerning the planting of an orchard on his estate at Treveliew in St Columb Minor.[5] In it, Corne explains that

> the orcharde ys plowed but not finished, they can not get cariges [carriages] men ar so busyed to plow, there ys no dounge broughte into neither gardin nor orchard. ... John Jenkyn ... hath ... sen the garden & orchard plats. He sayes your orchard will take vi score trees, he sayes more [that] ther must be as much good earth, dounge & sand be brought in to yt as must make yt two foot depe throughout, there can be no trees sett this yeare, he sayes more [that] it must be tyled [tilled] with beanes throughout for the losing [loosening] of the earth.

Carew provides further evidence for the cultivation of orchards in Cornwall in the late 16th century. In his *Survey*, started in 1586 though not published until 1602, he wrote:

> For Fruites ... longing [i.e. belonging] to the Orchard, as Peares, Plums, Peareplummes, Cherries, Mulberies, Chessenuts, and Wallnuts, though the meaner sort come short, the Gentlemen step not farre behind those of other parts [of the country].[6]

Carew omitted the apple from his list of fruit trees, but he did make one oblique reference to apple orchards, writing

> Not long sithence [since], there came a flocke of Birds into *Cornwall*, about Harvest season, in bignesse not much exceeding a Sparrow, which made a foule spoyle of the Apples.[7]

The evidence from the case of *Rolle* v *Blake*, relating to the payment of tithes in Sheviock on orchard fruits, likewise suggests that apple orchards could have been established here as early as 1598.[8] However, it was Carew's son, Richard, who was responsible for the large-scale planting of orchards in Sheviock and Antony a few years later. From his marriage in 1601 until he inherited his father's house at Antony in 1620, he lived in Sheviock, and probably resided at Sconner, which he bought in 1617. In the manuscript book he wrote for his children between 1628 and 1630, he stated that

> I ... fell to plantinge of fruite trees, makinge that my delighte, ... and I thanke god, as merily past [passed] my time therein, as if I had don it in hawking or huntinge, and mine apletrees I called my houndes, and my pearetrees, my hawkes, and I hope I can shew 20000 of them which have all passed through mine own handes, besides thousandes which I gave away.[9]

Richard Carew the younger married in January 1601 and was then granted the annuities that enabled him to set up his own household and to undertake this large-scale planting. By 1684, Edward Kneebone was reporting that there were 'throughout the whole [of the hundred of East] abundance of profitable orchards, whence syder [*sic*] as good as any unmixt elsewhere in the land is produced.'[10] A hundred years later, Marshall was writing that 'for the fruit markets, cherries, pears and walnuts are raised in great abundance'. He also observed that

> The orchards which succeed best in this district are situated in dips or hollows which are neither exposed to the bleak blasts from the north east, nor to the sea winds from the west and south west'.

This description perfectly fits many of the 29 acres of orchards that were shown to exist in Sheviock in the Tithe Redemption survey of 1840/41.[11] Although they were scattered all over the parish, the Sheviock orchards were invariably sited in valleys, dips or hollows, near houses. There were eight at Tredrossel, seven at Trewin, five at Trethill, five at Tredis, five at Polscoe Mill, four at Pool Farm, three at Kerslake, three at Haye, two at Horse Pool and two at the Glebe. In his will of 1815, Thomas Littleton of Trewin bequeathed to his younger son, Thomas, 'four hogsheads of cider to be selected by him out of my stock'.[12] There were other orchards in Sconner and on the holdings of the innkeeper, John Landrey, in Sheviock churchtown. The inns at Crafthole all had large orchards attached to them. Orchards at Tredis and Kerslake were described as 'gutter orchards' – that is, orchards straddling the bottom of a dip or valley. The guttering ensured that the grass growing below the apple trees was of the richest kind and would support flocks of grazing sheep. In Crafthole, many of the cottages had orchard plots attached to them, and the area called the Coombes was mostly given over to orchards.

The main purpose of the Sheviock orchards was to produce cider – some for sale, some to supply to the farm workers, and some for consumption by the farmer and his family. The cider-making process began with the maturation of the fruit. This took place either in the open air, where the apples would be piled in large heaps, or in the 'pound house'. The fruit was left piled up until it was sufficiently 'come' – i.e., until brown rot had begun to take place. Windfalls were just as apt for cider making as fresh-picked fruit. The 'pound house' was a building especially constructed for the operation of pounding or breaking

173 *Apples growing at Trethill House.*

174 *Painting at Cotehele by Mary Martin showing a horse working machinery to crush apples during the cider-making process.*

up the apples. Originally this was done by hand, a practice which persisted in Cornwall longer than in other counties. The apples would be thrown into a large trough or tub. Five or six people standing round the trough would then pound the apples with large club-shaped wooden pestles, whose ends were roughened and hardened with the heads of nails. By 1796, when Marshall wrote his *Rural Economy of the West of England*, hand pounding had largely given way to crushing in a horse-driven mill introduced from Herefordshire. The mill was a large circular trough with a smaller circular piece of stone in the centre.[13] This was called the 'trugg stone'. The space formed between the inner and outer walls of the trough was the track round which a vertically set millstone was rotated, drawn by one of the farm horses. The apples were shovelled into the trough to be pounded by the millstone. When the apples were sufficiently crushed, the resultant 'pomage' or 'cheese' was transferred to the cider press. Where water power was available, for example at Bag Mill in Trethill or at Polscoe Mill, the mill machinery could be altered from its usual operation of grinding corn to turning a wheel for crushing apples.

The press was a square container, on the bottom of which was spread a thin covering of unthreshed straw or reed, or sometimes sacking. The cheese was spread over this until it was three or four inches thick. Another thin layer of reed was spread over the cheese, and then another layer of pomage, and so on until it had reached the desired height. On the top, a wooden covering was laid. This was then depressed by a system of double levers to express the juice at the bottom. The juice was run off into large cisterns and the impurities were allowed to settle before the fermented liquor was poured into hogsheads of 63 gallons each, or sometimes 'pipes' – double hogsheads.

Cider-making at Blerrick and Kerslake in the 17th Century.

A law case that arose about the payment of tithes in 1669 and 1670 related in part to the orchards at Middle Blerrick, Lower Blerrick and Kerslake. The orchards that were marked on the 1840 tithe map probably stood on the same sites as those that featured in the case.[14] At Middle Blerrick in 1840 there were about three acres of orchard. According to Nicholas Sargent, one of the witnesses in the case, the defendant, Anthony Blake, occupied and enjoyed in 1669 and 1670 a tenement

> called Middle Blerrick conteyning by estimation about sixe or seaven acres of land on which the said defendant then had severall quantityes and bushells of Apples and peares which were worth for both the said yeares in this deponent's judgment at the least forty shillings. ... This deponent doth ... believe that [the defendant] did make use and convert the greatest part of these Apples into syder And this deponent saith that uppon the said tenement of Middle Blerrick there is and for many yeares last past hath beene an orchard, which is worth in the best of this deponent's judgement the sume of forty shillings at least.[15]

At Lower Blerrick in 1840, there were less than two acres of orchard surrounding the house. The witness, Nicholas Sargent, said that in 1669 and 1670, Blake 'was occupant and possessed of several orchards ... [at] Middle and Lower Blerrick' and that there were 'several quantityes of Apples and pears growen within the same, which this deponent is assuredly confident now worth foure pounds at least ...'

175 *The old apple pound at Trethill House, now used as an ornamental flower-bed.*

At Trethill and Kerslake in 1840, there were five orchards occupying some five and three-quarter acres of land. The biggest of these was over three acres in extent, and, though called Kerslake Orchard, was then part of Trethill Barton farm, as was 'Blarick Orchard' (just over half an acre). The other three orchards were at Kerslake and were called Gutter Orchard (three quarters of an acre), Orchard (just over an acre), and the tiny Maddock's Orchard. Although there were more orchards at Trethill and Kerslake than at Middle and Lower Blerrick, Anthony Blake apparently only occupied one of the orchards there, because according to another witness, Ann Bray, he only made one hogshead of cider from it and cut one acre of hay.

Cider-making offered employment to the women of the parish as well as to the men. The witness, Ann Bray, was one of those employed in the making of cider, as shown by her evidence to the court:

> att severall tymes within six or seaven yeares last past this deponent hath been employed by the defendant to gather and house severall quantityes of apples growen upon the tenement of Kesslake ... And accordingly this deponent hath gathered severall bushells of Apples growen upon the said tenement in each year some bushells of which Apples have been housed and sett to hoard and sundry other bushells thereof have been pownded up to make syder And this deponent believeth that the Apples made up into syder might make neere about a hogshead of sider each yeare one yeare with the other.

Cider-making in Later Centuries

The sale of cider was very profitable to the farmer. In 1800, for example, a hogshead fetched on average between one and three guineas (i.e. between £1 1s. and £3 3s.).[16] Good husbandry clauses in agricultural leases insisted on the replacement of apple trees. For example, in 1802, a clause in a lease of Chubb's tenement in Trewrickle provided that the tenant was to 'fetch bring carry plant dress prune and take care of all such young apple trees as shall from time to time be wanting to fill up the orchards on the premises'.[17]

Not all the effects of cider making were positive. William Marshall thought that 'the drunkenness, dissoluteness of manners, and the dishonesty of the lower class might well be referred, in whole or in great part, to the baleful effects of cider; which workmen of every description make a merit of stealing'.[18] Nevertheless, he recognised that the locals were 'more attached to it, even than those of Herefordshire. Their orchards might well be styled their temples, and apple trees their idols of worship'.[19] Sometimes a spirituous liquor was made from the dregs or 'snarlygogs'. This was called, with typical West Country humour, 'necessity'. Necessity continued to be made and sold in the West Country until the 1920s.[20] It was a cider spirit rather like a rough version of the Norman *calvados*.

Cider continued to be produced locally until well after the Second World War. Most farms produced just two or three hogsheads each year. This was consumed by the farmer and his family and friends, his staff and any casual labourers he employed. Tom Bersey remembers that at Sheviock Barton the cellar was kept locked, and the key was always taken into the kitchen at night. He recalls the occasion when a local lad called at the farm and struck up a conversation with him. During the course of it, the young man remarked that he had enjoyed the chat, but wished that his brother had been present. Tom Bersey, asking why, was told, 'If my brother had been here, he would have asked you for the key of the cellar; but I being very shy, don't like to'.

The largest cider-making farm in the parish was Tredrossel, with its eight apple orchards. Not surprisingly, therefore, Walter Hoskin at Tredrossel was the last farmer to have a working pound and press. During the war, when there was great pressure to grow more food, many of the old orchards were grubbed up; but schoolchildren from Sheviock School were still taken to see cider-making in process at Tredrossel.[21] Latterly the pound was worked by a machine rather than by a horse. Tom Bersey remembers that the other farmers would take their apples up to Tredrossel to use Walter Hoskin's cider-making facilities, until they were discontinued in the 1960s. Today the building that housed the old pound and press has been converted into a dwelling-house. It is called 'The Old Cider Press' and is owned by James and Karen Truscott. In recent times, apple orchards have been replanted at Trethill and Blerrick.

176 *Walter Hoskin operating his cider-press at Tredrossel, the last cider-making farm in Sheviock.*

177 *Harold Dawe (left) on his steam-driven traction engine with the blacksmith, Tom Ough, c.1938. These engines were driven from farm to farm to drive threshing machines.*

Chapter 25

Farming after 1800

During the 1700s and early 1800s, the price of corn was maintained at a high level by the Corn Laws, which protected British farmers from foreign competition. In 1828, a sliding scale of import duties was introduced. This meant that when domestic prices rose above a certain level, the duty fell by a corresponding amount. At the bottom end of the scale, when the domestic price fell below a certain level, the duty rose correspondingly. Until the end of the 1830s, protection was the official policy of both Whig-Liberal and Conservative governments. But at the end of that era both the Whig-Liberals and the moderate Conservatives led by Sir Robert Peel supported a low duty on corn imports in order to feed a rapidly rising population. In 1842, Peel altered the sliding scale to reduce the level of protection. In June 1846, he finally repealed the Corn Laws altogether, opening British markets to imports from the United States and elsewhere. Deprived of protection, the fortunes of farmers fluctuated considerably for the rest of the century. In 1847, shortages raised the price of grain, but in the following years it fell again. In 1850, a protectionist body called the East Cornwall Society for the Protection of Native Industry was formed. There were agricultural depressions in the 1850s and again in the 1870s. Rents were reduced by an average of 25 per cent.[1] Although the battle for protection was lost, tenant farmers continued to press for better contractual relationships with their landlords, for security for their investment in their farms, and for the reform of the Game Laws, which prohibited them from killing rabbits and hares. The opening of the Saltash railway bridge in 1859 was a boon for Cornish farmers and fishermen, because it enabled them to reach the important London market with their early crops of potatoes, vegetables and flowers, and their catches of fresh fish. By 1862, more than 2,000 tons of early potatoes and fish were sent from Cornwall to London by rail each year.

During the depression of the 1930s, farmers suffered very badly. Many commodity prices collapsed. The price of potatoes, for example, in the local markets went down from 10s. per cwt in 1924 to 4s. per cwt in 1929 and 1930. The price of hogs (young sheep, usually six to twelve months old, that had not yet been shorn), which had been

£2 to £3 each in 1926 and 1927, were down to just £1 in 1931. Fat steers, which had fetched 50s to 51s. per cwt in 1928, sold for only 41s. in 1931.[2] Some farms were let for just £1 per acre, and landlords had difficulty in finding tenants.

Potato Growing between the Wars

William Andrew, who was a mason by trade, possessed three fields to the west of Crafthole in the 1920s. These were Holloways (four acres) and Ring Burrows (nine acres) (formerly Lower and Higher Burrows) in Trewrickle, and West Field (15 acres) nearby. His daughter, Mrs Theodora Colwill, recalled the family's farming activities at this time:

> Our main living was growing potatoes and we grew the early ones in pieces cut out of the cliffs at the bottom of West Field. During the winter we went down to the harbour beach via Donkey Lane with our little donkey and baskets across his back to gather the horeweed [ore weed]. These are the long strands of seaweed and we put them in layers as we dug the ground over. In early January we started to dig the ground over again and prepare for the planting of the early potatoes. We had our little shed there, where we put the potatoes to bud, and of course it was a good shelter when it rained. When the potato leaves started to show it meant hoeing out the weeds, then banking them up.
>
> We dug our first potatoes around early or mid-April and they tasted good. They were put in one-stone boxes, all topped off nicely and covered with potato leaves. You then graduated to two-stone baskets, then four-stone maunds, never in bags.[3] Some were sold locally and others taken to market.[4] Then it was time to prepare Holloways for our main crop of potatoes.
>
> Dad had a little pony and trap and, of course, the donkey, but we needed a bigger horse along with a wagon and lots of other implements to work the ground. We also grew corn and various other vegetables. We kept pigs and a Guernsey cow, chickens, ducks, the odd goose, and all this was housed at the top of West Field. The Guernsey cow gave lovely milk, which was very rich. She had to be milked each day and the milk brought back home to Cosy Cot. Mum would put it to set, then scald in deep pans of water; when cooled the lovely thick cream would be skimmed off.[5] We never wasted any milk as any surplus would be taken back to the pigs and any cream left over we would make into butter.[6]

The fishing family, the Pengellys, also had 20 acres between Pool and Crafthole. Like the Andrew family, they used donkeys to bring up the seaweed to fertilise the potato fields, and later sold the potatoes in Devonport Market.

Agriculture in Sheviock during the Second World War

Towards the outbreak of the Second World War, farming changed dramatically. Prices recovered to pre-depression levels. Production of food became all-important and more machinery was introduced. Hedges were removed to accommodate larger and more efficient machines, and orchards were grubbed up to grow more food. Agricultural production doubled between 1939 and 1945. In consequence, more people were needed to work in agriculture. The Government formed a Land Army of women and girls to work on the farms. The survey carried out by Mrs Elsie Wilson of Lynher Villa in 1942 records two 'land girls', Mary Dawson and Ann Littleton, in residence at Hendra Farm (in St Germans parish); one, Grace Jenks, at Triffle (also in St Germans); and one, whose name is not recorded, at Crafthole Farm. It was also reported that another girl was about to take up residence at Trethill.

178 *Tom Ough on a horse-drawn mower cutting grass to make hay, perhaps at Sconner, before the Second World War.*

Horses continued to be used on farms in Sheviock until well after the Second World War. A survey carried out in 1942 by a local farmer, W.J. Holman of the Glebe Farm, showed that there were then 29 horses and 16 carts in the parish. Farmer Holman had a pony and trap. According to John Biles, who knew him, he was 'a barrel of a man' and when his cart was in motion, one corner was very low, with the rest seemingly in the air. Holman used this conveyance when he did his shopping in Torpoint. One day, after shopping, when he went to get into his trap, there was a dog sitting in the passenger seat. This was 'Timothy', whose owners lived in Sydenham House, Crafthole. They had accidentally left him behind when they had done their own shopping. According to Biles, 'At first, Mr Holman was afraid to get in, but as the dog was quiet, he did so, and they travelled together to Sheviock, when, without any ado, the dog alighted to walk up the hill to Crafthole.'

179 *Millicent Hoskin of Tredrossel driving a Ferguson T20 tractor c.1948.*

The first tractor arrived in 1935. It was a second-hand Fordson on iron wheels – 'very bumpy for the driver', according to Tom Bersey who drove it.

Rubber tyres on tractors did not come into general use until after 1938. There was a transitional period during which farmers adapted horse-drawn implements to the new source of power. Later, manufacturers introduced implements purposely made for tractors.

Recollections of an Evacuee

During the Second World War, older children who had been evacuated from London and elsewhere made themselves useful on the farms. Terry Leather, who had been evacuated from Catford in South London, soon found himself helping the Bean family at Lantic Farm.[7] His recollections of harvesting and catching rabbits have already been given. These are his other memories of life on the farm:

> Uncle Herb … had a big farm and was always appreciative of all the help he could get.[8] He was never short of [it], because we would get other boys from the village to help out. Working on the farm was a whole new experience for me, which I loved very much. There was so much to do. Over the years, I learnt to milk the cows and look after the horses. Most of the work on the farm was done with the horses. Due to fuel rationing there were no tractors. One of the horses, Tommy, was a moody horse, and if he played up, which he sometimes did – like not wanting to be harnessed to pull the cart – Uncle Herb knew just how to handle him. When he had dealt with him, he would do all that was asked. Uncle Herb had a marvellous way of handling animals.
>
> When it was time for digging up potatoes – approximately four tons a week would be the required amount – two tons were collected by lorry twice a week. As boys, we had many a spud fight while picking up potatoes. Ken was mostly in charge of the machines for digging and ploughing. The potato digger required two horses to pull it. Our job was picking them up in baskets and then bagging them into hessian sacks. The bags were then weighed and stacked up ready for collection. Although seed potatoes were brought in, we used to save some of our own for seed. I can remember all the potatoes placed on shelves in the seed shed. When it was time for planting, one of the jobs that had to be done was cutting the potatoes with a certain number of shoots on each. They were then placed very carefully in baskets to be taken out to the field that we ploughed ready for us to plant the new seeds. We used to plant early potatoes down in the cliff pieces, well down in the cliffs, which were the first early Cornish potatoes. It was a lovely farm to work on, and when we were planting early potatoes, I used to love looking out over the beach and the seashore. It used to get quite warm working down in the cliffs, particularly if the wind was blowing off land.

180 *Herbert and Florence Bean (above) farmed at Lantic on the border between Sheviock and St Germans during the Second World War.*

One day, while we were getting the cows in to be milked, one of the young heifers broke free from the herd and jumped a barbed wire fence and grazed its udders. This gave us all a big problem, because this cow still had to be milked. Although she hadn't hurt herself very badly, she did not take kindly to being milked. After several attempts to milk her without much success – with foot stuck in bucket – Uncle Herb decided the only way was to tie a rope around one of her back legs and then around her neck, and pull her back legs up. She didn't like that much either, but after a while it worked and we managed to milk her.

One morning, I arrived at the farm to find Uncle Herb and Ken very upset. During the night a fox had got into the chicken run and killed every chicken. I shall never forget the devastation caused by that fox – blood and chicken feathers were everywhere. Uncle Herb said to Ken, 'We are going to kill that fox'. After Prince, the dog, had picked up the scent from the fox, off they went both carrying shotguns. Lantic Farm was very near the cliffs and seashore. By midday, they both returned to the farm, having driven the fox down onto the beach where they shot it.

Sometimes, when it was school holidays, I used to stay and sleep on the farm. Chuffy and I used to have great fun.[9] We would go out rabbiting together with Prince, who not only caught rabbits but also used to go looking for and killing rats. On the farm we were up early, usually at 4.30 a.m. The first job was getting the cows in to be milked. All the animals had to be fed. These were the horses, pigs and chickens. When these jobs were done, we came in to breakfast.

One day up on the farm, Uncle Herb said to me, 'Tel, take Tommy the horse with the dray and drive over to Three Acre (that was the name of the field) and pick up five hundredweight of small spuds for the pigs' feed. And, Tel, go careful with

181 *Harvesting picnic at Trewrickle Farm c.1938. Mary Higman, the farmer's wife, has just brought tea to the 11 men needed to do the harvesting. The farmer, Hevan Higman, stands in the top row (centre) next to Tom Ough on his left. Tom's brother, Jack, stands at the end of the row. Seated, left, is Harold Dawe. His brother, Jack (with Trilby hat), is seated second from the end.*

> Tommy, because he's a bit frisky'. I was confident that I could handle him, as he was my favourite horse. The dray was a low platform trolley with two iron wheels on it.
>
> As we left the farmyard, the wheels on the dray were clattering away going along the road. I could feel Tommy's head pulling at the reins and wanting to gallop. As we got to the field, the gate was open, so we drove straight in. I loaded the spuds on the dray. Then, as we came back out of the field, lying close to the hedge was a sheet of corrugated iron. One of the wheels of the dray ran over it, which made a rumbling sound and startled Tommy. We came back out of the field a lot quicker than we went in! Tommy broke into a gallop. I was shouting at him, 'Whoa!' and 'Slow down!' At the same time, an army jeep with four American soldiers in it came up behind us and started sounding its horn. By this time, the spuds were spilling out over the road, and the Americans were laughing their heads off. I was holding on for all I was worth, and pulling on the reins to hold Tommy back. Suddenly, the reins broke and Tommy had a free head. How I managed to stay on the dray I don't know, but somehow I did. On hearing the commotion, Uncle Herb came out of the farm and grabbed the broken reins. Tommy then reared up, the dray spun round, and I fell off. The Americans were still laughing as they drove up the road.

Prisoners of War on the Farms[10]

In the later stages of the war, prisoners who were housed in the former U.S. Army camp at Bake, near Trerulefoot, supplied labour for seasonal work. The German and Italian prisoners were not forced to work on farms, but few objected. It was perhaps a welcome relief from the boredom of prison-camp life. One German prisoner of war, Matt Herbst, who was working at Crafthole Farm, a dairy farm run by Mr and Mrs Arnold Hoskin, fell in love with Anne Hoskin, the daughter of Mr and Mrs Reginald Hoskin of St Anne's in Crafthole. They met while he was waiting for the lorry to take him back to the camp, and she brought him a cup of cocoa.[11] Once he broke out of prison camp to visit her. After the ban on fraternisation had been lifted, he was allowed to spend Christmas with her and her family. Eventually, they got married. He settled in Cornwall and now lives in Torpoint.

Fred Paul, who was then a schoolboy living in Sheviock village, writes of the prisoners of war (P.O.W.s),

> In 1945, I would be waiting for the school bus to take me to Saltash school at the cross-roads at the end of Horsepool Lane nearly half a mile from Sheviock village. Some mornings an army lorry would drop off three or four P.O.W.s who would wait until a local farmer collected them for a day's work on his farm. They had no guards, were very polite, and most of them spoke fluent English. One of them would even check my maths homework. Some evenings a few of the P.O.W.s would be waiting by the churchyard steps for their lorry to take them back to camp. My grandmother, Mrs May, who said she hated all Germans, would load up a tray with cups of tea and freshly made scones and take them to them. Her excuse was, 'Well, I expect they have mothers somewhere worrying about them'.

Agriculture after the War

During and immediately after the war, agriculture developed rapidly with the introduction of milking machines, combine-harvesters, grain dryers, larger tractors and cultivating machinery. Chemical sprays were introduced for the control of weeds and diseases. New strains of cereals and plants were developed. All this led to a huge increase in yields per acre. During the 1950s and 1960s, many small farms were amalgamated into larger units. Farmers were encouraged to enlarge their farms by Government amalgamation grants. They were also given drainage and hedge-removal grants.[12] This made the farms more viable as commercial enterprises; but it fundamentally changed the character of Sheviock, by reducing the number of people employed in agriculture. Between 1840 and 2000, the number of farmers in Sheviock decreased from 19 to five, with Antony Estates taking over the direct running of many formerly tenanted farms, as shown by the table below.

SHEVIOCK FARMS 1840-2000

	Acreage 1840	Farmer 1840	Farmer 1940	Farmer 2000
1. Sheviock Barton	163	John Liscombe	T.Edgar Bersey	Antony Estates
2. Blazor: Quarters 1 and 3				
(Crafthole Farm)	79	William Lyne	Arnold Hoskin	golf course
Quarters 2 and 4				
(Cross House)	34	Mary Pynsent	Harold Bersey	golf course
3. The Glebe Farm	126	William Lyne	William Holman	Antony Estates
4. Haye Farm	111	Benjamin Cornish	Thomas Holman	Antony Estates
5. Kerslake	100	J W Angeer	Jim Giddy	Nicholas Rundle
6. Lantic (partly in St Germans parish)				
		–	Herbert Bean	Farmed with Trewrickle
7. Liscawn	70	Samuel Lyne	John Monksworthy	Farmed with Kerslake
8. Poole	57	John Batten		
	51	John Batten	William Rundle	Farmed with Trewrickle
9. Horse Pool	106	John Batten	Not known	Antony Estates
10. Sconner Farm	83	Robert Rickard	Harry Waycott	Farmed with Trewrickle
11. Tredis Farm (Higher)	96	William Lang	Albert Giddy	David & Cindy Rice
12. Tredis Farm (Lower)	105	Miss Pole	Ernest Baker	Peter & Helena Cade
13. Tredrossel	187	Anthony Spiller	Walter Hoskin	Farmed with Trewrickle
14. Trethill	151	Samuel Wallis Roberts		
			Col. Roberts	Farmed with Kerslake
15. Trewin	141	John Littleton	John Littleton	Keith Hoskin of Hendra
16. Trewrickle	71	Samuel Littleton	Hevan Higman	Kevin Andrew
	14	Edward Elliott		
	70	John Cock		
17. Vellands	47	John Trevan	Arnold Hoskin	Farmed with Kerslake

Farmed acreage 1,862

182 *A combine harvester working near Crafthole in 2008. The machine, driven by just one man, can cut and thresh the corn in a large field, in a few hours.*

Modern Diversification

In a move to add value to farm produce, Tom Bersey produced sheep's milk cheese at Sheviock Barton from 1984 to 1990. Three varieties were made: 'Sheviock', which was full fat; 'Ladywell', which was a soft cheese; and 'Port Royal', which was a mature blue cheese. The normal popular breeds of sheep do not produce large quantities of milk. Tom Bersey therefore introduced a new breed called 'British Milk Sheep' to his existing flock, by purchasing a few ewes and rams. The new breed gave much more milk. They were also very prolific, often producing quadruplets and sometimes quintuplets. The ewe lambs were required eventually for the dairy. Sheep only produce milk for two or three months after lambing. Therefore, to enable cheese to be made throughout the year, the milk had to be taken to a large freeze store in Plymouth. It was then released in small quantities each week to allow a continuous process. The transportation and freezing of the milk became very expensive and the business was discontinued in 1990.

In the 1990s Nick Rundle at Trethill Farm began to import Christmas Trees from the continent of Europe. These were stored near his barns at Trethill and then shipped to wholesalers around the United Kingdom and also sold retail from the farm. The Rice family at Higher Tredis have concentrated on egg production, selling through many local outlets, such the butchers' shop, Paul Bray at Tideford, and also selling retail from the farm.

Cornish Hedges

From the 1500s, the Cornish hedge has been a prominent feature of the landscape – serving not only to divide the fields or meadows, but also to give shelter and shade to cattle and sheep. The building and maintenance of these hedges is a very skilled craft. It former times it was usually carried out during the winter months, using turfs laid in rows on the outside and filling the centre with fine soil, consolidated with shovel and a 'bidix'.[13] Although this was very hard work, men took great pride in their skill and found great satisfaction in the finished work. A man was expected to build a 'land yard' in a day.[14] In modern times, Cornish hedges are usually built of stone. In earlier times, stone was not easily available, but all the materials for turf hedges were freely available on site. Early leases often specified whether the tenant had a right to cut turfs.

In rural areas, dustcarts were rarely seen until after the Second World War. Before the war, every parishioner was responsible for his or her own waste disposal. Tom Bersey remembers men setting off to build their hedges carrying small sacks containing tins and other non-inflammable waste objects which they subsequently buried in the hedges as they worked. Rubbish that would burn was thrown into the fire of the kitchen range.

183 *Threshed barley being unloaded onto a truck near Crafthole in 2008.*

PART VI

The Church

184 *The church of St Mary at Sheviock. The lower stage of the tower dates from the mid-1200s and the upper stage and steeple from the early 1300s.*

Chapter 26

The Early Church. The Medieval Fabric of St Mary's

The Early Church

Archaeological evidence has shown that Christians were living in Roman Exeter in the fourth century. From that time onwards Christianity had at least a toehold in the South West. It received a boost with the arrival of immigrants and missionaries from Ireland and South Wales in the sixth century. The nearest Celtic monastery to Sheviock was *Lannaled* or *Lanalet*, the modern St Germans. According to Susan M. Pearce it probably dates from the early sixth century, although this is conjectural.[1] The *lann* element of the place name is Cornish for a sacred enclosure, which usually incorporated a cemetery. The meaning of the second element, *alet*, is not certain, but recent scholarship suggests that it has a topographical meaning.[2] There is a River Aled in Wales, a place in Kenwyn parish (north of Truro) called Allet, and another in Brittany called Alet. The Welsh scholar, M. Richards, derives the Welsh river name, *Aled*, from the root *al*, meaning 'grow' or 'nourish', with a suffix, *-ed*.[3] *Lannaled* therefore probably means the churchyard of the nourishing river. The old name of the monastery of *Lannaled* has been preserved in a number of writings from about A.D. 950.[4] One of these, the *missa propria*, or special mass for St Germans, includes a collect which in translation reads:

> Favour, Lord God, all Christian people coming together from diverse parts of nations to one place so that they who desire … to visit the very famous and universally known place Lannaled, where the relics of Bishop Germanus are preserved, may certainly be freed from infirmities of soul and body.[5]

According to one authority, the Germanus in question was not the Bishop of Auxerre who came to extirpate the Pelagian heresy in the fifth century, but an earlier Celtic saint of the same name to whose shrine the monks were seeking to attract pilgrims.[6] By the time of Domesday Book (1086), the estate of St Germans consisted of 24 hides of land (2,880 English acres), the second largest religious estate in Cornwall.[7] By that time, too, the old name had been dropped in favour of St Germans. It was probably

185 *Springs were revered by the ancient Celts. Water from the spring at Ladywell was used for baptisms until the 1800s.*

the canons from Lannaled who first brought Christianity to the people of Sheviock. Religious centres like Lannaled (called minsters by the Anglo-Saxons, from the Latin *monasterium* or monastery) served very widespread communities. In the whole of eastern Cornwall there were only two such monasteries, Lannaled and *Lanscauetona* (St Stephens by Launceston). King Athelstan (924-9) made Lannaled the seat of a bishop and appointed a monk with the Cornish name of Conan as bishop. Conan's jurisdiction extended 'as far as the Tamar flowed'.[8] The monastery of Lannaled was served not by cloistered monks, but by canons, attached to the bishopric during the time that it was seated there. Early on, these were secular canons, living together as clergy, but not subject to a regular rule of conduct.[9] A minster, such as Lannaled, provided spiritual services to all the laity in its district:

> Celtic monasteries … acquired a pastoral role in their neighbourhoods from early times … Minsters became bases for evangelising the lands nearby. The clergy provided baptisms, confessions, masses, prayers and funerals for the public, either inside the minster church or out in the countryside. In return, the people were expected to look to their nearest minster for these services, and to support it with donations of food or money. A system of parishes grew up – territories accredited to each minster. They may have existed as early as the seventh century and were well established by the tenth.'[10]

186 *Monks from the priory of St Germans first brought Christianity to Sheviock. The entrance arches of the priory church probably date from the mid-1100s.*

The whole of the Rame Peninsula was within easy reach of the monastery. The canons could have brought the Christian message to the people of Sheviock, baptised them in the holy waters already venerated by the people (probably Ladywell), heard their confessions and said masses out in the open.[11] Crosses may have been erected at the regular meeting places, though none that still survive in the parish can be dated to this early period.

Sheviock, the Saxon Royal Family and Tavistock Abbey

There is no evidence that the Anglo-Saxons built a church in Sheviock, although it is generally thought that the division of Cornwall into parishes occurred in the tenth and eleventh centuries.[12] Aelfwynn, sister of King Edgar (959-75), was the first recorded Saxon owner of Sheviock. She certainly had the resources to build a church had she been minded to do so. The tithe laws of King Edgar of A.D. 960-2 relate to the payment of tithe revenues in circumstances where new churches had sprung up in territories previously served by minsters. They thus make it clear that by then many new churches had been built in Britain and were competing with the minsters for a share of local revenues. In 968, King Edgar founded a Benedictine abbey at Tavistock. His brother-in-law, Ordulf, Earl of Devon and husband of Aelfwynn, took over from his father, Ordgar, the supervision of the foundation, and Aelfwynn gave her estates in Sheviock, Rame and elsewhere as endowments for the abbey. In 1066, Antony was added to the endowments by their descendant, another Ordulf. In 981, the new King, Aethelred (978-1016), who was the nephew of Ordulf and Aelfwynn, issued a charter confirming the endowment of the estates to the abbey. Once Sheviock became an endowment of the abbey, the monks would have placed a 'sergeant' here to farm their lands and to ensure a regular supply of fish from the Tamar estuary and from their sea fishery at Portwrinkle. The base for their agricultural activities was probably the village of Sheviock. For more than one hundred years the whole manor belonged exclusively to the Anglo-Saxon monks. Charles Henderson credited the abbey with being the first builder of a church in Sheviock. However, he thought that they did so after the Norman Conquest and not before it. Sheviock's church, he wrote, 'was probably first built in Norman times by the Abbey of Tavistock'.[13]

The Norman Church at Sheviock at the time of Domesday Book

A charter issued by Bishop William Warelwast of Exeter (1107-1137) contains a reference to 'the churches of the honour of Sheviock'. The charter has been transcribed by H.P.R. Finberg and published in the original Latin.[14] In translation, it reads

> You should know that I have for good reason granted and confirmed to the monastery of Tavistock [the endowments of the] churches of the honour of Sheviock which

> Abbot Geoffrey and the abbey retained in their hands when they gave that land to Erbenald to hold by knight's service.[15]

The 'honour of Sheviock' consisted of six manors: Sheviock, Rame, Antony, Penharget in St Ive, Tolcarne in North Hill, and Trewornan in St Minver.[16] Sheviock was the seat of the holder of the honour. Abbot Geoffrey was abbot of Tavistock from A.D. 1082 to 1088, so any churches known to be within the honour of Sheviock at that time can date their foundation to the time of Abbot Geoffrey. In his study of Tavistock Abbey, Finberg stated that the churches in question were those of Antony, St John and Sheviock.[17] These churches were identified as belonging to Tavistock Abbey in a charter made between 1155 and 1160; so Finberg reasonably deduced that these must have been the 'churches of the honour of Sheviock' existing in Abbot Geoffrey's time. Although the church at Sheviock is not specifically mentioned in Domesday Book (1086), this does not mean that it was not then in existence; because Domesday Book omitted mention of all Cornish churches except the collegiate ones. Furthermore, the compilers of Domesday Book assumed that each 'vill' (nucleated settlement) would be able to provide a priest to give evidence to them, and also a reeve and six *villani*.[18]

The Dedication of the Church

The register of Bishop Veysey (in office 1519-51 and 1553-4), contains a copy of Pope Celestine III's bull of exemption and confirmation relating to all the churches and tithes of the monastery of Tavistock, dated 29 May 1193.[19] The bull includes the following words:

> Bishop Celestine, servant of servants, to the divinely beloved Herbert, Abbot of Tavistock, and to his lawful successors for ever: ... we adjudge to the monastery of Tavistock ... the care and absolute ownership (securing the privilege with these present writings) [of] the buildings and whatever possessions and whatever goods, both ecclesiastical and worldly, it may possess justly and according to canon law as a result of benefactions to the said monastery ... and they shall remain secure and undiminished to you and your successors. In which we number these properties expressly in words, namely ... Sheviock, and the church of blessed Mary founded there.[20]

187 *The unadorned font at St Mary's church was in place when the church was consecrated by Bishop Bronescombe in 1259.*

So we know that the original dedication of the 11th-century church was to St Mary, and that the church belonged to the abbey.[21] Another entry, in

188 *The windows of Exeter Cathedral constructed before 1300 set the style for many parish churches in Devon and Cornwall, including St Mary's.*

Bishop Bronescombe's register (for 22 March 1277), states that on the presentation of William Dawney, knight, the custody of *Ecclesie Beate Marie de Sevioch* (the church of Blessed Mary of Sheviock) was entrusted to a certain individual.[22]

The Endowments of the Church

From the moment when the abbot and convent of Tavistock granted the manor of Sheviock to Erbenald to hold by knight's service, all the temporal revenues of Sheviock belonged to the Dawneys, but Tavistock Abbey still owned the revenues deriving from the church. In legal parlance they were the owners of the 'spiritualities' or spiritual revenues. These revenues were also referred to as 'endowments'. They included the greater and lesser tithes, 'mortuaries' and burial fees and offerings at Christmas, Easter, Whitsuntide and the day of the patronal festival.[23] A mortuary was a gift to the rector from the estate of a deceased parishioner. In 1410-11, the rector's procurator received an ox, a cow, a sheep, two cocks and a hen as mortuary gifts.[24] Rent from the glebe was also part of the endowments of the church.

The charter naming Sheviock as one of the churches belonging to Tavistock Abbey was issued by Bishop Robert II of Exeter (1155-60). In translation, the bishop's charter reads as follows:[25]

> Sir Walter, Abbot of Tavistock, in our presence granted to Andrew of Petherwin, deacon, the endowments of the churches of Sheviock, Antony, and St John for his use, he giving in return each year to the monastery of Tavistock thirty shillings in three instalments: 10s. at the feast of St Rumon, 10s. at the Purification of St Mary, and 10s. at the birth of St John the Baptist.[26]

In this way, the abbot had farmed out the spiritual revenues of Sheviock, and the other two churches mentioned, in return for an annual fixed rent. Bishop Robert's charter shows that the annual value of the endowments of St Mary's was in excess of 10s. in the period 1155-60. In a valuation of church properties ordered by Edward I in 1291, the church was valued at £5 6s. 8d. In 1535, after Henry VIII had declared himself Supreme Head of the Church of England, he caused another valuation, called the Valor Ecclesiasticus, to be made. The entry for Sheviock reads in translation, 'The rectory [of Sheviock], including both the greater and the lesser tithes with the profits of the glebe [is worth] ... £26 14s. 6d.' At that time, the rector was also still paying an annuity of 3s. to the Abbey of Tavistock, the same amount that the rector's procurator, John Penhale, had paid as an annuity in 1410-11.[27] In 1840, the value of the tithes was given as £335 and the value of the glebe as £100.[28] The church at Sheviock possessed a large glebe, of more than 100 acres in extent, described in some detail by the rector's bailiff, John Penhale, in his account for 1410-11.[29]

Rectors, Parsons and Vicars

The person in legal possession of the endowments of a church was called the 'rector', being the person with the legal 'right' to them. Another name for the rector was 'parson'. A priest acting in place of the rector or parson was called the 'vicar'. We know from Pope Celestine's charter that Abbot Herbert of Tavistock was still in legal possession of the endowments of St Mary's in 1193, and so was in the position of rector. In these circumstances, the bishop would have insisted that the abbot presented a vicar or chaplain to look after the cure of souls in Sheviock. However, at some date between 1193 and 1279, the benefice of Sheviock became a rectory, with the full right to the tithes vested in the incumbent. In the Calendar of Patent Rolls of 1316, William de Lananta (Lelant), who was instituted in 1279, is referred to as 'parson' of Sheviocke, showing that the change had taken place by then.[30]

The Advowson of the Church

The right to appoint the priest, called the 'advowson', was another valuable incident of the ownership of a church. At the time of Domesday Book, the advowsons of Sheviock, Antony and St John belonged to Tavistock Abbey. But, sometime between 1174 and 1184, when Abbot Baldwin was in office, Henry Dawney contested the abbot's claim. According to another charter, the dispute was resolved in this way:

> Abbot Baldwin and the Abbey of Tavistock have conceded to Henry Dawney and his heirs the right of presentation to the churches of Sheviock and St John, and the said Henry proclaims for himself and his heirs forever that the church of Antony is [in the gift of] Tavistock Abbey, and he renounces for himself and his heirs forever all the falsehoods which he maintained against the abbot and the monastery concerning the advowson of this same church of Antony.[31]

This dispute was not the last concerning the advowson of St Mary's. Another erupted as a result of the minority of Nicholas Dawney, who lived from *c.*1280 to 1332 and was a great benefactor of the church, as well as being the founder of Crafthole.[32] According to the then Abbot of Tavistock, the right of presentation belonged to him because it arose during Nicholas's minority. According to the abbot, the advowson was attached to the tenement of Blereck (Blerrick), and he, the abbot, seized that tenement under the title of custody on account of Nicholas's minority. Although he handed the tenement back to Nicholas during the latter's minority, he reserved to himself the advowson that went with it until Nicholas should come of age. Nicholas counter-claimed that at the time of the vacancy he was of full age. The case was decided in Nicholas's favour.[33] Nicholas married Joan, daughter of Walter Langdon, and in 1330 presented John de Langedone as rector.

The Medieval Fabric of St Mary's

The Norman Church at the time of Domesday Book

Judging by the Domesday Book statistics, the population of the parish was between 100 and 125 in 1086. No traces of the Norman church built for this small community survive.

The Church Dedicated by Bishop Bronescombe

By the mid-1250s, the population had probably grown to about 250.[34] A new building was therefore begun. Walter Bronescombe, described by a medieval historian, William of Worcester (b.1415), as 'Walter le Goode', was then bishop of Exeter.[35] Early in his episcopacy (1257-80), Bronescombe inaugurated a wholesale programme of church dedications in the county. On 11 and 12 October 1259, he was staying at St Germans, where he had his own manor of Cuddenbeke. On 13 October 1259, he dedicated the church of the Blessed Mary at Sheviock.[36] The actual entry in the bishop's Register reads '*Anno eodem* [1259], *die Lune post Festum Sancti Dionisii* [13 October], *dedicavit Ecclesiam de Shevioke*.' (In the same year, on the Monday after the Feast of St Dionysius, he dedicated the church of Sheviock.) Over a period of three months, Bronescombe dedicated some 30 churches. Towards the end of his life, Bronescombe also conceived and planned the rebuilding of Exeter Cathedral.[37]

We can imagine the Bishop and his entourage of about 30 men and boys (the maximum permitted under canon law), coming in great state to the church. The bishop would have been greeted by the lord of the manor (probably Henry Dawney the younger), the parish priest (whose name has not been preserved), his clerk and assistants and the villagers. It would have been a rare opportunity for them to hear singing of a quality that was normally heard only in cathedrals and monasteries. Perhaps the bishop's chaplains and boys sang the eighth-century hymn, *Urbs beata Hierusalem*,

189 *The east window tracery at St Mary's was constructed in the early 1300s. The ogee-headed niche at its base is in the decorated style of the mid-1300s. The glass, inspired by the Oxford Movement, was made by William Wailes of Newcastle* c.*1850.*

which was the hymn sung throughout Europe at the dedication of a church.[38] The next day the bishop moved on to Antony, where he dedicated the church, and then on 15 October he dedicated the church at Rame. Only two parts of the church dedicated by Bishop Bronescombe at Sheviock survive: the lower stage of the west tower, and the font, still in situ. Churches had no pews in the 13th century, but moveable wooden benches were sometimes brought in.[39]

The Foundation of Crafthole and the Enlargement of the Church

In the early 1300s, the walls of the church dedicated by Bishop Bronescombe were taken down, leaving only the lower stage of the tower. The principal event that precipitated the re-building was the foundation of the borough of Crafthole by Sir Nicholas Dawney in 1314. The effect of this new foundation was to increase the population of the parish by about 100, making a total population of some 350 people. To feed the new residents, a huge new barn was built at Sheviock Barton. To grind enough corn to fill the barn, a new windmill may have been constructed at Gill Ball near Sheviock woods. To cater for the religious needs of the parishioners, an enlarged cruciform church was built with the elegant geometric window tracery that we still see today. However, to the parishioners at the time, the newly-enlarged church seemed still not big enough.[40] A village joke persisted down the ages relating to the smallness of the church compared with the hugeness of the barn. Carew tells the story in his *Survey of Cornwall*, published in 1602:

> There runneth … a tale amongst the parishioners, how one of these Dannyes ancestours undertook to build the Church and his wife the barne adjoyning, and that, casting up their accounts, upon finishing of their workes, the barne was found to cost three halfepence more than the Church: and so it might well fall out: for it is a great barne, and a little Church.[41]

The tale most likely refers to the buildings erected in the time of Sir Nicholas Dawney (lord of the manor from *c.*1286 to 1332) and his wife, Joan Langdon – for it was these two who were responsible for the foundation of Crafthole.[42] Sir Nicholas was noted for his piety as well as for his fighting qualities. According to the Calendar of Patent Rolls, he went on a pilgrimage to Jerusalem in 1309, and may have fought against the Moors.[43] In 1313, he went on another pilgrimage, this time to Santiago de Compostela. He and his wife may have been engaged in several building projects together. In a deed dated 11 July 1336, the Bishop of Exeter stated that Sir John Dawney's ancestors had erected the chapel dedicated to St Nicholas at West Looe. These ancestors were most likely the same Sir Nicholas and his wife, Joan. The Langdons had close connections with church dignatories. In the 1330s, Stephen Langdon was abbot of Tavistock and Baldwin Langdon was vicar of St Eustachius, the parish church of Tavistock.

A re-building date for the church coinciding with the foundation of Crafthole, and the lordship of Sir Nicholas Dawney, is supported by architectural evidence. According to Professor Pevsner, the south side of the nave, the south transept arch, the inner arches to all the south windows, the slender shafts supporting the inner arch

190 *The south transept window of St Mary's is in the Exeter style of the early 1300s.*

of the east window of the chancel, and the east window tracery were all 'early 14th century'.[44] This is the date of the windows at the east end of Exeter Cathedral, which contain both grouped lancet lights (like Sheviock's east window) and geometrical designs (like the big window at the end of the south transept of St Mary's). The main rebuilding programme at Sheviock would appear to have been completed in about 1321, when the spire and upper stage of the tower were most likely built. This was the year in which the similar spire at Rame is thought to have been erected.[45] According to Polsue, the stone used in the re-building of Sheviock's church was shipped over from Caen.[46] The original north transept window, identical in style to that in the south transept, was later moved to the west end of the north aisle.

191 *The sedilia for the parish clergy of Sheviock, dating from the early 1300s, provided seating for a priest, an assistant priest and a clerk.*

The Sedilia

Archbishop Stephen Langton (d.1228) stipulated that there should be three or four priests to every church with a large parish. Though Sheviock could hardly be described as a large parish, the three sedilia (stone seats for clergy) in the south wall of the chancel suggest that in the spirit of this provision, Sheviock had at least two priests and a clerk or holy-water carrier. The sedilia were probably constructed in the early 14th century. They were restored in 1850.

The East Window Niche

By the 1300s, canon law required that every church should install its 'principal image' – i.e. that of its patron saint – in the chancel, and this image was usually placed to the north of the high altar.[47] To comply with this law, the rector of Sheviock, or his patron, had the graceful ogee-headed niche built in to the north wall of the east window. It provided a glorious setting for the parish's image of the Blessed Virgin Mary. The 'decorated' style of this niche flourished between 1335 and 1348. The patron then was Sir Nicholas's son, Sir John Dawney (d.1346).

The Dawney Aisle (The South Transept)

Although it has long been known as the Dawney aisle, the south transept was originally built as a private chapel of the Dawney and Courtenay families. Under the window at the south end are the funeral effigies of Lady Emmeline Dawney and her husband, Sir Edward Courtenay. After the Reformation, the transept was brought into use as an additional aisle for the seating of the congregation. It is shown furnished with pews for such use in an engraving published in 1820.[48] But in the 1300s, when the transept functioned as a side chapel, an altar was positioned against the east wall. The piscina used by the priest to perform his ablutions is still perfectly preserved in the east wall of the former chapel. After the deaths of Lady Emmeline (in 1370) and Sir Edward (in 1372) an additional priest would have been paid to sing masses for their souls in the little chapel. When the rector, John Walle, died in 1427, he, too, left money for the saying of funerary masses for his soul.

192 *The piscina in the Dawney Aisle of St Mary's shows that the transept was originally used as a side chapel. An altar once stood next to it.*

The effigies of Lady Emmeline and Sir Edward lie under a groined canopy. The monument dates from about 1375 and was probably erected by their son. The canopy and effigies were once brightly painted. The plate armour of Sir Edward and the elaborate square head dress and ornaments on the breast of Lady Emmeline were gilded. Lady Emmeline's cote-hardie (a short jacket rather like a hacking jacket) was green and her dress was black.[49] The colour of her mantle (cloak) is not known. As befitted a country gentlewoman, two dogs lie at her feet. The one nearest to the wall is recognisably a spaniel, and the one on the open side is probably a pug. While these dogs may have been chosen simply to represent the virtues of faithfulness and fortitude, the bells on the collar of the pug rather suggest that they were Lady Emmeline's particular pets.

Gilbert wrote of the monument in 1820, 'the background is ornamented with a range of shields, each bearing a bend, charged with three annulets [rings], the arms of Dawney, and above the lady's head are the same arms, impaled with those of Courtenay.'[50] In a footnote, he added that 'these arms, which had been covered by white-washes, etc. as early as the time of Carew, were partially recovered, a few years since, by cleansing the walls, agreeably to the order of the right honourable Reginald Pole Carew.'[51]

Between the Dawney aisle and the chancel is a squint (opening in the masonry). The purpose of this opening was so that the priest saying mass and any family members in the side chapel could see the elevation of the Host (the consecrated bread) at the main altar during the celebration of high mass. This was the high point of the mass and was announced by the ringing of a little bell, called the 'sacring bell'.

The Effigy of a Knight: Various suggestions have been made as to the identity of the knight in the north aisle.[52] According to Carew, the knights in the north and south aisles 'are held to be father and sonne, and that the sonne slayne in our warres with Fraunce, was from thence brought home to be here interred'.[53] The father and son suggestion is certainly wrong, because the knight in the south aisle is known to be Sir Edward Courtenay, not a member of the Dawney family. But the idea that the lone knight in the north aisle was 'slayne in our warres with Fraunce' appears to be correct. Sir John Dawney, Lady Emmeline's father, went to France in 1346 in the retinue of Edward, Prince of Wales, the Black Prince. Sir John landed with the Prince's division in Normandy, but was killed or died of disease early in the campaign. It was common practice for the bones of knights slain in France to be brought back to England for burial. The medieval practice was to quarter the body and boil it until the flesh came away from the bones. The bones were then transported back to England in a simple chest to be buried in the family tomb.[54] The Victorian scholar, W.H.H. Rogers, first identified the effigy as that of Sir John. He wrote, 'The single effigy in the north aisle may be assigned to be Sir John Dawney … the father of the Lady Emmeline Courtenay.' [55] Originally, the tomb was in its own transept or side chapel, similar to the Dawney chapel in the south aisle. This, too, would have been provided with an altar and piscina for the saying of masses for the dead man's soul.

The effigy itself was probably commissioned by Sir John's grandson, Edward Courtenay, Earl of Devon, in about 1378. The dating evidence comes from the surcoat, sword-belt and armour that the knight is wearing.[56] The surcoat is a short close-fitting jupon, a garment that by this time had replaced the longer surcoat of the first half of the century. The low-slung sword belt, worn horizontally, is also a typical accoutrement of a knight of the later 1300s. The knight is fully encased in the highly developed plate armour of the late 1300s. The oval-shaped wings protecting the flanks of his knees, which are attached to his knee plates (poleyns), are an innovation of this time.

The Earliest Stained Glass: A fragment of stained glass in the south wall of the chancel shows the arms of Courtenay. It bears a three-pointed azure (blue) label as used by members of the family descended from the senior branch of the family. It, too, was probably installed by Lady Emmeline's son, Sir Edward Courtenay, when he erected the memorials to his parents and grandfather in the period 1372-8.

The South Door and Porch: During the Middle Ages, priests conducted parts of the sacraments of baptism and marriage at the south door. The door was also important in the processional life of the church. Porches came to be constructed around the door to give shelter to the participants in these ceremonies. The south porch was probably originally constructed along with the south aisle in the early 1300s.

The Rood Screen and Rood Loft

From early in the Middle Ages, screens were constructed to separate the nave from the chancel. They were placed underneath a sculptural group of Christ on the cross (the rood) flanked by figures of the Virgin Mary and St John. Hence the screen came to be known as the 'rood screen'. By the 1400s, church services came to be elaborated by part-singing. To accommodate the choir, and sometimes an organ, a loft was frequently built on top of the screen, in the aisle. It became known as the 'rood loft'. St Mary's Church had a rood loft of this kind. The stairway, which formerly led up to it, is still visible in the north wall. It was probably constructed in the late 1400s or early 1500s when the north aisle was built. A rood group of Christ, the Virgin Mary and St John, would have been erected on top of the screen in the centre of the nave. A similar arrangement may still be seen in Atherington, Devon. Lights (candles or oil lamps) would have been placed before the rood group.

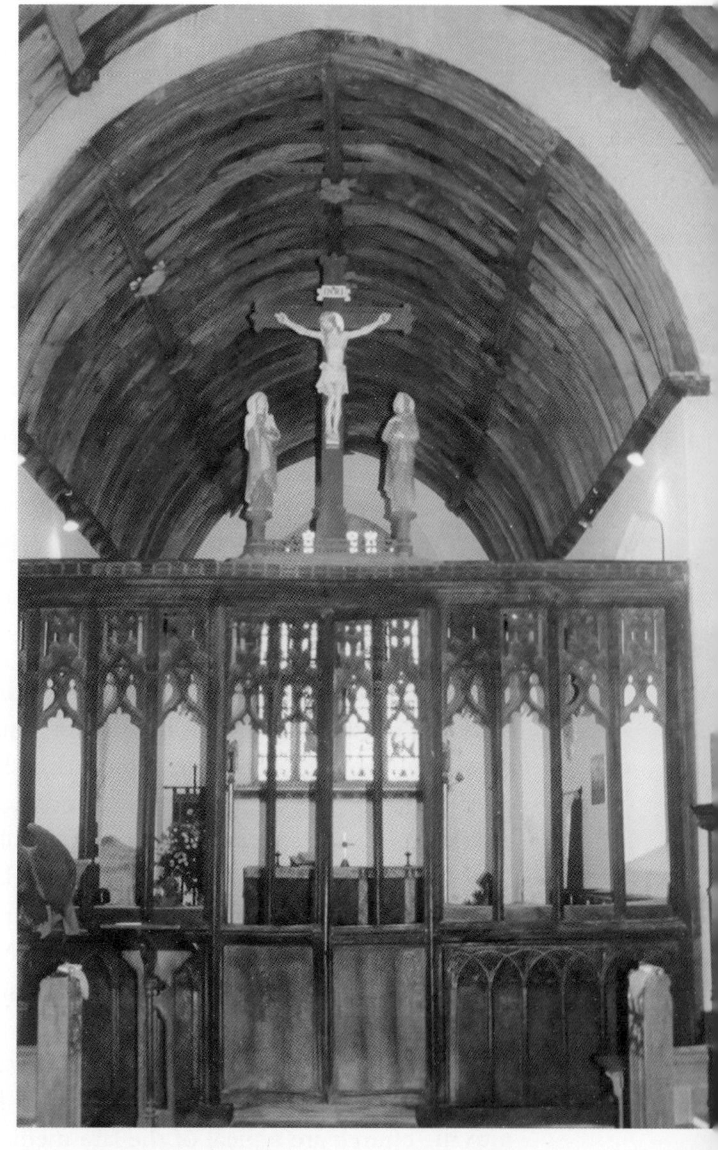

193 *St Mary's originally had a rood screen, like this one at Atherington, Devon.*

The North Aisle and North Porch

The Black Death of 1348-9 had probably reduced the population of the parish of Sheviock by at least one third. Over the next hundred years the population climbed back to about the pre-plague number (350). Pews had already begun to appear in the larger Cornish town churches, such as Bodmin, during the reign of Henry VII (1485-1509), so that educated members of the congregation could follow the Latin services through their Primers.[57] In the late 1400s, it was decided to build a new aisle in St Mary's on the north side of the church. The new aisle ran straight

194 *The head and shoulders of the Virgin Mary, dating from the late 1400s, are all that remains of the medieval religious glazing scheme at St Mary's.*

through the north transept of the 1300s, so the builders removed the traceried window from the north wall of the old transept, and re-erected it at the western end of the new aisle. The wagon roof in the north aisle is original work of the late 1400s. The north aisle has Perpendicular style windows and an arcade of six bays with 'Cornish standard piers and some decoration of the abaci'.[58]

Only a tiny fragment of medieval glass survives in the north aisle. But this tiny fragment, placed high up at the east end of the aisle, is a most important piece, because it shows the head of the Virgin Mary, to whom the church is dedicated. Stephen Clare, an expert in medieval stained glass, considers it to be English work of the late 1400s.[59]

The north porch is contemporary with the north aisle. Its roof has similar wooden bosses and ribs. The flattened stone arches leading from outside into the porch and into the church are typical of the late medieval and Tudor periods.

The Bells

Bells were probably hung in the church tower shortly after its construction. One of these bells was tolled at the elevation of the Host at the Sunday mass. After 1326, the papal authorities ordered that one of the bells should be tolled at dawn, noon and dusk to call the faithful to prayer. This was called the Angelus bell (from Angelus Domini, the angel of the Lord, who made the Annunciation to the Virgin Mary). The bells were also tolled at the time of burials and commemorative masses and on the eve of All Souls (All Saints' night).[60] The tolling was thought to rout demons and evil spirits abroad at these times.

The Medieval Church Plate

In 1551, the Government of Edward VI ordered an inventory to be taken of all the church plate in the country with a view to converting it to the king's use. The official charged with receiving the church plate was the Puritan, Sir Walter Mildmay. In 1553, the king rewarded him with the gift of a number of manors, including Sheviock. The inventory for East hundred has not survived, so we do not know precisely what plate and ornaments St Mary's possessed before the Reformation. However, there is a record of a 'challys part gilt' of 22 ounces being returned to the church in 1553. In that year, the new Catholic Queen Mary directed commissioners to return to the Cornish churches 'all such plate and other ornaments at this present [stored] in a castell by the haven of Falmouth'.[61]

195 *The north aisle and north porch of St Mary's were erected in the late 1400s.*

196 *A loaf was baked by the women of the parish in rotation and blessed by the priest for distribution to the congregation after High Mass on Sunday. This carved replica is on a bench end at St Winnow.*

Chapter 27

Church Life in the Middle Ages

At the centre of medieval parish life was High Mass on Sunday morning. This included a procession, the blessing of holy water and holy bread, the burning of incense and singing by the priests and choir. Matins took place before High Mass and evensong followed in the afternoon. All services were conducted in Latin and were said or chanted by the priest in dialogue with his deacon or clerk. The parishioners on the nave side of the screen did not join in the responses but, before the offertory, the priest came through the screen and asked people to pray for certain people, some living, some dead, and made announcements. Sermons were rare. On weekdays, 'low masses' were said at side altars. These were short services conducted by the priest without assistants and without singing. The first, held at dawn, was called the 'morrow Mass'. It was held for the benefit of servants, labourers and travellers. Requiem masses and masses in honour of particular saints also took place at these side altars. They were conducted by additional priests attached to particular churches and paid for by either chantry guilds or by bequests from wealthy testators, such as John Walle, rector of Sheviock, who died in 1427. These bequests might pay for a particular number of masses (as with Walle's bequest) or cover the wages of a priest for a certain time. The additional priests, who were often appointed because of their good singing voices, also assisted the rector or vicar by singing in the church choir.

The congregation only received communion once a year at Easter, following their annual confession, and then only in one kind (mass wafers). However, they were given unconsecrated wine to drink afterwards to ensure that they had entirely consumed the wafer. On ordinary Sundays, the clerk gave them the *pax* (a silver disc or rectangle bearing an image of the crucifixion) to kiss, and holy bread to eat after the service.[2]

Prayers and 'Bidding the Bedes'

Before the offertory at High Mass on Sundays, the priest came through the Rood screen and, in the vernacular, asked for prayers for the leaders of church and state and for those in special need, just as is done in church today. In Sheviock, any addresses would have been in the Cornish language until English became the vernacular. The priest also asked for prayers for the family who were supplying the holy loaf that week. Every Sunday, he also asked the congregation to pray for benefactors of the church and for the recently deceased. This was called 'bidding the bedes' (requesting the prayers). An early 16th-century roll listing benefactors who should be prayed for in this way has survived from Camborne. It uses the Latin format '[*Orate*] *pro anima*' ('Pray for the soul of') followed by the Latinised names of the benefactors. The Camborne roll, which may not be complete, lists 73 names. They were inserted on the list at various times in the 1400s and early 1500s.[3] The names were those of gentlemen, university doctors, masters of arts, non-graduate priests and men and women connected with the parish. Typically, they would have been people who had given offerings to the church, done good works in the parish or left bequests to the church or the poor of the parish, and had requested to be remembered in the prayers of the congregation. It was thought that the prayers of the living could help to release the souls of the dead from Purgatory.

The Saints

The medieval church recognised many saints, who were perceived as helpers and patrons. At baptism, the Christian child received as one of his or her names the name of the saint who was to be his or her particular patron. However, if he was a boy, his first given name was usually that of his Godfather, and if the child was a girl, her first given name was usually that of her Godmother. Some saints were revered by people in particular occupations. For example, St Nicholas, who was born in the ancient seaport of Patera in Lycia (in modern Turkey) in the fourth century, was venerated as the protector of fishermen and seafarers. Hence the St Nicholas chapels at West Looe and Saltash, and the chapel that formerly stood on St Nicholas' Island in Plymouth Sound. In the 1500s, Bishop Veysey of Exeter complained that 'fishermen and such as live by the sea' in the West Country 'will not go to the sea to fish for their living ... upon divers saints days'.[4] St Nicholas' Day (5 December) would have been one of these. The fishermen of Portwrinkle might well have maintained one of the side altars in St Mary's church as a shrine to St Nicholas. Blacksmiths revered St Loy (St Eligius in Latin) and would not shoe horses on his day (1 December). Farmers had particular affection for St Anthony who was thought to protect pigs and cattle from harm. His feast day was 17 January. St Margaret of Antioch, whose feast day was 20 July, was thought to protect women in childbirth. Altogether more than fifty days were kept as saints' days and images of saints adorned walls, windows, Rood screens and altars of most medieval churches. The candles that were kept burning before these images were among the heaviest expenses of the parishioners.

Easter Services

At Easter-time, every parish church had to provide an Easter sepulchre for the Holy Week ceremonies. This was a representation of Christ's burial chamber on carved or painted panels. This was set up at the north-eastern end of the church. In most churches, including St Mary's, the Easter sepulchres were constructed on a moveable wooden frame covered by a cloth, and so no trace of them remains today. In the wealthier churches, they were permanent architectural features and some of these have survived.[5] Sometimes, as at St Neot's church, Cornwall, the tomb of a wealthy donor doubled up as the Easter sepulchre.

On Maundy Thursday, the priest consecrated three Hosts, one for his communion on that day; one for his communion on Good Friday and one for the sepulchre ceremonies. After mass on Maundy Thursday, the altars were stripped and ritually washed. On Good Friday, a portable veiled crucifix was brought into the church and was slowly unveiled. Clergy and congregation then crept barefoot to the cross, which was held by two ministers, and went down on their knees to kiss its foot. This ceremony was called 'creeping to the Cross'. Members of the congregation kept a vigil before the sepulchre until Easter Day. On Easter Day, all the candles in the church were lit and a procession formed to the sepulchre. The Host was removed from it and hung over the High Altar. The crucifix was raised from the sepulchre and carried in triumph round the church while the bells were rung and the choir sang the anthem '*Christus Resurgens*'. The empty sepulchre remained a focus of devotion for the whole week, with candles burning before it during services, and was finally removed at the end of the week. [6]

Latin Books and Services

Because the services were conducted in Latin, the parishioners were expected to learn the essential parts of their faith by heart. In 1281, these were specified as the *Pater Noster* (Our Father), *Ave Maria* (Hail Mary) and *Credo* (The Creed). This was no easy feat for many country people, few of whom could read or write. For this reason, the Bishop of Exeter, Peter Quinil (1280-91), laid down that every parish priest should teach his parishioners the Creed in the vernacular. The congregation were also expected to know the Ten Commandments, and to understand what constituted the seven works of mercy, the seven virtues, the seven vices and the seven sacraments. The priest was required to explain these things to his flock four times a year. The church also employed various devices to imprint the Biblical stories on the minds of the parishioners. Works of art telling the stories were painted on walls or windows or movable panels; religious plays were performed; and Biblical scenes were enacted on particular days of the church calendar (such as the entry into Jerusalem, which was incorporated into the Palm Sunday procession).

197 *Medieval stone crosses, like this one at Crafthole, were the places where corpses were temporarily laid to rest en route for burial in the churchyard. Beside them, prayers were offered up for the deceased.*

Primers

Members of the congregation who could read, and could afford to buy books, were also assisted in following the services by manuscript books called 'primers'. With the arrival of printing in the late 1400s, huge numbers of these primers were produced. They were in Latin, but often included vernacular material as well. A primer always included 'The Little Office' or 'Hours of the Blessed Virgin Mary', and hence primers were often called 'Books of Hours'.[7] The Little Office included the gradual psalms (Nos.120-134) and lessons and collects celebrating the life and deeds of the Blessed Virgin Mary. Primers also included the Office for the Dead, consisting of Vespers (beginning '*Placebo*') and the special version of matins and lauds used for funereal occasions (beginning 'Dirige'). The '*dirige*' comes from the first word of the antiphon '*Dirige, Domine, Deus meus, in conspectu tuo viam meam*', which was a particular part of the Office for the Dead, and was chanted by the priest. The English word 'dirge' comes from it. Primers also included a calendar of the church year, marking the saints' days. They contained too the Litany of the Saints and particular prayers to seek the assistance of certain saints. There are windows in St Neot's church showing the donors kneeling at desks. The open books resting on the desks most probably represent these primers, and show how they were used. The primers included the four most used Gospel passages (John, Ch.1, vv.1-14 (*In principio* 'In the beginning'); Luke, Ch.1, vv.26-33 (*Missus est* '[The Angel Gabriel] was sent); Matthew, Ch.2, vv. 1-12 (*Cum natus est* 'When Jesus was born [in Bethlehem]'); and Mark, Ch.16, vv.14-18 (*Recumbentibus* '[He appeared to them] as they sat at meat'). These passages were read at mass on Christmas Day, the Feast of the Annunciation (Lady Day), Epiphany and Ascension Day. They were also the Gospels read aloud at the four points of the compass at the wayside crosses during the Rogationtide processions.

The Sacramentals[8]

In the Middle Ages, every aspect of parish life was touched by the teachings of the church. Objects blessed by the priest, called 'sacramentals', such as holy bread, holy water and blessed candles, were held to possess the power to ward off evil spirits and to cure ailments. Each week, one of the women of the parish was required to bake a loaf of bread. This she offered to the priest before matins on Sunday together with a candle. After High Mass on that day, the priest blessed the loaf, which was cut up in a basket and distributed to the congregation. A bench end at St Winnow's church in Cornwall, dating from the late Middle Ages, includes a fine wood carving of one of these holy loaves.

Also before mass each week, the priest mixed salt and water together and purified them with certain words and signs of the cross. Some of the water was kept in a stoup or bucket by the church door for parishioners to take away. What remained was under the care of the water-boy (who was also an assistant clerk). He was paid a fee for carrying it, when required, to particular households to sprinkle on the hearth to ward off evil, on to sick animals to cure them, or on to the fields or the marriage bed to produce fertility. Similarly, candles, which had been blessed at Candlemas, were lit to give protection during thunderstorms or to ward off sickness. They were also placed in the hands of the dying to ward off demons.

Processions

The all-pervasive influence of the church was expressed by the processions that were an important part of all religious ceremonies. Processions were formed every Sunday before High Mass. Priest and people processed round the church while the priest and his assistants sprinkled the altars and the congregation with holy water. Special processions were formed at Candlemas, on Palm Sunday, at Corpus Christi, at Rogationtide and on particular Saints' days.

Candlemas (2 February) was the feast of the Purification of the Blessed Virgin Mary. It would have been celebrated with particular devotion in Sheviock, whose church was dedicated to the Blessed Mary. Every parishioner was obliged to join the Candlemas procession carrying a candle. This was then offered, together with a penny, to the priest at mass. The candles were burned before the image of the Virgin in the church and others taken home as a protection against evil.[9]

On Palm Sunday, the priest blessed flowers and green branches (probably yew or willow in Sheviock). These were called 'palms' and were distributed to the people who processed out of the church following a painted wooden cross. They processed to a large cross (the 'palm cross') that had been erected in the churchyard at the north-east corner of the church, while the choir sang the appropriate anthems. When

198 *In the Middle Ages, crosses, like this one at 'Stumpy Cross', were sited at cross-roads and processional routes to and from the church.*

the procession returned to the church, the choir boys sang '*Gloria, laus et honor*' (Glory, laud and honour).[10]

At Corpus Christi (held on the Thursday after Trinity Sunday), the Host (the Blessed Sacrament) was again carried in procession by the parishioners. This was the time when the miracle plays – the Cornish *gwariow* – were performed by the various parish guilds.

Rogationtide (also called 'cross-tide') is the period of three days before Ascension Day. On these three days the rector, his deacon, and water boy led the members of the parish in a procession to and along the boundaries of the parish. They carried before them a cross and the parish banners. To scare away evil spirits, the marchers banged the boundary trees with sticks, rang bells and sang anthems. The procession also served to remind the parishioners of where the boundaries of the parish lay. Substantial householders with houses on the route were expected to provide food and drink for the marchers. Along the route, and at the parish boundaries, stone or wooden crosses were set up, and at these points the priest read out in Latin the passages from the Gospels.

In Sheviock, stone crosses have survived in the marketplace at Crafthole and at the crossroads near Polscoe. The latter originally stood at the centre of the crossroads and in the 1700s was called 'Stop or Cross' (also 'Stop a Cross' as shown on Thomas Pride's map of 1775).[11] That name became corrupted to 'Stump Cross' (1826) or 'Stumpy Cross'. Both Latin crosses are medieval, but they cannot be precisely dated. The will of Reginald Mertherderwa, Rector of Creed, who died in 1448, gives one example of how money was bequeathed to erect these wayside crosses:

> I will that nine crosses of stone be ordained and newly erected, at my costs and expenses … up to the church of Camborne, and let them be put in the places where the bodies of the dead being carried to burial are laid down for prayers to be offered there and for the alleviation of the bearers.[12]

A boundary stone has also survived at the westernmost boundary with St Germans on the coastal path near Lantic Farm. This, too, is of great but uncertain age. Field names recorded on Thomas Pride's map and on the Tithe Redemption map and survey of 1841 suggest that there were once several other standing crosses in the parish.[13]

Preparing for Death

We catch a glimpse of some aspects of life and death in Sheviock during the reign of Henry VI, through the will of the rector, 'Sir' John Walle, dated 29 September 1427.[14] Walle was not in fact a knight. By convention non-graduate priests were given the honorific title of *Dominus*, which was translated into English as 'Sir'.[15] John Walle began his church life as chaplain to the earl of Devon. His patron at Sheviock was Sir Hugh Courtenay, who was the second son of Edward, the blind Earl, who had been born in Sheviock.[16] Walle was instituted as rector of Stoke Damerel in 1410, but resigned in 1415 to become rector of Sheviock. He may have died at Plympton Priory, where he could have gone to be cared for by the monks in their infirmary.[17] This was a common practice at the time, for those who could afford it:

> The custom of old men taking the habit in their declining years, or even on their death-bed, was often a great financial asset to the monks. Not only was it a common belief that a monk stood a better chance of salvation than anyone else, but, in days when medical service was extremely primitive, by far the best hospitals were the infirmaries of the monks. But in order to enter the monastic infirmary a man must take the habit. Hence arose the custom known as *ad succurendum*, whereby a postulant paid a heavy price to enter the monastery[18]

Plympton Priory was re-founded for Augustinian canons in 1121 and was dedicated to St Peter and St Paul. It was one of the largest houses of the order in Britain. In 1329, a hospital for lepers, dedicated to St Mary Magdalen, was attached

199 *Crosses and boundary stones marked the boundaries between parishes. This one still marks the boundary between Sheviock and St Germans parishes.*

to the priory. It is to be hoped, for his sake, that John Walle spent his last hours in the infirmary of the priory rather than in the leper hospital. The rector's will was copied into the bishop's register at Exeter. Translated into English from the original Latin, the copy reads as follows:[19]

> In the name of God, Amen. I, John Walle rector of Sheviock, seeing myself in imminent danger of death, [and] being of sound mind on 29 September in the year of the Lord 1427:
>
> First, I bequeath my soul to God and my body to be buried in holy burial in the cemetery of the holy apostles Peter and Paul (*in cimiterio sanctorum apostolorum Petri et Pauli*) on the south side of the chancel of the same church.[20] Also I bequeath that on the day of my burial 20s be distributed to the poor and to children for the sake of my soul.[21] Also I bequeath to Master Walter Colle, 3s. 4d.[22] Also [I bequeath] to Joce Trevysa, 6s. 8d.[23] Also I bequeath to Sir Robert Ladycourth, 6s. 8d.[24] Also I bequeath to each priest celebrating divine service, serving in the same church on that day, 20d.
>
> Also I bequeath to the clerk of the town (*clerico ville*), 6d.[25] Also [I bequeath] to the deacon, 6d. Also I bequeath to each holy-water clerk (*aquebaiulo*) on the land, 4d.[26]
>
> Also I [will] that on the day of my obit there be distributed among the poor, 13s. 4d.[27] Also I bequeath to each priest of the same church present at dirige and mass on the day of my obit, 6d. Also [I bequeath] to each clerk of the same church present at the same time and being there, 2d.
>
> Also I will that from the day of my burial until the day of my obit, three masses should be said every day for my soul.
>
> Also I will that 100 masses should be celebrated with all haste after my death, wherever they can be said in Exeter and elsewhere.[28]
>
> Also I bequeath my horse to Richard atte Hellemar.[29] Also I bequeath to Joan, his wife, twelve silver spoons and one pair of sheets. Also I bequeath 10s. to be distributed to the poor.[30]
>
> Also I give and bequeath to Sir Joce Trevysa and Sir Robert Ladycourth the residue of all my goods not bequeathed above, and I ordain and constitute them my executors to distribute [my possessions] for the sake of my soul in the best way that they know or can.

Richard atte Hellemar and his wife, Joan, were most likely the couple who had looked after the rector and his bachelor household, consisting probably of himself, his clerk, and his holy-water boy. Richard was perhaps the rector's principal servant or manager of the glebe farm, for whom the bequest of the horse would have been appropriate. Richard's wife, Joan, may have done the cooking for him and taken care of his clothes and household linen – hence, the thoughtful bequest to her of spoons and bed linen. The rector's bequests give us a fleeting glimpse into the ordering of his daily life in the parish of Sheviock.

Most of the rector's will is concerned with the salvation of his soul. His life on earth was lived in a very troubled period. The Hundred Years' War had started some forty years before his birth and was to continue for nearly 30 years after his death. In 1461, a 'Walter Colle, clerk' was named along with several others as one of the victuallers of a carvel called *le Petir Courteney*, owned by Sir Hugh Courtenay.[31] It was alleged that the ship's crew seized *le Margarete* of Brittany when she was at Fowey, the principal port in Cornwall at that time, and illegally disposed of her cargo of wine and other goods.[32] The Walter Colle in question may have been the person named in John Walle's will, but as the incident occurred 34 years after Walle's death, it may have been a nephew or other relative who was involved.

Walle's testament shows him making strenuous efforts to atone for his failings on earth: money is to be paid out at his funeral service to clerics to say masses for his soul and to carry out the service in due form, and also to relieve the poor. A solemn dirige and mass are to be held on the anniversary of his death (his obit). Between his burial and his obit three masses are to be said every day. After his death no less than 100 masses are to be said for him as soon as possible at Exeter or elsewhere. The usual stipulation in wills of better off people was for 30 masses (the so-called 'Pope Trental', after Pope Gregory the Great). A stipulation for 100 masses suggests considerable wealth. Perhaps it also reveals a troubled conscience.

200 *The key of St Peter and the sword of St Paul were carved on this stone from Plympton Priory. Sir John Walle, rector of Sheviock, may have been cared for by the monks of the priory before his death in 1427.*

201 *The beeboles in the wall of Church House in Sheviock may once have housed the bees of 'the store of the blessed Mary of Sheviock'.*

Chapter 28

Church Administration in the Middle Ages. Medieval Rectors

The expense of maintaining the fabric of the church has been a continuing concern of parishioners both before and after the Reformation. The nature of many of the other parochial outgoings changed after the Reformation. In medieval times, the rector was expected to pay the wages of any assistant priests (except those reciting funerary masses, who were paid for by bequests from the deceased) and sometimes of the holy-water boy or clerk.[1] After the Reformation, there were no regular assistants and the expenses of the clerk were always borne by the parish. Before the Reformation, the parishioners spent much money on painting, gilding and decorating (sometimes with jewels) images of the saints. Groups of parishioners also paid for candles to burn before the Holy Rood set up on the rood screen and before other images of saints set up in the church. To sustain the poor, the medieval parish relied on the doles of money left by deceased parishioners and on alms distributed by the rector. Where gilds or chantries were in existence, they too often provided sustenance for widows and orphans. In the Middle Ages, only the priest, his assistants and the choir had need of books, and they were expected to provide these for themselves.[2] Wealthy parishioners might purchase their own primers, but this was a matter of individual choice.

Collecting Funds in the Middle Ages

Before the Reformation, church expenses were met principally by the accumulation of goods called 'stocks' or 'stores', which could be converted into cash (e.g. by selling or leasing them), and by the holding of church ales. Church stocks consisted of such things as cattle and sheep; or timber or loads of stone, which could be used for rebuilding the church, or sold for cash. Parishioners also left to the church crops of wheat, barley, or oats that could be converted into bread or ale that could be sold. They also left bushels of malt for brewing; beehives for the production of honey and wax; and barrels of salt and fish, which could be sold for profit. Members of an agricultural and fishing community, such as Sheviock, would possess many of these things, and as acts of piety would donate or bequeath them to the church. The will of the farmer, William Trenowyth of St Cleer, who died in 1400, provided that: 'I bequeath to the store of St Cleer, 3 sheep … Also I bequeath to the store of St Mary in the church of St Cleer, 2 sheep, and to the store of the Holy Cross there, one sheep, and to the store of St James there, one sheep.' [3] In Sheviock, the beeboles (recesses for bee skips) in the boundary wall of the churchyard are still preserved next to the former church house. In 1764, Philip Littleton confirmed that 'the Garden alongside the Church Yard belongs to the Church House'.[4] The bees that were once housed there would have formed part of the church stock. The wealthier parishioners might also give gold or jewels to adorn the images of the saints, or donate or bequeath land so that the church could enjoy an income from it.

Sheviock's principal church stock was known as 'the store of the blessed Mary of Sheviock'. This is known because Isabel, wife of Alexander Carew of Antony, left to it the sum of 6s. 8d. in her will of 1521.[5] In addition to the main store, there were often subsidiary ones. Particular groups of parishioners, such as the young men or young women of the parish, or the husbands or wives, often took on the responsibility for a particular task, such as maintaining the lights before St Nicholas or St Anthony or arranging a fund-raising event. Each group would have its own store, which it could put to a particular use as occasion arose.[6] At St Neot, the wives of the western part of the parish, the sisters (maidens) and the young men all had their own stores, which they used to pay for the beautiful stained glass windows still to be seen in the church.

Church ales were also an important method of raising funds for church expenses.[7] These were entertainments at which food and drink were sold for the benefit of the church. Ales were held regularly on certain of the church festivals and either on the dedication day of the church or on the principal feast of its patron saint. Additional ales were held when extra funds were required for church repairs and other special needs. Two people were chosen to act as wardens and masters of the feast. 'It was their duty to collect malt for brewing, corn for baking, and anything for the purpose of entertainment that they could persuade the householders to furnish.'[8] Ales were held sometimes in the churchyard, occasionally in the church, but, once the church house was built, usually in that building. The church house belonged to the parish and usually adjoined the churchyard.[9] According to a statement made by Walter Warren in 1764, a 'Little Brew House' belonging to Church House stood on the east side of Church House.[10] It was probably knocked down when Church House was rebuilt as an inn in 1786.

Church ales were sometimes known by the name of the time or tide at which they were held. Examples are May ales, Whitsun ales, Christmas Lord ales, Midsummer ales, Easter ales, Hallowmas ales, and Hocktide ales.[11] Sometimes they were known by the name of the principal characters who featured in the accompanying entertainments, such as Robin Hood or the three Kings of Cologne. Usually, a church ale lasted only for a day, but it could continue over several days. Parishioners from one parish were often invited to join in the ale of a neighbouring parish. Because the sale of drink played such a prominent role, ales were also called 'tavern ales' (in Latin *taberne cerevisiae*) or 'drinkings'. Robin Hood and Morris dancers were popularly included in the May or Whitsun ales, and minstrels were often hired for these and other ales. Hobby-horse dancing, which still survives at Padstow, was also often a part of the May festivity. Sometimes, too, there would be plays, and, if the ale was held outdoors, sports such as wrestling or 'throwing at kokes [cocks]'.[12] A Whitsun ale was nearly always presided over by a 'lord' and 'lady' chosen by the parishioners. Richard Carew, who must have attended many church ales in his home parishes of Antony and Sheviock, described them in his day:

> For the Church-ale, two young men of the parish are yerely chosen by their last foregoers, to be Wardens, who deviding the task, make collection among the parishioners, of whatsoever provision it pleaseth them voluntarily to bestow. This they imploy in brewing, baking, and other acates [*achats*, purchases], against Whitsontide; upon which Holydayes, the neighbours meet at the Church house, and there merily feed on their owne victuals, contributing some petty portion to the stock, which by many smalls, groweth to a meetly greatnes: for there is entertayned a kinde of emulation betweene these Wardens, who by his graciousnes in gathering, and good husbandry in expending, can best advance the Churches profit. Besides, the neighbour parishes, at those times lovingly visit one another, and this way frankely [freely] spend their money together. The afternoones are consumed in such exercises, as olde and yong folke (having leysure) doe accustomably weare out the time withall.[13]

By the late 16th century, as Carew recognised, church ales were under increasing attack from the Puritans. One of them, Phillip Stubs, wrote that those who attend ales drink until they 'be as dronke as rattes, and as blockishe as beastes'.[14] Under Puritan pressure, church ales gradually disappeared.

Medieval Incumbents[15]

There were five orders of priesthood below that of bishop: *presbiteri* (priests), *diaconi* (deacons), *subdiaconi* (sub-deacons), *accoliti* (acolytes), and *tonsurati* (tonsured). Only bishops and priests were qualified to hear confessions and administer the sacraments. Because of the value of the living of Sheviock, well-connected candidates who were only in minor orders were often put forward for the benefice. Bishops were reluctant to institute them unless they were sufficiently well educated to proceed to higher orders leading to the priesthood. Where individuals were nominated for the benefice, but were not graduates or priests, bishops would often license their absence from Sheviock to study at Oxford or Cambridge. Where the incumbent was not a priest or was non-resident, another salaried priest had to be appointed as vicar or curate to perform his parochial duties. Certainly up to 1193, and perhaps up to 1279, when the incumbent was first described as 'parson', he would have been simply a vicar or curate, receiving only a portion (usually a third) of the tithes of the parish for his own sustenance. Thereafter, incumbents of Sheviock were appointed as parsons or rectors, with full entitlement to receive the tithes. In 1410-11, in the absence of the rector, a chaplain, Robert Love, was appointed to look after the cure of souls. He was paid a salary of £5 6s. 8d.

*c.*1082-1269	No names have been preserved for these years.
1270-71	*John le Arceveske* [Archdeacon]. Instituted 11 January.[16] Patron, William Dawney the elder.
1278	William de Hautone (Halton). Instituted *sub pena concilii* 13 April. Patron, William Dawney the elder. De Halton was a deacon at the time. Sir John de Halton of St Dominic had married a certain Margery. After his death she married Nicholas Dawney. The incumbent no doubt belonged to that family, and may have been Margery's son by Sir John de Halton.
1279	*William de Lananta* (Lelant). Referred to as 'parson' of Sheviocke. (Cal. Pat. Rolls 1316).
1327	*Philip Risingdone.* He was a sub-deacon in July 1327, and was granted a two-year licence of non-residence in order to pursue his studium generale so that he could proceed to higher orders. This licence was renewed for the second year on 1 July 1328, and for a third year on 8 October 1329 until Whitsunday 1330. But he died on 23 February 1330 before completing his degree. Taxed at 10s.
1330	*John de Langdone.* Instituted 2 April. Patron Sir Nicholas Dawney, who was married to Joan Langdone. At this time Baldwin Langedone was vicar of Tavistock. John de Langedone was only an acolyte (and probably a child) when he was instituted. He was ordained sub-deacon in 1332 when he was granted licence of non-residence for two years in order to qualify for higher orders. When he died, sometime before 1371, there was a dispute as to who had the right of presentation to the living, the patron being a minor. Those claiming the right were the Bishop of Exeter; Edward, Prince of Wales; the Abbot of Tavistock; and Baldwin Langedone. The dispute was settled in favour of the Crown, 8 July 1372.
1331	*Walter Meuwy.* Mentioned as parson. In 1341, he was part of the entourage of John, Abbot of Tavistock (1334-49), who was accused of breaking open the pound of the earl of Gloucester at Lydford and releasing some cattle impounded there for trespassing.[17] The party was also accused of hunting over the earl's land after assaulting his servants. (Cal. Pat. Rolls 1342.)

1372	*Benedict de Eresby*. Instituted 28 July. Patron, King Edward III. He was admitted to both major and minor orders at the time of his institution, no doubt at the behest of the king. In 1375, he exchanged his living with Roger, parson of Lydlynch (Lidlinch) in Dorset. (Cal. Pat. Rolls.)
1375	*Roger*. By exchange with Benedict de Eresby.
1405-05	*John Godwyn*. He was chaplain to the earl of Devon. Instituted 23 March. Patron, Edward, Earl of Devon. He was granted licence of non-residence for two years, 3 October. He died next year.
1406-7	*Richard Donscombe*. Donscombe is perhaps Danescombe on the River Tamar. He was instituted as sub-deacon March 1406-7 and as priest, 17 December 1407. Patron, Edward, Earl of Devon. Granted licence of non-residence 1410 and 1412-13. Instituted to Northill, 1415.
1415	*John Walle*. He was chaplain to the earl of Devon. Instituted 13 September 1415. Patron, Sir Hugh Courtenay, son of Edward, Earl of Devon. The words of his will, as copied into the bishop's register, have led to uncertainty as to the original dedication of the church at Sheviock.[18] His will, reproduced in Chapter 27, left goods to a married couple, and money to the poor of the parish.
1427-8	*John Heydene*. On death of last named. The patron was then a minor, so the following acted as patrons: Sir Hugh Luttrell, John Fortescue, Thomas Henderson, Richard Aldryngton, William Dawney, Richard Bampfield, and Henry Fortescue. Heydene exchanged with Richard Strike, incumbent of Sherfield-on-Loddon, in the County of Southampton, in 1431. (Cal Pat. Rolls.) (Register of Bishop Edmund Lacy, Vol. X, Old Series, fol. 85[a].)
1431	*Master Richard Strike*. Patron, Ann, Countess of Devon. (Reg. as above, fol. 106[b].)
1449	John Hynde, chaplain to the earl of Devon. On death of the last. Patron, Sir Thomas Courtenay, Earl of Devon. He was still rector in 1457 (Henderson MS.). A Sir John Hynde was a Canon of Glasney Collegiate Church in Penryn.[19] His successor in that benefice was instituted 7 December 1473 on his death. (Reg. as above, fol. 243[b].)
1473	*Ralph Hynkes*. He died in December 1503.
1492	*John Payne*. See Henderson MS.
1503	*Master Owen ap Davi*. His patron was Henry VII. Both Henry VII and Henry VIII appointed Welsh incumbents when vacancies occurred in Sheviock. There was probably no better reason than that these were supporters of the Welsh dynasty for whom livings needed to be found. Henry VIII's muster roll of 1522 shows that Owen ap Davi was non resident 'because he is a stranger' and paid £6 to a curate, Nicholas Wenmowth. (Reg. Bp. John Arundell, Vol. XII, O.S., fol. 12[a].)

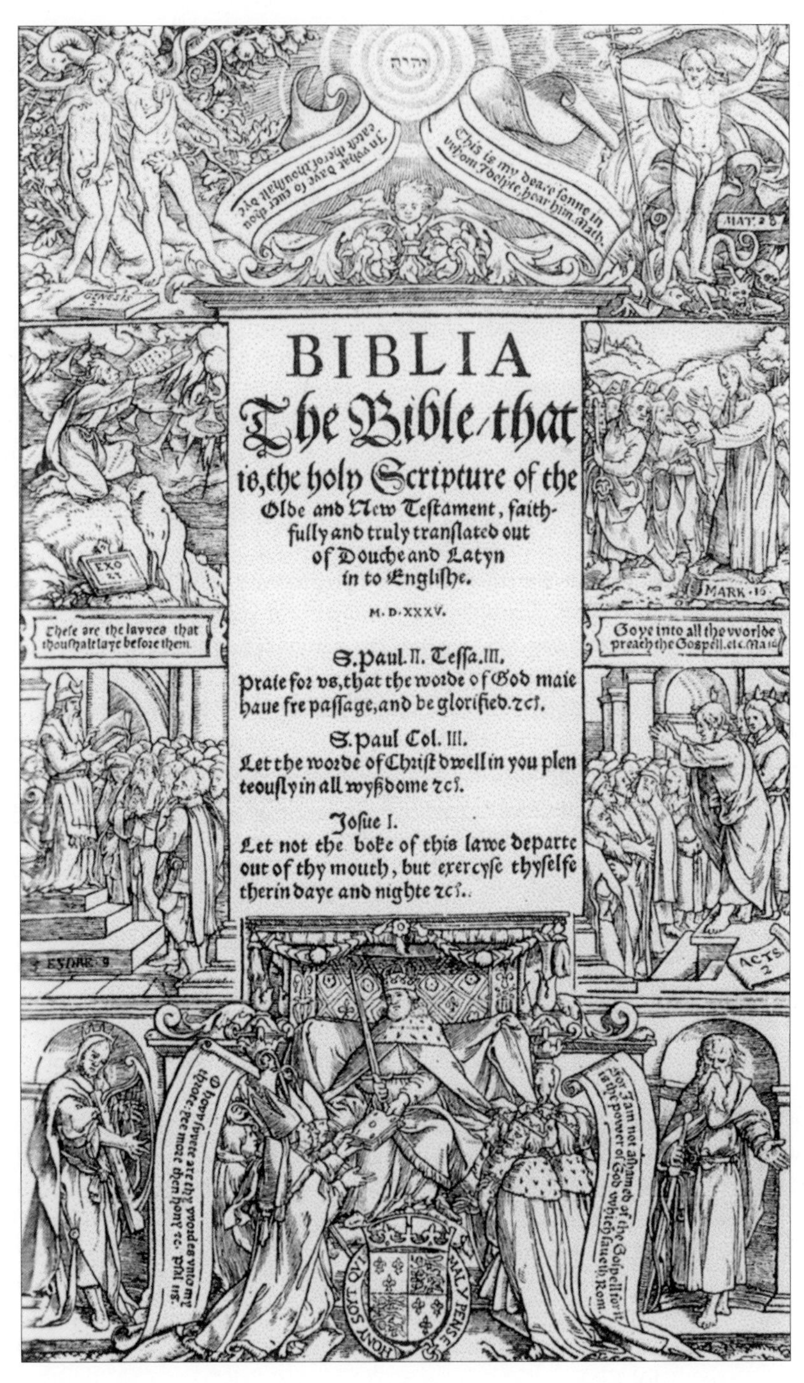

BIBLIA

The Bible/that is, the holy Scripture of the Olde and New Teſtament, faithfully and truly tranſlated out of Douche and Latyn in to Engliſhe.

M.D.XXXV.

S.Paul. II. Teſſa. III.

Praie for vs, that the worde of God maie haue fre paſſage, and be glorified. &c.

S.paul Col. III.

Let the worde of Chriſt dwell in you plenteouſly in all wyſdome &c.

Joſue I.

Let not the boke of this lawe departe out of thy mouth, but exercyſe thyſelfe therin daye and nighte &c..

202 *The title page of Miles Coverdale's* Biblia, *the first complete Bible in English, published in 1535.*

Chapter 29

The Reformation in the West Country

Henry VIII's breach with Rome in 1532-3 allowed the stream of Reformation thinking to seep gradually but with ever-increasing force into the worship and practice of the English church. In Henry's lifetime the outward forms of worship did not change drastically. The rood screen remained in place with lights still burning before it, and the priests continued to conduct the service of the mass in Latin. In 1534, the Act of Supremacy declared Henry to be the Supreme Head of the Church of England. In 1535, the king suppressed a number of priories including the one at St Germans.[1] In 1536, he reduced the number of saints' days, and between 1536 and 1539, he ordered the destruction of the monasteries and the transfer of their estates to the Crown. The Crown then sold most of them on to lay proprietors.[2] In 1538, Henry forbade people to go on pilgrimages and ordered images attracting veneration to be removed from churches. After the accession of Edward VI in 1547, the stream of reform became a torrent. The Reformers were opposed to many of the traditional practices of the church. William Tyndale listed his particular aversions as,

> penance, pilgrimages, pardons, purgatory, praying to posts, dumb blessings, dumb absolutions, their dumb pattering, and howling, their dumb strange holy gestures, with all their dumb disguisings, their satisfactions and justifyings.[3]

In its first year of office, the new Government of Edward VI prohibited all the ancient parish processions and the prohibition was given statutory force by the Act of Uniformity of 1549. Processions were briefly resumed in the reign of Queen Mary (1553-58), but, with one exception, were again prohibited by the Injunctions of Queen Elizabeth in 1559. Protestants particularly disliked the Latin incantations and sprinklings of holy water at particular places that were associated with the processions. As we have seen, William Tyndale heaped scorn on what he called 'praying to posts'.[4] In spite of these strictures, Queen Elizabeth allowed the Rogationtide procession to continue, but only as a religious thanksgiving for the fruits of the earth and as a means of preserving boundaries. The procession, commonly called 'beating the bounds', survived in Sheviock for many generations. The rector in the time of Queen Elizabeth and James I, Walter Arundell, has left a note recording how these processions were conducted in his day:

> The perambulations of the bounds are made yearly and many discreet children and youths of riper age are taken with the ould men and told which are the bounds.[5]

In 1548, Edward VI issued further proclamations banning many popular church ceremonies. He prohibited the burning of candles on Candlemas day, the strewing of ashes on Ash Wednesday, and the waving of palms on Palm Sunday.[6] Another proclamation compelled the removal of all images from the churches.

THE BIBLE IN ENGLISH[7]

While the Reformers railed against many of the old ways of traditional church life, they also argued passionately for one new development. That was the dissemination in English of the good news of the New Testament – called in Greek the *evangelion*. They thought that the Latin language had concealed this good news from ordinary people for too long. Furthermore, many of the leaders of the Reformation were Hebrew and Greek scholars of distinction, and they questioned the accuracy of the Latin version of the Bible, called the Vulgate, that was in general use. They therefore called for the Bible to be translated afresh from the original languages into English, and for church services to be conducted in English. English translations of the Vulgate had in fact been made in the late 1300s by followers of the Oxford scholar, John Wycliffe (*c*.1320-84). One of the principal translators was Nicholas of Hereford. But Wycliffe's views were declared heretical and his followers, called Lollards, were persecuted.[8] To suppress the populist doctrines of Wycliffe, the church had forbidden English translations of the Bible by the Constitutions of Oxford of 1409. The Constitutions were enforced by the draconian statute called *De heretico comburendo* (Concerning the burning of heretics), which had been passed in 1401. Because of this legislation, the early Reformers had to do their work of translation abroad.

William Tyndale was the first to translate the New Testament directly from Greek into English. Peter Schoeffer of Worms in Germany printed his English translation in 1526. It was printed in an octavo (pocket-sized) edition and smuggled into England in bales of cloth. The Bishop of London, Cuthbert Tunstall, and the Archbishop of Canterbury, William Warham, immediately ordered copies to be seized and burned. In 1534, Tyndale published a revised edition of his English New Testament. It was printed by Martin de Keyser in Antwerp and again smuggled into England. The copy owned by Anne Boleyn has survived and is now in the British Library. While Tyndale was working in Antwerp, a plot was hatched to have him arrested and tried for heresy by the Catholic authorities. The tragic result was that the learned and courageous Tyndale was burned at the stake at Vilvorde, outside Brussels, on 6 October 1536.

But Tyndale had not been alone. Other Reformers were also working abroad on translations. One of these was Miles Coverdale. In 1535, he published the first complete Bible in English, which he called *Biblia*. Martin de Keyser in Antwerp was probably once again the printer. Coverdale was not a scholar of Hebrew and Greek, so his edition of the Bible was based on the translations of others. These were Tyndale, who had translated half the Old Testament, as well as the New, before his death; Martin Luther's German Bible of 1532; another German version made by Huldrych Zwingli and Leo Juda in Zurich between 1524 and 1529; the Vulgate; and another Latin version. Coverdale's greatest achievement as a translator was his version of the psalms, which he turned into poetic English suitable for singing, and which later reappeared in the Great Bible of 1539 and in Archbishop Cranmer's *Book of Common Prayer*. While Henry VIII was conservative in many of the outward forms of religion, he was in favour of an English edition of the Bible. He therefore allowed Coverdale's Bible to be imported into England. The title-page, which was designed by Hans Holbein the Younger, included a portrait of the king himself.

203 *The title page of Henry VIII's* Great Bible *of 1539/40, probably the first English language Bible to be read in St Mary's church.*

After Tyndale's death, another Biblical scholar based in Antwerp, John Rogers, put together a complete Bible based on Tyndale's translation of the New Testament and the books of the Old Testament completed by him before his death. Rogers took the parts of the Old Testament not translated by Tyndale from Coverdale's *Biblia*. The London publishers, Richard Grafton and Edward Whitchurch, financed the work, which was printed in Antwerp by Matthew Crom in 1537. Because Tyndale had been condemned for heresy, the publishers could not use his name on the title-page. Instead they credited the translation to the fictitious 'Thomas Matthew' (from the names of two of Christ's disciples). This Bible was thereafter known as 'Matthew's Bible'. The Archbishop of Canterbury, Thomas Cranmer, and Thomas Cromwell, the king's 'Vicegerent for ecclesiastical affairs', both supported this translation. It was therefore able to claim on the title-page that it was 'set forth with the King's most gracious licence'. Cromwell urged the bishops to order copies for the parish churches. Though it is possible that this was the first English language Bible to be read in Sheviock church, this is unlikely because the number of copies printed fell far short of the 9,000 required for use in every parish church.

Cranmer and Cromwell therefore put in hand a new edition of Matthew's Bible. As before, it was to be published by Grafton and Whitchurch and it was to be printed by Francois Regnault of Paris. Miles Coverdale was selected as the editor of the new edition. The work was started in 1538 and 2,500 copies were soon printed. However, political difficulties between France and England led to the seizure of these copies and no further copies were printed in France. Eventually, the French authorities allowed the printed copies to be shipped to England, together with the type and unused paper so that the rest of the printing could be done in London – the first English-language Bible to be printed in England. Work commenced in London in April 1539 and was completed by April 1540. Cromwell had specified in his instructions that 'a Bible of the largest volume' was to be set up in the churches, and large it certainly was. The new work measured 14 inches by nine, and hence became known as 'the Great Bible'. On its title-page, the Great Bible stated that it was published '*Cum privilegio ad imprimendum solum*' – meaning that it was published under an exclusive royal licence. In 1540, Henry VIII appointed Rhys Lewys as the new rector of Sheviock. He therefore became the first rector provided with an English-language Bible from which to read the lessons.

In 1549, two years after the accession of Edward VI, the Latin mass finally gave way to a service entirely in English. By the Act of Uniformity, a new service book, the Book of Common Prayer, was made compulsory throughout the land. All the old service books were to be defaced and then burned. The new Protestant services were a modified version of the medieval ones, consisting of matins, the litany (omitting prayers for the intercession of saints) and the first half of the communion service in the morning, and evensong in the afternoon. The full communion service, a modified version of the old mass, now took place three or four times a year.[9] The new book was the work of Archbishop Cranmer. In the Introduction to it, he explained his reason for introducing the new services:

> And moreover, whereas S Paule would have such language spoken to the people in the churche, as they might understande and have profite by hearyng the same: the service in this Churche of England (these many yeares) hath been read in Latin to the people, whiche they understoode not, so that they have heard with theyr eares onely: & theyr hartes, spirite and minde, have not been edified thereby.

The Prayer Book Rebellion

The Council that governed England at the time had directed that the new English service was to replace the Latin mass in every parish church on Whitsunday, 9 June 1549. But in the West Country the imposition of this change, on top of all the previous prohibitions of traditional ways of worship and the confiscations of church property, provoked the armed insurrection known as the Prayer Book Rebellion. The uprising started at Bodmin on 6 June 1549, when some 6,000 people took up arms and gathered just outside the town to protest at the changes. Bodmin was the site of an old Celtic monastery and preserved the bones of St Petroc in a casket that is still in the church. These relics attracted many pilgrims, so the town would have been particularly hard hit by the Protestant reforms. Three days later, another angry congregation assembled at Sampford Courtenay in Devon and refused to let the vicar conduct the service in English as the Council had directed. When a local gentleman, William Hellyons, upraided the crowd for their conduct, he was attacked and killed.

The popular discontent was largely religious. But it was also fuelled by economic grievances. In 1549, at a time of high inflation, Parliament had levied a tax on goods in general and specifically a poll tax on sheep and a tax on woollen cloth put up for sale. The tax would therefore bite particularly hard in the West Country. It was rumoured among the rebels that 'after the payment for shepe they should paie for theyr geese and piggs and such like'.[10] The movement was essentially an uprising of the common people, supported by a number of parish priests (about twenty are known to have joined the rebels) and a very few gentlemen. The essence of their religious demands was the retention or restoration of traditional practices. The leaders who emerged in Cornwall were Humphrey Arundell of Helland (north of Bodmin), a younger son of the family of Lanherne, and John Winslade of Tregarrick, in Pelynt. Winslade was married to Jane, daughter of Sir John Trelawney of Pool in Menheniot. Another prominent rebel was a local man, Robert Smythe (or Smith) of Tregonack (today spelled Tregunnick), near the River Seaton, in St Germans parish.[11] St Germans, like Bodmin, would have suffered particularly from the proclamations against pilgrimages and the veneration of saints. Members of the Smythe family were the occupiers of Liscawn in Sheviock parish.

The rebels' demands, which they sent to the Council in London, included the following:

> we wyll have the Sacrament hange over the hyeghe aulter, and there to be worshipped as it was wonnt to be;
>
> we wyll have the Sacrament of ye aulter but at Easter delyvered to the lay people, and then but in one kynde;
>
> we wyl have holy bread and holy water made every Sondaye, Palmes and asshes at the tymes accustomed, Images to be set up again in every church, and all other auncient old ceremonyes used heretofore, by our mother the holy church;
>
> we wil not receve the newe servyce because it is but lyke a Christmas game, but we wyll have oure old service of Mattens, masse, Evensong and procesion in Latten, as it was before. And so we the Cornyshe men (wherof certen of us understande no Englysh) utterly refuse thys newe Englysh;
>
> we wyll have everye preacher in his sermon, and every Pryest at hys masse, praye specially by name for the soules in purgatory, as our forefathers dyd;
>
> we wyll have the Byble and al bokes of scripture in Englysh to be called in agayn, for we be enformed that otherwise the Clergye shall not of long time confound the heretykes.[12]

Through all these demands, except perhaps the last, we can hear the authentic voices of the rural people of the county, protesting at all that had been taken from them by the reforming government up in London. Only the last, demanding the withdrawal of the Bible and all books of scripture in English, does not sound as if it came from their own hearts and minds. The Great Bible had after all been in use in churches for the past ten years. English was widely understood in Cornwall by this time. The words of justification, 'for we be enformed, etc', suggest that this demand was inserted on the advice, if not the insistence, of the priests accompanying the rebel army. The most prominent of these may have been Robert Welsh, vicar of St Thomas outside Exeter.[13] He was a Cornishman from Penryn and had been appointed to his benefice by the last abbot of Tavistock. After the defeat of the rebels he was hung from his own church tower dressed in his priestly garments.

The Cornish rebels marched into Devon bearing aloft their banner of the five wounds of Christ, and accompanied by the priests carrying 'the pyx or consecrated host borne under a canopy, with crosses, banners, candlesticks, holy bread and water'.[14] The commander of the rebels, Arundell, despatched a strong force, probably under Robert Smythe from St Germans, to take Trematon Castle, and then to capture Plymouth. They were successful in both these objectives. Near Crediton the men of

Devonshire joined up with the main Cornish contingent. The combined force, now totalling some 10,000 men, proceeded to lay siege to the city of Exeter, having failed to persuade the mayor and aldermen to join them in rebellion.

The Council put together a strong force to oppose the rebels. The leader of the Royal forces was the Lord Privy Seal, John, Lord Russell. Other commanders were Sir Peter Carew and his brother, Sir Gawen, both supporters of the Reformation. Russell's force eventually included 1,000 German foot soldiers, 400 cavalrymen of mixed nationality, 150 Italian arquebusiers, as well as a strong English contingent, altogether totalling about 7,000 men. The first battle took place at Fenny Bridges, where the rebels were strongly entrenched. Russell eventually secured the position, but not before a charge by 250 Cornishmen under Robert Smythe temporarily routed the king's men. The rebels made another stand at Alfington, near Ottery St Mary, but were again defeated. Russell then continued his march towards Exeter and won further battles at Aylesbeare Common, Clyst St Mary, and Clyst Heath, killing hundreds of the rebel soldiers.[15] The rebels were forced to raise the siege of Exeter and fled westwards. Arundell conducted a fighting retreat through Sampford Courtenay and Okehampton, losing more men in the process. He and the other rebel ringleaders were captured at Launceston on 19 August, sent up to London for trial, and executed at Tyburn on 27 January 1550. Martial law had been declared on 16 July 1549, and after the victory of the royal forces, Sir Anthony Kingston, the Provost Marshal, proceeded through Cornwall to carry out a reign of terror. He executed the mayor of Bodmin, where the rebellion had begun, and others in a particularly cold-blooded fashion. Altogether the rebels lost about 4,000 men killed in action and about 1,000 people executed under martial law, about half of those who had originally taken up arms.[16]

The Bells after the Reformation

The ringing of bells was greatly reduced after the Reformation. Edward VI's Injunctions of 1547 forbade the ringing of bells during the Sunday services, except for one. This was to be rung before the Sunday sermon, again emphasising the importance of preaching the Gospel in English. The 1549 rebels had originally been summoned to march in defence of their faith by the sound of the church bells being 'rung backwards' – i.e. beginning with the tenor bell instead of the treble. The Council therefore instructed Russell to order the church bells to be taken down, except for the smallest one, which was to be retained to summon the parishioners to the sermons and divine service. Russell further ordered that the clappers of the bells that had been taken down should be removed from the parishes. The bells themselves were to be put in the charge of 'some honest men of the parish'. The king gave ownership of the clappers to two trusted Protestants in Devon, Sir Arthur Champernoun of Dartington and John Chichester of Hall, near Bishop's Tawton. When it seemed prudent for them to do so, at various times between 1551 and 1553, their agents sold the clappers back to the parishioners.

The Position of Sheviock during the 'Commotion'

It is not known how many of the people of Sheviock were involved in the rebellion, known locally as the 'commotion'. The leading role played by Robert Smythe of St Germans, who had relatives in Sheviock, would suggest that some at least of the parishioners had sympathy for the rebels' cause. Furthermore, the parish of Sheviock had been a possession of the earls of Devon for nearly two hundred years, with many of the local families owing their wealth and status to that connection. Henry Courtenay, Earl of Devon and Marquis of Exeter, had been an ardent Catholic, maintaining his adherence to the old religion throughout the reforms of Henry VIII. He was a possible claimant to the throne, through his mother Katherine, daughter of Edward IV. He was also related to the Pole family, whose most distinguished member, Reginald, had attacked Henry's ecclesiastical policy in 1536 and been created a cardinal by the Pope. The marquis criticised Thomas Cromwell and his Protestant colleagues with the words, 'I trust once to have a fair day upon these knaves which rule about the king; I trust to give them a buffet one day.' [17] Before he could do so, he was attainted for treason and executed in 1538. His estates were forfeited to the Crown. It is probably significant that the place where the 1549 rebellion broke out in Devon was Sampford Courtenay, an ancient possession of the Courtenay family.

By the year of the rebellion, the manor of Sheviock had belonged to the Crown for 11 years. Immediately after the execution of the marquis in 1538, Henry VIII had sent down one of his footmen, a Cornishman, Richard Tredery, as bailiff of Sheviock. Two years later he had appointed the Welshman, Rhys Lewys, as rector. Such men were likely to have been obedient to royal commands. They would have exerted a restraining influence on any militant Catholics, or loyal followers of the Courtenay family, resident in the parish. Whatever the local sympathies, Sheviock had to pay its part of the collective price for the commotion, because the orders about the church bells applied to the whole of Cornwall.

Further Advance of the Reformation

In November 1550, Edward VI's government ordered the old stone altars to be removed and replaced with a single communion table. This was to be placed in the body of the church. Lights before the rood were to be extinguished. Masses in side chapels and devotions before images were prohibited. The path was now set for the Dawney chapel in the parish church to become the Dawney aisle. In 1552, a second

Act of Uniformity was passed and a new more Protestant Prayer Book issued. In 1553, a commission was appointed in Cornwall with orders to collect from the parishes the gold and silver chalices, candlesticks and censers, leaving only one communion cup behind in each parish. The Commissioner in charge of this confiscation was Sir Walter Mildmay, who was rewarded by being given the royal manor of Sheviock.[18] But before the plate could be destroyed, the sickly king died, and the Catholic Queen Mary reversed his orders.

The Church under Queen Mary

Queen Mary attempted to undo most of the Protestant reforms, installing Cardinal Pole as Archbishop of Canterbury in 1556. She restored the Latin mass and ordered the church plate to be returned to the churches. She did not, however, order the restoration to the church of the monastic lands that had been given or sold to lay proprietors. Cranmer's Book of Homilies was replaced by another written by Bishop Bonner of London – although it actually included two written by Cranmer.[19] No further English editions of the Bible were made during her reign, and Protestants who were able to, including Miles Coverdale, fled abroad. The unlucky ones, such as John Rogers, were condemned and burned for heresy. Altogether, some 300 people were executed for heresy – a large number, but small compared with the 5,000 people killed or executed during the Prayer Book Rebellion of 1549. In 1554, Queen Mary appointed John Smyth, LLD as rector of Sheviock. Was he perhaps of the family of Tregunnick and Liscawn? He was to be the last incumbent appointed as a Roman Catholic. He appears to have accepted the Protestant reforms of the next monarch, Queen Elizabeth, and died in possession of his living in 1564.

The Genevan Exiles and the Geneva Bible

While they had been in exile during Mary's reign, many scholars, including Coverdale, had been based in the city of Geneva. This city was the seat of a university, called the Academy, founded by the Protestant divines, Jean Chauvin (John Calvin) (1509-64) and Théodore de Bèze (Beza) (1519-1605). The Academy, which had been established for the study of ancient texts, became a training ground for Protestant and Calvinist theologians. In 1558, Coverdale began work on a new English edition of the Bible there, making use of the work of the Genevan scholars. In 1560, Rowland Hall, another Marian exile, printed the new Bible in the city, whence it derived its name, the 'Geneva Bible'. It was sometimes referred to disparagingly as the 'Breeches Bible' because of its description of the dress of Adam and Eve in the Book of Genesis. It was printed in clear Roman type with numbered verses and many annotations, and became extremely popular among the Elizabethans, a copy being presented to the Queen herself.

The Elizabethan Church Settlement

In 1559, Queen Elizabeth repealed Queen Mary's religious statutes, and revived Edward VI's Act of 1552. She also recommended that the communion table should be kept in the east end, when not in use. The communion table was brought down into the body of the church only for the communion services, which now took place three or four times a year. The Queen reissued the Book of Common Prayer with one or two minor amendments and granted John Bodley (father of Thomas, founder of the famous library at Oxford) a seven-year patent for printing the Geneva Bible. Meanwhile, the English bishops under Archbishop Parker attempted to improve on the Geneva Bible with a new translation. This 'Bishops' Bible' was published in 1568. It was the only one licensed to be printed in England until the death of Archbishop Parker in 1575.

In 1564, the Protestant, Matthew Carew, was appointed rector of St Mary's, Sheviock. He later moved up to London, and in 1576 Walter Arundell was appointed rector. He was related to Juliana, wife of Richard Carew, the patron of the living. A letter, dated 10 April 1602, the last full year of the reign of Queen Elizabeth, has been preserved from Arundell.[20] It asks for help in procuring the bishop's licence to teach school and to preach the reformed religion.

The commotion of 1549 cast a long shadow over Cornwall. Richard Carew, who was aged four when Queen Elizabeth reversed the Catholic Acts of Queen Mary, recounts that the boys at the grammar school at Bodmin divided themselves into two factions or houses, each with its own captain. One of the houses was called 'the olde religion', and the other 'the new'. Matters got out of hand when one of the boys made a gun out of a candlestick and accidentally killed a calf with the projectile.[21]

The Church under the Stuarts

In 1604, following the Hampton Court Conference of church leaders, King James reissued the Elizabethan Book of Common Prayer with very few changes. As the Introduction explained, 'We thought meete … that some small things might rather bee explained than changed.' In the same year he launched a great project to revise the Bishops' Bible. Six companies of the most eminent scholars of the day were formed, based in Oxford, Cambridge and Westminster. For the New Testament, the scholarly teams relied heavily on William Tyndale's translation of 1534. The 'King James Version', as it came to be called, was published in 1611 and became the standard edition of the Bible in England and America for many generations.

In the reign of Charles I (1625-49), a conservative reaction set in. Archbishop Laud (1633-45) gave instructions that the communion table should be removed from the body of the church, and placed permanently as an altar at the east end. He also ordered that it should once more be adorned with candles. Laud also insisted that the clergy should wear proper vestments when taking divine service, rather than wearing just their surplices and preaching or 'Geneva' gowns. Gregory Arundell was appointed rector of Sheviock in 1622. We can infer that he welcomed these changes, because during the Commonwealth he was deprived of his living ostensibly for his Royalist and high church sympathies.[22] He died on 4 February 1654.

Damage to the Church during the Civil War and Interregnum

By 1650, the prevailing religious feeling in east Cornwall was Puritan, a feeling shared by the Carews of Antony, lords of the manor and patrons of the living of Sheviock. There is no wooden board containing the Letter of Thanks sent by Charles I to the County of Cornwall. He had issued this from Sudeley Castle on 10 September 1643, and ordered it to be put up in the churches.[23] In 1650-3, there was a major campaign of image-breaking in Cornwall. It was led by soldiers, who were motivated both by Puritan religious sentiments and an anti-Cornish agenda. 'It was well co-ordinated, exceptionally violent, and coincided with the third Civil War of 1649-51.'[24] In 1650, the soldiers took down the rood screen at Liskeard. It was probably at this time that Sheviock lost both its rood screen and most of its stained-glass, as the soldiers were targeting stained-glass in particular. About 1649 or 1650, the rector, Gregory Arundell, was ejected from his living, and a Puritan, John Gey, was intruded in his place. In 1655, following the death of Arundell the previous year, the trustees of Sir John Carew presented the living of Sheviock to another Puritan cleric and Carew relation, Richard Rolle.[25]

The Church after the Restoration

In 1660, the Church of the Elizabethan Settlement was restored. An Act of Uniformity was passed in 1662, requiring adherence to the established church. It was not until a year after the Glorious Revolution of 1688 that Parliament passed a Toleration Act allowing Protestant dissenters to set up, under licence, their own places of worship. The Methodists were the fastest growing of the dissenting groups from the 1740s onwards.

204 *The initials of the church wardens (CW), John Harvey (IH) and Sir William Carew (WC) were studded into the church door when it was replaced in 1723.*

Chapter 30

Church Administration after 1534. Post-Reformation Rectors

The habit of leaving sums of money to the poor of the parish to be distributed at the time of burial persisted for many years after Henry VIII's prohibition of common and open doles.[1] For example, when the farmer, William Brey, died in 1622, the first disposition of his will was: 'I give and bequeath unto the poore of the parish of Sheviock Five Shillings of lawfull money of England to be distributed at the tyme of my buriall.' Such bequests ceased only gradually, as compulsory payment of rates for poor relief took their place. The other medieval methods of raising money for the poor and sick and for church expenses continued to operate after the Reformation. Church 'stocks' continued to exist and church ales continued to be held, although they were under attack by the Puritans. In defending church ales from these attacks, the Bishop of Bath and Wells, William Pierce, wrote to Archbishop Laud in 1632, 'by church-ales many poor parishes have cast their bells, repaired their towers, beautified their churches, and raised stock for the poor'.[2] But these methods of raising money were no longer enough, so the rating of tenements according to their value became the usual way of raising money to cover church expenses. In 1614, Walter Arundell wrote a note explaining that when the church stock was insufficient to cover expenses, additional money was raised through these rates:

> The rate of our church hath been of long continuance … Certain [illegible] & some lands and tenements make up the stock & have sufficiently kept the church in repair until last winter [i.e. the winter of 1612/13] in which by the extreme winds the church was so much torne that the parishioners are to contribute somewhat more to the repair thereof.[3]

A receipt signed by the churchwardens, John Bloye and Richard Arundell, on 25 April 1694, accounts for five church rates paid by the trustees of Sir Richard Carew in respect of his holding at Sconner.[4] Those who refused or omitted to pay rates were presented to the bishop's court. For example, Phillip Blake, Edward Truscott, Peter Jefferye, William Rundle and Thomas Harry were all reported for non-payment of church rates. They all paid up before the Bishop's visitation court sat at Launceston in 1669.

Care of the Poor and Sick

In 1536, Henry VIII's Act prohibiting doles also provided that the churchwardens should establish a poor box to relieve the poor, sick and disabled. In 1598, an Act of Queen Elizabeth provided that compulsory church rates should replace voluntary contributions to sustain the poor and sick. It also provided that four overseers of the poor should be appointed and that they should use their funds to apprentice poor children and provide work for the unemployed.[5] In 1601, another statute required the overseers of the poor to purchase 'a convenient stock of flax, hemp, wool, thread, iron and other stuff to set the poor to work'. When, in 1618, the rector, Walter Arundell, built a house and workhouse for the employment of the poor he got into trouble with the jurors of the court leet at Crafthole, because he used the walls of the borough pound as the foundation for the new workhouse.[6]

Poor people were not allowed to move from one parish to another unless they had a pass for their journey issued by the parish constable. This was to prevent them from becoming a charge on another parish. This is the background to the entry in the Sheviock parish register for 13 February 1676/7:

> A certaine man having a passé was brought on horseback sick from one of the constabells of S. Germans and when hee was brought to the constable of this parish he was dead and was buryed here the 13th Feb.

To encourage the cloth trade, an Act of Parliament required people to be buried in woollen shrouds. This was noted in the Sheviock registers on 4 September 1678, as follows: 'Emm. Karle was buryed. He was the firste that was buryed heer in woolen.'

The overseer in 1693-4 was Philip Palmer. In that year, he issued to the trustees of the late Sir Richard Carew a receipt for the sum of 4s. 4d., 'being for on[e] Rate towards the Releif of ye poor, Assessed on Sconner'.[7] 18th-century overseers of the poor included Ferdinando Wallis (1719-20, 1727-8, 1732-3), who was High Sheriff of Cornwall in 1736, Philip Palmer (1719-20, 1730-1), Hugh Littleton (1721-2), Luke Taw, the miller (1726-7), Walter Warren (1727-8), John Dyer, a cooper (1728-9), Henry Short (1729-30), John Littleton (1731-2), Edward Elliot (1732-3), William Chubb and John Harvey (1745-6), John Hill and the Revd Mydhope Wallis (1760-1), Samuel Peter and Arthur Elliot (1765-6), Hugh Littleton and Samuel Peter (1767-8), Thomas Littleton and Samuel Peter (1787-8) and William Dunrich of Liscawn (1788-9). Thomas Buller and Thomas Bews were the overseers in 1833-4.

In the mid-1700s, the monthly disbursements of the overseers were usually about £2-3. For example, they disbursed £2 15s. 3d. in February 1745. Seven widows or single women were helped: Frances Avery, Ann Truscott, Elizabeth and Honor Avant, Mary Jory, Mary Hawkins and Sarah Spiller. They received a shilling a week unless they had children, in which case they received more. Thus Frances Avery received 6s. and

Mary Hawkins 8s. The overseers also disbursed 12s. 10d. for '11 yards of sarge [serge] at 14 pence per yard to make cloths [clothes] for the poore'; 2s. for '3 yards of canvas'; 2s. 2d. 'for thred and maken'; and 3s. 'for 4 yeards of cloth for Amy Williams'. In addition they gave 9d. 'to a boy that had the small pox' and 6d. 'to a soldyer in distress'.[8] In March 1745, they spent over £8. More than half of this was 'for keeping and clothing of Thomas Dyer'. They spent £1 on the constable's salary, and 8s. 9d. 'for the bueryell of John Hawkens the soon of Degery Hawkens', as well as making the usual weekly payments to the poor.

Churchwardens

The officers of the 'ordinary' (usually the bishop) in the parish are the churchwardens. There are normally two of them. Until recently, one was appointed by the incumbent and the other by the parishioners. Today both are elected annually by the parishioners.[9] Their rights and duties include the collection of alms, the maintenance of order, the allocation of seats in the church, the keeping of records relating to the church fabric, lands and possessions. In the early years of the reign of James I, the churchwardens were Amos Oddyarne (Odihorne) and William Sargent (the inn-keeper in Crafthole). In 1680, they were Hugh Hawkyn and Nicholas Rundle.[10] In 1694, John Bloye and Richard Arundell were the wardens. John Harvey and Sir William Carew were chosen in 1723. They had a new south door erected and left their initials studded in the door, where they may still be seen.

The Church Officials

The Clerk: After the Reformation, the role of the clerk was to assist the minister with the services and with the care of parish goods, such as the books and the communion vessels. Though a layman, usually with another principal occupation, he was expected to wear a surplice in church. John Jenkyn, parish clerk, died in 1732. The clerk in 1754 was William Bray. His salary was £3 per annum, but a supplement of 5s. or 6s. was paid for washing the surplices. In 1804-5, the task of washing the surplices was entrusted to the sexton's wife, or one of the other poor women of the parish, and the clerk's salary reverted to £3. The last full year in which there was a salaried clerk was 1850-1, when Henry Davey, also the village blacksmith, was paid his usual £3, plus 12s. for washing, so his perk had been

205 *Henry Davey, blacksmith, was also the last clerk of the parish of Sheviock.*

restored. In the following year, the clerk was paid just £1 10s. for half a year. Davey died on 31 August 1851 and is buried near the south door of the church.[11] There are no further entries of payments to the clerk in the churchwardens' accounts, the office having been made redundant.

The Sexton: The role of the sexton was principally to dig graves for the deceased and to keep the churchyard tidy. The sexton in the early 1700s was Joseph George, who died in 1711. In 1754, the sexton was William Roach, who was paid 10s. for his services. However, it was realised that this did not provide an adequate wage and so a supplement of 5s. 2d. was added for 'his care of the church leads etc'. This amount was then consolidated into his salary. Sometimes he was also paid extra for doing odd jobs or for doing a day's work at the rate of 1s. per day. In 1762, he was paid a supplement of 9d. 'for carrying 6 bushells [*sic*] of lime from George's House', a further 3d. 'for sand', a further 1s. 6d. 'for carrying 1,000 slate & [half a dozen] of raggs from George's House', and a further 1s. 'for his horse going to Tilland Quarry'.[12]

In 1788, a new sexton was appointed. The vestry minute sets out the reason for the appointment of this particular man:

> At a vestry held at Easter Monday the 24 March 1788 it was agreed by the parishioners then present that Wm. Beaver of this parish a poor man with a wife and five children & another now likely to be born soon shall stand sexton of this parish from the date hereof.

In 1797-8, Beaver was paid an additional sum of 1s. 6d. 'for cutting iveys [*sic*] round the church' and another 2s. 'For reparing [*sic*] the paths in the churchyard'. In 1799-1800, he was paid 3s. 6d. for 'cleansing the paths in churchyard' and a shovel was purchased for him, also for 3s. 6d.

By 1804-5, a new sexton, Thomas Stark, had been appointed. He was probably the son of the Thomas Stark who was rated 2d. for a tenement in Sheviock in 1754. His salary had gone up to 15s. 6d., and extra wages were now paid at a daily rate of 2s. Stark remained in post until at least 1813-14. In addition to his wages, he received 9s. for a pair of shoes in most years, and his wife was paid 3s. for washing surplices and an extra amount of 6s. 6d. in 1805-6 for mending them. In the same year, Stark provided '396 feet matting at ½d. per foot for the communion table' at a price of 16s. 6d. He also repaired the churchyard hedge for 4s. In 1807-8, he was paid 16s. (presumably eight days' work) for attending the mason. In 1808-9, he had to make a journey on horseback to Stoke church 'to forbid the banns of George Wolfe' for which he was paid 3s. in wages and expenses. In the same year, he was paid another shilling for 'destroying ivy around the church'. He did similar work in each of the next three years. In 1813-14, he did a total of 36½ days' work 'in church & churchyard'. This was probably in preparation for the victory celebrations at the conclusion of the Napoleonic wars.

Thomas Williams was sexton from 1845 to 1852 and William Keast from 1852 to 1861. Their salaries had gone up to £1 5s. From 1891 to 1894, Thomas Beaver, a descendant of the former sexton, took on the job.

Purchase of Books

After the Reformation, money was needed to purchase service books and hymn-books for the whole congregation as well as to replace the church Bible occasionally. Money was also needed to purchase prescribed prayers. In the 1700s, the bishop prescribed many occasional prayers for congregations to use. One of the churchwardens would make a journey to Liskeard to purchase these prayers, which initially cost a shilling each. The long years of war with the French, and periodic reverses, led to frequent calls by the bishops for the nation to fast. Parishes therefore had to obtain 'a book of prayers for the fast'. The churchwardens of Sheviock purchased these in 1756 and in every year from 1777-8 to 1781-2, from 1793-4 to 1796-7, and from 1805-6 to 1810-11. On the other hand, Nelson's victory at the Battle of the Nile in 1798 called for '2 forms of prayer of thanksgiving', and Wellington's victory at the Battle of Waterloo in 1815 called for 'forms of prayer for two general thanksgivings'. By this time the price of each prayer had increased to 2s.

The congregation also prayed for members of the Royal family, as they do today. A 'book of prayers for ye Queen' was purchased in 1772-3, and in each year from 1777-8 to 1780-1. Books of prayer for the king were purchased in 1788-9 and in 1789-90. In 1802-3, 'a form of prayer for the King's happy escape from assassination' was purchased. Next year, and again in 1810-11, forms of prayer were purchased for 'the King's recovery' from his bouts of mental illness.

In 1778-9, one of the churchwardens made a journey to Plymouth to purchase a new Bible costing £4. In 1805-6, Thomas Jay carried this Bible to Dock (i.e. Devonport) where it was re-bound. The cost of this and a new prayer book was £1 5s. Payments for music are detailed in Chapter 32.

Rectors after the Reformation[13]

1540 *Rhys Lewys*. Patron, King Henry VIII. He was the incumbent when the Great Bible in English was ordered to be placed in the church. Lewys was rector during the Prayer Book Rebellion (1549). (Register of Bishop John Veysey, Vol. XIV, O.S. fol.103[a].)

1554 *John Smyth, LLD*. On death of the last. Patrons, King Philip and Queen Mary (1553-1558). He was the last rector appointed as a Roman Catholic and may have been of the family seated at Tregunnick in St Germans and Liscawn in Sheviock.

1564 *(Sir) Matthew Carew, LLD.* Patrons, C. Copplestone and others, trustees of the will of Thomas Carew, who had purchased the manor of Sheviock in 1558 and died in 1564. Matthew (*c.*1531-1618), Thomas's brother, became a Fellow of Trinity College, Oxford, but took his doctorate in canon and civil law at Siena. He practised in the Court of Arches in London from 1573. He resigned the living of Sheviock in 1576 and moved to London, where he married a wealthy widow, Alice Ingpenny or Ingpen, daughter of Sir John Rivers, Lord Mayor of London. The Caroline poet, Thomas Carew (*c.*1595-1639/40), was one of their sons. Matthew became a Master in Chancery in 1577 and was knighted in1603. He was buried at St Dunstan's-in-the-West, where there is a memorial to him. (Register of Bishop William Alley, Vol. XVIII, fol. 85[a].)

1576 *Walter Arundell.* He was educated at Broadgates Hall, the precursor of Pembroke College, Oxford, which was popular with West Country students. The appointment of Walter appears to have been arranged as part of the marriage settlement between Richard Carew and Juliana Arundell, daughter of John Arundell, son of Sir John Arundell of Trerice.[14] Walter was a son of Nicholas Arundell and cousin of John Arundell. He appears to have been an exemplary parson. In 1602, he applied for a licence to teach. He also completed a glebe terrier in that year. In 1618, he erected a house (*domus*) and workhouse (*officina*) as places for the poor to live and work. He also bequeathed a capital sum of £32 10s., the profit from which (12d. a week) was to be given to the poorest every Sunday for ever as directed by the parson and wardens. The vestry records for 1761 show that some time before then the capital had been used to make loans to people. It was never recovered. He resigned in 1622 due to old age and infirmity. His descendants lived in the parish for several generations. (Register of Bishop William Bradbridge, Vol. XX, O.S., fol.36[b].) See also 'Arundell' in Appendix 1, *Families*.

1622 *Gregory Arundell.* In 1612, Walter Arundell purchased from Richard Carew the right to nominate the next rector of Sheviock. The consideration was an annuity of £30 payable to Sir Matthew Carew (see above) and Lady Alice, his wife, from whom Richard Carew had borrowed a large sum of money.[15] Gregory, the son of the previous rector, Walter, matriculated at Exeter College in 1599-1600. He took his BA from Broadgates Hall (later Pembroke College) in 1603. In 1613, he became rector of Ladock and continued to hold this living after being instituted to Sheviock. He had a poor relationship with the fishermen in the parish.[16] He was ejected from his living during the Commonwealth and was replaced by John Gey, whose tenure came to an end on Arundell's death in 1654/5. (Register of Bishop William Bradbridge, Vol. XXI, O.S., fol. 117[a].) See also 'Arundell' in Appendix 1, *Families*.

1655 *Richard Rolle.* His certificate of fitness is signed by his relations, Henry Rolle, Lord Chief Justice of the Upper Bench, and John Rolle, and by Hugh Fortescue and others. He matriculated at New Inn Hall, Oxford, in 1634, aged 18. He took his MA in 1642. He signed the Declaration of Conformity in 1662, and so held on to his living after the Restoration. He successfully sued a parishioner, Anthony Blake, for non-payment of tithes in 1673.[17] He was buried at Sheviock on 27 April 1680. In the Hearth Tax return of 1664, a 'Robert Warren clerk' is shown living in a house with three hearths 'and one other in a bakehouse'. He may have been Rolle's curate. For Richard Rolle's four marriages and children, see 'Rolle' in Appendix 1, FAMILIES.

1680 *Nicolas Kendall.* His uncle, Walter, had married Joan Carew, daughter of Sir Alexander and sister of his patron, Sir John Carew, in 1650. He was born in 1656, the son of Bernard Kendall of Pelyn in the parish of Lanlivery. He graduated from Oxford, and became a Fellow of Exeter College in 1678. He was appointed vicar of Lanlivery in 1681, Prebend of Exeter Cathedral in 1688, and Archdeacon of Totnes in 1713. In 1686, he married Jane, daughter of Thomas Carew of Harrowbarrow. She died in 1717 and was buried at Sheviock. He married secondly Hannah, daughter of John Snell, who survived him.[18] Of his 12 children, five were baptised in Sheviock: Walter 1689, Charles 1690, Jane 1693, James 1695, Mary 1696. James Kendall, clerk, buried March 6 1732, was his fourth son, the vicar of Altarnun. Nicolas's son, John, who married Elizabeth Tozer in 1764, had five children baptised in Sheviock. Nicolas's arms and motto are displayed in the plaster overmantel in one of the rooms of the former rectory, now Glebe House.[19]

On 1 May 1715, during Kendall's incumbency, the parish register noted that 'Joseph Kingston (a negro aged about 19 years) was baptised the first day of May being Sunday in the presence of hundreds.'

Kendall died in 1739 and is buried in Exeter Cathedral. There is a memorial to him in the church at Lanlivery. (Register of Bishop Thomas Lampleigh, Vol. II, New Series, p. 119.)

1740 *Samuel Deeble BA.* Patron, Sir William Carew. He was the son of John Deeble of Liscawn in Sheviock, who married Martha, heiress of the Smythes of Liscawn. His grandfather was Oliver Deeble of Wolsdon. He became vicar of Antony in 1726, and married there in 1747 Mrs Ann Sandford of Tiverton. They had two daughters, Ann baptised 1747, buried 1764, and Martha Smyth, baptised 1749. He was buried in Sheviock Church in 1750, aged 57. (Register of Bishop Stephen Weston, Vol. VII, N.S. p. 42.)

1752 *John Sandford BA.* Vicar of Antony. He was presented to the rectory of Sheviock under the terms of the will of Sir Coventry Carew, who described him as 'my friend'.[20] He was no doubt related to Mrs Sandford, wife of the previous incumbent. (Reg. Bp. George Lavington, Vol. VIII, N.S., p. 4.)

1753 *Josias Foot MA.* On cession of last. Under the terms of the will of Sir Coventry Carew, Foot followed Sandford successively as vicar of Antony and rector of Sheviock. He married Arabella, daughter of William Symons of Hatt.[21] (Reg. as above, p. 28.)

1781 *Duke Yonge MA.* University College, Oxford, 1782. On cession of last. Patron, the Rt. Hon. Reginald Pole Carew. Duke Yonge was the son of the Revd John Yonge of Puslinch, near Newton Ferrers. He resigned the living of

Sheviock the year after his institution to become vicar of Otterton, Devon, the seat of the Duke family. He married Cordelia, sister of the soldier, John Colborne, Lord Seaton. (Reg. Bp. John Ross, Vol. IX, N.S. p. 184.)

1782 *Edward Pole DD*. Fellow of All Souls. On resignation of above. Patron as before. His elder brother, Reginald, changed his name to Pole Carew on succeeding to the Carew estates. Edward and Reginald were two of the three sons of Reginald Pole of Stoke and Anne Buller of Morval. Their great-grandmother was Jane Carew, half-sister of Sir William Carew (d. 24 March 1743/4). Edward resigned from the living of Sheviock in 1796 and became rector of Lanreath in the following year. He died in 1837. (Reg. as above, p. 197.)

1796 *Joshua Jeans*. On resignation of the last. Patron as before. He was also curate of Antony. He died in 1807. (Reg. Bp. William Buller, Vol. X, N.S. p. 108.)

1806 *Duke Yonge*. Son of the rector appointed in 1781. Patron as before. Graduate of King's College, Cambridge. In 1811, he also became vicar of Antony, where he lived until his death *c*.1837. The novelist, Charlotte Yonge, was his niece. She described Yonge and his wife as 'very kind, merry, engaging people, who lived to promote happiness, and lived such an easy going scrambling life that they were said to be found dining at any hour from eleven to eight o'clock'.[22] (Reg. Bp. George Pelham, Vol. XI, N.S. p. 8.)

1824 *George Cumming Rashleigh MA*. Fellow of Winchester and New College. Patron as before. He was the son of Jonathan Rashleigh, rector of Silverton, Devon. He resigned in 1825. (Reg. Bp. William Carey, Vol. XI, N.S., p. 144.)

206 *The Revd Edward Pole, a nephew of Reginald Pole Carew, was for a short time rector of Sheviock. He died at Lower Tredis (Pen-Tredis), the home of his sister.*

1825 *Reginald Pole BA*. Patron, his uncle, the Rt. Hon. Reginald Pole Carew. He was the son of the former rector, Dr Edward Pole. He held the living in plurality with St Mary Tavy, of which he was rector 1826-39. He married, in 1836, Jane, daughter of Alexander Powell. He resigned and was re-instituted in 1837. (Patron, William Henry Pole Carew.) He finally resigned in 1839, when he became rector of Yeovilton, Somerset. He died in 1888. (Reg. as above, p. 164; and Bp. Henry Phillpotts, Vol. XII, N.S., p. 127.)

1839 *Edward Pole MA*. Patron, William Henry Pole Carew. He was the brother of the previous rector. He was also rector of Templeton 1833-79. He resigned the living of Sheviock in 1841. He married Mary, daughter of F.J. Chapman. He became rector of Rackenford, Devon in 1879 and died in 1890. (Reg. Bp. Henry Phillpotts, Vol. XII, N.S., p. 154.)

1841 *Gerald Pole Carew BA*. Matriculated at Balliol College, Oxford in 1832, aged 16. He became rector of Sheviock aged 25 on cession of above. Patron, William Henry Pole Carew, his brother. He was also vicar of Antony 1836-45. He married Harriet, daughter of John Buller. He built the new rectory in Sheviock churchtown, but was too ill to move there. He died in 1845 aged only 29. (Reg. as above, p. 167.)

1845 *John James Thomas Somers Cocks BA*. Brazenose College, Oxford. Patron as above. He was fourth son of the Hon. James Somers Cocks of Malvern Parva. His mother, Agneta, was a daughter of Reginald Pole Carew. Somers Cocks became an ardent follower of the Oxford Movement. At Sheviock, he was responsible for hiring the architect, G.E. Street, to restore the church and insert the magnificent new stained-glass window in the chancel. He also introduced many changes in the conduct of the Sunday services, making them more Catholic in spirit. He was responsible for pulling down the western gallery in the church, seating members of the choir in the chancel and dressing them in surplices. The churchwardens complained about the many innovations to Bishop Phillpotts, who compelled the rector to withdraw some of them. He resigned in June 1855 and seceded to Rome in 1856. (Reg. as above.)

1856 *Henry Carew Glanville*. Fellow of Exeter College, Oxford and Patron as above. he was the second son of Francis Glanville of Catchfrench, St Germans, and Amabel, daughter of Reginald Pole Carew. He took charge of the parish on the resignation of Somers Cocks in June 1855 and was instituted to the living in January 1856. He died on 20 June 1900 'much regretted by the parish in which he had ministered 45 years'. He left a bequest of £100 'the income of which to be distributed by the rector for the time being in gifts of coal and blankets to the poor of the parish of Sheviocke'. He also left a bequest of £300 to pay for dilapidations.

1900 *Gerald Pole Carew*. He was the son of the patron, W.H. Pole Carew. He was responsible for the restoration of the spire, tower and roof in 1902. He resigned in 1910. On the north wall is a memorial window to him (d.1922).

1910 *Herbert J.B. Walters*. Patron, Sir Reginald Pole Carew, KCB. Walters was a gifted musician and formed the Sheviock Band, taking rehearsals at the rectory.[23] His daughter assisted as a teacher at Sheviock school during the First World War. Walters resigned in 1918 due to ill health.

1919 *Bertram Lycett Lycett.* Patron as above. In the First World War he was temporary Chaplain to the Forces and served in France. He encouraged parishioners to purchase Lt-Col. G. A Kempthorne's *History of Sheviock* (*c.*1934). His long tenure as rector is still remembered by many in the parish. He took an active interest in the school and in the social life of the parish, founding the Recreation Club in Crafthole in 1920. He possessed a noisy motor cycle, from which he derived his nickname of 'Old Bang'. During the Second World War, he agreed to hold a stock of food in his rectory for distribution in the event of invasion.[24]

1955 *William John Hall.* One of his first acts as rector was to resolve the doubts about the name of the church by declaring it to be St Mary's.[25]

1965 *Bernard Walter Benskin.* He was ordained in 1919 and became curate of Antony in 1924. He graduated from St David's College, Lampeter, in 1925, and took a further degree from Keble College, Oxford in 1927. He was installed as rector of St John, where he lived, in 1938. He was made Hon. Canon of Truro in 1959 and Hon. Chaplain RNR *c.*1960.

1972 *Geoffrey Harper MA.* Hertford College, Oxford, 1952-5. Vicar of St Mark's Kingstanding, Birmingham, 1962-72. He was rector of Sheviock with Maryfield for a time and then also with Antony, and then with Antony only. He resigned from Sheviock in 1982 and was vicar of Paul until 1997. He initiated the glass screening of the Dawney Aisle.

1983 *Humphrey York BA.* Priest-in-charge, Luxulyan, 1966-83.

1994 *Kenneth Piper.* Non-stipendiary priest, house for duty, priest in charge. Diploma in Primary Education, University of Leeds. Teacher, 1953-62. Primary School Headteacher, 1962-87. Ordained 1983, Salisbury & Wells Theological College. Non-stipendiary priest, 1983-7. Chaplain to Norway; Anglican Chaplain at NATO – Allied Forces Northern Europe; Lay Training Officer for Scandinavia, 1987-9. Rector of Durrington (Larkhill Garrison), 1990-4. Founder member of the Children's Holiday Club held at Crafthole. Started Lent Lunches at Antony.

2000 Following the retirement of the Revd Piper, there was an interregnum. On most Sundays, services were taken by the Revd Nigel Fox (d.2007), formerly vicar of St Martin's by Looe.

2002 *Brian Anderson.* Prebendary of St Endellion. Assistant Priests: the Revd Christine Musser (2002-3); the Revd Jackie Johnson (2003-8).

Curates

The following are listed as curates (dates for their curacies are approximate): Francis Walters, 1754; Smart, 1756; William Neale, 1757; John Neilder, 1758-60; Mydhope Wallis, 1763-66; John Strode Foote, 1781; George Coryton, 1778-82; Bryan Roberts, 1776-89; John Bennet, 1789-93; William Williams, 1793-96; Hugh Littleton, 1802-11; Samuel Wallis Roberts, 1837-47; John Roberts, 1850-60.[26]

207 *The congregations of St Mary's church, Sheviock, and St James's church, Antony, in 2000. The Revd Kenneth Piper is flanked by the churchwardens of Sheviock, Peter England and Henry Pryn. The patron of the living, Sir Richard Carew Pole, stands next to his wife, Lady Mary, in front of the church tower. Susan and Neville Cusworth are in the back row, fourth from the left in front of the window. Tom and Mary Bersey stand at the extreme right.*

208 *This bench end at St Mary's is in the Renaissance style of the early 16th century.*

Chapter 31

St Mary's after the Reformation. The Tractarian Movement and afterwards

The fruits of victory for the religious Reformers included the destruction of religious images; the holding of church services and readings from the Bible in English; the regular delivery of sermons; and the transformation of the rite of the Mass into the Communion service. The entire congregation now partook of the sacrament in both kinds. These new forms of worship had a profound effect on the appearance and furnishings of St Mary's.

The Bench Ends

In 1540, Henry VIII ordered the new version of Matthew's Bible, known from its size as 'the Great Bible', to be read in every parish church. It then became essential to place pews in churches, so that the congregation could sit and listen to the readings.[1] In the same year, the king appointed Rhys Lewys as the new rector, the first incumbent certainly to be provided with an English-language Bible. The earliest surviving bench ends in Sheviock church may have been introduced under his ministry (1540-54). The first and last of each group of pews have bench ends carved with the classical motifs of putti (infant boys) and Roman vases. Though somewhat rustic in execution, these bench-ends are examples of the new art of the Renaissance.[2] Woodcuts in printed books, such as church Primers, picked up the new designs and were widely circulated.[3]

Church Plate

Queen Mary restored the old Catholic forms of worship for the six years of her reign (1553-58); but Queen Elizabeth, on her accession in 1558, reverted to the Protestant forms of worship introduced by Edward VI. Fewer pieces of plate were now required – a pyx for the reservation of the consecrated Host was no longer allowed, the pax to be kissed by the lay folk had been made redundant, and candlesticks and censers were discouraged. Whereas before only the priests drank the wine at mass, now all those confirmed drank from the cup at quarterly communions. So the old shallow chalice gave way to a more capacious cup.

During the incumbency of Walter Arundell (1576-1622), an inventory was made of the church plate. It was then of the simplest kind: 'A communion cup of silver and a cover. 2 pots of tyn for the wyne.' It was signed by the churchwardens, Amos Oddyarne (Odihorne) and William Sargent (the inn-keeper in Crafthole), and the 'sydeman', Laurence Blighe. This plate was stolen in 1824, and never recovered. New plate was purchased to make good the losses. The churchwardens' accounts for 1825-6 contain the entries:

A silver cup for the communion	£3 15s. 0d.
A silver plate for Do.	£6 9s. 0d.
Engraving 4s. Carriage 3s. 9d.	7s. 9d.

Lady St Germans and the Revd Mr Pole each subscribed two guineas towards the plate and the rest of the money came from the church funds.[4] Seven church rates were levied that year, each amounting to £4 15s. 5d.

In 1903, during the incumbency of the second Gerald Pole Carew (1900-10), another inventory was made which listed the 1826 communion cup and paten. By then, tastes had changed, and the rector referred to the 1826 cup as being of 'hideous egg cup shaped design'. This cup is still used as an additional vessel when, as at Easter, there is a large congregation. Gerald Pole Carew's dislike of the Georgian communion cup appears to have been shared by his predecessor, the Revd H. C. Glanville, who (according to Pole Carew) 'probably presented' the Victorian chalice that is still used at the regular Sunday communion. According to the inventory, 'it stands on a sixfoil foot, chased elaborately, has a silver gilt and chased knop with six square projections, on each a gilded cross floriated, alternately on red and blue enamel. On the bowl, gilded internally "Drink ye all of This for This is my Blood of the New Testament."' A new paten was presented at the same time.

THE GEORGIAN CHURCH

Raised Pews with Closed Doors

Two measures were taken to cope with an increase in population in the parish in the late 1700s.[5] Firstly, additional raised pews were constructed in the aisles and the south transept, now called the Dawney 'aisle'. The high-sided pews in that aisle can be clearly seen in an engraving made in 1820.[6] Secondly, a gallery was built at the west end of the church.

A note in the churchwardens' accounts, which must date from 1832, lists the ratepayers in the parish, together with the number of pews allotted to them and the number of seats in those pews, as follows:

John Littleton	(rate 15s. 1½d.; pews 4; seats 18)
William Laing	(rate 3s. 9d.; pews 1; seats 3)
Dr Pole	(rate 3s. 9d.; pews 1; seats 3)
Nathaniel Hawking	(rate 9s. 7d.; pews 2; seats 10)
Thomas Buttons	(rate 5s. 8d.; pews 1; seats 6)
John Liscomb	(rate 7s. 1d.; pews 2; seats 6)
Thomas Every [Avery]	(rate 6s. 3d.; pews 1; seats 8)
Samuel Lyne (Liscawn)	(rate 4s. 3d.; pews 2; seats 7)
Four sit in the Liscawn pew. Three for Edward's tenement at Crafthole)	
John Batten	(rate 4s. 9d.; pews 1; seats 3)
Robert Rickard	(rate 4s; pews 1; seats 3)
Thomas Hilman	(rate 6s. 9¼d.; pews 2; seats 6)
Thomas Bews	(rate 4s. 2¼d.; pews 1; seats 3)
Samuel Littleton	(rate 4s. 7d.; pews 1; seats 3)
Samuel Lyne rents the Glebe and sits in the chancel.	
Samuel Lyne for other farms	(rate 5s. 2d.; pews 1; seats 3)
	[Total 82 seats]

This was, of course, only a list of the most well-to-do parishioners, who paid church rates. The list may have been prepared in connection with a dispute that arose in 1832 between Samuel Lyne of Crafthole and Liscawn and Thomas Avery of Haye concerning the pews. Samuel Lyne's father, John Lyne senior, had built the Haye seat after taking up the tenancy of Haye in 1767. On his death in 1791, the use of the seat passed to his son, John, and then to his son-in-law, Robert Warren. Samuel Lyne, the younger brother of John Lyne junior, occasionally used the pew while Robert Warren and his sister were in occupation of Haye. Samuel Lyne had hoped that on Warren's death in 1832 the tenancy would pass to his own son, John. But he was thwarted and it went to Thomas Avery. Thereupon Samuel claimed to have a right to the use of Haye pew and persistently intruded himself into it, to the annoyance of Avery and his family. According to a member of the Pole family, who was a witness to the dispute,

> The seats in Sheviocke Church being partly open free seats and partly raised with closed doors, it has been the usual practice to appropriate the raised seats to the particular farms or tenements. In conformity with this custom a certain seat in the north east angle of the church has been appropriated to a farm called Hay.

While Lyne himself had alternative pews that he was entitled to use, by virtue of his holdings at Crafthole and Liscawn, it was pointed out that 'Should Mr Avery be deprived of this seat there is not another – excepting he sits with the paupers of the parish.' But Samuel Lyne was a difficult man – he was described by the Revd Reginald Pole of Tredis as 'old Sowerby' – and he would not give way until a legal opinion defeating his claim had been obtained from a senior church official called the Chancellor Master.[7]

209 *The Dawney aisle from C. S. Gilbert's* Historical Survey of the County of Cornwall *(vol. 2, 1820). The side chapel in the transept has been converted into an aisle with pews. The piscina has been omitted from the engraving.*

In addition to the raised seats, there were 150 free seats for the 'paupers of the parish'. Servants are not mentioned. But a proposed arrangement of seating in Antony church made in 1831, shows not only pews allocated to particular tenements, but also those set aside for servants. A pew in the nave was reserved for 'Horson' (one of the demesne farms of the manor of East Antony) and then behind them, 'Servants', and another for 'East Trelay' and then behind them 'Maid Servants'. The south gallery at Antony was to be disposed of as follows: 'Front seat – Lord Grave's [*sic*] Servts''; 'Second seat – Mr Bogers Do'; 'Three upper seats to the School Girls'; 'North Galery [*sic*] to the Labourers of the Parish'.

The Gallery

The growth in population led to the building of a gallery at the west end of St Mary's. The gallery also served to accommodate musicians. The churchwardens' accounts for 1782-83 state that £2 13s. 9d. was 'paid Mr Langmead for 43 feet of boulk at 15d. per foot'; that 5s. 2d. was 'paid Mr Hill for bringing up the boulk at George's House'[i.e. the house at George's Quay]; that a further 2s. 6d. was paid for 'drawing up the boulk to the church'; that 18s. 9½d. was paid to 'Mr Peter [Arthur Peter] bill for nails'; and that £2 5s. 0d. was paid the carpenter, John Billings. Although there is no certainty that the timber was used to support a gallery, it seems likely that this was the case.[8]

In 1819-20, £24 5s. was paid to 'John Billing for making a new gallery'; £1 15s. 6d. was paid to him 'for two pillars'; and 11s. and 8d. was paid to him 'for paint'. The new gallery survived Street's 1850 restoration of the chancel and installation of the choir seating. When the restored chancel was re-opened, a journalist wrote that, 'By the harmony of the choral service celebrated in the chancel, we are happy to find that the gallery is comparatively liberated from its former ill-disciplined frequenters.'[9] The gallery was probably removed at the time of Street's second restoration in 1872.

The Chancel and its Furnishings

According to a local newspaper, the chancel had possessed a plaster ceiling before its restoration by Street.[10] Such a ceiling would have been in keeping with Georgian taste. The Georgian furnishings had consisted of a high pulpit (with a sounding board over it) and a reading desk for the parson and clerk. The furnishings also included inscribed tablets containing the Lord's Prayer and Creed. Street lowered the pews and removed the pulpit, which was described by the newspaper as being 'cumbersome and ugly to an extraordinary degree'. Street may also have removed the stone tablets from behind the altar (their usual position) and re-erected them on the wall of the north aisle, where they still remain. These tablets had been commissioned in 1836-7. In the churchwardens' accounts for that year, it is noted that £2 15s. 8d. was paid 'Mr Prouse for engraving and putting up the Lord's Prayer and Belief [i.e the Creed] in church'.

210 *The churchwardens commissioned Mr Prouse to engrave and install the Creed and The Lord's Prayer on slate tablets in 1836-7.*

The South Door and Porch

In 1723, a new south door was inserted. The initials 'I H' and 'W C' studded into the door stand for the names of the churchwardens at the time. 'C W' (which must be read downwards), written after the initials, stands for 'churchwardens'. 'I H' was John Harvey, a local farmer, and 'W C' was Sir William Carew, the lord of the manor, who had completed the building of Antony House in 1720.

A local man made the sundial, which was placed in the gable over the south porch in 1780. In the churchwardens' accounts for 1780-1, it is noted that £1 was 'paid Mr. Bligh for a sundial'. He may have been a descendant of the Laurence Blighe, 'sydeman' who signed the inventory of the church plate in the 16th century.

The Bells

At least two of Sheviock's bells were recast after the Civil War of 1642-51, and it may be that the medieval bells were melted down to make into guns during that war. The Revd G. Pole Carew's inventory of 1903 describes the treble bell as being inscribed as follows: 'P.B: 1668 F.P'.[11] The tenor had been inscribed 'John Bloy. Richard Arundle

1693' but, as it had been badly cracked, it had to be recast in 1901. After recasting it bore the words 'G. Pole Carew Rector 1902 Edward VII R.I. "We Praise Thee O God"'. There had been a third bell, but this fell in 1820 and the metal was sold. It has never been replaced.

The Georgian Congregation

At this time the standard form of Sunday service was matins at 10.30 a.m. and evensong at 3.00 p.m. The priest wore a surplice for most of the time, but at many churches was expected to change into a black graduate's gown, sometimes called a Geneva gown, to deliver the sermon. Holy Communion was still only taken quarterly. The rector, the Revd Samuel Deeble (instituted 1740), stated in his reply to the Bishop's questions in 1745 that he had 24 communicants at Easter. Thirty-four years later, the number of communicants had declined, the rector, the Revd Josiah Foot (instituted 1754), stating that he had just 20 communicants.[12]

THE TRACTARIAN MOVEMENT AND RELIGIOUS REVIVAL

In the 1830s and '40s, a religious revival occurred known as the Tractarian or Oxford Movement. Its leaders were the Oxford divines, John Keble, John Henry Newman and Dr Edward Pusey, after whom the movement was sometimes known as 'Puseyism'. The doctrines of the movement were spread through 90 *Tracts for the Times* (1831-41). The Tractarians emphasised the importance of the Apostolic succession and sought to revive some of the practices of the early church, including the wearing of vestments, the burning of candles, the use of incense, processions, and the singing of hymns and anthems. To them, the behaviour of congregations brought up in the Georgian church was not up to the required standard. In describing what went on in Sheviock church before the reforms introduced by the Revd John James Somers Cocks (rector 1845-55), the local Conservative newspaper thundered:

> For years the people have been exhorted … to attend Divine worship regularly, to be in their places in proper time, and to join in, and love the social part of the services – but in vain. Empty benches in Church, and hostile contempt of her ordinances … seemed the result of ministerial efforts – for such singing as occasionally filled the aisles, there was little or no preparation – and therefore it produced irreverence rather than zeal.[13] While the western gallery, with many disorderly occupants, monopolised altogether the privilege of praising the most High, the congregation remained uninterested and unedified auditors.[14]

Somers Cocks had graduated from Brazenose College, Oxford, in 1843, and inspired by the Oxford Movement, he set about root and branch reform in the parish, beginning with the dedication of the church, moving on to the fabric of the building, and ending with the way services were conducted.

The New Dedication of the Church

An influential book, *Monasticon Diocesis Exoniensis* (Monasteries of the Diocese of Exeter), containing many of the Latin charters relating to the foundation of the monastic houses in the diocese, had been published in 1846. Its author was the Revd George Oliver, DD, a Catholic priest working in Exeter, who was given access to the Cathedral records. As a supplement to his book, Oliver included a 'Catalogue of the Parish Churches, and the Saints to whom they are dedicated, in Cornwall and Devon'. In the catalogue, Oliver attributed the dedication of the parish church of Sheviock to SS. Peter and Paul, and not to the Virgin Mary.[15] He gave as his authority Bishop Lacy's Register (1420-55), vol iii, fol. 501, which contained the will of the rector, John Walle.[16] The Tractarians were anxious to get back to the 'truth' of the early church. Somers Cocks therefore decided to follow Oliver and to re-dedicate the church to SS. Peter and Paul. The east and south walls of the chancel were rebuilt.[17]

The Windows

The beautiful stained glass in the east window was made by the firm of William Wailes of Newcastle.[18] Wailes (1808-81) had studied glass-making in Munich. The designer is thought to have been Francis Wilson Oliphant, RA (1818-59).[19] The window was described by the local newspaper as 'brilliant and sparkling to a wonderful degree' – an accurate and memorable description.[20] It is like a medieval altar-piece transferred from paint or stone onto glass. The central portion of the window contains full-size images of Christ and the saints, named not in English but in Latin, which had not been used in the Church of England since before 1549. They are, in the centre, the three figures which formerly stood on the rood screen, namely Christ, named *Salvator Mundi* (the Saviour of the World), *Sancta Maria* (St Mary), and *Sanctus Ioannes* (St John). At the extreme left and right are, respectively, *Sanctus Petrus* (St Peter) and *Sanctus Paulus* (St Paul), who were

211 *Under the influence of the Oxford Movement, the images of St Peter, St Mary, Jesus, St John and St Paul in the east window were named in Latin.*

held by Somers Cocks to be the patron saints of the church. The figures are contained in a canopied structure painted to look like stone, and within this structure are tiny figurines representing male and female saints. Below are scenes from the Passion.

On the north wall is a memorial window to another the Revd Gerald Pole Carew (d.1922), son of the patron, W.H. Pole Carew. He was rector from 1900 to 1910 and oversaw the restoration of the spire, tower and roof in 1902. The window was made by the firm of John Hardman of Birmingham, which commenced the manufacture of stained glass in 1845.

In the church tower is a rarity in a Church of England place of worship, for it shows the figure of John Wesley (1703-91). It was donated in memory of Florence Hart in 1960.

The Restored Chancel

G E Street restored the sedilia and a piscina in the south side of the chancel in the Gothic style.[21] On the north side, an old niche was restored and a new corbel set below it to serve as a credence.[22] The whole chancel was raised and paved with richly patterned encaustic tiles made by Minton.[23] The towering Georgian pulpit was replaced with a simple reading desk. Seats were installed for the church choir, which are still in use today, but no longer accommodate a choir. The seats were 'returned' at the west end, so that prayers could be said from the return seats on the north side.

The Re-opening of the Church

The building work on the chancel was completed, and the church re-opened, on 29 June 1850 (St Peter's Day). A service of re-dedication, a solemn Eucharist, was held to mark the re-opening. A procession was formed at the new rectory (completed in 1845). It consisted of men and boy choristers, in surplices, followed by the clergy, processing in pairs. The rector and the Archdeacon of Cornwall, Henry Phillpotts, junior, were followed by about a dozen clergymen from nearby parishes. They proceeded to the church chanting the 68th Psalm (Let God arise, let his enemies be scattered). When the procession reached the church, the congregation stood and joined in the singing. The Revd Somers Cocks celebrated, assisted by the Revd Reginald Hobhouse of St Ive and the Revd John Kitson of Antony as 'gospeller' and 'epistler'. Among the clergy present were the local men, the Revd Samuel Wallis Roberts, who lived at Trethill, the Revd James Crowley of St John, the Revd H.L. Jenner of Merrifield, and the Revd Augustus Cole, of Antony, not all of whom were in sympathy with the changes introduced by the rector.[24] The preacher was the Revd Arthur Tatham, rector of Boconnoc with Bradock.[25] The lessons were read by the Revd R. Martin of Menheniot and the Revd Richard Buller of Lanreath. Lay people in the congregation included Lord Graves and the architect of the restored chancel, G.E. Street. The singing was particularly praised by the local reporter, who observed that

> Mr Clarke, the schoolmaster of Sheviocke, led the choral services on the Seraphine, which he played with accuracy and ability; and who deserves the greatest credit for the admirable way in which he had made arrangements for the choral service, and for the manner in which the children of the school have been taught to sing[26]

Evensong followed at 3.30 p.m. The reporter concluded, 'The evening was closed with football and other rural games in the field adjoining the Rectory.'

In March 1851, nearly a year after the service of re-dedication, a national religious census of all places of public worship was carried out. Somers Cocks completed the return for Sheviock. He stated that the church had been 'consecrated before 1000', showing that he believed that the church had been originally founded by the Anglo-Saxons. He returned that there were 230 seats in the church (about 150 free and 80 paid), but that the average number of people attending services in the previous 12 months had been only 35 in the morning and 30 in the afternoon.[27]

'Puseyism at Sheviock'

The *West of England Conservative and Plymouth, Devonport and Stonehouse Advertiser*, from which the above reports were taken, was a high church and Tory newspaper, and gave an overly rosy view of harmony within the parish following the changes in worship introduced by Somers Cocks.[28] There were in fact many disaffected parishioners. Their subsequent actions were reported in the liberal newspaper, the *West Briton*, for 18 October 1850. The report was headed 'Puseyism at Sheviock'.[29] According to the report, the parishioners got the churchwardens to send a petition to the bishop objecting to the innovations. These they listed as:

> (1) a change in the position of the reading desk
> (2) dressing the clerk in a surplice
> (3) dressing the members of the choir in surplices and chanting the psalms
> (4) changes of place during the services, especially during communion
> (5) the frequent bowings by the rector during the services
> (6) changes in the administration of the Sacrament (with those vested being the first to be offered the sacraments)
> (7) removal of the rails round the altar
> (8) alterations to the communion table, and putting candles and candlesticks on it.

The Bishop of Exeter, Henry Phillpotts, father of the Archdeacon, was a conservative in matters of religious worship and disapproved of innovations without the consent of the parishioners. He ordered that the candles should be removed. Somers Cocks became increasingly unhappy, and in June 1855 resigned from his living. The following year he seceded to Rome.

The furore caused by Somers Cocks's innovations soon died down. In fact, many of the practices to which the parishioners so strongly objected in 1850 eventually became accepted usage in Sheviock. By 1869, the year of Bishop Phillpotts's death, the religious revival had proceeded to such an extent that communion was now being taken weekly. In 1874, a judgment of the Privy Council established the legality of sculptural ornaments in Church for the first time since the Reformation.

Further Victorian Restoration

In 1872, Street was once again employed on restoration work. He restored the nave, the north aisle, the Dawney aisle, the roofs and all the seats. He also replaced in Beer stone the tracery of all the windows except the Perpendicular ones in the north aisle and the east window of the north aisle.[30]

RESTORATION OF THE TOWER AND SPIRE

The engraving of 1820 in Gilbert's Historical Survey shows that at that time the top of the spire was missing.[31] Venning's Postal Directory for 1902 recorded that the spire had had its top shortened in repairing it; but did not state when that repair had taken place.[32] A big expenditure on masonry and helling (tiling) work was incurred in 1767-8, when it amounted to £14 13s. 5½d. John Spiller, and his assistants, William Francis and John Ford, were paid £7 1s. 4d. for mason's and hellier's work. Matthew Bartlett, the smith, was paid 17s. 11½d. One carpenter, James Prin, was paid 18s. 9d., and the other, Edward Hawkin, was paid 4s. 6d. The materials used were six bushels of lime, seven sheaves of reed (presumably for temporary thatching), six 'crest' or cresting tiles, eight hundred lathes, some timber supplied by the farmer, Mr Littleton, six thousand slates, and two dozen ragstones. A man and two horses fetched stones and slate; another two men and four horses fetched slate; and a man and two horses fetched helling sand. Another man was paid for loading a boat with slate and another man for carrying the slate in the boat. Clearly major work had been carried out on the church roof that year and it may be that this was when the spire was shortened.

The spire was finally restored, together with the tower, in 1902. At this time two oak floors were put in the tower. The oak was grown in the parish and parishioners carried out the work under the supervision of the architect, G.H. Fellowes Prynne. The bells were also re-hung and the bigger one was recast. The date 1902 and the initials 'G.P.-C.' in memory of the rector, Gerald Pole Carew, are stamped onto the top of the drain-pipes at the east end of the church. In the same year, a new oak pulpit in the international gothic style was erected as a memorial to the Revd Henry Carew Glanville.

The Re-naming of the Church

In 1903, when the rector, Gerald Pole Carew, was required to complete a 'List of Church Property and Inventory of Moveable Furniture', he added the words 'St Mary' after 'Sheviocke' (*sic*), indicating that he was aware of the original dedication.[33] However, neither he nor the next two incumbents took any formal steps to revert to it. In *c.*1934, Kempthorne referred to the situation as follows: 'The beautiful little church was originally dedicated to the Blessed Mary, but it is now known as the church of S. Peter and S. Paul'.[34] It was not until 1955 that the new rector, the Revd W. J. Hall, decided to go back to the original dedication. At a general church meeting held in the club room, Crafthole, on 2 November of that year, he proposed, and the meeting agreed, 'that the name of the Parish Church is St Marys' (*sic*).[35] There is no record of a special service of re-dedication having taken place.

The Modern Liturgical Movement

By the 1960s, there was a new movement within the Church of England for liturgical reform. This emphasised the Eucharist as the normal Sunday service. In 1980, an Alternative Service Book was introduced incorporating these liturgical reforms. This was itself replaced by a new service book, called Common Worship, in late 2002. In the same year, a new vicar, the Revd Prebendary Brian Anderson, was named as priest-in-charge to look after the cure of souls in St Mary's, Sheviock; St Philip and St James, Maryfield; St James, West Antony; and St James, Torpoint, together known as the 'cluster'. An assistant priest, the Revd Christine Musser, was also licensed to serve these parishes, and became the first woman priest to officiate at St Mary's. She left in 2003 and was succeeded by the Revd Jackie Johnson, who served in the cluster for five years.

212 *A Bevington organ now provides the main musical accompaniment to services at St Mary's. On the left of the organ can be seen the two doorways that once led to the rood loft of St Mary's. The choir would have sung from there in the late Middle Ages.*

Chapter 32

Church Music in Sheviock

The Middle Ages

The musical tradition in the western church goes back to the fourth century. The first composer of Latin hymns was St Hilary of Poitiers (*c*.320-68). St Ambrose of Milan (*c*.339-97) introduced metrical hymns alongside psalms and canticles. St Benedict (*c*.480-*c*.543) introduced Latin hymns, sung to plainsong melodies, into monastic services. St Gregory the Great (540-604) wrote many hymns and introduced the Gregorian chant. In England, the Venerable Bede (673-735) continued the tradition of Latin hymn writing. England was among the first countries to use the organ for Christian worship. According to St Aldhelm (d.709), the Anglo-Saxons ornamented their organs with gilding. In the tenth century, St Dunstan (924-88) reinvigorated monasticism and introduced the Rule of St Benedict into monastic life. He was a skilled metal-worker and organ-builder. He installed organs in Malmesbury and Abingdon Abbeys and many other places. Tavistock Abbey, founded during his lifetime, may well have possessed an organ to enrich the music of its services.

The first organ used for Christian worship in the Frankish church was installed in the chapel of Pepin, King of the Franks, at Compiègne *c*.757. Pepin had requested the instrument from Constantine Copronymus VI, Emperor of Byzantium. The Emperor sent a large pneumatic organ with lead pipes. Organs were also associated with gladiatorial combats, at which they had been played as part of Roman entertainments.[1] Following his father's example, the Emperor Charlemagne sent for an organ of Arabian manufacture that was placed in his chapel at Aix-la-Chapelle (Aachen) in 812. According to Arabic sources, there was a wonderful organ of gold and silver at the Cathedral of St Sophia in Constantinople in the mid-900s. However, organs were not in general use in the Orthodox Church, where the authorities held that the human voice was the only fit instrument for praising God.

By about 1100, the singing of hymns as part of the liturgy was established in parishes throughout western Christendom. St Bernard of Clairvaux (1091-1153) wrote the beautiful hymn *Dulcis Jesu memoria*. The congregation sang in Latin the

Kyrie, the *Gloria in Excelsis*, the *Credo*, the *Sanctus*, and the *Agnus Dei*, all to one simple plainsong setting.[2] The priest sang a psalm and antiphon (anthem), known as the Introitum, at the beginning of mass, and another psalm and antiphon at the end, known as the *Communio*.

Organs continued in use in English abbeys and parish churches after the Norman Conquest. The Lady Chapel in Westminster Abbey contained two organs in 1304, a small one standing on the choir step, and a large one fixed to the wall.[3] A passage in Geoffrey Chaucer's poem, *The Nun's Priest's Tale*, refers to an organ in use in a parish church:

> She had a yard that was enclosed about
> By a stockade and a dry ditch without,
> In which she kept a cock called Chanticleer.
> In all the land for crowing he'd no peer;
> His voice was jollier than the organ blowing
> In church on Sundays, he was great at crowing.[4]

It was at this time that churches began to install rood lofts for singers, and sometimes an organ, at the crossing between nave and chancel. Church services came to be elaborated by part-singing, also known as 'pricksong'. To sing the parts, men and boys formed a choir, and the choirmaster sometimes performed on a small organ. The singers' loft was built on top of the rood screen and usually at the side of the rood group. From its position next to the rood, it became known as the 'rood loft'. St Mary's Church in Sheviock had a rood loft of this kind, built probably in the late 1400s or early 1500s.[5] The stairway, which formerly led up to the loft, is still visible in the north wall.

CHURCH MUSIC AFTER THE REFORMATION

When Archbishop Cranmer translated and adapted the Latin service books for the new *Book of Common Prayer*, he may have intended also to translate the old Latin hymns. But the work remained largely undone until the religious revival of the mid-1800s. Instead, metrical paraphrases of the psalms replaced the singing of hymns in churches. In 1549, the year of the Prayer Book Rebellion, Edward Whitchurch (the publisher of Matthew's Bible in 1537 and the Great Bible in 1539-40) published *Certayne Psalmes, chosen out of the Psalter of David and drawen into English metre by Thomas Sternhold, grome of ye Kinges Maiesties roobes*. It contained 19 psalms without music. In the same year, a new edition was published with a further 18 paraphrases by Sternhold and a supplement of seven others by J. Hopkins. The first Psalter in English with musical notation appeared in 1553, just before the death in July of Edward VI. It was written by Francis Seagar and arranged for four voices. The publisher, William Seres, dedicated it to the same Lord Russell who had suppressed the Prayer Book Rebellion.

In 1556, Jean Crespin, a native of Arras in France and a compatriot and friend of the Reformer, Théodore de Bèze (Beza), published an edition of *Sternhold* in Geneva for the use of English Protestants who had fled there. It contained a separate tune for each of the psalms. English musicians wrote the tunes, many in imitation of the tunes they heard being sung by the French Protestants in Geneva. One such tune was later used for the hundredth psalm, 'All people that on earth do dwell', and became known as the 'Old Hundredth'. On the death of Queen Mary in 1558, a new edition of *Sternhold* was published and came into England. In 1559, the new queen, Elizabeth, permitted hymns and psalms to be sung in the churches. She stated in her injunctions to the clergy:

213 *The rood loft at Atherington, Devon, is a rare surviving example of a medieval rood loft. It stands on the screen in the north aisle beside the rood group, just visible in this photograph, in the centre of the nave.*

> For the comforting of such as delight in music, it may be permitted, that in the beginning or in the end of Common Prayer, either at morning or evening, there may be sung an hymn, or such like song, to the praise of Almighty God, in the best melody and music that may be conveniently devised, having respect that the sentence of the hymn may be understood and perceived.

In spite of this encouragement, there was no general revival of the use of organs in parish churches, though stringed instruments came into use in some places. In 1562, John Day published the first complete edition of *Sternhold and Hopkins*, containing all the psalms, evangelical hymns, and spiritual songs. It included 65 tunes. In the following year, he published a four-part setting of the psalms 'which may be song to al musicall instrumentes'. In 1592, Thomas East published a new Psalter that included tunes by Giles Farnaby, Richard Allison and John Dowland, all well-known for their writing of madrigals. In 1599, Richard Allison composed *The Psalmes of David in Meter, the plaine song being the common tunne to be sung and plaide upon the Lute, Orpharyon, Citterne, or Base Violl.*[6] The publication also included ten short tunes at the end 'for the use of such as are of mean skill, and whose leysure least serveth to practize'.

During the reign of James I, metrical versions of the psalms with music appeared in 1621 (with one tune composed by John Milton, father of the poet) and 1623. The first comprehensive hymn-book, George Withers' *Hymns and Songs of the Church*, also appeared in 1623. But overall there was a progressive decline in interest and skill in music during the reigns of James I and Charles I. When sung at all, the psalms were sung to only about half a dozen tunes. In 1643 and 1644, the overwhelmingly Puritan Parliament passed laws requiring the destruction of organs in places of worship.

The Restoration

The low ebb to which church music had sunk by the time of the Restoration was noted in a new publication, based on *Sternhold and Hopkins*, brought out by John Playford in 1671. It was entitled *Psalms and Hymns in Solemn Musick of Foure Parts on the Common Tunes to the Psalms in Metre: used in Parish Churches. Also Six Hymns for One Voyce to the Organ*. In his Preface, Playford stated that 'at this day the best, and almost all the choice tunes are lost, and out of use in our churches'. Because there were no trained trebles to be found after the Commonwealth period, Playford set the psalms for alto, countertenor, tenor and bass. In 1677, he brought out a new edition in a smaller format that proved so popular that by 1757 it had gone through 20 editions. The 1677 edition became the standard edition of *Sternhold and Hopkins*. In 1696, Nahum Tate and Nicholas Brady produced the so-called New Version of the Psalter. It included a supplement of 16 hymns. It was authorised by the Crown in 1700 and remained in use until the mid-1800s. By the later 1600s, some of the wealthiest parishes were re-introducing organs into their church services. Samuel Pepys first heard about an organ being played in a parish church when he went to Hackney on 4 April 1667. He noted with envy that it 'plays while the people sing; which I am mighty glad of, wishing the like at our church at London, and would give £50 towards it'.[7] The organ at Pepys's parish church, St Olave's, Hart Street, had been removed in 1644 as required by the new law and was not replaced until 1783. Until then the congregation sang unaccompanied, led by the parson or the parish clerk. A West Country contemporary of Pepys in favour of organs in church was John Newte, rector of Tiverton, who published *The Lawfulness and Use of Organs in the Christian Church* in 1696.[8]

The Revival of Hymn-singing

Hymn-singing was given a tremendous boost by the religious revival led by John and Charles Wesley. John Wesley's *Collection of Psalms and Hymns*, published in America in 1737, was the first designed for use with the service of the Church of England, though later editions were confined to Methodist use. During the rest of the century, all the hymn-books of the Church of England were based on Non-conformist originals. In the early 1800s, a number of popular hymn-books were produced, especially the *Hymns* (1827) published by Reginald Heber, Rector of Hodnet, Salop, and later Bishop of Calcutta. But the real revival came with successive editions of *The Hymnal Noted* (1852-4), which coincided with the Tractarian revival. The new hymnal included translations of ancient hymns from the Latin and Greek. J.M. Neale made beautiful English translations of hymns by St Ambrose (*c*.339-97) ('The eternal gifts of Christ the King'), St John of Damascus, who lived in the eighth century ('Come ye faithful raise the strain'), St Theodulph of Orleans, who died in 821 ('All glory, laud and honour, To thee, Redeemer, King'), and Peter Abelard, who lived from 1079 to 1142 ('O what the joy and the glory must be'), amongst many others. The proliferation of new hymn-books led, in 1861, to publication of a comprehensive collection, which became known as *Hymns Ancient and Modern*.

The Musical Revival in Sheviock

The first surviving record of expenditure on church music in Sheviock is an entry in the churchwardens' accounts for 1770, when 'strings for the bur' were purchased.[9] The 'bur' was almost certainly a bass-viol. Some 30 years ago the present organist, David Mashford, was asked to inspect an old wooden instrument in a barn that was part of one of the Crafthole Farms (perhaps originally Martin's Farm), then belonging to Stephen Grills. The instrument turned out to be a bass-viol with three strings. According to Mr Grills, the bass-viol had formerly been used in the musicians' gallery at St Mary's Church.[10] It would appear from the accounts that the bass-viol was the only instrument used in the church until 1814. A pitch pipe was used to keep it and the singers in tune. In 1773-4, 3s. 6d. was expended on 'a pipe for the singers' and in

1790, a further sum of 5s. was paid 'to a new pitch pipe'. In 1814-15, a violoncello was purchased from Mr Rowe of Plymouth for the sum of £5 12s. 6d. The player was probably William Cook, for he was paid 2s. 6d. 'for bringing home the instrument' in that year. A further sum was paid to Cook for 'strings for violincello' in 1829.

1814 was the year in which Britain emerged victorious from the wars with the French, and Napoleon was exiled to Elba. He escaped and ruled France again for 100 days until he was finally defeated at the battle of Waterloo in 1815. A concert seems to have been arranged to celebrate the victory. Eighteen singing books were purchased at a total cost of £1 2s. 6d. as well as eight pounds of candles and candle stands costing altogether 9s. 10d. In 1819-20, a violin was added to the little orchestra, for the accounts show that the sum of 10s. was paid to 'Willm. Cook for two strings for violin', Cook apparently performing on the violin as well as the 'cello. The orchestra was completed by the purchase of a second violin in or before 1822-3, for the accounts show that £1 was expended on 'strings for the two violins'. Interestingly, in view of the place of discovery of the bass-viol, the other violin player was John Martin. The accounts of 1829-30 show that 10s. was paid to 'John Martin for strings for violin'. He was the landlord of *Martin's Inn* (the modern *Finnygook*) in Crafthole, and also a small farmer.[11]

In an article written for the *West of England Conservative and Plymouth, Devonport and Stonehouse Advertiser* of 3 July 1850, a reporter had generalised that 'for such singing as occasionally filled the aisles there was little or no preparation'. This was untrue, or at least an exaggeration, as far as Sheviock was concerned, for most of the period from 1771 until 1850. Four choirmasters were engaged at Sheviock during this period, three at considerable cost. The first recorded in the account books was Nicholas Ham, who was paid £5 in 1771-2 'for teaching the singing'. He also supplied 'singing books' at a further cost of £1 4s. In five of the next ten years he was paid a guinea each year for 'keeping on the singing'. There was no recorded expenditure on music from 1780 until 1790. But in 1790-1, Mr Maurice was paid 18s. for music books, a new pitch pipe was purchased, Mrs Mullis of Crafthole was paid 5s. for 10lbs of candles (so that the singers and musicians could read the music after dusk), and Mr William Moon was paid £5 'for teaching the singing'.[12] Moon continued to be engaged by the parish for the next four years. In 1794-5, Andrew Kitt, was paid the lesser sum of 10s. 6d. 'for keeping the singin by order of the Easter meeting'. He continued to be engaged at this rate of pay for the next eight years until 1801-2. There was then another lull in expenditure on music until 1814-15, the year in which the 'cello was purchased. In that year the princely sum of £10 was 'paid Mr Coumbs [Coombe] for instructing the choir' and for 'twelve plain Psalm tunes'.[13] For the next 14 years, Coombe was engaged to attend the singers eight times each year at a fee of £4 per annum.[14] To put the expenditure on music in context: in 1771-2, at £6 4s. 11d., it constituted over a third of the total church expenditure. In 1790-1, at £6 8s., it constituted 41.5 per cent of total expenditure. In 1814-15, the first victory year over the French, the total musical costs soared to £17 4s. or 57.5 per cent of total expenditure. In 1815-16, the second victory year, the musical costs of £8 4s. constituted 40 per cent of expenditure. Thereafter, parishioners were spending more than £8 on music in every year from 1814-15 until the middle of the century.

The Singing Feast

The choir and orchestra in the Georgian era had two main duties. The first was to provide the fairly simple musical adornment of the Sunday services – hence the 'twelve plain Psalm tunes' purchased in 1814-15. The second was to give concerts on 4 and 5 November. Today, celebration of Guy Fawkes' night is a pale reflection of what it was in Georgian times. Its purpose then was to celebrate the deliverance of the nation's Protestant institutions – the king in Parliament – from the plots of its Catholic enemies. It must be remembered that James II had been chased off the throne for his Catholicism and that there had been two invasions from Scotland, in 1715 and 1745, designed to restore the Catholic Stuart monarchy. The new celebrations for the birthday of George II (30 October old style or 10 November new style) were combined with the old Guy Fawkes celebrations.[15] No wonder then that 4 and 5 November were celebrated with great enthusiasm and solemnity in every parish in the country. The celebrations began with a victory peal of the church bells on Guy Fawkes' Eve. There was another long ringing on Guy Fawkes' day itself. In almost every year for which the Sheviock churchwardens' accounts are preserved, payments were made to the bell ringers.[16] For example, 11s. was paid to them in 1754; 15s. in 1765-6; and 12s. 6d. in 1773-4 and 1774-5. By 1784-5, the expenses of the ringers had fallen to 6s. 8d. and they remained at this level until the mid-1800s.

But the main event of the celebration was the 'Singing Feast'. Most years' accounts simply record the payment of so much money 'To the singing feast'. However, in 1796-7, the accounts tell the whole story: 'To the singing feast fourth & fifth of November'. From 1791-2 until 1804-5, the cost of the singing feast was always £1 11s. 6d., plus varying amounts for candles – so that we know that the concert was held in the evening, perhaps ending with a gathering around a bonfire. In 1793-4, a payment of 2s. was made 'To Mrs Mullis for three pounds of candles'.[17] The singing feast was suspended from 1805-6 until the victory feast of 1814-15. In the victory concert of that year, William Davies was paid 8s. 8d. 'for 8 pounds of candles'. The cost of the singing feast in 1815-16 was £3 19s. 9d; in 1817-18, it was £4 and it remained at this level until 1822-3, when it dropped to £3. In the following year it increased to £3 5s., where it remained until the mid-1800s.

A New Musical Fashion

By 1850, when the Tractarian revival was at its height, the Georgian form of music-making with its little string orchestra had gone out of fashion. Instead, the parishioners purchased a seraphine as the musical accompaniment for the choir. As discussed in Chapter 31, this was played by Mr Clarke, the schoolmaster, who also trained the children to sing in choir.[18] In 1923, the seraphine was replaced by a second-hand Tucker pipe organ at a cost of £110.[19] The instrument was built by George Tucker of the Octagon, Plymouth. The church of St Mary's at Sheviock acquired it from a redundant Methodist chapel in Plymouth.[20] The organist in the 1930s was the farmer, Edgar Bersey. According to Kempthorne, there continued to be a violin accompaniment to the singing even after the installation of the organ.[21] This organ was repaired many times by Hele & Co. and W.N. Hosken of Plymouth. It was finally broken up on 12 February 1995. The lead pipework was melted down and given to Pete Goss to become part of the keel of his boat, *Aqua Quorum*.[22]

In November 1994, St Mary's purchased the present Bevington pipe organ from the now demolished East Hill Baptist church in Wandsworth.[23] The organ, which was then very dilapidated, was transported to St Mary's for restoration and installation. During the course of restoration, a hand-written paper label was found inside one of the soundboards, signed by Henry Bevington in 1808. Henry Bevington the elder had been apprenticed to the firm of Ohrmann & Nutt, who were themselves the successors to the business of the German organ builder, Johann Schnetzler (1710-1800). Schnetzler came to England in 1740, and in 1741 built for Georg Frideric Handel the organ upon which he first performed that great Protestant oratorio, 'Messiah'.[24] Bevington set up in business on his own account in 1794, and his business was continued by his sons, Henry and Martin, in Ohrmann's old premises in Rose Street, Soho, London. The label dated 1808 found in the organ may indicate the year in which the original five-stop instrument was enlarged to the magnificent two-manual organ in use today. After being transported to Sheviock, the organ was given a complete overhaul by W.N. Hosken. Church members undertook the refurbishment of the wooden casing. The organ was set up, fine tuned and first used for worship on Easter Day (16 April) 1995. The Venerable Rodney Whiteman, then Archdeacon of Bodmin, dedicated the organ on 7 October. The next day John Winter of Truro Cathedral gave the opening recital. The organ is one of only a few examples of Henry Bevington's work that have survived.[25]

CHAPTER 33

Tithes

The payment of tithes on agricultural produce can be traced back to the late 600s in the parts of Britain under Anglo-Saxon rule.[1] It was then called 'church scot'. King Edgar (959-75) issued an Ordinance enforcing the payment a 'tithe' or tenth thing, which was a form of taxation in kind. The tithes were payable to the 'rector', the person entitled to receive the tithes. Until 1215, a monastery as well as the local parish priest could be the rector. We know from a charter of Pope Celestine III (1106-98) that Abbot Herbert of Tavistock possessed the 'endowments' of St Mary's in 1193, and so was in the position of rector.[2] However, at some date between 1193 and 1279, the benefice of Sheviock became a rectory, with the full right to the tithes vested in the incumbent. In the Calendar of Patent Rolls of 1316, William de Lananta, who was instituted in 1279, is referred to as 'parson' (i.e. rector) of Sheviock, showing that the change had taken place by then. In spite of papal pronouncements to the contrary, lay people, called 'improprietors', often came into possession of rectorial tithes, paying a portion of them to the vicar or curate. By the late 1400s, more than half of the tithes from Cornish parishes had been appropriated by people other than the local incumbent.

Tithes were payable both on harvested cereal crops and hay, often called the great tithes, and on every other form of produce, called the lesser, small or minute tithes. Lesser tithes were paid for example on the increase of herds, or on the production of eggs, honey or cheese, or the vegetable crops from a cottage garden. Fishermen also had to pay tithes of fish from their catches. Needless to say payment of tithes was often much resented by the villagers. Dr James Whetter has drawn attention to the fact that Bishop Bronescombe of Exeter, the bishop who consecrated Sheviock church in 1259, was forced to issue regulations concerning certain ambiguities and abuses relating to the payment of tithes. The bishop also laid down the penalty of excommunication for those who tried to evade payment and those 'who maliciously bring the milk itself to church, and – what is more wicked still – finding there no man to receive it, pour it out before the altar in contumely to God and his church'.[3]

An account roll of the rectory of Sheviock, showing *inter alia* the payment of tithes from Michaelmas 1410 to Michaelmas 1411, was formerly preserved in the muniment room of Exeter Corporation. Although it was destroyed by enemy action in the Second World War, it was translated and printed by Kempthorne.[4] The rector at that time was Richard Donscombe, who had been granted licence of non-residence in that year. The account was prepared by his *procurator* (steward), John Penhale. It reads in part:

He also accounts for

61s. 4d. received for tithe of sheaves sold to John Sturr at Trewykkell		
55s.	"	John Bake of S. Germans at Resconern [Sconner], Trewyne, and Trenthest [Tredis]
27s	"	Roger Whiteforde at Pole
43s. 6d.	"	Robert Blerok at Blerok [Blerrick] and Carslake [Kerslake]
45s.	"	Simon Odyhorn at Drussell
33s.	"	Robt. Burnard and Roger Whiteforde at Truthill [Trethill] and Launstawen [Liscawn]
18s.	"	Peter Pyrok at Scheuokdoune [Sheviock Down]
23s.	"	Roger Campell at Blaser
70s	"	Ralph Icory.'

Because the incumbent was absent, all the great tithes were simply sold back to the farmers who had rendered them. However, some of the minute tithes were rendered to the steward in kind, probably for the benefit of the curate. Thus William Cornysch, John Scrogsden and Harry Blackaller each rendered a pig.[5]

A SEVENTEENTH-CENTURY TITHE CASE FROM SHEVIOCK

Resentment at having to pay tithes persisted down the centuries, and in 1669 and 1670 erupted into a major confrontation within Sheviock between the rector, the Revd Richard Rolle, and a local gentleman farmer, Anthony Blake. Richard Rolle (1616-80) was a kinsman of Sir Samuel Rolle MP, lord of the manor of Callington, who also owned some property in Crafthole. The Revd Rolle matriculated at New Inn Hall, Oxford, in 1634 and gained his MA in 1642. On 30 May 1655, he was appointed to the living of Sheviock by the patron, Sir John Carew, who was then a minor. Rolle was related to the Carews because a kinswoman, Grace Rolle, had become the second wife of Sir Richard Carew in 1621, and her younger sister, Jane, had married his son, Alexander. Sir Alexander was the late father of Rolle's patron, Sir John Carew.[6] Rolle's appointment was approved by the Commissioners for Approbation of Public Preachers as required by an Act of 1654. He must therefore have signed the Puritan Covenant found repugnant by so many ejected Anglican clergy. In 1662, he signed the Declaration of Conformity and thus was able to hold on to his living after the Restoration.

The Revd Rolle had four wives: Mary, by whom he had three children, Mary (baptised 1656), Richard (b.1657), who was destined for Oxford, and Margaret (baptised 1658). His second wife was Elizabeth, daughter of Thomas Smyth (almost certainly of Liscawn), whom he married in 1665. In 1668, Rolle married his third wife, Joan (d.1675), daughter of William Jane, the Sheviock Registrar appointed during the Commonwealth. The children born to the Revd Rolle and Joan were Joan (b.1668) and another Elizabeth (b.1671). Three years after the lawsuit, Rolle married for the last time, Mrs Joan Hitchens. In 1673, he commenced his suit against Anthony Blake in the Court of Exchequer at Westminster. The proceedings were recorded on parchment and are preserved at The National Archives in Kew.[7]

Anthony Blake (1632-1720) was the son of Philip Blake (1604-89) and Sibley, née Pope. The family belonged to the lesser gentry. According to the manorial rolls of the manor of Kerslake, which survive *inter alia* for the years 1636 and 1640, Philip Blake was then a free tenant of the manor.[8] The manor included the lands of Middle Blerrick, Lower Blerrick, Kerslake, Trethill, and Liscawn, and covered an area of approximately 500 acres. In 1640, the free tenants of the manor were Thomas Smyth of Liscawn, father of Rolle's second wife, Elizabeth; Philip Blake who is shown in the tithe proceedings to have lived at Lower Blerrick; Stephen Robyns; and William Sargent.[9] The latter two were tenants of Middle Blerrick and Trethill, respectively. There were also two conventionary (copyhold) tenants, Robert Williams and John Naunter. Probably they rented parcels of agricultural land without dwellings attached.[10] In 1607, one of the tenants of the manor had been a John Pope, so Philip Blake may have inherited his tenancy from his wife's father.

The Dispute

Anthony lived with his father, Philip, at Lower Blerrick. Philip had another son, John, who was seven years older than Anthony. It is likely that Philip (aged 65 in 1669) and his eldest son, John, farmed most of the fields and orchards attached to Philip's tenement and also another tenement in Sheviock churchtown, later known as Treise's tenement.[11] Anthony farmed 43 acres of land in Middle and Lower Blerrick and in

214 *At the centre of the dispute between the Revd Rolle and Anthony Blake about the non-payment of tithes in 1669-70 were these fields between Blerrick and Kerslake.*

Kerslake. According to the evidence, he occupied 'six or seven acres' of land at Middle Blerrick, 'six or seven acres of land meadow and pasture' in Lower Blerrick and '20 or 30 acres of lands, meadow and pasture' in Kerslake. On these lands, he had 'thirty or forty sheep', 'several ewes, at least 20, with lambs', 'several cocks and hens and chickens and several old geese and at least ten or twenty young geese', and 'several mares, nags … heifers, bullocks'. Small tithes were payable on the young of all these species and on the fleeces of the sheep. It was alleged that Anthony deliberately avoided paying the tithes on the sheep and lambs by driving them into the neighbouring parish of St John before they could be tithed. In effect, it was alleged, he had done a 'moonlight flit'. In addition to rearing the livestock, he cut hay and grew barley. Both these crops were subject to the 'great tithe'. The insulting way in which Anthony Blake was said to have declined to pay this tithe was one of the more inflammatory ingredients in the dispute. Anthony also had orchards on his tenements. The quantity of cider and perry made by Anthony from the fruit of the orchards was another disputed issue and it was alleged that Anthony had not paid tithe on any of it.

A number of factors caused the rector to bring the case. Firstly, there is evidence of deliberate fraud being practised against him. Secondly, he had a large and growing family, with one son intended for Oxford, and he may not have been wealthy, in spite of his family connections. His rectory was not then a large one. It had only four hearths, compared with Philip Blake's five.[12] Thirdly, there seems to have been an element of personal animosity between him and Anthony Blake. Fourthly, some of the villagers were aiming to establish a custom or 'modus', whereby only low or nil tithes were payable on orchard produce. The final point rendering the dispute intractable was that it was an argument between a parson with a history of Puritanism, and a small group of old-established Sheviock families with links to the Royalist cause. Alexander, the son of the former rector, Walter Arundell, gave evidence for the defendant. Alexander was a younger brother of the late Revd Gregory Arundell, Walter's son and successor, who had been ejected from the rectory of Sheviock during the Commonwealth. Their relative, Sir John Arundell of Trerice, had been a senior Royalist commander in the Civil War, and the hero of the siege of Pendennis Castle. The dispute therefore may have been inflamed by recent animosities between Puritan and Cavalier.

The case was started by the rector laying a bill of complaint before the Court in Westminster. Once the bill was laid, the court drew up lists of questions, called 'interrogatories' through which they aimed to establish the facts. They also appointed commissioners in Cornwall to take evidence under oath from local witnesses. The commissioners were Thomas Dandy, John Dyer, Hannibal Gryles, Robert Mutton, and Richard Tippett. All of them appear to have been Cornishmen. Thomas Dandy was probably the son of William Dandy of Trewren (or Trewen) in Lanreath, said to be descended from a younger branch of the Dawneys of Sheviock.[13] Hannibal Gryles was also from Lanreath. He was the son of the Revd Francis Gryles, the rector of Lanreath, and Martha Mayow of Menheniot.[14] Members of the Mutton family are commemorated in the windows of St Neot's church. The Tippetts are numerous in West Cornwall.

The witnesses for the complainant were Abraham Chubb, Thomas Gryles, Thomas Burdick, Ann Bray, Nicholas Sargent and Nicholas Gilberds.[15] The Chubb, Gryles, Bray, and Sargent families were long established in Sheviock parish. Thomas Gryles, who was 83 at the time of the case is described by the commissioners as being 'of the parish of Sheviock gent'. He spoke of his own father as 'being before his death aged at least eighty six years and constantly living in the … parish of Sheviock and having a considerable estate'.[16] A George Grilles was a conventionary tenant of Kerslake manor in 1636. In 1641 he married Annys Naunter.[17] The Naunters were also shown in the court rolls as being conventionary tenants of Kerslake manor from 1608 to 1640. A John Bray was listed as marksman with an 'harquebus' in the muster roll of 1569, and a Richard Bray was one of the guarantors for the building of the quay at Portwrinkle in 1612. Members of the Sargent family are shown as being first conventionary and then free tenants of Kerslake manor from 1565 to 1640. At the time of the lawsuit, Nicholas Sargent, was living in the neighbouring parish of Antony. He was described as a yeoman.

Thomas Burdick first came into the parish as a young man of about twenty, and apparently participated in the pilchard fishing industry, as he gave evidence about the payment of the tithe of fish. He was 'eighty yeares upwards' at the time of the case. Nicholas Gilberds worked for the rector in 1670 'being and living with [him] as his servant and agent to look after and save the tythes'. He appears to have been a professional agent and by the time the case was brought (1673) he had moved on and was then living in Boconnoc.

The witnesses for the defendant were Philip Blake, the defendant's father; John Blake, perhaps his brother; Alexander Arundell, son and brother of two former rectors; John Dodridge and David Dewstowe.[18] John Dodridge was a resident of St Germans by the time he came to give evidence, but for 35 years had lived and farmed at Trewin in Sheviock.[19] John Dodridge the younger was to marry Ann Blake, Anthony's sister; so the elder Dodridge's objectivity must be called into question. David Dewstow gave his profession as 'husbandman' or farmer and stated that he had known the defendant 'for twenty yeares last past and upwards'. What he did not say, but what one must suspect, is that he was related to the defendant. In 1637 a William Dewstowe married Pentecost Blake, and a Dowell Dewstowe married S. Blake.[20]

Issues relating to the Great Tithes

In relation to the great tithes of hay and corn, the tithe owner had a right to enter the farmer's land to take his dues. In many parishes the custom was for the farmer to give the tithe owner 24 hours' notice of the time he intended to cut his field. For his part, the rector's tithing man had to let the farmer know when he was ready to make or witness the tithing. Usually, the custom was for the farmer to harvest his entire crop in the normal way up to and including setting it up in sheaves. At this point, the tithing man, or sometimes the farmer, would mark every tenth sheaf with a green bough or the like, and then the rector's man would come back later to collect the marked sheaves.[21] Sometimes the custom of a parish would differ from this; but the evidence in this case was that the practice in Sheviock followed the normal pattern.

The Tithe of Hay: On the tithe of hay, Abraham Chubb testified that it was 'a general use within the ... parish to allott [i.e. mark] the tenth part or cock of hay after its cocking unto and for the Rector of the said parish.' Nicholas Sargent testified that in both 1669 and 1670 Blake 'did cutt [his field] and made and converted [the grass] into hay, which hay was worth ... at least ten shillings yearly'. Ann Bray testified that 'about one acre of grasse groweing upon ... Kerslake hath been severall tymes cutt and converted to hay within seaven years last past. And this deponent hath togeather with severall others beene payed for the making thereof'. Nicholas Gilberds said that in 1670 he 'saw severall shocks of hay in and upon the said premisses [of Kerslake]'. However, this testimony was too vague to satisfy the commissioners, and when they made their award they did not include any element for the tithe of hay.

The Tithe of Barley: The principal witness relating to the tithe of barley was the rector's tithing man, Nicholas Gilberds. According to him, in 1670, the defendant grew upon Lower Blerrick (6 or 7 acres) or Kerslake (20 or 30 acres) two or three fields of wheat, upon which he properly paid the tithes due in kind. But he also grew barley on another two fields containing four acres,

> And the barley ... was cut or mowed downe by the defendant or his order And the defendant gave the complaynant not above three or four hours warning to goe and see the same tythed wheruppon this deponent was forthwith sent by the ... complaynant to demand and receive the tythe thereof ... And this deponent and the defendant went into the said fields to tythe the same. But being come there found the same lying rudely and unbound in and uppon the said ground and not mowed upp or bound, as is constantly used not only within the said parish of Sheviock, but within and throughout the whole County of Cornwall, whereuppon and for that it is and hath always beene accustomed within the said County to gather bind upp mowe or shock all wheate rye barley and oats before the same are or ought to be carryed away and tythed And for that the defendant refused to bind upp the same into convenient sheafes or bundles as

> is usual, And has left ... neare halfe of the said corne scattered upp and downe these fields to the great abuse of the said complaynant ... this deponent did refuse to gather upp the said tyth and rent of the said barley or to take or carry away the same.

Gilberds also compared Blake's performance relative to the tithe of barley with that of the other inhabitants of the parish, who, he said, had put their corn 'into a fitt and convenient condicion to be carryed'. Gilberds then went on to state that the barley left on the ground 'was never afterwards gathered by the complaynant or ever came to his use but was spoyled by the defendant and his cattle'. He later deposed that the tithes payable on the barley were worth 'at least eight shillings'. David Dewstow confirmed Gilberds' statement, and the commissioners accepted their evidence as true. What Blake had done, therefore, was equivalent to the medieval farmer throwing the milk down before the altar. In one sense he could be said to have tendered his tithe, but in reality he had not, because the barley was not in the deliverable state that the custom of the parish demanded.

Issues Relating to the Small Tithes

The small tithes were even more problematical, firstly because they related to so many things. It was never easy to determine which things, or how many, had been produced by a parishioner in a particular year. The interrogatories included a fairly comprehensive list of what they might be: 'sheepe, wooll, lambs, cows, calfes, piggs, geese and henns, turkeys, ducks, chickens, eggs, pidgeons, bees, honey, wax, apples, peares or other fruites, turnepps, carrots and other roots.' The tithe was payable on the growth or increase of these things in the year, and the increase had to have taken place on land to which the tithe related.

Another difficulty was the issue of composition. It would obviously be hard for a rector to keep a tally of every tithable increase in these things throughout his parish, and even if he could, he may not have been able to consume or use all the individual items to which he was entitled. The practice, therefore, arose of accepting composition, or monetary payment, in lieu of tithe in kind. If such composition became standardised over a long period of time, and throughout the parish, it then became a 'modus' or customary payment or exemption. Once a modus was established it was difficult for the rector to revert to being paid in kind, or to increase the amount of monetary composition. To discover whether any modus was in operation in Sheviock, the interrogatory asked whether, if the tithe was not paid, it was 'for or by reason of any custome or customs to be exempted from the same'. The interrogatories also sought to discover whether no tithe was payable because the rector had agreed to accept a sum of money as composition in lieu of tithe. Finally, they sought to discover whether previous rectors had simply been negligent in collecting their tithes. If so, the tithe would still be legally payable.

Hens, ducks and geese: Nicholas Sargent deposed that in 1669 and 1670, Anthony Blake 'kept severall geese ducks and henns' on Lower Blerrick. In a second examination by Dandy and Gryles, at the inn at Sheviock churchtown kept by Daniell Sargent (who was probably a relative of Nicholas), Nicholas said that he knew that in those years Blake had several hens, geese, ducks, and other poultry most of which had young, but he did not know what their value was. Nicholas Gilberds deposed that in 1670 Blake kept 'several cocks and henns and chicken and severall old geese and at least tenn or twenty young geese' at Kerslake, and also 'kept severall hennes and ducks and geese which had several young' at Lower Blerrick. The commissioners accepted the evidence of Sargent and Gilberds and awarded the rector 2s. as the tithe due.

Sheep: Nicholas Sargent deposed that Blake kept at Lower and Middle Blerrick

> at least thirty or forty sheepe severall of them ewes which within the said time and yeares [i.e. in 1669 and 1670] did ewne [i.e. ween] and had lambs in and upon the same But were afterwards and within two or three dayes before they were shorne removed as this deponent was informed by William Rayne the defendant's owne servant ... into the parish of St John.[22]

Nicholas Gilberds deposed that in 1670 Blake kept at least 20 ewes at Blerrick and Kerslake

> which did ewne and have lambs ... and were there kept for a considerable time both before and after they soe ewned ... and ... some very short time before the usual time of tything the same, were by the defendant ... removed off from the said premisses ... into some other adjoining parish And then the said ewes and lambs were likewise shorne as this deponent hath heard and beleiveth and soe that the complaynant hath no tythe of the said ewes wooll or lambs so removed.

He went on to state that 'the said removal of the said ewes and lambs ... was on sett purpose to abuse the complaynant and to detayne the tythe thereof from him'. He estimated the value of the lambs and fleeces as at least £15. He also testified that tithe on such items was usually paid at the rate of 20 pence in the pound (i.e. 8.3 per cent), so that the tithes payable should have been 25s. Contrary evidence was provided by David Dewstow, who deposed that the defendant had in fact paid the tithes on the lambs and wool, but the commissioners accepted the evidence of Sargent and Gilberds.

Mares, nags, heifers and bullocks: Gilberds and Sargent deposed that in 1669 and 1670 Blake kept several mares, nags, heifers and bullocks in Sheviock, but did not know their value. However, Sargent then deposed that

> the usuall ... composition made by ... the neighbouring parishioners with their ... rectors ...is four pence for the small tythe of every acre of lands in tillage and six pence for every acre of ... lande when out of tillage for each year.

This composition would cover the mares, nags, heifers and bullocks. The evidence of Sargent was also to the effect that Blake occupied altogether 43 acres of lands within Sheviock, of which 20 acres were tilled and 23 were untilled. Dandy and Gryles accepted this evidence and thought that the rate of composition was 'very reasonable'. They therefore awarded the rector the sum of 13s. 4d. for the tilled acres and 23s. for the untilled ones, because, while the value of the tithes was uncertain, 'that uncertainty [was] occasioned by the ... defendant's owne contrivances'.

Orchard Fruit and Cider: According to the evidence of Nicholas Sargent, corroborated by Anne Bray, Anthony Blake had apple and pear orchards at Middle Blerrick, Lower Blerrick and Kerslake, from which he made cider, worth at least £2, but on which he did not pay the tithe.[23] The commissioners accepted this evidence.

The main grounds of Blake's defence for non-payment of tithe on orchard fruits and cider were that it was a custom of the parish not to pay tithes on fruits, and that a modus existed limiting the amount of tithe payable on cider. He produced Alexander Arundell, then aged 74, to speak for him. Alexander could also bear witness to what the custom had been in the time of his brother, Gregory (rector from 1622 until his death in 1654, though he was ejected from his living sometime before his death), and his father, Walter, who had been appointed rector as far back as 1576.

Alexander swore that his father and brother only received tithes 'for lambs wooll fish and corne', and that they:

> did always compound ... for the great as small and minuit tythes and never received the same in kinde but received the same in money (except tyth fish And once when his this deponent's father was Rector as aforesaid did take of one Richard Sarjant being a bad paymaster of the tyths due from him in kinde).

He went on to say that 'hee was imployed severall yeares by his said father ... in the collecting of all the tyths' and that the time when he was so employed was 'about fifty yeares since'. He then added that:

> he hath seen lately a paper book written in ... 1637 by his said brother Gregory Arundell ... [which he] believeth in his conscience to be all his said brother's own proper hand writing wherein he sayeth [he] had received three pence in leiw of each hogshead of syder and that hee had received the tyth of the said parish as his [father] had don for forty years befoure that tyme.

This information makes it possible to date the making of cider in Sheviock certainly to 1637, and possibly to 1598. If the earlier date is correct, it amplifies the evidence supplied by Richard Carew in his *Survey of Cornwall* (1602), which obliquely mentioned apple orchards, but not cider-making in the district.[24] The number of apple trees in the parish was hugely increased by Richard Carew the younger, who claimed to have planted 20,000 trees at various times before 1628.[25] Anthony Blake's other witness about the payment of tithes on orchard fruit was John Dodridge, then aged over 60, formerly of Trewin in Sheviock. He deposed that:

> he … did pay for every hogshead of syder made by him upon the said tenement of [Trewin] three pence in full leiw of the tyth thereof and that the … former Rector [Gregory Arundell] never demanded any thing in leiw for tyth of orchard fruit of this deponent during the said five and thirty yeares.[26]

However, contrary evidence was presented by Thomas Gryles, Abraham Chubb and Thomas Burdick. Gryles stated that he:

> never observed knew nor heard that there was or att any tyme has beene any particular customes of tything in the said parish untill now of som late years itt is pretended that there could be some custome by the defendant But this deponent hath constantly observed that all tythes [have] been and ought to be payed … in their proper kinde.

He went on to say that if any tithes had been detained from the rector, 'itt was not by pretence or couler of any custom whatsoever But by and through the negligence of the … Rector in not taking care to demand … and receive the same'.[27] He said that the same had been true in his father's time, and that his father had been before his death aged 'att least eighty six yeares'. The deponent, Chubb, concurred, swearing that 'all manner of tythes of anything growing within the said parish … have been always reported to be due and payable in kind or by composition to be made for the same with the parson or Rector'. Furthermore, he directly contradicted the testimony of Arundell, by stating that

> this deponent himself hath oftentimes payd the tythe of corne, wooll, lambs, calfes, bees, hay, honey in kind unto Walter Arrundel, Gregory Arrundel, John Gay and the Complaynant … And this deponent constantly paid all his tythes in kind unless he made composicon for the same with the said Rector or incumbent.

He went on to say that it was a:

> general use within the said parish … to carry [the Rector] a tenth parte of all honey in kind and to carry him apples in kind according to the severall quantities that every inhabitant … has growen upon each tenement he hath orchard.

Finally, Chubb swore that:

> this deponent never hath heard that there was, nor doth believe there is any custom whatsoever … to pay foure pence or any other sum whatsoever in liew of tythe for a hogshead or any other quantity of sider.

Thomas Burdick, who had been an inhabitant of Sheviock for more than 60 years, corroborated the evidence of Chubb. The commissioners chose to believe Gryles, Chubb and Burdick, to the effect that there was no modus in existence, in preference to Arundell and Dodridge.

The Judgment of the Court: The court ordered that:

> the defendant shall pay unto the plaintiff his tythes due unto him for the said years [1669 and 1670] unless the defendant shows cause to the contrary att the setting down of causes after this tyme paying five pounds costs before he be heard. And it is referred to the Auditor of the County of Cornwall to cast up the values of the tythes due to the plaintiff.

The whole amount owing according to the commissioners Dandy and Gryles was £2 14s. 8d.

Sheviock Life as Seen through the Case: The case of Rolle v Blake illuminates many aspects of life in Sheviock after the Restoration. It reveals that farming in the district was very intensive. Anthony Blake, with just 43 acres at his disposal, was raising and shearing sheep at least 'twenty ewes which afterwards had lambs', was cutting hay, was making 'three or foure hoggsheads' of cider each year, was keeping chickens and 'severall old geese and at least tenn or twenty young geese', was keeping horses, heifers and bullocks, and was also growing wheat and barley. The evidence of the witnesses shows that the other farmers around Blake were farming equally intensively, some also keeping bees. We also see how intermingled were the plots of land farmed by one person with those of the other farmers, so that the witnesses had difficulty in remembering just who was farming which plots. We also learn that apple growing and cider making were long established in the district – certainly going back to 1637 and possibly back to 1598. We learn that there was an inn at Sheviock churchtown in 1674, where the commissioners took some of the depositions. We also learn that it was usual to pay the tithe of fish in kind, and not to accept composition for it in lieu of tithes. Surprisingly, there is no mention of the raising of pigs.

The Later History of Tithes: In 1696, an Act of Parliament introduced a new process so that tithe owners claiming arrears of £2 or less could apply to two Justices of the Peace who could order payment on pain of distraint of goods.[28] Gradually payment by composition replaced the payment of tithes in kind, but even in 1791 payment in kind was still common. Agricultural prices boomed during the long period of war with France (1793-1815), with rental incomes from agricultural lands doubling in value, and the value of tithes increasing by almost the same amount.[29]

Following the Parliamentary Reform Act of 1832 the movement for tithe reform gathered pace, and in each of the parliamentary sessions from 1833 to 1836 a bill was introduced for the commutation of tithes into fixed monetary payments. Finally, on 13 August 1836, the Whig Prime Minister, Lord John Russell, steered the Tithe Commutation Act through Parliament. This provided that commutation was to be effected by substituting a monetary payment, known as a tithe rent charge, for the payment of tithe in kind. The amount of the rent charge could be agreed voluntarily between the parties, but if no agreement was reached it was to be imposed by the three Tithe Commissioners. Their calculation was based on the average value of the tithes over the previous seven years for wheat, barley and oats.[30] The biggest problem for the Commissioners and their assistants was the apportionment of the rent charges between the tithe payers. Local landowners appointed tithe 'apportioners' to settle their differences. The Commissioners had completed the main bulk of their work by the late 1850s. One of the incidental benefits of the Act to future generations was the making of the great maps for every single parish. These, with their accompanying lists of local landowners and tenants, now repose in county record offices throughout the land. The map for Sheviock, made in 1840 and 1841, is in the County Record Office in Truro.

There was a huge increase in investment in agriculture between 1840 and 1870.[31] This was the so-called 'Golden Age' in English farming. Most of the great barns and farm buildings still visible in Sheviock – e.g. at Trethill Farm (now converted into houses), Sheviock Barton, Glebe Barn, Liscawn (converted into hotel suites), Tredis and Trewin – date from this period. There was a collapse in grain prices in the 1880s brought about by competition from Canada and the U.S.A. In 1891, a new Tithe Act enacted that no rent charge could exceed two-thirds of the annual value of the land. Prices went up again during the First World War but slumped again after the war. In 1918, a new Tithe Act held the tithe rent charges to 1918 levels for a period of six years. After 1924, the charges were to be based on a moving 15-year average of grain prices. With the fall in corn prices and rents after 1921, there were further demands for tithe reform. The Tithe Act 1925 lowered the basis of the rent charge from the 15-year average and established a sinking fund to redeem rent charges owned by the church. The Great Depression of 1929-1931 further intensified the pressure for reform, and a Royal Commission was appointed in 1934 to report on the whole matter. Their Report led to the Tithe Act 1936. This extinguished all tithe rent charges immediately. Owners of rent charges were compensated with gilt-edged three per cent Government stocks redeemable at par after 60 years. Landowners paid to the Government an annuity over the same 60 years. Both expired in 1996 and brought to an end the long and tortuous history of tithes.

215 *This stained glass memorial in the tower of St Mary's contains a fine image of the founder of Methodism, John Wesley.*

Chapter 34

Crafthole Methodist Chapel

On 16 January 1795, five people put their names to a request to the Bishop of Exeter in these terms:

> We whose names are hereunto subscribed do hereby certify that we have appropriated and set apart a room on the ground floor of the dwelling house of Mrs Elizabeth Mullis situate in the village of Crafthole in the parish of Sheviock in the county of Cornwall and diocese of Exeter for worship of Almighty God by a congregation of his Majesty's Protestant subjects dissenting from the Church of England which we humbly desire may be registered pursuant to an Act of Parliament in that case made and provided.

The five signatories of the letter were John Trevethick, Edward Moon, Thomas Moon, Joseph Mallett and Elizabeth Mullis. John Trevethick came from Stoke Damerel in Devon, but was married to Joanna Bews of Sheviock. Joseph Mallett was renting a house and garden in Portwrinkle for 10s. in 1817. He was then aged fifty. He had a son, George, then aged 29 and a daughter, Mary, aged twenty-seven.[1] Elizabeth Mullis (b.1752) was the widow of Philip Mullis junior (b.1742). He was the farmer of an 89-acre holding in Antony parish, called Scraesdon and Brockhole.[2] Their son, John, was born in 1775 and their daughter, called Elizabeth after her mother, was born two years later. Philip Mullis was dead before 1793. In 1795 his widow, Elizabeth, took a reversion of the farm leases in favour of her two children.[3] She was still the tenant in 1807.[4] As a widow, Elizabeth Mullis lived not on her tenements, but in Crafthole, and no doubt her son, John, actually ran the farm. Her house stood on the south side of the road leading into Crafthole from Antony, more or less opposite the present Methodist church. She kept a shop and supplied candles to the parish church of Sheviock for the annual Singing Feast held on 4 and 5 November.[5] By 1818, her son, John, had moved to London and was described as a 'gentleman' and her daughter, Elizabeth, had become Mrs Peter of Torpoint.

On 23 January 1795, the bishop's official endorsed the request of the five applicants with the magisterial words, 'Let this room be registered'. This was the beginning of the organised practice of Methodism in Crafthole. After the death of John Wesley, a number of dissenting groups had seceded from the main Wesleyan movement, but the Crafthole Methodist society always remained true to the original Wesleyan tradition.[6]

The Launceston Circuit register for 1800-26 records the full membership of the Society a few years after the room was registered. Only two of the people who had signed the original request were still shown as members. These were Edward Moon, who was named as class leader, and Elizabeth Mullis.[7] New members were Ann Moon (who is shown as occupying a house and garden in Crafthole in the Tithe Redemption Survey of 1840), Peter Kitt, who was a farmer and also ran the inn at Crafthole (now the *Finnygook Inn*), Mary Mirand, Elizabeth Trevor, John Warwick (deputy class leader), Ann Warwick, Thomas Wilcox (or Wilcock), probably the tenant of a quarter of Blazor in 1820-1, and Thomas Sone.[8]

The First Chapel (1819)

The first purpose-built Methodist chapel was licensed by the Bishop of Exeter on 9 August 1819. The site of that first building is not recorded. In 1821, in his replies to the questions asked at the Bishop's Visitation, the rector, Duke Yonge junior, reported that the Methodists met at the house of Thomas Wilcox. He went on to say that 'a few others occasionally attend a small Calvinistic chapel in the village of Crafthole'. This may have been the building licensed in 1819.

The Second Chapel (1843)

Within twenty years or so, the congregation had outgrown its first home. In 1843, Samuel Perry, a boot and shoe maker from Devonport, registered a new building at the Bishop's registry. The new building stood a few houses to the east of the present building. It has been converted into a dwelling and is now called Old Chapel Cottage. According to the religious census of 1851, there was then a Sunday school at the chapel. In the 12 months prior to 30 March 1851, the Sunday school taught 30 children in the morning and 11 in the evening.[9] The religious census also showed that the 1843 chapel was operating at full capacity. According to the steward who prepared the return, there were 108 seats in the chapel (81 paid and 27 free seats) and the average size of congregation for the evening service was 105 in the 12 months prior to 30 March 1851.

The New Chapel (1867-8)

The Society therefore decided to build a larger chapel. Trustees were appointed to purchase the building land. The leading trustee was Joseph Simpson of Callington. He was the superintendent preacher of the circuit in the Methodist Connexion in which the Crafthole chapel lay. Other trustees were Robert Hancock of Crafthole, described as a cordwainer (leatherworker or shoemaker); Nicholas and Richard Parsons, of Antony, yeomen; John Coade, John Pengelly, junior, William Stanton, and William Vosper of St Germans, yeomen; John Bray of Trematon, St Stephens by Saltash; Samuel Roseveare of Leigh, Quethiock, yeoman; Charles Woolcock of Newton, St Mellion, yeoman; and three men from Callington.[10] These three were Edward Nicolls, described as a gentleman, Amos Doidge Davey, a druggist, and William Dingle, a tanner. On 16 January 1862, the trustees purchased the land from John Melchesidic Rogers of Antony. He was probably the son of the Melchesidic Rogers who had purchased the lease of Scraesdon and Brockhole from the Mullis family in 1818. A yearly high rent of 6d. was payable to the lord of the manor of Sheviock. The purchase price was £150.[11]

The land purchased was bounded on the east by land formerly occupied by William Davey (the blacksmith's shop); on the west by land of John Bogers Esq.; on the south by the King's highway; and on the north by the route leading to Crafthole Coombe. William Davey's son, John, was then the Crafthole blacksmith. The land conveyed included orchards and ruins formerly in the possession of Joseph Shepherd

216 *The present Methodist Chapel, built in 1867-8, is the third purpose-built chapel in Crafthole.*

and John Kitt. The trustees commissioned the Plymouth architects, Dwelly and Son, to draw up detailed plans, and the central Wesleyan Chapel Committee approved these on 9 July 1867. On 3 August 1867, at 3.00 p.m., Mrs Hancock, wife of one of the trustees of the building project, laid the first stone, and the Revd J. Brewster of Plymouth preached a sermon. Tea was served at 5.00 p.m. to some 300 people. After this, John Bray of Trematon presided over a public meeting, whose object was to raise the funds to complete the project. The speakers were the Revd R.P.Davey, the Revd T. Hicks of Woolwich, the Revd J. Brewster again, Mr Nanscawen and Samuel Roseveare of Quethiock.[12]

217 *The congregation of the Methodist Chapel at the centenary celebration in 1967.*

The cost of the new chapel was £500, of which £370 was paid off within the first year, as stipulated by the Wesleyan Chapel Committee. The trustees were given another ten years to pay off the remaining £130. The chapel took less than six months to build, and the new building was dedicated on 14 January 1868. At the service of dedication, which started at 11.00 a.m., the Revd E. A. Telfer preached on the Song of Solomon, Chapter 6, verse 10, 'Who is she that looketh forth as the morning, fair as the moon, clear as the sun, and terrible as an army with banners?' The service lasted two hours and at 1.00 p.m. lunch was served. In the afternoon, there was another service that started at 3.00 p.m., with the Revd N. Boyns as preacher. At the insistence of the Revd Telfer, a prayer meeting followed and then afternoon tea. There was another service in the evening at which the Revd Telfer was again the preacher. The congregation was so large that, notwithstanding the increased capacity of the new building, many people could not get inside it.

There were 13 trustees for the 1867 building project: Robert Hancock, John Coad, William Stanton, William Vosper, Nicholas and Richard Parsons, John Bray, Edward Nicholls, Amos Davey, William Dingle, Samuel Roseveare, Charles Woolcock and John Pengelly.

Up until the First World War, the travelling Methodist preachers often arrived on horseback, and the chapel would arrange to pay someone to look after and feed the preacher's horse at 5s. a time. These payments were discontinued in February 1919. In 1918, the schoolroom was first used for meetings of the Parish Council, which continues to meet there. Electric lighting was installed in 1938. The mines that fell on Crafthole in August 1940 caused some damage to the chapel, which was repaired the following year.

Care and attention continues to be devoted to the fabric of the church, which is in regular use. A kitchen and toilet were installed in 1985. An electric organ was also purchased in 1985. All the windows in the church were replaced in 1987-8, and in November 1988 two stained glass windows were inserted on top of the new north windows. They were made by the monks at Buckfast Abbey.

See also for the Methodist primary school, Chapter 38, *The School in Sheviock and other Local Schools*.

PART VII

The Parish in Arms

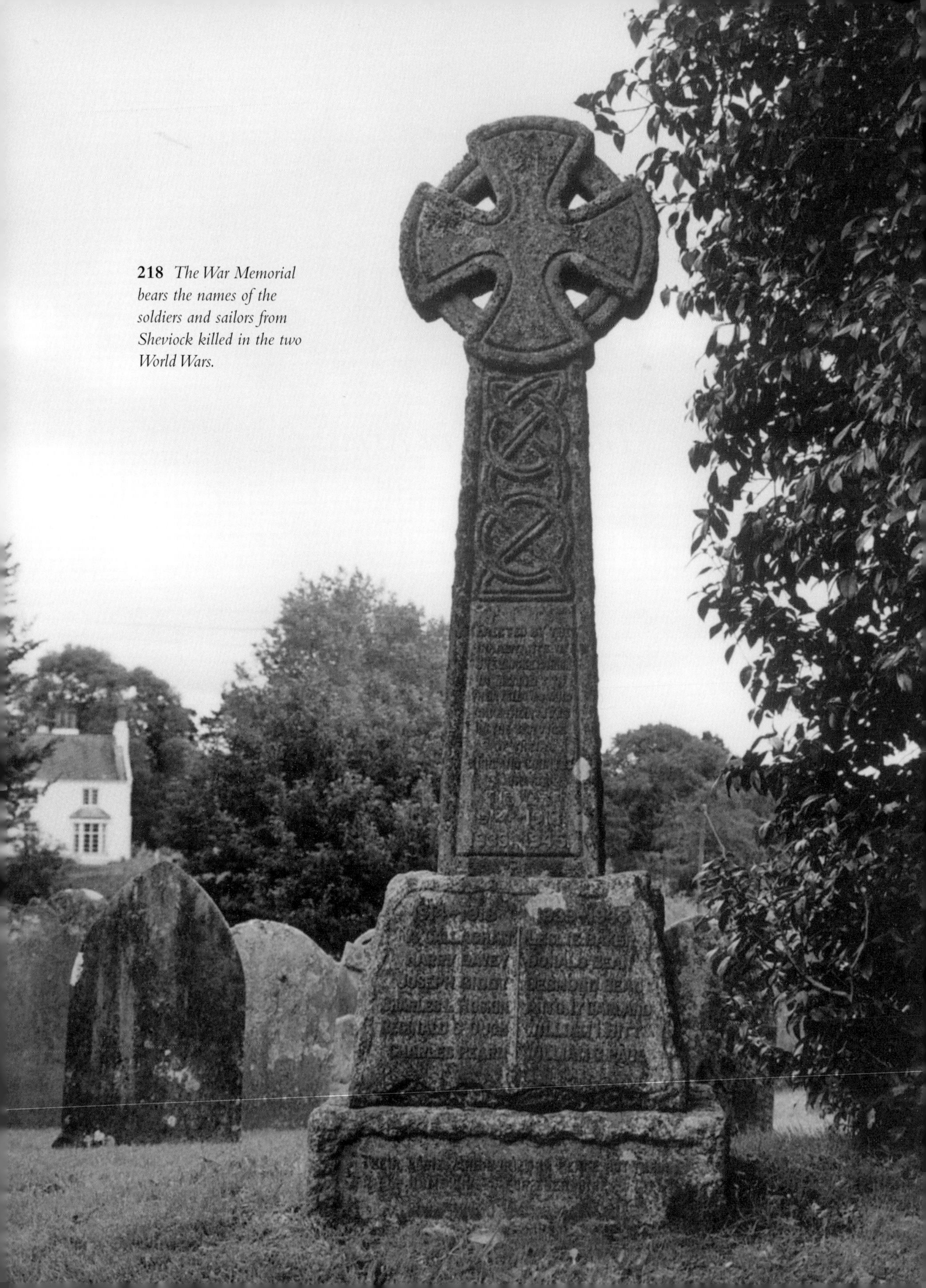

218 *The War Memorial bears the names of the soldiers and sailors from Sheviock killed in the two World Wars.*

Chapter 35

The Norman Conquest to the Reign of Charles I

After the Norman Conquest of 1066-8, the Saxon warriors based in militarily sensitive areas, such as Sheviock, either fled or were killed. But many Saxon ecclesiastical landowners, such as Sihtric, Abbot of Tavistock, remained in office.[1] Attacks on the coast continued and in 1069 the sons of the slain King Harold raided the south Devon coast in search of plunder. In response to such incursions, in 1070 King William made the feudal obligation known as 'knight service' compulsory for bishoprics and abbeys as well as for his lay tenants. The Abbot of Tavistock was required to maintain 15 knights, and the endowments to support them were to be taken from the abbey lands. Probably, Sihtric hired mercenaries to fulfil his obligations in 1070.[2] But by 1086, Sihtric's successor, the Norman Abbot Geoffrey, had completed landholding arrangements for the permanent maintenance of the Abbey's own knights.[3]

The most important of them on the Rame Peninsula was Erbenald, the ancestor of the Dawneys, who was given the estates of Sheviock, Antony, Rame, Trewornan (in St Minver), Tolcarne (in North Hill), Penharget (in St Ive), and half a virgate (i.e. about 15 acres) on Tavistock manor (probably at Taviton).[4] Together the estates were valued at £12 3s. 4d., and extended to several thousand acres. Erbenald was expected to maintain three other knights beside himself from these estates.[5] The responsibility of the Dawneys for the protection of the Rame peninsula was increased by the grant to them of the Royal manor of Pendrym (on which was built the castle of East Looe), and the acquisition by them of the estate or manor of Tregantel (formerly part of the manor of Trematon), perhaps in 1270. The Bishop of Exeter later licensed St Michael's chapel on top of Rame Head to their heirs, the Courtenay earls of Devon.[6] The chapel served as a lookout point and the site of a beacon, which was lit in times of danger. The linkage of the four knights with the original estates granted by the abbey continued until the close of the Middle Ages. In 1303, Nicholas Dawney was shown in a list of feudal aids as liable for the provision of one man-at-arms (i.e. knight) on account of his manor of Sheviock, another for Tregantel, and three others. John of Rame, who held a knight's fee in Rame under the manor of Sheviock, and was probably a descendant

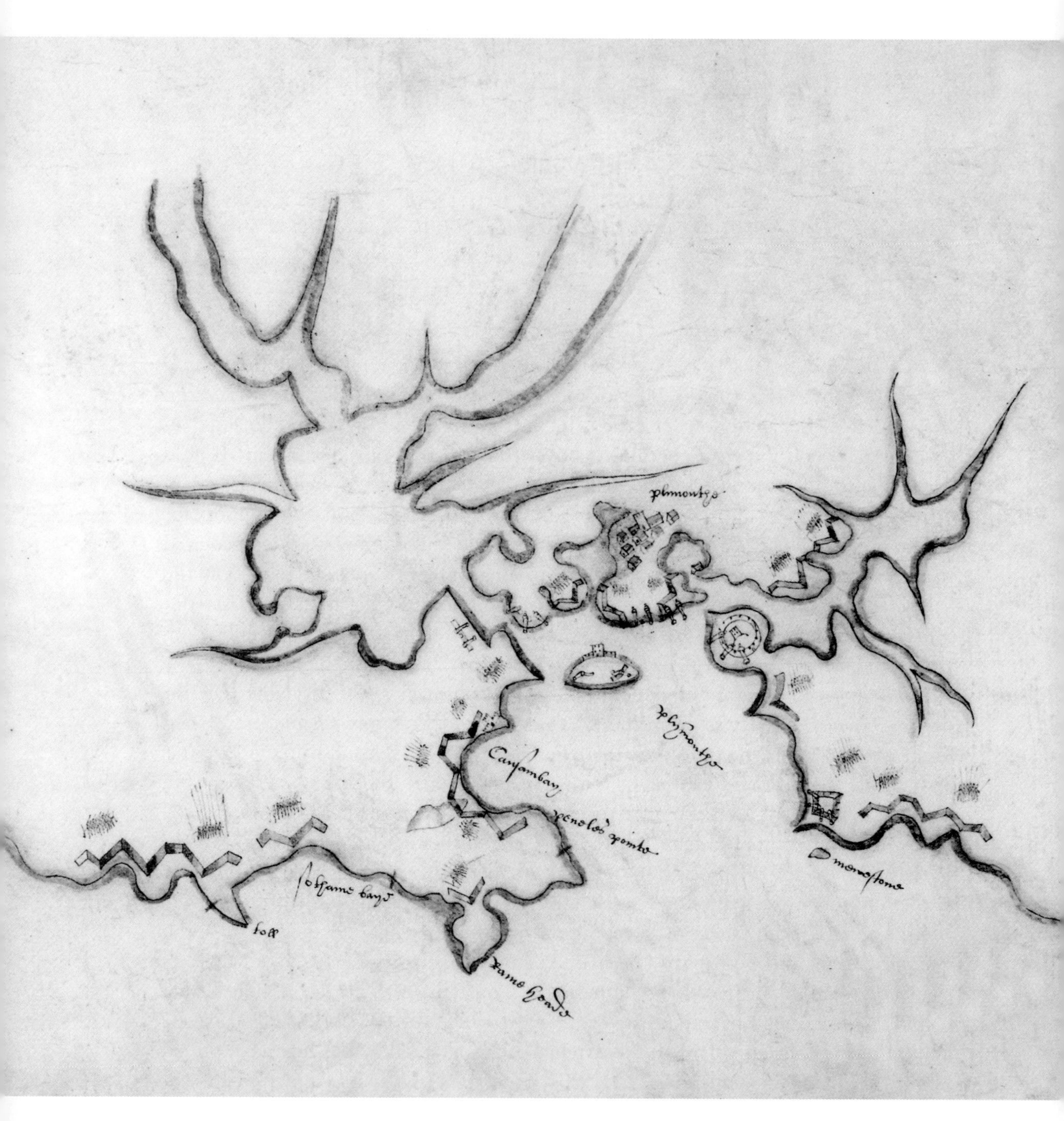

219 *'A plott of all the coast of Cornwall and Devonshire, as they were to be fortyfied in 1588'. Detail showing the Rame Peninsula, the mouth of the Tamar and Plymouth at the time of the Spanish Armada.*

of one of the original Dawney knights, was named as one of these.[7] Baldwin and John Walrond, co-occupiers with two others of half a knight's fee in Churleton in St Ive, by knight's service and suit of court to the earl of Devon in the late Middle Ages, may also have been descendants of one of the original Dawney knights.

The property in Taviton would have enabled Erbenald to provide accommodation for himself and his knights, and no doubt his wife, Deintedosa, as well, on his frequent visits to Tavistock. For, like the other knights, he was required to present himself at the abbot's court on the quarter days to do homage for his fiefdom, and to receive instructions for performing his knight's service. These services were usually to be performed locally, such as doing garrison duty at Exeter castle. But sometimes the knights had to go on campaign elsewhere. For example, in 1223, in the reign of Henry III, the knights were ordered to take part in a campaign in Wales. In 1314, Nicholas Dawney was commissioned to raise troops in the west to fight against the Scots. In 1324, the local levies were ordered to France to help defend Aquitaine.

The Defence of the Coast

The local commanders had a responsibility not only for levying troops when attack was imminent, but also for maintaining the warning system of beacons. Sherds of medieval pottery were recovered from Beacon Hill, formerly known as Round Burrows, in Sheviock, when the Bronze Age burial mound at the top of the hill was excavated in 1982.[8] Several instances of medieval orders to prepare beacons have survived. In September 1224, when there were fears of a French invasion, John of Bayeux was made keeper of the coasts of Devon and Cornwall, and was instructed to provide beacons in every parish on the coast.[9] As lord of Sheviock and Rame, the Abbot of Tavistock and his knights had a special duty to protect the Tamar estuary from Channel pirates. This role was extended in the 1200s by the establishment of the Benedictine Priory of St Nicholas in the Isles of Scilly, as a daughter house of the abbey.

Trematon Castle

Trematon Castle was built at the confluence of the Tamar and Lynher rivers. Richard Polwhele in his *History of Cornwall* (1803) suggested that a Cornish earl, Condorus, built the first castle there before the Conquest. Be that as it may, it was rebuilt after the Conquest, and 50 slaves were working there in 1086, probably on the fortifications. The castle was the property of Robert of Mortain, Earl of Cornwall, and it was held under him by Reginald de Valletort. In 1270, Reginald's grandson, Roger, sold the honour, castle and manor of Trematon and the manor of Calstock, with 60½ knights' fees, to Richard, Earl of Cornwall (1209-1272).[10] It may have been at this time that the manor of Tregantel, on the Rame Peninsula, was sold to the Dawneys. Trematon castle has remained part of the earldom and (from 1366) the duchy of Cornwall since its acquisition by Earl Richard in 1270. The Dawney lords and their supporting knights would have looked to Trematon as the key strongpoint for the defence of the area. Signal fires erected on Beacon Hill would have been visible at Trematon, and vice-versa. The Dawneys and their tenants had certain obligations towards the honour and castle of Trematon, in return for which they also received certain privileges and exemptions. The Caption of Seisin 1337, a description and account of the newly-formed duchy of Cornwall, put it thus:

> John de Alneto [Sir John Dawney] holds four knights' fees, crosses the passage [of the Tamar at Saltash] at the [privileged] rate of John de Ferar [John de Ferrers] and does similar services.[11]

During the Hundred Years' War (1337-1453), the French often raided the English coast. In times of crisis, the king would order the Abbot of Tavistock, who was required to keep a permanent store of arms, to arm his tenants and station them on the coast. In 1338, for example, Sir John Dawney and two other commanders were ordered to array all men between Saltash and Fowey to resist a threatened French landing.[12] Sir John was the last male of his line to live in Sheviock. He died on active service in France on 9 August 1346, just before the battle of Crécy. His daughter, Emmeline, married Sir Edward Courtenay, another knight who fought under Edward III. Sir Edward died in 1372, and his effigy, clad in the armour of his time, can be seen in the south transept of the church, next to that of his wife.

Payment for the Defence of the Realm

As the Middle Ages wore on, it became possible to avoid performing knight's service in person by paying money, called 'scutage', instead. With this money, the king was able to hire professional soldiers.[13] To pay for defence, ordinary people with valuable lands or goods were also subject to periodic 'assessments' (taxation). In 1327, in the first year of the reign of Edward III, all subjects who had goods of the value of 10s. or more were taxed at the rate of one-twentieth of their value for defence against the Scots.[14] The armour, jewels, horses, and robes of knights and gentlemen, as well as their vessels of gold, silver and brass, were excluded from the value of their assets. In Sheviock, those with goods worth more than 10s. were: Nicholas Dawney, assessed at 6s. (implying goods worth £6), John de Kolecomb, assessed at 3s. (goods worth £3), Henry de Orr and Roger Pole,[15] both assessed at 2s. (goods worth £2), Baldewin Casset,[16] assessed at 1s. 6d. (goods worth £1 10s.), and Roger de Pole,[17] assessed at 1s. (goods worth £1). Peter Pekoket, Thomas Tusket,[18] Roger Skaner,[19] and Walter Huta were all assessed at 9d. (goods worth 15s.). Roger Longa was assessed at 7d. (goods worth 11s. 8d.). The remaining four subsidy payers, Thomas Farwel, Simon Hara,[20] Richard Tyk,[21] and Nicholas Warde, were all assessed at 6d. (goods worth 10s.).

Tudor Soldiers

In 1522, Henry VIII launched a war against the French. Writs were issued to the justices of the peace in the coastal parishes to resist any French landing and to prepare beacons.[22] Again, this would have included the beacon on Round Burrows above Trewrickle Farm. Cardinal Wolsey, the king's chief minister, raised a forced loan to finance the expedition. As the basis for this, a muster roll of all able-bodied men between the ages of 16 and 60 was compiled. The roll recorded the capital value of each man's land and goods. It then assessed his annual income as a percentage of the capital value.[23] From this assessment, it calculated the amount of arms and armour that each man should be able to provide. All those assessed at £5 or more were required to make a loan of that amount to the king. The Sheviock roll contained 57 names. Of these, 15 men were required to make loans: John Whiteford, £20; Henry Hancoke, £12; John Hancoke, £12; John Davy, £10; Robert Leskawen,[24] £10; William Mathew, £10; William Bonne, £8; John Gryllys, £8; John Bony, £6; William Chubbe, £6; Walter Harry, £6; Richard Peter, £6; John Davy jun, £5; Edward Meryng, £5; Thomas Spyller, £5.

In addition, the muster roll itemised the arms and armour that each man possessed. The six wealthiest men all had 'full harness'.[25] They were John Whiteford, Henry and John Hancoke, John Davy, Robert Lescawen, and William Mathew. William Chub(b)e had a 'sallet' (a short brimmed helmet) and a 'brigandine'.[26] Richard Peter had a 'bill' (a blade with a long wooden handle), a 'coat' (similar to a brigandine), and 'splints' (pieces of metal used for protecting the forearms). John Benett (£4) had a bill, coat and sallet. John Sargent (£4) had a sallet and splints. John Josep (£3) had a coat and sallet. William Bray (£2) had a bill and sallet. It is not known whether any of the men of Sheviock actually saw service in France.

In 1544, Henry VIII ordered another assessment.[27] This time there were 51 names on the list, including two widows, Joan, probably the widow of John Sargent; and Alice, presumably the widow of Henry or John Hancock, who both paid 2s. on their goods. There were also two other women, Margery Harry, who paid 2s., and the wealthy Dionisia Odyhorne, who paid 9s., the fourth highest assessment in the parish. The wealthiest men were John Crefylde, who paid 15s.; William Mathew (Mathie) and John Wallis, who both paid 12s; and Robert Lescoyn (Smith of Liscawn), Richard Bone, John Whytford, and Thomas Grylles, who all paid 8s.

In the following year, King Henry required his wealthiest subjects to grant him a 'benevolence' for the defence of the realm. The three men who had to pay were John Creffeylde, who paid 10s., and William Mathew and William Wallys, who both paid 8s.

The Militia [28]

In 1558, Philip and Mary repealed the medieval statutes that had laid down the weapons that every man must keep according to his wealth.[29] They replaced them with new liabilities based on a scale of ten bands of wealth rising from £5-£10 per annum to £1,000 or more. The wealthiest men provided the cavalry, and varying quantities of arms and armour. Every man with *goods* valued at £10-£20 was required to possess a long bow, a sheaf of arrows, a steel cap or scull, and a bill or halberd. A sheaf contained 24 arrows. The archers also carried a short sword and dagger. Like the Welsh, the men of Cornwall were particularly noted for their archery, and used longer arrows than normal, suggesting a stronger pull.[30]

Those who had *land* valued at £5 to £10 had to provide bow and arrows and the steel cap, but instead of the bill were required to be equipped with a brigandine or plated coat. Those who had land valued at between £10 and £20 had to provide the same as the lesser landowners, plus a 'haquebut' (also spelled hackbut and harquebus or arquebus), an early form of portable firearm, which was supported on a forked rest (OED) and a 'morion' (a helmet with a ridged crest, which originated in Spain) or a sallet. From about 1570 to 1670, parish armour was usually kept in the church, together with powder, bullets and match.

The Musters

Queen Elizabeth adopted the banding system of Philip and Mary and passed a new Act for the taking of 'musters'. The general muster was an inspection by the Queen's officials in each county to ensure that the provisions of Philip and Mary's Act had been complied with. If the arms were not as prescribed or not in a fit state, they did not 'pass muster', and had to be produced again. The general muster was followed by a combined exercise. In 1569, war broke out between England and Spain. The government immediately ordered musters to be taken in every parish. All the 'able men' of the parish were included. The return for Sheviock showed that there were 27 of them, 30 fewer than in the reign of Henry VIII. Three of the men had no arms or armour at all. These were Water [Walter] Salmon, John Smythe, and Robert Trigge. They may have been younger sons rather than poor men. Five possessed bows and arrows and bills, as required for men with goods worth £10-£20. These were John Okwyn, Harry Spiller, John Harry senior, Richard Bake and William Grill (who also had a 'jack' – a leather, canvas or quilted sleeveless jacket reinforced with small plates).[31] None of these men is listed as possessing steel caps, which they should have done. Walter Sum (Sonne), who did have a sallet as well as his arrows and bill, had no long bow. All men over 17 were required to keep bows and arrows, and seven possessed just these weapons. They were Walter Burges, Edmond Eliott, Water Peter, Richard Peter,

John Skynnerd junior, Thomas Skynnerd, and Robert Stephen. Six men were armed only with bills. These were William Charke, William Clenyck, John Blighe (who also had a sallet), John Blighe junior, John Peter (who also had splints), and Davy Blake. Finally, there were five men armed with harquebuses. These were the principal men of the parish, whose wealth was assessed at more than £10 per annum. They were John Braye, junior, Thomas Hancock, Humfrey Ryxton, John Vallys (i.e. Wallis) and Jesper (i.e. Jasper) Whitford. Thomas Hancock and Jesper Whitford were probably the sons of the men who had been most highly assessed by Cardinal Wolsey's officials in 1522. As well as the arms possessed by the able men, the parish had a residual store of 22 bills, 17 bows, five sheaves and one jack. There were no horsemen in the parish.

The Trained Bands

In the 1570s, the government took measures to improve military training.[32] Firstly, they decided only to muster the most able-bodied men, who were to be given proper training at special musters. In 1573, they introduced payments, at the rate of 8d. per day (increased to 1s. by 1600). Another 8d. a day was allowed for powder, match and shot. This was the beginning of the 'trained bands'. The government also recalled experienced soldiers from the Low Countries, and sent them as 'muster-masters' to train the men in the coastal parishes. The government specified three periods of training a year: four days commencing on Easter Monday, four commencing on Whit Monday, and two days after Michaelmas Day. The parishes were combined into groups of three, and muster-masters visited each group to train the soldiers. Each 'hundred' then combined to form a company. Although the Government still required all men over 17 to keep bows and arrows, these weapons were really obsolete, as firearms were coming into general use. In quick succession the harquebus was superseded by the 'caliver' (a light kind of harquebus, fired without a rest) and, by the late 1580s, the caliver was superseded by the musket. Among other exercises, the soldiers learned to 'shoot at boards'.

The Elizabethan Beacon

Carew wrote, 'Of Beacons, through the neernesse to the sea, and the advantage of the hilly situations, welneere every parish [in Cornwall] is charged with one, which are watched …' At the time of the Spanish Armada, Beacon Hill, above Trewrickle Farm, was once more manned. The deputy-lieutenants for Cornwall, of whom Richard Carew was one, reported that the 'beacons are sufficiently erected and watched'.[33] When the Spanish ships came into view in 1588, they were lit. The Elizabethan beacon system was quite sophisticated. The beacon was set up on a high hill with a commanding view out to sea. The iron brazier for the signal fire was erected on top of a very high pole – a tree trunk, in fact. According to Sir Richard Knightley of

Kent, 'I think you must set down more than three [trees] to a beacon'.[34] The reason for this was that two subsidiary poles were set up against the main pole, to serve as supports and as ladders for the men serving the braziers. The beacons were normally watched from March until October or November. The two men who served each signal station were paid wages of 8d. for a day and a night. The parishes had to levy a rate to provide the money, which was paid by the churchwardens. On key sites – and Sheviock may have been one – there were three beacons. Once the local JP had given permission for the beacons to be fired, one beacon would be lit to signal a hostile fleet of 20-30 sail, and two would be lit to signal a fleet of 30-50 sail. All three were lit if the fleet consisted of more than 50 ships (or if a landing was thought to be imminent).

The duty of keeping watch was shared between the villages in rotation. The Justices selected the individual watch keepers from among the most reliable and prosperous inhabitants. The watch keepers worked in pairs, and were armed. For their shelter a little hut was provided, with wood for a fire and candles. But the hut was kept deliberately spartan: 'without any seates or place of ease lest they should fall asleepe; only to stand upright in with a hoale towards the beacon'.[35] No dog was allowed in case it should distract the men. To prevent false alarms, the beacons were not to be fired without the authorisation of the local JP or military captain, who was to be summoned by one of the watch keepers as soon as a suspicious force was sighted. To signal the general alarm, all the church bells were clashed together. To avoid confusion, after 1583 the bells were otherwise kept silent, except for a single one which was tolled at christenings, weddings and funerals. Winston Churchill gave a similar instruction in the Second World War. The warning system provided by the beacons was supplemented by pinnaces watching at sea, and messengers on land. Each parish had to provide horse and foot posts, with the messengers on call and preferably living near the parish church.

Sir Richard Grenville, who was given responsibility for the defence of Cornwall in 1587, laid down a new defensive strategy. Whereas in earlier times the only defence was the hastily assembled local force that would rush down to the beaches to try to prevent a landing, now well-trained mobile forces were assembled at a distance to shadow the enemy's fleet and then to concentrate on any major port at which they attempted to land. A thin screen of local defenders still manned the ramparts erected on the beaches.

The Spanish Armada

In 1586, the lord lieutenants were directed to make up their musters of men and of arms. The deputy-lieutenants were directed to brief their captains as to their posts and to cover these posts by batteries, to dig pits and plant stakes to stop the progress of the enemy if he landed.[36] The deputy-lieutenants for Cornwall reported that they had 'erected the bulwarks and defences on the sea-coast'.[37] In the following year, orders were given to the commanders in the maritime counties to make a survey of the places where the enemy might land, and to provide means to convey the forces to resist him. Directions were again given to raise ramparts, erect beacons and place men near them to watch the movements of the enemy's ships.[38] The Government also supplied heavy guns and ammunition. A plan of the coastal defences made in 1588 has survived. It shows precisely where the ramparts were erected and the men and guns positioned along this part of the coast.[39] There were extensive ramparts along the beach at Downderry guarded by two companies of soldiers. There was another at Portwrinkle, described on the plan as 'Cobland baye' with another company. There was another at Polhawn guarded by a company. Cawsand Bay was defended from one end to the other by ramparts, manned by three companies, and ending at Picklecombe, where a fort was built. Guns were positioned at Cremyll and there was another company of soldiers at Mount Edgcumbe. St Nicholas's Island (Drake Island) was fortified and protected by cannon. There was a fort at Mount Batten defended by cannon, and Plymouth itself was protected by ramparts, cannon and companies of soldiers.

The Spanish fleet was first sighted on Friday, 19 July. A.L. Rowse has described what happened:

> Fifty ships of the Armada were spied off Scilly hovering in the wind as it seemed to attend the rest of the fleet. That night Howard [40] got the news at Plymouth of their having been seen off the Lizard: the whole Armada ... coming slowly up-Channel in unbroken formation, a great coloured crescent moon.[41]

There were 166 ships in the Spanish and allied fleet: 40 great hulks, 60 galleons, 30 great ships, four galiasses, eight galleys, and 24 pinnaces. There were more than 27,000 troops on board accompanied by 180 friars. Richard Carew, who saw the ships himself, referred to them in his *Survey* as 'the Spanish floating Babel', an allusion both to the towering height of the ships (similar to the tower of Babel) and to the multinational composition of the fleet.[42] To quote Rowse again,

> Next day the (English) fleet warped with difficulty against the wind out of the harbour, under the lee of Mount Edgcumbe, and about three in the afternoon Howard first got sight of the Spaniards. That day and night the English ships hugged the coast of Whitsand Bay, until they caught up with the Armada off Looe, having recovered the wind of the Spaniards. At nine o'clock on Sunday morning they first gave fight, when the two fleets were thwart of Plymouth: a spectacle which the mayor and citizens beheld for themselves, sending out reinforcements and victuals as they could.[43]

Had the Spanish attempted to land at Plymouth or nearby, Grenville's plan was to mass a force of 19,200 men to resist the invasion. In the days that followed, the Armada was pounded by the English fleet, scattered by fire ships, and wrecked by storms. The Spanish Admiral, the Duke of Medina Sidonia, was forced to abandon his mission. He had lost more than a third of his fighting strength.

Spanish Raids

In 1589, Philip gave orders to prepare a new Armada. In October 1590, 3,000 Spanish troops occupied parts of Brittany threatening once again the coasts of Cornwall. The Government ordered Plymouth and the Scilly Isles to be re-fortified. Fighting continued in Brittany for several years. Then, on 23 July 1595, four Spanish galleys raided the Cornish coast, setting fire to the villages of Mousehole and Paul. The Spaniards landed at Newlyn and attacked Penzance, causing the inhabitants to flee in panic. Before the English commanders could organise effective resistance, the Spaniards set fire to both Penzance and Newlyn. Once again the Government was compelled to take action. In the words of Carew,

> By direction from the Lords, order was taken, that upon any alarum, the next [44] Captains should forthwith put themselves with their companies, into their assigned seacoast towns, whom the adjoining land-forces were appoynted to second and third, as the opportunity of their dwellings affoorded best occasion.[45]

Carew was put in command of five companies of soldiers, numbering 500 men altogether, consisting of 300 musketeers, 170 armed pikemen, and 30 men with calivers. The military preparations were necessary, because in March 1597 a Spanish pinnace sailed into Cawsand Bay and sent a raiding party ashore to set fire to the village, but an alert defender chased them off with a caliver and removed the barrels of inflammable material.[46] This was the last attack by the Spaniards on the Rame Peninsula, but not the end of the Spanish threat. The pinnace was probably on a scouting expedition, and in October 1597 a Spanish invasion fleet was heading for Falmouth, but was dispersed by gales. In 1599, another Armada was prepared, consisting of 70 galleys and 100 ships, and carrying 15,000-16,000 soldiers, but in the end it did not land.

220 *The Elizabethan blockhouse at Mount Edgcumbe was armed with cannon from the time of the Spanish Armada until the early 1800s.*

The Reign of James I

The early part of the reign of James I (1603-25) was marked by a policy of non-aggression towards Spain. As part of this policy, James repealed the Elizabethan statutes for the taking of musters and the keeping of horses and armour. But, by 1612, relations with Spain had again deteriorated, and annual general musters were resumed together with special musters for training. These actions were taken under the authority of the revived medieval statutes and the Royal Prerogative. In 1613, a Spanish invasion was feared and the beacons were rebuilt. In Cornwall, because of its proximity to Spain, the system of mustering only the fittest men was abandoned in favour of mustering the entire male population. The Thirty Years' War in Germany, which commenced in 1618, led to renewed alarm and increased military preparations. Attempts were made to introduce improvements in, and greater standardisation of, arms and armour. Drill-books were issued to the muster-masters in an attempt to produce greater 'exactness' in their deployments.

The Reign of Charles I

One of the first actions of Charles I after his accession was to issue an Ordinance for the creation of an exact or perfect militia. In March 1625, an expedition was assembled at Plymouth for an attack upon Cadiz in Spain. Ten thousand men were billeted in and around Plymouth, including 2,650 in Cornwall. Sir Richard Edgcumbe and Sir Richard Carew of Antony (son of the historian) were among those placed in charge of the billeted men. In August, the Council, which now feared an invasion by the French, ordered all coastal defence forces to be mobilised. Early in 1626, the government brought in from the Low Countries 84 sergeants to train the militia in the latest continental fighting techniques. Ammunition was distributed to all the parishes and the militiamen were ordered to perform regular target practice. All the beacons were once again prepared for lighting.

In the same year, Sir James Bagg (or Bagge) of Saltram, on Government orders, completed a survey of the shipping of Devon and Cornwall to assess what resources were available for naval expeditions. In September 1627, 2,000 troops were billeted in Devon and Cornwall, this time for an attack on the Ile de Ré (or Rhé) near La Rochelle in France. In October, Bagg was authorised to impress ships to provide transport. Sheviock had one ship, the *Dayestarr* of 50 tons burthen, but it was not impressed for service.[47] The Ile de Ré expedition was a disaster, and when the survivors returned at the end of November, 4,750 soldiers were billeted in Devon and Cornwall. 1,300 of the soldiers were sick or injured, and many of these were billeted along the Tamar Valley (particularly in Saltash) and on the Rame Peninsula. Sheviock would have taken its share of the sick survivors, but St Germans was exempted. The parishes had to bear the full cost of accommodating and caring for the soldiers.[48] Many complained bitterly. For example, in a list of grievances sent up to the government by John Connocke of Treworgey and others in St Cleer, the eight wealthiest parishioners complained,

> That his Majestie oweth them three hundred poundes, for Billitting souldiers, Cote [coat] and conduct, which returned from the last Cales aition (Calais action) and the Ile of Ree, over and above their voluntarye Loane of 5 intire subsidies, which is a great part of their present want and povertye.[49]

Coastal Piracy

During the 1600s, pirates infested the Cornish coast, just as they had done during the Middle Ages. This time, most were based at the so-called 'Barbary' ports of Salé, in Morocco, and Algiers and Tunis, then part of the Ottoman Empire. Dunkirk, in the Low Countries (now part of France), was also an infamous haven for pirates. The main target of the pirates was people, whether men, women or children, who would be taken to North Africa and sold into slavery. These human prizes would either be taken from ships at sea or, sometimes, were snatched from fishing villages. For example, a pirate fleet of 20 ships captured 60 people from Mount's Bay, and 80 fishermen from Looe, in particularly daring raids in the summer of 1625. Other pirates occupied Lundy Island and used it as a base to snatch people from Padstow and other villages on the north Cornish coast. By the end of the year the mayor of Plymouth estimated that 1,000 fishing craft had been destroyed and about the same number of people carried into slavery.[50] In 1627, the Scilly Isles had to be fortified against the 'Turks', recalling medieval times when knights were stationed there at the cost of Tavistock Abbey to deal with the menace of piracy.

Sporadic attempts were made by the government to suppress the evil. In February 1637, an expedition under the brilliant leadership of Captain William Rainsborough blockaded the port of Salé and forced it to surrender, releasing more than 200 captives.[51] Rainsborough's fleet had been paid for by the ship money which so enraged the inland parishes immediately before the Civil War. Sometimes collections were made in the parishes to ransom the captives – the going rate was £38 for a male, but much more for a female slave. The Sultan of Morocco from 1672 to 1727 was Moulay Ismail, and during his long reign piracy again became a menace. It continued, with occasional intermissions, under his successors. Finally, at the end of the Napoleonic Wars, the Foreign Secretary, Lord Castlereagh, despatched a strong force under Sir Edward Pellew (later Lord Exmouth) to bombard Algiers and force its surrender. After a hard-fought battle that took place in late August 1816, he was successful. 1,642 slaves from many European nations were released, and Algiers, Tunis, Tripoli and Morocco renounced slavery for ever.

CHAPTER 36

The Civil War to the Reign of Queen Victoria

In 1641, fearful of the restoration of Catholicism, the government required every parish to compile a list of all able-bodied men over the age of 18 who professed the Protestant faith. The Sheviock list contains 156 names. Several of the first names on the list are taken from the Old Testament, reflecting the heightened religious feeling of the times – for example, Abraham Chubb, Amos and Esay (Esau) Odiorne, Abraham and Amos Palmer, Baltasar Snell and Daniell Sargent. Of the families encountered in the 1522 and 1569 muster rolls and the 1544 tax subsidy roll, the families of Bray, Chubb, Grylls, Harry, Odiorne, Peter, Pope, Rundle, Sargent, Smyth, Spiller, Truscott and Wallis reappear on the Protestation roll. The Hancock, Skinner and Whitford families have disappeared, although the Hancock family was still resident in St Germans parish and re-appeared in Sheviock later. But many new families appear for the first time, including those of Arundell, the family of the rectors appointed in 1576 and 1622, Hocken (Hoskin?), Pryn (still present in the parish) and Wills.

Apart from the Arundells of Sheviock, who were High Church and Royalist, we know the political allegiances of only a few of the parishioners. Sir Samuel Rolle, one of the principal property owners in the borough of Crafthole before the Civil War, and a major investor in the Devon cloth trade, supported the Parliament. William Condy, a Tavistock clothier, owned a number of properties in the borough after the Civil War and is also likely to have supported the Parliament. On the other hand, Joseph Hunkyn, another owner of property in Crafthole, may have been related to the 'John Hunkyn, gent.' of Liskeard, who was fined £1 6s. 8d. in 1650 for his Royalist activities during the war.[1] Toby Langdon, who owned property in Crafthole and also lived there, may have been related to Walter Langdon of Keverall, one of the senior Royalist leaders in Cornwall during the war.[2]

In south-east Cornwall, many of the local gentry sided with Parliament. Leading Parliamentarians included Sir Richard Carew (d.1643), his sons, Alexander and John, Sir Richard and Francis Buller of Shillingham, John and Edward Eliot of St Germans,

221 *Sir Alexander Carew (1609-44) fought courageously for Parliament at the start of the Civil War, but he was later executed for planning to surrender St Nicholas Island to the Royalists.*

and Sir Anthony and Francis Rous of Halton Barton in St Dominic. The leader of the Parliamentary cause in Cornwall was Lord Robartes of Lanhydrock, further west. Plymouth strongly supported the Parliament, as did Saltash. The navy, which had been badly neglected in the reign of King James, also came out for Parliament. Leading Puritan clergy included John Fathers of St Stephens, whose patron was Sir Richard Buller, Charles FitzGeffry of St Dominic, whose patron was Sir Anthony Rous, and Jasper Hicks of Landrake.

Although the manor of Sheviock had belonged to the Carews since 1558, the most densely populated part of the parish, Crafthole, then belonged to the Crown. An examination of the court rolls immediately before the Civil War does not reveal particularly harsh treatment of the tenants by the Crown at this time, though this apparently happened in some other places.[3] Those Sheviock residents with strong naval connections, or strict Puritanical views, would have been for Parliament. Many families may have tried to avoid taking sides until it became unavoidable, for example by armed occupation of their lands and property. The author, Anne Duffin, has suggested that it was only the Royalist advance on Millbrook and Mount Edgcumbe in October 1642 that decided Piers Edgcumbe to declare for the king.[4] He subsequently became a commander of one of the Royalist regiments. Further west, a majority of the Cornish gentry were for the king. They included Warwick, Lord Mohun of Boconnoc and Lanteglos near

Fowey, Sir William Wrey of Trebigh in St Ive, Sir John Trelawney of Trelawne near Pelynt, Sheriff John Grylls of Lanreath, Charles Trevanion of Caerhayes, and Sir John Arundell of Trerice. Sir John's much younger cousin, Gregory Arundell, was rector of Sheviock. He was unpopular with the fishermen of the parish and this, as well as his political and religious leanings, may have been a factor in his ejection from his living during the Commonwealth period.[5]

The Rame Peninsula during the Civil War

In June 1642, the king issued a commission of array for Cornwall, summoning the trained bands to the defence of the county. Various commissioners were also named, whose task it was to raise and lead the troops. The commissioners included the Royalists mentioned above together with Sir William and Sir Peter Courtenay, Sir Nicholas Slanning and Sir Bevill Grenvile. In March, Parliament had passed its own Militia Ordinance authorising the raising of troops in its interest, and on 27 July Sir Richard and Francis Buller, Alexander Carew and others were ordered to execute it. Matters came to a head at the assizes held in Launceston on 5 August. The High Sheriff, John Grylls, proclaimed his intention to execute the king's commission of array calling the trained bands to arms in the king's service and refused to read the Militia Ordinance. The vicar preaching the assize sermon and the assize judge also spoke in favour of the commission of array. Both sides continued with their recruitment drives. According to Sir Ralph Hopton, by the end of September,

> Sir Richard Buller and his [Parliamentarian] Confederates had much increased their numbers having drawn to them most of the able men of the East Division of Cornwall.[6]

The Parliamentarians garrisoned and fortified Launceston. Meanwhile, Sir Ralph Hopton and a Royalist force of 110 horsemen and 50 dragoons crossed over from Devon and stationed themselves at Bodmin. The Royalists recruited nearly a thousand men from the two western hundreds of Powder and Pydar. At the Michaelmas Quarter Sessions at Lostwithiel, the Parliamentarians brought in a Bill of Indictment against Hopton and his forces for breaching the peace, and in reply the Royalists brought in a Bill against Buller and Carew 'for a rowte and unlawfull assembly at Lanceston'.[7] The grand jury found for the Royalists and ordered the High Sheriff, John Grylls, to raise the 'posse comitatus' (county force) to disperse the unlawful assembly and apprehend the rioters. The Bill against Hopton was thrown out by the jury when the Sessions resumed at Truro.

By 4 October 1642, the Royalist infantry, which included the posse raised by the sheriff, 'a gentleman very well affected' [8] and the soldiers recruited in the west, consisted of 'about three thousand foote well arm'd under severall coulors, and divers others with clubbs'.[9] They assembled at Moilesbarrow Down near Lostwithiel. Sir Ralph Hopton, who had fought in the service of the Elector Palatine on the Continent during the Thirty Years' War, assumed command. He 'set the Posse in as good Order as they were capable of'[10] and advanced towards Launceston. The forces of Buller and Carew, who were by then heavily outnumbered, abandoned the town and withdrew into Plymouth. They took with them 700 men, including 200 Scots and the garrison of Saltash, leaving that town also to be occupied by the Royalists. The Royalists then began to recruit proper army regiments. Lord Mohun of Boconnoc was the commander of one of the new regiments and he made preparations for securing the Rame Peninsula for the Royalists. According to Hopton,

> Upon the desire of the well affected people of the parts about Milbrooke and Mount Edgcombe, Coll: Walter Slyngesby (then Major of the Lo: Mohuns Regiment) was commanded thither with Capt. Cosowarth's new leavyed dragoones, where at their first entrance into Milbrooke, Mr Edgecombe and Mr Stephens came to him, and declared themselves for the King.[11]

A lieutenant and a troop of dragoons were placed as a guard below Millbrook, but Sir Alexander Carew:

222 *A cannon guarding the approach to Plymouth harbour. Mount Edgcumbe was fortified and garrisoned by the Royalists at the start of the Civil War. Plymouth and St Nicholas Island (centre right) were in Parliamentary hands.*

> with Muskettiers from Plymouth landed thereabout, and tooke him and some of his men prisoners, which enforced Major Slingsby and those that were with him to retreat to Craft-Hole, leaving twenty men to secure Mount Edgcumbe house.[12]

On news of this threat, Sir Ralph Hopton, Capt. Jonathan Trelawney and Capt. William Arundell and their companies marched up from Bodmin

> and being arrived there the same day, found the good high Sheriffe Mr. Grills (*sic*) with five hundred of the Posse newly drawen together, and advanced by him that verie day. With those forces Sir Ralph Hopton advanced to Mount Edgcomb-house, and settled guards at Cromwell-Passage [Cremyll] over against Stone-house, at Impecombe, and at Milbrooke and having put all things in order left Major Slingsby there to command that quarter, and those men.[13]

Shortly afterwards, Parliamentary forces from Plymouth crossed over secretly by night in 36 boats and again assaulted the Royalists' positions at Millbrook. Although Major Slingsby had not yet finished constructing his barricades, his troops successfully beat off the attackers and took several prisoners, including one of the leaders, Major Fortescue. According to Hopton, the rest retreated 'in great fright and disorder.'[14] After these actions, the posse, whose use was limited because it had no authority to enter Devon, was discharged. Sir Beville Grenvile, Sir Nicholas Slanning, Col. John Trevanion, and Col. William Godolphin proceeded to raise new regiments of foot to augment the Royal army.

Meanwhile, the Parliamentary forces in Devon, reinforced by troops from Somerset, Dorset and other eastern counties, and now led by Colonel Ruthin, threatened to take Saltash. Hopton withdrew his forces from there and Major Slingsby withdrew from Millbrook. Part of the Royalist army assembled at Liskeard and Lostwithiel and part at Bodmin. The posse was reconvened. These forces assembled once again on Moilesbarrow Down and advanced into Boconnoc Park. In January 1643, the opposing forces met at Braddock Down, west of Liskeard, and the Royalists won their first significant victory in the West Country, leading once again to the stationing of Royalist troops at Saltash and Mount Edgcumbe[15] The battle was followed by another major Royalist victory at Stratton in May. In July, the Royalists captured Bristol and in September, Exeter. By December, virtually the whole of the South West, except Plymouth, was in Royalist hands, and Plymouth was besieged. In July 1644, a Parliamentary army led by the Earl of Essex, marched into Cornwall, apparently swayed by the advice of Lord Robartes. They took Saltash and Mount Edgcumbe, but were heavily defeated at Lostwithiel and Fowey in September. The Royalists then recaptured and reinforced Saltash and Mount Edgcumbe and besieged Plymouth once more.

But, by the end of 1645, the Royalist cause in the South West was on the point of collapse. On 1 October, General Fairfax and his new model army began their westward advance. In December, the Royalists abandoned the siege of Plymouth and began to retreat into Cornwall. On 16 February 1646, the Parliamentary army defeated Hopton at the battle of Torrington in Devon, and what remained of the Cornish Royalist armies fled across the Tamar. Fairfax captured Launceston on 25 February. In March, Colonel Edgcumbe surrendered Mount Edgcumbe. Finally, on 16 August, the aged Sir John Arundell, together with his depleted band of Royalists, including Sir John Grylls and his son, Charles, were forced to surrender Pendennis, the last Royalist bastion in Cornwall.[16]

The Financial Burden of the War

As the war progressed, the financial burden became very heavy, not only on the gentry who had to sell their plate, but also on the parishes, who were required to make contributions to support the army and the various garrisons. Sheviock, along with ten other parishes, was required to make a contribution of £32 19s. 7d. per week to maintain the Royalist garrison at Pendennis.[17]

From the beginning of the Civil War until after the Restoration, many rents went unpaid. These included both rents owing to the Carews for the manor of Sheviock and rents owing to the Duchy of Cornwall for premises in the borough of Crafthole. On the manor of Sheviock, for example, by 1656, Richard Lavers, who leased a house and fishing premises in Portwrinkle for 16s. a year, owed the manor £6 4s., showing that rent had not been paid for seven years and nine months – i.e. since 1648. Thomas Austen, who also leased premises there at that rent, owed the manor £6, showing that rent had not been paid for seven years and six months. The worst case was that of Isaiah Odihorne, who had not paid any rent since 1641, a lapse of 15 years.[18] In 1660, the bailiff of the manor, John Rawlings, was ordered to levy distress for the amount of the debt on these three and sixteen other tenants, including Joan Odihorne and George Winnacott. George was the tenant of a fishing cellar in Portwrinkle and of a cottage on the quay by the River Lynher. From the execution of Charles I in 1649 until 1660 the borough of Crafthole belonged to the Commonwealth. The Commonwealth authorities had some difficulty in collecting their rents. A note on the Parliamentary Survey of 1649 reads: 'The rent [of the borough] being per annum £1 11s. 8½d. hath not been paid by the said tenants for these last two years.' The borough was restored to the Duchy at the Restoration.

The Dutch Wars

Britain was at war with the Dutch Republic, apart from a few peaceful interludes, between 1652 and 1674.[19] Trade was the main source of friction between these two maritime powers, both seeking to achieve naval dominance. The First Dutch War, during the Commonwealth period, lasted from 1652 until 1654, and ended in a

British victory. The Second lasted from 1665 to 1667 and ended with the destruction of much of the English fleet in the River Medway in 1667, the greatest defeat ever suffered by British naval forces. The war was brought to an end by the Treaty of Breda in the same year. In the Third Dutch War, which lasted from 1672 to 1674, and was entirely fought in Dutch coastal waters, Britain and its ally, France, failed to accomplish their intended destruction of the Dutch fleet. This last war was brought to an end by the Treaty of Westminster. The naval wars against the Dutch were fought either in the waters lying between England and Holland or far away and so had little direct impact upon the parish of Sheviock.

Sheviock during the American and French Wars

When in the next century Britain was at war with the American colonies (from 1776 to 1783), the French made a determined effort to win from Britain control of the seas, and formed an alliance with Spain. In 1778, the French fleet menaced the Channel. Admiral Keppel failed to defeat them in a battle off Ushant. In the following year, the French fleet, reinforced by the Spanish, threatened the invasion of Britain. Just as Richard Carew and his contemporaries had watched the Spanish Armada threatening England's shores in 1588, so now another generation watched the enemy's ships preparing to attack. James Chubb, then living in St Germans, but probably a member of the family that had resided in Sheviock in the 1500s and 1600s, was a witness. He wrote in his diary:[20]

> In 1779 August 17th in the morning most people here was much alarmed on account of a very large enemy's fleet supposed to be the French and the Spaniards. I rid to Crafthole about eight o'clock and saw a large fleet supposed to be our great fleet, chasing the French. But about 11 o'clock the Ardent coming from Portsmouth unluckily fell in with them and sustained a running fight for almost two hours and then struck. I trembled to hear the guns firing supposing that many of our fellow creatures had hardly time to say the Lord have mercy on them before they were like water spilt on the ground. The French and the Spanish fleet is supposed to be more than 100 sail and 60 upwards of the line. They were in sight of our land 15th, 16th, 17th and 18th instant. Most that saw them thought they intended to land. But the God of Jacob was on our side, it was a mallancolly [*sic*] sight and great number of women and children removed from Kingsand, Dock, etc, making great lamentations.

The combined enemy fleets did not in fact make a landing but the threat had been real. Peace was concluded eventually at the Peace of Versailles in 1783.

Following the outbreak of the French Revolution, France declared war on Britain in 1793. Apart from brief interludes in 1802 and 1814, Britain was then at war with France continuously until the Peace of Paris, which was concluded after the battle of Waterloo in June 1815. During this period the site of the old beacon on Beacon Hill once again came into use. But this time it was converted into a flag signal station[21] and later a semaphore station[22] to communicate with another one situated on Maker church tower. The chain of signalling stations stretched all the way from the Lizard to the Admiralty in Whitehall.

In 1797, the Government offered incentives to those who formed volunteer corps. Lord Eliot of St Germans and Reginald Pole Carew both took up the challenge. In July of that year Pole Carew had formed the East Cornwall Voluntary Cavalry (the Antony Yeomanry Cavalry), consisting of 50 troopers. To help pay for their maintenance, local people made voluntary contributions. In March 1798, the Revd Joshua Jeans, who was rector of Sheviock and curate of Antony, reported to Pole Carew:

> Our farmers behav'd very well, particularly Pike,[23] who wished to make five guineas the common mark from them all. Others thought three enough. I put down £25 to set them an example. Mr E Roberts followed with £5.[24] I suppose that both the parishes will raise fifty or sixty guineas. Jeffries [*sic*] and Lyne[25] go round to collect from house to house, & I inculcated the idea the poor man's mite … shou'd be receiv'd with as much respect as the rich man's bank note.[26]

Among the campaigns of that war was the Peninsular Campaign of 1808-14, in which Wellington's troops drove Napoleon's armies from Portugal, and later (1812-13) helped to expel the French from Spain. In 1811, the British and Portuguese under General Beresford, defeated a French army under Marshal Soult in a bloody battle at Albuera near Badajos. In that battle, Lt-Col George Henry Duckworth was killed while gallantly leading the 48th Regiment of Foot. There is a memorial to him in Sheviock church, because he was related to the owners of Trethill through his mother, Ann Wallis. His grandfather, John Wallis of Stoke Damerel, had died at Trethill in 1780 while on a visit to the then owner, the Revd Mydhope Wallis. At the time of the French wars, three church bells hung in Sheviock church tower. These were rung for British victories on land and sea. On those occasions when our forces were defeated, the Government would order days of fasting and humiliation.[27]

A Costly Battle for the Empire

In Sheviock church is a memorial to Alphonse de Morel, killed in India in 1849. It reads as follows: 'To the memory of Alphonse Charles de Morel, Ensign in the XXX Regt. Of British Native Infantry. He fell in the battle of Chillianwallah on the 13 January, 1849; aged 23. He was the eldest son of the Count de Morel & Charlotte Jemima his wife, eldest daughter of the Rt. Hon. Reginald Pole Carew, of Antony.' The battle of Chillianwala was part of the Punjab Campaign of 1846-9 against the Sikhs.[28]

Chapter 37

The Parish in the Two World Wars

The First World War

Lt.-Col. Gerard Kempthorne, author of the first *History of Sheviock*, which was privately published about 1934, moved into the parish after the First World War. He was a doctor who had served in France with the RAMC, and was awarded the DSO. On his retirement in 1931, he moved to Lynher Villa in Crafthole. He would have heard about wartime life in the parish from his neighbours, and he devoted a short but valuable passage to it:

> it is certain that the precautionary telegram of August 1914 found some at least of the [Tregantle] fort staff at golf at Whitsand Bay.[1] Within a few hours the Coast Guard and the Naval Reservists belonging to the village were embarked in wagonettes and cheered as they got under weigh.

Walter Andrew from Portwrinkle and two of the sons of Joseph Pengelly, Walter and Wilfrid, joined the Royal Naval minesweeping service.[2] In June 1917, Wilfrid was on H.M. Trawler *Carew Castle* as a leading deckhand and (the only) gunner. The ship was based at Milford Haven and patrolled the Bristol Channel as far as the Irish coast. On 12 June, she struck a mine and sank in four minutes. After jumping overboard, Wilfrid caught his foot in a coil of wire rope and was dragged under with the ship, only managing to free himself after being dragged down to a considerable depth. In August, he joined a new trawler, the *George Borthwick*. In April 1918, she sailed from Falmouth to the Mediterranean and was based at Taranto in Italy. The trawlers formed a hydrophone barrage across the Adriatic between Italy and Albania to trap submarines. Wilfrid remained there until the Armistice was declared. Walter's flotilla of minesweepers at first swept for mines in British waters and later moved to the Mediterranean, patrolling between Italy and Egypt.

A bizarre incident occurred in Whitsand Bay towards the end of the war. Whilst Joseph Pengelly and his eldest son, Theophilus, were fishing in their boat, *Onward*,

223 *Wilfrid Pengelly survived the sinking of the minesweeper on which he served during the First World War.*

in misty weather, they were shelled by a Portuguese merchant ship. It is thought that she mistook the *Onward*'s mizzen sail for the conning tower of a German submarine. Fortunately, they were not hit. Some of the shells landed on the foreshore at Portwrinkle; one landed at Lantic; and another fell at Sow Park, in Crafthole.

About the army, Kempthorne wrote: 'To the regular army the parish sent a much more modest contribution [on the day that war was declared], but, as the war developed, Sheviock bore its due share in providing recruits for the New Army.' William Andrew of Crafthole (Walter's cousin) was one of the early recruits. He joined the Royal Engineers in late 1914 and was sent to fight in France, winning the Military Medal for bravery in the Battle of the Somme. His daughter, Mrs Theodora Colwill, remembered going to Raglan Barracks in Stonehouse in the late 1920s to see the medal being presented to him.

Soldiers from other parts of the country and from the overseas Dominions were stationed in the parish at various times during the war, and the army paid for troops to be billeted in the pilchard cellars at Portwrinkle (1914) and the Methodist chapel schoolroom (1915). Kempthorne wrote that:

> In the early days of the Great War our people watched the long line of ships which brought the Canadian contingent to England from the same cliffs where their ancestors had followed, though with very different feelings, the course of the Great Armada through Whitsand Bay.

Kempthorne also mentions the uses to which Tregantle Fort was put, stating that, 'A territorial unit was encamped on its slopes when the Great War broke out, and later its casements afforded accommodation for a training battalion of the Worcestershire Regiment'.[3] Seven men from the parish lost their lives in the War.[4] A memorial to them was put up in the churchyard, and is inscribed: 'Erected by the inhabitants of Sheviocke Parish in memory of their fellows who gave their lives in the service of their King and country during the Great War.'[5]

THE SECOND WORLD WAR

The Second World War commenced on 3 September 1939. Charles and Ernestine Bean of Fernleigh in Crafthole, were among the first in the parish to suffer from the war. Their son, Desmond, was drowned when his ship, the aircraft carrier HMS *Courageous*, was sunk by a U-boat in the Bristol Channel on 17 September. In the spring of 1940, the British and French armies were defeated in France. The evacuation from Dunkirk took place between 29 May and 4 June. The British army lost all its equipment, but more than 330,000 soldiers were saved. One of the sailors on the 'little ships' that took part in the evacuation was Walter Pengelly's son, Lester. At the beginning of the war, he was based at Lowestoft on minesweepers and fast patrol boats. He formed part of a skeleton crew that took a motorised barge across the Channel. Though attacked many times by German aircraft, they survived and rescued many soldiers.

224 *Petty Officer George Paul on his wedding day in 1929. He went down with his ship, HMS* Dorsetshire, *when she was sunk by the Japanese in 1942.*

France surrendered on 25 June. In the same month, the Home Guard was formed in Britain. There was real fear of invasion. Defences were constructed all around the coast and coastal regions were declared prohibited areas for unauthorised personnel. At Portwrinkle, the beaches were covered with what looked like scaffolding as anti-invasion devices.[6] The *Whitsand Bay Hotel* and the Chalet were both requisitioned by the army. Pill-boxes were erected. Two of these can still be seen: one near the Chalet at Portwrinkle and the other at the end of Trethill Lane. A wall was constructed at the bottom end of Ladywell to prevent enemy vehicles getting on to the main road to Torpoint. A perforated metal pipe was also stretched along the A374. It was linked to an oil tank somewhere on the Trethill estate. In the event of invasion, the oil would have been allowed to flow through the pipes onto the road where it would have been ignited.[7] An American mobile anti-aircraft gun was positioned in Cross Park in 1944. There was a heavy anti-aircraft battery at St Winnolls, in St Germans parish. Barrage balloons, floating at the end of cables up to a height of 10,000 feet, appeared above Plymouth. The late Henry (Hal) Whittaker, an engineer who worked in Plymouth, but lived with his parents-in-law, Arnold and Mollie Hoskin, at Crafthole Farm, and was a member of the Home Guard, described these balloons:

> [They] were moved from place to place ... The cables were wound onto drums on heavy lorries and, depending on the direction of the wind, the lorries moved one side or other of the perimeter they were to protect ... The balloons were ... about 30 to

> 40 feet in length and 15 feet in diameter when inflated. They were rather pear-shaped with fins on the tail. [They were] constructed of non-porous fabric without any strut or framework to maintain [their] shape ... They were filled ... with hydrogen, helium or plain ordinary gas. On the bottom of each balloon, for the purpose of maintaining its direction into the wind, was a sort of scoop with an open end towards the front, bulbous end, of the balloon.'[8]

One evening, one of the balloons broke away from its moorings with a length of cable trailing from it. Whittaker described what happened next:

> Shortly after I got home to Crafthole ... I was told the balloon was blowing away, had come into sight, and seemed to be coming down over the village. So out I went, with about a score of others [from the village], to try to recapture it ... We found it up on the golf course where it had actually landed among a whole lot of brambles. Now, because it was still bulging, inflated with some of the gas that had been in it, some people wanted to slash holes in it to let the gas escape. But, having made sure no one was smoking, ... I walked on top of the balloon, pressing it down and forcing the gaseous contents out through the scoop. I was just about rendered unconscious by being enveloped in gas so that I couldn't breathe. However we got it all out before anyone was injured or the balloon was badly damaged and we tied it up with the rope that had been hanging from it. I suppose someone notified the barrage balloon people where it was and asked them to come and fetch it.

On 16 July 1940, Hitler ordered operation 'Sea Lion'. This was to be a seaborne invasion launched from the French Channel ports between Calais and Brest. In England, the attack was expected somewhere on the coastline from Harwich right round to Portsmouth, Portland or even Plymouth, but centring upon Kent and Sussex. For the Germans to be successful, they needed control of the Channel, both in the air and on the sea.

The Battle of Britain and the Mines that Fell on Crafthole

The German attempt to control the airspace took place in three separate phases. In the first, from 10 July to 18 August, German bombers attacked the southern ports from Dover to Plymouth and also convoys proceeding up the Channel. Two casual bombs were dropped on Crafthole on 21 July 1940, but did no damage.[9] The Germans also dropped mines in an attempt to deny the Channel to allied shipping. Crafthole sustained severe damage from two of these mines, which were dropped by a German seaplane on a bright moonlit night, 16 August 1940. John Kentisbeer, then aged 14, was living at No 1 the Terrace. Between 10 and 10.30 p.m., he saw the silhouette of two mines coming down. They were intended for Whitsand Bay, but, because of the strong on-shore wind, they had drifted inland. The mines exploded almost simultaneously. One fell on the golf course. Everyone was in bed. John's window caved in and the ceiling fell in on his parents, Reginald and Violet, in the bedroom next door. The whole village turned out. Some villagers went into the meadow called Judas Park.[10] In this meadow there were 20 or 30 metal cages containing chickens. Many had been turned upside down with the fowls inside. The villagers righted them. Some fowls had been killed, but many survived. The second mine fell near what is now Burns View.[11] It completely demolished High House and the butcher's shop attached to it. High House had been one of the oldest dwellings in the village.[12] The occupier, Albert Bersey, and his wife, Violet, were uninjured.

John Biles was then living with his mother and father at Carclew, the home of Gerald Crispin and his wife.[13] That night he happened to be fire-watching in the centre of Plymouth, where he worked. He returned to Crafthole next morning. As he wrote, 'I left one scene of utter devastation to return to another'.[14] He remembered the effect of the explosion on Jessie, wife of the farmer, Harold Bersey.[15] The Berseys lived in Cross House opposite High House. Biles recalled that Mrs Bersey 'was very proud of her butter pats, but sadly, after the mines exploded, they were all dotted around the walls and ceiling of her dairy'.[16]

BOMBS FALL AT SOUTH-WEST VILLAGE

... and dislodged slates formed the bulk of the damage in the main street of a South-West village when two German bombs fell on Friday night.—"The Western Morning News" Photograph.

PROBLEM | WAR MINISTER | SOLDIER DROWNED

225 *Two German mines fell on the golf course near Crafthole on 16 August 1940, destroying High House and damaging the roof of Cross House (*WMN *18 August 1940).*

When the mines fell on Crafthole, the windows of Carclew were blown out and landed on the front lawn. John Biles's mother told him that, on the night in question, she had been saying her prayers by her bed, and suddenly found herself huddled at the other end of the room, following the explosion. The point of a very large dagger of glass was deeply embedded in the headboard, exactly where her head would have been. Biles also learned that Edward (Eddy) Callaghan, the golf professional, had been on duty with his pitch-fork when the German aircraft released the two sea mines.[17] Eddy was said to have phoned headquarters to report that 'the bloody Germans had landed'.

At this time, there were also many evacuees in the village. Faced with the threat of heavy bombing raids on London, the Government had made arrangements for children to be evacuated into the countryside in the early summer of 1940. One of the evacuees, Terry Leather (aged eight), who was staying with his sister, Vera (aged seven), at the home of Mr and Mrs Hearn, at the *New Inn*, had a lucky escape from the mines. Mrs Hilary Lee recollected the event, [18]

> On the evening of 16 August 1940, my husband and I were in bed when we heard a German plane overhead. There was this tremendous flash and Wilfred pulled the bedclothes over our heads. When we pulled them back we were looking at the sky, our bed covered in debris, the roof rafters resting on top of the wardrobe. My mother and father were still downstairs with some friends. The men scrambled up the stairs terrified at what they might find. Vera was awake and crying, but Terry was still asleep.[19] My father picked him up to carry him downstairs. He met mother coming up and told her, 'I think this boy is dead, Hyld'.[20] Then Terry opened his eyes and said 'What's up, Unk?' He hadn't heard a thing, and although both children had the ceilings on their beds, neither had a scratch on them.

The only fatalities were several sheep grazing on the golf links, a farmer's dog, which was blown straight out of a window, and the chickens mentioned above. A headline in the *Cornish Times* read, 'And Terry slept'.[21] Some time later, many local evacuees also sought shelter in the village. People would come out from Torpoint every evening to sleep in Crafthole and Sheviock away from the dangers of the bombs aimed at the dockyards in Devonport. For example, when the oil tanks in Torpoint were hit and on fire, No.1 the Terrace, Crafthole, accommodated no fewer than 16 people. Reginald and Violet Kentisbeer, their son, John, and their baby, Ronald, slept in one bedroom; three other members of Violet's family slept in the second bedroom; a family of five from Torpoint slept in a downstairs room; whilst another refugee family of four sheltered in the kitchen.[22]

The Second Phase

Between 24 August and 6 September 1940, the Germans switched the direction of their attacks. They now attempted to eliminate the RAF and its installations, attacking airfields all along the south coast. From 7 to 27 September, they targeted London. The crucial battle, and the turning point in the campaign, was the battle fought on 15 September, when the RAF destroyed 56 German planes for the loss of 40 British ones. On 17 September, Hitler decided to postpone Operation Sea Lion indefinitely, and, on 12 October 1940, definitely cancelled it for that year.

226 *Sir John Carew Pole, DSO (1902-93), painted by Oswald Birley in 1944. Sir John served in Normandy, France, Belgium, Holland and Germany in 1944-5.*

The Third Phase

The third and final phase of the battle took place from October 1940 onwards, when the Germans launched indiscriminate bombing attacks on London and other industrial cities. From 7 September to 3 November 1940, an average of 200 German bombers attacked London every night. It was during this phase, on 11 October 1940, that St Germans Rural District Council, which included Sheviock parish, launched a Spitfire Fund, to raise money over a two-month period to build more Spitfires. Sheviock, largely through the efforts of the Recreation Club and the Women's Institute, raised £17 0s. 4d. On 20 and 21 March, and from 21 to 29 April 1941, German bombers mounted heavy attacks on Plymouth. The attacks continued sporadically throughout the summer. Decoy fires were lit near Erth Barton on the other side of the River Lynher. As a result many bombs were dropped in and around Sheviock woods and the surrounding fields. One landed near Cote Farm damaging the nearby cowshed and also the east window of Sheviock church. Fred Paul writes about another:

> Mr A. Carpenter, who lived with his wife at No 4 the Terrace, Sheviock village, next door to my mother and Gran, brought home an unexploded bomb that he found out in Sheviock woods when helping to put the fires out after the woods had been bombed one night. On occasions … he would place the bomb in a vice in his shed and with a punch and hammer would try and unscrew the cover… About 30 years later in the seventies he died. His relations came to sort out his property and one of them marched into my mother's house to say that they had found a bomb in his shed. They phoned the bomb disposal people who took it away and in a field near Torpoint, which was temporarily cordoned off, they blew [it] up. He could have destroyed Sheviock!

After May 1941, the raids on London ceased (although they started again in 1944). On 22 June 1941, Hitler invaded Russia, and in July 1941 he again postponed Operation Sea Lion until the spring of 1942. On 13 February 1942, he finally abandoned the idea of invading Britain. This was not, however, known to the British Government at the time, and preparations for dealing with the expected German invasion continued until the autumn of 1943.

Sheviock Prepares for Invasion

In 1941, local Civil Defence Committees were formed throughout the country to feed and succour the civilian population in the event of invasion, which then appeared imminent. On 20 August of that year, William Rundle of Pool Farm was nominated as Chairman of the Civil Defence Committee for Sheviock. Meetings were held every other month in the evenings in the schoolroom at the Methodist Chapel in Crafthole. The original members of the committee included Mrs H.L. Coursens, headmistress of Sheviock School, Mrs Eileen Crace of Trewin, Miss Winifred Roberts of Trethill House, and Mrs Elsie Wilson of Lynher Villa. Male members were Edward Callaghan (golf professional and ARP warden) of the Cottage, Crafthole, John Crace (retired Eton schoolmaster) of Trewin, Gerald Crispin (parish clerk, rating officer, and voluntary food organiser for the district) of Carclew, in Crafthole, Steven Grills (farmer and special constable) of Sydenham House, Crafthole, William Grills (farmer) also of the Cottage, Crafthole, Police Sergeant James from St Germans, and Edgar Richards (insurance agent) of Keyham Cottage, Crafthole. Extracts from the minutes of the meetings of the committee are set out in Appendix 3.

The Home Guard

A platoon of the Home Guard was formed at Crafthole. The officer in charge was Lt Rivett, who lived at Blerrick. His sergeant was Clifford Hoskin of Holmleigh in Sheviock village. The platoon's night-time duty was to watch the beaches to prevent secret enemy landings. Hal Whittaker was a member of the four-man unit stationed on Tregantle beach. They worked in shifts of two hours on watch and two hours asleep. Hal remembered being on the beach there on the night of 5-6 June 1944 and hearing the sound of the D-Day invasion of Normandy coming across the Channel.[23] Harold Bersey's unit was stationed on Portwrinkle beach. The whole Home Guard unit paraded once a week or once a fortnight, and possessed a small calibre field gun. William Rundle of Poole Farm was the detachment's quartermaster as well as being chairman of the Civil Defence Committee.[24]

The Auxiliary Coastguards

During the Second World War the auxiliary coastguards manned their watch house day and night (assisted by local, mostly elderly, volunteers). They were armed with

Ross .303 rifles, a Sten gun and a Thompson sub-machine gun (Tommy gun). They made armed arrests on two occasions. In October 1941, two men dressed as Polish officers landed from a small motor boat on the beach below Liscawn. Wilfrid Pengelly, the volunteer-in-charge, armed with a rifle, went to investigate. He questioned the men but was not satisfied with their answers; so he escorted them to a searchlight unit at the top of the cliffs, where he handed them over to a corporal. He in turn took them to an army base at Triffle, where they were interviewed by an officer. Ten weeks later a local man discovered, near the place where the men had landed, a suitcase and cans of petrol and water. The suitcase contained civilian clothes and a map of the coast of Brittany. The men were detained for the rest of the war.

Early on the morning of 30 April 1944, a German bomber was shot down over the sea about two miles south and east of Portwrinkle. Verey lights were seen coming from the scene of the crash. Wilfrid Pengelly informed the police and, armed with a Tommy gun, led the constables down to the beach at Helstor point. The Luftwaffe pilot had swum towards the coast and landed on the Helstor Rock. Pengelly saw him preparing to jump into the water again to swim across the deep gulley to the shore. He fired a shot into the air to make the man stay put. He then helped him cross the gully and handed him over to the waiting policemen.

The Royal Observer Corps at Portwrinkle

The Germans mounted 'hit and run' air raids on South Coast targets from 1942 to 1944. To give warning of these raids, the Royal Observer Corps, a uniformed civilian organisation under the operational control of R.A.F. Fighter Command, set up satellite stations in southern areas, working from dawn till dusk. One of these satellite stations was set up in Portwrinkle. It was in constant communication with the regular 24-hour posts throughout Cornwall, and with Group H.Q. At the end of 1943, Valerie Powell, from Cheshire, a Leading Observer, was put in charge of this post on a full-time basis.[25] She was assisted by three local women, who worked part-time. This was the only all-women post in the Group, so its call sign 'Sugar 4' was appropriate. Valerie recalls her time at Portwrinkle:

> When the post was first set up there was a Mr Botterell there from another full-time post, to whom we had to apply for our uniform. Annoyingly, we had to give clothing coupons in return. Uniform was air-force blue battledress jacket, skirt or trousers, plus a good warm raincoat. We wore a black beret with a circular metal badge showing a standing figure in Elizabethan dress waving a flame from an adjacent bonfire, with ships in the distance. Although universal to the Corps, the badge was particularly appropriate to the South West.[26] Around the edge of the badge was inscribed the motto, 'Forewarned is Forearmed'. On the jacket there was also a circular embroidered badge, showing a pair of wings with 'ROC' in the centre.

> Our duties were to recognise and report on height and direction of aircraft, and also, by a code name, merchant shipping convoys seen. No actual post had been built when I arrived, and until this was remedied we had to share the existing Coastguard hut above the harbour. This caused some concern and apprehension amongst the older residents. A woman – and a young one at that – inside the previously male-only stronghold! The three Pengelly fishermen brothers, Theo, Walter and Wilfrid, were joined by some local older men to share regular duties in the hut.[27] They were able to gauge the correctness of reports, apparently to their satisfaction, using what now seems to be rather primitive gear. Eventually, a brick post was built quite close to the Coastguard building. It was open to the elements, save for a small cupboard-type space for books etc.
>
> On one occasion when I was on duty, I remember that towards dawn I spotted a flare sent up from a distant beach on Whitsand Bay. I alerted Wilf and the others, who set out … to bring in a young German airman whose plane had come down a mile or so offshore. He had swum ashore in his full kit in the night and had waited until first light hoping for rescue. I saw him being marched past my post.
>
> My father … arranged for me to stay with Mrs Edna Davey and her small daughter, Pauline, at 3 Coastguards Cottages, Portwrinkle. Mrs Davey's husband, Alec, was then serving abroad in the army. … I continued to serve with the Corps at my post in Portwrinkle until after VE Day, when the Corps was disbanded [7 May 1945].

U.S. Forces on the Rame Peninsula

In 1943 and 1944, thousands of US troops were encamped on the Rame Peninsula. Tregantle Fort was the Headquarters of the U.S. 29th Infantry Division, where the champion boxers, Joe Louis (heavyweight) and Jackie Wilson (lightweight) were stationed. Bake House in St Germans was also requisitioned by the U.S. Army and there was a large encampment near the house. After the landings, this camp was used to house German prisoners of war. One of the German prisoners, Matt Herbst, married a local girl, Anne Hoskin, and stayed in Cornwall after the war.[28] There was a US Army repair camp in St Germans at the top of Barn Hill, and amphibious vehicles called DUKWS were tested near Heskyn Mill.[29] In Sheviock parish, a pioneer battalion of black US soldiers was encamped in the fields belonging to Pool Farm (on the site of what is now the Memorial Hall and the field below it).

The US troops used to drink at the *New Inn* and also attended the Saturday night 'hops' at the Recreation Club.[30] One of them, Lt William Hitt, married Susan Channings, who lived at Marlborough House in Crafthole. Henry Pryn remembers seeing his Jeep decorated with white ribbons on the day of his wedding. He was killed in Normandy shortly after D-Day, and is commemorated on the war memorial in Sheviock churchyard. Around the time of D-Day, 6 June 1944, all the US troops, who were part of V and VII Corps of General Omar Bradley's 1st US army, departed for the invasion of France.[31] Many were killed during the invasion or the subsequent battles in Normandy.

Life of the Evacuees

The children evacuated from London in 1940, sometimes accompanied by their mother or a female relation, were sent in a group to a particular village, and then collected from the local billeting station by the villagers who had volunteered to take them. Brothers, sisters and cousins often travelled down to the country together, but then found themselves split up once they reached their destination. In the case of Sheviock, on arrival at the village hall at Crafthole, several families found that they were to be separated.[32] But sometimes it was possible to keep the children together.[33] In one case, two related families, called Leather, from Catford in Lewisham, made arrangements to evacuate all seven of their children. The mother of one of the families also came down. Mrs Leather and one of her daughters, Eleanor, lived at 1 Council Cottages with the Worthington family. Three of her other children, George, aged 13, Jean aged eight, and Donald, aged six, lodged with the butcher, Albert Bersey and his wife, Violet, after they had relocated to Moor View, Crafthole. The youngest daughter of the family, Thelma, aged three, lived with her two cousins, Terry and his sister, Vera, at the *New Inn*, Crafthole.

Recollections of an Evacuee

This is Terry Leather's story. It is probably typical of many such recollections, although Terry does seem to have been an unusually happy child. It is told in his own words, recollected 60 years later.[34]

> *Leaving London*
>
> I remember my sister and I being with thousands of other children standing on Paddington station in London with our gas masks in a box strung around our necks and a label pinned to our coats with our names and addresses on. Mother and father were at the station with many more parents to see us off. We were told by mother that we were not to be separated.
>
> After about five hours on the train, we finally arrived at a small countryside station [St Germans]. We were then taken by bus to the village hall at Crafthole where, upon arrival, we were met by the local authorities and people from outlying villages.[35] The people were very kind to us and gave us refreshments. Eventually we were approached by Auntie Hilary (Mrs Lee) and Auntie Loveday (Miss Hearn).[36] They were looking to take in two boys, and when asked if I would like to be one of those boys, I quoted mother's instructions that we were not to be separated. They then agreed to take my sister and me. We were then taken to meet Auntie Hylda and Uncle Bill (Mr and Mrs Hearn).
>
> [They] owned the village pub, the *New Inn*, and the village shop.[37] Uncle Bill was working in the pub and came out to meet us. Later that day we met Uncle Wilfred (Mr Lee). He worked in the dockyard in Devonport. On our first morning I recall my sister and I were upset because we were now missing our Mum and Dad. We were

comforted and assured that everything would be all right, then afterwards we were taken down to the local beach at Portwrinkle. I remember the tide was out and so we were able to go among the rocks looking for crabs and sea creatures in the rock pools. It was great fun and we enjoyed it immensely. From that moment on I was to enjoy a most happy childhood.

Uncle Bill had a very big garden where they grew their own vegetables. There was always lots of work to do in the garden. Uncle Wilfred used to do most of it and I loved helping him. There were also lots of fruit trees and bushes to attend to so we had lots of fresh fruit. There was also a big meadow with an orchard down one end. It was great fun when it was time to pick the apples. … Uncle Bill also kept chickens so we had plenty of fresh eggs and now and again we would have a chicken for dinner. I used to love feeding them and collecting the eggs.

Auntie Hylda was a very good cook. I used to love her Cornish pasties and pasty pie.[38] Auntie Hylda, Auntie Hilary and Auntie Loveday would all help out in the shop which was always quite busy. It was a very busy household, what with the pub to run as well as the shop. My sister Vera used to help out in the kitchen which she enjoyed.

During the war there were lots of soldiers and sailors on duty in that area and they would come to the pub in the evenings for a few beers. Many a tale was told by them about the near misses and the damage that was done by the German planes to Plymouth and Devonport dockyard. Many of the soldiers used to man the ack-ack guns and search-lights high up on top of the Cornish coast, and would tell us about the German planes they had shot down during the night.

227 *Evacuee children, Terry and Vera Leather, having fun on their soapbox with their young cousin, Thelma.*

Out in the Countryside

Auntie Hylda would always take us out in the car for short trips somewhere, because as the seasons came around there was always something to do. … In the summer, we would go picking blackberries and she knew just where to go. We would come home with baskets full. She would then set about making bramble jelly jam. That used to taste so good. I can remember we used to pick wild strawberries, which were very small but lovely and sweet to eat.[39]

In the autumn, Auntie Hylda would take us in the car to a place where we [went] to look for chestnuts. … During the long nights we would roast the chestnuts on a shovel over an open fire. When we had the snowfalls in winter we used to have great fun going out with our toboggans and sliding down the hills near the golf course. … In the summertime, we would get up very early and go out into the fields to collect mushrooms.

Air Raids

I remember how during the blitz of Plymouth and Devonport I used to lie awake at nights listening to the drone of the German planes passing overhead and in the distance the sounds of the bombs exploding. I also remember the sound of the ack-ack guns banging away at the German planes.

The Shipwreck

One night, one of the coastguard men came into the pub for a drink, and told us that a cargo boat had been torpedoed off the Lizard and was trying to make Devonport harbour.[40] The ship was gradually sinking and was reported to be jettisoning its cargo. Unfortunately, it didn't quite make the harbour and sank in Whitsand Bay, near Rame Head. The next morning, many people from the village went beach combing. I can remember lots of large pieces of timber being washed up, together with large tins of paint and various other things. The farmers were out with their horses and long ropes and chains, which were used to haul the timber from the beach up over the cliffs.

I also remember we came across large sacks of flour that had washed up. As they had been in the water, the bags had sealed themselves with a thick crust, which resulted in the flour on the inside being in good condition. Auntie Hylda said we should carry the sacks up above the tide line, then return tomorrow with pillow cases to take some of the flour home, which we did. Everyone in the village then set about making fresh home-made bread.

The End of the War

When the war was over, it was time for my sister and I to go home. I can remember how upset we both were, because we didn't want to go home. We were so attached to the Cornish way of life and didn't know anything else. That was one of the saddest

228 *The Liberty ship,* James Eagan Layne, *which was sunk by the U1195, on 21 March 1945. Some of her cargo, including timber and flour, washed up in Sheviock and was salvaged by the parishioners.*

> times of my young life: to start all over again in a very different lifestyle was very hard indeed. We had become so attached to Auntie Hylda and Uncle Bill. They were as upset as we were.

Vera Leather eventually married and settled in Saltash in Cornwall. Terry Leather lives in Basingstoke, Hampshire. But he still returns to Cornwall regularly to visit the Hearn sisters, and to indulge in his favourite sport of sea fishing. He visited the author to show him some of the places mentioned in his narrative.

The Sheviock Roll of Honour

In 1946, Mrs Colwill and the WI organised a 'Welcome Home' event for returning servicemen and women. At about the same time, Gerald Crispin, the parish clerk, compiled a roll of honour of all connected with the parish who served in HM Forces between 3 September 1939 and 14 August 1945.[41] Fifty-five people from Sheviock served in the armed forces during the Second World War. Six members of the parish were killed in action or died of wounds and their names were added to the war memorial in the churchyard.[42]

PART VIII

Education and Commercial and Social Life

229 *Inscribed tablet commemorating the building of the school at Antony in 1766, in accordance with the will of Sir Coventry Carew.*

Chapter 38

The School in Sheviock and other Local Schools

In the Middle Ages, parents undertook a lot of the teaching of their children. There were schools in cities and large towns, whose teachers were probably laymen.[1] Plympton had a school under the protection of the earl of Devon in 1263. Professor Orme has found evidence for schooling at Launceston probably by 1342.[2] He has also found evidence for a school at Bodmin probably by 1472 and definitely by 1524.[3] Monasteries and parish clergy also sometimes kept schools. The boys at all these schools learned to read and write Latin. In the 12th century, they translated between Latin and French, and, from the 1300s, between Latin and English. If clever enough, and with sufficient funds to maintain themselves, they then entered Oxford or Cambridge to study theology and civil and canon law. They could also study arts or medicine if they did not intend to enter the church. Benedictine monasteries, such as Tavistock Abbey, were supposed to pay for one student a year at university, but they often neglected this duty. Tavistock was fined by the Chapter for not supporting a student in 1423, 1425 and 1426.[4]

Once ordained, a young man might find employment as a chaplain or other official in a noble household. He might also accept a post as a chantry priest, which sometimes required him to teach, as well as say masses for the soul of the founder of the chantry. If he was lucky enough to be appointed rector or vicar of a parish, his duties would include teaching the elements of the Christian faith to his parishioners. In particular, he was required to teach them the *Paternoster*, the *Ave Maria* and the Creed by heart. He was also encouraged by the bishop to train up a boy as a holy-water carrier and to teach him to sing and to read so that he could sing the responses in the church services.

An incumbent might be required to teach the children of the local squire to read and write. He might also be willing to teach these subjects to other local children. One of the most celebrated of these priest-teachers was Gilbert of Sempringham in Lincolnshire (*c.*1083-1189). After obtaining his Master's degree in France, he returned to his native village and began to teach the village children, both boys and girls.[5] One example survives of such local teaching in east Cornwall, right at the end of the Middle Ages. The historian John Hooker recorded that he 'was brought up to school' at Menheniot, where he was taught by the Revd John Moreman, who was instituted as vicar there in 1529.[6] Hooker learned enough from Moreman to go on to Oxford, eventually to study civil law.

Local Schools in Tudor and Stuart Times

After 1556, incumbents were required to have a licence from the bishop in order to teach. Because of this requirement, we know that Walter Arundell, who was appointed rector of Sheviock in 1576, kept a school there – or at least applied to do so. A letter from him, dated 10 April 1602, asks an acquaintance to help him procure the bishop's licence to teach and to preach the reformed religion:[7]

> I pray if you may to procure my Lord's favour to grant unto mee licence to teache and preache in myne owne cure and no where els. I cannot bury my simple talent & as I ought I would be doing that the bloud of my flocke may not be required at my hands/good Mr Mychell get me some comfort herin to healpe me to goe onwarde to thend and I will thanke you & god.[8]

The teaching provided by Walter Arundell may have been no more than basic literacy and the elements of the Christian faith. But two of his own sons went on to Oxford University, so he may also have taught Latin grammar.[9] Probably he wanted to teach local children along with his own, and hence the need for the bishop's licence.

There were also a few schools in nearby towns to which boys could be sent away to learn. As we have seen, there were schools at Plympton, Bodmin and Launceston. Schools are mentioned in Plymouth in 1507 and in Tavistock in about 1530, though both probably had them much earlier.[10] Saltash had a stipendiary priest serving St Nicholas' chapel and teaching at a school there sometime before 1546.[11] The mayoral accounts show that Liskeard had a grammar school in 1574–5, and was paying the schoolmaster £4 a year. The school was held within the precincts of the former castle, which led to a Latin motto being inscribed on the castle wall, *olim Marti, nunc arti* (formerly [used] for war, now for the arts). There was also a famous boarding school at Week St Mary, established between 1506 and 1512 by Dame Thomasine Percival (née Bonaventure), who had been born in Week. She was the widow of the Lord Mayor of London, Sir John Percival. Her school was mentioned approvingly by Richard Carew in 1602.[12]

The number of literate persons in Sheviock grew slowly during the 1500s and 1600s. Factors stimulating the increase in literacy were the Reformation, with its emphasis on the study of the Bible in English, and the increase of trade and commerce. Commerce required literate merchants, and ships' officers able to read charts. Four mariners are recorded in Sheviock in the early 1600s. Three of them, Elias Burne, George Carkeeke, and Robert Hoskins were officers on the *Dayestarr.* Elias Burne and George Carkeeke both lived in Crafthole and both died in the same year, 1633. The fourth was William Harry, who died tragically young in 1626. All these men could have been taught to read and write by the Revd Walter Arundell, who lived until 1622, or could have attended one of the schools mentioned above.

However, the total number of literate people in Sheviock remained small throughout the 1600s. Professional men (such as the scrivener Robert Honney) usually had to be engaged when a written document was needed, such as a will, an inventory of goods, or an account for presentation. Many quite substantial parishioners were obliged to sign documents with a mark, often just a cross, but sometimes a more elaborate sign. An inventory of the goods of John Naunter, a fisherman, made in 1648, was drawn up by a professional person, but Amos Palmer, Daniel Sargent (the Sheviock village innkeeper), and Richard Beare, the three parishioners who valued the goods, were all illiterate and witnessed the document with their individual marks.[13] In 1692, Mathew Stanton, who was a skilled mason with a servant, acknowledged payment for work done on the quay at Porwrinkle, by making his sign, similar to a modern 'hache' mark.[14] The bailiff of the manor, however, Thomas Harvey, was literate and wrote out the wording of the acknowledgement for Stanton to sign. In 1657, Nicholas Hony (who may have been related to the Crafthole scrivener, Robert Honney) founded a school at St Germans and endowed it with land. In 1814, this land was still generating an income of £10 10s.[15]

Another clergyman who taught school locally in the late 1600s was the rector of St John, the Revd Robert Eare. He taught Sir Richard Carew until 1695, when, aged 12, he was considered old enough to be sent away to Winchester College.[16] In 1703, the young Sir Richard died, and his younger brother, William, inherited the baronetcy. From the age of 12, Sir William was a pupil at the grammar school at Plymouth, of which the Revd John Bedford was then headmaster.[17] There both he and his manservant, John Pockard, contracted the smallpox. They recovered with the aid of effective but very expensive medical treatment. In autumn 1704, Sir William entered the school of the Revd Christopher Furneaux in Whitchurch near Tavistock. Furneaux was a graduate and fellow (1680-8) of Exeter College, Oxford.

In 1701, Sir Robert Jeffery, who was born in Landrake, but prospered in London as an East India merchant, endowed a free school at Landrake. He entrusted the governance of the school to the Ironmongers' Company of London, who continue to run it to this day. In 1713, John Buller of Shillingham founded charity schools in Saltash, Liskeard, Looe, Penzance and Grampound. The schools were to teach poor boys to 'read, write, and cast accounts' and to give them religious instruction.[18]

Local Schools in Georgian Times

Sir William Carew's son, Sir Coventry Carew, who died in 1748, left £200 in his will for a school to be built at Antony to teach ten poor children 'either boys or girls' to read and write 'but no further'.[19] The interest on a further sum of £200 was to be used for repairs and for the salary of a 'fit and able person, who hath good Morals' and was a member of the Church of England, to serve as schoolmaster. The school and dwelling for the master were completed in 1766. Sir Coventry enjoined his heirs 'to cloath the Children once during the term of three years … in such sort and manner as other Charity Children are cloathed.' A seating plan prepared for the south gallery of Antony church in 1831 reserved 'Three upper seats [pews] to the School Girls'.

By 1761-2, most of the Sheviock parishioners signing off the churchwardens' accounts were literate. Of four signatories of the accounts that year, just one, William Stevens, was obliged to sign by making his mark. Daughters of the more well-to-do families were also being sent away to school. In 1785, Dr William Borlase, wrote to

230 *The school endowed by Sir Coventry Carew at Antony.*

the young John Bennet, then studying at Cambridge, about the education of his young sisters. Bennet was related to the Wallis family of Trethill and served as curate of Sheviock from 1789 to 1793. 'Your Uncle at Fowey', Borlase wrote, 'has proposed that place for the residence of your sisters; it may perhaps be a little cheaper than Truro, but its … not so convenient for the Teaching the little ones, there not being I'm told so good a school there.'

The National School

A National Society was formed in 1811 to promote 'the education of the poor in the principles of the established church'. The Society gave financial support to elementary schools funded by voluntary subscriptions. It became a condition of attendance at National Schools that the pupils should attend the Sunday services of the local Church of England. A National School was built at Antony in 1822 and another may have been started in Sheviock at about this time.[20] The *West of England Conservative and Plymouth and Devonport Gazette* for 3 July 1850 mentions with approval the musicianship of 'Mr Clark, the schoolmaster of Sheviock'. The 1851 census shows that this was Edward Clarke, aged 22, who is listed as both choirmaster and schoolmaster of what was presumably a National School. Clarke was assisted at the school by a 'pauper', Elizabeth Davey (62) and Harriet Mary Knight (18), who lodged with her at the school house. *Kelly's Post Office Directory* for 1856 and Harrison, Harrod & Co.'s *Directory of Devon and Cornwall* for 1862 list a National School in Sheviock. In 1861, the school house was occupied by William Keast, described as a groom and sexton, his wife, Thomazine, two of their children and a grandchild.

The Methodist School

The Wesleyan Conference had approved a national school building policy in 1833 and recommended the opening of 700 additional primary schools in 1843.[21] A Methodist school was opened in Crafthole sometime between 1843 and 1873. In the latter year, William Petherick was the schoolmaster and his wife, Mary, the schoolmistress. They retired in 1888 and were succeeded by Mrs Lydia Williams, who was a lodger at Trewrickle Farm. Although the schoolroom below the chapel was built to accommodate 150 children, the average attendance was forty. In 1915, the army paid the school trustees £14 11s. 6d. for billeting troops in the schoolroom, and another £3 for damage caused by the soldiers. Electric light was first installed in the schoolroom in 1939.

Sheviock Elementary Church of England School

In 1902, a new Education Act extended state aid to Anglican and Roman Catholic primary schools. In 1903, Major General Sir Reginald Pole Carew made an agreement with his brother, the Revd Gerald Pole Carew, rector of Sheviock, for the Church of

England to lease a building in Sheviock churchtown at a rent of £6 a year.[22] The building was to be used for the elementary education of children 'of a labouring manufacturing and other poorer classes in the ... parish of Sheviocke'.[23] According to the agreement, the head teacher was to be a bona fide member of the Church of England. The school was to be conducted according to the principles of the Incorporated National Society for Promoting the Education of the Poor in the Principles of the Established Church. There were to be four Foundation Managers, consisting of the rector and three other members of the Church of England. Those nominated were: Thomas Hoskin of Crafthole, farmer; Thomas Bersey of Crafthole, butcher; and Stephen Pyne of Sheviock churchtown, carpenter. At a managers' meeting held on 13 November 1903, two other people were added to the committee.[24] They were Colonel J. D. A. Roberts of Trethill, who was named as 'parish manager', and James Hoskin, who was named as 'council manager'.[25] The District clerk was also in attendance to explain a County Council circular relating to managers' duties. The staff consisted of the headmistress, Miss M. E. Hancock, and the school cleaner, Miss Ough.

At the beginning, it was envisaged that the school would close at lunchtime, when all the children would return home to eat. However, early in 1904 the managers instructed the headmistress to allow one of the two schoolrooms to be used at midday by the children who brought their 'dinners' with them. The school holidays were originally the whole month of August, 11 days at Easter and seventeen days at Christmas. Occasionally, special holidays were granted – for example a half holiday on 23 June 1905, a whole day on 30 April 1906, for the purpose of a school 'show day', and a whole day on 10 July 1906 'as a steamer party would take away most of the children'. In 1904, Colonel Roberts asked for the use of the schoolroom at the end of the Christmas holidays so that he could, at his own expense, give a party for the children. This became an annual event for many years.

The boys and girls entered the school each morning through two separate porches. The school day began with prayers and hymn singing. By 1908, the school harmonium was in need of repair. Religious instruction was a key part of the curriculum and in 1907 the school acquired two dozen bibles. This was the Edwardian era, when people prided themselves on the number of countries that came under British rule. In 1908, the school requested the purchase of a map of the British Empire.

The older children were taught by the headmistress, and the infants, housed in a gallery, were taught by an assistant teacher. The first of these was Ann Bray; but in December 1906, some unexplained problem had arisen with regard to her, and she was asked to go. As the minutes coyly record, 'The Chairman explained the difficult situation with regard to the teacher ... to the best of his ability, and the managers approved his action.' In July next year, the managers asked Lily Cole to serve temporarily 'at a nominal salary' in her place. The normal age for infants entering the school was five, but it was tempting for some to enter younger children. In 1911, the managers resolved 'that Henry Ough be asked to keep his son James at home until he has reached his fifth birthday'. The attendance was said to be about sixty in 1910.[26]

Miss Hancock left the school at the end of 1912 and in January 1913 a supplementary teacher was put in charge.[27] In 1914, Miss Louie Trenary, previously headmistress of Zennor School was appointed head. The headship of Miss Trenary, which lasted for 15 years, and is remembered by parishioners alive today, was quite successful in terms of the results achieved by the pupils in their academic studies and very successful in teaching the religious curriculum. Miss Trenary also organised sales of work done by the pupils and thereby contributed to the school funds. But her tenure as headmistress was marred by outbursts of violence.

Her appointment coincided with the outbreak of the First World War. The only written reference to the war in the school records is in 1916, when the managers noted in relation to the assistant teacher that 'Miss Snowdon's resignation was approved, also the temporary assistance of Miss Walters under the present difficult circumstances'. Miss Walters was the daughter of the rector, the Revd Henry J. B. Walters. In fact, life was so difficult that the school managers could not often get a quorum together. In June 1916, only the rector was present and in July of the following year only the rector and William Bennett (the farmer at Tredrossel, who had replaced the late Thomas Hoskin on the committee). In 1918, no minutes at all were kept.

It was not until the end of 1919 that the situation returned to normal, following the institution of the Revd B. L. Lycett as rector. The other managers were Col Roberts, William Bennett, W. Grills, and Henry Ough. A programme of refurbishment was begun, following the dilapidation of the war years. Edith Ough of Cote Cottage was appointed assistant teacher in March 1921, but gave notice in September. Marion Andrew, a young woman of gentle disposition, replaced her in October. She had no previous experience and the school inspector suggested that she spend some time in a good infants' school to gain some. Mr Burden, the District Education Officer, commented, 'I think three weeks will be quite sufficient for this'. Marion Andrew taught the infants at the school for the next ten years. A piano was purchased for the school in 1922.

In July 1923, H.M. Inspector, W. M. Page, reported that

> There are 42 children in the books, 19 of these are in the upper standards taught by the Head Teacher and 23 are infants in Standard I and are taught by the Supplementary ... The infants are kindly managed and the teaching is fairly effective ... Both the teaching and the children's activities are hampered by the presence of an awkward gallery which it would be well to remove.

The local carpenter and undertaker, George May, removed the gallery in the Christmas holidays 1923. The District Education Committee also asked the managers to consider starting a school garden. The managers replied that this was 'quite unnecessary for the children of Sheviocke Village' – nearly all of whom lived on farms or smallholdings. Nevertheless, the managers did introduce a best-kept garden competition for the boys – the gardens being a patch of ground attached to the headmistress's house. The pupils achieved consistently excellent results in religious studies. They competed in an annual prize called the Bishop Phillpotts Prayer Book Prize Examination. In 1928, a sewing machine was purchased.

In October 1925, the first of two allegations of violence committed by Miss Trenary came to the notice of the managers. William Andrew of Crafthole, wrote to them to complain that his daughter, Dora, had come home with her ears all red and bruised. Years later, Dora, who became Mrs Colwill, wrote in the Sheviock parish newsletter that, as a result of the blows, she became very ill. She never went back to Sheviock School, but stayed with her aunt and attended a school at St Budeaux. Although Miss Trenary was reprimanded for her conduct, she did little to mend her ways. In February 1929, Hevan and Mary Higman, who farmed at Trewrickle, felt obliged to keep their children, Ena May and Roy, away from school, and wrote a letter to the

231 *Sheviock School in 1924. Marion Andrew, who taught the infants, stands on the left, with the stern headmistress, Miss Trenary, on the right. The five-year-old Tom Bersey sits in the front row on the right.*

rector explaining the reason. The managers interviewed Miss Trenary, who admitted shaking the child in class but refused all blame for the bruises. No further action was taken, but at this time Miss Trenary applied for and was offered a post on the County unattached staff. She left at the end of October 1929. The reported acts of brutality by her were only a few of the many remembered by the pupils.[28]

Miss Trenary was replaced by Miss Darton, who quickly fell out with the school governors, and especially the Revd Lycett. In 1932, the governors sought to have her removed on the grounds, principally, that she had lost her voice on several occasions, 'which militated against her proper conduct of the school'; that there had been a serious drop in the number of pupils, with some parents preferring to send their children to Torpoint; and lastly that the report of the diocesan inspector was not satisfactory. There had also been a confrontation between her and the Revd Lycett. On one occasion, the headmistress told the monitress (assistant teacher) to bring the infant class to sit with her in the main schoolroom. When Lycett remonstrated with

232 *Sheviock School in 1932. The teachers are Miss Gwen Bersey (left) and Mrs Coursens, the headmistress. The pupils are L to R: Back row: John Gardener, Charlie Sparks, Russell Greenaway, Nicholas Collins, Kenneth Collins, Bert Pengelly, Festant Greenaway. Middle row: Reg. Greenaway, Frances Collins, Joan Lobb, Biddy Bean, Millicent Gardener, Pat Bober, Mary Channings, Sue Channings, Derek Bean; Front row: Henry Pryn, Harold Sparks, Darrel Bean, Eileen Greenaway, unknown, Sheila Channings, Arthur Dawe, David May.*

the headmistress, she said that that was 'a matter for me to decide'. A deputation from the Local Education Authority, led by no less a person than Sir Arthur Quiller-Couch, visited the school. They decided that Lycett was in the wrong and that there was no evidence that the teaching was inefficient. They therefore did not approve the dismissal of the headmistress. By 1933 the number of pupils had dropped to about twenty.

An Evacuee's Recollections of his Schooldays

Terry Leather, a war-time evacuee from London, found the teaching at the school 'limited', but, as he wrote, he had a very happy time there: [29]

> My sister and I … used to go to school in the village of Sheviock, and to get there we had to walk half a mile. Many other evacuees also went to the same school.[30] I remember we used to have lots of fun walking to and fro. There used to be a little tuck shop where we could purchase sweets for a penny near the school.[31]
>
> When we were at school we would go on nature trails. … We used to pick lots of different wild flowers. I can remember the teacher took us all to one of the farms which used to make cider.[32] All the apples were placed on a bed of straw and built like a sandwich within the cider press which was screwed down to crush all the apples. The juice then ran into a big stone trough. It was then tapped into barrels. I can remember we all used to have a little taster.
>
> My schooling was very limited. I remember going home for lunch one day and saying to Uncle Bill, 'This afternoon we have got to do country dancing and dance around the Maypole.' Uncle Bill said, 'I've got better things for you to do at home here, so you can stay home this afternoon to help me.'

One of the teachers at the school in the 1940s was Lois, daughter of Arnold Hoskin and his wife, Mollie. She was appointed temporary head in 1943, and was still working there in 1947. She married Henry (Hal) Whittaker, the engineer in charge of laying the new water mains in Crafthole in 1939 and 1940.

Following the heavy bombing of Bristol, a teacher, Dorothy Stafford, brought a group of evacuee children from there to Crafthole. She lived at the Cottage with the Callaghans and taught the children in Coombe Barn (later the Recreation Club), because the school at Sheviock was full.[33]

In 1947, Sheviock C. of E. School became a 'Voluntary Primary School' and in 1955 it became a 'Civil Parish Controlled School' under the new Education Acts. In June 1966, when the number of pupils in the school had dropped to seven, the pupils were transferred to Antony C. of E. School and Sheviock School was closed.

Chapter 39

Trades and Crafts

Fishing and farming apart, detailed information on the occupations of residents of Sheviock begins only in the 1600s. In 1640, Sir Richard Carew let a cottage and 60 perches of land near to Crafthole to William Reepe of Sheviock, 'weaver'.[1] A lease of property in Sheviock made in the same year between Richard Chubb, a farmer, and Daniell Sargent describes the latter as a 'saylor' – he later became an innkeeper. Wills, though rarely made by poorer people, also sometimes give occupations, such as that made by John Blighe, 'saylor', in 1607. The records of the borough of Crafthole, preserved from the late 1500s, also give information on the occupations of some of the residents. Churchwardens' accounts, which have been preserved from the mid-1700s, contain information about craftsmen who supplied goods or services to the church. The descendants of some of the craftsmen mentioned in these accounts, such as the glaziers, John Andrew and Richard Holman, and the carpenter, Edward Hawkin, are later recorded as farmers. The descendants of others, such as the mason Philip Goard, the blacksmith Henry Davey, and the miller John Clapp, continued to practise the same crafts as their ancestors for several generations. Many tradesmen and craftsmen were also small farmers or involved with the fishing industry in Portwrinkle. We can infer that anyone possessing a lease of a cellar or palace in Portwrinkle was involved with fishing, either as an active fisherman or as an investor in the fishing business. In Crafthole and Portwrinkle, from the Middle Ages until the early 1800s, probably the majority of livelihoods were connected with the sea – many of the young men working as sailors or as fishermen.

But in the parish as a whole, until after the Second World War, agriculture was the biggest employer of labour. We see the first of these labourers enumerated in Domesday Book, though none is named. In the churchwardens' accounts of the 1700s and 1800s, most of the indentures of apprenticeship relate to 'husbandry' (farming). Thus, William Hoyle of St John, aged only nine, was apprenticed to John Stephens, farmer, in 1815, and Robert Collins Geach of Cawsand, aged ten, was apprenticed to the farmer James May, junior, in the following year.

Both men and women worked on the land. In a law case of 1673, one of the witnesses, Ann Bray, testified that she 'hath togeather with severall others beene payed for the making [of hay at Kerslake]'.[2] Her employer was Anthony Blake who also paid her at harvest time to gather up apples. Many back-breaking agricultural jobs were done by women. In April 1731, the 'hind' or farm manager of the Carew estates paid a number of women for 'Harrowing, leasing [releasing] stones etc.' [3] In March the following year, he paid more women for 'gathering stones & picking turneps'. Whereas men were generally paid 1s. a day for agricultural work at this time, the women were paid only 4d. Women also earned money curing pilchards in the 'palaces' at Portwrinkle, but no accounts of payments for this work have survived. Women's occupations are hardly ever mentioned in the manorial leases, except as shopkeepers. Nor do they often appear in the churchwardens' accounts. But their occupations are sometimes given in legal proceedings, when they appear as defendants or witnesses. Presentments in the borough courts of Crafthole show that many women baked bread not only for their own consumption but also for sale.[4] The baking activity of these women accounts for the fact that no-one living in the borough in the 1600s and 1700s was described as a 'baker'. Many young unmarried women worked as servants in the houses of the better-off. In 1815, Catherine Hoyle of St John, aged 12, was apprenticed in 'housewifery' to William Bickford, the miller at Polscoe. Mary Hawkins (b.1821) is recorded working for Catherine Serpell, an innkeeper, in Crafthole in 1841. Mary Pearn, 'Servant Sheviocke Rector' witnessed a lease for the rector in 1881.[5] Laura Pengelly (aged 17) worked as parlour maid for the Littleton family at Trewin in 1901, while her sister, Florence (aged 15), worked in the same household as kitchen maid.[6]

The entries below give many of the trades practised in the parish from the late 1500s to the mid-1800s. The names of fishermen and farmers are not included here, but many of their names can be found in Parts IV and V of this book. The names of some sailors are listed below, and many others will be found in Chapter 16, *The* Dayestarr *and her Crew*. Cross-references to other trades listed in this chapter are indicated by **heavy type**.

Agricultural Implement Makers

John Davey (1814-76) began life as a **blacksmith** in Crafthole, but developed his business into that of an agricultural implement maker. He employed three men in 1861 and 12 in 1871. He developed and patented the 'Excelsior Plough' at a new workshop at Polscoe, on the site of the former Sheviock Mill. At one time, he and his wife lived at Lynher Villa in Crafthole. On his death, he left his business premises, machinery and stock-in-trade at Polscoe to his foreman, William Sleep, who was married to his niece, Ann. Sleep moved the business to Plymouth before 1891.

William Brenton was working as a blacksmith by 1878. He started the firm of William Brenton Ltd, East Cornwall Iron Works, at Polbathic. The firm is described in *Venning's Directory* as 'agricultural implement makers, engineers, millwrights and patentees'. Among many successful products were 'Reliance' drills and sheep racks; cutters for roots, turnips and weeds; hoppers; hay sweeps; manure distributors; lamb shelters and creeps.[7] The firm also made sack trolleys and patented a type of bolt, still to be found in many houses in the parish. William Brenton attended the World Exhibition in Paris in 1889. The company won many prizes at agricultural shows for its products, including a gold medal for the Reliance drill. After a century in business, Brentons closed in December 1979.

Agricultural Labourers

From the earliest times, more people were employed doing agricultural labour than any other work, but few names are recorded. The census shows that, in 1841, 54 men and women were employed as agricultural labourers out of a total population (in 1847) of 567. Of these, two were women living in Crafthole: Mary Westlake (b.1796) was a widow with two young children; another, Susanna Bickford (b.1781), also took in lodgers to make ends meet. Richard Parsons (b.1816), was an agricultural labourer living in Crafthole with his wife, Sarah, in 1834.[8]

233 *A horse-drawn spreading machine, early 1900s, manufactured by William Brenton Ltd of Polbathic.*

Bakers

Because many village women baked and sold bread, no specialist bakers appear in the records until the 19th century. In 1841, Hester Littleton (b.1811), who lived in Portwrinkle with her two young children, and was probably a widow, gave her occupation as 'baker'. Nathaniel Bolt (b.1841) was a baker and confectioner living in Polbathic in 1891.

Bargemen (See also **Carriers**, below)

Bargemen were operating in the Tamar-Lynher estuary and the adjacent coastal waters from at least the 1300s. They delivered sand for 'sweetening' the soil of agricultural land, and also conveyed heavy building materials such as stone, timber, and slate. The earliest-known bargeman resident in Sheviock was one 'Chark', a neighbour of Richard Carew the younger who lived in the parish before 1620. William Charke (*sic*), who may have been his father, was entered on Henry VIII's muster roll for the parish in 1569. Members of the Grills family of Sheviock and St Germans were also occupied as bargemen from the early 1700s to 1871. In 1841, Thomas Stephens, bargeman, aged 50, was living at Polbathic with his wife, Jane, and two children.

234 *The sailing barge,* Shamrock *(built 1899), moored next to the lime kilns at Cotehele Quay. Barges like this delivered lime and other products to farms along the Tamar estuary from the 1200s to the early 1900s.*

Blacksmiths

In 1698, William Condy and his wife let a cottage and herb garden in Crafthole to Thomas Waite, 'blacksmith'.[9] It stood on the south side of the main road, with the house of Henry Richards on the east, and the 'shopp heretofore of one John Earle Blacksmyth' on the west. The rent was 8s. The premises had previously been let to Anthony Wallis, a **mariner**. Waite was able to read and write. In 1705, the Condys let another cottage in Crafthole to Waite at a rent of 6s.[10] In 1710, the Condys granted Waite a new lease of: (1) the 'Cottage house, and the Smiths-Shopp and Garden' commonly called 'Roaches Tenement' and (2) the cottage that had been in the possession of Mary Sargeant.[11] Simon Waite succeeded his father as blacksmith. In 1730, he sold the freehold to Sir William Carew, but leased it back again.[12] In 1745, Mary Sargent's former premises were let to John Williams, blacksmith (age 35).[13]

Matthew Bartlett was paid 5s. by the churchwardens in 1760 for 'repairing the bells' and another 9s. 2d. in 1761 'for smith's work [on the] bells'. Bartlett's mother, Deborah, lived in the former Church House in Sheviock churchtown. Bartlett appears in the accounts in most years until 1789. In addition to his work on the bells, he mended the leads on the church roof in 1779-80 and 1786-7. He also supplied 'rag nails' (7d. for 2 doz.) in 1762 and 1780-1 and 'rigge [ridge] nails' in 1775-6. The surveyors of highways paid him for work done at Easter 1767, October 1768, and in 1769. The work presumably related to repairs to the road plough and to picks and shovels. The surveyors of highways paid James Prin 5s. 3½d. for blacksmith's work in September 1768 and 6s. 4d. for work done in 1769.[14] In 1774-5, the churchwardens paid him and his son, James, 1s. 1d. for one day's work repairing the 'hupe [i.e. hoop] of ye little bell'. See also **Carpenters** below.

The churchwardens paid Henry Davey (1746-1825) 1s. 6d. 'for iron work on the bells' in 1780-1.[15] He carried out further work on the bells or did other unspecified ironwork in each year from 1788-9 to 1795-6. His son, Henry (1775-1851), was working in Crafthole in 1841.[16] Henry Davey junior was paid 1s. 6d. for work in 1800-1 and 6s. 1d. for work in 1813-14. He sold the church a new hammer and nails for 2s. 9d. in 1821-2. He repaired a lock (for 1s.) and sold a new chisel to the church (for 3d.) in 1824-5. John Davey (1814-76), Henry's son, continued the blacksmith's shop in Crafthole, but also expanded into other premises as an **Agricultural Implement Maker**.[17] Henry and his father were also the last paid parish clerks.

In 1791, Reginald Pole Carew let a cottage and garden that stood near the corner of West Lane and the road to St Germans to Joseph Bickford (b.1761) of St Germans, blacksmith.[18] It is probably the house marked 'Warrens' on the 1825 map of Lord Clinton's property, for it had once been occupied by William Warren. The rent was 8s. Bickford was illiterate. During the period 1802-3 to 1811-12, he was the main contractor to the church for smith's work and was the brother of the miller at Polscoe, Jonathan Bickford (b.1764).[19] See also for members of this family, Chapter 42, *Mills and Millers*.

In 1815-16, Robert Bath did work for the church valued at 2s. 7d. This included sharpening an implement and mending the key of the church. In the following year he repaired the church lock for 2s. In 1820-1, he supplied a lightning conductor for the church.[20] He was born in Sheviock and lived in Crafthole. By 1851, when he was 64, he described himself as retired.

The family of Rowe did both blacksmith's work and carpentry work for the church. In 1820-1, John Rowe was paid £1 3s. for a new vane. Richard Hoskin (b.1811) was described as a blacksmith living in Polbathic in the 1841 census. He is also listed as such in *Kelly's Post Office Directory* (1856) and Harrison, Harrod & Co.'s *Postal Directory* (1862).

Brick Makers

The 1861 census first mentions the existence of a brickworks in Sheviock. The contractors who operated the site were Henry Cullis, from Chippenham, aged 39, and his brother William (38). William lived with his wife and son in Crafthole. The works employed more than a dozen mostly skilled men, brought in from elsewhere. There was apparently accommodation for most of the men at the works. Only the 15-year-old George Bonney came from Sheviock. Harrison, Harrod & Co.'s *Postal Directory* for 1862 lists the brick works of Messrs. 'Harvey and Roach' as being within Sheviock. The works were located on land at Haye Farm to the east of the farm house. The brickworks may have been needed in connection with the forts at Scraesdon and Tregantle, which were constructed between 1858 and 1865.

Butchers

In March 1705, Henry Richards, husbandman, let, and then sold, half of a property in Crafthole to Mark Barrett, butcher, for £27.[21] The witnesses were Jane Jenkyn, Emanuell Martin and Anthony Blake. Blake signed in a most beautiful hand, and had clearly been to a good school.[22] The property stood on the south side of the main road through Crafthole. Henry Richards had purchased it from the Kingsand baulker (rope maker), Naphtaly Salmon and his wife, Peternell. There was a field called Barrett's Park in Trethill.

In 1774, Reginald Pole Carew leased to John Tawe (also Taw) (b.1718) of St Germans, butcher, the 'dwelling house garden and premises situate at Crafthole being the corner house between the Saint Germans and Looe Roads'.[23] The house, which was also his butcher's shop, stood in what is now the eastern corner of the garden of Lynher Villa. It had formerly been let to the **blacksmith**, John Williams. The lease was on Taw's own life and those of his two daughters, Elizabeth (19) and Jane (16). The rent was 6s. The house to the west had been let to the yeoman, John Searle, and his wife, Mary, in 1739, at a rent of 8s.[24] See also for the Taw family, Chapter 42, *Mills and Millers*.

John Landry (1777-1853), butcher, originally of St Germans, married Ann Clinnick of Sheviock whose parents had leased the old Church House from Reginald Pole Carew. John Landry continued to occupy Church House after his marriage and presumably ran his butchery business from there. He ceased that business when he became an innkeeper. See further Chapter 41, *Inns and Innkeepers*. Joseph Landry (b.1811) lived and worked as a butcher in Crafthole in 1841.

Before the Second World War, Albert and Violet Bersey ran a butcher's shop from their premises at High House (rebuilt as High Hopes). It was destroyed by a German mine in 1940.[25]

Carpenters

In 1679, William and Frances Condy and Benjamin Sparkman, all of Tavistock, granted a building lease to Israell Pope of Crafthole, carpenter.[26] Israell could read and write. The new cottage stood on the site of the present Post Office. A little cote house was attached to it on its western side, once in the possession of Mary Pope. The lives named were Israell and Richard Pope, Israell's sister, Grace, and his eldest son, also called Israell. The rent was 12s. Richard Pope was described as a 'husbandman' in the conveyance of the freehold to Sir William Carew in 1711.[27] Israell Pope junior was described as a 'joyner' in a new lease of the property granted to him in 1722 on the lives of his daughters Bridget (age 35) and Grace (age 33).[28] In 1706, William and Frances Condy let a dwelling house and 'splatt of ground' in Crafthole to 'Richard Pope of Crafthole carpenter'.[29] The lease was on the lives of Richard's son, Esdras, and his daughters, Patience and Jane. The rent was 2s. per annum. Pope signed with his mark. A witness was 'John Andrew'.

The carpenter, Edward Hawkins (also spelled Hawkin, Hawking and Hawkings), of Crafthole, was married to Frances, daughter of Gilbert Stark, a **thatcher**. According to the churchwardens' accounts, Hawkins was paid 5s. in 1760 'for repairing the bells'. He was paid a little more in 1761 'for carpenter's work on the bells', and he did similar work in the following year. In 1768, Hawkins was paid 9d. 'for putin [*sic*] in of two seats and mending the communion taable'. The unusual spelling of 'table' accurately reflected the local pronunciation.

In 1764, James Prin (also spelled Pryn), who lived in Crafthole, joined Hawkins and the two were the principal carpenters employed by the churchwardens from that year until 1786.[30] He married Joan, the second daughter of the innkeepers, William and Ann Lord, in 1771. In 1764, the sum of £2 7s. 6d. was paid to Prin for '30 deal boards'. James Prin's son, another James, began to assist him with his work in 1771-2. In 1769-70, Prin was paid 9d. for mending the churchyard gate. In 1774-5, he was paid a further 3d. for 'staven the church lader'. He was also a blacksmith and, in 1774-5, he and his boy were paid 1s. 1d. for one day's work repairing the 'hupe [i.e. hoop] of ye little bell'. See also **Blacksmiths** and **Sailors**.

From 1780 until 1811, the carpenter principally employed by the churchwardens was John Billing, who was paid 8s. 8d. in 1780-1 'for repairing the frames of the bells' and another shilling 'for puting barrs to the window'. In 1782-3, he was paid £2 5s. This fairly large sum may have been for putting up a western gallery in the church (see **Timber Suppliers** below). Thereafter, he was paid various lesser sums in each year from 1788-9 to 1797-8. In 1794, Robert Billing was paid £1 7s. 6d. 'by bill for boards & laths'. This was a year when the mason, Philip Goard, had to do a lot of work replacing tiles on the roof. John Billing continued to be employed on small jobs in most years until 1803-4. In 1804-5, another large sum was paid 'To John Billin's bill' and a further £2 17s. 3d. 'To John Billins the timber merchant' – presumably the timber merchant's bill passed on by Billing. In 1810-11, the roof must have been completely renewed because the massive amount of £157 18s. and a halfpenny was paid 'to Mr Billing as per bill of carpenter's work'. The tradition of carpentry lasted a long time in the family. Samuel Billing (b.1796) was listed as a carpenter in Crafthole in 1841 and 1862.[31]

Edward Moon appears in the churchwardens' accounts doing small jobs as a carpenter between 1800-1 and 1810-11. In 1809-10, he was paid the quite large sum of £8 0s. 6d., no doubt in connection with the massive repair job on the roof, for which John Billing was the main contractor. He also did glazier's work in 1807-8 (see **Glaziers** below). The William Moon who was paid £5 'for teaching the singing' in 1790-1 and the straw bonnet maker, Elizabeth Moon (b.1816) may have been related to Edward.[32]

The family of Rowe did both carpentry work and **blacksmith**'s work for the church. In 1859-60 Thomas Rowe was paid £2 3s. 'for timbers and labour'. He submitted another bill in 1862-3.

In the early 1900s, Stephen Pyne, who lived in Sheviock churchtown, worked as a carpenter and undertaker. He was one of the first managers of Sheviock C. of E. School. George May (b.1866), who lived at 3 the Terrace, Sheviock, married into the family and entered the business, building a workshop on top of the old village pound in Sheviock. The business was continued by his son, Walter, whose stationery described him as 'carpenter, wheelwright, funeral director, house decorator, etc.' Among other activities, he carried out repairs on the Chalet at Portwrinkle in 1947.

Carriers

Building materials were generally heavy – rags and slates from the quarries; lathes, deal boards and balks of timber from the timber merchants – and often they had to be transported a considerable distance. Sometimes the contractor delivered the goods himself, but more often separate carriers were employed. When the materials were delivered by barge from Plymouth or elsewhere to one of the quays in the parish, someone – usually a different person – had to be paid to harness a horse or two to drag the materials from the quay to the place where the materials were required. George's Quay at the end of George's Lane was used to deliver building materials for the church. In 1762, the sexton, William Roach, was paid 9d. 'for carrying 6 bushells of lime from George's House', 3d. 'for sand', and 1s. 6d. 'for carrying 1000 slate & [half] dozen of raggs from George's House'. He was paid another 1s. 'for his horse going to Tilland Quarry' (a mile or so north of Tideford).

In 1756, sums of 8s. 4d. and 15s. were paid to an unnamed carrier 'to carting lime & sand stones from Bedford under Cliff etc'. In 1769-70, Samuel Jane was paid 8s. 3d. for 'carrying 3 thousand of slates'. The high cost again indicates that the slate must have travelled some distance. In 1767-8, William Shilling was paid 3s. for 'carrying of 3 thousand of slate' and William Warren was paid the same amount for 'fetching of raggs'.[33]

In 1819-20, John Andrew was paid 2s. 'for bringing the stone in the boat' – probably from Devonport to George's Quay. In 1821-2, James Johns was paid 3s. 'for the water carriage' of slate supplied by Mr Rickard and, in 1823-4, he was paid 6s. for the carriage of slate. Members of the Rickard family were involved in quarries and lime kilns in various parts of the Tamar valley. In the following year, Andrew Johns was paid 9s. for the carriage of slate and rags and another 5s. for drawing it 'from the water to the church'.[34]

Coopers

The development of the fishing industry beginning in the tenth century caused a demand for wooden casks in which to store and carry pickled or salted fish.[35] It is estimated that upwards of 20,000 hogsheads were required each season. Demand was further increased by the growth of cider-making in the 16th century.

In 1603, John Harry, yeoman, sold two plots of land in Crafthole to William Jeffery or Gefferie 'couper'.[36] In 1632, Richard Mitchell, **farrier**, was fined a shilling for making a pile of dung in front of the 'inn of William Jeoffrey'. Jeffery was therefore an innkeeper as well as a cooper. The two trades were highly compatible. Jeffery had a daughter, called Agnes, later Mrs Coombe.[37] Jeffery also appears to have had a son, also called William, who married Grace.[38] Their son, another William (died before 1716), did not learn the cooper's trade, but became a **sailor** or **mariner**.

In 1610, Richard Avery, gentleman, of St Germans granted another lease to Jeffery of one quarter of a tenement near the town well at the top of Well Lane.[39] This tenement was described in a conveyance of 1716 as 'two orchards ... commonly called the higher and lower orchards ... in Crafthole Coombe'.[40] It had previously been attached to the village tavern, which had been taken over by Jeffery. Robert Honney, **scrivener**, and Amos Bone of Sheviock acted as agents for Avery.

In 1715, Sir William Carew let a house and palace in Portwrinkle to John Dyer, cooper, for 9s.[41] The lives named were his own and those of Mary, his wife, and his son, John. The premises had formerly been in the tenure of David Reed and Hugh Hooper, deceased, so they, too, may have been coopers. In 1741, he also leased to Dyer the field called Britton.[42] Dyer was also an active fisherman.[43]

In 1729, Sir William let two fields to the west of Portwrinkle called North Down and Monk's Meadow, and also another meadow, to the cooper, 'William Michell'.[44] The rent was 6s. 5½d. The lives named were those of his son William (age 29), John Pope, son of Amos Pope, deceased, and Mary, daughter of John Husband of St Neot.

Cordwainers (Leatherworkers)

The term 'cordwainer' derives from the Spanish city of Cordova (Cordoba), famed for its leatherwork. Cordwainers undertook all kinds of leatherwork, in particular, in an agricultural and fishing community like Sheviock, the leather traces and harnesses for horses and the leather sleeves for oars. They also made shoes.

George, the son of 'Peeter Jeffery of Sheviock Cordwainer', was named as a life on a lease of 1648.[45] The lease was for the ground in Sheviock woods on which George Winnacott built his house.

Robert Hancock (b.1833), cordwainer, rented a dwelling house and garden containing about 22 land yards on the south side of the road running east and west through Crafthole in 1865.[46] The rent was £2 4s. Messrs Kelly and Westlake occupied the house next to it on the east side. Hancock also rented an orchard in the Coombes. He was one of the trustees for the building of the new Methodist chapel in Crafthole in 1862 and 1867. His wife, Emma Mullis Hancock (b.1816), was probably a granddaughter of the Methodist, Elizabeth Mullis. In 1871, Robert erected three dwelling houses on a 42-yard plot of ground between his house and that formerly occupied by Kelly and Westlake (and later by William Pengelly).[47] See further, **Shoemakers**.

Engineers (See **Agricultural Implement Makers**)

Farriers (See also) **Blacksmiths**

A farrier is a shoeing-smith – a blacksmith who specialises in shoeing horses. Crafthole, being on the main road from Cremyll to Liskeard, and also at the heart of an agricultural parish, is likely to have had farriers in residence from the tenth century until the advent of the petrol engine. In 1601, John Smyth of Liscawn let houses and lands in Crafthole to John Mychell, farrier, and Richard Mychell 'son of the said John'.[48] The rent was probably 6s. 8d. At a court held in April 1619, Richard Mitchell confessed to digging up the street (probably Well Lane) to divert the stream of water. In 1632, he was fined a shilling for making a pile of dung in front of the inn of William Jeoffrey, a **cooper**. In 1841, William Trevan, farrier (1777-1846), was living in Sheviock village with his wife, Jane.

Glaziers

Ralph Harry of Tiverton, who is famed for his work at St Neot's church, may have been the glazier of the original late 15th-century windows in the north aisle of St Mary's church. His employer and patron was the marquis of Exeter, who was also the lord of Sheviock manor. Except for one small image of the Virgin Mary, these windows were destroyed either at the Reformation or during the Civil War. Throughout the 1700s, the church windows were repaired in nearly every year. As the glaziers were local men, one may assume that they supplied plain glass. The first glazier mentioned by name is John Andrew. His name appears in the churchwardens' accounts intermittently, though often every year, from 1756 to 1797. In most years, to judge by the small sums paid to him, he was engaged on minor repairs to the windows. For example, he was paid 6s. 3d. in 1756; 13s. 10d. in 1769-70; and 5s. 6d. in 1773-4. However, more extensive work was done in 1761, 1764 and 1772-3, when each of his bills came to more than a pound. The John Andrew who was carrying slate by water in 1819-20 may have been a descendant (see **Carriers** above).

In just one year, 1766-7, the name of 'Richard Holman the glazier' appears, when he was paid 12s. 6d. In 1780-1, the churchwardens paid to an unnamed glazier £4 1s, the largest sum recorded to date. In 1785-6, they paid a glazier £2 0s. 6d. In 1796-7, money was paid 'To the glazer [*sic*] for repairing the church windows' and a further sum of 2s. was paid 'To meat & liquer [*sic*] for the glazer'.

In 1783-4, the name of John Chubb appears in the accounts, when he was paid £1 0s. 6d. He appears again in 1790-1 ('To Mr John Chubb for glass work 7s') and 1794-5 ('To Mr John Chubb by bill for glass work 14s'). Edward Moon, who earned most of his living as a **carpenter** (see above), was paid the large sum of £13 12s. 4d. in 1807-8 'as per bill, glazier's work'.

Helliers

'Hellier' is an Old English word for someone who lays slates or tiles. In 1707, Robert Harry, yeoman, let certain premises in Crafthole to 'David Pepperell, helliar'.[49] Pepperell also had a lease for 900 years of land on the south side of the main road through Crafthole.[50] The property stood to the east of Mrs Mullis's house. In 1711, he sold the lease to a gentleman named Hawkins Beere. A sailor on the *Dayestarr* in 1626 was named Thomas Peperel. He may have been an ancestor. Three members of the Peperel family were shown in Bagg's survey of shipping as coming from Dartmouth.

Innkeepers (See Chapter 41, *Inns and Innkeepers*)

Labourers
From 1764 to 1784, the churchwardens paid small sums, at a rate of 1s. per day, to Edward Carlyon for work about the church and churchyard. In 1764-5, he was paid 1s. for assisting the **mason**, Philip Goard. In 1780-1, he was paid 2s. 'for putting reed on the church'. In 1783-4, he was paid his shilling 'for making a road in the churchyard'. In 1823, Reginald Pole Carew let a dwelling house and two orchards 'commonly called the Higher and Lower Orchard otherwise Jeffery's Orchards' to James Keast (b.1797), labourer.[51] It had lately been in the occupation of Richard Keast, perhaps his father. The rent was £2 2s. and the lease was on the lives of himself, his sister Ann (age 28) and his brother, William (18). William Waddleton, labourer, leased a dwelling house, garden and orchard in Crafthole in 1824.[52] The rent was £4 10s. He may have come from Stoke Damerell, where his brother, John, lived.

Lime Burners
Since Roman times, burnt lime has been used to make the lime mortar used in construction work. A charter of Tavistock Abbey dating from 1230 refers to a 'furnace' at Morwelham Quay, and it has been suggested that this may have been a lime kiln.[53] In liquid form, lime wash or whitewash has been used for hundreds of years to paint the insides and outsides of buildings, especially those that could become contaminated, such as pantries, privies, or pigsties. When roofs were slated, lime was also used on the underside of the slates to help secure them, a process called 'torching'.[54] In the context of the church, lime would have been used for construction work and, after the Reformation, for whitewashing the interior of the church and for torching the roof tiles. In 1810-11, for example, the churchwardens of Sheviock paid a Mr Betesworth the sum of £1 17s. 6d. 'for mixing the lime'.

Lime was also used intensively on the land to increase fertility. The limestone was imported in barges from the Cattedown quarries near Plymouth. The barges unloaded the stone at specially-constructed quays, where lime kilns were erected to burn the lime, thus reducing it to the state required for agricultural or building purposes. In Sheviock, two of these quays and limekilns are still extant on private land. One is in the garden of Polgreen in Polbathic.[55] The lime burners' cottages connected with this kiln also survive to the west of the kiln. This kiln was probably constructed in the early 1700s. The other, obscured by trees, is at Sconner, and is referred to in a lease of 1696. The kiln at Sconner is shown on Thomas Pride's map of the manor of Sheviock made in 1775 and the field in which it stands is called Kiln Parks.

The first reference suggesting that lime was being burned in the parish is in the hearth tax return of 1664. The taxpayer was Henry Odiorne, who was assessed for two hearths. According to the collector, Henry 'returned two short whereof one is a kiln'. Henry Odiorne was tenant of the agricultural holding of Haye in 1689-90 (at a rent of £1 16s.).[56] He was reeve of the manor in 1690. Henry was no longer tenant in 1691.

In 1696, Dame Mary Carew and other trustees of her late husband, John Carew, let 'all that Messuage and Tenement & Lime-Kill [*sic*] ... called ... Skonner' to John Dodridge of Tideford, yeoman. The consideration was the hefty sum of £550, payable in three instalments. The rent was 53s. 4d. plus two capons or 2s. According to a new lease issued in the following year, the premises had been 'late in the tenure of John Wallis Gentleman'.[57] Wallis was the farmer at Sconner.

In 1789-90, the churchwardens paid 2s. to 'Mr Short Peter for lime & carriage'; in 1790-1, they paid him 4s. 'for three bushels of lime and carriage'; and, in 1794-5, they paid him 11s. 'for six bushells of lime and carriage'.[58] He seems to have occupied the limekilns at Polbathic. Thomas Peter was rated for a tenement at Polbathic in 1809-10 and 1820-1. William Tapson, who also worked the limekiln at St Germans Quay *c.*1840, was rated for the Polbathic limekilns from 1858 to 1860. Mr Keast was rated for them in 1861. In 1860-1, the churchwardens paid him 5s. for five bushels of lime and a further 1s. 3d. for carriage. William Keast had operated the limekiln at Morvah Quay, Tideford from 1791. William Barnett was a limeburner living in Polbathic in 1861. The limekilns and their associated quays continued in operation until the early 1900s.

Masons (*see* also Hellyers)

In 1692, Matthew Stanton (Stonton or Stenton), a stonemason, gave a receipt to Thomas Harvey, the bailiff of Sheviock manor, for 3s. 8d. 'for three dayes work for my selfe and my sarvent, on ye key at port wrinkle.'[59] In 1715, Thomas Stanton, together with his son, Thomas junior, and John Stanton and Thomas Bray spent a total of 10½ days erecting a new bollard at the quay.

Amos Tinney, mason, leased the property that had been in the possession of David Pepperel, hellier, from the heirs of the Gennys family in 1751.[60] The property was situated on the south side of the main road through Crafthole.[61]

For about one hundred years – from 1755 until 1858 – the name of Philip Goard appears more frequently than any other in the list of masons entered in the Sheviock churchwardens' accounts. The entry for 1764-5 'Paid Philip Goard & his son' shows that father and son both worked in the trade. They were both called Philip. At the end of the period, the name of James Goard replaces that of Philip. Philip Goard first appears in the accounts in 1755, when he received 4s. for unspecified work. Judging by the frequent payments for slates, he spent most of his time working on the church roof. For work of such a nature masons often work with an assistant, and there are instances in the accounts of the employment of two masons on the same job. For example, Goard worked with John Spiller in 1761-2. The largest payments to Goard were in 1756 (£4 15s. 9d.); 1794-5 (£4 5s. 6d.); 1798-9 (£4 6s. 10d.); 1801-2 (£5 6s.); 1804-5 (three bills totalling £8 8s. 11d.) and 1809-10 (£4 4s.). But not many years went by without the Goards being employed on the roof on some task or other. Substantial quantities of roofing materials were purchased throughout this period. For example, in 1762-3 (1,000 slates); 1765-6 (2,000 slates); 1767-8 (seven sheaves of reed, 800 lathes, 9,000 slates); 1769-70 (1,000 lathes, 3,000 slates); 1772-3 (1,000 lathes, 3,000 slates); 1780-1 (two bundles of lathes, seven sheaves of reed, slates to the value of £2 18s. 6d. – perhaps 7,300 – see **Slate and Ragstone Suppliers** below) and so on. The quantities of slate purchased not only reveal the force of the gales that were battering the church, but also suggest that the roofing timbers were nearing the end of their natural life. The replacement of those timbers in 1810-11 prevented the chance of a disaster. The roof of the Dawney's barn, perhaps originally constructed at the same time, collapsed in 1837, nearly killing some farm workers. Philip Goard, was also responsible for 'Fixing the Guide post and for Repairs of the New Quay' in Portwrinkle in *c.*1792. He was paid 8s. 5½d. In 1775, Philip Goard married Jane, the youngest daughter of the innkeepers, William and Ann Lord.

John Spiller first appears in the accounts in 1761 when he worked as a mason with Goard. He next appears in 1766-7, when he was paid £1 1s. 9d. In 1767-8, he worked with William Francis and in the following year with John Ford, when together they were paid £4 5s. 7d. In 1768-9, Spiller was paid 1s. 6d. 'for covering a grave'. In 1772-3, he submitted three bills totalling £5 12s. 4d. He is last mentioned by name in 1778-9. See also for Spiller, Chapter 41, *Inns and Innkeepers* and Appendix 1, *Families*.

In 1735, William Ford of Sheviock, 'mason', leased the 'messuage ... in Crafthole formerly ... in the possession of one Joseph Prin and ... lately in the possession of Jane Sunn now deceased'.[62] The rent was 4s. The lives named were his wife, Patience and his daughter, Joan. John Ford, mason, did work on the church with John Spiller in 1768-9.

In 1810-11, the hefty sum of £72 0s. 6d. was paid 'To Mr Betesworth as per bill of mason's and hellier's work'. This was the year when the church roof was renewed (see also **Carpenters** above). He was paid a further sum of £1 17s. 6d. 'for mixing the lime'.[63]

Millers (See Chapter 42, *Mills and Millers*)

Milliners and Bonnet Makers

In the 1841 census, Elizabeth Moon (b.1816) is listed as a straw bonnet maker and Ann Hole (b.1821) is listed as a milliner. Both lived in Crafthole.

Mole Catchers

James Giddy senior, then aged 82, avowed the useful occupation of mole catcher in the 1861 census.

Potters

In the Middle Ages, St Germans was a famous centre for making pottery, and several pieces are preserved in the museum of the Royal Institution of Cornwall in Truro. Pottery was still being made there in the 18th century. William Bond of Earth let some land in Newport Street, St Germans, to 'Nicholas Bennett of St Germans potter' in 1637; and 'Nicholas Bennett junior, potter' let a tenement in that street to a spinster of St Germans in 1665.[64] Sheviock had a pottery in 1856, perhaps in Polbathic.[65] The manager was William Willmore.

Plumbers

In 1780-1, Edward Philp was paid 3s. 'for mending the lead' of the church. In 1793-4, he was paid 11s. 'for repairing the leads of the church'. In the same year 3s. was expended on 'meat and licker [*sic*] for Mr Philps sons' and another 8d. 'to wood for heating their irons'.

Sailors

In 1601, John Smyth of Liscawn let a house and land in the borough of Crafthole to Richard Pryn of the parish of Sheviock, 'sailor'. The rent would appear to have been 6s. 8d. John Blighe made a will in 1607, in which he described himself as a 'saylor intending by the grace of god a voyage at sea'. He died on the voyage. A lease of premises in Sheviock to Daniell Sargent in 1639, describes him as a sailor.[66] However, he changed trades to become an innkeeper. Alnutt Pryn of Sheviock, 'saylor', rented a 'cellar, pallace and courtlage' in Portwrinkle in 1646.[67] In 1710, William Condy the elder, and his son, William, let certain premises in Crafthole to Anthony Wallis of Crafthole, sailor.[68] William Jeffery, son of William and Grace Jeffery, became a sailor, rather than entering the cooperage and inn-keeping trades of his grandfather and father.[69] See also Chapter 16, *The* Dayestarr *and her Crew*.

Salters

Until the mid-1100s, the salt used to cure fish caught along the coasts and estuaries of the South West was produced at local saltings. However, with the marriage of Henry II to Eleanor of Aquitaine in 1152, the salt used in the curing process came largely from the productive salt pans of the northern part of the Bay of Biscay. There the salters were able to use the warmth of the sun to evaporate the water, rather than burn fuel to do so. Bay salt was therefore produced much more cheaply than English salt. As a result of the Napoleonic Wars, there was a revival of salt-making in the South West in the late 1700s and early 1800s. In Sheviock, at the surprisingly late date of 1833, the miller, William Coombe, took a lease on the mud-flat at the head of Trethill Creek apparently to create a salt-pan. See further, 'Denny Bowl Mill' in Chapter 42, *Mills and Millers*.

Scriveners

A scrivener performed many of the functions of the modern solicitor. Until the 1700s, a high proportion of the parishioners were illiterate, so the scrivener was engaged whenever some transaction had to be recorded in writing. From 1603 to 1640, Robert Honney was the most active scrivener in the parish.[70] He rented properties in Crafthole and Portwrinkle and was a juror in the borough court in 1629, 1632, 1633, 1635-1637, and 1640. See further Chapters 11 to 13 in Part III, *Crafthole*.

Sextons (See under 'The Church Officials' in Chapter 30, *Church Administration after 1534*)

Shoemakers (also called **Cordwainers**)

Samuel Drew was apprenticed to a shoemaker in Crafthole in 1775, according to an account written by his son. During this period, Drew became involved with other residents of Crafthole in smuggling. He later achieved fame as a Methodist preacher and author, becoming known as 'the Cornish metaphysician'.[71]

Nicholas Cole (b.1771) was a shoemaker living in Crafthole in 1841. Thomas Williams was a shoemaker living in Polbathic in 1841.

In 1834, Thomas Leane, shoemaker, then aged 26, rented a dwelling house and garden in Crafthole on the lives of himself, his wife Jenny, 25, and son, Felix, aged one.[72] The rent was £1 10s. The house stood at the corner of West Lane and the road to Looe. Thomas Giddy (b.1811) was described as a shoemaker in the 1841 census. John Cock (b.1811), who lived in Crafthole, was also a shoemaker.

Shops and Shopkeepers

Although purpose-built shops in towns have a long history, going right back to classical times, in villages, craftsmen and farmers would often simply sell from their homes or workshops goods that they produced as a side-line from their main activity. Thus the smith, Henry Davey, sold hammers and chisels which he had made (see **Blacksmiths** above); bee-keepers sold candles made from the wax from their hives; and farmers sold milk, cream, butter, cheese and eggs. The village shop, a repository of general goods made by people other than the shopkeeper, as well (sometimes) as the shopkeeper, is first recorded in Sheviock in the 1600s. A survey dated 1691 shows that Judith and Mary Prin (or Pryn) were renting 'a shopp' from the Carews on the life of Philip Prin. The rent was 2s.[73] For shops in Crafthole, see Chapter 13, *Houses, Shops and Farms in Crafthole.*

Specialist items sold by shopkeepers within the parish include the following:

Bell-ropes. These appear to have been supplied by the blacksmiths who repaired the bells. In 1774-5, Mr Colmer was paid 15s. 'for bellrope'. In 1780-1, he was paid 9s. 6d. 'for a set of bellropes & spun yearn [i.e.yarn]'. He sold more bell-ropes in 1783-4, 1786-7 and 1788-9 for prices between 10s. and 14s. In 1791-2, Christopher Davey sold 'three bell roaps' to the churchwardens for 11s. and the same number in 1793-4 and 1794-5 for about the same price. Richard Bath sold bell-ropes to the value of £1 11s. 3d. in 1801-2 and for a little more in 1804-5. Richard Morecomb sold bell-rope in 1846 for 7s. 6d. By 1880, the price of a single bell rope (paid to Mr Sale) had risen to 17s.

Candles. People who supplied candles in the 1700s and 1800s almost certainly kept bees. Between the years 1793-4 and 1799-1800, the churchwardens purchased their candles for the 'Singing Feast' from Elizabeth Mullis. Mrs Mullis supplied between one and a half and three lbs of candles each year, and charged 8d–10d. per lb. She was the widow of Philip Mullis who had farmed at Scraesdon and Brockhole in Antony from 1773, but had died before reaching the age of fifty. His widow continued to lease the 89 acres of land, probably farmed by her son, John (born 1775). Her daughter, Elizabeth, was born in 1777. From a plan of Lord Clinton's property in Crafthole, made in 1825, Mrs Mullis is shown to have moved to a house owned by him at the east end of the village outside the turnpike gate.[74] In 1795, the front room of her house became the first licensed meeting place for the Methodists.

In 1814-15, William Davey (also spelled Davies) sold no less than eight lbs. of candles (at 1s. 1d. per lb.) to the churchwardens to light the great Singing Feast held that year to celebrate the end of the Napoleonic Wars. In the following two years, he sold only two lbs. of candles each year at just 10d. and 9d. per lb. Davey, who was a **blacksmith** by trade, lived in Crafthole, on the east side of the land on which the Methodist chapel was later built. His land then included orchards and a garden suitable for housing bee-hives.

The Landry (also spelled Laundry) family were involved in many commercial activities in Sheviock in the early 1800s, first as butchers, then in running the inn, the *Carew Arms.* They were also active in the fishing industry.[75] There were recesses (called bee-boles) for bee-skeps at the side of their property in Sheviock. These had originally been part of the medieval Church House and are still preserved. Landry family tradition holds that members of the family kept bees.[76] They also supplied candles to the church. John Landry sold two lbs. of candles in 1821-2; three lbs. in 1824-5; four lbs. in 1825-6; and two lbs. again in 1829-30. The prices ranged from 6d. to 8d. per lb.

Nails. Mr Streeck supplied the church with nails to the value of 8s. 9d. in 1772-3. Arthur Peter is recorded as a supplier of nails in 1782-3, 1794-5, 1800-1 and 1804-5. The lowest amount he was paid was 9s. 7d. in 1794-5 and the highest was £1 0s. 8d. in 1800-1.[77]

Nets, Hassocks and Canvas. In 1795-6, Joseph May was paid 9s. 'for six sets for the church at 1s. 6d. per set'. Possibly these 'sets' were hassocks, because in 1806-7 he was paid 12s. 'for six hassocs (*sic*) at 2s. ea.'. In 1796-7, he was paid 3s. 'for making a nett'. This may have been to catch birds that had flown into the church or to catch rabbits in the churchyard.

Sweets. Between 1910 and 1920, a small wooden hut in the front garden of Myrtle Cottage (the modern Tirada) was used for the sale of sweets.[78] During and after the Second World War, Mrs Kate Carpenter ran a sweet shop from her house at 4 the Terrace, Sheviock village, near the school, where children could purchase sweets for a penny.[79]

Slate and Ragstone Suppliers

Nicholas Rickard was paid 13s. 6d. for 3,000 slates in 1769-70. He was paid another £3 3s. 3d. in 1772-3, but what was delivered is not specified. If it were slates, it could have been as many as 14,000. In 1780-1, he was paid £2 18s. 6d. for slates. At the following year's price (an increase of 77 per cent on the 1769-70 price) he would have supplied some 7,300 slates. In 1782-3, he was paid £1 12s. for 4,000 slates. Members of the Rickard family operated the quays (and lime kilns) at Halton in St Dominic and at Cotehele in 1796.[80] John Rickard was the tenant of Sconner Farm from 1833 to 1861. There was a lime kiln at the quay at Sconner. There may also have been a slate quarry on the land at Sconner.

Tailors

In 1777, the house of the mason, Amos Tinney, was leased and later purchased, by a tailor, Richard Hole.[81] His eldest son, William, continued to run a tailoring business from there, but mortgaged the house for £40.[82] Ann Hole (b.1821), who became a milliner in Crafthole, may have been William's daughter or niece. The house stood on the south side of the main road through Crafthole on the east side of Mrs Mullis's house. William's brother and heir, Richard, a labourer of Stoke Damerel, sold the premises for £145 to William Avery in 1804.[83] He in turn sold it to a well-to-do Sheviock farmer, Thomas Bews, in 1808 for £153.[84]

In 1723, Sir William Carew let to Walter Warren 'of the parish of Sheviocke ... Tailer' the 'cottage (now fallen down) with a garden plot thereunto adjoyning in Sheviocke ... adjoyning to the house where John Warren now dwells, late in the tenure of Jane Palmer'.[85] The rent was 2s. The lives named were Walter, his brother, Robert, and Christian, daughter of John Nichols of St Germans, 'Tailer'. John Warren was also a tailor, and had two sons, Gregory and Richard, who were lives named on a lease granted to George Warren, yeoman, in 1742.[86]

John Wain (b.1771) was working as a tailor in Crafthole in 1841. Robert Pawley (b.1796) was a tailor in Crafthole in 1841. John Pawley (b.1816), also a tailor in Crafthole in 1841, was probably his son.

Thatchers

The steward of the manor of Sheviock in 1726 noted in his accounts that he had paid 2s. for the 12 sheaves of reed needed to repair Ann Winnicot's house at Wrinkle, 9d. for 300 spars, and 1s. to 'John Clinnick for thatching the same'. John Clinnick may have been a specialist thatcher; but competent agricultural labourers were expected to be able to thatch a roof as well as a hay rick – hence the payment of 2s. to the labourer, Edward Carlyon, in 1780-1 'for putting reed on the church' (see also **Labourers** above).

In 1759, Jonathan Rashleigh of Menabilly, trustee appointed by Sir Coventry Carew, let a small plot of ground on the south side of the main road through Crafthole to Gilbert Stark (b.1702), thatcher.[87] Stark was obliged to build a new house on the plot within 12 months to replace one that had fallen down. The rent was only 1s. The house stood behind the modern post office. It had the house of Thomas Holman on the east and the house and shop of William Toser on the west. Stark's wife, Anne, was then fifty. Their daughter, Frances (b.1729), was married to Edward Hawkins, **carpenter**, of Crafthole. The sexton, Thomas Stark, who was rated 2d. for a tenement in Sheviock in 1754, may have been Gilbert's brother.

Timber Suppliers

In 1782-3, Mr Langmead was paid £2 13s. 9d. 'for 43 feet of boulk at 15d. per foot', probably for a western gallery for the church. John Langmead was the tenant of Cote Farm and of the land at Polscoe Mills from 1858 to 1861.

Toll-House or Turnpike Gate Keepers (See Chapter 40, *Markets, Highways and Turnpikes*)

Weavers

Weavers were among the more prosperous members of the parish.[88] The exercise of their trade required them to have enough capital to purchase looms and ancillary furniture, to buy regular supplies of wool, and to rent the workshops in which to house them. In 1585, Richard Carew had granted John Bonne (also Bonny) a 99-year lease of a cottage and 60 perches of land near to Crafthole. The lease was on the lives of himself, Diones, his wife, and George, their son.[89] John Bonne may have been a weaver. In 1640, Richard Carew granted William Reepe of Sheviock, 'weaver', a 99-year lease of this same 'cottage neere adjoyning to Crofthole and certen landes to the same adjoyning conteyning by estimcon threescore perches of land.'[90] Reepe's lease was on the lives of himself, Thomas, his son, and Joan, his daughter. The rent was 2s. On 17 July 1697, the steward of the Carew estates paid John Holman £1 16s. 10d. for 'repairing Reeps house in Crafthole'.[91] In the 1700s, members of the Reepe family were living in Antony churchtown.

Members of the Bray family were involved with the fishing operations at Portwrinkle and were also weavers. Emanuel Bray was the father of a Richard Bray (b. *c.*1630). In 1657, this Richard married Joan, daughter of the weaver, William Reepe. A William Bray is shown as renting a 'cottage and 60 perches' in Crafthole for 4s. in rentals of 1634 and 1691.[92] In 1711, Sir William Carew leased to William Bray of Crafthole, weaver, a 'House Garden and a Little Meadow containing ... about twenty yardes [i.e. 60 perches] of land'.[93] The rent was 4s. These were most likely the same premises as those originally leased to the Brays in 1634. The site was at the north end of West Lane, with the meadow on the west of the Lane and the cottage on the east. William Bray was reeve of the manor in about 1775.[94]

Chapter 40

Markets, Highways and Turnpikes

In the Middle Ages, the main road through the parish, used by parishioners travelling to other market towns, and by itinerant tradesmen, merchants, pilgrims and others, was given a special status as the 'the king's highway'. Not all roads were classified as such, but only those that led from one market town to another. The king's highway along the coast crossed the Tamar by a hazardous ferry-crossing at a place called Barnpool (*Bar-an-pol*, meaning the top of the cove) on the Cornish side, nearer to the sea than the present crossing at Cremyll.[1] Celia Fiennes described her experience in crossing over to Cornwall in 1695, recording that it was 'a hazardous passage by reason of three tides meeting. I was at least an hour going over; those ferry boats are so wet that I never fail to catch cold, as I did this day'.[2] Once on the Cornish side, the route into the county passed through Millbrook and then through Crafthole to Looe or Liskeard. The road to Looe went via Lantic, Triffle, Narkurs, Carracawn Cross and Hessenford. A branch from this road, called the southern road, descended from Triffle to Downderry and Seaton. The road to Liskeard went via Polscoe, Tredis, Buttarvilly (Butter Villa) Farm, Polbathic, Treboul, Trerule Foot, Catch French and Menheniot. At Polbathic there was a turning to St Germans.

Market Fairs and the Roads to them

St Germans, Liskeard, Bodmin and Menheniot

Journeys to Market

The nearest important local market to Sheviock in Saxon times was the Prior's market at St Germans. This was said to be 'reduced to nothing' after the Norman Conquest, as a result of the Count of Mortain's newly-created market at Trematon.[3] St Germans was still without a market in the 18th century.[4] Carew, writing in 1602, said that a fair was held at St Germans each year on 1 August.[5] By the 19th century, the Fair had been moved to the end of May. The *Cornubian* for 3 June 1831 reported that 'an excellent supply of fat and store bullocks' was available at the fair that year. The fair continued until the 1950s. Tom Bersey remembers selling cattle at the St Germans May Fair in the 1930s. The cattle were sold by auction in the village square next to the blacksmith's shop. The cattle were penned into adjoining streets until it was their turn to enter the ring and the streets became very foul as a result.[6]

The most important market for the whole of east Cornwall, certainly from Saxon times, was the one at Liskeard. In 1086, when Domesday Book was compiled, it belonged to Count Robert of Mortain and it was situated under the protection of his castle there. The market was worth 4s. to him annually. In the 1600s, Liskeard became a major centre for the production of leather goods, such as boots, gloves, purses, etc.[7] Cattle would find a ready market in Liskeard for their hides as well as their other properties. Train oil, a by-product of the fish-curing process that was carried on at Portwrinkle, was used to soften the leather. Liskeard also had a wool market and was the main centre for the production of the 'cards' used for the spinning of wool by hand.[8]

The accounts of the Carews' steward, John Treis, note many payments for purchases of livestock at Liskeard. The fair was traditionally held on St Matthew's day, 21 September, but other fair days were added. For example, Treis paid £20 for four oxen purchased at Liskeard Fair in March 1694. The following June, he paid

235 *Farmers buying cattle at Liskeard Market, November 2008.*

£19 7s. 6d. for another four bought there. In the five years May 1727 to May 1732, the Carews' farm manager used the road to or through Liskeard more than any other. He bought bullocks, oxen, sheep and honey at Liskeard Fair in December 1727, September and October 1729, and May 1732.

In the 1950s, the weekly market at Liskeard gradually replaced the local village markets, such as the one at Antony. By this time, local farmers could easily hire lorries to transport livestock. The advantage of going to Liskeard was that many more buyers were present there than at local village markets, so that prices were driven up. The Liskeard market is now held once a fortnight on Thursdays.

At Bodmin, the historic fair had been held on St Nicholas's day (25 December). But fairs also came to be held on other days as well. Two of John Treis's men attended the fair at Bodmin in June 1694, where they bought 70 sheep for £43 10s. 6d. They spent a day at the fair, a day getting there and another day driving the sheep back along the highway. The tolls at the fair and the men's wages came to another 6s. The Carews' farm manager bought numerous sheep, bullocks and oxen at Bodmin Fair in May 1727, June 1731, and May 1732.

In 1487, John Trelawney of Pool in Menheniot was granted a market and fair there.[9] The fair was on 11 June.[10] Two of Treis's men went there on horseback in 1694, returning with two oxen that cost together £13 17s. 6d. The Carews' farm manager again bought two oxen at Menheniot Fair in June 1727 for £11 12s.

236 *Mileposts, like this one at the bottom of Ladywell Lane, were erected along the length of the turnpike road built in 1826.*

The West Country has always been renowned for rearing cattle to be sold as 'stores'. Many buyers came from further up country to buy stores for further finishing on pastures more suitable for the final fattening. According to Tom Bersey, during the 1960s and 1970s, St Ive became a very popular monthly 'store' market, with hundreds of animals passing through the auction ring. It eventually closed because the facilities did not meet the latest animal health and welfare requirements.

The market at Crafthole licensed in 1314 took place on Wednesdays and later Fridays as well.[11] The annual fair took place on the vigil (eve), feast and morrow (following day) of St James (25 July). A cattle fair was later licensed on Lady Day (25 March) and a holiday fair on Easter Tuesday.[12] The markets and the fair on St James's day had disappeared before 1872, and the cattle and holiday fair were then said to be 'passing away'.

Pilgrimages

People using the highways to go on a pilgrimage would have been a common sight in medieval England. Chaucer's pilgrims travelling to the shrine of St Thomas à Becket at Canterbury, were typical travelers in that age of faith. If you lived in Devon or certain parts of east Cornwall, Crafthole was en route to the shrine of St Germanus, Bishop of Auxerre, at St Germans, and to the shrine of St Petroc at Bodmin. It also lay on the east-west route to St Michael's Mount. In 1155, the English Pope, Adrian IV, granted a release from a third part of their penances to all people who visited the church of St Michael on the Mount with oblations and alms.[13] Until 1390, the Mount was also one of the places from which pilgrim ships left for Santiago de Compostela.[14] In 1313, just a year before he founded his new borough of Crafthole, Sir Nicholas Dawney had himself gone as a pilgrim to Compostela.

Antony, Millbrook and Plymouth

Thomas Carew of Antony had purchased the manor of Sheviock in 1558. The Carews' steward kept his office at Antony House and the bailiff of Sheviock had to make many journeys there to report on manorial affairs.

In 1816, Reginald Pole Carew started a wool market in Torpoint, though this only survived for a few years. In the 1900s, a market was held at West Antony every fortnight until the 1950s. Tom Bersey remembers driving his cattle along the road from Sheviock to Antony in the late 1940s and early 1950s. The cattle to be sold were held on a farm with a large courtyard near to Antony crossroads until the time came for them to be auctioned. Pigs were transported by horse and cart and were sold in the cart, the vendor delivering the pigs to the purchaser.

There was a market at Millbrook in Elizabethan times.[15] The Justices of the Peace were also seated there. It was the main ship-building and repairing centre of the Rame Peninsula, and an important fishing port in Elizabethan and Stuart times. Sheviock fishermen often went there to sell their fish.[16]

Plymouth had become a flourishing port in the 1300s and was a major collecting centre for the export of fish. The fish merchants from Plymouth would come to Portwrinkle and 'greedily and speedily' take the 'larger remainder' of the catch, after the local people had taken their share and filled up the panniers on their horses.[17] Numbered among these fishing merchants from the early 1500s to the mid-1600s were members of the Brooking and Trevill families. The Brooking family acquired freehold property in Crafthole and must have been frequent travellers between the two places. William 'Brokyn' was a juror of the court leet of Crafthole in 1605.[18] The Trevills, who owned property in Antony parish, also acquired Rame Barton, and many members of the family are buried in Rame church.

Trematon, Saltash, Tavistock and Callington

After the Saxon conquest of Cornwall in the ninth century, the Saxon royal house gave the manor of Sheviock, with its important fisheries, to Tavistock Abbey. This gift meant that the direct route northwards from Portwrinkle to the abbey would have been much used. From Portwrinkle the track led to a ford or (at high tide) a river crossing, across the River Lynher at the bottom of the lane, later called George's Lane. From there the land route led to Tavistock via Trematon, Hatt and St Mellion. Goods could also be loaded onto barges at the riverside quay and taken to the abbey along the Lynher and up the Tamar and Tavy rivers to Morwelham Quay, which served as the port of Tavistock from the 1100s onwards. An alternative route to Trematon was through Antony village then northwards through the park at Anthony House to cross the Lynher at the place later called Jupiter Point.

In Saxon times, the route to Tavistock would also have been important for the abbot's sergeant or reeve at Sheviock to report to his officials on the affairs of the manor and on any sea-borne attacks by enemies.[19] After the Norman Conquest, this same route would have been much used by the Dawneys, who held their lands in return for knight's service rendered to the abbey. The lord of Sheviock had to present himself regularly at the abbot's court to do homage and to receive

237 *Farmer William Holman (right) in his 'Jingle' at Glebe Farm. The other passenger is the blacksmith, Tom Ough.*

238 *Farmer William Holman in his 'Sunday best' at Glebe Farm.*

instructions concerning the military duties he was obliged to perform.[20] The Dawneys owned property in Tavistock until about 1200 when they exchanged it for two acres of land used by the abbey's fishermen at Portwrinkle. Trematon, *en route* to Tavistock, also became an important destination. The Count of Mortain built a castle there shortly after the Norman Conquest. It was occupied by his military tenant, Reginald de Valletort.[21] The Dawney knights would have made many journeys there. The count's market at Trematon also made it an important destination for Sheviock farmers.

In 1105, the Abbot was licensed to hold a weekly market in Tavistock and, in 1116, he was licensed to hold an annual fair there.[22] Tavistock became the destination of people from all over south-east Cornwall and Devon at the time of the fair (29 to 31 August). In 1472, John Glyn, under-steward of the duchy of Cornwall, was murdered near his home in Morval as he was setting out for the fair at four o'clock in the morning.[23] But by the 1700s, the farm managers of the Carew estates rarely purchased livestock at Tavistock Fair. In the five years from May 1727 to May 1732, only four oxen were purchased there (in September 1729).[24]

The fair at Callington was traditionally held on the feast-day of the Nativity of Our Lady (8 September).[25] The farm managers of the Carew estates purchased oxen, sheep and bullocks at Callington Fair in October 1729 and in September 1730. The fair at Saltash was traditionally held on St James's day (25 July), the same day as the fair at Crafthole.[26] The Carew farm managers purchased 20 sheep at Saltash Fair in July 1729 and another 20 in July 1730, together with two fat oxen.

The Wool and Cloth Trades

In the early Middle Ages, wool was an important export from Devon and east Cornwall. Later on, woven cloths became the chief export. The principal centres of manufacture were Tavistock, which became noted for coarse cloths called 'Tavistocks', and Exeter, which became the regional centre for the production of kerseys and serges. All the main towns in east Cornwall had wool markets in the 1600s, and Devonshire clothiers would travel there to buy it.[27] Many householders had pairs of 'cards' and

spindles to turn the wool into yarn. Spinning was especially the occupation of women and poor people. In the early 1600s, the most important markets for yarn were at Launceston and Liskeard. In the second half of the century, Callington was described by Edward Kneebone as 'well frequented for the yarn trade'.[28] Sir Samuel Rolle, who was lord of the manor of Callington, played a key part in developing the trade. He held six cottages and one other house in Crafthole, and was no doubt energetic in collecting the wool and yarn from farmers and cottage workers in Sheviock parish. His son, Samuel, who was born in Maker, was elected portreeve of the borough of Crafthole in 1713.[29] Weavers leasing property in Sheviock manor included William Reepe (1640) and William Bray (1711).

THE HIGHWAYS AND THEIR MAINTENANCE

Until the 1700s, road traffic was mostly by foot or on horseback. John Moyse of Penimble, Port Eliot, St Germans, writing in 1760, stated that 'untill within forty years last past there were very few wheell Carriages in this part of ye Country and as I am informed, not three pairs of wheels in ye parish of Antony except at Sir Wm Carews'.[30] Goods as well as people were transported on horses, and when necessary by strings of packhorses. George Lipscomb, who journeyed through Devon and Cornwall in 1799, described how alarming these strings of horses were to other road-users, when driven at speed:

> These [packhorses] are not secured with traces, but run loose in troops, consisting of five or ten, having either one or two [people] mounted upon other horses to drive them. When they are in small numbers the driver is commonly seated on the top of the load, and trots, or sometimes, even gallops along, with the greatest unconcern, up hill and down, and over the roughest ground … Loads of straw, hay, wood, and furze, are all conveyed in the same manner, and the horses which carry them are no small annoyance to any unfortunate passenger whose steed may happen to be restiff [restive], or who may, by chance, approach too near the crooks, which in these narrow roads it is very difficult to keep clear of ….[31]

When livestock needed to be taken to new pastures or to the marketplace, it would be driven on the hoof along the highways. It was thus a common sight for the traveller to pass herds of cattle, sheep or pigs, or flocks of geese or other fowl being driven along the highways, churning up the surface. In the spring, herds of 'store' cattle were driven into Devon for fattening, and thence to London for slaughter. Cornwall was also noted for its pig production. Pigs were driven to the London markets via various staging posts where the pigs were fed en route. Pig street in Axminster, Devon, was one of these staging posts.

Medieval law imposed the duty of highway maintenance upon the manor, and the lord of the manor passed this duty on to the whole body of tenants. Compliance was enforced by the court leet. The duty of repairing the road surfaces was shared between all the able-bodied men of the parish. Each man served compulsorily for a certain number of days without pay.[32] The parishioners not only provided all the manual labour gratuitously, but also all the necessary tools, horses and carts.

In 1555, an Act of Philip and Mary regularised the performance of these duties. For each plough-land (20 acres) that he cultivated, whether as arable or pasture, the farmer had to provide one wain or cart, with its draught animals. He also had to send two able-bodied men along with the cart. Any other person keeping a draught of horses or plough in the parish was subject to the same service. Every other male householder, cottager or labourer (except hired servants) had to present himself for work on the roads, or to send someone else in his place. Each of these people had to appear on the roads on the date and at the hour fixed by the parish's surveyor of highways. The labourers were summoned to work by notice in church. Their obligation was to work for eight hours a day under the surveyor's direction for four consecutive days during the year. In 1563, when the 1555 Act was made permanent, the number of days was increased to six. This 'statute labour' or 'team duty' provided the main resource for road maintenance until 1835.

The highways of Sheviock parish first enter the record books in 1608, when Richard Prynne and John Moreshed were fined 2d. each at the court leet of the borough of Crafthole for allowing the main street in Crafthole to fall into disrepair. In December 1639, Maria, wife of John Sonne, and her daughter, Elizabeth, were also brought before the court. The Sonnes lived on the main thoroughfare running through the borough, and John was several times elected a juryman of the court. The jury 'presented' his wife and daughter for assaulting Ralph Holman while he was repairing the *via regale* – the 'king's highway'.[33] The women were found guilty, and in the following April, John placed them at the mercy of the court, where they, too, were fined 2d. each.

Each year, the parish surveyors compiled a list of all the occupiers of lands, and of all the inhabitants between 18 and 65 years of age, who were liable for work on the highways. In 1768-9, the occupiers listed were Hugh Littleton of Sheviock Barton (one plough and three men), the Revd Mydhope Wallis of Trethill (one plough and two men), Samuel Peter of Tredis (one plough and four men), John Hill (three ploughs and three men), Samuel Littleton, brother of Hugh (two ploughs only), William Dunrich of Liscawn (one plough and one man), Edward Andrew (one plough only), John Lyne of Haye (one plough and one man), and William Taylor (one plough and two men). The total number for whom these occupiers were liable was 16 men. The other 14

occupiers were liable only for the provision of between one and four men, making a total of 30 men. In addition there were 23 inhabitants who were not occupiers of land and were therefore only liable to contribute their own labour. The total workforce available to work on the roads was thus 69 men.

Parishioners were able to commute their labour services by payment of a fine. Acts of 1766 and 1773 imposed a national scale of commutation. In the year 1768-9, John Lyne paid £1 8s. by way of composition, the Revd Mydhope Wallis paid 16s. for two men and two ploughs, William Dunrich paid 4s. for one man, Henry Taw paid 8s. for two men. Richard Darley and Samuel Peter each paid 16s. for four men, Richard Lavers paid 4s. for one man, and William Stephens paid 10s.

The Act of 1555 required each parish to appoint its own surveyor of highways to superintend the work on the roads. He was nominated by his fellow parishioners and formally appointed by the local Justices of the Peace at special Highways Sessions. It was the surveyor's duty to view all the roads in the parish at least three times during the year, and to report upon their condition to the local JP. It was also his duty to report to the justices anyone who failed to supply the labour or materials required of him. The justices had the power to fine defaulters, and these fines were to be spent on highway maintenance. The justices could also levy a rate of 6d. for the purpose of highway maintenance or construction.

Until the 1800s, all roads were essentially 'dirt roads', whose surfaces had to be levelled from time to time. As we have seen, these surfaces might be churned up by animals, or, with the big increase in wheeled traffic in the late 1700s, by the wheels of carriages and carts. To mend the highways, teams from the parish would plough them up, casting the furrows towards the centre of the road, and then harrowing it to create a level surface. The plough used was a special 'road plough' of enormous dimensions strengthened with iron. Work on the plough may account for some of the blacksmiths' bills paid by the surveyors of Sheviock between 1767 and 1769. There were payments to Matthew Bartlett of 11s. 2d. for work done at Easter 1767, 5s. 1d. for work done in October 1768, and 6s. 2d. for work done in 1769. The surveyors also paid James Prin, blacksmith and carpenter, 5s. 3½d. for work done in September 1768 and 6s. 4d. for work done in 1769. It took teams of six or eight powerful horses to pull the road plough. In January 1768, John Lyne sent two men and his plough team to work on the parish roads for two days.[34]

Some of the work on the roads could be done by men working with picks and shovels. The parish surveyors paid a contractor, George Row, £2 9s. 1d. 'for 45½ journies [*sic*] on the highways of Sheviocke near Portwrinkle', and they paid Samuel Littleton 5s. 10d. 'for raising stones near Sheviock'. The basic rate for manual labour on the roads in the years 1767-9 was 1s. per day. Thus, in 1769, John Spiller was paid

15s. for 15 days, work in addition to the six days he was obliged to work gratuitously, and Nathaniel Grills was paid 16s. for 16 days' additional work. In the same year, the surveyors also had orders printed for pruning the hedgerows. The printing cost them 1s., and they probably had the notices posted in the church porch. Sometimes more drastic action was required, and in August 1768 the surveyors paid a contractor 4s. 'for blowing up a Rock near Portwrinkle'.

In 1767 and 1768, the surveyors of highways were the Revd Mydhope Wallis of Trethill and Samuel Peter of Tredis.[35] The same two individuals were also appointed Overseers of the Poor. As happened in many other places, the parish had combined oversight of road repair with that of poor relief, so that male paupers could be put to work repairing the roads.

Crossroads

A statute of 1698 required sign-posts to be erected at crossroads. One of these would certainly have been at the junction marked by the medieval cross called in 1775 'stop or cross', and in 1826 'stump cross'. Field names incorporating the word 'cross' indicate fields close to either medieval crosses or sign-posts erected in accordance with the Act of 1698. Thomas Pride's map of 1775 and the map produced in conjunction with the Tithe Redemption survey of 1841/2 show many such field names.[36]

TURNPIKES

The Liskeard Turnpike Act 1760

In and near to London, wheeled traffic started to increase significantly in the 1600s. But it took another century before wheeled traffic became commonplace in Cornwall. Coaches with springs were first introduced into England in 1754, and this ushered in the era of stage coaches and coaching inns. The coach from Devonport to London took 24 hours to cover the distance of 227 miles (9.5 miles per hour). The medieval system of road maintenance by statute labour and team duty in each separate parish still survived, but it was no longer sufficient to create and maintain the long stretches of straight, hard and level roadways that the stage coaches required. The solution that was found was the establishment of trusts empowered to construct and maintain specified stretches of road and to levy tolls on those stretches. The trustees could pay for contractors to work on the specified road, using toll receipts to do so, or, with the sanction of the local justices, by imposing sixpenny rates on parishioners. They could also make use of the old statute labour and team duty imposed on the inhabitants of the affected parishes.

The first Turnpike Act affecting Sheviock was that passed in 1760 (1 Geo. III, cap. 25) entitled 'An Act for repairing and widening the Road from the East End of West Taphouse Lane, to the Borough of Liskeard … and also the Road from … Liskeard to Crafthole and from thence to Crimble Passage and Tar Point, and from Crafthole aforesaid, to Saint German's Beacon'. To make use of the compulsory statute labour, the trustees had to give notice in writing to the parish surveyors concerning their labour requirements, and then the parish surveyors were 'required and directed to give publick notice thereof, and summons, on the Sunday before, either in the church immediately after divine service, or by affixing such notice on the church door'. The trustees were given power to erect toll-houses, turnpikes and gates for the purpose of collecting the tolls from the different classes of road users. They were also empowered to measure the roads and set up 'stones or posts ... at the distance of one mile from each other'. Most of these mile-posts still survive in the parish.

The trustees under the Act of 1760 included John Blake of Antony, Michael, Thomas, Edward and William Hoblyn, Hugh Littleton of Landjore in St Germans, Hugh Littleton of Sheviock, Hugh Littleton of Intown in St Germans, Samuel Littleton, John Littleton, John Lyne, the Revd John Lyne, Philip Lyne, Samuel Lyne of Antony, William Morshead, the Revd Edward Morshead, and the Revd Mydhope Wallis. All these men occupied lands or tenements that yielded £40 or more a year, or were the heirs to lands or tenements worth £100 a year, or had considerable personal possessions. The trustees were empowered to erect two compulsory turnpikes, one of which was to be 'in the village of Crafthole'. Thomas Pride's map and survey of 1775 shows that the 'Turnpike House and Garden' were situated on the site of the present post office. It had originally been occupied by the farmer, Charles Bligh. The tolls that Bligh and his wife were permitted to charge were laid down as follows:

For every horse [etc.] drawing any carriage	three pence[37]
For every yoke of oxen drawing any waggon, cart [etc.]	four pence[38]
For every horse, mare, gelding, mule [etc.] laden or unladen and not drawing	one penny.
For every drove of oxen, cows or neat cattle	ten pence per score,
and so in proportion for any greater or lesser number.[39]	
For every drove of calves, hogs, sheep or lambs	five pence per score,
and so in proportion for any greater or lesser number.	

Numerous journeys were exempted from tolls. In particular, those of any horses or carts carrying manure or sand or lime to spread on parish farmland, or carrying hay or corn from the fields to the farmyard, or teams drawing ploughs or cattle going to pasture. To protect the local cloth and tanning industries, horses that were used to carry serges, woollens or hides to local manufacturing centres were also exempt. Horses carrying the mail were exempt, as were horses carrying the goods of soldiers on the march. Horses carrying materials for road-mending were of course also exempt. People riding to church on Sunday were exempt, as were people riding to

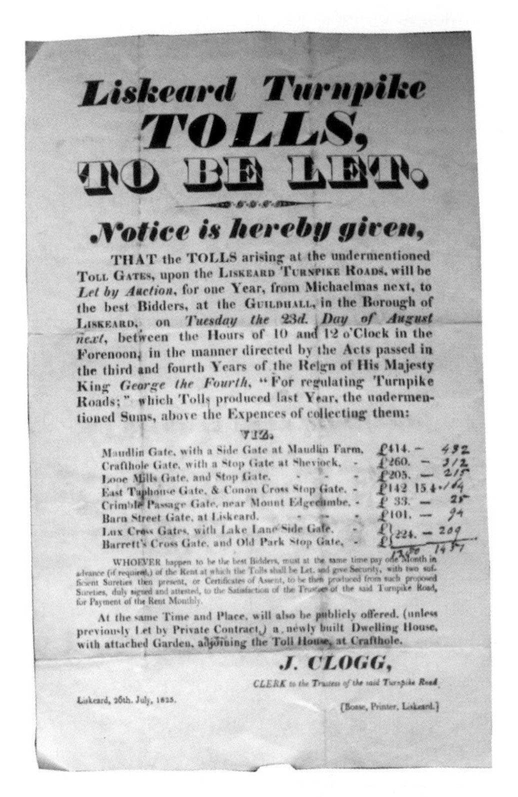

Liskeard Turnpike
TOLLS,
TO BE LET.

Notice is hereby given,

THAT the TOLLS arising at the undermentioned TOLL GATES, upon the LISKEARD TURNPIKE ROADS, will be *Let by Auction*, for one Year, from Michaelmas next, to the best Bidders, at the GUILDHALL, in the Borough of LISKEARD, on *Tuesday the 23d. Day of August next*, between the Hours of 10 and 12 o'Clock in the Forenoon, in the manner directed by the Acts passed in the third and fourth Years of the Reign of His Majesty King *George the Fourth*, "For regulating Turnpike Roads;" which Tolls produced last Year, the undermentioned Sums, above the Expences of collecting them:

VIZ.

Maudlin Gate, with a Side Gate at Maudlin Farm,	£414. –	492
Crafthole Gate, with a Stop Gate at Sheviock, -	£260. –	312
Looe Mills Gate, and Stop Gate, - - -	£205. –	215
East Taphouse Gate, & Conon Cross Stop Gate, -	£142 15 4	164
Crimble Passage Gate, near Mount Edgecumbe, -	£ 33. –	25
Barn Street Gate, at Liskeard, - - -	£101. –	94
Lux Cross Gates, with Lake Lane Side Gate, -	£ 224. –	209
Barrett's Cross Gate, and Old Park Stop Gate, -	£	

WHOEVER happen to be the best Bidders, must at the same time pay one Month in advance (if required,) of the Rent at which the Tolls shall be Let, and give Security, with two sufficient Sureties then present, or Certificates of Assent, to be then produced from such proposed Sureties, duly signed and attested, to the Satisfaction of the Trustees of the said Turnpike Road, for Payment of the Rent Monthly.

At the same Time and Place, will also be publicly offered, (unless previously Let by Private Contract,) a newly built Dwelling House, with attached Garden, adjoining the Toll House, at Crafthole.

J. CLOGG,

CLERK to the Trustees of the said Turnpike Road.

Liskeard, 26th. July, 1825.

[Bone, Printer, Liskeard.]

239 *Turnpike tolls were let at auction for one year at a time. This notice advertises an auction to be held at Liskeard on 23 August 1825. The amounts inked in are the actual amounts that were fetched at the auction.*

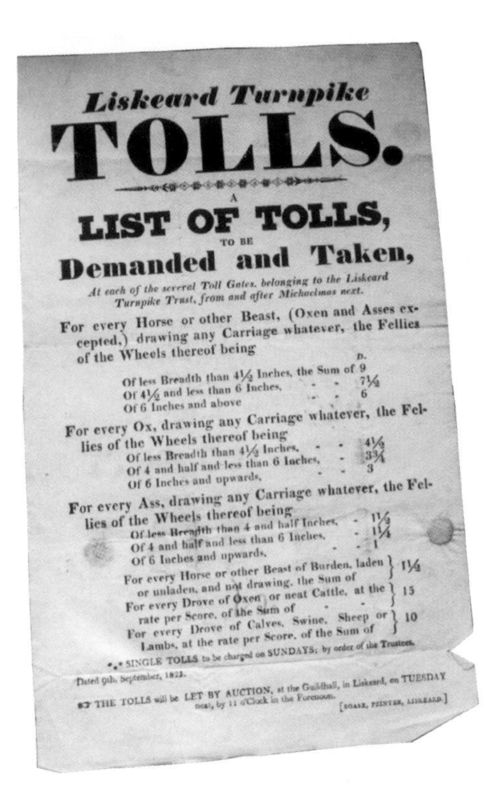

Liskeard Turnpike
TOLLS.

A
LIST OF TOLLS,
TO BE
Demanded and Taken,

At each of the several Toll Gates, belonging to the Liskeard Turnpike Trust, from and after Michaelmas next.

For every Horse or other Beast, (Oxen and Asses excepted,) drawing any Carriage whatever, the Fellies of the Wheels thereof being

	D.
Of less Breadth than 4½ Inches, the Sum of	9
Of 4½ and less than 6 Inches, - -	7½
Of 6 Inches and above - -	6

For every Ox, drawing any Carriage whatever, the Fellies of the Wheels thereof being

Of less Breadth than 4½ Inches, - -	4½
Of 4 and half and less than 6 Inches, -	3¾
Of 6 Inches and upwards, - -	3

For every Ass, drawing any Carriage whatever, the Fellies of the Wheels thereof being

Of less Breadth than 4 and half Inches, -	1½
Of 4 and half and less than 6 Inches, -	1¼
Of 6 Inches and upwards, - -	1

For every Horse or other Beast of Burden, laden or unladen, and not drawing, the Sum of	1½
For every Drove of Oxen or neat Cattle, at the rate per Score, of the Sum of - -	15
For every Drove of Calves, Swine, Sheep or Lambs, at the rate per Score, of the Sum of	10

*** SINGLE TOLLS to be charged on SUNDAYS; by order of the Trustees.

Dated 9th. September, 1823.

☞ THE TOLLS will be LET BY AUCTION, at the Guildhall, in Liskeard, on TUESDAY next, by 11 o'Clock in the Forenoon.

[BOASE, PRINTER, LISKEARD.]

240 *The turnpike trusts were empowered to set the amount of toll for each type of horse or other beast using the turnpike road. This list of tolls dates from 1823.*

attend a funeral. In 1770, an amending Act was passed to tighten enforcement of the tolls.[40] It authorised the erection of 'one side-gate in a certain lane near to Sheviock church' to prevent travellers avoiding the toll-gate. The use of the turnpike increased considerably when the Torpoint Ferry was opened on 4 July 1791. The roads had been much improved for the use of wheeled traffic by the employment of professional surveyors and, under their supervision, the creation of more durable surfaces.

Until April 1794, the Royal Mail for Liskeard from eastern counties travelled by way of Tavistock and the bridge at Gunnislake. As a result of the opening of the ferry, it crossed at Torpoint from 9 April in that year.[41] A stage coach, called the Royal Cornish, was started in February 1796 to carry passengers and goods from Torpoint to Liskeard and Bodmin.[42] The coach had to ascend the steep hill at Antony and make the circuitous journey through Crafthole and Tredis to Polbathic, and from there climb up another steep hill at Treboul in St Germans and so on to Liskeard. However, the mail still went on horseback until about 1805-6, when it too was carried by the stage coach starting at Torpoint.[43] In 1836, when a second ferry was added, the mail was carried over into Cornwall on the same coach used in Devon, called the Quicksilver, or Devonport Mail.[44]

The Liskeard Turnpike Act 1826 [45]

The difficulties of the terrain were not overcome until 1826, when a new Act was passed to create firstly 'a new piece of road diverging from Anthony (*sic*) Green, through Brockhole, along Wacker Lake, Trethill, Kerslake, and Sheviock, to join the present road near stump cross'; secondly 'a new piece of road diverging from Polscove by the side of Sconner Lake, through Trewin and Sconner, and along the side of Polbathick Lake, to join the present road near Polbathick Lime Kilns'; and thirdly 'a new piece of road from Polbathick up the valley through Treskelly, to join the present road at Trerule Foot'. The 1826 Act thus created the parts of the A374 passing through the parishes of Antony, Sheviock and St Germans with which we are familiar today. With one exception, the old stretches of turnpike road still remained in use and were subject to lower tolls than those charged on the new stretches. For example, the new toll for a horse drawing a carriage was 9d. on the old stretches, but 1s. on the new ones. The stretch of road leading from Crafthole to St Germans Beacon was declassified as a turnpike, and reverted to the care of the parishes of Sheviock and St Germans.

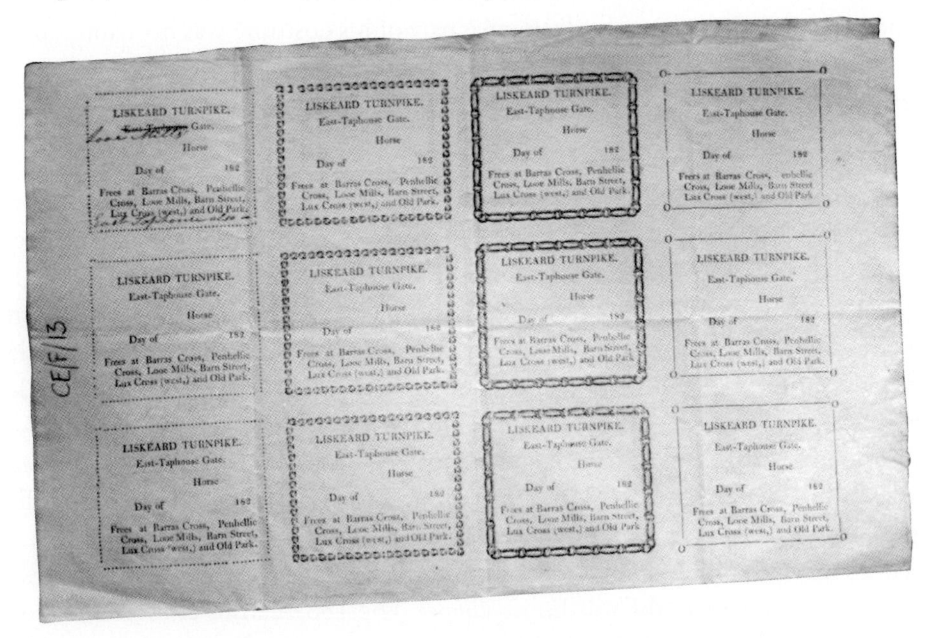

LISKEARD TURNPIKE.
Gate.
Horse
Day of 182
Frees at Barras Cross, Penhellic Cross, Looe Mills, Barn Street, Lux Cross (west,) and Old Park.

LISKEARD TURNPIKE.
East-Taphouse Gate.
Horse
Day of 182
Frees at Barras Cross, Penhellic Cross, Looe Mills, Barn Street, Lux Cross (west,) and Old Park.

LISKEARD TURNPIKE.
East-Taphouse Gate.
Horse
Day of 182
Frees at Barras Cross, Penhellic Cross, Looe Mills, Barn Street, Lux Cross (west,) and Old Park.

LISKEARD TURNPIKE.
East-Taphouse Gate.
Horse
Day of 182
Frees at Barras Cross, Penhellic Cross, Looe Mills, Barn Street, Lux Cross (west,) and Old Park.

LISKEARD TURNPIKE.
East-Taphouse Gate.
Horse
Day of 182
Frees at Barras Cross, Penhellic Cross, Looe Mills, Barn Street, Lux Cross (west,) and Old Park.

LISKEARD TURNPIKE.
East-Taphouse Gate.
Horse
Day of 182
Frees at Barras Cross, Penhellic Cross, Looe Mills, Barn Street, Lux Cross (west,) and Old Park.

LISKEARD TURNPIKE.
East-Taphouse Gate.
Horse
Day of 182
Frees at Barras Cross, Penhellic Cross, Looe Mills, Barn Street, Lux Cross (west,) and Old Park.

LISKEARD TURNPIKE.
East-Taphouse Gate.
Horse
Day of 182
Frees at Barras Cross, Penhellic Cross, Looe Mills, Barn Street, Lux Cross (west,) and Old Park.

LISKEARD TURNPIKE.
East-Taphouse Gate.
Horse
Day of 182
Frees at Barras Cross, Penhellic Cross, Looe Mills, Barn Street, Lux Cross (west,) and Old Park.

LISKEARD TURNPIKE.
East-Taphouse Gate.
Horse
Day of 182
Frees at Barras Cross, Penhellic Cross, Looe Mills, Barn Street, Lux Cross (west,) and Old Park.

LISKEARD TURNPIKE.
East-Taphouse Gate.
Horse
Day of 182
Frees at Barras Cross, Penhellic Cross, Looe Mills, Barn Street, Lux Cross (west,) and Old Park.

LISKEARD TURNPIKE.
East-Taphouse Gate.
Horse
Day of 182
Frees at Barras Cross, Penhellic Cross, Looe Mills, Barn Street, Lux Cross (west,) and Old Park.

241 *A proof copy of toll tickets. A ticket was issued at the first gate entered. This allowed the traveller to pass through the other gates listed on the ticket without further charge.*

The trustees appointed under the new Act included Reginald Pole Carew, Lord Eliot, John Coryton Roberts of Trevol, the Revd Duke Yonge, the Revd John Lloyd Lugger of Freethy (*sic*), John Boger of Wolsdon, the Revd Hugh Littleton, the Revd Henry Grylls, Thomas Hoblyn, William Glencross, John Littleton of Trewin and the Revd Reginald Pole [of Tredis].

The Toll-House Keepers

As shown by the lease of Bligh's house in Crafthole, the toll-houses were leased to the trustees of the turnpikes, and they in turn employed the individuals who inhabited them and collected the tolls. Their usual wage was 10s. or 12s. a week. Many toll-house keepers were illiterate and could not keep proper accounts. To avoid losses to the trust, it became common practice for a year's worth of tolls to be sold at auction for a fixed sum. A handbill in the Cornwall Record Office dated 17 July 1829 gives notice that the tolls at the Crafthole toll-gate and the (new) Sheviock toll-gate would be let either together or separately. In the previous year the two gates together had yielded net receipts of £251, and a note in ink on the handbill suggests that the successful bidder paid £261. The toll on horses not drawing carriages had by then been increased to 1½d. and it was to be further increased to 2d. in the following year. The toll-house keeper, or 'pikeman', usually wore a distinctive uniform. According to Charles Dickens, 'A pikeman … wore a tall black glazed hat and corduroy breeches, with white stockings. But the most distinctive part of his costume was his white linen apron'.[46] Women as well as men could act as toll-house keepers, and they, too, wore the distinctive white apron.

The Toll-house in Crafthole

Charles Bligh first took a lease on the property that later became the toll-house in Crafthole, in 1744, at a rent of 12s.[47] The house had been built by the carpenter, Israel Pope in 1679. In another 1744 lease of a small orchard in the Coombes, Charles Bligh is described as a 'husbandman' or farmer.[48] Bligh's lease was renewed in 1757.[49] In 1770, he was still paying the 12s. for his house and garden, plus another 2s. for his little orchard, plus another 2s. for 'House and Garden Turnpike'.[50] When Thomas Pride made his survey and map the house was leased to the Commissioners of the Turnpike Road for the life of Ann Bligh, then aged seventy. The Act creating the turnpike road through Crafthole had been passed in 1760, and the use of Bligh's house as the toll-house presumably dates from that time. A dwelling-house adjoining the toll-house was described as 'newly built' in an auction of the tolls in 1825. The 1851 census shows Maria Growden, aged 55, as the toll-house keeper. The 1861 census does not include any toll-house keepers and in 1871, 'Toll Gate House', as it was called, was occupied by James Carpenter, described as an 'agricultural labourer' and his wife and son.

The Toll-house in Sheviock Churchtown

In 1825, while the new Turnpike Act was in preparation, the trustees of the Liskeard Turnpike Roads took a 99-year lease of a cottage in Sheviock churchtown to serve as a toll-house.[51] In 1841, William Henry Pole Carew and his trustee granted to Edward Hoblyn Pedler of Liskeard, gentleman, a lease of 'all that dwellinghouse now used as a Toll House or Turnpike Gate House situate near the village [of Sheviock]'.[52] Pedler was the treasurer of the trustees of the turnpike. The consideration for the lease was the fact that the trustees had erected a new toll-house and outbuildings on the site. That house still stands. It was apparently built by T.H. Lakeman, the contractor chosen to build the new stretches of turnpike road. In a letter of 3 April 1820, he had quoted a price of £250 for each of the two toll-houses situated on the new road.[53] The rent was 5s. 6d. The 1841 census shows William Body, then aged 50, as the toll-house keeper. He was married to Mary Ann, aged 45, and they had four children. Ten years later, the census shows John Maynard as the keeper. He was a widower, aged 69. According to the 1871 census, the resident of Toll Gate House was James Ough (55), described as a mason, and his wife, Elizabeth (49). In the photograph of the *Carew Arms* taken in *c.*1875, a woman is standing outside the inn wearing a small hard hat and a long white apron. As stated by Charles Dickens, these aprons were the distinctive dress of toll-house keepers, so this woman may have been the toll-house keeper in Sheviock. The income from the Liskeard Turnpike Trust increased rapidly after the new stretches of road were completed. It stood at £1,250 in 1822/3 and rose to £2,850 in 1853.[54]

The Pounds

'Pounds' (enclosures to hold straying sheep and cattle) had been a feature of manors and boroughs since time immemorial. With the construction of turnpike roads and fast-moving stage-coaches, there was a new urgency to prevent accidents and obstruction from strays. Accordingly, an Act of 1824 (3 Geo. IV) provided that if any 'horse, ass, sheep, swine or other beast or cattle of any kind' should be found 'wandering, straying or lying about any Turnpike Road' it could be seized and impounded in the common pound of the parish. The owner of the stray had to pay 5s. to whoever impounded the animal, as well as the costs of its keep. The manor pounds of both Sheviock and Antony were located near the village greens of each place, and both were close to the new stretches of turnpike constructed in 1826.[55]

The price paid for the new stretches of turnpike was a heavy one, in that the village greens of Antony and Sheviock, marked on Thomas Pride's map of 1775, were both sacrificed. Furthermore, the two villages continue to pay a price in suffering the roar of motorbikes along what is now the A374. In addition to the loss of the village green at Sheviock, a number of private occupiers sacrificed parts of their holdings.

These were listed in the Act as 'three gardens at or near Polbathick cottage' owned by Thomas Short Peters and occupied by William Holman and William Geake; another garden nearby occupied by William and Daniel Couling; 'an orchard at Sconner' owned by Reginald Pole Carew and occupied by Robert Bickford; 'a plantation [of trees] at or near Trewin' owned and occupied by John Littleton; 'a garden near Polscove', and also a nearby orchard, owned by Reginald Pole Carew and occupied by Henry March; 'two orchards and a garden, at or near the village of Sheviock' owned by Reginald Pole Carew and occupied by John Trevan (who farmed at Sheviock Barton); 'a garden at or near Sheviock village' owned by Reginald Pole Carew, leased to Ann Roberts and occupied by John Landrey (the butcher and later innkeeper); and 'a rick yard on the Sheviock Glebe', owned by Reginald Pole Carew and occupied by the farmer, Samuel Lyne.

242 *The toll-gate house, Sheviock churchtown, built by T.H. Lakeman in c.1825.*

THE 19TH CENTURY AND AFTER

Local Government Changes in the 1800s

The obligation of male parishioners to render service in kind, by performing manual labour or team duty on the roads, was finally abolished by the General Highway Act 1835.[56] The care of roads not entrusted to a turnpike trust was then entrusted in each parish to the ratepayers assembled in Vestry. The Vestry was authorised to nominate a surveyor, who might be a salaried officer, and to levy a rate to pay his salary and the cost of maintaining the roads. By the Highways Act 1862, Justices in Quarter Sessions were empowered to combine parishes into Highway Districts, and by 1865 most Cornish parishes were combined in this way. The Highways and Locomotives Act 1878 required the justices to make these Districts coincide as far as possible with the new Rural Sanitary Districts. The Local Government Act 1894 then merged the Highway Districts and Highway Parishes into Rural Sanitary Authorities, thus finally ending a parish's responsibility for its own roads.

The Arrival of the Railway and the Motor Car

Most of the income of turnpike trusts came from stage-coaches. Each stage-coach paid £7 a year in tolls for each mile of turnpike that it traversed. As soon as railways covered the same routes, stage-coaches ceased to be profitable. The last stage-coach between Plymouth and London ran in September 1847. Brunel's railway bridge across the Tamar was constructed in 1859, signaling the beginning of the end of stage-coaches in Cornwall. According to a timetable of 1850, the journey from Plymouth to London, Paddington, by train took just over ten hours.[57] The demise of the stage-coach soon led to the winding-up of the turnpike trusts. The trustees of the Liskeard Turnpike Trust surrendered their lease of the toll-house in Sheviock churchtown to Reginald Pole Carew in October 1881, marking the end of the era of stage-coaches and turnpikes in Sheviock.

Petrol-driven motor cars were introduced into England in 1894. At first they traveled over the same roads that had served the stage-coaches. But their greater velocity meant that in the summer they raised clouds of dust and in wet weather they scattered mud and became bogged down. The problem was addressed by the introduction of tar-spreading machines, which were tried out successfully in the Home Counties in 1907 and gradually came into use throughout the country. But there was still no tarmac finish to minor roads and lanes in the 1930s. As John Biles remembered, 'in dry mid-summer, the hedges would be white with dust, while the occasional car or charabanc would leave behind a cloud of choking intensity'.[58]

243 *A 'cloamy' pot made at St Germans, which was an important centre of pottery-making in the Middle Ages.*

Chapter 41

Inns and Innkeepers

During the Middle Ages there was a flourishing trade in wine, which was imported from France in exchange for Cornish tin and woollen products. In fact, more wine was consumed than ale. The ale did not taste good, since, at this time, it was made from oats, often without the flavouring of hops.[1] Cider does not appear to have been widely drunk, except in monasteries, where there is evidence of considerable production. In 1327, cider was being produced on the Bishop of Exeter's manor at Cuddenbeke in St Germans. It was recorded that one dole of cider produced there was sold for 10s.[2] There was a great increase in the number of taverns in Cornwall in the 13th century. In the eastern part of Cornwall, 15 wine wholesalers were recorded in 1201 and 18 in 1302. St Germans had none in 1201 but two in 1302.[3]

In 1592, the court leet of the borough of Crafthole granted licences to seven residents of the borough to brew ale. These were Richard Hearle (or Harle), Elizabeth Pryne, John Chubbe, Mathewe Battyn, William Charke, Oliver Hancock, and another John Chubbe (perhaps the son of the former). Each licence cost 6d. The innkeeper, Ferdinando Spiller, who died in 1607, is not mentioned in the list. However, as an innkeeper, he must also have brewed ale, and in his will he left all the utensils necessary for the purpose. He may have already obtained a licence, or his brewing activity may have taken place at his windmill above Sheviock woods, so that he would not have gone to the court leet of Crafthole for a licence.

Many other parishioners possessed implements for brewing ale, and were occasionally caught selling it without a licence. At the court leet held in Crafthole in October 1617, Thomas Wilmote was fined a shilling for selling drink without a licence, and Ralph Symon was fined 6d. for doing so on behalf of his wife, Maria, who had no doubt made it. On 30 March 1633, the Sheviock parish constables, John Blake and Arnott Odiorne, and the churchwardens, George and Edward Grills, presented six parishioners to the justices at the Petty Sessions held at Millbrook 'for selling of ale without lycins'[4] The six presented were Emmanuel Bray, Richard Searle,

Toby Langdon, John Bath, George Winnacott and Jone Sampson. George Winnacott, after whom 'George's Lane' is named, was the tenant of a cottage at the quay on the River Lynher, and he was no doubt selling his ale to travellers crossing the river by ferry and also to the crews of barges and fishermen calling at the quay. Each defendant was given the heavy fine of 20s. The money was given to the poor of the parish.[5]

Inns at Sheviock Churchtown

Wallis's Inn: A law case from the 13th century records that Roger Chapman of Shevyek (*sic*) and his brother, Henry, killed John Walecu (perhaps Wallis) in his house in Sheviock. This house, according to Dr James Whetter, was probably a tavern.[6] If so, the unfortunate Wallis is the first recorded innkeeper in the parish. At that time the sign of a bush or leaves distinguished a common tavern.[7] Taverners sold wine by the gallon, pottle (half gallon), quart or pint.[8] Some of the containers would have been pottery jugs made at St Germans, a great centre of pottery production from the Middle Ages until well into the 18th century. Others would have been made of pewter or leather.[9] An inventory of the goods of William Harry of Sheviock, who died in 1626, includes 'pewter & clommye vessells' valued at 20s. 'Clommye' or cloamy meant made from clay. Richard Harvey, a Sheviock farmer who died in 1645, left implements upon which to hang and rest pots and one 'clommiy cupp' together valued at 1s. 6d. The medieval wine trade collapsed at the end of the Hundred Years' War (1453), when the English were expelled from Gascony.

Daniell Sargent's Inn: It is recorded in the law case of *Rolle* v *Blake*, that the commissioners, Thomas Dandy and Hannibal Gryles, examined the witness, Nicholas Sargent, at the inn of Daniell Sargent on 25 April 1674.[10] In 1639, Daniell Sargent had taken a sub-lease of premises in Sheviock churchtown from the farmer, Richard Chubb. Sargent had previously been a sailor. Chubb himself was the tenant of Richard Carew the younger. The premises leased were 'the whole dwelling house … or cottage' and 'the whole herbe garden lyeng on the North side of the said dwelling house' together with part of a 'plot of ground [with] stone floors or town place which hath been lately used by … Gabriell of Sheviock … husbandman for a Reeke [rick] place.' Sargent also leased the 'Courtlage belonging unto the said Cottage on the South side of the same'. But part of the rick place and a strip of land nine feet in breadth and running along the entire frontage of the house 'known by the name of the Church of Shevoc house [i.e. Church House]' was reserved out of the sub-lease by Richard Chubb. From this description it would appear that Daniell Sargent's inn stood to the east of the old Church House.[11]

The rent of the head lease was 5s., which was to be paid by the sub-tenant, who also paid an additional 4d. to Chubb. The lease was on the lives of Richard

Chubb, Margaret his daughter, and Agnes Hawkes (or Hawke) of Sheviock. Agnes was probably Richard's married daughter. Margaret may have become Daniell Sargent's wife. The witnesses to the lease were William Odyorne, William Sargent (probably related to Daniell) and the Crafthole scrivener, Robert Honney. In a manorial survey made in 1691, Daniell Sargent's house and garden is shown as being in the occupation of Edward Hawke, at a rental of 6s. 8d.; but there is no indication as to whether Hawke continued with the inn-keeping business.[12]

According to a statement made by Walter Warren in 1764, a 'Little Brew House' belonging to Church House stood on the east side of Church House. It stood between Church House and 'the Little House where Wm Smith now Lives'.[13] The 'Little House' may have been the former *Daniel Sargent's Inn*, and the little brew house may have been used by him. It was probably knocked down by Clinnick when he rebuilt Church House as an inn.

The Carew Arms: Before the introduction of church rates in Queen Elizabeth's reign, churches raised funds partly through the 'church ales' that were held in a building known as 'Church House'.[14] Church house was used both for holding the ales and for the official business of the parish – such as meetings of the vestry. By about 1600, Puritans were attacking the holding of church ales. Richard Carew defended them, but recognised that they were unpopular with many of his Puritan contemporaries.[15] With the introduction of church rates as the main means of raising money, the church house could be said, in part at least, to have become redundant. Sheviock's church house had ceased to be used for regular parish business sometime before 1706. In that year, it was leased to Henry Austen and was described as 'old, ruinous and decayed'. In 1764, it was leased to Mrs Deborah Bartlett, a widow then aged sixty. She was paying a rent of 6s. In 1779, Matthew Bartlett, the smith, who was Deborah's son and heir was the tenant. He let it to Joseph Clinnick (1735-1802), yeoman.[16]

In 1786, Reginald Pole Carew granted Joseph a new 99-year lease limited by three lives. Joseph and his wife, Ann, both died in 1802, leaving a daughter, Ann, and two sons. Ann, who continued to live in the house, married John Landry (1777-1853), butcher, first of St Germans, then of Sheviock. In 1830, John obtained a new lease at an annual rent of £1 10s.[17] It was a condition of the lease that the house should, within five years, be pulled down and rebuilt 'in a good strong and substantial manner' and covered with 'Mill hill or other good blue slate'.[18] This is the building that still stands today, but now converted into two separate dwellings. The new turnpike road, completed in 1826, ran right by the house, and so Landry opened the new premises as an inn, called the *Carew Arms*, sometime before 1835. In 1838, he also rented another cottage on the road leading up to Crafthole (Barn Cottage), and may have lived there.[19] Until his death in about 1850, John ran the inn with his wife and two younger unmarried sons, John Peter Landry (1812-72) and Richard (1815-81). Ann died in 1853 and John Peter became the innkeeper as well as farmer of 20 acres of land. The inn also served as a post office, and Richard was described as sub-postmaster in the 1861 census and post-master in 1871. On the death of John Peter in 1872, Richard ran the *Carew Arms* alone, whilst continuing as postmaster. At about this time his niece, the widowed Mary Jane (Polly) Weihtner (née Landry) moved in as housekeeper.

Copies of a photograph of the *Carew Arms* taken in 1875 have survived. The central figure in the doorway is Richard Landry and the tall lady next to him is Polly. The child at the window above is her four-year old child, Lily. Some of the windows are broken, perhaps as a result of a brawl when clods of earth were used as ammunition. Polly remembered the incident and passed the story on to members of the family. With the death of Richard in 1881, the lease expired. William Pole Carew granted a new lease of the property to his nephew, the rector of Sheviock, the Revd Henry Carew Glanville.[20] The witness was the rector's servant, Mary Pearn. The rent was £1 9s. 3d. One of the conditions of the new lease was that the tenant should not keep it, or permit it to be kept, as an inn. Local tradition is that the rector wished to put and end to the practice whereby the bell-ringers, having done their job on Sunday, would repair to the inn for refreshment instead of attending divine service.[21]

244 *The* Carew Arms *in 1875. The innkeeper, Richard Landry, stands in the doorway next to his niece, Polly Weihtner.*

Inns at Crafthole

The Inn at the top of Well Lane

Bryant Hayes (Spiller's Inn): In 1555, Henry Spiller, his wife Elizabeth, and son Ferdinando, possessed a newly-built house called Bryant Hayes in Crafthole.[22] Ferdinando, who died in 1607, also operated the windmill at Gill Ball near Sheviock Woods.[23] When he died his effects included '2 brewing keeves, barrels & other wooden vessles' valued at £1 10s. and 'canns & beere barrels' valued at 6s. 8d.[24] This inventory suggests that he was running Bryant Hayes as an inn, as well as supplying the bargemen and fishermen using the quay on the River Lynher (the predecessor to George's Quay) with corn, bread and ale. *Spiller's Inn* at Bryant Hayes would have been one of the inns at which the momentous events of 1588 – the descent of the Spanish Armada upon our shores – were discussed as the topic of the day.[25]

Spiller's Inn later came to be called *Jeffery's Inn*. The holding is located at the top of Well Lane, on the north side, and includes the two orchards called the higher and lower orchards. It is a steep hillside site. The enclosures surrounding the upper and lower orchards, were termed in English, 'hayes'. Ferdinando did well out of his windmill and his tavern. When he died he left money and goods worth £64 1s. 6d., a substantial sum. In 1649, Elizabeth Spiller (born in 1586), wife of William Spiller (deceased), and her surviving son, George (born in 1608), still lived in Bryant Hayes, with its half acre of land, but by then the ownership had been divided and William Jeffery was running the inn. The house on the site today is called *Tirada*, a Spanish word meaning beer that is drawn from a barrel – a happy choice recalling both the Elizabethan Inn and the Spanish Armada.

There are two pieces of written evidence connecting Spiller's Bryant Hayes with *Jeffery's Inn*. A 1730 sale and leaseback of a 'messuage or tenement with two orchards ... commonly called the higher and lower orchards', were said on the sale document to have been previously in the tenure of 'Grace and Roger Jeffery'.[26] Roger Jeffery was a cousin of William Jeffery the younger (deceased). On the lease, the two orchards were described as having been 'heretofore in the possession of one Spiller deceased'.[27] In addition, a 1722 lease of a 'little orchard ... sometime heretofore in tenure of one William Jeffery' is marked on the back 'late Spiller's land'.[28]

Jeffery's Inn: In 1603, John Harry, yeoman, sold two plots of land in Crafthole to William Jeffery or Gefferie 'couper' (cooper).[29] The location of these plots is not specified in this document. But in 1610, Richard Avery of St Germans sold to Jeffery a quarter of a tenement 'between the lands of John Smith esq.' (he farmed at Liscawn) on the east and Jeffery's two plots on the west. These two plots had been 'lately separated' from the tenement a part of which was now being sold. The tenement lay between the land of Alnett Harry (John Harry's son) to the north, and 'the waie leading to the towne-well' to the south (i.e. Well Lane). In 1716, Grace Jeffery leased and then sold this same quarter to the blacksmith, Thomas Waite.[30] The lease describes the tenement as a 'messuage … and two orchards … commonly called the higher and lower Orchards … in Crafthole Coombe'.[31] It is known from a law case in the borough of Crafthole that the cooper, William Jeffery, also kept an inn. This case is recorded in 1632, when the farrier, Richard Mitchell, was fined a shilling for making a pile of dung in front of *Jeffery's Inn*.[32]

William Chubb became the tenant sometime before 1755, and probably continued to run the place as an inn. In 1755, he passed the tenancy on to his daughter, Joan Harris, and after her death to his grandchildren, Robert (b.1727) and Mary Warren (1740-96). The Warren family occupied Bryant Hayes until about 1775.[33] It must have been a good outlet for smuggled liquor. Robert Warren, who also rented premises at Portwrinkle, was the tenant of half of Blazor from 1809 to 1821 and of Haye Farm from 1792 to 1832.[34] In 1823, Haye was publicly identified as being an assembly point for smugglers' landing parties.[35]

Bryant Hayes and its orchards were occupied by Simon Waite in 1775, and are so marked on Thomas Pride's map of that year. In 1776, Reginald Pole Carew let the 'messuage … with two orchards … commonly called the higher and lower orchard otherwise Jeffery's orchards' to Gregory Warren at a rent of 5s. In 1823, he leased the same property to James Keast (b.1797), labourer. The property may have ceased to be an inn at this time. Keast also had a house on the other side of the main road.[36] (Elizabeth Warren had become Mrs Keast, James's mother.) Conditions of the 1823 lease were that Keast should 'convert the Pound House on the said premises into a good and convenient dwelling house' and replace any dead or dying apple trees. The pound house was the structure within which apples were pounded to make cider.

The Inn on the site of the old Manor-house

The Finnygook Inn (Sargent's Inn): C.S.Gilbert, writing in 1820, described Crafthole as 'A mean village with two small inns'.[37] One of these was probably *Jeffery's Inn* in the last few years of its existence. The other was what is now the *Finnygook Inn*, which was known in the 1600s and 1700s as 'Sargent's tenement'. The Sargent in question was William Sargent, who was leasing the premises from John Smith of Tregunnick before 1622 when Smith sold the head lease to Richard Wallis of Sconner.[38] William Sargent was an innkeeper. This is known because at the court leet held in Crafthole in November 1620 he was fined 4d. for selling wine in an un-measured quantity.[39] William may have been related to the innkeeper at Sheviock churchtown, Daniel Sargent, mentioned in the case of *Rolle* v *Blake* in 1674. Sargent's tenement consisted of 'a messuage (house) stable and garden', the field containing the Dawney's culver house, known as Culver Park, another field going down to the sea, called Crooked Park, a barn and yard, and banks and waste by the sea. It also included a small orchard in the Coombes. The whole tenement amounted to just over nine acres.

In 1711, Sir William Carew purchased 'Condey's Lands in Crafthole', including Sargent's tenement.[40] In 1718, he let Sargent's tenement, except for the dovecote, to John Edwards junior, grandson (through his mother, Grace) of Richard Wallis of Sconner, on the surrender of Edwards' earlier lease.[41] The rent was 26s. 8d. John Edwards had been 'the Hyne' (hind or principal farm manager) for the Carew family in the years around 1706.[42] He may have continued to keep the inn going, but he was also a farmer, leasing a quarter of Blazor. He died in 1735. Sir William then let Sargent's tenement to another 'innholder', William Lord (*c*.1704-60), at the same rent. In 1741, Lord took on a new lease at the same rent. The fine or premium for the lease, paid over seven years, amounted to £151 6s. 9d., including interest.[43] The lease was on the lives of William, his wife Ann (born *c*.1706), and Thomas Westcott, their nephew, son of the shipwright Richard Westcott of Topsham.[44] The Lords had three daughters, all of whom married Sheviock men. Frances (b.1742) married Sampson Trevan, a farmer; Joan (b.1747) married James Prin, a carpenter; and Jane (b.1752) married Philip Goard, a Mason.[45]

In 1752, William Lord was also renting Harvey's house, orchards and eight acres of land north of Crafthole.[46] In a general rental of 1770, it was noted that the lessee was to lay out £20 in repairs to Sargent's tenement and to 'plant young apple trees'. From 1763 to 1765, when Ann Lord was running the inn, the manorial courts of the manor of Sheviock were held at her inn.[47] They were also held there from 1772 to 1780 (George Westcott, innkeeper); in 1781 and from 1785 to 1796 (William Crocker, innkeeper); 1797-1800 (John Binney, innkeeper), 1801-3 (Elizabeth Binney, innkeeper); 1804-7 (Andrew Kitt, innkeeper, and Elizabeth) and 1807- (William Bews and Elizabeth). The latter two 'Elizabeths' could be the former Elizabeth Binney now re-married. A map of 1825 shows the inn as then being in the possession of Dinah Kitt, perhaps the daughter of Andrew and Elizabeth.[48] Members of the Kitt family had farmed at Blazor in 1741 and also at Hearle's Parks in 1770.[49]

Martin's Inn is first mentioned in a rating list dated 1833-4. The rating lists for the church rate in 1833-4 and 1845-6 show John Martin (b.*c*.1793) as the occupier of 'Martin's tenement and Inn'. It is the same holding as the earlier Sargent's tenement and inn. *Martin's Inn* must have been a lively establishment, for John Martin, the landlord, also played the violin in the church orchestra.[50] He and his wife, Elizabeth, had seven children. On the 1840 Tithe survey and map, he is shown as occupying two houses in Crafthole. One of these is the inn itself. Martin also occupied the 'Long

Orchard' (to the north of the higher and lower orchards) and a smaller orchard in the Coombes. He also cultivated some seven acres of land on the north-east side of the road leading from Crafthole to Sheviock churchtown. In the 1851 census, John Martin still described himself as 'innkeeper and farmer'.

The New Inn; the Finnygook Inn: *Martin's Inn* changed its name to the *New Inn* sometime before 1861, when the new name first appears in the census. The innkeeper then was Thomas Clements, age 47, the son of a local farmer. He was married to Christian. His daughter, Helen, aged 17, worked as the bar maid. The name probably indicates that the premises had recently been rebuilt. Clements was still there with his wife in 1871, assisted by his younger daughter, Ann. The licensee of the '*New Inn* and East Park' before 1895 was Joseph Channings. In 1895, Edward Tabor of Reading, auctioneer and estate agent, and Robert Bath of Brighton, gentleman, took over Channings' leases and also leased Long Orchard.[51] During the Second World War, the *New Inn* was run by William and Hylda Hearn.[52] Sir John Carew Pole (1902-93) was responsible for changing the name of the *New Inn* to the *Finnygook* in *c*.1950.[53]

Audit Dinners: An agreeable custom of Sheviock manor, as of many other manors, was the holding of audit dinners, in October, when rents and other payments owing to the manor were settled up by the tenants. This may well have been a survival from the 'scotale' of medieval times.[54] Originally all the tenants were required to attend the gathering and make their payments. This was part of the duty known as 'suit of court'. In the 1700s, the lord of the manor was paying more than half the total costs of the dinners, but everyone present still contributed the sum of 6d. each, at a time when the

245 *Left to right, the evacuees, Thelma, Vera and Terry Leather with Hilary Lee outside the entrance to the* New Inn, *Crafthole,* c.*1940, after the inn was damaged by German mines.*

246 *William and Hilda Hearn, who ran the* New Inn *during the Second World War, with their granddaughter, Heather Lee.*

average daily wage of an agricultural labourer was 1s. The dinner was held at an inn at Crafthole. Although the name of the inn is not recorded, it is likely to have been the old *Sargent's Inn*, then in the tenancy of Ann Lord.

Several accounts of these dinners have been preserved. At the dinner held on 19 October 1763, the 37 people present ate beef costing £1, a goose (2s. 6d.), which was 'dressed' (i.e. cooked) for an extra 4s., bread (3s.), and greens and butter (1s. 6d.). To drink, they had punch (12s. 6d.), ale (8s.) and wine (1s.). In May 1764, the 31 people present ate roast beef, bread, greens and butter, but no goose. They drank 23 quarts of ale (7s. 3d.) rum (2s.) brandy (2s. 8d.), perhaps smuggled in from France, wine (2s.), and cherry brandy (6d.). One of the spirits was flavoured with 'lymons suger' at a cost of 1s. In October 1766, when 40 people attended, goose was again on the menu as well as beef and also 'puden' (1s.). The tenants drank 42 quarts (whether of ale or cider is not stated) (10s. 6d.), two quarts and 1 pint of brandy and rum (7s. and a few pence), and cherry brandy (6d.).[55] Only one account (undated, but probably 1765) specifically mentions that cider was consumed. At that dinner, attended by 42 tenants, '42 quarts Ale Syder' were drunk at a combined cost of 10s. 10d. A tip of 3s. was always given to the servants at the end of the meal.[56]

Tavern at Portwrinkle

In 1731, Mary Horwell submitted an invoice to the steward of the manor of Sheviock for 18s. 2d. for delivering beer 'to the men that worked one [on] the key'. She may have been related to 'Pearce Horel' who was one of the workmen referred to. Mary may also have been keeping a tavern in Portwrinkle from which she could supply the beer. She was renting a house there for 8s. 8d. in 1770.[57]

Whitsand Bay Hotel (See Chapter 43, *Leisure, Sport and Tourism*)

The Inn at Liscawn

Liscawn was one of the tenements on the manor of Sheviock, but in the 15th century it came into the possession of the Smythe family of St Germans, and may then have become attached to their manor at Tregunnick.[58] In the 1950s, the house was converted into a private club. In 1963, W.H. Williams opened a licensed restaurant there, and took in paying guests. In 1969, Mr Wilkes obtained a full licence and opened Liscawn as an inn. The current landlords, Paul and Fiona Ingall, acquired the property in 1995.

247 *The Ingall family outside the* Liscawn Inn *in 2008. The farmhouse at Liscawn was turned into a club in the 1950s and opened as an inn in 1969.*

Chapter 42

Mills and Millers

Six mills are known to have existed in Cornwall at the time of Domesday Book (1086), though none of them was in Sheviock. The first document mentioning a mill at Sheviock dates from 1286, when Sir William Dawney made a contract with Warrin de Herth (Erth). This allowed Sir William to make and maintain a watercourse through Warrin's lands at Tredrossel, in order to carry water to his mill at Sheviock.[1] This was the manorial mill at Polscoe (also Polscove). The name may derive from Cornish *pol*, meaning stream or creek, plus *skawenn*, meaning elder tree, or more likely, *skath*, meaning large boat or barge.[2] The mill at Polscoe could have been built at any time between 1086 and 1286. It entered the records in 1286 only because it was then found that there was insufficient power to drive it efficiently throughout the year, so an additional source of water was needed. There was another watermill in the parish, further east at Kerslake, but it is not known when this was first built.[3] A windmill was also constructed in the parish, at some time between the early 1300s and the 1500s, on a high hill above Sheviock woods. In the 19th century, there was also a tidal mill at Denabole on Trethill Lake.

One of the incidents of feudal servile tenure on a manor was that the tenant had to grind his corn at the lord's mill. Leases in the Antony archives show that this obligation continued on tenancies of Sheviock manor right up to the 18th century. A lease of Cote, dated 3 December 1674, between Dame Mary Carew and Tristram Harry, yeoman, required of the tenants 'doing suit to the mill, called Sheviock Mill, with all their corn and grain that shall be spent in and upon the said premises'.[4] This obligation was also imposed on the tenants of Holmans, Blazor, Crowstone Parks, Peakes Park and many other tenements of the manor until the late 1700s.

Sheviock Mill

This was the mill belonging to the lord of the manor of Sheviock sited at Polscoe. Sir William Dawney made a contract with his brother-in-law, Warrin de Herth (Erth), allowing him, William, to take water through Warrin's land at Tredrossel '*ad aquam ducenda molendino suo de Sevioc*' (to the water driving his mill at Sheviock), in 1286. The contract was made '*in vigila pentecosten*', on the eve of Pentecost (Whitsun), at Sheviock, probably in William's manor-house at Blazor. The consideration for the right to take the water was 1s. per annum. The occupier of Tredrossel received his shilling each year so long as the mill at Polscoe continued to function. An Antony estate survey made in 1691 includes the entry: 'To James Bond Esq. for a watercourse from Tredrossell to Sheviock Mills pa – 1s.'[5] A receipt from J. Keest, dated 2 December 1725, states, 'recd of Sir William Carew Bart by the hand of John Andrew one shilling in full for one yeares rent for a water course thorough my Barton of Tredrussel to Sheviock Mills'. A general rental for 1770 contains the entry: 'Sheviock Mills – To the heirs of John Neels for a watercourse from Tredrosell – 1s.'[6]

There is an oblique reference to the manorial mill in another charter of Sir William Dawney also dating from about 1286. When he granted 15 acres of his wood called 'Hey(wode)' at Sheviock to the prior and canons of St Germans, in return for them giving up certain rights to take wood, he made it a condition that they should not build any sort of mill.[7] The purpose of this clause was no doubt to protect his mill at Polscoe.

248 *The mill at Polscoe (Sheviock Mill) first enters the records in 1286. All the copyhold tenants of the manor were bound to grind their corn there.*

In the late 1600s, the tenant of Sheviock Mill was Walter Boteler (also Botler or Butler).[8] He was repaid for expenses he had incurred on the mill in 1696 and 1697.[9] The mill had a thatched roof, which was repaired with 'one hundred of reed' in March 1705.[10] Anthony Mitchell, the thatcher, charged 18s. 1d. for the job. Luke Taw, miller, of St John, succeeded Boteler in 1715. The lease was on the life of himself, his wife, Elizabeth, and his son, Thomas, who died in about 1753.[11] The rent was only £1 10s. plus two capons or 2s. But the entry fine was £140, which he paid over the four years 1716-19. A heriot of the best beast was payable on deaths of named lives. Taw was paying the same rent in 1726. In February 1729, he and Henry Lavers were drowned. His widow, Elizabeth, must have carried on the business after his death, because she was rated 2s. for the mill in 1754. The actual work of milling was carried out by her son, Thomas. Sheviock Mill was still known as 'Taw's Mill' after the Taws had given it up. Arthur Bartlett (who also operated Wacker Mill) took out a lease on Sheviock Mill in 1767.[12]

249 *Water was the source of power for most of the mills in Sheviock parish. This waterfall at Trethill powered the ancient Kerslake Mill, later called Bagmill.*

The churchwardens' accounts for 1768-9 show the entry 'I crave alouence for Poulscow Mill 4s.'; for 1770-1 'an allowance for Taw's Mill 6s.'; and for 1771-2 'I crave allowance for tawsmills 6s.'. There is no information as to what the churchwardens bought at Polscoe. However, each year they had to make four journeys to Liskeard to attend the Bishop's visitation court. It may be therefore that they were claiming for bread and ale for themselves, and/or oats or bran for their horses, just as today officials might claim for subsistence and petrol allowances. Arthur Bartlett was still the tenant of Sheviock Mill in 1774, but appears to have sub-let the mill to Abel Marks in 1770.[13] Bartlett bequeathed his lease to his son, William. William died before 1821, leaving nine children, who each inherited a ninth part of the lease.

Jonathan Bickford was rated for Sheviock Mill in 1809-10 and again in 1820-1. The smith, Joseph Bickford, was his brother. One of William Bartlett's children, Thomas, had agreed to sell his share in the mill to William Bickford, who was the miller around 1815.[14] However, with Bickford's consent, he assigned this share instead to

Henry March (b.1781), in about 1820. In 1823, Henry married Elizabeth Trevan at Sheviock. He was still operating the mill in the 1850s, but by 1861, aged 83, he was described as 'retired'. John Langmead succeeded him. When the premises ceased to be profitable as a mill, in the late 1800s, they were converted into the workshop of Davey, Sleep & Co., agricultural implement makers. That company remained there until the 1890s. This is why the house on the site today is called 'The Old Forge'. However, the 1891 census shows that John Maynard (b.1834) was then living there, and he gave his occupations as 'miller and farmer', so perhaps milling continued on the site for some time longer.

Kerslake Mill (also Bog Mill or Bag Mill)

A mill for grinding corn was built at the bottom end of the valley at Kerslake. It was driven by a strong stream that wells up below Blerrick. The mill was an overshot one – i.e. the water passed over the top of the waterwheel driving the mill. The ruins of the mill and the torrent which powered it are still visible on the Trethill estate. Robert Blerok was holding the tenements of Blerrick and Kerslake in 1411, but it is not known if the mill had been built by then. A list of the fees of Edward Courtenay, earl of Devon, was made during his lifetime or just after his death in 1419.[15] It includes Kerslake among the fees of the earl's manor of Sheviock. Sometime afterwards, Kerslake was effectively, if not legally, separated from the manor of Sheviock, and

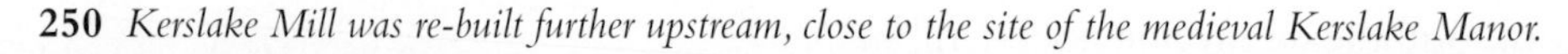

250 *Kerslake Mill was re-built further upstream, close to the site of the medieval Kerslake Manor.*

separate court rolls survive for the manor of Kerslake for the years 1565-1640.[16] The lord of the manor of Kerslake mentioned on the court rolls of 1607 and 1608 was Stephen Medhop (Mydhope) of St Martins by Looe.

According to a map drawn by Thomas Pride in 1775, the mill at the bottom of the valley was originally called Kerslake Mill.[17] However, because it was built on boggy ground, it came to be called 'Bog Mill', later corrupted to 'Bag Mill'. A mill was certainly functioning there in the late 1600s. The mill was let by Henry Wallis of Trethill, together with 'pasture in the coppice adjoining Bag Wood' to Andrew Gregory of Bickleigh, in 1700. The lease describes it as having been 'lately held by Thomas Clap miller, decd.'[18] A Thomas Clap (also Clapp) was also the miller at Wacker Mill in the period 1691-1726.[19] Thomas had two sons, John and Thomas, who were the millers at St John's mills.[20] On 26 May 1772, the Revd Mydhope Wallis and his second cousins, John and Samuel Wallis (to whom the estate was next entailed), let 'Bagge Mill' and premises in Sheviock to John Clap for the lives of John, Jane and William Clap. John Clap was rated for this mill in 1809-10 and 1820-1, when the rate was set at 7d. John was paying a rent of two guineas per annum to the heirs of Mydhope Wallis in 1814. 'Mr Coombs' [William Coombe] was rated for Bag Mill in 1833-4. He also built and operated Denabowl Mill (see below). Richard Clements (b.1811), described as a miller, was the occupier in 1841. He was rated for the mill from 1858 to 1860 and was still there in 1861.

In 1809, another waterwheel was constructed further upstream on the site of the old Kerslake manor. The lower mill was already known as Bag Mill by then, so the higher one was given the name Kerslake Mill.

Denny Bowl Mill (also Denabole Mill)

The Tidal Mill: 'Denny Bowl' is probably a corruption of 'Dawney Bowl'. Tidal mills were known to be in use in England in the 13th century (e.g. at Dartmouth), but there is no evidence for the existence of a mill at Denny Bowl until the 19th century. By lease dated 1 August 1833, but with effect from 29 September 1834, Reginald Pole Carew let 'a Mill called Denny Bowl' to William Coombe on the lives of the lessee (age 39) and his sons, John (age ten) and William (age eight).[21] The mill apparently had two pairs of stones driven by an undershot wheel. The lease included,

> all that Lake called or known by the name of Denny Bowl Mill Pool as the same is now divided off from Wacker Lake by the new Turnpike road from Torpoint to Liskeard together with the Mill House with the Appurtenances called Denny Bowl Mill *lately erected* [italics supplied] by the said William Coombe on the north east end thereof also all that field or close of land called Denny Bowl containing about half an acre of Land adjoining and forming part of the north east boundary of the said Mill Lake.'

251 *The mill pools at Bagmill and Denny Bowl. The lower mill at Denny Bowl was tidal, powered by the water of Wacker Lake.*

The combined yearly rent for the mill and two closes of land was £4. William Taylor (age 45) was the miller in 1851. The Ordnance Survey Map of 1906 marks the spot where the mill once stood with the legend 'Denny Bowl Mill (disused)'.[22]

The Saltings: In addition to the Mill House, Mill Pool and half an acre of land, Coombe also leased, 'a piece of mud land containing … about three acres and fourteen poles being the western extremity of Wacker lake together with the coppice lying on the south thereof and bounded on the south by the Turnpike road.' Coombe was obliged to enclose this piece of mud and coppice 'in a substantial manner and face the outside of the embankment forming such inclosure [*sic*] sufficiently with stone and so construct the same as to properly let off the Freshet [fresh water stream].' Coombe clearly did his work well, because this embankment is still there. The purpose of leasing this mud land appears to have been to create saltpans and produce salt. The Ordnance Survey Map of 1906 designates the land simply as 'Saltings'.

The layout of saltpans on the Axe estuary has been the subject of a recent study.[23] They were created by Sir John Trevelyan at Seaton, Devon, in 1704. To make the salt, rectangular saltpans were dug in the soil down to estuarine clay. The sea water was let into the pans at high water of spring tides, and then the tide was shut out by a sluice gate. During the summer months the sun evaporated the water to form a concentrated brine. The brine was boiled until the salt crystallised. Wood or furze was used as the fuel to avoid cracking the pans. At Sheviock, William Coombe could have obtained wood from the coppice that he leased and furze from the cliffs above Crafthole.

Wacker Mills

Although not in Sheviock parish, these tidal mills are worth mentioning here, because the millers who operated them sometimes ran them in tandem with other mills on the Rame Peninsula. Wacker Mills are first mentioned in 1348 when they formed part of the dower of Sibella, widow of Sir John Dawney.[24] The first miller whose name is preserved is Pasco Sibley, who was an occupier in the mid-1600s.[25] Thomas Clap is named as the occupier in 1691 and 1726. He also operated St John's Mill and Bag Mill in Sheviock. Jonathan Rashleigh, one of the trustees of the estate of Sir Coventry Carew, was the occupier of both Wacker and St John's Mills in 1764.[26] In 1767, Arthur Bartlett, then aged 19, took out a lease on these mills and also on Sheviock Mill.[27] Wacker Mills continued in operation until the 1940s. Tom Bersey and Brian Roseveare of Wolsdon remember the miller coming round on his horse and cart and selling flour. By then, the mill was driven by a petrol engine.

252 *In 1833, William Coombe was making salt in saltpans dug at the western end of Wacker Lake. The tide was controlled by this embankment, which had a sluice-gate at its southern end.*

The Windmill at Gill Ball

A windmill once stood on the high ground above Sheviock woods to grind corn to provide bread for the bargemen and fishermen who used the landing place on the River Lynher.[28] A mill erected in connection with a ferry and landing place was recorded at Starcross (the cross by the stair) in Devon as early as 1240.[29] The Sheviock mill was constructed on a five-acre field, known since the late Middle Ages as 'Gill Ball'.[30] The date of construction of the first mill on this site is not known, but the name of the tenement may be connected with an Elizabethan official, John Gill, who witnessed the grant of a lease in the Coombes in Crafthole in 1580. The presence of the windmill explains the existence of this isolated holding, carved out of Sheviock woods, and adjacent to, but not included in, Treise's tenement.

It is known that the mill at Gill Ball was wind-driven, because it was still functioning in the reign of James I, when it was mentioned in the will of the tenant, Ferdinando Spiller. He died in 1607, and his effects included 'bunting haches & other necessaries for the myll' (valued at 20s.). The bunting and hatches indicate that the mill was driven by the wind, unlike the other water-driven mills in the parish.[31] Amongst Ferdinando's other effects were '2 barrs of yron & beels for the myll'. A 'beele' was a small pickaxe with two sharp points. The miller used this tool to score grooves in his millstones. Like Chaucer's miller in *The Miller's Tale*, Ferdinando sold 'bread and ale' from his mill. His brewing equipment included '2 brewing keeves, barrels & other wooden vessles' and 'canns & beere barrels'.[32] As well as serving the crews of vessels that called at the quay and travellers using the ferry between Sheviock and Erth Barton, Ferdinando also had customers to look after at his tavern, called 'Bryant Hayes' in Crafthole.[33] By 1663, the mill had gone and the field in which it stood was let to Richard Holman (age 50), a farmer at Trewrickle, at a rental of 3s. 4d.[34]

Chapter 43

Leisure, Sport and Tourism

Tourism has become the most important commercial activity in Cornwall accounting for 16 per cent of jobs and ten per cent of total income.[1] In Sheviock, tourism now employs more people and probably brings in more income than agriculture. Even Sheviock Barton, once the farmhouse of the demesne farm of the Dawneys and the Carews, has found a new purpose as a bed and breakfast establishment.[2] In addition, the parish boasts two inns, an hotel, and many 'holiday lets', from which summer visitors can enjoy the sandy beaches of Whitsand Bay and the 18-hole golf course which surrounds the historic culverhouse of the Dawneys.

Richard Carew mentions two sports as being popular in east Cornwall in his day. These were 'wrastling' [wrestling] and 'hurling to goales'.[3] The Cornish were famous as wrestlers and Henry VIII took some Cornish wrestlers over to France with him to compete with Bretons when he met Francis I at the Field of the Cloth of Gold in 1520.[4] Hurling to goals was in some respects similar to lacrosse in that a hard silver ball was used; in some respects to soccer, in that the aim was to get the ball through the opponents' goal posts; and in others to rugby, in that the players could use their hands. Like these modern games, an 'off side' rule applied.[5] Carew wrote that 'These hurling matches are mostly used at weddings, where commonly the ghests undertake to encounter all commers.' Matches were also played on Shrove Tuesday, and, until the Reformation, on Saints' days. After the Reformation, there were fewer holidays, but probably the traditional sports and pastimes still took place at Hocktide (Easter Monday and Tuesday), May, Whitsun, and Midsummer, when the church ales were held. Carew mentions one particular exhibition of physical strength by John Bray, one of his tenants. This probably took place at a gathering on one of the parish holidays:

> For strength, one John Bray (well knowne to me as my tenant) carried upon his backe, at one time, by the space welneere of a Butte length, sixe bushels of wheaten meale, reckoning 15 gallons to the bushel, and the Miller a lubber of foure and twenty yeres age, upon the whole.[6]

Modern Sports

There are very few flat spaces in the parish, and so there have never been any permanent football or cricket pitches. Scratch games have been organised from time to time in farmers' fields. The Victorian restorations of the parish church were followed by football games for the children in the field beside the rectory. The Sheviock Parish Recreation Club, discussed below, organised cricket matches against neighbouring villages until its demise in 1962. After the Second World War, a football team comprising some players from Sheviock, and some from Torpoint, competed in the Plymouth and District League. The cricket and football teams played on Fred Rundle's field at the corner of Trethill Lane and the coast road (on the western side). Today a Table Tennis club meets at the Old School Room in Crafthole and a Badminton club meets at the Memorial Hall.

The Whitsand Bay golf course was laid out in 1905. Formerly it had its own little clubhouse next to the *Whitsand Bay Hotel*, but today the hotel serves as the clubhouse. John Biles remembered the Duke of Gloucester playing there with the professional, Eddy Callaghan, in the 1930s. After the round, the duke presented his ball, signed 'Henry', to Callaghan.

Cruises along the Tamar

In the early 1900s, when steam boats called at St German's Quay and George's Quay, local people enjoyed an outing to Calstock to feast on strawberries and cream. Wilfrid Pengelly recalled walking from Portwrinkle to Downderry to collect his sweetheart,

253 *The* Whitsand Bay Hotel, *built as a private house by Lord Graves in 1871, was removed from Thankes to its present site in 1909-11. This photograph dates from the 1920s.*

and future wife, Annie, and then catching the 8.30 am steamer to Calstock for the feast. The boat arrived back at St German's at 10 pm.

Seaside Holidays

The attractions of Sheviock as a holiday destination were first recognised in 1788, when Lord Eliot of Port Eliot converted some old fishing premises in Portwrinkle into a 'bathing shed'. This happened just a year after the Prince of Wales had instructed the architect, Henry Holland, to convert a farmhouse at Brighton into a Marine Pavilion.[7] According to a handwritten note by Reginald Pole Carew, the premises at Portwrinkle had formerly consisted of a 'Fishing Cellar, & Palace & a Dwelling or Room over the Cellar'. As a fishing cellar and palace, the premises had been successively in the occupation of Philip Blake of Landrake, Thomas Edwards, and Richard Warren.[8] Warren, who was then nearly 70, gave this information in person to Reginald Pole Carew.[9] The conversion of the premises had, however, been done without the knowledge or licence of Pole Carew. Therefore his steward, Charles Rashleigh, wrote to Lord Eliot on 30 August,

> I have … to repeat to your Lordship that Mr Carew claims as within his Right all the soil where your Lordship has erected your Bathing Machine (*sic*) … [He] is desirous of accepting any trifling Acknowledgement for your Lordships Trespass by this Machine … any Acknowledgement paid at the Manor Court will be sufficient.

Lord Eliot wrote back,

> With regard to the Bathing Shed at Wrinkle, I am surprised beyond measure, at your seeming to think it possible that I should have the most distant idea imaginable of calling into question, or of doubting the least in the world; of Mr: Carew's Manorial Right over that Spot. When you mentioned it to me some time since; I am very confidant that I referred myself entirely to Mr: Carew's good will & pleasure, & gave Directions immediately afterwards to Turner to pay whatever acknowledgment, you should be pleased to desire, at the Court.

At a meeting at Port Eliot a few days later, Lord Eliot acknowledged to Pole Carew, in the presence of his son, the Hon. John Eliot and the Revd Mr Penwarne, curate of St Germans, that the bathing shed was a trespass and agreed to pay an annual acknowledgement at the court of Sheviock manor. Pole Carew left a note of that meeting and of the witnesses present.[10] From then onwards, Portwrinkle and the surrounding area became a popular holiday destination, with many local families taking in paying guests for the summer holidays. John Biles remembered Michael Redgrave, the actor, holidaying with his family in Mollie Hoskin's cottage next to Crafthole Farm in the 1930s.

The Beach Hut in St Germans

In the late 1800s, the Earl of St Germans decided to build a beach hut on his own land near Downderry. The 'St Germans Hut' as it became known, was used not only by the Eliot family, but also by other visitors, as reported by a local newspaper:

> By the kindness of the Earl of St Germans visitors have for several years past had placed at their disposal an ornamental chateau, at which provision is made for their comfort by convenient rooms, with dinner and tea services and hot water at a nominal charge.[11]

Unfortunately, some people abused the earl's hospitality and thereafter would-be visitors had to obtain prior permission from the earl's steward, Mr Newport, at Port Eliot. However, as the paper encouragingly pointed out,

> To persons whose respectability is a guarantee for the propriety of their conduct such permission is never refused, and few will leave the charming spot, whence they can watch the passing of vessels up and down the Channel, and the breakers rolling in on the magnificent sandy beach, without in their hearts thanking the noble proprietor for permitting access to so beautiful a retreat.

Some time afterwards a stable and coach-house were added to the two-storey chalet, and also a dairy to provide fresh milk. A housekeeper was also installed.

The Chalet in Portwrinkle

The Chalet on Portwrinkle Beach was built for Lady Beatrice Pole Carew in 1908. The builder was George Hoskin of Crafthole. In 1920, the house was put up for sale by auction in Plymouth, but was not in fact sold then. The particulars of the house

254 *The Chalet at Portwrinkle, built for Lady Beatrice Pole Carew in 1908, was acquired by the Elmhirsts in 1928. Note the pill box at its foot, built during the Second World War.*

prepared for the auction describe it as 'A charming seaside residence. Substantially built in masonry in the Swiss style … beautifully situated in its own secluded grounds … and embracing an area of about one acre and 32 sq. poles.'[12]

In 1928, Dorothy and Leonard Elmhirst of Dartington Hall bought the Chalet from the Pole Carews as a weekend and holiday retreat. The immediate members of their family were their children, William (Bill) and Ruth Elmhirst, and Whitney and Michael Straight, Dorothy Elmhirst's children by her first marriage to the American, Willard Straight.[13] In 1940 or 1941, the house was requisitioned by the army for coastal defence purposes. It was restored to the family in 1944, but much damage had been done. In 1947, the carpenter, Walter May of Clicker, repainted the Chalet and carried out extensive repairs. In 1952, the house was transferred by deed of gift to William Elmhirst. In 1966, it was reported that owing to exceptional rainfall a large portion of the eastern terrace had slipped down the cliff face.[14]

Despite its windswept position on the cliff face, the Elmhirsts experimented with many species of plants in the grounds of the Chalet. In 1965, they planted a dozen *pinus muricata* (Bishop's pines), purchased from the Forestry Commission and said to have come from the Royal estate at Sandringham. Most of these still survive. In the same year, William Elmhirst commissioned a sculpture of welded phosphor-bronze to be placed near the cliff top on a plinth of granite from Bodmin Moor. The sculpture, by Sean Crampton FRBS, was a life-sized figure of the third horseman of the Apocalypse. It was removed when William sold the Chalet in 1972. Michael Straight's autobiography, *After Long Silence*, contains one oblique reference to the Chalet. Leonard Elmhirst's affection for the Chalet was expressed in a letter he wrote to a friend in 1954, 'Apart from the oil on the beach,[15] it is a wonderful place for a five-year old, with lots of pools to explore, and perhaps a little shrimping. The best place for this is … a quarter of a mile east of the Chalet'.[16] Some of the Elmhirst holiday snaps are preserved in the Dartington Hall Trust Archive. They show canvas awnings put up on the beach to cover stalls from which the Portwrinklers sold tea to visitors. To improve access to the beach, Leonard wrote to Cornwall County Council to get them to construct a ramp. This was completed in 1965. The Elmhirsts employed local people to manage the house for them when they were away, and to look after them when they were in residence.

Music before and during the First World War

The rector from 1910 to 1918 was the Revd Herbert Walters. He was a gifted and enthusiastic musician and led, if he did not form, the Sheviock Band. He held rehearsals in the living room of the rectory and was reputed to be able to play all the instruments himself better than the players. He also composed pieces such as the 'Crafthole Waltz',

255 *The band formed by the Revd Herbert Walters became known as the 'Sheviock Prize-winning Band' after winning a competition in 1913.*

256 *Col. Roberts of Trethill (right) and his wife, Hyacinth, with John (Jack) Littleton of Trewin, at a meeting of the East Cornwall Hunt on Bodmin Moor, in 1922.*

257 *The Sheviock Parish Recreation Club in 1920. On the steps: Mrs Marks, two children and an unknown woman. L to R, standing back row: Jack Davey, Dick Pryn, Revd Bertie Lycett Lycett (the driving force behind the club's foundation), Hedley Bastard, Edgar Bersey, Bert Davey. Standing, centre: Harold Hoskin, William Holman (partly obscured), Revd Hindley of the Methodist Chapel, Mrs Holman, W. Grills (partley obscured), unknown woman, Albert Bersey, Mary Hancock, Charles Foster, Charles Symonds (who leased one of his barns to the club at a peppercorn rent), Mr Soady, Bill Bennett, Molly Hoskin, Harold Bersey, Arnold Hoskin, Custi Callaghan, George Pryn, Fred Dawe, Mr Bean. Seated, Mrs Beryl Bennett, Mrs Grills, Mrs M Davey, Mrs Soady, Mrs R. Andrew, Mrs Lycett, Mrs Symons (with bouquet), Miss Lycett, Miss Edie Ough, Miss Marion Andrew, Mrs Violet Bersey, Miss Babs Hill, Mrs Jessie Bersey.*

the 'Trewin March', and the 'Black Row Polka'. The band was very successful, entered Cornish and South West brass band competitions, and won at least one prize, in 1913. Thereafter, it was known as the Sheviock Prize Band. Among other players, Arnold Hoskin played a cornet and Harold Bersey played a trombone.[17]

Walters also formed an orchestra. The string section included women players, such as Jessie Bersey on the viola and Jane Channings on the violin. Some players from the brass band also played stringed instruments, including Arnold Hoskin on the violin, and Harold Bersey on the double bass. The band and the orchestra did not survive the departure of Walters in 1918, but during the war a dance band was formed, with Jessie Bersey playing the piano.

258 *The Women's Institute c.1939. The members are L to R: back row: Mrs Rita Grills, Mrs Giddy, Nancy Bean, Mrs Hobson, Mrs Richards, Mrs Byles, Miss Bersey, Mrs Nance Foster, Gwen Bersey, Mrs Mary Bersey, Mrs Annie Pengelly, Mrs Johnson (the doctor's wife). Middle row: Mrs Lois Whittaker, unknown, Mrs Ri Davey, Mrs Edith Hoskin, Mrs Crispin, Mrs Marian Bolt, Miss Hooper, Mrs Elsie Hancock, Enid Chapman, Mrs Johnson, Mrs Soady, Mrs Adele (Dolly) Channings, Mrs Mabel Grills (carrying Frances). Front row: unknown, Nurse Fletcher, unknown, Mrs Millicent Hoskin (carrying Christopher), Mrs Winnie Dawe, Miss Winifred Roberts (of Trethill), Mrs Crace (of Trewin, President), Mrs Theodora Colwill (holding Julian), Emily Hancock, Mrs Rose Andrews, Mrs Edna Davey, with her daughter, Pauline (standing next to her) and Helen Johnson (in front).*

The *Whitsand Bay Hotel*

The *Whitsand Bay Hotel* was formerly Thankes House, built by Lord Graves in 1871 on the River Tamar at Torpoint.[18] Sir Reginald Pole Carew sold it to a Plymouth syndicate who demolished it and rebuilt it as a hotel at Portwrinkle in 1909-1911.[19] Lord Graves was a descendant of Admiral Graves, victor of the Battle of The Glorious First of June, off Ushant, in 1794. The battle is commemorated in a stained glass window over the staircase in the hotel. During the 1920s and 1930s, a Mr Garland was the managing director and he operated a hotel bus for the convenience of his visitors. From the 1960s to the early 2000s the hotel was managed by the Earle family. The hotel today boasts many rooms and chalets, an indoor swimming pool, and an 18-hole golf course.

Sheviock Parish Recreation Club [20]

The Revd Bertie Lycett Lycett arrived in the parish in 1919, following service as an army padre in the First World War. Soon after his arrival, he formed a planning

259 *Henry Pryn (left) and Arthur Dawe on the beach at Portwrinkle c.1935. Note the stall in the background from which visitors could hire deckchairs and buy refreshments.*

committee with two parishioners, Charles Symonds and Charles Foster, to raise the £200 necessary to start a recreation club and to finance the costs of a clubhouse. Symonds offered his own barn in Crafthole village for use as the clubhouse, at a peppercorn rent.[21] The barn was on the site of what is now Coombe Barn Cottage. The clubhouse was officially opened in August 1920, and a photograph taken outside the clubhouse on the opening day hangs in the lounge of the new Memorial Hall. The village carpenters, George and Walter May, enlarged the club premises by erecting a single storey wooden extension with a corrugated iron roof. Water came from the village pump nearby and lighting was provided by army surplus oil lamps. A flight of wooden steps outside led up to a billiards room on the first floor, which was for men only. There, a fire was lit every day in winter and a newspaper was provided.

A Ladies Committee organised whist drives, socials, flower shows, children's carnivals and dances. The village dances, or 'sixpenny hops', were extremely popular – especially towards the end of the war, when British and American troops were stationed in and around the parish.[22] Sometimes two dances were held each week. Theodora (Dora) Colwill usually played the piano, accompanied by her father playing a large triangle, with Leonard Harris playing drums. Sometimes, when he was home from the Army, Alec Davey played the piano. After the war, the Revd Lycett donated a Bechstein grand piano to the club following the death of his wife. When the Crafthole and District branch of the Women's Institute was formed in 1941, the two institutions shared the work of organising events and any profits arising from them.

260 *Leonard Elmhirst with his son, Bill, and daughter, Ruth, at the Chalet at Portwrinkle in the 1930s.*

After the war, members took part in local billiards and snooker leagues, and a Youth Club was started. Village sports days and carnivals were re-started and Wilfred and Hilary Lee organised weekly whist drives. In 1953, the committee organised special events to celebrate the Coronation of HM the Queen, and used the funds generated to start a New Hall Memorial Fund. The Recreation Club remained a centre of village life until 1962, when the widow of Charles Symonds died, and the club was given notice to quit. The Memorial Hall was opened in 1976.

261 *Teeing off from the ladies' tee at the Whitsand Bay Golf Club in 2008, with the Dawneys' culver house and Whitsand Bay in the distance.*

Appendix 1

Families

Internal cross-references to families mentioned in this appendix are indicated by **heavy type**. For biographies of lords of the manor, see Chapter 5.

Andrew (also Andrews)

John Andrew witnessed William and Frances Condy's lease of a dwelling house and 'splatt of ground' in Crafthole to 'Richard Pope of Crafthole carpenter' in 1706.[1] John Andrew is mentioned as a glazier in the churchwardens' accounts intermittently, though often every year, from 1756 to 1797. A fisherman, John Andrew (b.1771) was living in Portwrinkle in 1841. Another John Andrew (b.1801) described as an agricultural labourer, also lived there, and was perhaps his son.

In 1819-20, a John Andrew was paid 2s. by the church wardens 'for bringing the stone [for mending the church] in the boat'. This may have been the father of the John Andrew who died in May 1905. The latter had six sons, William, Thomas, James Henry, George Walter, John, and Albert Edward, and one daughter, Elizabeth, who married Westlake. John senior left money to John and Albert Edward to buy their boats at Cawsand. He left all his shares in the Portwrinkle Mackerel Seine, together with his boats and tackle, nets and crabpots at Portwrinkle to his sons, James Henry and George Walter. He named George Walter as his executor and left him his pony and trap and household goods. George is seen in the photo of the *Poor Man's Endeavour* fishing seine in Chapter 17. John senior left personal property and money to William, Thomas, and Elizabeth, and to his other sons. William 'Skipper' Andrew was born in a thatched cottage next to the modern Post Office in the late 1800s. A mason by trade, he was employed in re-building Thankes House as the Whitsun Bay Hotel in 1909-11. His descendants still live in the parish.

Archdeacon See **L'Erchdekne**

Arundell

Sir Thomas Arundell of Tolverne (in Philleigh) was second son of Sir John Arundell of Lanherne. He married Margery **L'Erchdekne** (Archdeacon) (d.1420) through whom he inherited the manor of East Antony. He held half a knight's fee in Sheviock in 1428.[2] The inheritance passed to Margery's sister, Philippa. She married **Sir Hugh Courtenay of Haccombe** and their daughter, Joan, was the heiress. Joan married Sir Nicholas Carew, who thus came to possess both Haccombe and East Antony.

Sir Renfrey Arundell of Tremodret (in Roche) (d.1505) was the son of Sir John Arundell and Eleanor Lamborne and nephew of Sir Thomas of Tolverne. He was steward to the earl of Warwick and servitor to King Edward IV. The king made him sheriff of Cornwall and gave him a financial interest of £40 in Sheviock, Antony, and the advowson of Antony.

Walter Arundell (*c.*1538-1622) was a son of Nicholas Arundell and cousin of Sir John Arundell of Trerice. Richard Carew, who was married to Sir John's daughter, Juliana, presented Walter to the living of Sheviock in 1576. According to Polsue (Lake, Vol. IV (1872), p. 147), Walter's grave in Sheviock churchyard was once marked by the following inscription:

> Here lieth the body of Walter Arundell, descended of the house of Trerice, was parson here 44 years, lived 84 years, builded two almshouses, and gave £32 10s., the profit of which, being twelve pence a week, is to be given to the poor every Sunday for ever, by the direction of the parson and wardens.

Walter and his wife, Dorothy, had at least five sons, Gregory, George (1583-after 1649), Gabriel, Emanuel and Alexander. Emanuel was to become rector of Sheviock in the event of Gregory's death.[3] Dorothy, George and Alexander were entered in the court roll of Crafthole of 7 August 1612 as copyholders of High House.[4] They moved there in 1622.

Gabriel Arundell (d.February 1655/6). Gabriel had five children, Walter II, Gabriel, Samuel, John, and Dorothy. Three of these were named on a lease of 1640.[5] Gabriel was not wealthy. In his will, he gave Walter 1s. and all the goods within the house in which he lived (except the press (bookcase)) in the chamber over the hall. He gave £10 to Gabriel. He gave just 1s. to Samuel, and another 1s. to John, together with 'the bedstead with the bed furnished whereon I now lye in the little Chamber over the ground roome commonly called the parlour'. He gave the rest of his possessions to Dorothy.

The Revd Gregory Arundell (*c.*1584-1654) matriculated at Exeter College, Oxford in 1599-1600, but took his BA degree from Broadgates Hall (later Pembroke College) in 1603.[6] In 1613, he became rector of Ladock, a living which he continued to hold after he was presented to the living of Sheviock in 1622. Sometime after 1622, Hancock's tenement in Kerslake, consisting of some 88 acres, was let to the Revd Gregory. After his death in February 1654/5, the holding passed to his son, Richard, and after that to Richard's daughter, Edith.[7] The court roll of Kerslake manor shows that Gregory held another tenancy of the manor in 1636.[8] His son, John, continued that tenancy.[9]

As rector, he was entitled to receive tithes, and according to the evidence of his brother, Alexander, he kept a manuscript book in 1637 in which he entered all the payments made to him. Gregory was ejected from his livings by the County Committee of Cornwall at some time between 1646 and 1649.[10] He was also unpopular with the local fishermen. He was replaced at Sheviock by John **Gey** and succeeded by Richard **Rolle**. He married (1) Dorothy and (2) Edith, sister of Sir Richard Crane. Gregory and Dorothy had one son, David (b.1624).[11] Gregory and Edith had three sons: John, Richard **I** and Francis, and two daughters: Dorothy and Mary.

John Arundell, Gregory's second son, was married three times. His first wife was Elizabeth, by whom he had a son, Gregory, who was left 20s in the will of his uncle, Richard, in 1654. He married, secondly, Ann Skelton (in 1661), and thirdly Ursula Hocken (in 1662 or 1663). He lived at Cote Cottage, Sheviock churchtown. John and Ursula had a daughter, Amy (b.1664), and a son, John (b.1668). John junior married Mary Cole, widow in 1700, and had two daughters who survived infancy (Mary, b.1701, and Elizabeth, b.1704).

Richard Arundell I (*c.*1615-after 1654), Gregory's elder son, leased the larger part of Poole, consisting of some 60 acres in 1653, when he was 38. His wife was a daughter of Thomas **Hoblyn**, lord of the manor of Kerslake, where Richard lived.[12] In his will, he left 20s to the poor of the parish. He left to his daughter, Charity, some money due to him from his father-in-law and from his friend, George Kendall, and £100 to be made from the sale of some manors. He gave to his nephew, Gregory, 20s. He gave other small bequests to his friends, Trehane Scawen, John Beauchamp, and Walter Arundell and to their children, and to the children of his brother-in-law, Francis Reynoles. He left to his son, Francis, all the land within the parish of Sheviock that he had inherited from his father. To his younger son, Thomas, he left lands in another parish.

Alexander Arundell (1599-after 1673) was a joint copyholder of High House in Crafthole. He took over the tenancy of Cross Parks from his father, Walter, probably on the latter's death in 1622. In 1663, he was presented by the reeve to the borough court at Crafthole 'for suffering his house to be ruinous & in decay' and he was fined 13s. 4d.[13] He was a key witness in the case of *Rolle* v *Blake* (1673) when he was 74 years old.

Walter Arundell II (*c.*1630-) was a son of Gabriell. He married Jone in about 1656 and they had a son, Richard, the following year, and another, Walter, who died in infancy, in 1665.

Richard Arundell II (1657- before 1707), son of Walter II, married (1) Bridget *c.*1683. The couple had seven children, Walter (b.1684), Jone (b.1685), Amie (b.1686), Richard (b.1689), Bridget (b.1692), and the twins, Gregory and John (b.1693). Richard had to pay a heriot of £2 10s. on account of Bridget's death in 1693 or 1694. He was probably one of the churchwardens in 1693. The tenor bell in the church had been inscribed 'John Bloy. Richard Arundle 1693'.[14] Richard married (2) Joan, by whom he had a son, Gregory (1695-after 1731) and a daughter, Mary, b.1700. His children by his first wife, Walter and Jone, were lives named in a lease of property in Crafthole in 1699 to John Balsey, yeoman.[15] By then, Richard had lost his status as a gentleman, being described as a 'yeoman'. His son, Gregory, sold barley and oats to the steward of Sir William Carew in 1731.

Blake

Richard Blake was assessed for goods in Sheviock in 1544. According to Kempthorne, the Sheviock Blakes were connected with those of St Erney.[16] Some were classed as gentlefolk; some as yeomen. Blake's Plantation, on the site of the present spinney overlooking Kerslake stream was named after the family.[17] The field name, 'Black-a-ball Pasture', in Trethill and Kerslake, and the section of coast called 'Blackyball' may also refer to the Blake family.

John Blake married Sibil **Holman** in 1591, and after her death, Phillipa **Grilles** in 1603. In 1605, he and Richard **Harry** were partners representing 'Blake's company' in the building of the quay at Portwrinkle. John and Phillipa were most likely the parents of Philip.

Philip Blake (1604-1689) was the head of a household in Sheviock. In 1624, William Uppeton let a dwelling and tenement in Trethill to Philip Blake, yeoman. Philip married Sibley Pope in the same year. In 1663, Philip let a tenement in Lower Blerrick to William **Sargent** for a consideration of £90.[18] This was probably the tenement called 'Sargent's Tenement' conveyed by James Gibbs, MD to Mrs Elizabeth Wallis, widow, in 1706 for a consideration of £90.

John Blake II (b.1625), probably Philip's eldest son, married Grace Smith *c.*1663. On 6 May 1663, **Thomas Smith** (of Liscawn) entered into an agreement with Philip for settling several premises in Sheviock on John II prior to his marriage with Grace.[19] John II and Grace had a son, Philip II (b.1664) and a daughter, Mary (b.1665). John II testified in the law case of *Rolle* v *Blake* (1674).[20]

Philip Blake II (1664-after 1722), son of John II, married Mary of St Erney and they had a son, John III (b.1691). A survey of the manor of Sheviock made in 1691 shows Philip and Anthony Blake as the tenants of 'Hay and Pryor's Wood' for the lives of Henry Blake and Anne Dodridge (née Blake).[21] Philip II was Anthony Blake's nephew. In 1722, Philip was renting four cellars and two palaces in Portwrinkle.

Anthony Blake (1632-1720), second son of Philip, farmed 43 acres of land in Lower Blerrick and Kerslake in 1669 and 1670. He withheld payment of tithes on them and was forced to pay up.[22] In 1684, he and a widow, Elizabeth Bageley whom he later married, let Trethill and fields in Trethill for a year. In 1689, Anthony inherited land in Kerslake and Trethill. He died in 1720.

Bray

Henry Bray was named as one of the victuallers of the carvel called *le Petir Courtenay* of Fowey in an action for piracy brought in 1461. The carvel belonged to **Sir Hugh Courtenay of Boconnoc**, who was related to Thomas Courtenay, Earl of Devon, the lord of Sheviock manor.[23] Walter **Colle**, clerk, was also named as one of the victuallers in the action.

William Bray was listed in Henry VIII's muster roll of 1522 as armed with a bill and sallet.

John Bray. In Queen Elizabeth's muster roll of 1569, John Bray junior of Sheviock was listed as armed with an harquebus, and was therefore worth more than £10 per annum. This John, or his son, was one of the few residents of Sheviock to be described by Richard Carew in 1602.[24]

William Bray II (Brey). The William Brey (*sic*) who was described as a 'yeoman' in his will of 1622 may have been the son of the above John. William's wife and executrix was Thomasine, the widow of one Harvy. His first-named son in his will was also 'John Brey.' The other three, to whom he left £7 apiece, were Oliver, Ferdinando and Amos. He also had two adult daughters, Dorothie and Johane (Joan), and two daughters under 18, Grace, and Alice. He left £10 to each of them, hopefully an adequate portion for each of them to find a husband. He also left £3 6s. 8d. to his step-daughter, Johane Harvy. He was clearly a successful farmer, but the name of his holding on Sheviock manor is not recorded. A lease granted by Richard Carew in 1605 of land and tenements in Portwrinkle names William Bray as lessee of a 'cellar and palaice' there.[25]

Richard Bray was the leading member of 'Braye's Company', one of the three seining companies that stood as guarantors for the building of the quay at Portwrinkle in 1612. He was perhaps the son of the above William.

Emanuel Bray was the father of another Richard Bray (born about 1630). This Richard married Jone, daughter of the weaver, William Reepe, in 1657.

William Bray III (*c.*1615-*c.*1700), is shown as renting a 'cottage and 60 perches' in Crafthole for 4s. a year in rentals of 1634 and 1691.[26] In 1691, he was renting the property on the lives of Joan Bray (his sister, who became Joan **Prin**); William Bray IV**;** Patience Bray and Margaret Kneebone. In a rental of 1634, he is also shown as paying 4d. per annum, probably for a cellar in Portwrinkle.[27]

William Bray IV (1688-after 1775). In 1711, Sir William Carew let a house, garden and meadow containing about twenty yards of land to 'William Bray of Crafthole weaver'.[28] His tenancy was 'for the life of William Bray aged 87 in 1775'.[29] William Bray's house in Crafthole stood on the site of 'The Cottage' next to Crafthole House. His small meadow lay on the other side of West Lane on the site of what is now Sydenham House.[30] In 1722, William Bray IV was also renting a cellar and palace in Portwrinkle at 9s. a year for his fishing operations. The William Bray who was parish clerk in 1754 may be the same person.

William Bray V was reeve of Sheviock manor in about 1775. In that year he is shown as the tenant of the Net Park in Portwrinkle 'by virtue of his office being Reeve of the Manor.'[31]

Alexander Carew [32]

He was the fourth son of Sir Nicholas Carew (d.1469) and Joan Courtenay, who inherited Haccombe, south of the River Teign, and other estates in Devon and Cornwall.[33] Having fallen out with her eldest son, Joan distributed her estates to her younger sons. Alexander (*c.*1439-1492) inherited the manors of East Antony, 'Shoggebroke' (Shobrooke Barton near Crediton), and 'Landegy' (Kea near Truro). He married Isabel (née Hatch). Their son, John (b.1470), married Thomasine Holland, by whom he had a son, (Sir) **Wymond**.

Sir Wymond Carew

Sir Wymond (*c.*1493-1549) was Treasurer of Henry VIII's last Queen, Catherine Parr. He married Martha Denny (*c.*1524), a sister of the Protestant courtier, Sir Anthony Denny, an intimate of King Henry VIII. Wymond was knighted at the coronation of King Edward VI, and was elected MP for Peterborough in the same year, 1547. Sir Wymond and Martha Denny had a son, Thomas, who resided at Antony and purchased the manor of Sheviock.[34]

Chubb(e)

William Chubb was listed in Henry VIII's muster roll of 1522 as armed with a sallet and brigandine.

John Chubb (born *c.*1570) served as deputy portreeve of the borough of Crafthole in 1592, 1593, 1595 and 1596.

William Chubb II (b.1593) rented a 14-acre holding in Trewrickle, later called 'Chubb's' for 10s. 4d.[35] He had two sons, William and John, who were each fined 6d. at the court leet of the borough of Crafthole in October 1619 for attacking and wounding John Bone.[36]

Richard Chubb was a farmer who let premises in Sheviock churchtown to the innkeeper, Daniell **Sargen**t in 1639. Chubb himself was the tenant of Richard Carew the younger.

William Chubb III (born *c.*1635) married Martha, daughter of Tristram and Joan **Harry**. He became a co-tenant of Tristram Harry's quarter of Blazor, which he and Martha managed together when the ageing Tristram Harry moved to Cote in 1694.[37]

William Chubb IV (born *c.*1660) became the sole tenant of this quarter of Blazor after the death of Tristram Harry sometime before 1719.[38] He was still renting it in 1726 when he was also renting one-third of the enlarged Peake's tenement together with John **Littleton** and John **Edwards**.[39]

William Chubb V (born *c.*1710). The court roll of the borough of Crafthole shows William Chubb as living in the borough in 1730. His tenancy of a quarter of Blazor was renewed in 1747 on the lives of his daughters, Joan (Mrs Harris) and Martha.[40] Martha was in occupation of two quarters of Blazor in 1766. Her co-tenant was Joan Phillips, probably her sister.[41] In about 1750, Chubb was the occupier of three tenements in Crafthole: Odiorne's (or Warrens), Bryant Hayes (the former Spiller's inn), and High House. In 1755, he passed these tenancies to his daughter, Joan Harris, widow, and then to his grandson, Robert Warren, husbandman, and his grand-daughter, Mary Warren, spinster.[42]

William Chubb VI is shown as the tenant of 15 acres of Blazor in 1772 on the life of Martha. Matthew Warren was the tenant of this quarter in 1775 on the life of Martha Chubb, then aged 72.[43]

Abraham Chubb appeared as a witness for the complainant, Revd Richard **Rolle**, in the tithe case of *Rolle* v *Blake* (1673).[44] He was a small farmer and paid tithes in kind to Walter **Arundell**, Gregory Arrundell, John **Gey** and the complainant, Revd Rolle. He lived in a house with one hearth in 1664.

Colle (also Cole and Coles)

Sir Adam Cole was steward of the household of the earl of Devon in 1381-2.[45] His duties included administration of the earl's estates in Sheviock.

Walter Colle, clerk, was a friend of John Wall, rector of Sheviock (d.1427) and was left money in his will. In 1461, Walter Cole, clerk, either the same person or a relative, was one of the victuallers of *le Petir Courtenay*, a carvel of Fowey, which was involved in piracy. The ship was owned by **Sir Hugh Courtenay of Boconnoc**, a cousin of Thomas Courtenay, Earl of Devon.[46] Members of the Cole family settled in Sheviock. One of the windows in Sheviock church at one time contained the arms of Cole impaling **Kingdon**'.[47] Anthony Kingdon was the bailiff of the earl of Devon in Sheviock.

Sir Hugh Courtenay of Ashwater and Boconnoc

Sir Hugh (killed 1471) was the son of **Sir Hugh of Haccombe** by his third wife, Maud. He married Margaret Carminow through whom he came into possession of Boconnoc in Cornwall. He owned the carvel, *le Petir Courtenay* of Fowey, which was involved in piracy in 1461. His second son, Hugh, was one of the victuallers of the carvel. In 1471, Sir Hugh joined Queen Margaret at Exeter to oppose King Edward IV. Shortly afterwards, the Queen's forces were defeated at Tewkesbury, where Sir Hugh was killed. His eldest son, Edward, succeeded to the earldom of Devon in 1486 after the accession of King Henry VII.[48]

Sir Hugh Courtenay of Haccombe

Sir Hugh (d.1425) was the younger brother of Edward, the blind earl of Devon. Earl Edward gave to this brother the manors of 'Gotherington' (Goodrington), Stancombe-Dauney and South Allington in Devon, which had come to him through their mother, Emmeline Dawney. Sir Hugh married (1) Elizabeth, daughter of Sir William Cogan, *c.*1393; (2) Philippa, daughter and co-heir of Sir Warrin **L'Erchedekne** of Haccombe; and (3) Maud, daughter of Sir John Beaumont. The inheritance of his second wife, Philippa, included the manor of East Antony. This later passed to his daughter, Joan, who was married to Sir Nicholas Carew.

Davey

Morice Davy. In 1533, 'Morice Davy Joan his wife & Richard their son' became the tenants of Blazor.[49] The bailiff who signed the lease was **Robert Kingdon**.

Henry Davey (1746-1825) first appears as a blacksmith in the churchwardens' accounts for 1780-1, when he was paid 1s. 6d. 'for iron work on the bells'.[50] He was parish clerk of Sheviock until 1811. His eldest son, Henry (1775-1851), married Frances Trevan (1780-1852), daughter of Sampson Trevan and Frances (née Lord), at Sheviock in 1800. Henry succeeded his father as blacksmith and as parish clerk, and remained in office as clerk until his death. His second son, William (b.1776), married Mary Ann Trevan (b.1783), sister of Frances, at Sheviock in 1802.

John Davey (1814-76), the eldest son of Henry and Frances, continued the blacksmith's business in Crafthole with his brothers, Joseph and David.[51] He married Elizabeth Moon in 1841. He developed the business into that of agricultural implement maker. He established a new workshop at Polscoe on the site of the former Sheviock Mill. There he developed and patented 'The Excelsior Plough'. His success enabled him to move into Lynher Villa, where he and his wife were living in 1871, with their servant, Eliza Opie. On his death, he left his business premises, machinery and stock-in-trade to his foreman, William Sleep, who was married to his niece, Ann (daughter of his brother, William Davey, 1805-53). Under the name of Davey, Sleep & Co., the business remained there until sometime before 1897.

John Henry Davey (1846-1923), son of William, also an agricultural smith, took over the smithy in Crafthole in 1876 and continued the shop there until 1909. He was the last blacksmith in Crafthole. He married Eliza Rickard (d.1943). Their grandson, Alec John (1909-71) and his wife, Frances, had two daughters, Pauline (b.1939) (Mrs Thomas Kemp) and Susan (b.1948) (Mrs Barry Irving).

Edwards

Edwards' Parks was an 11-acre holding between Crafthole and Sheviock.

John Edwards married Grace, daughter of **Richard Wallis** of Sconner in the late 1600s. He became the hind of the Carew estates in Antony and Sheviock in 1706.[52] He rented a quarter (13 acres) of Blazor in 1691, on his own life and those of his wife, Grace, and Henry **Blake**. He was leasing the same quarter in 1721 and 1726. In 1710, he was sharing a tenement of 25 acres (Dell's) with John **Littleton**. Between 1710 and 1726, he was also leasing a third (ten acres) of Holman's tenement in Trewrickle. In 1721, he also took on a half share of Peake's enlarged tenement in Trewrickle. In 1726, he shared this tenancy with John Littleton and William **Chubb**. In the early 1700s, he took on a number of big leases in 'late Cundy's' tenement in Crafthole. These were 'Sargent's tenement', including eight acres of land and a house (an inn); and another two houses and gardens there. In 1691, John Edwards also leased a house and garden in Portwrinkle on the life of his son, Thomas, and sometime afterwards he took over Robert Vinton's house and garden in Portwrinkle. In 1710, he was leasing a fishing cellar in Portwrinkle. In 1721, this was marked as 'down'.

Thomas Edwards and Thomas Ellery leased a cellar and palace in Portwrinkle and a field nearby, called Crowstone Park, between 1691 and 1726. Thomas had two daughters, Elizabeth and Joan (born in 1710). In 1691, he rented half of 'Warren's Tenement' in Trewrickle jointly with two others. In 1726, he was renting four cellars and two palaces and another house and cellar in Portwrinkle. He was dead by 1762. His house was converted into a 'bathing shed' by Lord Eliot in the summer of 1788.[53]

Elmhirst

In 1928, Dorothy and Leonard Elmhirst of Dartington Hall bought the Chalet in Portwrinkle as a seaside holiday home.[54] They had two children together, William (Bill) and Ruth; and Dorothy had two children by her first marriage to the American, Willard Straight: Whitney and Michael **Straight**. The family spent many holidays at the Chalet and some of their holiday snaps are preserved in the Dartington Hall Trust Archive at Dartington. Leonard took an active interest in the fishing at Portwrinkle, the upkeep of the quay and access to the beach. Although not a churchgoer, he made a donation towards the restoration of the Sheviock church organ. In 1969, he was elected a vice-president of the golf club. He declined, but gave a donation.

Foster

Kimberley George Foster (1896-1979) was born at Buckfastleigh, Devon. He married (1), in 1916, Hazel Penwarden (d.1938), by whom he had two children, Delphine and Pam; and (2), in 1940, Gertrude Mills (d.2005), by whom he had four sons, Paul, John, Antony and Nicholas.[55] He was appointed surveyor to St Germans District Council in 1916 and lived at Tideford and then at Landrake. Hazel was governess to the Steed children at Poldrissick. In 1924, Foster began to acquire interests in road building and in 1927 founded British Tarmacadam. In the following year, he acquired a quarrying business from the Steed family and Treluggan Manor from the Langford sisters. In the same year he founded the West of England Road Metal Company. In 1935, the company was merged with others to become the Amalgamated Roadstone Corporation Ltd, one of the country's largest suppliers of granite roadstone. During the Second World War, the company built airstrips throughout the UK and after the war made paving slabs used in the re-building of Plymouth. The company was later acquired by Consolidated Gold Fields, which merged it with another company to form Amey Roadstone Construction (ARC). In September 1945, Foster purchased Trewin and its lands from John Littleton. He lived there until his death. He retired as a director of ARC in 1952. Foster was elected to St Germans RDC in 1931 and later to Cornwall County Council, of which he became chairman (1963 to 1973) in succession to Sir John Carew Pole. He was a magistrate from 1946 until 1966 and was awarded the CBE in 1971. He was a keen player of hockey and cricket, founding both the St Germans and Plymouth hockey clubs, and playing for Cornwall at both games. He captained the Cornwall hockey team 50 times. Kimberley Foster Close in Crafthole is named after him.

Grills (Grylls)

John Grylles of Sheviock was entered on Henry VIII's muster roll of 1522 and Thomas Grylles was listed in his 1544 subsidy roll.

Farmers

Edward Grylles married Elizabeth Spyller on 30 October 1604. (On 29 October 1604, William **Spyller** had married Elizabeth Grylles.) Edward rented a tenement in the manor of Sheviock in the period 1656-60 at a rent of 10s.[56] Edward and George Grylles were both churchwardens in

March 1633.[57] George was married to Margaret and they had a son in 1624. They joined with the parish constables in presenting six parishioners to the justices 'for selling of ale without lycins'.[58] In the court roll of the borough of Crafthole, dated October 1640, a little garden and orchard situated at the eastern end of the borough was called 'Grylles walles' otherwise 'Gillhays'. This is the field later known as 'Wellhay', down Well Lane. Thomas Grylles was a witness in the law case of *Rolle* v *Blake* in 1673/4. He was apparently farming at Kerslake and Trethill. A lease made in 1744 describes a tenement as 'commonly called by the name of Grills his fields'.[59] This is probably the field called 'Grills Park' shown on Thomas Pride's map of 1775 and running eastwards from Trethill Lane. Grills descendants still live in the parish.

Fishermen, Sailors and Bargemen

Richard Grills was renting a 'house and garden' in Portwrinkle in 1710 and 1726.[60] In 1727, 'widow Grills' owed 16s. for property in 'Trewinkle' for ¾ year. Four generations of the Grills family of Sheviock plied the trades of mariners or bargemen.[61] The first on record is Philip Grills, mariner, who was born in Sheviock in 1690, married Dorcas Prin in 1725 and died at sea two years later. His son, Philip, orphaned when only a year old, became a bargeman. He married in 1759 and their son, Philip, born in 1766, followed in his father's footsteps. He married Elizabeth Geach, and their son, another Philip, was born in 1793. He too became a bargeman and died in 1871. William Grills, leased a house in Wilcove in Antony in 1722.[62] In 1732, he was one of three barge masters paying a rent of £2 4s. for use of the sand quay at Wilcove.[63]

Hancock (also Hancocke and Handcock(e))

The Hancock estates lay mostly in the southern part of St Germans. Their principal seats were at Hendra (west of St Winolls) and Kelly or Treskelly (north-west of Polbathic). Four members of the family were resident in Sheviock in 1522: Richard, William, John and Jerry. The value of the goods of the last two was £12 each. William, who married a Scawen, held Hendra *c.*1590. The Hancocks were also tenants of land on Kerslake manor from before 1565 to after 1609. Alexander Hancock held land in Sheviock in 1605. He was a tenant for three lives of Kerslake manor, and records exist of rental payments by him from 1607 to 1609. The lord of the manor then was Stephen **Mydhope** (Medhop). The rent was £4 per annum, implying a holding in excess of 60 acres.

Robert Hancock. In 1647, Arthur **Peters** of Sheviock sold to Robert Hancock of Hendra lands at St Winolls, Menawithen and Lancolling. The will of Robert Hancock, who died in 1663, is among the Henderson papers in the library of the RIC in Truro.[64] He had six sons: William, Robert, Humphry, John, Nicholas, and Arthur. William predeceased his father, but Robert entailed to William's son, another William, 'Bedreda' (i.e. Padreda), South Padreda (i.e. Higher Padreda), Triffle, and Tregunnick (on the east bank of the River Seaton). (As to Tregunnick, see **Smythe of Tregunnick** below). William the younger was in possession of North Padreda (i.e. Lower Padreda) in 1688.

William Hancock. In 1690, William Hancock of Hendra, in view of an intended marriage between him and Grace Rolle, daughter of Alexander Rolle of Parkgate in Devon, settled on her Hendra Barton, Triffle and Eglarooze the Higher (except that part still held by his mother, Ann, in dower). Grace died and William then settled those properties on Philippa Sprye, widow and relict of George Sprye, in view of his intended marriage to her.[65]

In 1692, William settled lands in Sheviock on Henry **Wallis** in anticipation of the latter's marriage to Elizabeth Hodge.[66] Hancock's Hill, situated along the western side of the slope bordering Kerslake stream, may have been part of this settlement.

Robert Hancock II. In 1660, Robert, second son of Robert the elder, became rector of St Martins by Looe. His father left him *inter alia* Eglarooze the Lower and '£10 to buy him a nagge'.

Nicholas Hancock. Robert I left to his fifth son, Nicholas, Treskelly, Padreda (for two lives), his lease of 'Venegook Close' in Sheviock, and £10 for life out of Lancolling.

Arthur Hancock. Robert I left to his youngest son, Arthur, £600 to be raised out of Cobland and Lancolling.

Arthur Hancock II. In 1768, Arthur Hancock and his wife Susanna sold Hendra and other parts of the Hancock estate to Edward Eliot for £8,665. In 1799, he also sold to the Eliots: Cobland, St Winolls, Higher Hendra, Lancolling, Padreda, Cair, Narkurs, Eglarooze, Lower Padreda, Triffle and Frogmere. Samuel Hancock was joint occupier with William Clements of a small orchard in Crafthole in 1840. Members of the Hancock family still live in Crafthole.

Harry (or Harys)

Anthony Harry was the bailiff of Henry Courtenay, Marquis of Exeter (1512-1538) for his manor of Sheviock.[67] Two fields in the demesne farm of Blazor, Harry's Ball and Harry's Ball Meadow, were named after the family. Both are now incorporated into the golf course. Members of the Harry family may have occupied what is now Cross House in Crafthole.

John Harry I was assessed for goods valued at £2 in 1521. John married Margaret, and the couple had a copyhold tenancy in Crafthole, where they were living with their son, Tristram, in 1570.[68]

Tristram Harry occupied a holding in Blazor, in the reign of Queen Elizabeth (1558-1603). He also became the tenant of a holding near Crafthole called Hearle's Parks (9 acres).[69] He lived in Crafthole and was portreeve in 1609 and 1622. He was a juror of the borough court from 1628 to 1637.[70] He had a wife, Jane (née Dawe), and a son, John, born in 1603. When he died, in 1638, he left goods and chattels valued at £76 3s. 10d. The bulk of his wealth consisted of his corn crops, valued at £25. But he also had livestock valued at £18 15s. These included three 'keene' [kine or cattle] which gave him his milk, and four bullocks. He had only one horse, a 'nagge' valued at £3 6s. 8d. His furniture and household goods were valued at £18 19s. 4d. On his death 'ye provision of the house in flesh fish butter & cheese' was valued at 5s. He also left 'table cloathes & napkins', valued at 5s., 'ye silver spoons', valued at 8s, and pewter, valued at 15s. He had tools in his workshop valued at 10s. and husbandry tools and other iron stuff valued at 4s. His weapons were a pike, sword and dagger, valued at 6s. 8d. As a young man, he may have been one of Richard Carew's 170 armed pikemen summoned to resist a threatened Spanish invasion in the years 1595-7.

John Harry II (b.1576) was entered on the Crafthole court roll of 1612 as a copyholder of Wilhays. He was also a free tenant of Kerslake in 1608-9.

Alnet Harry (b.*c.*1580) was portreeve of Crafthole in 1606 and 1617 also renting property in Portwrinkle.

John Harry III (b.1603), Tristram's son, was renting premises on the manor of Sheviock in 1634.[71] John and his wife, Joan, were renting one quarter of Blazor from the Commonwealth authorities in 1653.[72] John attended a vestry in Sheviock in the same year.[73] He had a son, Robert, and a brother, George.[74] It may have been this John who married, secondly, Margaret, from whom was descended Tristram Harry III.

Tristram Harry II (b.1643), son of John and Joan, took over the tenancy of the quarter of Blazor and Hearle's Parks previously held by his grandfather.[75] He was also the tenant of the larger part of Poole.[76] Tristram II also married a Joan, and they had a daughter, Martha, who married William **Chubb**. Chubb became a co-tenant of Tristram's quarter of Blazor.[77] In 1692, Tristram was appointed reeve and collector of rents for the Carews.[78] He took over the tenancy of Coate in 1694 and left Blazor to be managed by William and Martha.[79] Tristram was dead by 1719 when William Chubb junior became the sole tenant.[80]

Tristram Harry III, was a descendant of John and Margaret Harry who were the copyhold tenants of Willhays cottage, garden and orchard in Crafthole. He died before 1730 when, at a special court, his widow, Martha, surrendered her lease of those premises to the Prince of Wales, lord of the manor of Crafthole, on condition that he granted a new lease to Amos Pope and his two children, Amos and Mary.[81]

Walter Harry was assessed for goods valued at £6 in 1521.

Richard Harry, who may have been the son of Walter, married Margery **Sargent** in 1570.[82] He was portreeve of the borough of Crafthole in 1604 and was one of the guarantors for the building of the quay at Portwrinkle in 1612.

William Harry, son of Richard and Margery, held a tenancy in Portwrinkle. He died in 1626, tragically young – at the time of his death, his wife, Priscilla, was pregnant.[83] William and Priscilla had a son, Robert. In his will, William is described as a 'mariner' (ship's officer). He left 'sea instruments and bookes', valued at £3.[84]

Robert Harry, son of William I and Priscilla, became a substantial farmer in Sheviock, at one time farming over 200 acres. In 1653, a holding called Blight's (also Bligh's) in Trewrickle had been let to Elizabeth May at a rent of 20s 8d. and two capons.[85] In 1691, the 41-acre holding was let to Robert Harry on the life of Elizabeth May.[86] In 1708, he agreed to pay £220 for exchanging one life and adding two lives on Bligh's Tenement.[87] He was also the tenant of 'the two Hayes Tenements in Sheviock' in 1705.[88] These tenements amounted to 100 acres and were part of the demesne lands of the Carews. Robert was also the tenant of part of Poole (perhaps 48 acres) and of one third of Peake's half tenement (perhaps 18 acres). In the same year he paid more than £39 as a fine for the reversion of Warren's tenement (48 acres). By Michaelmas 1707, Robert owed more than £115, secured by bonds and notes. In 1708, he sold his rights in Peake's to Tristram Harry and John Pope.[89] Robert also inherited his father's fishing tenancies in Portwrinkle and in 1691 was jointly renting ten yards of premises there with Katherine Odiorne, to whom he was related. In 1707, Robert let to one David Pepperell, 'helliar', a house, garden and meadow on the south side of the road leading from Tregantel to Crafthole.[90] Tristram Harry junior was a witness to the lease.

Thomas Harry was a cousin of Richard Truscott, husbandman, who had been in his youth (*c.*1626) a sailor on the *Dayestarr.* When Truscott died in 1655, the beneficiaries of his will were Thomas Harry, Thomas's sister, Joane, and his daughter, Joane.

William Harry II was renting premises for 4s. per annum in Portwrinkle in 1634 on the life of his sister, Elizabeth. He and Elizabeth also had another tenancy on the manor of Sheviock for which they were paying 6s. 8d.[91]

Harvey

In 1691, John Harvey was renting a cellar and palace in Portwrinkle for 1s. a year by the life of his son Thomas. Thomas Harvey was bailiff of Sheviock manor in 1691-3.[92] His bond on his appointment has survived.[93] In the same year, he jointly rented a cellar and palace in Portwrinkle for 2s. He witnessed a lease in 1699.[94]

In 1715, Sir William Carew leased to John Harvey II a cellar and palace then in the tenure of Thomas Harvey (his father), and previously in the tenure of Marjory Warren.[95] The rent was 1s. The lives named were his own and those of Amy, his wife and Samuel, his brother. In 1719, Sir William let the two fields called Crafthole Parks to John.[96] The lives named were himself, his wife, Amy, and his daughter, Mary. In 1723, John was one of the Sheviock churchwardens. His initials, 'I H', are still studded into the church door. His fellow warden was his employer, Sir William. By 1775, his house, garden and orchard in Crafthole (which stood to the north of the modern Tirada) were in the hands of Jane Harvey.[97]

Helman (Hillman)

In 1812, Reginald Pole Carew let to Thomas Helman of Sheviock, yeoman, 'a Messuage Tenement or Dwelling House and Garden' in 'the Village of Wrickle' at a rent of 5s. a year. Helman may have been a smuggler. The house, now called 'Smuggler's Cottage', has the initials 'TH' and the date '1795' carved above the door. It was probably the same Thomas 'Hillman' who was the tenant of Net Park in 1809-33 and of part of Trewrickle in 1820-1. He paid the church rate for Net Park and for Finnygook and North Down in Trewrickle in 1810.[98] He was dead by 1834. The 1812 lease of the cottage was on the lives of Helman (age 65), his wife Elizabeth (49), and William Stephens Helman (19), their son.

Hill

Simon Hill (1823-98) was born at St Martins by Looe. He worked as farm bailiff for the Roberts family of Trethill from 1851. There he met his wife, Emeline Giles (1830-1915), from Walkhampton, Devon, who was working for the Roberts family as housemaid. By 1881, he was farming at Liscawn and employing eight men. Simon and his second son, William (1861-1926) were both musical. Simon discovered the beaker burial on the fields at Trethill in 1880. His eldest son, John (1859-1946) married Clara Walker. John and Clara had five daughters, Mary (Mollie) (m Arnold Hoskin), Peg (m Carlos Loretto), Jane (aka Adèle, m Gerald Channings) and became postmistress in Crafthole, Violet (m Albert Bersey, butcher of Crafthole), and Ena (m Athelston Daw).

Hitchins (Hichens, Hichen, Hitchin, Hitchens, Hitchen)

In the church of St Stephens by Saltash there is a memorial with coat of arms to a William Hitchins, who died in 1593. In the early 1600s, a John and Joan Hitchins were farming at Sheviock Barton.[99] John was dead by 1613, when his widow, Joan, occupied Cote and Crafthole Parks.[100] Among their children were another Joan, William and Randolph. In his will, John left £80 to his daughter, Joan. The terms of the bequest were varied in 1621 when William Hitchens, husbandman, perhaps her brother, and owner of the barque, *Dayestarr*, undertook to maintain and keep her and provide her with 'apparell & other necessaries according to [her] degree and calling'. The scrivener, Robert **Hunny**, was a witness to the variation. William died in 1635 and passed the tenancy to his fourth son, John.[101] John farmed Sheviock Barton and also Crafthole Parks. He also had a tenement in Stockaden in St Stephens by Saltash. He died in 1648. His entire estate was valued at £393 11s.

In 1653, at the age of 32, another 'Jehon' (John?) 'Hichen' was the tenant of Sheviock Barton.[102] The rent was £4 and 2 capons (or 2s.) a year, the most expensive holding on the manor.[103] John Hitchins the younger was dead by 1676. In that year, Joan Hitchin, perhaps his widow, married the rector of Sheviock, Richard **Rolle**.

Thomas Hitchin (then aged 34) was named as a life in a lease of a 32-acre holding to Honor Blake in 1653.[104] In a lease of 1678, 'Thomas Hutchins the sone of William Hutchins of [Sheviock] ... merchant', was referred to as a life named on an earlier lease granted to Henry **Blake**.[105]

A Colonel Hitchins of the U.S. army called at Sheviock Barton when it was being farmed by Tom and Mary Bersey in the 1950s, and declared that it was the home of his ancestors.

Hoblyn

Thomas Hoblyn was taxed 10s. for land in Sheviock in 1521. The Hoblyns were related to the Carews through John Carew, younger son of Richard Carew, the historian, and John's wife Alice (née Hillman of Drewsteignton, Devon). Three of John Carew's daughters were married to Hoblyns: Agnes to Richard of Antron in Sithney, Grace to Robert of Nanswhyden in St Columb, and Bridget to Edward of Bodmin.[106] Until 1704, Edward Hoblyn was steward to Sir William Carew and acted as his lawyer in law suits in London.[107] He died before 1708, when his widow and administratrix, Mrs Damaris Hoblyn, repaid a loan of £1,737 8s. ¾d to the Carew estate. Richard Arundell, son of Gregory Arundell, rector of Sheviock, married a daughter of a Thomas Hoblyn in the second quarter of the 17th century. A Robert Hoblyn was instituted as vicar of Maker in 1683.

The manor of Kerslake, which had belonged to the Mydhope family from 1607 to 1640, came into the possession of the Hoblyn family. An indenture dated 8th October 1750 shows the then owner, Miss Damaris Hoblyn of Croan, converting the entail into a fee simple. On 27 November 1751, Miss Hoblyn conveyed the manor to Francis Kirkham on her marriage to him.[108] In 1760, four members of the Hoblyn family became trustees of the turnpike roads running through the parish. They were Michael, Thomas, Edward and William.

Holman

Sibil Holman married John **Blake** in 1591. A survey of the manor of Sheviock made in 1653 shows that a 45-acre tenement in Trewrickle, later called 'Holman's tenement', was then let to Richard Holman (age 40) on his own life and that of his son, John (age 20). John was named as a life on a lease of a cellar and palace in Portwrinkle to John Reed in 1669. In 1691, the tenement in Trewrickle was let to John Holman on his own life and that of John Holman of Tresmeer. The house and garden that went with it were let to Blanch Chubb on the lives of Dorothy and Blanch Chubb; and later they were let to John Holman on the lives of Katherine and Catherine Holman. The rent was 4s. From 1710 to at least 1726, John Holman was farming two thirds of the tenement at a rent of 18s. 6d.[109] The dwelling house of Thomas Holman in Crafthole is mentioned in a lease of 1759 to the thatcher, Gilbert Stark.[110] It stood to the east of the present post office. A Mrs Holman was living there within living memory.

Honney (also Honey, Hunny, Hunnye)

Robert Honney was a 'scrivener', akin to a modern solicitor. From 1613 to 1636, he was the tenant of a house, with a garden and meadow attached, on the south side of the main road through Crafthole.[111] He frequently acted for Richard Carew. In 1603, he witnessed a lease of premises in Crafthole to the cooper and innkeeper, William Jeffery.[112] In 1610, he witnessed a lease of other premises to Jeffery, and acted as attorney for the landlord, Richard Avery of St Germans.[113] In 1612, he was one of the witnesses of the deed whereby Richard Carew granted the next presentation of the living of Sheviock to the rector, **Walter Arundel**. He also witnessed the will of **William Bray** in 1622. He appears as a juror of the borough of Crafthole between 1607 and 1640.[114] At one time he had been the tenant of a cellar and palace in Portwrinkle. In 1726, this was said to be 'washed down'.

In 1657, Nicholas and J Honey left land valued at £13 p.a. to maintain a school in St Germans.[115] Robert Honney may have been related to them. William Honey, perhaps a descendant of Robert, leased a house and 60 perches of land in Crafthole in 1777.[116]

Hoskin

Thomas Hoskin (1830-1908), who was born in Landrake, originally spelled his name 'Hosking'. He was a builder and monumental mason as well as a substantial farmer. He built Crafthole House *c.*1860, which was known as Crafthole Farm while he and his descendants carried out their farming operations there. He was also at one time the tenant of Sconner Farm. He and his wife, Jane (née Heath) (1833-1927), born in St Germans, ran a grocer's shop from one end of Crafthole Farm, and built a cottage at the other end for Jane's mother, Philippa. They had three children. The youngest, Harry (b.1857), married Elizabeth, daughter of William Brooks (1824-88), chief boatman (Coastguard) at Portwrinkle. He farmed at Cross Farm. Harry and Elizabeth's daughter, Jessie, married Harold Bersey. Their son, (Harry) Arnold (1886-1969), married Mary (Mollie) Hill (1891-1983) of Liscawn. The Berseys took on Cross Farm, while Arnold and his wife continued to farm at Crafthole Farm. Arnold and Mollie's daughter, Lois (1916-91), was head of Sheviock C. of E. School 1943-7. She married (Henry) Hal Whittaker, hydraulic engineer (d.2002). Arnold and Mollie's son, John (b.*c.*1918), married Dorothy.

Walter Hoskin of Tredrossel Farm, noted for its cider production, was a cousin of the above Arnold. Clifford Hoskin, Walter's son, married Millicent (d.2008).

Kempthorne

Gerard Ainslie Kempthorne was born in 1876 at Wellington College, Somerset, where his father, Revd Philip, was an assistant master. His maternal grandfather was Lt-Gen. G. R. Ainslie, formerly Governor of Domenica. After school at Winchester, Gerard went on to St John's College, Cambridge, and graduated BA in 1898.[117] He qualified at St Thomas's Hospital, London, as MRCS and LRCP in 1902. In 1902 and 1903, he worked as a house surgeon at the Derbyshire Infirmary. In 1903, he was commissioned in the RAMC and served in India from 1905 to 1910. He was posted back to the UK between 1910 and 1914, during which time he obtained his Diploma in Public Health. He served with the British Expeditionary Force in France from 13 August to 12 November 1914. He was wounded in action at Nailly, Aisne, on 14 September 1914, and was mentioned in despatches. He was recuperating in hospital in the UK between November 1914 and January 1915. In May 1915, he returned to France as commander of 6 Field Ambulance and was mentioned in despatches again on 24 December 1917. In January 1918, he was awarded the DSO. He returned to India in 1919. In March 1923, he was posted first to Edinburgh and then to Colchester. He was promoted lieutenant-colonel in June 1926, and retired on 10 May 1931. He may have moved to Lynher Villa in Crafthole at the suggestion of his friend, Revd B.L. Lycett, rector of Sheviock, whom he could have met on active service in France. He is the author of the *History of Sheviock* published *c.*1934. In 1936, he published 'Notes on the Cornish Priories' in *Old Cornwall.* He died at St Austell on 4 December 1939.

Kingdon (Kyngdon)

John Kyngdon appeared in records at Plympton in 1355. From 1394 to 1399, Richard Kingdon was portreeve (mayor) of Liskeard. One branch of the family settled in Launceston, another in Lawhitton and another at Trehunsey in Quethiock. Roger Kyngdon (1393-1472) was a member of the Quethiock branch, and there is a brass in the church there to him. He and Joan, his wife, had 11 sons and five daughters. His eldest son, Walter (d.1516), was a fellow of Exeter College, Oxford (1456-68), canon of Crantock, vicar of St Cleer (1473-98), and rector of St Martin's by Looe (1515). At this time the living was in the gift of the marquis of Exeter.

Robert Kingdon was bailiff for the manor of Sheviock when it belonged to Henry Courtenay, Marquis of Exeter (1512-1538). In 1533, he signed a document granting Morice Davy and his wife and son the tenement of Blazor.[118] Thomas Pride's map of 1775 shows a small field in Blazor called Kingdon's Park. His name also appears on a number of fields in the parish of Antony. According to Kempthorne, the window at the east end of the south aisle of the church contained at one time the arms of Cole impaling Kingdon.'[119]

Langdon

In about 1300, Sir Nicholas Dawney married Joan, daughter of William Langdon. John de Langdon was rector of Sheviock in 1330, no doubt as a result of this marriage. At about this time Stephen Langdon was Abbot of Tavistock and Baldwin Langdon was vicar of Tavistock. In the 1600s, the main branch of the family lived at Keveral, on the west bank of the River Seaton, in the parish of St Martins by Looe. Walter Langdon of Keveral was one of the senior Royalist leaders in Cornwall during the Civil War.[120] There is a screen in the church of St Martins that bears the family coat of arms. The tomb of Walter Langdon, who died on 16 February 1676, describes him as the last of the male line.[121] His only daughter married John Buller.

Toby Langdon lived in Crafthole in the early 1600s. He had a hot temper. At the end of April 1616, he attacked the scrivener, Robert **Honney**, and was fined for hitting him on the head with a stone. He insulted him again the next year, for which he was fined 1s. 6d, and he was fined another 1s. for a further insult offered to him. In October 1621, Toby was fined 6d. for attacking John Bone.[122] In October 1623, he was fined 6d. for attacking Richard **Sargent**. He was fined for non-attendance at the court leet of the borough in 1633 and 1640. He was also presented to the justices at the petty sessions at Millbrook in 1633 for 'selling of ale without lycins'. In the same year, Richard Carew the younger granted him a lease of a large property with adjoining 'palace' in Portwrinkle.[123] The property was 140 feet long and 41 feet wide. The lives named in the lease were his son, John, John's wife, Honor, and their son, Toby. Toby senior died in 1654. Honor Langdon is shown in John Rawling's account of the manor of Sheviock of 1656-7 as owing the sum of £1 13 4d. in unpaid rent.[124] Mrs Phillis Langdon was buried in 1719. Roger Langdon, a gentleman, described as a 'riding officer or waiter', and who may have been her husband, was buried in 1723. A riding officer was a customs official. See further, C.S. Gilbert, *Historical Survey of the County of Cornwall* (1820), p. 183 and plate XVI (coat of arms).

Lavers

In 1649, Henry Lavers, fisherman, leased nine yards of ground in Crowstone Park in Portwrinkle on which he was to erect a 'dwelling house' with 'courtlage' and garden.[125] The lease was on his own life and those of his wife and daughter, both called Sibella. A 'John Lavers of Lantick', which is in St Germans parish, but on the western boundary of Sheviock parish, was drowned on 20 June 1650 along with a John Rooby.[126] The two men had been shipmates on the *Dayestarr* in 1626. Members of the Lavers family were involved with fishing in Portwrinkle for several generations. In 1656, the Commonwealth authorities noted that Richard Lavers owed rent of £6 4s. and was to be distrained.[127] John Lavers the younger shared a tenement in Portwrinkle with George **Winnacott** (Winnicot). Simon, Henry and Richard Lavers all signed the Protestation Roll of 1641, and Richard is shown as being one of the Overseers of the Poor. In the Hearth Tax roll of 1664, Simon and Richard Lavers are both shown as living in houses with two hearths. Eleanor Lavers, widow, married Oliver **Wallis** in 1670. She appears to have died shortly afterwards, because Johan (Joan), daughter of Henry Lavers, married Oliver Wallis in 1671. In 1672, John and Mary, children of John Lavers of St Germans parish (perhaps the fisherman drowned in 1650), were lives named on a lease of a tenement called Britton, adjacent to Lantic.[128] In 1729, Henry Lavers was drowned at sea.

L'Erchdekne (Also Archdeacon, Archdekne, Erchdekne)

Members of the family are depicted in liveried garb in a window of *c*.1300 at St Winnow. The arms are 'in a field Argent, three chevronels Sable'. The family possessed the manor of East Antony. Sir Warrine Archdeacon, left two heiresses, Philippa and Margery. Margery married Sir Thomas **Arundell** of Tolverne in Philleigh. She died without issue in October 1420 and is buried in Antony church. Phillipa, who eventually inherited all the estates, married **Sir Hugh Courtenay of Haccombe** (in Devon) and Boconnoc (in Cornwall). Their younger daughter, Joane, married Sir Nicholas Carew of Haccombe (living in 1449), with whom she had six sons. Having fallen out with her eldest, she distributed her estates to her younger sons. **Alexander Carew**, the fourth son, inherited the manor of East Antony and two others.[129]

Littleton

The Littleton family of Sheviock and St Germans appear to be descended from a cadet branch of the family of Sir Henry de Littleton of Lanhydrock.[130] Hugh Littleton (1603-92) lived at Boslymon, Lanlivery. His second son, Hugh (1655-98), lived at Strickstenton, Lanlivery. This Hugh's son, also Hugh (1682-1761), settled in Lanjore, St Germans, and achieved gentry status. He may also have acquired Trewin in Sheviock for his son, John (d.1764), who was living there in the 1750s. A cousin, also called Hugh (d.1788), lived at Intown, St Germans.[131] Lanjore was the ancient seat of the Prynne or Resprinne family. In the early 1700s, it was used as a place for Quaker meetings.[132] Intown is near Triffle. Hugh of Intown, a yeoman, married his cousin, Jane (1710-73), daughter of Hugh of Lanjore (1682-1761), gentleman.[133] They were married in St Germans and Jane was buried in Sheviock.[134]

A John Littleton of Sheviock, who married Dorothy Bloye there in 1698, was the farmer at Haye, where he re-thatched the barn in 1732.[135] He died in Sheviock in 1735 and was illiterate, signing his will with a mark. Their children, Elizabeth (1699-1716), John (1701-2), John (b.1702), Philip (b.1705), Hugh (b.1710) and Samuel (b.1712), were all born in Sheviock. Samuel married Grace Martin in 1738. The John, Philip, Samuel and Hugh Littleton who paid church rates of 1s. each in 1748 were probably these same brothers. Their relationship to the yeoman family at Intown and the gentry family at Lanjore and Trewin is unclear, but as they were classed as yeomen they may have been closer to the Intown branch. In his will, John left to his son, Hugh, 1s; and to his son, Samuel Littleton, 'one younge orchard lying at the Bottom of the Millpool Parke'. He left the remainder of his estate, goods and chattels to his three sons, John, Phillip and Samuel, who were also named joint executors. The inventory included two 'chattell estates' worth £240, farm stock and barley in the ground. The witnesses were Frederick Wallis and Pearce Horwell. Horwell was a labourer who worked on repairing the harbour walls at Portwrinkle in 1723.[136] In 1794, Thomas Littleton, who then owned both Trewin and Tredrozell, nominated Hugh Littleton of Sheviock as gamekeeper, illustrating the differences in fortune between the two families.[137] The Samuel Littleton who was farming 71 acres at Trewrickle in 1841 may have been a descendant of the Littletons of Sheviock village.

In 1718, Sir William Carew let Sheviock Barton and its fields to Hugh Littleton of St Germans, yeoman.[138] He may have been of the Intown family. The lives named were Hugh and his sons, Hugh and Thomas. Hugh (the son probably), was paying the church rate (7s. 3d.) for Sheviock Barton and Horse Pool (7d.) in 1748 and was probably living at the Barton.[139] Hugh Littleton was named as the tenant of 'Treises tenement' (one of the Carew demesne farms) in leases from 1733 to 1766, and was still there in 1770.[140] Hugh Littleton was also farming at Sheviock Barton in 1770 and 1772.

In 1760, five members of the Littleton family were trustees of the turnpike roads running through Sheviock. They were Hugh of Lanjore, Hugh of Sheviock [Barton], Hugh of Intown, Samuel, and John.

The John Littleton who had lived in Trewin died without issue in 1764, leaving the estate to his nephew, Thomas (1747-1815), son of his brother, Hugh. Thomas had taken over Trewin from John's widow Jane (née Boger) by September 1771.[141] In 1772, he married Theophila, only daughter of **John Roberts** (the younger) of Lifton in Devon and Trevol (or Treval) and Carbeile in Antony. She was the sister of **Revd Bryan Roberts** of Drewsteignton. Roberts was a descendant of Revd Richard Wightwick, co-founder of Pembroke College, Oxford. This marriage enabled the Littletons to claim 'founder's kin' status at Pembroke. Their son, (Revd) Hugh (1776-1830), became a Scholar of the college in 1789, and a Fellow in 1797, both on the Wightwick Foundation. He graduated BA in 1796 and took holy orders. He was bursar of Pembroke from 1798 to 1800 and curate of Sheviock from 1802 to 1811. John Littleton, son of Thomas and Theophila, lived at Trewin from 1815 until his death in 1849. John's nephew, also called John, the son of his brother Revd Hugh, lived there until his death in 1869. He was succeeded by his son, John (1859-1910), who was a pupil at Cheltenham College and then, in 1878, became a student at Magdalene College, Cambridge.[142] He married Catherine Williams in 1883. He was succeeded by his son, John (1886-1953).

Mydhope (also Medhope and Medhoppe)

Members of the Mydhope family were seated at Trenant in Duloe parish.[143] The family also acquired Penhale near the River Seaton in the parish of St Martins by Looe. They were said by Hals to be descended from the Mydhope family of Essex. They were lords of the manor of Kerslake from at least 1565 until *c.*1640, as shown by the court roll.[144] The lord in 1607-9 was Stephen Mydhope. He had three sons, Stephen, Thomas and John. In 1640, John succeeded his brother Thomas as lord. Stephen the elder (d.1636) was rector of St Martins by Looe. His son, Stephen, was said (by Polsue) to have succeeded his father as rector, but to have resigned in order to become a Baptist preacher in Looe. He died in 1652.

Francis Wallis (b.1678) of St Germans married a daughter of Roger Mydhope of Duloe, through whose inheritance he acquired Penhale in St Martins by Looe. **Revd Mydhope Wallis**, their son, was born there in 1719. He graduated from Balliol College, Oxford in 1738 or 1739. On the death of his aunt, Ann Wallis, in 1760, Mydhope inherited the Trethill estate. He became curate of Sheviock in 1764.

Mullis

Philip Mullis was the tenant farmer of Scraesdon and Brockhole in Antony parish in 1728.[145] In 1773, his son, also Philip (b.1742) and Philip's wife, Elizabeth (b.1752) took a reversion of the tenancy.[146] Their son, John, was born in 1775 and their daughter, also called Elizabeth, in 1777. Philip Mullis junior was dead before 1793. In 1795, his widow, Elizabeth, took a reversion of the leases in favour of her two children.[147] She was still the tenant in 1807.[148] As a widow, Elizabeth Mullis lived not on her tenements, but in Crafthole. Her house stood on the south side of the main road through Crafthole, more or less opposite the present chapel. She kept a shop and supplied candles to the parish church for the annual Singing Feast held on 4 and 5 November. On 16 January 1795, Elizabeth was one of the five people who requested the Bishop of Exeter to license a room in her house in Crafthole as a Methodist meeting place. In 1818, the Mullis children surrendered their interests in the leases of the two tenements in Antony to Melchisedec Rogers.[149] By then, John had moved to London and was described as a 'gentleman' and Elizabeth had become Mrs Peter of Torpoint. Emma Mullis, perhaps John's granddaughter, married Robert Hancock, who was 17 years younger than her, in about 1860.

Odiorne (also Odyorne, Odyhorn, Oddyarne and Adyone)[150]

Simon Odiorne is shown as the tenant of Drussel (Tredrossel) in an account roll of the rectory made by John Penhale in 1411.[151] He and Richard Odyhorn also leased part of the rector's glebe.

Thomas Odiorne was assessed for goods in 1522. Joan Odiorne, who had been born in 1562, became a copyholder in Crafthole in 1612.

William Odiorne was assessed for goods in 1571, when his goods were valued at £4.[152]

John Odiorne was buried in 1605 leaving goods worth £94 15s. (CRO: AP/0/6). He appears to have had two sons, William II, and Amos.

Laurence Odiorne was a juror of the court leet of Crafthole in 1590.[153]

Christiane Odihorne, widow, sued the fisherman, Thomas Briggett, for an unpaid debt of 13s. 4d. in 1618.[154] A widow, 'Joan Odyarne', had married Thomas Briggett in 1612 or 1613, so the litigants were related.

William II (d.1609), son of John and brother of Amos, was a considerable farmer and fisherman, leaving an estate worth £128 17s. 10d. His livestock included three oxen, three cattle for milking, six bullocks, 40 sheep and 30 lambs. He left 18 acres of growing wheat, barley, oats and peas.

To carry the crops he had two horses, 'a paire of wheele and a wayne'. He was armed with two muskets and a 'fouling peece'. He also owned a cellar at 'Wrinkell Clyffe' and a 'Boate and her furniture'. His widow, Katherine, married Robert Harry.

Amos Oddyarne was a churchwarden in the reign James I (1603-25). He married Thomasine Symons in 1611 and was apparently tenant of Haye. When he died in 1645, his goods were valued at £96 12s. 8d. (CRO: AP/0/141). He leased a cellar and palace at Portwrinkle (value £10). His livestock and corn were valued at £30. Thomasine, then aged 70, was the tenant of Haye in 1653.[155] The couple had at least two sons, Isaiah (Esay) and John, and a daughter, Phillipp(a), who married Oliver Pope.

William Odiorne III was named as a life on a lease to Emanuel Harry of some property in Portwrinkle in 1634.[156] In a rental of 1634, he is shown as renting a tenement for 6s. 8d. The other two lives on the lease were his brother, John and his sister Emblyn.[157] William married Agnes, whose brother, William Hitchens, owned Sheviock's fishing barque, the *Dayestarr*. The couple had eight sons, William, Henry, Stephen, Francis, Jacob, Nathaniel, John and Philip. In 1640, William was one of the two valuers of the goods left by Mary Hitchens, widow (his sister-in-law), in Portwrinkle. William, 'sonne of William Odiorne of Sheviock' was one of the lives on a lease to William Dewstow of a cellar and palace in Portwrinkle in 1635.[158] In 1649, William Odyorne, 'husbandman', acquired a tenancy of ten yards of land and gardens in Crowstone Park in Portwrinkle in connection with his fishing activities. The lease was on the lives of his sons, John, Stephen and Francys.[159] John and Philip went to America, where they are recorded in 1655 and 1656. A William Odiorne owed £2 15s. 4d. as a copyholder on the manor according to an account of 1656–60.[160] William III died in 1662.[161]

William 'Adyone' married Margaret Wilshman at St Keyne in 1659.[162] According to a rental of 1663, he was the tenant of a 30-acre holding called Wayland in Northill parish, which was part of the manor of Sheviock. The rent was 14s. and 2 capons yearly.[163]

Arnott Odiorne was one of the two constables of Sheviock manor in 1633. Annys Odiorne was a copyholder in Crafthole in 1649. Joan Odiorne owed the manor of Sheviock £1 15s. for rental arrears in 1634 according to an account of 1656-60. She was fined 10s. in 1658. In 1691, she had taken over Bridget Lavers' old cellar and linhay at Portwrinkle.[164]

Henry Odiorne, son of William III had been assessed for two hearths in the assessment of 1664. According to the collector, Henry 'returned two short whereof one is a kiln'. It is likely that this was a lime kiln.[165] He was reeve of the manor in 1690 and the tenant of Haye in 1689-90.[166] He was dead by 1691.[167] There was a meadow at Haye called 'Odiorne's' (1775). By 1840, this had been corrupted to 'Addyham's'. Anthony Blake took over a meadow in the borough of Crafthole called Odiorne's *c.*1700.

Stephen Odiorne, son of William Odiorne III, husbandman, had two children: William, and Margaret. In 1669, they were named as lives on a lease of a cellar and palace at Portwrinkle.

Richard Odiorne was named as a life on a lease of Friday's Parks in 1691.

Isaiah Odiorne, a son of Amos, owed £3 for arrears of rent on a property according to an account of 1656-60. In October 1660, officials ordered that the goods of both Joan and Isaiah Odiorne should be distrained to pay their debts. He had a son, Isaiah, who went to North America.

Katherine Odiorne, widow of William II, and Robert Harry rented 10 yards of ground in Portwrinkle on the life of John Odiorne in 1691.[168] Katherine and Robert later married.

Pengelly

A fishing family established at Portwrinkle in the late 1800s. The family also rented 20 acres of land, of which ten acres were planted with potatoes. They kept two horses and later acquired a 'Trusty' tractor.

Joseph and Mary (d.1908) Pengelly lived at Smuggler's cottage together with their children, Theophilus (d.1961), Walter (d.1960), Wilfrid (b.1894) and Edna (1899-1953), and also Joseph's bachelor brother, Theophilus, senior, known as 'Off' or 'the Skipper', because he was skipper of one of the Portwrinkle mackerel seine-fishing boats. Theophilus junior married Ellen Leah from Gulval, Penzance, who later ran a grocer's shop in Portwrinkle. Walter married Margaret Hawke of Sheviock and Wilfrid married Annie Couling of Polbathic. Walter had one son, Lester (d.1999). Edna married Jack Stephens of Polbathic. Joseph and Mary were Wesleyans (Methodists). Joseph and his son, Walter, were both Superintendants of the Sunday School at Crafthole. Theophilus junior was educated at the Methodist school there. He left at 12 to join his father in his fishing operations. Walter, Wilfrid and Edna went to Sheviock School, the boys leaving at 13 or 14 also to go fishing. Joseph and his brother wore canvas fishing smocks and black bowler hats.

Wilfrid had a son, Bert, and a daughter, Margaret (Mrs Bartlett). In 1911, Wilfrid joined the rocket party as a volunteer.[169] His life-saving activities were interrupted by war service in the First World War. From 1932 to 1961 he was the volunteer-in-charge of the auxiliary Coastguard station at Portwrinkle. In 1949 he was awarded the British Empire Medal for his work for the Coastguard during the Second World War and for his lifesaving activities.

Peter (also Peters)

The Peter family purchased Lower Tredis when it was divided into two in the late 1500s or early 1600s.

William Peter. In 1594, one William Holleford was presented in the court leet of the borough of Crafthole for causing an affray and shedding the blood of William Peter. Peter was also presented, because he had insulted Holleford in the first place. Peter was a juror of the court leet of Crafthole in 1590, 1592-4 and 1596.

John Peters was one of the guarantors for the building of the quay at Portwrinkle in 1612.[170] He was born about 1576. He left £40 to his grandson, Arthur, who was living in his father's house at Lower Tredis in the early 1600s. Arthur died at sea in 1651 and left his bequest of £40 to his sisters, Anne and Tabitha.[171]

Oliver Peter was a juror of the court leet of Crafthole in 1608, 1611, 1616, 1618, 1621, 1623-30 and 1632-8. He was a sailor on the *Dayestarr* in 1626.

Amos (Amias) Peter was a sailor servant on *Dayestarr* in 1626 and a juror in 1624 and 1629.

Walter Peter. An account of 1726 shows that a cellar and palace belonging to Walter Peter in Portwrinkle was 'in decay'.

Symon Peter. In 1691, the larger part of Poole (60 acres) was let to Symon Peter and John Dell.

Arthur Peter was rated for part of Poole in 1754. In 1787, Philip Rashleigh demised part of Poole to Arthur Peter, yeoman.[172]

John Peter II was owner of Lower Tredis in 1754.

Samuel Peter was one of the Overseers of the Poor of Sheviock in 1765-6, 1767-8 and 1787-8. This duty was combined with that of Surveyor of Highways. He succeeded John Peter II as owner of Lower Tredis in 1754.[173] It was probably Samuel who sold Lower Tredis to Revd Edward Pole, DD, rector of Sheviock from 1782 to 1796.

Thomas Peter was rated for a tenement at Polbathic in 1809-10 and 1820-1.

Henry Short was the tenant of Sconner and Friday's Parks in 1726. His daughter, Mary, married into the Peter family. Between 1789 and 1795, the churchwardens paid 'Mr Short Peter' various sums for 'lime & carriage', showing that he was operating a lime kiln, probably the one at Polbathic.[174]

Pole

Revd Edward Pole, DD, was the younger brother of Reginald Pole Carew of Antony. He was rector of Sheviock from 1782 to 1796 and purchased Tredis farm from the **Peter** family. In 1760, when the turnpike road was created, a stretch ran through the hamlet of Tredis where there was a turnpike gate. The Revd Pole incorporated the toll-keeper's lodge into a new house that he built on the opposite side of the road from the farm. From his new house he was able to see his church in the distance. The gothic-arched windows of his house proclaimed his status as a clergyman. He died in 1837.

Revd Reginald Pole, Edward's elder son, was rector of Sheviock from 1825 to 1839. In 1831, he received permission from the bishop, on account of illness, not to live in the rectory but 'in the house of my father ... about a mile distant from the church.'[175] He was also rector of Mary Tavy (1826-39) and then of Yeovilton. He was a trustee of the turnpike road under the Liskeard Turnpike Act 1826.

Revd Edward Pole, brother of Revd Reginald, succeeded him as rector of Sheviock from 1839 to 1841. He had two other livings, Templeton (1833-79) and Rackenford (1879-1890). In 1861, a Miss Pole, perhaps a sister, occupied 'Tredis Farm'.

Henry and Jane Pole. In 1889, Henry and Jane were responsible with other members of the Primrose league for erecting a small obelisk in the grounds of Tredis farm.

Pryn (also Prynn, Prynne, Prinn and Prin)

When first mentioned in parish records, the Pryns were connected with seafaring.

Richard Pryn. In 1601, John Smyth of Liscawn let a house and land in Crafthole to Richard Pryn of Sheviock, 'sailor'.

Mary Prynne. John Blighe, who described himself as a 'saylor', made his will in 1607 'intending ... a voyage at sea', from which he did not return. In his will, he left 'unto Mary Prynne ... spinster my best chest with all such things as now are therein' and also 'my best hatt my best breeches and my best jacket'. These bequests suggest that Mary (probably related to the sailor, Richard Pryn) was

Blighe's sweetheart. She was one of the witnesses to his will along with fishermen, William Hellyer, Dowell Dewstowe and John Lytheby, who were all fishermen on board the *Dayestarr* in 1626.

Alnutt Pryn. In 1646, Alnutt Pryn of Sheviock, 'saylor', leased a 'cellar, pallace and courtlage' in Portwrinkle.[176] The premises were already in the 'use and occupation of Alnutt Prynn'. The lease was on the lives of Alnutt's son, also called Alnutt, and Judith and Mary, his daughters. In 1691, when Judith leased Sheviock's old church house, she was described as a 'shopkeeper'. The rent was 2s. 4d. to the lord of the manor and another 3s. 8d. to the church.

John Prin. In 1718, John Prin was drowned with three others.

John Prynn. In 1736, Sir William Carew let a house in the village of Trewrickle to John Prynn (aged 48), on his own life and those of his wife, Grace (age 43) and his daughter Margaret (age 16).[177]

James Prinn. Sometime before 1764, James Prinn was leasing a house in Crafthole, later let to Thomas Bews.[178] He assisted Edward Hawkins with carpentry work at St Mary's church from 1764 to 1786.

Henry Prynn, who formerly worked as an engineer at Brentons in Polbathic, was one of the churchwardens of Sheviock church in 2008.

Roberts

The Roberts family first appears in Devon in 1680, when John Roberts moved to Lifton from Little Braxted in Essex. John's wife, Joyce Bourne, provided the Roberts family with kinship to Revd Richard Wightwick, co-founder of Pembroke College, Oxford. As a result, at least four Robertses became Fellows of the college. John Roberts' son, another John (1702-71) first acquired an interest in land in Cornwall. He married an heiress of Coryton and through her acquired the estates of Trevol or Treval and Carbeile in Antony. He had a son, Bryan (b.1753) and a daughter, Theophila, who married **Thomas Littleton** of Trewin.

Revd Bryan Roberts, DCL (1753-1808), one time Fellow of Pembroke College, Oxford, was Rector of Drewsteignton in Devon and St John in Cornwall. The Carews were the patrons of both livings. He was curate of Sheviock in 1776-89. The Revd Bryan and his wife, Ann Wallis, continued to live at Drewsteignton after she became joint owner of the Trethill estate. He was one of the Justices of the Peace for the county of Devon.

Revd Samuel Wallis Roberts (1793-1863), one time Fellow of Pembroke College, inherited Trethill on the death of his mother in 1836. In 1837, he was appointed as curate of Sheviock by Revd Reginald Pole, to hold until Gerald Pole Carew was old enough to take orders and be inducted as rector. Gerald died, aged only 29, in 1845. Samuel and his brother, John, continued as curates for at least ten years.[179] In 1837, Samuel was living in Antony in leased accommodation, and the rector had to apply to the Bishop of Exeter for a licence of non-residence for his curate.[180] On account of his inheritance, Samuel was obliged to resign his Fellowship, which he eventually did in April 1839. Following his departure from Oxford, Revd Samuel set about building a new house for himself and his two brothers and sister at Trethill. He presided over a bachelor household. Like his brother, Wightwick, he was opposed to some of the Tractarian innovations introduced by the new Rector, Revd Somers Cocks after 1845.[181]

Anne Roberts (1796-1883) inherited Trethill on the death of her brother, John, in 1881. During her period of ownership great excitement was occasioned by the discovery of a Beaker burial on the estate.[182] On her death, the property passed to her first cousin, twice removed, John Dobree Anderson Roberts. It therefore bypassed the cousins of one remove, including Richard Wightwick Roberts, a Fellow of Pembroke College, and John Coryton Roberts.[183]

Revd John Roberts (1797-1881), brother of the foregoing, had been a Wightwick scholar at Pembroke College, but was sent down in 1816 before taking his degree. His offence was 'sleeping out of [his room] and with [another man]'.[184] Notwithstanding this setback to his career, he later took holy orders and for a time acted as curate of Sheviock. He inherited the Trethill estate on the death of Samuel in 1863.

Wightwick Roberts (1799-1872), the youngest member of the family, became a solicitor in Plymouth. He was churchwarden during the incumbency of Revd J.J. Somers Cocks. He complained to the bishop on behalf of the parishioners about the alterations to religious practice in St Mary's church introduced by Somers Cocks. His complaint was in large part successful.

John Dobree Anderson Roberts (1860-1945) began life as a regular army officer. In 1879, he joined the First Brigade RA in Bombay and then Aldershot. In 1887, he was transferred to the auxiliary list. In 1890, he was a captain in the Cork Artillery on retired pay and then transferred to the Duke of Connaught's Own, Sligo Artillery. These were territorial regiments, and for the most part Roberts was able to reside at Trethill. He was prominent in local affairs. In 1898, 'Captain Roberts of Trethill sent a hamper of toys etc' to the children in the St Germans Union Workhouse at Torpoint.[185] He eventually attained the rank of Lt.-Col. (Reserve). He married Hyacinth, daughter of Revd J.H. Kirwan of St Feock, by whom he had one daughter. He kept a stable of eight hunters and a pack of foxhounds at Trethill, and hunted with the East Cornwall on Bodmin Moor. In about 1905, he built a hunting lodge and stables at Tregarrick, west of Minions. He eventually replaced the foxhounds with bloodhounds, which he sometimes loaned to the police to hunt escaped prisoners on Dartmoor. The staff at Trethill consisted of a gardener, William Gardener, a kennel man, a groom, and a handyman, Albert Doney. The kennel man also reared pheasants. The handyman cleaned the boots and shoes, filled the grates, milked the house cows, looked after the mule that pulled the carts, and helped the gardener look after a grass tennis court. From 1903 to 1934, Roberts was 'Parish Manager' of Sheviock C. of E. School. In 1920, the new rector, Revd B. Lycett Lycett, elected him as rector's warden of St Mary's, a position which he retained until his death 25 years later. William Gardener's daughter, Millicent, joined the household as cook in 1934, and remained there until she married Clifford Hoskin of Tredrossel in 1940.

Winifred Roberts (1894-1957), daughter of the above, succeeded her father as rector's churchwarden in 1945. She resigned on leaving the parish in 1948. She was a leading light in the Women's Institute. Like her father she was a passionate horsewoman and rider to hounds, and a good painter of horses.

Rolle of Heanton Satchville, Devon

Robert Rolle (*c.*1560-1633) was married to Joan Hele (d.1634) and was seated at Heanton, near Okehampton. His father, Henry, had married Mary Yeo, heiress of Heanton (d.1591). Robert and

Joan had three sons, (1) Sir Samuel (b.1588); (2) Sir Henry, Judge of the King's Bench; and (3) John.[186] The couple also had three daughters, Joan, Grace and Margaret. In 1621, Grace became the second wife of Sir Richard Carew (son of the historian), and in 1631 Joan married Sir Richard's son and heir (by his first marriage to Bridget Chudleigh), the ill-fated Sir Alexander Carew. Margaret married Hugh Boscawen of Tregothnan. The Rolles were a zealously Puritan family who followed an austere lifestyle.[187]

Sir Samuel Rolle (b.1588, knighted 1620) eldest son of the above, married (1) Margaret Wise, and (2) Anne, daughter of the historian, Richard Carew. He was educated at Oxford and at the Inner Temple. Perhaps as a result of his marriage to Anne, he came to live in the parish of Maker, where his son, Samuel, was baptised in 1632.[188] He was a Puritan and Parliamentarian during the Civil War. He was lord of the manor of Callington, and proprietor of its profitable market. He increased the prosperity of the town by developing the yarn trade. The yarn was sent to Exeter, then the principal place for the manufacture of serges.[189] In 1640, Rolle was returned as MP for Callington. In 1649, he was listed as the owner of 'six cottages in one burgage in the borough [of Crafthole] by the yearly rent of two shillings six pence'. He also held 'one other messuage there for which he payeth yearly … the some (*sic*) of one shilling.'

Samuel Rolle, son of Sir Samuel Rolle, was baptised in Maker church in 1632.[190] The Samuel Rolle who was elected portreeve of the borough of Crafthole in 1713, and died in about 1719/20, may have been the same man or his son.

Richard Rolle (1616-1680) was the son of Richard Rolle of Cookburye, Devon, gent, and a cousin of Samuel. He was appointed to the living of Sheviock by the patron, Sir John Carew, then a minor. His certificate of fitness was signed by Sir Henry Rolle, Lord Chief Justice of the Upper Bench (see above), John Rolle (see above), and others.[191] He had four wives: (1) Mary, by whom he had three children, Mary (baptised 1656), Richard (b.1657), who matriculated at Oxford in 1674, and Margaret (b.1658); (2) Elizabeth (married 1665), daughter of Thomas **Smyth** of Liscawn. Their daughter, Elizabeth, was born in 1664 and probably died soon afterwards along with her mother; (3) Joan (m.1668; d 1675). She was the daughter of William Jane, the Registrar of Sheviock during the Commonwealth and parish clerk after the Restoration; (4) Mrs Joan **Hitchins** (m 1676; d 1683). The Hichens family were the tenants of Sheviock Barton, close by the rectory. Their son, George, was baptised in 1679. He died the following year and was buried on the same day as his father.

Sargent

Richard Sargent. In 1612, Richard Sargent and his partner, Thomas **Warne**, were members of a fishing syndicate that gave a guarantee to Richard Carew and his son for the building of the quay at Portwrinkle. In 1634, he rented a property in 'Wrikell' for 6s. 8d.[192] The other lives named on the lease were his son, William, and his nephew, John.

Henry Sargent. In 1613, Walter Pryn of Harberton, Devon, let a house and 20 acres of land in Blerrick to Henry Sargent of Sheviock, yeoman. Three years later Henry let the same property to his son, William, on a 99 year lease for a rent of 20s.[193] The lives named were William Sargent, and Elizabeth Prynn, daughter of Thomas Prynn of Antony, deceased. The house let to Henry may have been the property later known as Middle Blerrick.

William Sargent, who could have been the son of either Richard or Henry, leased the inn at Crafthole (the modern Finnygook) from John Smith of Tregunnick sometime before 1622.[194] At the court leet held in November 1620, he was fined 4d. for selling wine in an un-measured quantity.[195]

Daniel Sargent was an innkeeper in Sheviock churchtown in the mid-1600s. His inn stood on the east side of Church House. In 1639, Daniel took a sub-lease of other premises in Sheviock from a farmer, Richard **Chubb**. The lease was on the lives of Richard Chubb, Margaret his daughter, and Agnes Hawkes (or Hawke) of Sheviock. The witnesses were William **Odyorne**, William Sargent and Robert **Honney**. In the case of *Rolle* v *Blake*, commissioners examined Nicholas Sargent as a witness at Daniel Sargent's Inn in Sheviock village on 25 April 1674.[196] Before becoming an innkeeper, Daniel had been a sailor.

Thomas Sargent held a tenancy in Blerrick (perhaps Higher Blerrick) in the early 1600s. He died before 1630 and left his lease to his daughter, Joane, who married first Hodge (perhaps John) and then George Seccombe. When, in 1630, Joane's son, John Hodge, married Thomasine Jacob of Antony, this holding was left in trust to provide maintenance for Joane and then a widow's portion for Thomasine in the event of John's death.[197] The scrivener, Robert Hunny, was a trustee.

Smythe (also Smyth or Smith)

The senior branch of the family was established at Tregunnick, near the River Seaton in St Germans. Robert Smyth of Tregunnick was one of the leaders of the Prayer Book Rebellion of 1549. Another branch lived at Liscawn in Sheviock from the 1400s to the early 1700s. The Smiths owned property in the borough of Crafthole and in the 1600s often paid fines for absence from the court leet. If elected to the office of portreeve, they paid deputies to serve for them.[198]

Richard Smyth held land in Sheviock in 1428.[199]

Thomas Smyth was living at Liscawn before 1461.[200] In that year his widow, Joan, granted lands there to her grandson, John, and to his heirs by Joan, daughter of Robert Lankynhorne.[201]

John Smythe. In 1488, John Smythe granted lands in 'Lanscawen' to Sir John Halywell, **Alexander Carew** and John Payne, clerk.[202]

Robert Smyth. In 1522, Robert Smyth was assessed for land in the parish, and in 1528 was admitted at the manor court to 'Bellond's' (i.e. Velland's) tenement, which adjoins Liscawn.[203] In the Subsidy roll of 1544, Smyth was ranked in the third wealthiest group.[204]

John Smyth LLD. In 1554, the Catholic Queen Mary appointed a John Smyth LLD as rector of Sheviock. It is not known whether he was related to the family of Liscawn.

John Smythe. According to Kempthorne, a floor memorial in Sheviock church marked the grave of 'John Smythe gent, 1598' and bore the arms of the Tregunnick family, viz., 'azure a saltire argent between four mantlets or'.[205]

John Smyth. In 1602, Smyth made grants for life of houses and lands in Crafthole to John Mychell, farrier, and Mychell's son, John, and to Richard Prynn, tailor.[206]

Oliver Smyth was renting premises on the manor of Sheviock (probably in Portwrinkle) for 1s. per annum in 1634.[207] The other lives on the lease were his nephew, Thomas, and his sister, Julyan.

Thomas Smith, gent, married Mary Arundell in 1610. They had at least two sons, Francis (born 1625) and Nicholas. Smith held three cottages in Crafthole in 1649.[208] In 1652, he had his goods sequestered as a supposed delinquent, but they were later restored.[209] Smith and his business partner, Nicholas Carkeek, rented four cellars and two palaces under the cliff and within the key at Portwrinkle *c.*1670.[210]

Nicholas Smith, son of Thomas, married Martha Hitchens in 1651. They had a son, Samuel, in 1655 and a daughter, Martha, in 1658. In 1669, another son, John, matriculated at Exeter College.[211] In September 1673, Nicholas succeeded to his father's property in Portwrinkle.[212]

Samuel Smith. In 1716, the parish register states that 'Mr Samuel Smith was buried, being a gentleman.' He was the last male of his line to live at Liscawn. The property passed to his sister, Martha, who was married to John Deeble.

Spiller (also Spyller)

Henry Spiller. In 1555, Henry Spiller, his wife Elizabeth, and son, Ferdinando, had a copyhold called Bryant Hayes in Crafthole, which became an inn.[213]

Ferdinando Spiller died in 1607. His effects included '2 brewing keeves, barrels & other wooden vessles' and 'canns & beere barrels', the necessary equipment for inn-keeping.[214] The inventory of his goods, and his tenancy of the five acres of the wind-swept Gill Ball, also showed that he operated a windmill.[215] He was probably bailiff of Sheviock manor, as he was tenant of Bailiff's Meadow. On his farm land, he grazed two cattle and ten sheep and kept ten hogs. He also undertook a little arable farming, leaving in his will, '2 harrowes', 'betaxes, drills and shovels'. He was a man of many parts – innkeeper, miller, farmer, bailiff, huntsman, fisherman and soldier. At his death, his goods included 'a rapier, dagger, musket & pike'. Like his younger contemporary, **Tristram Harry**, he could have been one of the pikemen recruited by Richard Carew to resist the Spanish invasion in 1595-7. Ferdinando and his wife, Margery, lived in comfort. His goods included '4 feather beds their boulsters and pillowes', '6 counterletts', '3 payre of blankets & 2 paire of sheets', 'a dozen of table napkins', 'sixe cushions', '6 sylver spoons', and many pewter dishes as well as numerous beds and other pieces of wooden furniture. He possessed a nag and a mare, two yearlings and 'a hackney, saddle & side saddle'. Ferdinando died leaving money and goods worth £64 1s. 6d, a substantial sum, even though some of the money had to be used to pay off his debts. He owed £11 to Mr Trelawny (*sic*) of Plymouth; £6 to John Bligh (perhaps the sailor of that name who also died in 1607); and £13 to Nicholas Collinges. On the credit side he was owed money by Mr Silvester of Plymouth; his relation, Elias Spiller, Philip Wallis, and one Edwards. One of his friends, David **Blake**, though illiterate, helped to compile the inventory of his goods. Oliver **Wallis**, who lived at Trewin, also helped. Other witnesses to his will were Revd Gregory **Arundell** and the churchwardens, Edward and George **Grylles**, who were related to Ferdinando. On 29 October 1604, William Spyller, son of Ferdinando and Margery, married Elizabeth Grylles, and on the next day their younger daughter, Elizabeth, married Edward Grylles. After Ferdinando's death, Margery moved into Cote Cottage, which included seven acres of land, and she also farmed the eight acres of Crafthole Parks.[216] Margery died before 1613.

William and Elizabeth Spiller had three sons, Ferdinando II, Henry II and George (b.1608). Elizabeth and her sons, Henry and George, became copyholders of the inn at Bryant Hayes in 1608.[217] Henry also owned three other cottages and 'a quarter part of a fourth part of a house in one burgage'.

Sir Henry Spiller, MP, of Laleham, Middlesex, was a cousin. He was an Exchequer clerk in the Lord Treasurer's Remembrancer's office, and was knighted by James I. He amassed great wealth, and when he died in 1653, left property to his cousins, with the bulk of it going to Henry II.[218]

Henry Spiller II. In June 1660, Henry II sold to Sir John Carew for £60 a 'messuage, lands & tenements ... gardens orchards and stirpes [strips] of land common and common of pasture meadowes pasture and feedinges ... in Crofthole'.[219] He had moved to Ebbisfield in Hampshire and was described as a gentleman.

Mary Spiller, daughter of Ferdinando and Margery, married William Bond of Earth in 1599.[220] In 1576, Mary and her father had taken a reversion of the rights to fish and hunt water birds in Thankes Bay and Pengelly Bay and half the fishing rights in St Peter's Bay, St John's Bay and Wacker Lake.[221] According to John Norden's *Survey*, Mary was still paying a rent of 2s. 8d. for these rights in 1615.[222] Regrettably, the records do not show whether Mary was an Elizabethan 'roaring girl' who tucked her petticoats into her belt and herself shot and fished, or whether she merely enjoyed the economic benefits of her property until they passed to her husband in 1599.

Ferdinando II married Margaret *c.*1664, and they had a son, Henry III, born in 1665. In 1691, Ferdinando II, his wife, Margaret, and John Deeble were the tenants of the 60 acres of Berry Wells and Berry Down.[223] The rent was £4. Ferdinando was buried at Sheviock in 1710.

Henry III was farming at the demesne farm of Haye from 1694 to 1696. He was paid for 'Repairs of Hay-Tenements' in August 1694 and again the following February.[224] Descendants still live in the parish.

Straight

This is the family name of Dorothy **Elmhirst**'s two sons, Whitney and Michael, by her first husband, the American, Major Willard Straight (1880-1918). The Elmhirsts acquired The Chalet in Portwrinkle in 1928.

Whitney Willard Straight (1912-1979) was born on Long Island, NY, but moved to Dartington, Devon, in 1926 after his mother's marriage to Leonard Elmhirst. In 1929, aged seventeen, he obtained a pilot's licence. In 1931, he went up to Trinity College Cambridge. In the early 1930s he acquired a number of racing cars, which he raced at Brooklands, setting up a lap record in 1934 and winning the South African grand prix in the following year. In 1935, he married Lady Daphne Finch-Hatton, elder daughter of the Earl of Winchilsea and Nottingham. They had two daughters. On his marriage, he quitted motor racing and formed the Straight Corporation, which acquired and built aircraft and operated eight airfields, including Exeter Airport. In 1936, he designed and built a two-seater light aircraft, called the Miles Whitney Straight. It was probably one of these that he landed on the golf links at Whitsand Bay in the 1930s, as remembered by John Biles.

Straight became a British citizen in 1936, joined the RAF and was awarded the MC in 1940 for action in Norway. During the Battle of Britain, he flew Hawker Hurricanes and brought down four enemy aircraft. In August 1941, he was shot down and captured in Vichy France. He was awarded the DFC. In the following year, he escaped and returned to England. He commanded No 216 (Transport) Group in the Middle East, and was promoted to Air Commodore. In 1944, he was made a CBE. On the formation of BEA in 1946, he became MD and deputy chairman. He moved to BOAC as managing director the following year. He was chairman of BOAC from 1971 to 1976 and was appointed Executive Vice-Chairman of Rolls Royce in 1976.

Michael Straight (1916-2004) attended the school founded by his mother and stepfather at Dartington, and then went on to study economics at the LSE and Trinity College, Cambridge. At Trinity, he became a member of the Apostles, a society that included Guy Burgess and Anthony Blunt. Like them, he was recruited to spy for the Russians, on whose instructions he went back to the USA to work in the Office of the Economic Adviser in the Department of State. In 1940, he left to work on *The New Republic*, a liberal journal founded by his parents. At this time he and his first wife, Belinda (Binny) (née Crompton), became friends with Jessica Romilly (née Mitford) and her first husband, Esmond.[225] The Straights had five children. After service in the US Air Force, he returned to *The New Republic*, of which he was first publisher and then editor. In 1963, President Kennedy asked him to become chairman of the newly-formed Advisory Council on the Arts, a post that would have involved a security check by the FBI. Straight made a voluntary confession about his contacts with the Russians. His statement provided the first hard evidence of the spying activities of Burgess and Blunt. However, Blunt's spying activities were not made public until 1979, when Mrs Thatcher made her famous statement in the House of Commons unmasking him as a traitor. In 1973, President Nixon appointed Straight deputy chairman of the National Endowment for the Arts, from which he retired in 1981. After divorce, Straight married (2) Nina Auchinchloss (née Steers) and (3) Katherine (née Gould), who survived him. His many writings include three novels and a play. His autobiography, *After Long Silence*, was published in 1983. Amidst all the political revelations, it contains one oblique reference to the Chalet at Portwrinkle. See also Chapter 43, *Leisure, Sport and Tourism*.

Wallis

The name, Wallis, is common in Cornwall, since it was the name by which first the Saxons and then the Normans referred to native Britons. The first Wallis mentioned in Sheviock is 'Robertus le Waleis', Robert the Briton, who is mentioned in a charter of Henry Dawney between 1174 and 1206. A law case from the 1200s records that Roger Chapman of Shevyek (*sic*) and his brother Henry killed John Walecu (perhaps Wallis) in his house in Sheviock. This house, according to Dr James Whetter, was probably a tavern.[226] No Wallis is mentioned in Sheviock in the survey and loan list of 1521. In the subsidy roll list of 1544, there is a John Wallys. In the muster roll of 1569, a John Vallys (Wallis) is listed as armed with an harquebus. He was therefore a man of some means. John Wallys married Susanna Carkeete in 1610. Ferdinando Wallis married Mary **Peter** in 1616.

Wallis of Trewin

Oliver Wallis. In 1572, an Oliver Wallis married Margaret **Sargent**.[227] This is the 'Olyver Wallys of Shevyocke yeo.' who made an agreement with Richard Carew in 1605 to erect a pilchard cellar and palace in Portwrinkle. In a list of the free tenants of the manor of Landrake dated 1578 there is a reference to 'the lands of Ralfe Wallis and Oliver Wallis [of] Trewinna [Trewin] in Sheviock'.[228] Trewin was a manor.

Oliver Wallis II married Catherine and they had a son, Peter, in 1626. The Protestation Roll of 1641 lists an Oliver Wallis.

Oliver Wallis III. In 1670, an Oliver Wallis married Eleanor **Lavers**, widow. In 1671, Oliver Wallis married Joan, daughter of Henry Lavers. The Lavers family, who were involved in the Portwrinkle fishing industry, and rented property there, also farmed at Lantic, not far from Trewin. In 1691, Oliver Wallis married Elizabeth Austen, widow.

John Wallis. Edward Kneebone, in his survey of East Hundred (1684), described Trewin as 'the seat of John Wallis, gentleman'. In about 1655, John Wallis married Mary. They had six children, Richard (1656-before 1667), Mary (b.1657), Elizabeth (b.1663), John (b.1665), Richard (b.1667) and Arthur (b.1672).

Wallis of Sconner and Crafthole

Richard Wallis (*c.*1581-1653) married Ursula. Their children included: John (b.1613), Anne (b.1625), Richard (II) (b.1626), Edward, Joan, and Mary. A survey of the manor in 1653 showed Richard Wallis as the tenant of Sconner, on his own life and that of his eldest son, John. The holding at Sconner consisted of 88 acres.[229] Richard Wallis was an investor in building the quay at Portwrinkle in 1612. He may also have been a lawyer, because he was one of the 'attorneys' who had witnessed the sale of Sconner to Richard Carew the younger in 1617. In 1653, 'Mr Richard Wallis of Skonner was buryed'.[230] In his survey of East Hundred (1684), Edward Kneebone included Sconner in his list of 'seats of note'.

In his will, proved in 1654, Richard left one pound to the poor in each of the parishes of Sheviock, Rame and St Germans, indicating the breadth of his interests as lawyer and merchant. He left the bulk of his estate to his eldest son, John; a bequest of £120 to Edward, and £2 to Richard. He also left £300 to his daughter, Mary, and £2 each to his married daughters, Joan Walter and Anne Hobbes. He left £1 to Jane Budge, perhaps a trusted servant. Finally, he left small bequests to each to his three grandsons.

The Old Manor-house at Blazor (Crafthole). Probably in the reign of King James, John Smith of Tregunnick had acquired from the Duchy of Cornwall the site of the Dawneys' ancient manor-house and dovecote at Blazor, above Crafthole. This property was held in free tenure and was legally part of the borough of Crafthole. In 1622, Smith sold the head-lease of this extensive property to Richard Wallis of Sconner for £104. Richard was fined for non-attendance at the court leet of Crafthole from 1628 to 1630. In 1638, he was one of the jurors of the court.[231] In a Parliamentary Survey of 1649, he is shown as holding seven cottages in five burgages in Crafthole.[232] In 1650, he let that part of the property called 'Sargent's tenement', to his son, Richard II, and his wife, Isott (daughter of Willyam Sparkman of St Germans), for life; and after their deaths to their daughters, Grace and Mary.[233]

John Wallis. Richard bequeathed the head-lease in the Crafthole property to his eldest son, John. In 1661, Sir John Carew let Sheviock Barton, Berry Down and Berry Wells to John Wallis of Sconner and William Hitchins of Sheviock, both described as gentlemen.[234] The consideration was £280. In May 1667, John Wallis sold his lease of the Crafthole property, subject to the sub-leases, to Willyam Sparkman junior for £250. Sparkman then let some of it back to John's brother, Richard II.

Richard Wallis II was married to Sparkman's sister, Isott.[235] Sparkman had a daughter, Frances, who was married to a clothier of Tavistock, called William Condy. He also had a son, Benjamin, who is described as 'of Tavystock yeoman' in a lease of 1679.[236] Benjamin Sparkman and Frances (Condy) were co-heirs to William Sparkman. In 1694, William and Frances Condy let that part of Condy's tenement known as 'Sargent's' to Mary Wallis, spinster.[237] The tenement included Culver Park, but the dovecote standing in the park was excluded from the lease. Mary became Mrs Cole sometime before 1702.

Richard Wallis II and his wife, Isott, were the tenants of 'Sargent's tenement' from 1650. In 1653, Richard also leased two quarters, or 28 acres, of the adjacent holding called Blazor.[238] Richard was a juror of the court leet of the Borough of Crafthole in 1663.[239] Another juror was Anthony Wallis (see below). In the Hearth Tax roll of 1664, Richard Wallis, 'gentleman', is shown as occupying a house with four hearths. 'Richard Wallis the sone of Richard Wallis of Sheviock,' was described as a merchant in a lease of 1678.[240]

Richard and Isott's daughter, Grace, married (1) a certain Popplestone, who was dead before 1694, and (2) **John Edwards**.[241] Mary Wallis sold her share in the Crafthole properties to Edwards who, in 1702, sold his interest to William and Frances Condy and then leased most of it back.[242]

Anthony Wallis

Anthony Wallis married Annis Pe[ter?] in 1640. They had a son, John, in 1656. Anthony is shown as possessing a house with one hearth in the 1664 roll.

Anthony 'Wallace' II married Grace Sargent, widow, in 1689. In 1698, William and Frances Condy leased to Thomas Waite of Sheviock, blacksmith, a 'cottage dwelling house and herb garden' on the main road through Crafthole. It had previously been in the tenure of Anthony Wallis. The rent was 8s.[243] The house lay between the house of Henry Richards on the east and the shop once occupied by John Earle, blacksmith, on the west.

Anthony Wallis married Elizabeth Avery in 1697. In 1710, William Condy and his son, William, let a house and garden in Crafthole to Anthony Wallis of Crafthole, 'sayler'.[244] The house had been let to Thomas Avery of Crafthole in 1679. The lease was on Anthony's own life and the lives of his wife, Elizabeth, and his daughter, Agnes. The rent was 4s. The property was situated on the south side of the main road, west of Thomas Hollman's house in the east and behind the late William Toser's shop to the north. In 1759, the same premises were let to the thatcher, Gilbert Stark, and are marked on Thomas Prides map of 1775.[245]

Philip Wallis. In 1620, the claim by a Philip Wallis, perhaps the Philip Wallis of Lanlivery who became tenant of Hearle's Parks in Sheviock in 1640, to register his arms and pedigree at the Herald's Visitation was disallowed. Philip Wallis is shown in an inventory of goods compiled on the death of **Ferdinando Spiller** in 1607, as owing him £5.

Wallis of Trethill

In the early 1600s, a John Wallis moved to Trewall, north east of Downderry, in St Germans parish. He apparently came from Fentonwoon in Lanteglos-by-Camelford.[246] John married Francis Jory of Lanjore, east of Trerulefoot and south of Heskyn, also in the parish of St Germans. They had a son, Ferdinando (1620-1687). He, together with Robert Hancock and four other overseers of the poor in St Germans, were entrusted with land purchased under the will of James Neilder (or Nylor), dated 20 June 1649. Rents from the land were to be used for certain charitable purposes. Ferdinando left land in St Germans to his elder son, Ferdinando (*c.*1640-1692), and land in Nether

Blarrick, also called Nether Sheviock to his second son, Henry. This became part of the core holding of the Trethill estate.

Henry Wallis married Elizabeth Hodge of St Germans in 1692. On 26 October 1692, in anticipation of their marriage, William Hancock of Hendra, who owned Trewall and most of the land in the southern part of St Germans, settled several premises in Sheviock on the young couple. 'Hancock's Hill' on the Trethill estate may be one of these settled lands. In January 1693, Henry purchased freehold land at Trethill in Sheviock from Anthony **Blake**, gentleman, and his wife Elizabeth, where he built 'a convenient mansion'.[247] The site may have been the place where the coach house of Trethill House stands today. The price of the land was £605 7s. 6d.[248] In January 1706, five years after Henry's early death, his widow purchased from James Gibbs, MD another tenement in Trethill, formerly Sargent's tenement, for £90. A grave tablet in the church, which is no longer visible, was inscribed,

> Here lyes the body of Henry Wallis of this parish, gent. who died the 12th of Oct., 1701; aged 49 years. Also John Wallis, his 2nd son, who died the 30th of October, 1714; aged 19 years. Also Ferdinando Wallis, his eldest son, who was Sheriff of this county in 1736; and died the 14th of July, 1738; aged 44 years. Also here lyeth the body of Elizabeth Wallis, wife of the aforesaid Henry Wallis, of Trethill in this parish, who died the 7 of November; in ye 86 year of her age 1743.

Ferdinando Wallis (1694-1738), Henry's eldest son, was High Sheriff of Cornwall in 1736. He died two years later, aged 44.

Ann Wallis (1697-1760), Henry's daughter, inherited Trethill and bequeathed it to her first cousin once removed, Revd Mydhope Wallis. According to the accounts of Miss Damaris **Hoblyn** of Croan, who owned the neighbouring manor of Kerslake, Mrs Ann Wallis, probably this same Ann, rented from her a house and land in Kerslake and Trethill in 1754/5.[249] The rent for this property for £4 13s, suggesting that it included the 88 acres of Kerslake that had been leased by Alexander Hancock from the Mydhopes in 1607. Ann's rights under the lease passed to John Wallis the younger of Callington (and formerly of Camelford).

Revd Mydhope Wallis was born in 1719. His father, Francis (b.*c.*1678) was the son of Ferdinando Wallis of St Germans (*c.*1640-1692). His mother was a daughter of Roger Mydhope of Duloe who inherited Penhale in St Martin's by Looe. Mydhope matriculated at Balliol College in 1735 and graduated in 1738/9. He is said to have been an excellent classical and Hebrew scholar. In 1759, he was appointed headmaster of the Grammar School at Plymouth. On the death of Ann Wallis, his father's first cousin, in 1760, he inherited Trethill and gave up his teaching post. He married Elizabeth, daughter of Philip Palmer the younger of Sheviock. She was then living in Sheviock churchtown, in a house that had been leased to her father, and Mydhope went to live there.[250]

In 1757, Elizabeth Palmer had taken out a lease on Bailiff's Meadow. The lives named were her own (she was then 26) and those of Thomas Littleton (aged 9) and Philip Palmer, presumably a younger brother or nephew (aged 4). A son was born to Mydhope and Elizabeth in 1761, but he lived for only a few weeks.[251] In September 1766, Mydhope renewed the lease on the house and garden in Sheviock on the lives of himself and his wife and his eight-month old daughter, Jane, who died sometime before 1777.[252] Revd Mydhope Wallis was churchwarden of Sheviock in 1762-3 and curate from 1766 until 1774. In the latter year, he was again listed as the tenant of both 'house and garden' in Sheviock and Bailiff's Meadow. His house in Sheviock would have been a convenient residence for him as curate. Mydhope and Elizabeth had two further daughters, Ann, who married Revd Bryan Roberts of Drewsteignton, Devon, and Elizabeth, who married Revd John Bennet, curate of St Mary's, Sheviock, 1789-1793. A Mrs Wallis, who could have been Mydhope's wife, Elizabeth, died in 1779 or 1780, and he himself died in 1791.

In 1760, Mydhope became a trustee of the turnpike road running through Crafthole. In 1767 and 1768 he was appointed Overseer of the Poor and Surveyor of Highways for the parish. Revd Mydhope Wallis was rector of St Endellion from 1753 to 1774. In 1776, he became rector of St John. On 26 May 1772, together with his cousins and next heirs, John and Samuel, he let Bagmill to the Clap family for three lives. On 28 and 29 September 1783, he leased some land from Mrs Damaris Kirkham (née Hoblyn). On Mydhope's death in 1791, the Trethill estate passed to his cousin, Captain Samuel Wallis RN.

Of Mydhope and Elizabeth's four children, only two daughters survived into adulthood. Ann married **Revd Bryan Roberts**, and Elizabeth married Revd John Bennet, curate of Sheviock 1789-1793. Elizabeth died in 1805 and Ann in 1836. In 1795, on the death of the then proprietor, Captain Samuel Wallis, Trethill passed into the co-ownership of Ann and Elizabeth. On Ann's death in 1836, the estate passed to her eldest son, **Revd Samuel Wallis Roberts**.

John Wallis of Fentonwoon (1713-1780) was the elder brother of Capt. Samuel Wallis. Both brothers were born in Fentonwoon (also called Fenteroon) in Lanteglos-by-Camelford. Their father was John Wallis (1680-1768) of Fentonwoon and their mother was Sarah Barrett (d.1731). Their father's mother was Mary Wallis of Trewall in St Germans. She married a cousin, John Wallis of Fentonwoon. John probably inherited the family seat of Fentonwoon, because he is described by Polsue as 'the last of the family of this place'. The family representatives sold the estate in 1801. John married Ann – and lived in Stoke Damerel. They had a daughter, Ann, who married Captain John Thomas Duckworth, RN, & Colonel, Royal Marines. There is a memorial to their son, Lt.-Col. George Henry Duckworth in St. Mary's church, Sheviock. Henry Wallis, who had acquired Trethill in 1693, was the great-uncle of John and Captain Samuel Wallis. John died at Trethill while staying with his cousin, Mydhope. John's wife, Ann, died in 1806.

Captain Samuel Wallis RN, the younger brother of John, was born in Fentonwoon in Lanteglos-by-Camelford. He married Betty Hearle of Penryn. He achieved lasting fame through his circumnavigation of the globe in HMS *Dolphin* between August 1766 and May 1768. In the course of this voyage he discovered Tahiti and other South Sea islands. The Wallis and Futuna Islands are named after him. After his voyage he was appointed a Commissioner of the Navy. According to Polsue, he at one time resided at Trelissick in Feock, where his portrait was painted by Clifford. Copies were hung at Tregenna Castle and at the home of a Mr Prater of St Austell. On the death of his cousin, Mydhope, in 1791, he inherited the Trethill estate. He died in London in 1795.[253]

Samuel and Betty had a daughter, Betty, who married Samuel Stephens of Tregenna Castle, St Ives. Stephens was elected MP for St Ives, and became High Sheriff of Cornwall in 1805. He died before 1838. Betty Stephens was said to be still living in 1842.[254]

Warne (also Warren)

According to the subsidy roll, two men called 'John Waren' were living in St Germans parish in 1544 as well as a 'William Waryn' and a 'Reynold Waryn'. In 1608, William Waren, perhaps a descendant of William of St Germans, married Elizabeth Wallis of Sheviock parish. Ezekiel Warren was a sailor on Sheviock's fishing vessel, the *Dayestarr*, in 1626. Robert Warren was shown as a 'clerk' inhabiting a house in Sheviock with three hearths 'and one other in a bakehouse' in 1664.[255] There was a holding in Trewrickle called 'Warrens'. It contained some 48 acres stretching between Trewrickle and Tredrossel. It also included a house, which may have been the one with three hearths referred to above. Sometime before 1653, the holding was divided into two more or less equal portions.

Thomas Warne. In 1612, Thomas Warne and his partner, Richard Sargent, were members of a fishing syndicate that gave a guarantee to Richard Carew and his son for the building of the quay at Portwrinkle.[256] In a rental of 1634, Thomas Warne is shown as paying a rent of 4d. per annum to the lord of Sheviock manor and Margery Warne is shown as paying a rent of 1s.[257] The lives named on the lease were her children, Thomas and Mary.

Gregory (b.1719), *George* (b.1724), and *Richard Warren* (b.1727) were brothers. All three were named on George's lease of Higher Clicker and a tenement in Crafthole, formerly in the possession of one **Odihorne**, in 1742.[258] George was described as a yeoman. Thomas Pride's map and survey of 1775 show Gregory Warren as tenant of an 'orchard at Crafthole' at the bottom of Well Lane and Richard Warren as tenant of Higher Clicker. In 1798, three properties in Crafthole were described as constituting 'Warren's tenement'. One was Odiorne's tenement, probably the house originally built by Walter Sonne and then occupied by Joan Odiorne under a copyhold dating from 1612. It was some 16 perches in extent. The map showing Lord Clinton's property in Crafthole *c.*1825 shows this dwelling house and garden designated as 'Warren's'. In 1776, Gregory also took a lease (to commence after the death of John Truscott of Sheviock) on Jeffery's higher and lower orchards at the top of Well Lane.[259] The lives named were Mary (age 18) and Elizabeth Warren (age 12). Mary became Mrs Elliott and Elizabeth became Mrs Keast.[260]

Robert (b.1727) and *Mary Warren* (1740-96). William Chubb was the tenant of Bryant Hayes in Crafthole sometime before 1755, and probably ran the place as an inn. In 1755, he passed the tenancy on to his daughter, Joan Harris, and after her death to his grandchildren, Robert and Mary Warren.[261] The Warren family occupied Bryant Hayes, a convenient outlet for smuggled liquor, until about 1775. Robert Warren was the tenant of a house and garden in Portwrinkle c.1775. Robert Warren was the tenant of part of Blazor from 1809 to 1821, and of Haye Farm from 1792 until his death in 1832.[262] The farm became an assembly point for smugglers' landing parties.

Matthew Warren was the tenant of a quarter of Blazor (29 acres) in 1775 on the life of Martha Chubb, then aged 72.[263]

William Warren (b.1722) occupied the dwelling in Crafthole marked 'Warrens' on the 1825 map of Lord Clinton's property.[264] He also leased a little orchard in the Coombes in 1783 for 10s. 6d.[265] The lives named were his children William (age 21), Robert (age 18) and Elizabeth (age 16).

Walter Warren. In 1723, Sir William Carew let to Walter Warren 'of the parish of Sheviocke … Tailer' the 'cottage (now fallen down) with a garden plot thereunto adjoyning in Sheviocke … adjoyning to the house where John Warren now dwells, late in the tenure of Jane Palmer'.[266] The rent was 2s. The lives named were Walter, his brother, Robert, and Christian, daughter of John Nichols of St Germans, 'Tailer'.

Winnacott

In 1648, 'George Winnacott of Sheviock husbandman' was the builder and tenant of a cottage in Sheviock woods by the River Lynher. The rent was 2s.[267] George's Quay (now gone) and George's Lane are named after him. George was probably a son of John Winnacott, who had been a sailor on the *Dayestarr* in 1626. The account of the bailiff, John Rawlings, made between 1656 and 1660, shows that George also shared a tenement in Portwrinkle with Joan Lavers. In 1656, they owed rent of £2 17s. 1d. and were to be distrained.[268]

Another son of John Winnacott was probably the John Winnacott, husbandman, who leased ten land yards in Crowstone Park (big enough for a fishing cellar) for 10s. in 1649.[269] Mary Winnacott, perhaps the younger John's wife, had a house in Portwrinkle. A life on the lease was that of Richard Winnacott, probably her son. He died in 1693 and Mary had to pay a heriot of 10s.

Appendix 2

Jurors of the Court Leet of the Borough of Crafthole

Jurors from the Reign of Queen Elizabeth to the Reign of King Charles II [270]

Arrundle (Arundell), Gregory, clericus, 1630
Avery, Robert, 1591, 1592, 1596-7
Avery, John, 1636, 1639, 1646

Bambery (Burnebery), John, 1612, 1617
Battyn, Mathew, 1590, 1591
Beard, Peter, 1623, 1630
Beare, Richard, 1619-21, 1623-5, 1628-30, 1633, 1635, 1638-9, 1641, 1643
Bickdon (Bickham), Philip, 1617, 1619-20 (d.1624)
Bickdon (Bickton), Francis, 1627, 1629
Blighe, John, 1594, 1596
Blighte (Blighe, Bligh), Thomas, 1593, 1596, 1604
Bone, Robert, 1591-2, 1596-7
Bonney, Richard, 1609
Bowhay, Emanuel, 1630, 1632
Braye (Bray), Emanuel, 1624, 1627-9, 1633-4
Braye, Henry, 1663
Bray, John, 1622, 1632-3
Bray, John jun., 1630
Bray (Braye, Braie), Richard, 1594, 1596-7, 1604-14, 1617, 1619-21, 1624-5
Bray, Richard, 1633-6, 1638, 1643, 1663
Briggett (Bridgett), Thomas, 1617, 1622, 1632-3, 1626, 1628, 1633, 1635-7, 1639-40, 1643
Broade (Brode), William, sen., 1622, 1628, 1630, 1632, 1634-9, 1641
Broade, William, jun., 1643
Brooking (Brokyn), William, 1605, 1608, 1616-17 (d.1618)
Buller, Thomas, 1597, 1605, 1612, 1614-17, 1619-24
Burne, Peter, 1593, 1597, 1606, 1609-12, 1614-15
Burne, Elias, (Elizeus, Ellizeus) 1606-12, 1616, 1619, 1626-30

Carhath (Carharth), John, 1625, 1627-9, 1632
Carkeeke, George, 1627-8, 1630-2, 1636
Charke, John, 1590
Charke, William, 1590, 1593-4, 1596-7
Chubbe (Chubb) John, sen., 1591-3, 1596, 1617
Chubb, John, 1623, 1628-9, 1631, 1634-6, 1640
Chubb, William, 1613-14, 1617, 1619, 1623-4, 1626-7, 1629-30, 1632, 1634-7, 1639-41, 1643
Coffyn, William, 1631
Collor, William, 1592
Coller, William, 1612, 1616
Combe, James, 1636
Cornishe, Robert, 1615
Creffell (Crefeilde, Creffeilde, Creffille), John, 1591-2, 1596-7
Crosse, John, 1608, 1613
Crosse, Richard, 1627 (d.1627)
Curle, John, 1618

Dart, Roger, 1634
Dawe, John, 1610, 1616
Dewstowe (Dewstow), Dowell, sen., 1609-13, 1615-16, 1618, 1621-2, 1625-38, 1640
Dewstowe, Dowell, jun., 1640-1, 1643, 1646
Dewstowe, William, 1633-4
Dony, John, 1636, 1639, 1644, 1646
Downing, Digory, 1620, 1625
Dweane, Wimond, 1607
Dweane, Christopher, 1627, 1630

Earle, John, sen., 1606, 1609-12, 1614, 1619-21, 1624-7, 1634, 1636-40
Earle, John, jun., 1640-41, 1643, 1663
Enne, Thomas, 1597
Enne, Walter, 1596 (d.1597)

German, William, 1604
Henry, Glidden, 1622
William, Gliddon, 1611

Hancocke, Oliver, 1592, 1594, 1596
Hancocke, William, 1617-18
Harell, Gabriel, 1629
Harell, John, 1625
Haresdon, John, 1621
Harrell, Tristram, 1631
Harrle, Henry, 1594
Harle (Harrell), Richard, I, 1590, 1593, 1596-7
Harle (Harell, Harrell), Richard, II, 1604-6, 1608-10, 1630-2 ? or III
Harle (Harell, Harrell), Richard, Harle (Harrell, Hearle), III, 1609-11, 1613-19, 1621, 1623-4, 1626, 1633-4, 1636-41, 1644
Harle, William, 1633
Harris, John, 1623
Harry, Alnett (Alnet), I, 1606, 1612, 1615-18 (d.1622)
Harry, Alnett, II, 1630
Harry Christopher, 1604
Harry (Harrye), John, 1597, 1620, 1627, 1629, 1631-6, 1639-40, 1644, 1646
Harry, Martha (admission to roll only), 1682
Harry (Harrye, Harrie), Richard, 1592, 1594, 1596, 1604, 1606-25
Harry, Richard, 1630-8, 1640, 1643-4
Harry, Robert (admission), 1682
Harry (Harrye), Tristram, I, 1592-4, 1596, 1605-9, 1611-22, 1624-6
Harry, Tristram, II, 1627-32, 1635-8
Harry, Tristram, III, 1682
Harvey, John, 1663
Hellyar (Hellier), William, 1608, 1610, 1614, 1616, 1619-26, 1629, 1630, 1632
Hickes (Hicks), Richard, 1626, 1628, 1631, 1634
Hoblyn, Richard, (admission), 1682
Hollman, Radolphus (Ralph), 1636, 1639, 1643-4
Honnye (Honny, Hunny, Honney), Robert, 1607, 1609, 1611-13, 1615, 1618, 1620-1, 1623-9, 1631-3, 1635-7, 1640
Hoskyn, Leonard, 1604-5, 1608-9, 1613
Hunkyn, John, 1627

Jenkyn, George, 1638
Jeofford, William, 1608, 1629
Jeoffry, George, 1637
Jeoffrey, Roger, 1634, 1636
Jeoffrey (Jeffry, Jeffery), William, I, 1606-8, 1610-25, 1627-8, 1631-5 (d.1636)
Jeoffrey, William, II, 1622, 1625, 1635, 1637-9
John, William, 1609-11
Jooles (Geeles, Jeoles), William, 1623, 1625, 1627, 1633, 1635, 1640
Jory, George, 1635,1640
Joary, Henry, 1663
Jorye (Jorey), Richard, 1606, 1609, 1611-12, 1621

Kinge, Thomas, 1592

Langdon, Richard, 1604
Langdon, Tobias, gent, 1611-16, 1621-3, 1625-6, 1631-2, 1634, 1637, 1640, 1644, 1646
Lethiby, William, 1619, 1624
Lockwoode, Henry, 1641
Lugger, John, 1596-7, 1604, 1607-9
Lugger, William, 1610
Lugger, Walter, 1608

Lyne (Line), Richard, 1627, 1631

Maister, Oliver, 1624, 1631
Maister, Samuel, 1619-20, 1622-3
Mathewe, Walter, 1607, 1609, 1616, 1621, 1624-6
Mathew, William, 1623
Michell, Geoffrey, 1590-2, 1596-7, 1604 (d.1606)
Michell (Mitchell), John, 1596, 1606, 1617, 1622, 1624-5, 1627, 1628, 1631, 1634 [271]
Mitchell, Paul, 1636
Mitchell, Richard, 1618, 1624-7, 1634-8, 1640-1, 1646, 1663
Mitchell, Tobias, 1663
Mitchell, William, 1631
Moreside (Moresyde, Moreshed, Moreshedd) John, I (son of Thomas M.), 1596-7, 1604-12
Moreshed, John, II, 1612, 1615, 1619, 1621, 1623 (d.1624)
Moresyde (Moreside), Thomas, 1591-3 (d.1596)
Moreshead (Moreshedd, Mooreshed), Edward, 1626, 1629

Naunter, Henry, 1618, 1626, 1627-8, 1633, 1639
Naunter, John, 1612 [High House]

Odihorne, John, 1610-11
Odihorne, Laurence, 1590, 1610

Palmer, Thomas, 1597, 1605-6
Palmer (Pallmer), Abraham, 1634, 1636-8, 1640, 1663
Peake, Walter, 1635, 1643, 1646
Peter, Amos (Amias), 1624, 1629
Peter (Peeter), Oliver, 1608, 1611, 1616, 1618, 1621, 1623-30, 1632-8
Peter, William, 1590, 1592-4, 1596
Pollerd (Pollard), John, 1611, 1613-15, 1617-18, 1620-1, 1623-8, 1630-1
Pollard, Roger, 1628
Poplestone, James, 1612, 1615-18, 1620-1, 1624-5, 1627-8, 1630
Poplestone, Richard, 1625
Procter, Ambrose, 1634-7, 1640-1, 1644, 1646
Prynne, Richard, 1610, 1612

Rowe, Simon, gent., 1629
Ruby (Rooby), John, 1628
Rundell, John, 1641
Rundell, Richard, (sen), 1627, 1635, 1640, 1641
Rundell, Richard, (jun.) 1644
Rundell, David, 1620
Rundell, William, 1608, 1615-20, 1622-3, 1629, 1630-1
Rundle, William, 1596

Samnell, Oliver, 1625
Sarell (Scarell), John, 1643-4
Sargeant, Henry, 1596
Sargent, Luke, 1637, 1639
Sargent, Richard, 1606, 1609, 1619, 1623, 1629
Sargent, Thomas, 1631-3, 1640-1
Sargent, William, (sen), 1604-21, 1623-6
Seacell (Seawell), Simon, 1615, 1618
Scawne, John, 1592
Scawen, John, 1618, 1623
Short, John, 1663
Skynnerde (Skynnarde), John, 1591-2, 1594, 1596-7, 1609
Smith (Smythe), John, I, gent., 1591-4, 1596 (d.1599)
Smith (Smythe), John, II, gent., 1604, 1606-7, 1609-17, 1619-20 (d.1635)
Smith, Thomas, gent. (son of Robert S., d.1592), 1631 1634, 1638
Sonne, John, 1604-7, 1612-15, 1617, 1619, 1623-6, 1630-8, 1640-1, 1643-4, 1646
Sonne, Peter, 1646
Sonne, Philip, 1644
Sonne (Sone, Sonn), Thomas, 1590, 1592, 1604-20, 1622-9 (d.1630)
Sonne, Walter, 1590-4
Spiller, Ferdinando (son of Henry S. d.1596), 1593-4, 1596, 1604-6 (d.1607)
Spiller, Henry, 1630 (d.1636)

Spiller, William, I, 1608 (d.1610)
Spiller, William, II, 1633-5, 1637, 1644, 1646
Sweane (Swayne), John, I, 1591, 1592, 1596-7, 1604 (d.1604)
Sweane (Swayne), John, II, 1605
Symon, Ralph, 1610-14, 1619-20, 1622

Tancking (Tankyn, Tamkyn, Tanckyn), John, 1623, 1625, 1628, 1634
Tundell, John, 1640

Valtorte, Walter, 1613, 1618

Wallis, Anthony, 1663
Wallis (Wallys), Oliver, 1612-13
Wallis, Richard, 1630, 1638, 1663
Warne, Elizeus, 1618
Warne, Ezechiel, 1620
Warne, John, 1604-6, 1608, 1610-11, 1613, 1615, 1621, 1623-4, 1626
White, Walter, 1593
Williams, Jeremiah, 1619
Wilmotte (Willmott, Willmote), Thomas, 1596, 1606-7, 1609, 1611-15, 1617-19
Woodman, David, 1615-16

Jurors of the Combined Court in the reigns of Queen Anne and George II

Jurors of the Combined Court in 1712 and 1713

Blake, Anthony, 1712-13
Harry, Tristram, jun., 1712
Harvey, Tristram, 1713
Holman, Thomas, 1712
Jane, Peter, 1712-13
Jenkin, John, 1713
Jorey, Henry, 1713
Pirrey, Edward, 1712
Stephens, John, 1712
Waite, Thomas, 1712-13

Jurors of the Combined Court in 1730

Biddick, Thomas
Chub, William
Edwards, John
Harvy, John
Heatton, John
Jenkyn, John
Marten, George
Pit, John
Pope, Amos
Searl, John
Waite, Simon
Waite, Thomas
Warren, John
Warren, Robert

Appendix 3

Proceedings of the Civil Defence Committee (Invasion Committee)

20 August 1941–12 October 1943

The committee came into existence on 20 August 1941, when William Rundle of Pool Farm was nominated as Chairman. The first meeting took place on 29 September of that year. The minutes, which are kept in the CRO in Truro, read as follows:

'The Chairman … pointed out that should invasion take place we may have to become a self supporting unit … First of all comes the question of food supplies and the Voluntary Food Organiser of the District will explain his needs.

The Voluntary Food Organiser stated that he only had to act on his own initiative should this district be cut off from the Food Office at Saltash, if this occurred he was then responsible for husbanding and rationing all available food. He suggested that all householders should be asked to store at least a week's supply of flour. With regard to milk it was not considered that any great difficulty would arise considering that this was a dairy farming district, and it was also considered that the question of meat supplies would not prove insurmountable. If the need arose there was a slaughterhouse in the parish and orders would be given to kill any animal required.[272]

Cooking

Here the question of fuel supply was important, it was pointed out that there was every possibility of the electric supply being cut off and it was suggested that a local coal depot would be invaluable. If coal could not be obtained it would be possible to get fuel from the neighbouring woods.

Lighting

Here again a difficulty would arise should the electric supply be cut off and it was suggested that a supply of paraffin should be stored locally for use during an emergency.

Water

Water supplies in most of this area were obtainable from two sources – first through the Council's mains and secondly from wells or streams. It was suggested that it might be wise if every householder kept a few bottles of water (freshly drawn daily) in readiness for an emergency.

Distribution of Food

It was imperative that the Voluntary Food Officer should have at least four assistants* to help in the supply of foodstuffs. It was pointed out that no food would be delivered and everyone would be expected to fetch their share.

*It was resolved to ask Mesdames W.A.Hearn, [273] A. Carpenter,[274] S. Grills,[275] and H.A. Hoskin.[276]

Survey of the District
As it was essential that the number of persons resident in the district should be known to the Voluntary Food Officer it had been arranged to take a complete survey. Mrs Wilson, Lynher Villa, agreed to undertake the organising of this important matter.[277]

Labour Organiser
All able bodied persons may be required to assist the military authorities in digging trenches, putting up barriers etc., and it was advisable to organise as far as possible those persons most suited to this work and it was resolved to ask Mr J. Triscott to undertake this work.[278]

Transport Organiser
Sergeant James representing the Police stated that during an emergency all private motor vehicles would be immobilised and the petrol filling station put out of action and it was therefore advisable to take a survey of all the horses, carts etc. which could be used for transport.[279] It was resolved to ask Messrs. W.J.Holman[280] and T.E. Bersey[281] to carry out this important task.[282]

School Children
Mrs Coursens, Head Mistress of Sheviock School, stated that the teachers were instructed that should there be immediate danger all children were to be sent home at once.

ARP[283]
The question of decontamination should a gas attack occur was raised and it was resolved that the St Germans Rural District Defence Committee be asked to make available sufficient chemicals for this purpose.'

At its next meeting on 17 November 1941, Mrs Wilson's daughter, Lina, who was a nurse, joined the committee. So did John Hoskin, who was the senior fire guard as well as being a farmer[284] He was the son of Arnold and Mollie Hoskin of Crafthole Farm, and lived at the farm. The third new member was Clifford Hoskin, son of Walter Hoskin of Tredrossel Farm. He was a sergeant in the Home Guard. He was married to Millicent. Mr and Mrs Crace, who lived at Trewin, were both elected vice-chairmen of the committee.

John Hoskin, the senior fire guard, asked for a supply of sandbags, and also reported that the trailer pump crew had had difficulty fixing the hose to the hydrants, because the couplings were of different dimensions. It was resolved to ask for a hydrant stand.

At the next meeting on 12 January 1942, Mr Crispin was named as clerk to the committee.[285] It was also reported that the trailer pump had been removed and taken to Plymouth, but that a hydrant stand had been delivered. With this, water could be pumped into a collapsible tank from whence it could be used to douse a fire. The sandbags requested in November had still not been delivered, so Mr Crispin would send a reminder to the RDC. It was resolved to ask people to store extra coal and oil and to keep in a good supply of flour. Miss Winifred Roberts of Trethill undertook to give a talk at the Women's Institute about the storing of provisions in case of an invasion.[286] It was agreed that the public should be made to realise that there was a real possibility of an invasion.[287]

Nurse Wilson was put in charge of the first aid equipment, which included a stretcher. It was decided to use the recreation room in Crafthole as a casualty station. However, it was pointed out that when the time came, this might have been destroyed so other temporary facilities would have to be found. Water would have to be easily obtainable, because 'in the case of Mustard Gas lots of hot soapy water would be needed'. There was no official cleansing station, but householders with baths were asked to make them available to the general public during an emergency.[288] A long discussion took place on setting up a messenger service, and John Hoskin was asked to set one up.

A letter from Mr P.B. Govett, surveyor to St Germans RDC, was read out concerning the collection of waste paper. John Hoskin said that boy scouts and girl guides already collected waste paper, which was stored in his barn before being sold to a Mr Nicholls of Plymouth. It was agreed that this should be made available to the RDC. It was also agreed to put up notices in each village to let the public know when the salvage lorry would come round to collect the waste paper.

At the next meeting on 16 March 1942, it was reported that the RDC had agreed to set up a static water tank at the bus stop at the crossroads in Crafthole. It was reported that the sandbags had still not been delivered. Mrs Crace said that the matter of home storage of flour had still not been brought up at the WI, but that Miss Roberts still intended to do so. It was also reported that emergency stocks of food had been delivered and were stored in equal quantities at the Rectory, Sheviock[289] and in Lynher Villa, Crafthole. On 11 March, the clerk to the St Germans RDC, J. Percival Heath, who was also the food executive officer for the district, had issued Mr Crispin with forms for the distribution of the emergency food stocks. In the event of an emergency, the shops would be closed and the 'coastal belt emergency rations' would be issued. It was reported that 32 tins of biscuits had been delivered to Lynher Villa in error, and this fact had been reported to the RDC. Nurse Wilson proposed that Mrs Lee should be appointed a deputy food officer, and this was agreed.

One of the instructions that came from the Ministry of Food was that 'During an invasion all shops will be temporarily closed *for the purpose of stocktaking by the Ministry of Food*.' Such an instruction could only have been carried out in parishes far removed from the invasion beaches. It was also stated that 'All roads will be blocked – the general public will not be allowed to travel by road. Persons can only be evacuated by the military. The order to "stay put" must be carried out.'

On 18 March 1942, the committee recommended that every household should be issued with a reference card showing:

1. Name and address of the voluntary food organiser.
2. Depot from which the emergency food ration would be issued.[290]
3. Nearest first aid post.
4. Nearest warden's post.
5. National Fire Service station and telephone number.

At the committee meeting held on 8 June 1942, Walter G. Pengelly (fisherman and market gardener) of 5 Coastguards Cottages, was added to the committee. It was reported that Nurse Wilson had left the district. There was a complaint that the fire guards were not taking sufficient interest in their work, because at a recent demonstration only seven out of the 35 fire guards had turned up.[291] It was reported that 70 sandbags would soon be delivered, but that the regional commissioner had refused permission for the static water tank as requested by the RDC. Every household was urged to keep at least four gallons of water in buckets. Miss Roberts stated that she had raised the matter of storage of flour, coal, oil, etc. at the WI. John Hoskin said that the following people had agreed to act as messengers: Reginald Greenaway,[292] John Kentisbeer, Sheila Channings,[293] Hilda and Jean Joyce.[294]

At 8.30 p.m., the meeting was opened to the public and Revd B.L.Lycett and Mr C.J.Clark, a retired schoolmaster who was staying with him at the Rectory, attended. The chairman informed the meeting that communication exercises would be held on 20 and 21 June, when the headquarters (the schoolroom at Crafthole) would have to be manned. Revd Lycett wished to know how many persons present had their gas masks with them – with the exception of the police, he turned out to be the only person in the room with one. The clerk drew attention to the fact that although some people still carried a gas mask very few ever troubled to wear them and he suggested that everyone should be encouraged to do so at frequent intervals.

Revd Lycett also wished to know who gave authority for the ringing of the church bells in the event of invasion. This was a good question. Two years earlier, on 7 September 1940, the code-word 'Cromwell', which meant that invasion was imminent, but not in process, had been issued by Home Forces command to the eastern and southern commands. On this, in some parts of the country, the Home Guard commanders, acting on their own initiative, called out the Home Guard by ringing the church bells. The Government therefore ordered that in future church bells were to be rung only by order of a Home Guard who had himself seen *as many as 25 parachutists landing*, and not because other bells had been heard or for any other reason.[295] The answer given to Revd Lycett was that only the military or the police were authorised to order the ringing of the bells.

The difficulty of organising a labour gang was discussed. The clerk said that 'he had always found that people in this area were reluctant to being organised but that they were always on hand when really required.' Mrs Crace suggested that there should be practices of the first aid services, etc. The clerk responded by suggesting that the WI and the WVS might arrange a number of incidents.[296]

At the next meeting on 10 August 1942, the Civil Defence Committee became the Sheviock Invasion Committee. A new nurse, Nurse Treglown, who had moved into Sydenham House, replaced Nurse Wilson as the person in charge of the first aid party.

At a meeting held on 29 September, Mrs Edith Bucknell (domestic science teacher) of 2 the Terrace, Portwrinkle, Mrs Annie Pengelly (housewife) of Gavina, Portwrinkle, Mrs J. (Annie) Bean (housewife) of Ubena, Crafthole, and Mr William Andrew (mason) of the Bungalow, Crafthole, joined the committee. Mr Andrew became the new labour organiser.

At the September 1942 meeting, the committee was joined by the military area commander, Commander W.G. Manfield, who reported on the communication exercises (code-named 'Ajax') which had been held on 22 and 23 August. He said that 'as far as he was concerned this Committee was one of the best he had visited, there were of course many errors but none serious, and he assured the Committee that if they adopted the proposed scheme (with one or two minor alterations) they would have one of the finest committees in the County.'

Less happy news was that the first aid party had never booked the recreation room as a first aid post. Instead the county council had procured it as a rest centre. The committee therefore had to reorganise their affairs, and resolved that Mrs D. Smith of Trewin should be appointed organiser of a first aid party; the Methodist Sunday school would be booked as the first aid post; and minor first aid posts would be arranged in Portwrinkle and Sheviock village.[297] It was also agreed that, with the consent of the postmaster (i.e. postmistress), the headquarters of the committee would be moved to the post office. At this time, the post office was at Marlborough House, and Mrs Adele Channings was the postmistress. Reginald Kentisbeer, who ran the ironmonger's shop, 'David Sales', at Devonport, but was then living at No 1 the Terrace, Crafthole, was elected to the committee and appointed liaison officer.

Shortly after the meeting held on 29 September 1942, a memorandum was issued setting out the committee's current arrangements. New members of the committee were Walter J. Hoskin (farmer) of Tredrossel and Miss L Hoskin, who had moved into Liscawn. Members were instructed that they had to attend at HQ 'fully prepared' – i.e. with gas masks, steel helmets (if available), blankets and sufficient food. Their duties were to receive communications from all services and to pass on all information so received to the officers concerned. The services were the Home Guard, the ARP, the Fire Guard, and the Police. Lt. Rivett, who was stationed at Blerrick Farm, was in charge of the Home Guard, and the local representative was Sgt. Clifford Hoskin, then living at Holmleigh, Sheviock village. The ARP consisted of Eddy Callaghan and William J. Grills (farmer), who lived with the Callaghans at the Cottage, Crafthole. The senior fire guard was John Hoskin, who had three street captains and fifty other fire guards reporting to him. Sgt. James of the police was based in St Germans, but he was assisted by four local special constables: Steven Grills of Sydenham House, Crafthole; Mr S. Griffin (bus driver) of Sea View, Crafthole; Harry Ough (mason) of 2 the Orchard, Sheviock village; and Arthur Holman (farmer) of the Glebe Farm, Sheviock.

By this time, Nurse Wilson had returned, so she once more became organiser of nursing and first aid, with eight people to help her. Miss Roberts was listed as being in charge of the WVS. The designated rest centres were the recreation room, Crafthole, and the Church of England School at Sheviock. Mrs J (Annie) Bean of Ubena, Crafthole, was the organiser of the rest centres. She had six helpers, and had the use of 100 blankets, 20 mugs and plates, two dozen knives, forks and spoons, and various other essential items. The memorandum included the instruction that 'The Committee must make all possible plans to ensure that every householder is convinced that it is its inescapable duty to provide food and shelter for any homeless person. Refugees must be directed to the Rest Centre and billeted from there.'

It was proposed to dig a number of slit trenches, since they were 'invaluable during bombardments, they are about 4 feet deep, 2 feet wide at the base and 3 feet at the top'. Mr Crispin was named as 'mortuary superintendent'. The golf links tool shed was designated as the mortuary.

The next meeting was held on 11 December 1942. The committee were once again meeting in the Methodist schoolroom, but it was laid down that during exercises and in the event of an invasion, the headquarters would be at Mr H.A. (Arnold) Hoskin's house. He lived at Crafthole Farm. It was also agreed that he would be paid a retaining fee of five shillings per quarter for the right to use his telephone when required. The charge for any calls would be paid in addition. The clerk pointed out that there was no proper black out material in the Sunday school. It was therefore agreed to pay to the trustees of the Methodist chapel one-third of the cost of providing it. It was reported that very little had been done about first aid training and Nurse Wilson promised to do her utmost to get the first aid party 'on a proper footing'.

The next meeting was probably held in February 1943, though the minutes in the CRO are undated. At that meeting it was reported that the county deputy controller had intimated that the proposal to pay a retaining fee to Mr Hoskin and to contribute to the black out material could not be sanctioned by his authority. It was therefore proposed to hold an entertainment later in the year to raise the money. The committee had also been asked to put on an entertainment to raise money for the 'Wings for Victory' campaign, and an ad hoc committee was formed to organise this. The clerk had written a letter tendering his resignation, but was persuaded to withdraw it. The clerk also read out instructions on what to do in the event of an enemy commando raid:

> The general public must be informed that when the church bells ring they will be expected to remain off the roads preferably in their homes … the main function of the civil population will be to keep out of the way, but ready to help the military if asked to do so.

Mr Kentisbeer proposed that an application should be made to the county ARP to lay on a supply of water to the Sunday school, since it was the first aid post. Nurse Wilson seconded the resolution.

The next meeting was held on 17 April 1943. It was noted that no contribution had been given to the trustees of the Methodist chapel in respect of the black out, and it was resolved that Nurse Wilson should organise a whist drive to raise the money. Nurse Wilson reported that the WVS had stated that the Sunday school was to be requisitioned for use as a rest centre. The clerk pointed out that it had already been earmarked as a first aid post and was shown as such in the 'war book' (official log). 'He had received no information from an official quarter that the WVS intended to take this room, but as soon as he did he would oppose this encroachment and suggested that if this Committee was to be constantly overridden it may as well resign en bloc.'

The war book was amended by the addition of Pte R Hoskin as a member of the Home Guard.[298] Another long memorandum was read out on what to do in the event of enemy commando raids. Warnings would be issued, but only by senior officers, containing the code words 'Bouncer', meaning 'raid – stand to' (amended at the next meeting to mean 'expect Bugbear'), or 'Bugbear', meaning 'raid – action stations'. If civil defence personnel were the first to discover the raid, they should immediately inform Lt. Rivett or the police. It was resolved that the committee should take part in the 'Salute the Soldier' savings campaign, and an ad hoc committee was formed to do this.

Mrs Theodora Colwill remembered that during the war 'Everyone was working for the war effort, making shirts, etc. for the Red Cross and hospitals, knitting socks, etc for the troops, and selling National Savings stamps'. She herself was in charge of this last operation. During Warships Week in 1941 or 1942, the residents of Crafthole raised £3,781 4s. 5d; those of Sheviock village £1,769 3s. 11d; and those of Portwrinkle £1,494 3s. 11d.

The Women's Institute organised the sending of parcels and money orders to serving members of the forces who came from the parish. Mrs Colwill preserved her accounts for those activities in 1943 and 1944. For Christmas 1943, she sent 37 postal orders for 14 shillings each, and a number of parcels, to the service personnel. The total cost of £26 8s. 3d. was met by sales of produce, raffles (for which the prizes were a sugar sifter, two cakes and two dolls) and a whist drive. For Christmas 1944, she sent 42 postal orders of 13 shillings each, and a number of parcels to the service personnel. The total cost of £28 0s. 4d. was met by a 'bring and buy' sale, which included a cake raffle and games, a whist drive, which included a cigarette raffle, and a dance (at which 4 shillings' worth of potatoes were sold). Mrs Colwill also remembered that the WI organised auctions on behalf of the war effort. The monies collected were put into National Savings certificates and shared between the various organisations of the parish.

At a meeting of the Sheviock Invasion Committee held on 12 October 1943, Walter Hoskin of Tredrossel was elected to the committee to represent the war agriculture committee. Nurse Wilson was unable to attend through sickness, but sent a message that she would shortly arrange the whist drive in aid of funds. She also sent a message that at last a number of persons were undertaking a course of home nursing. Unsurprisingly, the county deputy controller had written stating that as the first aid post was not a recognised one, he could not sanction any expense to lay on a water supply.

The October meeting is the last for which Sheviock Invasion Committee minutes have been deposited at the CRO. It may indeed have been the very last, for the minutes record that 'an invasion was not so imminent as it was'. This was undoubtedly true. In August, the plans for the allied invasion of Europe, operation 'Overlord', had been approved by President Roosevelt and Winston Churchill at their meeting in Quebec. In September that year, Italy had surrendered to the allies. It is satisfying to record that the last paragraph of the Sheviock Invasion Committee minutes notes that the chairman of the district invasion committee, Mr Rogers, had examined the Sheviock 'war book' and judged it 'excellent'.

Appendix 4

The Sheviock Roll of Honour in the Second World War

Originally composed by Mr G. Crispin, parish clerk, with amendments as marked.

Surname	***Christian Name***	***Home Address***	***Service***	***Rank & No.***	***Service Address***
Adams	Peggy	Lower Tredis House, Nr. Crafthole	ATS	Private Demobbed	
Baker	**Leslie**[299]	Sydenham House, Crafthole	Army	[Trooper Royal Tank Regt.]	**Killed in Action**
Ball	Clarence	Kerslake, [Antony]	RAF	LAC. 1244884	
Ball	**Roy**[300]	Kerslake, [Antony]	Army		**Killed in Action**
Bean	Derrick	Ubena, Crafthole	Navy	ERA	RNATE, Torpoint
[Bean	**Desmond**	Fernleigh, Crafthole	Navy		**Killed in Action]**[301]
Bean	**Donald**	Portwrinkle	Army	Lieutenant	**Died of Wounds**
Bean	Dudley	The Cottage	Navy	PO Stwd D/LX 21549	RN Party 1763 Naval Base, Belgium
Bean	James William	Laburnum Cottage, Crafthole	Navy	Naval Storehouseman	c/o Redirection Officer, Br. Pacific Fleet
Bean	Lewis	Laburnum Cottage, Crafthole	Navy	L. Sea. 13697	Demobbed
Bean	Sydney	Old Chapel Cott., Crafthole	RAF	Sgt. 1415858	Demobbed
Bean	William, D.	Freden, Crafthole	Navy	Sto. PO KX82549	Demobbed
Bersey	Mary J.	The Orchard, Sheviock	ATS	L/Cpl.	Demobbed
Bersey	Thomas	The Orchard, Sheviock	Army		Demobbed
Biles	John	Carclew, Crafthole	RAF	LAC. 1702590	–
Bishop	Alexander C.	Portwrinkle	Navy	PO MX57073	–
Bishop	William C.	Portwrinkle	Navy	AFE FX90180	–
Channings	Gerald H.	Marlborough House, Crafthole	RAF	LAC. 1298979	5721 M&E Flt. att. to BFHQ, Aden MEF
Chapman	Thomas	The Terrace, Crafthole	Navy	AB D500	Demobbed
Colwill	Garfield H.	The Bungalow, Crafthole	Army	Sgt.47755175	Demobbed
Davey	Alec J.	Portwrinkle	Army	Private 14374460	–
Davey	Herbert J.	West Lane, Crafthole	RAF	LAC.1850827	Demobbed

Davis	Owen L.E.	Fernleigh, Crafthole	Navy	PO Wtr. DX34	Demobbed
Dyer	Gerald H.	Sheviock	Navy	Shipt. D/MX62782	Mess 22, HMS *Girdleness* c/o GPO London
Dyer	Patricia	Sheviock	WRNS	PO	
Freathy	William N.	Ubena, Crafthole	Navy	CERA	
Garland	**Anthony E.**	Portwrinkle	Navy	(FAA)	**Killed in Action**
Garland	Eugene	Portwrinkle	RAF		Demobbed
Greenaway	Russell	West Lane, Crafthole	Navy	AB (CO) P/JX428730	Demobbed
Greenaway	William F.	West Lane, Crafthole	RAF	ACI 1318353/7	Demobbed
Griffin	Honor F.M.	Sea View, Crafthole	WRNS	Wren 49384	Demobbed
Haimes	Cyril	The Cottage, Crafthole	Navy	D/MX70759	–
Haimes	Patience	The Cottage, Crafthole	WRNS	Wren	Demobbed
Haimes	Sydney	The Cottage, Crafthole	Navy	Chief Sto. 310009	Demobbed
Hancock	Frederick	West Lane, Crafthole	Army	Driver 42166	Demobbed
Harris	Gerald	Portwrinkle	RAF	LAC	Demobbed
Harris	Leonard	Portwrinkle	Army	CFN10554739	REME A Coy. 23ASP RAOC, Bedall
[Hitt	**William I.**[302]		US Army		**Killed in Action]**
Hobson	Walter	Serena, Crafthole	Navy	PO JY 1289954	Demobbed
Hoskin	Anne	St Anne's, Crafthole	WRNS	Third Officer	Demobbed
Hughes	Charles	The Terrace, Crafthole	Navy	PO Sailmaker	HMS *Alaunia*
Jasper	Charles E.	Laburnum, Crafthole	RM	CSM	Offrs. Trg. School Thurlestone
Johnson	Douglas H.	Portwrinkle	Navy	Surg. Lieut.	Demobbed
Kelly	Desmond J.	Portwrinkle	Army	Capt.	
Kent	Thomas J.	9 Thornhill Rd. Mannamead Plymouth	Army	Sgt.	Demobbed
Kentisbeer	John	Lynher Villa, Crafthole	Army	Cpl 2667210 Coldstream Guards	
Lansallas	Betty	Pinetum, Sheviock	WRNS	L/Wren23376	–
Lansallas	Graham	Pinetum, Sheviock	Army	Fusilier 14622371	–
Page	Thomas F.	Portwrinkle	Navy	AB	Demobbed
Paul	**George**[303]	The Terrace, Sheviock	Navy		**Killed in Action**
Pengelly	Lester	Portwrinkle	Navy	Ldg. Sea.	L4 Mess, HMS *Turtle* Poole, Dorset
Sealey	Kenneth	Cockles Peep-out, Crafthole	RAF	AC2 1836851	Demobbed
Shannon	Mary	Langley, Slough	WAAF	Cpl	Demobbed
Smelt	Frank	Crafthole	Army	Bandsman 4343090)	Maintenance Party (Depot E. Yorks Regt Beverly, Yorks.
Vercoe	Dennis L.	Portwrinkle	RAF	S/Ldr.	Demobbed
Westlake	George	Hay Farm, Crafthole	Army		

Endnotes

English Currency Units

For most of the period covered by this book, the principal units of English currency were pounds, shillings and pence. These units were abbreviated to '£' (preceding the number of pounds) from the Latin *libra* (singular) or *librae* (plural); 's' (following the number of shillings) from the Latin *solidus*; and 'd' (following the number of pennies) from the Latin *denarius*. Where sources used for this book refer to the old currency, I have retained the '£ s. d.' abbreviations and made no attempt to give the decimal equivalents.

Before the decimalisation of the currency in 1971, the pound was divided into 20 shillings. There were twelve pennies in a shilling. The coins issued included half-crowns (2s. 6d.), two-shilling pieces (also called florins), shillings, sixpenny pieces and three-penny pieces. These were all originally silver coins. But later the three-penny piece was made of nickel-brass. A penny was divided into two half-pennies or four farthings. All penny coins and their fractions were made of bronze.

In the Middle Ages, gold coins issued were the pound, the mark (two-thirds of a pound: 13s. 4d.) and the noble (one-third of a pound: 6s. 8d.), sometimes called an angel from the design stamped upon it.

On 15 February 1971, the old units of currency were replaced by a new decimal system, in which the pound was divided into 100 pence. The old ten-shilling note was replaced by a 50p. piece. The new 10p. piece was equivalent to the old florin and the new 5p. piece was equivalent to the old shilling.

Abbreviations

CA/, CD/, CE/ CM/, CP/, CZ etc.	Documents cited thus are from the archives at Antony House, which may be accessed via the CRO in Truro
Cal. Pat. Rolls	Calendar of Patent Rolls
CRO	Cornwall Record Office, in Truro
DCNQ	*Devon and Cornwall Notes and Queries*
DRO	Devon Record Office, in Exeter
EHR	*English Historical Review*
H.24/226 etc.	Documents cited thus are from the Henderson papers in the Courtney Library of The Royal Institution of Cornwall in Truro
IPM	*Inquisitiones post mortem*. See, *A Calendar of Inquisitiones post mortem for Cornwall and Devon from Henry III to Charles I (1216-1649)*, Exeter (1906)
JRIC	*Journal of the Royal Institution of Cornwall*
RIC	Royal Institution of Cornwall
TNA	The National Archives, in Kew
VCH	*Victoria County History*

Chapter 1, *From the Stone Age to the Roman Invasion*

1 Stephen Oppenheimer, *The Origins of the British: A Genetic Detective Story* (2006), p. 174.
2 Stephen Oppenheimer, *The Origins of the British: A Genetic Detective Story* (2006), pp. 37, 38, 42, 57.
3 *De excidio et conquestu Britanniae* translated as *The ruin of Britain* by Michael Winterbottom (1978).
4 S. Oppenheimer, *The Origins of the British: A Genetic Detective Story* (2006), p. 265.
5 See report in *The Times*, 11 February 2003. See also *Past*, the Newsletter of the Prehistoric Society, No 41, July 2002.
6 *Timewatch*, BBC 2, 27 September 2008.
7 Another group of three archers buried at Boscombe Downe, near Amesbury, was buried with similar grave goods to the Amesbury Archer; but their skeletons showed them to have originated in Wales or the Lake District: see Wessex Archaeology: The Boscombe Bowmen (Internet).
8 The finds were deposited in the Plymouth Institution (now the Plymouth Museum), but were lost or destroyed by enemy action in the Second World War.
9 R I C Journal 1881.
10 A. Fox, *South-West England 3,500 BC-A.D. 600* (revised ed. 1973), p. 100.
11 A similar one was excavated at Ringlemere in Kent in November 2001: see *Past*, the Newsletter of the Prehistoric Society, No 41. I am grateful to Cynthia Gaskell Brown for drawing this to my attention.
12 As to Bronze-Age agriculture, see Chapter 20, *Early History of Agriculture*.
13 See J. King, *Kingdoms of the Celts* (1998).
14 A. Fox, *South-West England 3,500 BC-A.D. 600* (revised ed. 1973), pp. 131-2.
15 Information supplied by the Cornwall Archaeological Unit, Cornwall County Council.
16 Information supplied by Cynthia Gaskell Brown.
17 See C. Thomas (ed.), *An Archaeological Survey of the Rame Peninsula* (1974).
18 See H. Quinnell, *Trethurgy. Excavations at Trethurgy Round, St Austell: community and status in Roman and post-Roman Cornwall* (2004).
19 G. A Kempthorne, *A History of the Parish of Sheviock* (c 1934), p.vi.
20 See O. J. Padel, *A Popular Dictionary of Cornish Place-names* (1988).
21 See A. Fox, *South-West England 3,500 BC-A.D. 600* (revised ed. 1973), p130. According to Charles Thomas, the name *Dumnonii* may be derived from the fact that they were 'worshippers of the God Dumnonus'. See 'The importance of being Cornish in Cornwall', Institute of Cornish Studies, Redruth 1973, p. 4, quoted in *Cornwall*, by Philip Payton (1996), p. 65.
22 *The Conquest of Gaul*, III,1.
23 The fort at Restormel was discovered in 2007 and that at Calstock in 2008. I am grateful to Peter Nicholas for information on these discoveries.
24 A. Fox (1973), p. 171.
25 P. Payton, *Cornwall* (1996), p. 65.
26 See further H. Quinnell, *Trethurgy. Excavations at Trethurgy Round, St Austell: community and status in Roman and post-Roman Cornwall* (2004).
27 This Lady Carew was Mary (née Bampfylde), widow of Sir Coventry Carew.
28 These coins are now in the Royal Cornwall Museum in Truro. I am most grateful to Anna Tyack of the Museum for showing me the coins and obtaining the information about them.
29 See further Chapter 20, *Early History of Agriculture*.
30 See N. Orme (ed.), *Unity and Variety: A History of the Church in Devon and Corn*wall (1991), p. 1.
31 *Cornish Church Guide* (1925), p. 17.
32 See A. Fox (1973), p. 195.
33 www.channel4.com/history/microsites/T/timeteam/2008/padstow.

Chapter 2, *The Celtic Kingdoms, the Saxon and Norman Conquests*

1 See R.C. Barrowman, C. E. Batey and C. D. Morris, *Excavations at Tintagel Castle, Cornwall, 1990-1999* (2007).
2 For example, a sixth-century trading vessel that foundered off the coast of southern France was carrying a 3,600-gallon cargo of wine and oil amphorae from North Africa and the eastern Mediterranean: reported in *The Times*, 9 June 2004.

3 See John Keast, *The Story of Fowey* (1950).
4 *Cornish Church Guide* (1925), p. 18.
5 C.Thomas, *Celtic Britain* (1st pb. edn. 1997), pp. 68, 69.
6 A. M. Kent, *The Literature of Cornwall* (2000), p. 24.
7 See P.Payton, *Cornwall* (1996), p. 82.
8 See Della Hooke, *Pre-Conquest Charter Bounds of Devon and Cornwall* (1994).
9 See I.N. Soulsby, *A History of Cornwall* (1986), p. 25.
10 P. Payton, *Cornwall* (1996), p. 82.
11 A discussion of these grants is to be found in 'Celt, Saxon and Norman in the Rame Peninsula', a lecture given at Millbrook 16 March 1962 by Dr W.G. Hoskins as part of the University of Exeter Extra-Mural classes at Millbrook and Cawsand, presented to the Earl of Mount Edgcumbe on his 90th birthday (1963). Peter Nicholas drew to my attention a typescript summary of this lecture.
12 See the essay by Charles Henderson in the *Cornish Church Guide* (1925), p. 25.
13 *Anglo Saxon Chronicle.*
14 See I.N. Soulsby, *A History of Cornwall* (1986), p. 25. The sub-division into hundreds goes back to Roman times. The word Trigg derives from the Latin *Tricorios* '(area of) the three war bands', Pydar from one of four quarters of mid-and west Cornwall: see K. Branigan and P.J. Fowler (eds.), *The Roman West Country: Classical Culture and Celtic Society* (1976), p. 207.
15 In 1963, the Rural District Council recommended that some 30 properties in Polbathic should be transferred to St Germans; in 1986, the whole of the populated area around Polbathic was transferred to that parish. See Sheviock Parish Council Minute Books for 4 March 1963, 5 August 1985, 4 August 1986.
16 A virgate was about 30 acres (a quarter of a hide).
17 *Anglo Saxon Chronicles.* See also H.P.R. Finberg, *The Formation of England 550-1042* (1976), p. 181.
18 See D. Bates, *William the Conqueror* (pb. edn. 2004), p. 115.
19 Vivian's *Visitation of Cornwall* uses the spelling 'Dauney', not Dawney. The Viscounts Downe, who are descendants of this family, use the spelling 'Dawnay', which must therefore be presumed to be the correct spelling. However, as the usual spelling in the parish today is Dawney (as e.g. in Dawney Terrace), the local spelling has been preferred in this book.
20 The manor of Pendrym was in the hands of the King at the time of Domesday Book (1086). At this time it had been reduced in size by the removal from it of certain estates by Count Robert of Mortain. In its reduced state, Pendrym still embraced roughly half the parish of St Martin by Looe. In the early 1200s the manor came into the hands of Lucy Russel and then of her descendants, the Bodrugans. The Dawneys became high lords of the manor at an unknown date. The Bodrugans were paying the Dawney lords ¼ knight's fee for the borough of East Looe alone, or ½ knight's fee for the borough with its parent manor of Pendrym: see 'East Looe Corporation MSS. Part I. The Rentals', *DCNQ* 1941, p. 88. The Bodrugans were still receiving rentals from the borough of East Looe and the manor of Pendrym in 1468: RIC Henderson Mss. Edgcumbe Papers AI, quoted in J. Whetter, *The Bodrugans* (1995), at p. 14.
21 See W. M. M. Picken, 'The Earliest Charter of East Looe', *JRIC* 1981, pp. 350-7.
22 IPM 18 February, 2 Ed. II. An entry in the book of tenures of Edward, Earl of Devon (d.1509) states that 'Richard Cergeaux holds for the term of his life of the inheritance of Botrigan [Bodrugan] one knight's fee in Pendryn, by knight's service and owes common suit at the court of Sheviock as often as it shall be held there.' Pendrym was still shown as part of Sheviock manor in a rental of 1691 (CM/F2/158). The heirs of Lord Brook were then the tenants.
23 Kempthorne (*c.*1934), pp. 12, 13.
24 In October 1642, during the Civil War, Royalist forces again used Crafthole as a defensive base.
25 The leases are CD/AH/3 (1622), 8 (1667), 10 (1679), 13 (1694), 17 (1702), 28 (1711) and CD/AI/12 (1825). The argument showing that the Dawneys' manor-house was sited at Blazor is more fully set out in the author's article 'The Dawnays' Dovecote and Manor-house: A lost relationship re-discovered' in JRIC (2005), at p. 16.
26 Juliet Barker, *Agincourt: the King, the Campaign, the Battle* (pb. ed. 2006), pp. 118, 119. In the fifth century a Hunnish warrior required a string of ten horses, so that he could rotate them and always ride a fresh horse into battle: Peter Heather, *The Fall of the Roman Empire* (2005), p. 328.

27 This was coincidentally the number of horses on the manor of Bodrugan in 1426: J. Whetter, *The Bodrugans* (1995), p. 21.
28 See further Chapter 4, *The Manor of Sheviock*.
29 Transcribed by H.P.R. Finberg in 'Some Early Tavistock Charters', *EHR* July 1947, Vol. LXII, No.244, pp. 352 *et seq*.
30 The two acres were right down by the seashore where fishing and smoking operations were carried out. The field became known as Cross-stone or Crowstone and the field to the west of it was called Monks Park. Poldreisoc is the modern Poldrissick, in Landrake-St Erney. Poldrissick Farm was part of St Germans Priory estate. The feast of St Giles (St Egidius in Latin) is on 1 September. The perambulation therefore took place on 2 September.
31 See Chapter 29, *The Reformation in the West Country*.
32 *Tavistock Abbey* (1951), p. 11.
33 O.J. Padel (private correspondence).
34 I am grateful to Jeffrey Hackney of Wadham College, Oxford, for help in understanding these charters.
35 This charter is also dated between 1174 and 1206.
36 The Cornish acre was a variable amount depending on the quality of the land. English acres, too, were of variable size at this time, though generally smaller than Cornish ones. Finberg, in *Tavistock Abbey* (1951), p. 11n, gave a range of 15 to 300 English acres to a Cornish acre, but 50 acres seems to have been the usual approximation in the Middle Ages (see e.g. Dr Whetter, *The Bodrugans* (1995), p. 31, n 6).
37 See Kempthorne (*c*.1934), p. 18.
38 CD/AE/8.
39 For the later history of these estates and those discussed below, see Chapter 9, *Outlying Farms and Houses*.
40 The Inkpenne family possessed the manor of Halton in St Dominick from 1304 to at least 1351 (see *Lake*, Vol. I, p. 299). In 1390, that manor belonged to the Fychets (*ibid*.).
41 Thomas had inherited the estate from his mother, Ricarda, who was the daughter of John Inkpenne. Sir Thomas Fychet, who died in 1336, was lord of Spaxton in Somerset. Thomas junior, who inherited the estate, died in 1395. His sister and heiress married Robert Hill. In 1411, the tenant of the half fee was John Bake of St Germans. Robert Hill's son, William, was mentioned in *Feudal Aids*, as holding land in Sheviock in 1428.
42 RIC, Truro: H.24/226.
43 CP/FX/11.
44 CD/AE/4. See also 'Haye' in Chapter 4, *The Manor of Sheviock*.
45 CD/AF/40. The document of sale gives the history of the properties before the time of the Reformation.
46 See Kempthorne (*c*.1934), p. 18 and *Feudal Aids*.
47 See the fine brass to her in Antony church.
48 The manorial accounts of the manor of Sheviock for 1721 show receipts of 1s. each from Kerslake, Trethill and Trewin, showing that they had originally been part of Sheviock manor. The amounts received for Kerslake and Trethill related to a plot of land 'half an acre Cornish'. That for Trewin, then tenanted by John Cock, stated expressly 'and suite to Court'.

Chapter 3, *The Cornish Language on the Rame Peninsula*

1 *Celtic Britain* (1st pb. edn., 1997), p 17.
2 Stephen Oppenheimer, in *The Origins of the British: A Genetic Detective Story* (2006), p.215, surmises that during the Neolithic period (4,500-2000 B.C.) Celtic could have been 'the new trade-net language allowing people who already had ties of culture and genes to exchange prestige materials such as copper, gold and beaker pots more easily'.
3 See generally, Kenneth Jackson, *Language and History in Early Britain* (1953) and P. Beresford Ellis, *The Cornish Language and its Literature* (1974).
4 Information on the Middle English form of the name Kerslake and on the names of the bishop *c*.959 courtesy of Dr O.J. Padel.
5 O.J. Padel, *A Popular Dictionary of Cornish Place-Names* (1988), p. 8.

6 CD/AE/3. The phrase is '*viam rationabilem ad boscum suum cariandum de bosco suo de labiricome usque ad terram suum de Tredrusel*' ('a reasonable passage to his (William Dawney's) wood allowing [the wood] to be carried from his wood of (the) Biricome to his land of Tredrossel').
7 O.J. Padel (private correspondence).
8 See the *Carta Henrici Regis de mercato ville de Tavistock* in H.P.R. Finberg's 'Some Early Tavistock Charters' in *EHR*, July 1947, Vol. LXII, No. 244, at pp. 352 et seq.
9 In 1465, for example, Sir Hugh Courtenay of Boconnoc commissioned a carvel called le Petir Courtenay as a privateer operating out of Fowey. One of the boatswains was John Blake and the victuallers included Walter Colle, clerk, and Henry Bray. All three families had connections with Sheviock. The rector of Sheviock, John Walle, a protegé of the Earl of Devon, had left money to Walter Colle, clerk, in his will of 1427. Members of the Blake and Bray families were engaged in the Portwrinkle fishing business for many generations. See further J. Whetter, *The Bodrugans* (1995), p. 98.
10 The original MS of Penhale's account was destroyed by enemy action in the Second World War. This translation is taken from Kempthorne (*c.*1934) at p. 36.
11 In *c.*1819, a carpenter, John Billing, was paid for erecting a gallery in St Mary's church. In 1723, John Andrew, the reeve, paid for work to be done on Joan Symons' house in Portwrinkle: CM/B/98. Members of the Symonds family were still living in Portwrinkle (at Channel View) in the 20th century. Mr Charles Symonds let Coombe Barn in Crafthole to the Recreation Club in 1920.
12 The Act, 36 Edw. 3, st. 1, c.15, provided that after 1362 arguments on pleadings in court should be conducted in English rather than Norman-French, though the written records, the Year Books, continued to be written in Norman-French.
13 See P. Beresford Ellis, *The Cornish Language and its Literature* (1974), pp. 47-9.
14 P. Beresford Ellis, *The Cornish Language and its Literature* (1974), p. 59.
15 F. Rose-Troup, *The Western Rebellion of 1549* (1913), p 408.
16 P. Beresford Ellis, *The Cornish Language and its Literature* (1974), pp 64, 65. A page from Tregear's translation is reproduced in that book (plate 4). See also Diarmaid MacCulloch, *Reformation: Europe's House Divided 1490-1700* (2003), p 284; and Brian Murdoch, *Cornish Literature* (1993), Chapter 6.
17 F. Rose-Troup (1913), p 228, and John Norden, *Speculi Britanniae* (1584).
18 *Survey* (1602), p 56 r. The Cornish phrase should properly be '*My ny-vynnaf cows sawsnek*' meaning 'I do not want to speak English' (F.E. Halliday, *Richard Carew of Antony* (1953)).
19 In 1585, he contributed £198 to equip three horsemen for the defence of the kingdom against the Spanish.
20 The phrase should properly be '*Mollath Dew yn dha las*', meaning 'The curse of God in thy guts' (Halliday).
21 *Survey* (1602), p 56 r.

Chapter 4, *The Manor of Sheviock*

1 See further, Chapter 2, *The Celtic Kingdoms, the Saxon and Norman Conquests*, and the sections on Kerslake, Trethill, Tredis and Trewin in Chapter 9, *Outlying Farms and Houses*.
2 Such holdings were usually referred to in manorial accounts as 'scattered lands'. The scattered lands of the manor of Sheviock are not considered in the present work, which is concerned solely with those lying within the parish of Sheviock.
3 Letters and Papers H.VIII 1540; Kempthorne (*c.*1934), p. 25.
4 The letter authorising the taking of possession by Sir Walter is in the Antony archives: CD/AE/6. Sir Walter Mildmay was the founder of Emmanuel College, Cambridge (1583-8).
5 CD/AE/9.
6 Writers who have accepted this assumption include C.S. Gilbert, in *Historical Survey of the County of Cornwall*, Vol II, p. 401; Davies Gilbert, in *The Parochial History of Cornwall*, Vol III, p. 439; G.A. Kempthorne, *A History of the Parish of Sheviock* (*c.*1934), p. 15.
7 See also the author's article, 'The Dawneys' Dovecote and Manor-House: A Lost Relationship Re-discovered' in *JRIC* 2005, p. 16, which sets out more fully the argument for this conclusion.

8 The first certain date for the property being an inn is 1620. At a court leet held on 3 November in that year, the tenant, William Sargent, was fined 4d. for selling wine of an unmeasured quantity: TNA: SC/2/158/39. In 1741 the property was let to the 'innholder' William Lord (born *c.*1704): CD/AH/44. For the holding of audit dinners at the inn in 1763-6, see Chapter 41, *Inns and Innkeepers*.
9 See Kempthorne (*c.*1934), pp. 11,12.
10 *The Birds of Cornwall and the Isles of Scilly* (1978), p. 385.
11 W.E. Tate, *The Parish Chest*, 3rd edn. (1969), p. 178.
12 See J. Whetter, *The Bodrugans* (1995), p. 22.
13 Mrs Theodora Colwill recalled that it was used to light the coppers on wash days.
14 See R. Penhallurick, *The Birds of Cornwall and the Isles of Scilly* (1978), p. 385.
15 This is Penhallurick's calculation (presumably based on the following calculation: 52 weeks divided by the six weeks of the rearing cycle equals 8.7, multiplied by two for the two eggs, equals 17, less three for accidents and replacement of adults).
16 Polydora Baker, *The Archaeologist* No, 59, pp. 26, 27, quoted in *The Times*, 27 March 2006.
17 Minutes of Parish Council meetings of 29 May 1961, 7 March 1972, 5 June 1973.
18 R. Penhallurick (1978), p. 390. A potence has been reconstructed inside the late mediaeval culverhouse at Cotehele. Its footings may be glimpsed through the low doorway into the building.
19 CD/AH/17.
20 CD/AH/28A & B.
21 Sir William Carew's steward paid various sums of money to James Lellek 'on account of Mr John Moyle for building ye pigeon ho.' in May and June 1719 and in January of the following year. Moyle also made the bricks used in building it.
22 Juliet Barker, *Agincourt: the King, the Campaign, the Battle* (pb. ed. 2006), pp. 118, 119.
23 Ten was also the number of horses kept by each Hunnic warrior of the fifth century: see Peter Heather, *The Fall of the Roman Empire: A New History* (2005), p. 328. Henry VIII is also said to have worn out ten horses on a full day's hunting.
24 Information obtained by Mrs P.A. Halliday, Master of the Worshipful Company of Farriers (2006-7), Chief Commoner of the City of London (2007-8).
25 Kempthorne (*c.*1934), p. 36.
26 CD/AE/7. Robert Kingdon, who executed and signed the lease, appears to have succeeded Harry as bailiff of the marquis.
27 See further, as to these quarters, Chapter 8, *Holdings on Sheviock Manor.*
28 The widow, Mary Jory, was a life named on a lease of a quarter of Blazor in 1691: CM/F2/158. The tenants were John Dell and Symon Peter.
29 As to Mrs Mullis's house, see 'The Scrivener's House; Mrs Mullis's House' in Chapter 13, *Houses, Shops and Farms in Crafthole.*
30 CD/AE/26; CM/B/97.
31 CM/F2/158.
32 CM/B/18.
33 CM/F2/158.
34 CM/B/156.
35 CM/F2/158.
36 CA/HI/3.
37 CD/AE/33B.
38 CD/AE/28A. See further Chapter 8, *Holdings on Sheviock Manor.*
39 CM/B/97.
40 CM/F2/158.
41 CM/F2/158.
42 CM/B/97, 98.
43 CD/AE/43.
44 CD/AE/33.

45 CE/G/23.
46 See further Chapter 15, *The Landing Place and Quay at Portwrinkle.*
47 The Anglo-Saxons were great beer drinkers, and they needed sizeable enclosed places to keep the barley prior to fermentation. The word 'barn' comes from the Anglo-Saxon *bere-erne*, also meaning place for barley.
48 Kempthorne (*c.*1934), p. 36.
49 See further Chapter 6, *Courts and Officials of the Manor.*
50 CD/AE/21.
51 CM/B/18.
52 Kempthorne (*c.*1934), p. 63.
53 CM/B/97.
54 CD/AE/22.
55 CM/F2/158. Ferdinando was probably the grandson of the Ferdinando Spiller who ran the mill at Gill Ball and the inn at Crafthole in Elizabethan times. See further Chapter 41, *Inns and Innkeepers.*
56 CD/AE/23.
57 Kempthorne (*c.*1934), p. 72.
58 CM/B/156.
59 *Survey of Cornwall* (1602), p. 108v.
60 Kempthorne (*c.*1934), at p. 14, credits Emmeline Dawney, Sir John Dawney's daughter, as the builder of the barn. But her husband, Sir Edward Courtenay, could hardly be described as 'one of these *Dannyes* ancestours'.
61 Strictly speaking, it was not a 'tithe' barn, because the Dawneys never impropriated the great tithes of the parish, which belonged, from about 1200, to the rector.
62 A third part, consisting of 30 acres, was attached to Prior's Wood.
63 CM/B/97.
64 CRO: CM/B/97. I am grateful to Ellan Odiorne Derow for this reference and information on the Odiornes.
65 CM/B/98.
66 CA/HI/2.
67 CA/HI/4.
68 In 1742, Sir William Carew let to George Warren a 'dwelling house garden and little meadow commonly called by the name of High Clicker ... and part of a certain tenement ... formerly in the possession of one Odihorne': CD/AG/47. For Higher Clicker, see 'Clicker' in Chapter 10, *Sheviock Churchtown.*
69 CA/HI/8.
70 CD/AF/34.
71 CE/G/23.
72 See CM/F2/158.
73 See Chapter 2, *The Celtic Kingdoms, the Saxon and Norman Conquests.*
74 CD/AF/40. The document of sale gives the history of the properties before the time of the Reformation.
75 See also 'Sconner Farm and Lime Kiln' in Chapter 8, *Holdings on Sheviock Manor.*
76 CM/F2/158. The total area of Haye and Prior's wood in 1770 was 30 acres, hence the presumption that Haye and Prior's wood together encompassed 30 acres: see CM/F2/160A.
77 See further Chapter 42, *Mills andMillers.*
78 CE/C/18.
79 CA/HI/6.
80 CD/AF/28.
81 CM/B/18.
82 See Chapter 10, *Sheviock Churchtown.*
83 Glebe Terrier in the Devon Record Office.
84 CM/B/97.
85 CM/B/98.

86 The Plan is catalogued as CP/FX/11 and the Survey as CM/B/101.
87 CD/AE/17.
88 CD/AG/1A.
89 CM/B/98.
90 CM/B/18.
91 CD/AG/2.
92 CD/AG/3.
93 CD/AG/4A.
94 See CD/AG/4A.
95 CM/F2/160A.
96 CE/C/18.
97 CM/B/98.
98 Phillip Blake's mother was Phillipa Grills.
99 CM/F2/158.
100 CA/HI/6.
101 CD/AE/18.
102 See further 'Officials of the Manor' in Chapter 6, *Courts and Officials of the Manor.*
103 CM/B/18.
104 See 'Orchard Cottage' in Chapter 10, *Sheviock Churchtown.*
105 CD/AE/19A&B.
106 CD/AE/20.
107 This right is specifically mentioned in the deed of sale of the manor to Thomas Carew in 1558: CD/AE/9.
108 CM/B/98.
109 CM/B/98.
110 CA/HI/8.
111 CD/AG/52.
112 The Revd Walter Arundell had done the same thing to the pound at Crafthole, 300 years earlier: see 'Unauthorised Works and Public Nuisances' in Chapter 12, *Courts and Officials of the Borough of Crafthole.*

Chapter 5, *Lords of the Manor*

1 See further 'The Dawney Aisle' in Chapter 26, *The Early Church.*
2 In this book I have used the spelling 'Dawney' because it is the one current in the parish today.
3 See P.L.Hull (ed.), *The Caption of Seisin of the Duchy of Cornwall (1337)*, DCRS new ser. 17 (1971).
4 Lake, Vol. IV (1872), p. 148.
5 K.S.B.Keats-Rohan, *Domesday People* (1999), p.190.
6 Also transcribed by H.P.R. Finberg in 'Some Early Tavistock Charters', *EHR*, July 1947, Vol. LXII, No. 244, at pp. 352 *et seq.*
7 Trewornan is situated on a creek of the River Camel, which separates St Minver from Egloshayle: see Lake, Vol. III (1870), p. 370.
8 K.S.B.Keats-Rohan, *Domesday Descendants* (2002), p. 276.
9 *Ibid.*
10 Lake, Vol. IV (1872), p. 148.
11 CD/AE/1.
12 Kempthorne (c.1934), p. 10.
13 CD/AE/3.
14 Thomas married the heiress of John Newton of Snaith and settled at Escrick in East Yorkshire. He is the ancestor of the Viscounts Downe. See J.T.Ward, *East Yorkshire Landed Estates in the 19th Century* (1967), p. 28.
15 Calendars of Patent Rolls, 13 August 1309.
16 Calendar of Close Rolls, May 1330.

17 I.P.M. 26 Sep, 6 Ed. III. See also Calendars of Close Rolls, Oct 18 1332.
18 Cal. Pat. Rolls, 18 Ed. II, Pt. 1, m. 22.
19 Calendars of Inquisitions, 20 Edward III.
20 Kempthorne (*c.*1934), p. 10.
21 I am grateful to Lady Katherine Watney, sister of the earl of Devon, for help with this section.
22 The main published source for this section is Ezra Cleaveland, *A Genealogical History of the Noble and Illustrious Family of Courtenay, etc.* (1735). Cleaveland was a Fellow of Exeter College, Oxford, and later rector of Honiton, Devon.
23 Kempthorne (c.1934), p. 33.
24 See 'Sir Hugh Courtenay of Haccombe' in Chapter 44, *Families.*
25 See Martin Cherry, 'The Courtenay Earls of Devon: The Formation and Disintegration of a Late Medieval Aristocratic Affinity', *Southern History*, Vol I (1979), p. 80.
26 He appointed proxies for every Parliament after May 1400: *ibid.*, p. 93.
27 Ezra Cleaveland, *A Genealogical History of the Noble and Illustrious Family of Courtenay, etc.* (1735), p. 204.
28 These were Waddesden, Hillesden and Waninton.
29 The Dorset manors were Iwerne-Courtenay, Ebrighton and Corstan.
30 These were the manors and hundreds of Crewkerne and West Coker, and the manors of Hannington, Hinton and Modeford.
31 These were the borough of Limington and the manor of Bremer.
32 These were the manors and hundreds of Exminster, Plympton, and Tiverton; the hundreds of Woneford, Harridge, Culliton, and West Budley; the manors of Topsham, Twilebear, Okehampton, Sampford-Courtenay, Chirbear, Duelton, Chimleigh, Caverly, Newnham *juxta* Chitlehamsole, Ex-Island, Kenn, Whimple, Ailesbear, Huntsbear, Whitwell, Cullsomb, Whitford, Musberry, Farway, Godmington (?Goodrington), Stancomb, South-Allington, and Shapton; the hamlet of Newton-Popleford; the boroughs of Tiverton, Chimleigh, Caverly, Kenford, and Culliford; the honour of Okehampton; and the castles of Plympton and Okehampton.
33 These included Radford, Sheviock, Antony, Tregantel, Trelewin, Porthlooe, Treluggan, Landilip (Landulph), Leigh-Durrant, Landren (Landrake?), Northill, Treverbyn, Tregamur, and the borough of Porthpighan (borough of West Looe), Croftholeborough (Crafthole), and Landile.
34 For the decline in power of the earls of Devon during this long minority, see Martin Cherry, 'The Courtenay Earls of Devon: The Formation and Disintegration of a Late Medieval Aristocratic Affinity', *Southern History*, Vol. 1 (1979), pp. 71 et seq.
35 See 'Sir Hugh Courtenay of Ashwater and Boconnoc' in Appendix 1, *Families.*
36 Alison Weir, *Henry VIII, King and Court* (2001), p. 350.
37 Ezra Cleaveland, *A Genealogical History of the Noble and Illustrious Family of Courtenay, etc.* (1735), p. 251.
38 On his attainder, the king annexed to the Duchy of Cornwall the manors of West Antony, Porthlooe (East Looe) and the borough of Porthpighan (West Looe), Northill, Landrane [Landrake?] Trelowyn, Treganor, Tregulan, Croftoleborough (borough of Crafthole), Treverbyn-Courtenay, Landulph, Leigh-durant and Tinten.
39 E. Cleaveland (1735), p. 251. As to the *Dirige* and trental of masses, see Chapter 27, *Church Life in the Middle Ages.*
40 See Joanna Mattingly, 'Stories in the Glass – Reconstructing the St Neot Pre-Reformation Glazing Scheme', *JRIC* 2000, p. 21.
41 The present earl is the 18th of the new creation.
42 TNA: E315/414 (Misc. Bks. Augn. Office).
43 Calendars of Close Rolls.
44 D. and S. Lysons, *Magna Britannia*, Vol. III, Cornwall (1814).
45 For example, Syon Abbey.
46 *History of the Worthies of England* (1662).
47 J. L. Vivian and H. H. Drake, *The Visitation of the County of Cornwall in the year 1620* (1874), p. 28.

48 See 'Alexander Carew' and 'Sir Wymond Carew' in Appendix 1, *Families.*
49 For the descent of the manor of East Antony from the L'Erchdekne (Archdeacon) family to Sir Nicholas Carew, see 'L'Erchdekne' in Appendix 1, *Families.*
50 CD/AE/9.
51 See 'Sconner Farm and Lime Kilns' in Chapter 8, *Holdings on Sheviock Manor.*
52 CZ/EE/32.
53 Jane, daughter of his younger son, Thomas of Harrowbarrow in Calstock, married the Revd Nicholas Kendall, who was instituted rector of Sheviock in 1680.
54 E. Cruickshank, S. Handley and D.W. Hayton, *The House of Commons 1690-1715*, Vol. III (2002), p. 464.
55 On leaving the Revd Eare's school in July 1695, Sir Richard presented him with a silver tankard, costing £6 10s.: CA/HI/2.
56 CM/B/98.
57 CA/HI/2. Parson Kendall was the rector of Sheviock. 'Dominus Carew', the Latin for 'Sir [Richard] Carew' is entered on the long rolls of Winchester College for the years 1695, 1696, 1699 and 1701: information supplied by Ms Sarah Shawcross of the Wykehamist Society Office.
58 CA/HI/3. The cost of his schooling and board and lodging for himself and his manservant came to £6 5s. per quarter.
59 They cost 16s.: CA/HI/3.
60 Joseph Foster, *Alumni Oxonienses (1715-1886)* (1888); and information supplied by Dr John Maddicott, Librarian and Archivist, Exeter College.
61 E. Cruickshank, S. Handley and D.W. Hayton, *The House of Commons 1690-1715*, Vol. III (2002), p. 466.
62 CA/HI/5A.
63 CD/AH/28A &B.
64 CM/B/96.
65 See Crispin Gill, *Plymouth: A New History* (1979), Vol. II, p. 86.
66 CA/HI/5A.
67 CD/AE/28A.
68 Oliver Garnett, *Antony*, for The National Trust (2002), p. 32.
69 Oliver Garnett, *Antony*, for The National Trust (2002), p. 35.
70 The passage from Tonkin is reproduced in *Lake's Parochial History of Cornwall* (1867), Vol. I, p. 23.
71 CA/HI/8.
72 CM/A/6/1-70.
73 The information in this and the following two articles is taken, with permission, from Professor Edwin Jaggard's *An Exceptional Man: Reginald Pole Carew of Antony* (2008).
74 See Crispin Gill, *The Park and Gardens of Antony House* (unpublished), pp. 10-16.
75 See Crispin Gill, *The Park and Gardens of Antony House* (unpublished), p. 17.

Chapter 6, *Courts and Officials of the Manor*

1 See H.P.R. Finberg, *Tavistock Abbey* (1951), p. 239.
2 The prohibition was imposed by the Council of London: see R. Lennard, *Rural England: 1086-1135* (1959), p. 157.
3 See further, T. Plucknett, *A Concise History of the Common Law* (5th edn, 1956), pp. 86 *et seq.*
4 CD/AE/9.
5 CD/AE/7.
6 E.g. until 1866 in Bradninch, Devon: *DCNQ* XV (1928), p. 202.
7 See *DCNQ* XV (1928), p. 203.
8 CM/A/18, 28, 65, 69.
9 CM/A/6.
10 CE/C/24. See further 'Receipts from Wreckage and the Lord's Right to Great Fish' in Chapter 7, *Manorial Revenues.*
11 CE/C/24.

12 CA/HI/8.
13 CM/B/55.
14 CD/AG/44.
15 CA/HI/7.
16 CM/B/55. For the audit dinners held in connection with these courts, see Chapter 41, *Inns and Innkeepers*.
17 G.R.Y. Radcliffe and G. Cross, *The English Legal System* (3rd edn. 1954), p. 23.
18 S. and B. Webb, *The Manor and the Borough* (1908), pp. 14, 15.
19 For court baron records of East Antony from 1719 to 1806 (with some gaps), see CM/A/6.
20 CM/B/90. The 1806 court baron of the manor of East Antony still included as its first presentment, 'We present all the ancient Customs of this Manor to be good and laudable': CM/A/6.
21 This was also the case on the other Carew manors of Drewsteignton and Notter. The last combined court for Notter was held at Antony Passage House in 1763. At that court the rents were received, but it was noted that 'no Court has been held for the said Mannor for many years': CM/B/155.
22 CM/B/55.
23 A John Prinn or Prynn occupied what is now Smuggler's Cottage in Portwrinkle according to Thomas Helman's lease of the premises executed on 29 September 1812.
24 See CM/A/18, 65, 69.
25 CE/C/24.
26 I have found only one instance of the lord presiding at his own court. This was Reginald Pole Carew, who presided at the court baron of East Antony in 1782: CM/A/6.
27 CM/A/3.
28 CM/A/3/2.
29 The spelling 'Kelleway' is the one used on his memorial in Branscombe Church. The name is also spelled Kaylway, Caylwaye, Calway, Callaway and Calloway. As to the earl, see Chapter 5, *Lords of the Manor*.
30 On 3 November 1492, John 'Kaylway' and others were given messuages, lands, tenements, services etc., at a place called Smythston, in the parish of Berrynarbor, near Ilfracombe in Devon: Wiltshire Record Office: 413/134. On 26 July 1511, John 'Cayleway' and others witnessed a grant by Thomas Payne of Hutton of the manors of Uphill and Shipston and other lands in south-west Somerset to John Row, sergeant at law, William Wadham, and others as trustees for himself and his wife, and after their deaths, for his heirs: Bristol Record Office: AC/D/11/41. I am grateful to Mrs S.M. Laithewaite of the Devon Record Office for this information.
31 See further as to Kelleway, Chapter 12, *Courts and Officials of the Borough of Crafthole*.
32 See Joanna Mattingly, 'Stories in the Glass – Reconstructing the St Neot Pre-Reformation Glazing Scheme', *JRIC 2000*, pp. 21, 41, 42.
33 CD/AF/26. For Brooking, see further Chapter 11, *The Borough of Crafthole*.
34 Joanna Mattingly, op. cit., p. 21.
35 See W.H.H. Rogers, *The Antient Sepulchral Effigies and Monumental and Memorial Sculptures of Devon* (1877), p. 171.
36 See A.L. Rowse, *Tudor Cornwall* (1941), p. 235.
37 His own coat (in quarters 1 and 4), is 'argent, a saltire sable between four pears pendant gules'. His first wife (in quarter 2) may be a member of the Trethurf family. Joan's coat appears in quarter 3.
38 The epitaph to this monument reads 'Here lieth intombd the body of a virtuous & antient Gentlewoman descended of the antient House of the Plantagenets sometime of Cornwall, namely JOAN one of the daughters & heirs unto John Tregarthin Esq. She was first married unto John Kelleway Esq who had by her much issue. After his death she was married to John Wadham of Meryfield in the county of Somerset Esq & by him had several children. She lived a virtuous & godly life & died in an honourable age + September in the year of Christ 1583.'
39 The portion was part of the marriage settlement made when Sir John's daughter, Rachel, married Ambrose Manaton in 1690: CA/HI/2. She was the second daughter of his first wife, Sarah Hungerford.
40 CA/HI/2.
41 CA/HI/2.

42 CA/HI/2.
43 His payments book up to 24 June 1734 ends with the word 'Finis': CA/HI/8.
44 CA/HI/8.
45 CM/B/55; CM/A/6.
46 CD/AF/43B.
47 CD/AF/43A.
48 See May McKissack, *The 14th Century: 1307-1399* (1959).
49 CD/AE/7.
50 John Kyndon, perhaps Robert's son, was an official of Queen Elizabeth, leasing property in the borough of Crafthole, in 1580: TNA: E315/414.
51 CM/A/1.
52 See Chapter 4, *The Manor of Sheviock.*
53 Account entry for 7 October 1696: CA/HI/2.
54 CA/HI/3.
55 CA/HI/8.
56 CA/HI/8.
57 CA/HI/8.
58 On the Duchy manor of West Antony, 'Three Tenements (viz) Trelay, Hole and Scrasdon have been accustomed to do the Office of Reeve in their turn to collect the Lord's rents Heriots etc and be accountable for the same at the Princes audit': Spry's *Survey of the Manor of West Antony* (1793), CM/A/76.
59 CM/B/98.
60 CM/B/98 is the source for much of the information in this paragraph.
61 CM/B/55.
62 CM/B/98.
63 See the survey of 1775 (CM/B/101) which shows William Bray as the tenant of the Net Park in Portwrinkle 'by virtue of his office being Reeve of the Manor.'
64 CM/B/98 and CM/F2/158.
65 The lease was kindly shown to the author by the present owner, Mrs Margaret Bartlett.
66 CD/AE/13.
67 CM/B/98.
68 CM/B/55.

Chapter 7, *Manorial Revenues*

1 CM/A/23.
2 CM/A/6.
3 CM/B/98.
4 Account entry for 14 December 1697: CA/HI/2.
5 CM/B/97.
6 CE/C/18.
7 CE/F2/158.
8 CM/B/98.
9 CM/B/98.
10 CM/B/98.
11 CD/AE/43b
12 CD/AE/3.
13 See Harold Fox, *The Evolution of the Fishing Village: Landscape and Society along the South Devon Coast, 1086-1550* (2001), p. 67.
14 CE/C/24.
15 M. Kowaleski, *The Havener's Accounts of the earldom and Duchy of Cornwall 1287-1356* (2001), p. 20.
16 See Harold Fox, *The Evolution of the Fishing Village: Landscape and Society along the South Devon Coast, 1086-1550* (2001), p. 53.

17 See also for 'great fish', the section 'Receipts from Wreckage' below.
18 CE/C/24.
19 Palmer was bailiff of the manor in 1725 and became the tenant of Bailiff's Meadow as well as Treise's tenement. See further Chapter 4, *The Manor of Sheviock.*
20 CE/C/24.
21 CE/C/24.
22 CE/C/24.
23 'Mr Carew' must be Coventry Carew. In 1738, his father, Sir William, removed to Bath, and Coventry was put in charge of the Antony estates. In 1744, on the death of his father, he inherited the baronetcy.
24 CA/HI/5B.
25 CE/C/24.
26 CA/HI/6.
27 CA/HI/6.
28 See further Chapter 18, *The Village of Portwrinkle.*
29 CE/C/24.
30 *Parochial Memoranda.* British Library MS Egerton 2657.
31 CM/B/98.
32 CA/HI/2.
33 CM/B/98.
34 CA/HI/2
35 CE/C/20.
36 See further, Chapter 11, *The Borough of Crafthole.*
37 See Kempthorne (*c.*1934), p. 63.
38 CD/AF/26.
39 CE/E/2.
40 Philip Palmer was the bailiff in that year.
41 CD/AF/29.
42 CA/HI/8.
43 CD/AF/30.
44 CRO: Edgcumbe MS B manorial accounts 1460, quoted in J. Whetter, *The Bodrugans* (1995), p. 22.
45 See J. Whetter, *The Bodrugans* (1995), p. 22.
46 CM/A/73.
47 See Lawrence Blair, *English Church Ales* (1940), p. 17: 'By the 13th century, the scotale, an entertainment given by the lord of the manor-house to his tenants and lower dependants, which their fealty bound them to attend, each with his "scot" or set contribution in hand, had become a universal custom on manorial tenures in England'.
48 There are eight gallons in a bushel.

Chapter 8, *Holdings on Sheviock Manor*

1 For the demesne farms, see Chapter 4, *The Manor of Sheviock.*
2 See Surveys of 1691 (CM/F2/158), 1698 (CM/F2/159), *c.*1762 (CM/F2/160), 1770 (CM/F2/160A), 1797 (CM/F2/164), 1816 (CM/F2/165).
3 CP/FX/11 (map); CM/B/101 (Survey).
4 'Readen' is sometimes spelled 'Roaden'.
5 'Slade' means ground too marshy to cultivate.
6 In Pembrokeshire, according to a report by Simon de Bruxelles in *The Times*, 9 August 2004, 'large tracts of the rugged and remote clifftops where sheep once used to graze are now covered with the creeping menace. The plant is spreading across Britain at the rate of 3 per cent a year, killing everything in its path.' Because the terrain was too dangerous for tractors, the landowner, the National Trust, imported a mule from America to draw the heavy rollers needed to crush the roots of the plant.

7 'Survey of the Freehold Lands of the Manor of Landrake made by Wm. Samuell Reeve of the same' (1578): H24/225.
8 CD/AF/1.
9 TNA: E315/414.
10 CD/AH/4.
11 CE/C/18.
12 CM/F2/158.
13 CM/B/18.
14 CD/AE/42.
15 See John Rawling's Account of Sheviocke 1656 to 1660: CM/B/98.
16 CM/F2/158.
17 CD/AE/43A.
18 CM/B/18.
19 CM/B/156.
20 CD/AE/42.
21 CE/C/18.
22 CM/F2/158.
23 CM/B/98.
24 CD/AH/57.
25 CD/AE/12.
26 CD/AE/44.
27 CM/B/18.
28 Kempthorne (*c.*1934), p. 72.
29 CD/AE/46A and B.
30 CD/AI/33B.
31 CD/AI/33B.
32 CD/AE/15.
33 CD/AF/12.
34 CD/AF/13.
35 CM/B/98.
36 CD/AF/14A&B.
37 CM/B/98.
38 CM/B/101
39 CA/HI/3.
40 CM/F2/158. John Balsey also rented Friday's Parks. In 1707, he also rented a house and orchard in Crafthole for 4s. on the lives of Amy and Mary Arundell, spinsters, daughters of Richard Arundell (deceased), yeoman, and Joan Arundell, his widow.
41 CM/B/18.
42 CM/B/101.
43 As to the origin of the name, see further Chapter 21, *Field Names in Sheviock.*
44 CE/C/18.
45 CM/F2/158.
46 CA/HI/5B.
47 CM/B/18.
48 CD/AI/33B.
49 CD/AE/27.
50 CD/AE/27.
51 CM/F2/158.
52 CD/AE/28A.
53 CM/B/18.

54 CD/AE/29.
55 Samuel Madock, a Plymouth merchant who died in 1713, is buried in Tamerton-Foliot church: see W.H.H.Rogers, *The Antient Sepulchral Effigies and Monumental and Memorial Sculpture of Devon* (1877), p120.
56 CE/C/18.
57 CD/AF/1.
58 CD/AF/2.
59 CM/B/18.
60 CD/AF/3.
61 CD/AF/5.
62 CD/AF/7.
63 CD/AE/1.
64 Kempthorne (*c.*1934), p. 36. For 'Trethill', see Chapter 9, *Outlying Farms and Houses.*
65 CD/AF/19.
66 CM/B/97.
67 CD/AF/20.
68 CA/HI/4. See further 'Haye' in Chapter 4, *The Manor of Sheviock.*
69 CM/B/18.
70 CD/AF/22A&B.
71 CM/B/156.
72 Richard also inherited an 88-acre tenancy in Kerslake after the death of his father in 1654.
73 CM/F2/158.
74 See CD/AF/21.
75 CD/AF/21 and CM/B/18.
76 CD/AF/21.
77 CM/B/156. For the Peter family, see also 'Tredis' in Chapter 9, *Outlying Farms and Houses.*
78 CP/FX/11 (map); CM/B/101 (Survey).
79 CD/AF/25B.
80 CD/AF/25.
81 Kempthorne (*c.*1934), p. 36.
82 CD/AF/40. The document of sale gives the history of the properties to before the time of the Reformation. See also Chapter 4, *The Manor of Sheviock.*
83 CM/B/97.
84 Sheviock register of burials; Kempthorne (*c.*1934), p. 61.
85 CD/AF/42.
86 CM/B/98.
87 CM/B/18.
88 CA/HI/7.
89 CM/B/156.
90 CD/AF/43B.
91 CD/AF/43A.
92 CD/AF/44.
93 CD/AF/45
94 CD/AF/46.
95 CD/AF/47.
96 CD/AF/48.
97 CD/AF/49.
98 CD/AF/50.
99 See E. Jaggard, *An Exceptional Man: Reginald Pole Carew of Antony* (2008), p. 105.
100 *Cornwall* in Pevsner's Buildings of England series (2nd ed., revised by Enid Radcliffe, 1970), p. 213.

101 D.E.Pett, *The Parks and Gardens of Cornwall* (1998), pp. 240, 241.
102 'Vel' implies deep soil, and a velling ploughshare was an exceptionally wide one used to strip off the greensward prior to beat-burning. There was a field at Vellands called 'Furse Park'. For 'beat-burning', see Chapter 23, *The Soil and Crops*. See further Robin Stanes, *The Old Farm* (1990).
103 CE/C/18.
104 CM/B/18.
105 Penhale was the rector's *procurator* (steward). The original MS of his account was destroyed by enemy action in the Second World War. For Kempthorne's translation of the main provisions, see Chapter 33, *Tithes*.
106 CD/AG/9.
107 CD/AG/16.
108 CD/AG/18.
109 CM/B/97.
110 CM/F2/158.
111 CM/B/18.
112 CD/AI/37B.
113 CD/AE/3.
114 CD/AG/12.
115 CD/AG/14.
116 CM/F2/158.
117 CM/B/18.
118 CD/AG/28.
119 CM/B/97.
120 CM/B/97.
121 CD/AG/15.
122 CM/B/18.
123 CD/AG/34.
124 CM/B/156.
125 CD/AG/32.
126 CD/AG/41A.
127 CD/AG/42A.
128 See further Chapter 2, *The Celtic Kingdoms, the Saxon and Norman Conquests*.
129 E.g. in 1637 to Richard Hockyn (CD/AG/9) and in 1681 to John Holman (CD/AG/16).
130 CM/F2/158.
131 CM/B/18.
132 CM/B/101.
133 CD/AI/23.
134 CD/AJ/45. See further Chapter 18, *The Village of Portwrinkle*.
135 CD/AG/12.
136 CM/B/98.
137 CD/AG/13.
138 CM/F2/158.
139 CD/AG/21.
140 CD/AG/36.
141 For the meanings of these Cornish words, see Chapter 21, *Field Names in Sheviock*.
142 CD/AF/16.
143 CM/B/98.
144 CD/AF/17A&B.
145 CM/B/156.
146 CD/AF/18A&B.
147 CM/B/18.
148 CD/AG/33.

149 CM/B/156.
150 See further 'Reginald Pole Carew's New Leases' in Chapter 18, *The Village of Portwrinkle.*
151 CD/AE/13.
152 CM/B/18.
153 CM/B/156.
154 See Chapter 15, *The Landing Place and Quay at Portwrinkle.*
155 For 'Tredrossel', see Chapter 9, *Outlying Farms and Houses.*
156 CD/AG/22.
157 CM/B/156.
158 Walter Peake was a sailor on Sheviock's deep-sea fishing vessel, the *Dayestarr*, in 1626. Peake owned property in the borough of Crafthole, where he was a juror on the court leet in 1635 and 1643. William Peake was described as a yeoman of St Germans in a lease of 1681 (CD/AG/16). He married Elizabeth Hocken, daughter of Richard Hocken, who farmed at Trewrickle.
159 CD/AG/23.
160 CM/B/18.
161 CD/AG/25.
162 CD/AG/51. William Mitchell was living at Trewin in 1753: see CD/AG/56.
163 CM/F2/158.
164 CD/AG/24.
165 CD/AG/40.
166 CD/AG/35A.

Chapter 9, *Outlying Farms and Houses*

1 *Historical Survey of the County of Cornwall*, Vol. II (1820), p. 402. For Poole and Sconner, see Chapter 8, *Holdings on Sheviock Manor.*
2 Kempthorne (*c.*1934), p. 35.
3 Thomas Pride's Map and Survey of 1775 show the location of Higher, Middle and Lower Blerrick. See CM/B/101 (Map) and CP/FX/11 (Survey). In 1798, Reginald Pole Carew purchased the manors of West Antony and Crafthole from the Duke of Cornwall for the combined price of £11,240: CZ/AV/7.
4 'Survey of the Freehold Lands of the Manor of Landrake made by Wm. Samuell Reeve of the same' (1578): H24/225.
5 CD/PP/30.
6 CD/PP/35.
7 See further 'Weavers' in Chapter 39, *Trades and Crafts.*
8 CD/PP/41.
9 CD/PP/43.
10 CD/PP/49.
11 CD/PP/36.
12 CD/PP/44.
13 CD/PP/34.
14 See Kempthorne (*c.*1934), p. 44.
15 CE/F/5.
16 Now in the CRO: WH 5074.
17 Hearth Tax roll, 1664.
18 CM/F2/158.
19 As to Kerslake, Bog and Denabole Mills, see 'Mills and Millers' in Chapter 39, *Trades and Crafts.*
20 See Kempthorne (*c.*1934), p. 18.
21 CD/AE/8.
22 For the manorial rolls, see CRO: WH 5074.
23 It is marked on early editions of the Ordnance Survey Map.

24 An 'indenture' is a piece of parchment or vellum cut into two by a wavy line, thus creating two separate documents. When the two documents are brought together it can be seen that the two parts were cut from the same piece of material, so that the parties must have been together at the time it was agreed. Each party kept his piece of the indenture.
25 CD/AE/58 (dated 24 April 1688).
26 Map: CP/F1/19.
27 CD/AE/63A&B. See also CZ/AV/7.
28 CP/FX/11. Presumably it was included on the estate map of the manor of Sheviock because the sale was then in contemplation.
29 CD/AF/37.
30 CRO: WH 5074.
31 These were described as Hancock's Orchard and Hancock's Hill (divided into Upper, Lower, Little and Outer Hancock's Hill) on a map of 1742: CP/F1/19. Today they are all woodland. They abut the A374 below Trethill.
32 CD/AE/59.
33 CD/AE/59.
34 CD/AE/62.
35 CD/AE/62.
36 CE/F/5.
37 CM/B/101 and CP/FX/6. For an account of farming at Lantic during the Second World War, see Chapter 25, *Farming After 1800*.
38 Kempthorne (*c.*1934); Sloan MS xxxiii, 13.
39 Kempthorne (*c.*1934), p. 36.
40 Kempthorne (*c.*1934), p. 67.
41 See pedigree of the Smiths of Tregunnick, in J.L Vivian, *The Visitations of Cornwall, comprising the Heralds' Visitations of 1530, 1573 and 1620* (1887).
42 He is shown as the landowner on the Tithe Redemption Survey of 1840/41.
43 Run by Paul and Fiona Ingall. See further 'Liscawn Inn' in Chapter 41, *Inns and Innkeepers*.
44 Kempthorne (*c.*1934), p. 68.
45 Kempthorne (*c.*1934), p. 60. Add. MSS. BM 13060.
46 Thomas had inherited the estate from his mother, Ricarda, who was the daughter of John Inkpenne. Sir Thomas Fychet, who died in 1336, was lord of Spaxton in Somerset. Thomas junior, who inherited the estate, died in 1395. His sister and heiress married Robert Hill. In 1411, the tenant of the half fee was John Bake of St Germans. Robert Hill's son, William, was mentioned in *Feudal Aids*, as holding land in Sheviock in 1428.
47 Kempthorne (*c.*1934), p. 59. H. 7/4A.
48 H. 24/226.
49 See Chapter 15, *The Landing Place and Quay at Portwrinkle*.
50 Will of Arthur Peters in the National Archives.
51 CE/F/5.
52 Letter dated 21 December 1831 in the DRO.
53 Lake, Vol. IV, p. 149.
54 CE/F/5.
55 J. Manco, *The History of Trewin House, Sheviock, Cornwall* (2008), commissioned by D. and A. Leighton-Squires.
56 CD/AE/3. 'Socage' means in return for services, other than knight's service. These services were often converted into a rental payment.
57 Possibly this was furze wood from the fields.
58 CD/AE/3.
59 H. 7/4A.
60 Kempthorne (*c.*1934), pp. 36, 61.
61 CD/AH/21.

62 Kempthorne (*c.*1934), p. 62.
63 See further Chapter 24, *Fruit and Orchards.*
64 CM/A/73.
65 H 28/44.
66 Anthony Blake was accused of moving his sheep from Middle and Lower Blerrick and Kerslake to this property in St John's to avoid paying the tithes on them: see Chapter 33, *Tithes.*
67 Sir John Maclean, *Parochial and Family History of the Deanery of Trigg Minor, in the County of Cornwall* (3 vols. London and Bodmin, 1872-79).
68 He wrote that, south of his two closes called Ladywell, he had another two closes 'divided by mee, called the south downe, conteyning 16A (acres) [bounded] in the East with Joseps land, *Sergiants land*, and Mr Stitchens lande'.
69 CE/F/5.
70 *Historical Survey of the County of Cornwall*, Vol. II (1820), p. 402.
71 I am grateful to Rosamund Reid for giving me sight of her thesis 'The Work of George Wightwick (1802-1872): Architect, Writer and Critic' (1996), submitted for the degree of Master of Philosophy in the University of London. I have made use of this thesis in preparing this section.
72 CD/AF/37.
73 She died in 1957.
74 H.7/10A.
75 J.B. Gover, *Place Names of Cornwall* (collected between 1922 and 1927; July 1948; typescript in Royal Institution of Cornwall Library, Truro).
76 The Inkpenne family possessed the manor of Halton in St Dominick from 1304 to at least 1351 (see *Lake*, Vol. I, p. 299). In 1390, that manor belonged to the Fychets (*ibid.*).
77 Kempthorne (*c.*1934), p. 36.
78 Kempthorne (*c.*1934), p. 59. Thomas had inherited the estate from his mother, Ricarda, who was the daughter of John Inkpenne. Sir Thomas Fychet, who died in 1336, was lord of Spaxton in Somerset. Thomas junior, who inherited the estate, died in 1395. His sister and heiress married Robert Hill. In 1411, the tenant of the half fee was John Bake of St Germans. Robert Hill's son, William, was mentioned in *Feudal Aids*, as holding land in Sheviock in 1428.
79 H.24/226.
80 See Chapter 33, *Tithes.*
81 Kempthorne (*c.*1934), p. 59.
82 C.S. Gilbert, *Historical and Topographical Survey of the County of Cornwall*, Vol. 2, p. 402.
83 Kempthorne (*c.*1934), p. 72.
84 This lease was referred to in a later lease of 1792: CD/AG/56.
85 Information from Nicholas Foster, previous owner of Trewin.
86 Letter of 24 November 1832 from Samuel Lyne to Reginald Pole Carew.

Chapter 10, *Sheviock Churchtown*

1 For the demesne farms, see Chapter 4, *The Manor of Sheviock.*
2 See further Chapter 28, *Church Administration in the Middle Ages.*
3 See Joanna Mattingly, 'The Dating of Bench-Ends in Cornish Churches', *JRIC* 1991, p. 58.
4 *Survey of Cornwall* (1602), p. 69r.
5 CM/B/98.
6 CM/F2/158.
7 CD/AE/38, 39.
8 CM/B/18.
9 Information about the *Carew Arms* and the Landrey and Clinnick families supplied by T.G. Gregory-Smith, a descendant of the Landry family.
10 See further Chapter 41, *Inns and Innkeepers.*
11 TNA: E178/6177.

12 CM/F2/158.
13 CM/B/18.
14 CD/AG/47.
15 Information supplied by Fred Paul, grandson of George May.
16 See also 'Cote' in Chapter 8, *Holdings on Sheviock Manor.*
17 English Heritage.
18 CD/AE/42.
19 CD/AF/27.
20 CB/B/98 – MAN 10/1.
21 CM/B/98 – MAN 8/16.
22 CD/AJ/17.
23 See Chapter 4, *The Manor of Sheviock.*
24 The Plan is catalogued as CP/FX/11 and the Survey as CM/B/101.
25 The family of Treis or Treise were anciently the owners of the manor of Tremain; see Lake, Vol. IV (1872), p. 240.
26 Blake's rent was £2 0s. 7d.: CM/B/97.
27 CM/B/98.
28 See Kempthorne (*c.*1934), p. 69.
29 CM/B/98.
30 CM/B/18.
31 General rental of the manor dated 1770: CM/F2/160A.
32 Rentals of 1770 and 1772.
33 CD/AG/57.
34 See also on the Landreys, Chapter 41, *Inns and Innkeepers.*
35 CD/AG/52.
36 CD/AE/14.
37 CD/AF/15.
38 CD/AE/16.
39 CD/AG/45.
40 See Henderson MS, *Materials for a Parochial History of East Cornwall* (begun 1924) in the RIC Library, Truro (Ref H79 (Sheviock)).
41 The original document is in the CRO, Ref. TER/573. The terrier was countersigned by the two churchwardens, Hugh Hawkyn and Nicholas Rundle. See also Richard Potts, *A Calendar of Cornish Glebe Terriers 1673-1735* (1974).
42 Meaning 'suppressed virtue rises again'.
43 The author is indebted to Rex and Anne King for allowing him to see the plastered chamber.
44 Letter dated 21 December 1831 in the DRO.
45 See Chapter 9, *Outlying Farms and Houses.*
46 Ed. J. Wallis (1847).
47 See also 'The Endowments of the Church' in Chapter 26, *The Early Church.*
48 The original MS of Penhale's account was destroyed by enemy action in the Second World War. This translation is taken from Kempthorne (*c.*1934) at p. 35. See also Chapter 33, *Tithes.*
49 CRO: TER/573. See also Richard Potts, *A Calendar of Cornish Glebe Terriers 1673-1735* (1974).

Chapter 11, *The Borough of Crafthole*

1 O.J. Padel (private correspondence).
2 CM/B/90.
3 *Survey of Cornwall* (1602), p. 108v.
4 O. J. Padel, *Cornish Place-Name Elements* (1985), p. 74.
5 The other place, called simply 'Hole', lay to the east of the village of West Antony.
6 See further, this chapter, 'The plan of the New Town'.

7 The figures are taken from M. Beresford, *New Towns of the Middle Ages* (1967), p. 303.
8 The arms of the Bodrugan family were incorporated into the town's seal.
9 See A. Ballard and J. Tait, *British Borough Charters 1216-1307* (1923).
10 Thomas Bond, *Topographical Sketches of the Boroughs of East and West Looe* (1823), pp. 54-56; Cal. Pat. Rolls 18 Ed II, Pt. I, m. 22.
11 Lake, Vol. III (1870), p. 163.
12 Lake, Vol. II (1868), p. 179.
13 See H. Spencer Toy, *The History of Helston* (1936), pp. 39, 438, 439.
14 Lake, Vol. II (1868), p. 179.
15 Lake, Vol. III (1870), p. 85.
16 Cal. Pat. Rolls 8 Ed. II; Kempthorne (*c.*1934), pp. 11, 24. For the manor of Sheviock, see Chapter 4. See further on markets, Chapter 40, *Markets, Highways and Turnpikes.*
17 John Penhale's account of the tithe of sheaves made in 1410-11 shows that the farm at Blazor was producing the second smallest harvest of corn in the parish. Most of the land was probably used as grazing for cattle or sheep at this time. By 1775, when the manor was mapped by Thomas Pride, the number of productive acres in Blazor had increased substantially.
18 See further Chapter 2, *The Celtic Kingdoms, the Saxon and Norman Conquests.*
19 Samuel's brother, Oliver, was a sailor on the fishing barque, *Dayestarr.* For the Court records, see TNA: SC/2/158/39.
20 See further Chapter 12, *Courts and Officials of the Borough of Crafthole.*
21 However, the Dawneys' manor-house was eventually replaced by farmhouses.
22 CP/FX/11.
23 For example, the juror Alexander Arundell lived in High House and the juror Richard Wallis owned Cross House.
24 The tenure of a 'burgage plot' entitled the holder to the privileges of the burgh (borough).
25 Similarly, Reginald Pole Carew donated building materials to the builders of the new pilchard cellars at Portwrinkle in 1792.
26 See CM/B/101.
27 TNA: E317 Corn 10. For a copy made in 1798, see CM/A/75.
28 Ground rents in the borough of Saltash were even cheaper, at 6d. A 1729 rental of the borough of Crafthole shows that the 9d. ground rent was then in effect: CM/B/92.
29 J. Whetter, *Cornwall in the Thirteenth Century. A Study in Social and Economic History* (1998), p. 90.
30 See further Chapter 3, *The Cornish Language on the Rame Peninsula.*
31 Harold Fox, *The Evolution of the Fishing Village: Landscape and Society along the South Devon Coast, 1086-1550* (2001), p. 22.
32 See further, Chapter 39, *Trades and Crafts.*
33 See M. Beresford, *New Towns of the Middle Ages* (1967), pp. 194, 195. See also Christopher Dyer, *Making a Living in the Middle Ages* (2002).
34 See further Chapter 39, *Trades and Crafts.*
35 Letters and Papers H.VIII 1540; Kempthorne (*c.*1934), p. 25.
36 Edward VI had already granted the manor of Sheviock to Sir Walter Mildmay. In 1558, Thomas Carew of Antony purchased the manor from him: CD/AE/9.
37 The record of this court and other 16th-century courts relating to property transactions in Crafthole were copied into one of the Miscellaneous Books of the Augmentation Office: TNA E315/414.
38 TNA: E317/Corn 10.
39 CD/AH/28.
40 CD/AG/44.
41 CA/HI/7.
42 Though ground rent was still payable to the Duchy of Cornwall.
43 CD/AH/66.

44 See Peter Ackroyd, *London: the Biography*, p. 553: 'the watermen of the Thames, from the 13th century to the 19th, were known for their insulting and foul language.'
45 He slew his rivals for the throne and defeated a Roman army in Numidia in 110 BC. He was eventually betrayed by a neighbouring king, Bocchus, and taken to Rome. In 105 BC, he was put to death there like a common criminal.
46 TNA: E317/Corn 10.
47 Misc. Books LR 207 66; quoted in Kempthorne (*c.*1934), p. 24.
48 See Chapter 39, *Trades and Crafts.*
49 TNA: E317/Corn 10.

Chapter 12, *Courts and Officials of the Borough of Crafthole*

1 18 Edward II. See further R.D. Connor, *The Weights and Measures of England* (1987).
2 S.&B.Webb, *The Manor and the Borough* (1908), Vol. I, p. 21.
3 For court records up to April 1612, see TNA: SC/2/158/38.
4 CD/AH/21.
5 Section 35 of *Magna Carta* is set out in Chapter 6, *Courts and Officials of the Manor.*
6 TNA: SC/2/158/39. The original pound was converted into a poorhouse by the rector, Walter Arundell, in 1618: CM/B/96.
7 CM/B/93.
8 G.R.Y.Radcliffe and G.Cross, *The English Legal System* (3rd edn. 1954), p. 23.
9 J.H.Oaten in *The Oxford History of the Laws of England* (ed. Sir John Baker), Vol.VI, p. 316.
10 S. and B.Webb, *The Manor and the Borough* (1908), Vol. I, pp. 14, 15.
11 CM/B/90.
12 Peter Jane may have been a descendant of William Jane, the parish Registrar appointed during the Commonwealth. William became parish clerk after the Restoration.
13 He was born in Maker in 1632.
14 J.H.Oaten in *The Oxford History of the Laws of England* (ed. Sir John Baker), Vol.VI, pp. 312-14. See also G.R.Y.Radcliffe and G.Cross, *The English Legal System* (3rd edn. 1954), pp. 239-41.
15 See Chapter 15, *The Landing Place and Quay at Portwrinkle.*
16 Lake, Vol. III (1870), p. 63.
17 Lake, Vol. III (1870), p. 146.
18 See F.B.Kingdon, *The Kingdon Family* (no date), p. 81.
19 CD/AI/12.
20 The first certain date for the property being an inn is 1620. At a court leet held on 3 November in that year, the tenant, William Sargent, was fined 4d. for selling wine of an unmeasured quantity: TNA: SC/2/158/39. In 1741, the property was let to the 'innholder' William Lord (born *c.*1704): CD/AH/44. For the holding of audit dinners at the inn in 1763-6, see Chapter 41, *Inns and Innkeepers.*
21 Also Kaylway, Caylwaye, Calway, Callaway and Calloway.
22 CD/AF/26. William Brooking, who was probably the son of the merchant of 1514, inherited property in Crafthole from one Edwards, and was nominated as Portreeve in 1596. He paid John Chubbe to deputise for him. He was a juror of the court leet of Crafthole in 1605, 1608, and 1616-17. He died in 1618. Members of the Brooking family also resided in Totnes and St Stephens by Saltash in the 17th century: see A. J. Jewers, *Heraldic Church Notes from Cornwall* (London, after 1886), p. 149.
23 Edward VI had already granted the manor of Sheviock to Sir Walter Mildmay. In 1558, Thomas Carew of Antony purchased the manor from him: CD/AE/9.
24 TNA: E315/414 (Misc. Bks. Augmentation Office).
25 TNA: SC/2/158/38.
26 CD/AE/26.
27 CM/A/73.
28 CM/B/93.
29 S. and B.Webb, *The Manor and the Borough* (1908), Vol. I, pp. 23, 24.

30 See further Chapter 41, *Inns and Innkeepers.*
31 The Statute of Winchester, 13 Edw. I (1285) specified which arms were to be taken up.
32 In 1606, Laurence Odihorne was himself put at the mercy of the court for failing to produce John Odihorne (perhaps his brother), James Poplestone and John Moreshed, who should have been jurors at the assizes.
33 John Creffell, had been Honney's landlord in Crafthole in 1628.
34 CM/B/90.
35 CM/B/93.
36 *Historical Survey of the County of Cornwall*, Vol. II (1820), p. 402.
37 Records of the Court Leet survive for 1576 and for 10 of the last 14 years of Queen Elizabeth's reign – that is, from 1590 to 1601, except for 1595 and 1598: TNA: SC/2/158/38. They also survive for most years of the reign of James I (1603-25) and for some years of the reign of Charles I: SC/2/158/39-40. The court records for November 1628 to April 1644 (except 1642), and for 1663, 1682, 1712, 1713 and 1730 are preserved in the Antony archives: CM/B/77-91 and 93.
38 John Hunkyn, a gentleman of Liskeard, was fined £1 6s. 8d. in 1650 for his Royalist activities during the Civil War: see M. Coate, *Cornwall in the Great Civil War and Interregnum 1642-1660* (Oxford, 1933; 2 ed. Truro, 1963), p. 370.
39 CM/B/98.
40 William 'Brokyng' was a merchant of Plymouth. In 1515, he and Richard Huntingdon of Plymouth bought for 40 marks (£26 13s. 4d.) all the mature oaks and ashes growing between the Greenaway and Fenton Ogglake in Sheviock Woods: CD/AF/26.
41 Tobias Langdon may have been related to Walter Langdon of Keverall , one of the senior Royalist leaders in Cornwall during the Civil War. For Walter, see M. Coate, *Cornwall in the Great Civil War and Interregnum 1642-1660* (Oxford, 1933; 2 ed. Truro, 1963), pp. 31, 216, 356 and 371.
42 TNA: SC/2/158/39.
43 CP/FX/11.
44 CM/B/93.
45 See further 'The Town Well' in Chapter 11, *The Borough of Crafthole.*
46 For 'train-oil', see 'Curing and Exporting the Fish' in Chapter 17, *The Fishing Industry at Portwrinkle.*
47 TNA: SC/2/158/39.
48 TNA: SC/2/158/39
49 Attachment was the legal process by which goods were taken in lieu of unpaid debts. I am grateful to Professor Sir John Baker, Q.C., of St Catherine's College Cambridge for this translation, and to Ellan Odiorne Derow for the information on Briggett's marriage.
50 CD/AJ/21.
51 There were two members of the Hoblyn family (one illegible, the other Richard), two members of the Ernle family (Joshua and Johib), Josie Tozer, Willy Tooker, Ralph and Anne Lamb and their son, Ralph.
52 CD/AH/28.
53 CM/B/93.
54 In 1714, Thomas Lampen of Liskeard, clerk, was paying rent of £1 0s. 9d. to Sir William Carew for 'his house and garden' in Crafthole.
55 CM/B/92.
56 CM/B/94.

Chapter 13, *Houses, Shops and Farms in Crafthole*

1 CM/A/75.
2 William Brookinge was one of the co-heirs of Edwarde, who had owned a burgage in Crafthole, and died before 1591. Brookinge was elected as portreeve in 1596, but got John Chubbe to serve the office for him: TNA: SC/2/158/38. William 'Brokyn', probably the same man, was a juror of the court leet in 1605: TNA: C/2/158/39.
3 CD/AH/3.

4 CM/B/98.
5 TNA: SC/2/158/38.
6 CRO: WH 5074.
7 See CD/AH/17. In 1657, William Sparkman contracted a civil marriage with Mrs Mary Wallis.
8 CA/HI/3.
9 On the assumption that they were located in the two gardens that were let to Andrew Kitt for 10s. in 1804.
10 CD/AH/28A&B.
11 CA/HI/5A.
12 CD/AG/44.
13 See e.g. Mrs Ann Lord's payment to the reeve, Matthew Phillips, on 1 October 1766: CM/B/98.
14 CA/HI/7.
15 CD/AH/44.
16 CM/B/55. For the 'audit dinners' held at her inn, see Chapter 41, *Inns and Innkeepers.*
17 CD/AG/50A.
18 See further, Chapter 11, *The Borough of Crafthole*, and Chapter 41, *Inns and Innkeepers.*
19 The Rt. Hon. Robert Cotton Saint John Trefusis, Baron Clinton and Saye of Heanton Satchville Hall.
20 CD/AI/12.
21 Probably the two houses let by the Condeys to John Edwards in 1654 had once stood in these gardens.
22 See further 'The Demesne Farms and Buildings (Blazor)' in Chapter 4, *The Manor of Sheviock.*
23 CM/F2/158.
24 The map is in the CRO: EM20/4.
25 See further 'Blazor' in Chapter 4, *The Manor of Sheviock.*
26 Information from Ian Whittaker.
27 Jessie was the sister of Arnold Hoskin, who took over Crafthole Farm (see below).
28 Information from Ian Whittaker.
29 For damage to Cross House in the Second World War, see 'The Battle of Britain and the Mines that Fell on Sheviock' in Chapter 37, *The Parish in the Two World Wars.*
30 TNA: E315/414. See also 'Bonne's Parks' in Chapter 8, *Holdings on Sheviock Manor.*
31 TNA: SC/2/158/39.
32 CM/B/94, 95.
33 The other two were Bryant Hayes and Walter Sonne's cottage.
34 CM/B/95.
35 For the destruction of High House in the Second World War, see 'The Battle of Britain and the Mines that Fell on Sheviock' in Chapter 37, *The Parish in the Two World Wars.*
36 CD/AH/15.
37 CD/AH/26.
38 CM/B/98.
39 CD/AH/18.
40 CD/AH/42.
41 CD/AH/59.
42 CD/AH/65 & 65C.
43 CRO: EM 20/4.
44 CD/AI/11.
45 CRO: EM 20/4.
46 See also 'The Blacksmiths' Cottages and Shops' above and 'Agricultural Implement Makers' in Chapter 39, *Trades and Crafts.*
47 They both served on the Sheviock invasion committee: see Appendix 3.
48 TNA: E315/414.
49 For the mill, see Chapter 42, *Mills and Millers.*
50 For the meaning of Bryant Hayes, and later occupants, see Chapter 41, *Inns and Innkeepers.*
51 CM/B/95.

52 The other two were High House and Walter Sonne's cottage.
53 CM/B/95.
54 TNA: E315/414.
55 In 1639, John and Maria Sonne were living in a different property on the main thoroughfare running through the borough: CM/B/85. The jury presented Maria and their daughter, Elizabeth, for assaulting Ralph Holman while he was repairing the king's highway.
56 CM/B/95.
57 The other two were High House and Bryant Hayes.
58 TNA: E315/414.
59 TNA: E315/414.
60 CM/B/92.
61 CM/B/94.
62 CD/AI/3.
63 CD/AH/21.
64 CM/B/95. As to Mrs Mullis, Appendix 1, *Families*.
65 CM/B/98 and CM/F2/158.
66 CM/B/98 and CM/F2/158.
67 CD/AH/29.
68 See the survey of 1775 (CM/B/101) which shows William Bray as the tenant of the Net Park in Portwrinkle 'by virtue of his office being Reeve of the Manor'.
69 CM/B/18 and 98.
70 CM/B/101.
71 CP/FX/11.
72 See further 'Blazor' in Chapter 4, *The Manor of Sheviock*.
73 Information from his descendant, Ian Whittaker.
74 See Harrison, Harrod & Co., *Postal Directory* (1862).
75 Her father, William, was chief boatman in the Coastguard at Portwrinkle.
76 Information from Ian Whittaker.
77 See 'Liscawn' in Chapter 9, *Outlying Houses and Farms*.
78 See Harrison, Harrod & Co., *Postal Directory* (1862).
79 Information from Ian Whittaker.
80 Information from John Biles.
81 See further, Chapter 37, *The Parish in the Two World Wars*.
82 Information supplied by Mrs Margaret Bartlett.

Chapter 14, *The Quay at the Riverside and Fishing in the Lynher and Tamar Rivers*

1 The meaning of *Lynher* is uncertain, but it may be connected with the Cornish *lei*, meaning to flow or glide (O.J. Padel, *A Popular Dictionary of Cornish Place-Names* (1988)). It was written *Linar* in the late 11th century. 'The suffix *-ar* is presumably the same as in the River Tamar' (ibid.).
2 The monks were forbidden to eat meat; see further Chapter 15, *The Landing Place and Quay at Portwrinkle*.
3 See in relation to Rame, unpublished notes from a lecture given by Dr W.G.Hoskins, at Millbrook 16 March 1962; and in relation to Exmouth, H. Fox, *The Evolution of the Fishing Village: Landscape and Society along the South Devon Coast, 1086-1550* (2001), p. 48.
4 CD/AE/4.
5 CD/AF/33.
6 See Lake's *Parochial History* (1872-3), Vol. IV, p. 146.
7 'Caption of Seisin' means the 'Taking of Possession'. This document of 1337 listed all the hereditary possessions of the earldom of Cornwall that were to be transferred to the Duchy when Edward Woodstock, eldest son of Edward III, was created Duke of Cornwall in March of that year.
8 The fields were called Inner and Outer Portroy: see further 'Treise's Tenement' in Chapter 4, *The Manor of Sheviock*.

9 CD/AF/27.
10 Information from the late Bert Pengelly of Portwrinkle.
11 J.L.Vivian, *The Visitations of Cornwall, comprising the Heralds' Visitations of 1530, 1573 and 1620* (1887).
12 CM/F2/158.
13 CM/F2/159.
14 Liz Luck, *Green Lane walks in South-east Cornwall*, p. 48.
15 See H. Fox, *The Evolution of the Fishing Village: Landscape and Society along the South Devon Coast, 1086-1550* (2001), p. 85.
16 Tavistock and Ashburton were the two stannary towns of Devon.
17 See M. Kowaleski, *Local Markets and Regional Trade in Medieval Exeter* (1994).
18 See E. Cleaveland, *A Genealogical History of the Noble and Illustrious Family of Courtenay, etc.* (1735), pp. 137, 138. The source of Cleaveland's story was Richard Izacke who wrote a MS entitled *Antiquities of the City of Exeter* in 1677. See also *Gleanings from the MS of R Izacke's Antiquities etc.* by Prof. Walter J Harte (Wheaton, Exeter, 1929).
19 The livery gown was 'crane-coloured' – ashen grey: see A.L. Rowse, *Tudor England* (1941), p. 235.
20 M. Kowaleski, *Local Markets and Regional Trade in Medieval Exeter* (1994), p. 81.
21 M. Kowaleski (ed.), *The Havener's Accounts of the Earldom and Duchy of Cornwall 1287-1356* (2001), p. 307.
22 TNA: Rot. Cart. 8 Edw. II.
23 See D. and S. Lysons, *Magna Britannia, Vol. III, Cornwall* (1814), p. 283, note h.
24 See M. Kowaleski (ed.), *The Havener's Accounts of the Earldom and Duchy of Cornwall 1287-1356* (2001), p. 201.
25 The Havener was the Duchy official responsible for exploiting the economic resources of the coastline of Cornwall. In the 14th century he resided at Place in Fowey. See M. Kowaleski (ed.), *The Havener's Accounts of the Earldom and Duchy of Cornwall 1287-1356* (2001), p. 202.
26 *Survey* (1602), p. 100r.
27 P. L. Hull (ed.), *The Caption of Seisin of the Duchy of Cornwall, 1337* (1971), p. 119.
28 CA/HI/3.

Chapter 15, *The Landing Place and Quay at Portwrinkle*

1 This was the *Mesolithic* or Middle-Stone-Age period.
2 I. N. Soulsby, *A History of Cornwall* (1986), p. 85.
3 *Finnygook* derives from the English 'fenny' (marshy), plus dialect *gook*, meaning inlet. *Partickle* is a corruption of Portugal pump and point. At this point, the sea rushes in and out between two big rock formations. As the tide ebbs, it makes a noise like a pump. *Blackyball* is *Black-a-ball* on the 1840 Tithe Map. The name may be connected with the Blake family who farmed and fished in Sheviock from the 1500s to the 1700s, and were guarantors of the building of the quay. There are several local field names ending in ball, which simply means a ball-shaped piece of land.
4 Until the 1800s, farmers used these sandways to transport sand on the backs of horses or donkeys to fertilise the fields above. Donkey Lane in Portwrinkle was used for a similar purpose.
5 For the village of Portwrinkle, see Chapter 18.
6 For text of Henry's grant, see Chapter 2, *The Celtic Kingdoms, the Saxon and Norman Conquests*.
7 The names 'Torcross' and 'Starcross' in Devon indicate the sites of similar coastal crosses.
8 See also 'Crowstone Park' in Chapter 8, *Holdings on Sheviock Manor.*
9 The list of orders in the archives at Antony is in Richard Carew's own hand: CE/C/24. I have preserved the original spelling and most of the punctuation, except that I have omitted the full stops after abbreviations.
10 TNA: SP 16/34. See further Chapter 16, *The* Dayestarr *and her Crew.*
11 Edward Kneebone, *Description of East Hundred, co. Cornwall* (1684), BM Add. MS 33420 f. 126. There is a copy in the Library of the RIC in Truro. See also Liz Luck, *South Cornish Harbours*, 3rd edn. (1995), p. 120.
12 See T. Gray, *Early-Stuart Mariners and Shipping* (1990), p.xi.

13 *The Booke of M^as Richard Carew* (1628-30): CZ/EE/32. Richard Carew the younger was then living in Sheviock parish (probably at Sconner Farm) with his wife and family. Hence the reference to 'my parish' meaning Sheviock, not Antony.

14 CD/AJ/1.

15 CE/C/24.

16 The holding of Richard Wallis (*c.*1581-1653) at Sconner consisted of 88 acres. The rent was £2 13s. 4d. John Peters was the grandfather of Arthur Peters, who was living in his father's house at Lower Tredis when he died in 1654. Philip Wallis is shown in an inventory of goods compiled on the death of Ferdinando Spiller in 1607, as owing him £5. Philip Wallis of Lanlivery leased Hearle's Parks in Sheviock from Richard Carew the younger in 1640. Hearle's Parks consisted of only eight acres. His claim to register his arms and pedigree at the Herald's Visitation in 1620 was disallowed. Alexander Hancock held a tenement of Kerslake Manor at a rental of £4, plus two capons per annum, suggesting a holding of 80-100 acres. Rental receipts are entered in the roll book for Kerslake manor for 1607-9 (CRO).

17 Richard Bray was renting a property, probably a cellar, from Sheviock manor for 3s. 4d. in 1634 (CM/B/98). At the same date Richard Bake, perhaps John Bake's son, rented two premises, again probably cellars, at a shilling each; Richard Sargent rented a property in 'Wrikell' for 6s. 8d. Thomas Warne rented a property there for 4d. (ibid.). He may also have occupied the 48-acre tenement, called Warren's or Warne's in Trewrickle. If so, he was probably more an investor in the fishing syndicate than an actual fisherman.

18 CA/HI/7.

19 By 1695, the price per barge had been increased to 5s.: CA/HI/6.

20 William 'Charke' is shown as resident in the parish of Sheviock and armed with a bill in Henry VIII's muster roll of 1569. He or his son was resident in Crafthole in the 1590s and served as a juror on the court leet for many years: TNA: SC/2/158/38. Mr Porter does not appear to have been resident in the parish. John Chark was a tenant of a 30-acre holding in Trevol in East Antony in 1608: CM/A/73.

21 F. E. Halliday, *A Cornish Chronicle* (1967).

22 A gold coin, also called a noble, bearing the device of the archangel Michael slaying the dragon, and worth 6s. 8d.

23 See Richard Grylls: *Grylls and Grills: the History of a Cornish Clan* (1999), Vol II, p. 127.

24 CA/HI/7.

25 CA/HI/7. By then the cost of a barge-load of sand had risen from 10s. to 15s.

26 The words 'At Sheviock' suggest that the negotiating meetings were held in the house of Richard Carew the younger in Sheviock parish, probably at Sconner, and not at his father's house in Antony. In modern reckoning, 'March 1611' would be March 1612. The draft for the agreement was dated 23 December 1611, when the first negotiation probably took place.

27 I take 'Sayners' to mean seining groups put together by the parishioners, as distinct from the three bigger seine companies that contributed towards building the quay. The next clause covers these bigger companies.

28 I take 'Company' to mean each of the three companies contributing towards building the quay – namely Bray's, Blake's and Warne's. The amount of fish payable is specified in the next clause.

29 'Carry' in this context must mean fetch water from inland springs and carry it to the boats or wherever it was needed. The nearest freshwater spring would have been at Blizer's Well, a little way up the hill going up to Crafthole.

30 Carew had five sons: Richard, John, Hobye, George, and Wymond.

31 'Causon' was the fishing port of Cawsand on the Rame peninsula. The meaning of 'within Causon middle price' is obscure. It may mean that the prescribed price of xii^d per last relates to fish of a certain size – namely those falling within the middle price range at Cawsand.

32 For 'trayne water', see 'Curing and Exporting the Fish' in Chapter 17, *The Fishing Industry at Portwrinkle*.

33 The 'Courte' was the court leet (law court) of the manor of Sheviock, held twice a year.
34 CW/GG/5.
35 CE/C/24.
36 The 'shaming' would probably have been by means of a period spent in the village stocks.
37 See further Chapter 33, *Tithes*.
38 CM/B/98.
39 CE/C/24. The men were William Goard, John and William Ford, John Ridols, Richard Earle, Amos Pope and Pearce Horel (Horwell). Horwell was a witness to the will of John Littleton in 1735: CRO AP/L/1401.
40 CA/HI/7 (entry for 20 May 1724).
41 CA/HI/6.
42 CE/C/24. The other men were George Marton, John Prynn, Gilbert Starke and Fohn Foard.
43 CA/HI/8.
44 CD/AJ/49A.
45 See Chapter 18, *The Village of Portwrinkle*.
46 CE/C/24.
47 *The Cornwall Register 1848* (1847), p. 313, and 1858 Survey by Captain G. Williams & J. L Wells, Master RN.
48 Bowden's reply, dated 25 June 1932, is held in the Dartington Hall Trust Archive.
49 Letter dated 31 May 1938, Dartington Hall Trust Archive.
50 Parish Council Minute Book 25 June 1984.

Chapter 16, *The* Dayestarr *and her Crew*

1 J.J. Beckerlegge, 'Plymouth Muniments and Newfoundland', *Report and Transactions of the Devonshire Association for the Advancement of Science (Transactions)*, 18 (1936-7), 3-23.
2 Millbrook was a shipping centre as early as 1351. On 2 February of that year, Benedict Chikston, the owner of a cog called the *Seynt Marie* of 'Millebrok' had to pay export duty on a cargo of hides. The master was William Alas. See M. Kowaleski (ed), *The Haveners' Accounts of the Earldom and Duchy of Cornwall 1287-1356* (2001), p. 213.
3 See T. Gray, *Early-Stuart Mariners and Shipping* (1990), Table 4, p.xxiii.
4 T. Gray, *Early-Stuart Mariners and Shipping* (1990), pp. 61, 65.
5 William left 40s. 'unto the childe that is nowe in the wombe of my wife'.
6 T. Gray, *Early-Stuart Mariners and Shipping* (1990), pp. 65, 111.
7 T. Gray, *Early-Stuart Mariners and Shipping* (1990), p. 61.
8 T. Gray, *Early-Stuart Mariners and Shipping* (1990), pp. 110, 111.
9 T. Gray, *Early-Stuart Mariners and Shipping* (1990), p. 47.
10 W.B. Stephens, 'The West Country ports and the struggle for the Newfoundland fisheries in the 17th century', *Report and Transactions of the Devonshire Association for the Advancement of Science (Transactions)* 88 (1956), p. 90.
11 See N.C. Oswald, 'Devon and the Cod Fishery of Newfoundland', *Transactions*, 115 (1983), p. 24.
12 H.A. Innis, *The Cod Fisheries: The History of an International Economy* (1940). Line fishing from dorys lasted until the early 1920s, when the practice was superseded by trawling with nets. A cameraman employed by the French philanthropist, Albert Kahn, recorded for posterity the last days of the dory line fishermen. It was shown on BBC 2 on 10 March 2008.
13 M. Kurlansky, *Cod* (1998), p. 72; N.C. Oswald, 'Devon and the Cod Fishery of Newfoundland', *Transactions*, 115 (1983), p. 21.
14 M. Kurlansky, *Cod* (1998), p. 79.
15 *Survey of Cornwall* (1602), p. 33r.
16 N.C. Oswald, 'Devon and the Cod Fishery of Newfoundland', *Transactions*, 115 (1983), p. 26.
17 The names of the constables in 1626 are not recorded. In 1633 they were John Blake and Arnott Odiorne.

18 Spellings have been standardised as far as possible on those used in the official court records of the borough of Crafthole. Where these differ from those used by the constables for Sir James Bagg's survey, I have included the constables' spellings in brackets where the name first occurs.
19 CD/AE/15.
20 CD/AJ/6.
21 From 1590 to 1597: TNA: SC2/158/38.
22 CD/AJ/7.
23 CM/B/98.
24 A. Jewers, *Heraldic Church Notes from Cornwall* (after 1886), p. 26.
25 CD/AJ/21.
26 CD/AJ/21.
27 CD/AJ/21.
28 CE/C/18.
29 TNA: SC/2/158/38.
30 See Chapter 12, *Courts and Officials of the Borough of Crafthole.*
31 A William Peter had served on the jury in the reign of Queen Elizabeth: TNA: SC/2/158/38.
32 John Wicot is probably the same as John Winnicot. Ann Winnicot's house in Wrinkle was in need of re-thatching in 1726.
33 Thomas Moresyde was a juror in 1591-3 and John Moresyde in 1596-7 and 1604-7.
34 TNA: SC/2/158/39. I am grateful to Professor Sir John Baker, Q.C. of St Catherine's College Cambridge for elucidating this passage.
35 CM/F2/158.
36 CM/B/98.
37 TNA: SC/2/158/39.
38 CRO: WH 5074.
39 CM/B/98.
40 The goods were appraised by Amos Palmer, Richard Beare and the Sheviock innkeeper, Daniel Sargent. All of them were illiterate and signed the inventory with their marks.
41 CRO: N 223/1.
42 The tenement included the property now known as the *Finnygook Inn* and the field containing the Dawneys' Culverhouse, in about 1622, when the freehold was sold by the landlord, John Smith of Tregunnick, to Richard Wallis of Trewin and Sconner. Because the property had been in the occupation of William Sargent it was usually referred to in 17th- and 18th-century leases as 'Sargent's tenement'. In 1620, William Sargent was running the place as an inn. A William Sergeant is also shown as a free tenant of the manor of Kerslake in Sheviock parish in surviving rentals of 1608, 1609, 1636 and 1640. He may have been cultivating apples there to make into cider.
43 Members of the Truscott family are included in Henry VIII's list of able-bodied men of Sheviock in 1522. They also appear on his subsidy roll of 1544. In the list compiled for the Hearth Tax in 1664, 'Edward Trescott' is shown as living in a house with two hearths.
44 CM/F2/158.
45 CD/AJ/17.
46 CM/B/98 – MAN 10/1.
47 CD/AF/27.
48 See T. Gray, *Early-Stuart Mariners and Shipping* (1990), p.xxii.
49 See J. Whetter, *Cornwall in the 17th Century* (1974), p. 156.
50 Kneebone's original MS is in the National Archives. There is a copy in the Library of the RIC in Truro. See also Liz Luck, *South Cornish Harbours*, 3rd edn. (1995), p. 120.

Chapter 17, *The Fishing Industry at Portwrinkle*

1 See H. Fox, *The Evolution of the Fishing Village: Landscape and Society along the South Devon Coast, 1086-1550* (2001), p. 60.

2 M. Kowaleski, *The Havener's Accounts of the Earldom and Duchy of Cornwall 1287-1356* (2001), p. 49.
3 I.N. Soulsby, *A History of Cornwall* (1986), p. 86.
4 *The Booke of M*[as] *Richard Carew*: CZ/EE/32.
5 *The Booke of M*[as] *Richard Carew*: CZ/EE/32.
6 Edward Kneebone, *Description of East Hundred, co. Cornwall* (1684), BM Add. MS 33420 f. 126.
7 D. and S. Lysons, *Magna Britannia*, Vol. III, Cornwall (1814), p. 283.
8 CA/HI/5A. Dried whiting was known from its hardness as 'buckhorn'.
9 I.N. Soulsby, *The Cornwall Domesday* (1988), p. 9.
10 J. Whetter, *Cornwall in the 17th Century. An Economic Survey of Kernow* (1974), p. 66.
11 *Fuming* means smoking.
12 *Survey* (1602), p. 33r.
13 A 'house built for the nonce' means a house built specially for the purpose of smoking. The practice of smoking fish on long sticks in temporary smoke houses was probably the medieval method of preserving the fish. See the reference to *cured* hake and conger in the document of 1202 (Whetter, p. 66). In 1306, King Edward I asked for a supply of 'five thousands of *hard fish*' from Cornwall, probably another reference to fish cured by smoking (ibid.). The local Cornish term for preserved fish, whether smoked or pressed, was 'fairmaids', a corruption of the Spanish *fumados*.
14 *Survey* (1602), p. 33r.
15 See A.R.Bridbury, *England and the Salt Trade in the Later Middle Ages* (1955).
16 During the Napoleonic wars, salt was imported from Portugal.
17 See further Chapter 15, *The Landing Place and Quay at Portwrinkle.*
18 See J. Whetter, *Cornwall in the 17th Century. An Economic History of Kernow* (1974), p. 92. Liskeard was the principal centre for manufacturing leather goods in south-east Cornwall.
19 *Rambles beyond Railways* (2nd edn, 1851), p. 161.
20 See further Chapter 23, *The Soil and Crops.*
21 In the 1500s, a hogshead might contain any number of pilchards between 5,800 and 9,600 (see Cyril Noall, *Cornish Seines and Seiners* (1972)). In the 1700s, the contents became standardised at about 3,000.
22 *Survey* (1602), p. 33r. 'Ventred' means sold. 'Staunch' means not leaky.
23 The cellar was built in 1794: see Chapter 18, *The Village of Portwrinkle.* When the contents of the Portwrinkle cellar was auctioned in 1834, the sale included 90 tons of new and 30 tons of old salt.
24 They could still be seen in 2000.
25 CM/A/3/3.
26 See Lake's *Parochial History*, Vol IV, p. 109.
27 CD/AJ/29.
28 See Chapter 16, *The* Dayestarr *and her Crew.*
29 See J. Whetter, *Cornwall in the 17th Century. An Economic History of Kernow* (1974), p. 200.
30 *Cornwall in the 17th Century. An Economic History of Kernow* (1974), p. 102.
31 *Cornwall in the 17th Century. An Economic History of Kernow* (1974), p. 101.
32 Skippers who sailed to Naples liked to have their brigs painted in the Bay of Naples with Vesuvius spouting in the background (see C. Noall, *Cornish Seines and Seiners* (1972), p. 51).
33 The seine boats were sometimes named after these Italian ports. For example, there was an *Ancona* at Gorran Haven, and a *Venice* at St Ives (C. Noall, *Cornish Seines and Seiners* (1972), pp. 91,130). One of the seines at Porthleven was called *The Pope* (Noall, p. 137), since it was his edicts about the fast days that created the markets for the Cornish fish.
34 C.S. Gilbert, *An Historical Survey of the County of Cornwall* (1817), Vol I, p. 331.
35 C.S. Gilbert, *An Historical Survey of the County of Cornwall* (1817), Vol I, p. 331.
36 CRO: N223/1.
37 CA/HI/2.
38 A.K. Hamilton Jenkin, *News from Cornwall* (1951), p. 75.

39 See H. Fox, *The Evolution of the Fishing Village: Landscape and Society along the South Devon Coast, 1086-1550* (2001), p. 123.

40 In the reign of James I, an Act of Parliament gave 'huers' an unfettered licence to practise their calling on any part of the seashore. The seiners also had licence to land their catch on any part of the coastline. See Noall, p. 19.

41 'Cundeth' is an Old English word perhaps derived from the German *kundgeben*, to inform. The huer was also called sometimes at this period the 'condor'. His cry on first sighting the shoal was 'Hevva! Hevva! Hevva!' C. Noall, *Cornish Seines and Seiners* (1972), p. 29. *Hevva* is Cornish for 'shoaling'. 'Wheazing' means making.

42 *Survey* (1602), p. 32v.

43 Richard Bray was renting a property, probably a cellar, from Sheviock manor for 3s. 4d. in 1634. At the same date Richard Bake, perhaps John Bake's son, rented two premises, again probably cellars, at a shilling each; Richard Sargent rented a property in 'Wrikell' for 6s. 8d. and Thomas Warne a property there for 4d. (CM/B/98).

44 A. Jewers, *Heraldic Church Notes from Cornwall* (after 1886), p. 26.

45 See further, 'Wrecks before 1900' in Chapter 19, *Smuggling, Coastguard and Wrecks*.

46 CD/AJ/49A.

47 CE/C/24.

48 Steedman charged two shillings per yard, plus the cost of the explosives.

49 A volyer was originally a very nimble eight-oared boat with the speed of a racing eight. Because it was so fast, it could outrun the coastguard cutters and was much favoured by smugglers. The Government therefore prohibited the manufacture of eight-oared volyers in 1721, but allowed a four-oared version. See Tony Carne, *Cornwall's Forgotten Corner* (1985; 2nd ed. 1990), p. 64.

50 See C. Walker and J. Smith, *The Spirit of Rame: Rowing in the Waters off the Rame Peninsula* (1995), pp. 23, 24.

51 Printed handbill: CE/C/24.

52 The word 'seine', variously spelt seine, seyn or sean by the fishermen, originally referred to the large net used to catch the fish. But it also came to mean the syndicate that held shares in the enterprise making use of a particular seine. There were always 16 shares in a seine, with individuals owning varying numbers, including fractions, of them. Some shareholders were fishing members of a seine, others were not. In 1849, each share cost £5, so that the working capital of the seine was £80.

53 The discoloration of the sea indicated the shoal. The practice of huing persisted at Portwrinkle, for shoals of bass, until 1962. Mrs Margaret Bartlett, née Pengelly, remembers acting as huer for the family; but this was a rare event, for it was a superstition among fishermen that women did not take part in the fishing expeditions. Another superstition was that you never said 'rabbit' on the boat.

54 This is the Charles Dawe who was a shareholder in the *Fox* in 1875.

55 Named after Leonard and Dorothy Elmhirst. Dorothy Elmhirst named the boat with a bottle of cider from the Dartington estate on Easter Monday 1951. The Elmhirsts were the founders of the Dartington complex in Devon. They bought the Chalet in Portwrinkle in 1928. It still stands on Portwrinkle beach, but has been renamed the Beach House. The Pengelly family supplied fish, especially shellfish, to Lady Beatrice and then to the Elmhirsts when they were on holiday.

56 Sand eels are also called 'launce' or 'sand-launce', a fish of the genus *ammodyte* (OED).

57 'Uncle Wilf' was Wilfred Lee who lived at the *New Inn* with the Hearns, who had taken in Terry and his sister as evacuees.

58 'Chuffy' was Terence Bean, aged eight in 1940, who lived with his parents at Lantic Farm. He now lives in Crafthole.

59 'Aunt Hylda' was Mrs Hearn; 'Uncle Bill' was William Hearn, landlord of the *New Inn* (now the *Finnygook Inn*).

60 Herbert Bean, who farmed at Lantic, was the brother of Hylda Hearn.

61 See further 'Potato Growing between the Wars' in Chapter 25, *Farming after 1800*.

Chapter 18, *The Village of Portwrinkle*

1 For a study of the process by which full-time fishermen in fishing villages in South Devon replaced 'fishing farmers', see H. Fox, *The Evolution of the Fishing Village* (2001).
2 CD/AJ/2.
3 CD/AJ/5.
4 CE/C/18.
5 Records of a number of Devon manors in the 1500s also give their dimensions. The Devon cellars were smaller than the Portwrinkle ones.
6 CD/AJ/2.
7 There were similar pilchard cellars, now in ruins or converted to other uses, at Cawsand, Penlee, Polhawn and Sharrow Point, in neighbouring parishes.
8 CM/B/98.
9 CD/AJ/5.
10 CD/AJ/4.
11 CM/B/98.
12 CM/B/98.
13 CM/B/98.
14 CD/AJ/6; CM/B/98.
15 William's son, also called William, was one of the lives named in the lease.
16 CD/AJ/21.
17 In 1676, this was let to his widow, Susan (née Deeble, daughter of John Deeble of St Germans), on the lives of her daughters, Elizabeth and Agnes.
18 She may have been claiming under the lease granted to Richard Lavers on 15 May 1633: CD/AJ/4.
19 CD/AJ/27.
20 CD/AJ/31A &B. The premises had formerly been in the possession of Nicholas Smith gent deceased.
21 CM/F2/158.
22 No doubt the same one leased to Richard Lavers in 1633: CD/AJ/4.
23 CM/F2/157.
24 CM/F2/157.
25 CM/F2/158.
26 CD/AJ/30.
27 CD/AJ/32.
28 CD/AJ/48.
29 CD/AJ/33.
30 CD/AJ/35B.
31 CM/B/156.
32 CD/AJ/34. A 'baulk' was the stout rope by which fishing nets were fastened one to another (OED).
33 CD/AJ/35A.
34 CD/AJ/37.
35 CD/AJ/37.
36 CM/B/156.
37 CM/B/18.
38 CM/B/98.
39 CD/AAJ/39.
40 CD/AG/27.
41 CM/B/156.
42 CM/B/98.
43 CM/B/156.
44 CM/B/101 (Survey) and CP/FX/11 (Map).
45 The Net Park took its name from the place where the fishermen dried and mended their nets. Thomas Hillman (Helman?) was the tenant of the Net Park from 1809 to 1833; William Pengelly in the 1840s; and John Pengelly from 1858 to 1861.

46 CM/B/98.
47 See further, Chapter 43, *Leisure, Sport and Tourism*.
48 CD/AJ/40A &B.
49 CD/AJ/41.
50 CD/AJ/42A.
51 These concessions were designed to ensure that the contractors did not use cob for the building of the cellars, which had been their original intention.
52 Information from the late Bert Pengelly. Each hogshead contained approximately 3,000 pilchards.
53 Information from the late Bert Pengelly.
54 They included an oil merchant, a tallow chandler, and two attorneys-at-law: CD/AJ/53A.
55 CD/AJ/56.
56 Information from the late Bert Pengelly.
57 It is now the home of Margaret Bartlett, née Pengelly.
58 According to John Biles, a resident of Crafthole for many years, the initials stand for Thomas Hearne, reputed a great smuggler; but this attribution is not supported by the surviving leases. Members of the Hearne family ran the *New Inn* during the Second World War.
59 See further Chapter 19, *Smuggling, Coastguard and Wrecks*. For the *Whitsand Bay Hotel* and Golf Club erected in 1909-11, see Chapter 43, *Leisure, Sport and Tourism*.
60 Information from Margaret Bartlett, niece of Mary Ellen.

Chapter 19, *Smuggling, Coastguard and Wrecks*

1 *A Journey into Cornwall* (Warwick, 1799).
2 The written account is included in Paul White's *The Cornish Smuggling Industry* (Redruth, 1997).
3 Drew was born in St Austell in 1765. His father was a farm labourer. At the age of 10, he was apprenticed to a shoemaker. He was working as a shoemaker in Crafthole in 1784, when he was involved in the smuggling episode. The following year, he moved back to St Austell to pursue his trade as a shoemaker. He taught himself to read and write and joined the Methodists, becoming a class-leader and preacher. In 1802, his essay on 'Immateriality and Immortality of the Soul' earned him the title of 'the Cornish metaphysician'. In 1814, he completed a *History of Cornwall* begun by F. Hitchins. He later moved to Liverpool and London as editor of the *Imperial Magazine*. He died in Helston in 1833.
4 Kempthorne (*c*.1934), p. 53. Letters from Lord Teignmouth in the *Western Morning News* (pre 1934).
5 CE/G/23.
6 CM/B/94.
7 Kempthorne (*c*.1934), p. 53; Letters from Lord Teignmouth in the *Western Morning News* (pre 1934).
8 John Foot was born in Kingsand in 1781, His brother, William, and son, John, were both members of the Coastguard service by 1828. Father and son were both still in service at Cawsand in 1841; but John senior had retired by the time of the next census in 1851: see Jack Spence, *The Smugglers of Cawsand Bay* (2007), p. 109.
9 The *Harpy* was a Revenue cutter that patrolled the waters around Plymouth and the Rame peninsula.
10 In 1831, a 15-year-old boy, Sampson Trevan Davey, son of William Davey and his wife, Mary Ann (née Trevan) was living in Crafthole.
11 Lt. The Hon. H. Shore, RN, *Smuggling Days and Smuggling Ways* (1892), pp. 114, 115.
12 Much of the information in the sections on the Coastguard, Lifesaving and Wrecks comes from the journal of Wilfrid Pengelly, who for many years served as 'volunteer-in-charge' of the auxiliary coastguard at Portwrinkle. The journal was kindly loaned to the author by his daughter-in-law, Peggy Pengelly.
13 Other Station Officers were: Lt. James Stephens, RN (1856), George Cock (1894), James Hayman (1898), Charles Wroth (1910-20), Charles Parker (1920-21), Charles Stoyles (1922-24), E.J. Reed (1924-28), and H. Cox (1928-32).
14 Other Chief Boatmen were: Philip Perry (1833), William Brooks (1881-83), born at Plymstock, John Trevett (1883-92), Henry Stimpson (1899), Edmund Colwill (1901), and Charles Bennett (1902-4).
15 This was re-erected at the Bin Down Golf Club (Looe) in *c*.1935 after the closure of the station.
16 It was replaced in 1954. In 1985, the watch house was demolished and the site was converted for use as a

public viewing platform. In 1995, South West Water built a sewage pumping station on the site.

17 The horses were hired from the farmer at Trewrickle.

18 Sailing Vessel (SV) *Arethusa*, 1872; SV *Auguste* (German), 1882; SV *Pride of Fleetwood*, 1882; Fishing Vessel (FV) *Water Lily* (of Portwrinkle), 1883; SV *Gypsy* (French), 1901; *Torpedo Boat No 108* (French), 1902; Steam Ship (SS) *Daisy* , 1903; SS *Panama Transport* , 1915; SV *Mary Peers*, 1923; SV *S M Neilson* (Danish), 1926; SS *Treverbyn*, 1930; Yacht *Sus*, 1931; SV *Katie*, 1932; SS *Chancellor*, 1934; A small sailing boat from Looe, 1934; Aircraft (Wellington Bomber), 1942; Motor Vessel (MV) *Three Brothers*, 1946; SS *Empire Chamoes*, 1947; SS *Sadikoglu* (Turkish), 1957; Yacht *Defender*, 1957; MV *No 1547*, 1957; MV *Lapwing*, 1958; MV *Eutarte* (French), 1958; A small rowing boat (from Portwrinkle), 1959; MV *Gazalle* (Dutch), 1960 . List compiled by the late Wilfrid Pengelly.

19 The late Wilfrid Pengelly noted four in the 17th century, eight in the 18th, and more than 40 in the 19th century. The increase in numbers was due partly to the general increase in shipping and partly to better record-keeping.

20 C. Walker and J. Smith, *The Spirit of Rame: Rowing in the Waters off the Rame Peninsula* (1995), p. 35. Elizabeth Hurrell may have been related to Pearce Horel who effected repairs to the quay at Portwrinkle in 1723 and to Mary Horwell, who supplied liquor to the workmen at the quay in 1731.

21 The wreck has been described by Peter Mitchell and Roy Roseveare in their book *Shipwrecks Around Plymouth Sound* (1984), from which this account is partly taken.

22 McNeil's service No. was R 66037.

23 Marine Accident Investigation Branch: *Report on the investigation of the cargo shift, abandoning and grounding of the mv* Kodima *in the English Channel 1 February 2002.*

Chapter 20, *Early History of Agriculture*

1 See Chapter 1, *From the Stone Age to the Roman Invasion.*

2 See generally on Bronze-Age farming, Aileen Fox, *South-West England 3,500 BC-A.D. 600* (1964; revised ed. 1973), pp. 100 to 112.

3 As to this structure, see Chapter 1, *From the Stone Age to the Roman Invasion.*

4 See K. Branigan and P.J. Fowler (eds.), *The Roman West Country: Classical Culture and Celtic Society* (1976), p. 201.

5 The mouldboard was introduced by the Anglo-Saxons.

6 As to the beat-axe, see Chapter 23, *The Soil and Crops.*

7 Examples of Roman shares, axe-mattocks, and iron-edged rectangular spades are preserved in the Museum of London.

8 See K. Jackson, *Language and History in Early Britain: A Chronological Survey of the Brittonic Languages 1st to 12th c. A.D.* (1953), p. 76.

9 H.P.R. Finberg, *Tavistock Abbey* (1969), p. 32.

10 Cf. Welsh *trosel* 'a plashed or plaited fence': Gover.

11 CP/FX/11.

12 Cf. Old Breton *Iudhael* meaning 'generous lord': Gover.

13 For Cornish field names, see Chapter 21, *Field Names in Sheviock.*

14 Charles Thomas (ed.), *An Archaeological Survey of the Rame Peninsula* (1974), p. 33.

15 According to Charles Thomas it means in Cornish 'hound of the sea'; see *Britain and Ireland in Early Christian Times A.D. 400-800* (1971). But Gover gives the meaning as 'great chief'.

16 Except that it lost its village green when the turnpike came through it in 1826: see Chapter 40, *Markets, Highways and Turnpikes.*

17 The Council of London in 1102 prohibited monks from acting as reeves: see R. Lennard, *Rural England: 1086-1135* (1959), p. 157.

18 The original is in Latin. Published by Alecto Historical Editions (London, 1988) in facsimile with translation and commentary. Each county is covered by a separate three-volume set.

19 King Edward is Edward the Confessor, who ruled from 1042 to 1066.

20 See D. Bates, *William the Conqueror* (1989) (pb ed., 2004, p. 254).

21 i.e. Domesday Book 'of Exeter' (*Exoniensis* in Latin). The Exon. Domesday is kept in the library of Exeter Cathedral, from which it takes its name.
22 The parish comprised 2,433 acres in 1930: Kempthorne (*c.*1934), p.v.
23 By 1769, there were at least 13 ploughs in the parish: CRO:P208/21/1.
24 H.P.R. Finberg, *Tavistock Abbey* (1951), p. 32.
25 R. Lennard, *Rural England 1086-1135: A Study of Social and Agrarian Conditions* (1959), pp. 372, 375.
26 See Chapter 2, *The Celtic Kingdoms, the Saxon and Norman Conquests.*
27 I.N. Soulsby, 'An Introduction to the Cornwall Domesday' (p. 7), in *The Cornwall Domesday* (1988).

Chapter 21, *Field Names in Sheviock*

1 For Thomas Pride's Map, see Antony archives, CP/FX/11. The 1840 Map is kept in the Cornwall Record Office.
2 As to these tenements, see Chapter 8, *Holdings on Sheviock Manor.*
3 See J. Whetter, *Cornwall in the Thirteenth Century. A Study in Social and Economic History* (1998), p. 45.
4 Richard Mabey, *Flora Britannica* (1996), p. 228.
5 See further Chapter 17, *The Fishing Industry at Portwrinkle.*
6 See Robin Stanes, *The Old Farm* (1990), p. 97.
7 See Kempthorne (*c.*1934), p. 63, and Liz Luck, *South Cornish Harbours* (Revised Edn., 1995), p. 130.
8 R. Stanes, *The Old Farm* (1990), p. 80.
9 J. Field, *A History of English Field Names* (1993).
10 R. Stanes, *The Old Farm* (1990), p. 144.
11 *A History of English Field Names* (1993).
12 *The Old Farm* (1990), p. 80.
13 CA/HI/8.
14 See also 'Vellands Parks' in Chapter 8, *Holdings on Sheviock Manor.*
15 For a place name in Mullion possibly deriving from *an velin*, see 'Vellan Head' in O.J. Padel, *A Popular Dictionary of Cornish Place-Names* (1988).
16 O.J. Padel, *A Popular Dictionary of Cornish Place-Names* (1988), pp. 18, 85.
17 In March 1705, Henry Richards leased, and then sold, half of a property in Crafthole to Mark Barrett, butcher, for £27: CD/AH/19A and B.

Chapter 22, *Livestock*

1 *The Rural Economy of the West of England* (1796), Vol. I, p116.
2 J. Whetter, *Cornwall in the Thirteenth Century. A Study in Social and Economic History* (1998), p. 10.
3 A Roman iron prod is preserved in the London Museum.
4 TNA: Prob 11/1581.
5 *The Rural Economy of the West of England* (1796), Vol. I.
6 Tone Carne, *Cornwall's Forgotten Corner* (1985), p. 117.
7 See J. Whetter, *Cornwall in the 17th Century* (1974), p. 28.
8 *General View of the Agriculture of the County of Cornwall* (London, 1811).
9 Information from Tom Bersey, who farmed in Sheviock for all his working life.
10 M. Kowaleski (ed.), *The Havener's Accounts of the Earldom and Duchy of Cornwall 1287-1356* (2001), pp. 36, 38.
11 J. Whetter, *Cornwall in the Thirteenth Century. A Study in Social and Economic History* (1998), p. 10.
12 See 'Modern Diversification: Sheviock Cheese' in Chapter 25, *Farming after 1800.*
13 R. Stanes, *The Old Farm* (1990), p. 144.
14 See J. Whetter, *The Bodrugans* (1995), p. 21.
15 William Condy, a 'clothier' from Tavistock, was a free tenant of land in Blazor in 1691: CM/F2/158.
16 Carew, *Survey* (1602), p. 23v.
17 *The Hundred of East. Described by Ed. Kneebone of Westcot [gentleman]. Ann. D. 1684* (R.I.C., Truro).
18 CA/HI/2.

19 CA/HI/2.
20 TNA: E178/6177. See also Chapter 33, *Tithes.*
21 CM/F2/158.
22 See Helen Clarke, 'Agriculture in Late Anglo-Saxon England' in *Domesday Book Studies* (1987), p. 47.
23 Today the main species of trees in the woods are oak, beech, chestnut, elm and larch: see R.D. Penhallurick, *The Birds of Cornwall and the Isles of Scilly* (1978), p. 13.
24 H.P.R. Finberg, *West Country Historical Studies* (1969), p. 97.
25 Dawlish Warren in Devon had a similar location.
26 CA/HI/5A.
27 'Ken' was Kenneth Bean, son of Herbert Bean of Lantic Farm. 'Chuffy' was his younger brother, Terry.
28 I.e., the ferret's mouth was tied up.

Chapter 23, *The Soil and Crops*

1 See Oliver Rackham, *The History of the Countryside* (1995), p. 332.
2 CM/F2/159.
3 H.P.R. Finberg, *Tavistock Abbey* (1951), p. 92.
4 The beat-axe seems to have been descended from the Roman axe-mattock. In later times the axe was replaced by two prongs, but it continued to be called a beat-*axe*. The beat-axe still survives under the name 'bidix', a corrupt form of beat-axe. For its use in modern times, see Chapter 25, *Farming after 1800.*
5 Carew, *Survey* (1602), p. 20v.
6 CA/HI/8.
7 See R. Stanes, *The Old Farm* (1990), p. 110.
8 See H.P.R. Finberg, *Tavistock Abbey* (1951), p. 89.
9 The words of the confirmatory Charter, read in translation; 'for the common advantage of the land of Cornwall, allowing all the inhabitants to take sea sand without payment and to keep the sand on their lands, and to cast it throughout Cornwall for the fertility of their lands by a proper road assigned or to be assigned' : see J. Whetter, *Cornwall in the Thirteenth Century. A Study in Social and Economic History* (1998), p. 30. Sanders Lane was no doubt the 'proper road assigned' in Sheviock.
10 CD/AE/3.
11 *Survey* (1602), p. 27r.
12 M. Kowaleski (ed), *The Haveners' Accounts of the Earldom and Duchy of Cornwall 1287-1356* (2001), p. 307.
13 *Survey of Cornwall* (1602), p. 19v.
14 CM/F2/159.
15 See R. Stanes, *The Old Farm* (1990), p. 118.
16 CM/B/98.
17 Borlase MSS. Morab Library, Penzance. Original Letters V/7.
18 *Survey of Cornwall* (1602), p. 27r and v.
19 See Chapter 25, *Farming after 1800.*
20 CD/AG/42A.
21 See R. Stanes, *The Old Farm* (1990), pp. 120-3.
22 CM/F2/159.
23 *Survey* (1602), p20r.
24 See J. Whetter, *Cornwall in the 17th Century* (1974), p.50.
25 See H.P.R. Finberg, *Tavistock Abbey* (1951), p. 96.
26 See H.P.R. Finberg, *Tavistock Abbey* (1951), p. 97.
27 CM/F2/159.
28 See Carew, *Survey* (1602), p. 20r.
29 CM/F2/159.
30 CM/F2/159.
31 W. Marshall, *Rural Economy of the West of England* (2 vols. 1796), Vol. I, p. 166. The crooks were the wooden supports strapped onto the back of a packhorse.

32 CA/HI/2.
33 The 'arrish' was the stubble field created by the operation of harvesting.
34 *The Natural History of Cornwall* (1758), p. 88. Borlase included an impression of these arrish mows, looking rather like wigwams, in the engraving of Enys House opposite that page.
35 See further Chapter 1, *From the Stone Age to the Roman Invasion.*
36 See further 'Cider-making in Later Centuries' in Chapter 24, *Fruit and Orchards.*
37 W. Marshall, *Rural Economy of the West of England* (2 vols. 1796), Vol I, p. 176.
38 See R. Stanes, *The Old Farm* (1990), p. 131.
39 CM/F2/159.
40 CM/F2/159.
41 W. Marshall, *Rural Economy of the West of England* (2 vols., 1796), Vol. I, p. 184.
42 CM/F2/159.
43 CA/HI/8.
44 *Historical Survey of the County of Cornwall*, Vol. I, p. 350. The 'Baker' in question may have been William Baker, who was advertising threshing and winnowing machines in the *Reading Mercury* in May 1808.
45 Information supplied by Tom Bersey, who operated the machinery in his youth. See also 'Agricultural Implement Makers' in Chapter 39, *Trades and Crafts.*
46 See further S. Wade Martins, *Historic Farm Buildings* (1991), pp. 45, 50.
47 'Uncle Herb' and 'Auntie Flo' were Herbert and Florence Bean, the farmers at Lantic.

Chapter 24, *Fruit and Orchards*

1 Carew, *Survey* (1602), p. 20v.
2 J. Whetter, *Cornwall in the Thirteenth Century. A Study in Social and Economic History* (1998), p. 40.
3 *Register of the Bishop of Exeter*, edited by F.C. Hingeston-Randolph (1889).
4 See H. Fox, *The Evolution of the Fishing Village: Landscape and Society along the South Devon Coast, 1086-1550* (2001), p. 109.
5 *JRIC* 2001, pp. 62, 63.
6 Carew, *Survey* (1602), pp. 20v and 21r.
7 Carew, *Survey* (1602), p. 25v. The birds were probably bullfinches.
8 See further, Chapter 33, *Tithes.*
9 CZ/EE/32.
10 Quoted in J. Whetter, *Cornwall in the 17th Century* (1974), p. 130.
11 Before the 'Act for ... improving certain roads to and from Liskeard' of 1826 (7 Geo IV cap 84), there were even more orchards. That Act authorised the removal of one orchard at Sconner, one at Polscoe, and two in Sheviock village.
12 TNA: Prob 11/1581.
13 An example is preserved at Trethill House. According to the late Fred Rundle, his father, John Rundle, on the orders of Col. Roberts, removed it from its original location in the orchard at Kerslake to its present location. The removal took place in the late 1930s.
14 See further, Chapter 33, *Tithes.*
15 The premises in question were replanted with apple trees in 2003.
16 W. Marshall, *Rural Economy of the West of England* (2 vols. 1796), p. 233.
17 CD/AG/42A.
18 Marshall (1796), p. 234.
19 Marshall (1796), p. 237.
20 R. Stanes, *The Old Farm* (1990), p. 70.
21 See the recollection of the evacuee, Terry Leather, in Chapter 38, *The School in Sheviock and Other Local Schools.*

Chapter 25, *Farming after 1800*

1 I.N. Soulsby, *A History of Cornwall* (1986), p. 100.

2 Information supplied by the Alger brothers of Herodsfoot from their own farm records.
3 A maund is a large two-handled basket.
4 Usually Devonport Market. Market days were Tuesdays, Thursdays and Saturdays.
5 Mum was Mrs Rosina Andrew (née Bennett).
6 This extract was first published in the Sheviock Parish Newsletter, Issue 54 (September 2005).
7 For the story of his arrival in Sheviock with his sister, see Chapter 37, *The Parish in the Two World Wars*.
8 Herbert Bean's farm, Lantic, in the west of the parish, was some 170 acres in extent.
9 'Chuffy' was Terence Bean.
10 Information supplied by Tom Bersey.
11 Information from Matt Herbst.
12 Information from Sir Richard Carew Pole Bt.
13 This is the 'beat-axe' of earlier times.
14 An old measure equal to three and a half linear yards.

Chapter 26 *The Early Church. The Medieval Fabric of St Mary's*

1 *The Kingdom of Dumnonia* (1978), p. 105. However, Professor Orme points out that there is no evidence for it before the tenth century.
2 Lynette Olson, *Early Monasteries in Cornwall* (1989), p. 64.
3 *Atlas Meirionydd*, p. 200; cited with approval in O. J. Padel, *Cornish Place-name Elements* (1985) and followed by the Cornish Bard, Craig Weatherhill, *Cornish Place Names & Language* (1995), p. 78.
4 On folio 1 of the *Codex Oxoniensis Posterior* there is part of a *Missa propria Germani episcopi* which refers to the church of a place called *Lannaled* in Cornwall. The Codex is in the Bodleian Library in Oxford: MS Bodley 572 (S.C. 2026). Another manuscript, called the Lannalet Pontifical, includes (at folios 183r-184r) a formula of excommunication which begins (in translation), 'The bishop, by the assent of the divinity, of the monastery of Lanalet to all the faithful of the holy church of God: let it be known, etc.' The manuscript is in the Bibliothèque Municipale in Rouen: MS A. 27 (368). See Olson, pp. 60-2. See also *Pontificale Lanaletense*, ed. Doble, London, H. Bradshaw Soc., 1937, p.xii.
5 L. Olson, *Early Monasteries in Cornwall* (1989), p. 60.
6 C.A. Ralegh Radford, 'The Church of Saint Germans', *JRIC* 1975/6, p. 190. The Bishop of Auxerre had made two visits to Britain in A.D. 429 and 447. Relics of the saint were donated to the monastery in A.D. 1358, by which time the earlier saint had apparently been forgotten.
7 Only the minster of St Petroc, originally at Padstow, later at Bodmin, with its 37 hides, was bigger.
8 In a letter written by Archbishop Dunstan to King Aethelred between 980 and 988 appears the statement: 'Then it happened that King Athelstan gave to Cunun the bishopric as far as the Tamar flowed', followed by a reference to the seat of the bishop of Cornwall at St Germans in King Eadred's time (946-55). See L. Olson, *Early Monasteries in Cornwall* (1989), p. 63.
9 It was not until the time of Leofric, Bishop of Cornwall and Crediton (1046-50), and later of Exeter (1050-72), that a college of regular (Benedictine) canons was established in place of the secular ones. Bishop Bartholomew of Exeter (1161-84) replaced this rule with the Augustinian one.
10 N. Orme, *Unity and Variety: A History of the Church in Devon and Cornwall* (1991), p. 12.
11 The dedication of the spring to Our Lady may have occurred at the same time as the dedication of the church to her. Like many other holy wells in Cornwall, Ladywell was probably the site of a pre-Christian cult. The Revd H.C. Glanville (rector 1856-1900) left a note relating to this well at the beginning of the volume of early churchwardens' accounts, which he had bound up in 1896. He wrote: 'When I first came into the parish I was told that the water for Baptisms used to be brought from the well in former days.' This book is now in the CRO.
12 See N. Orme, *Cornwall and the Cross* (2007), p. 21.
13 *The Cornish Church Guide* (1925), p. 195.
14 See 'Some Early Tavistock Charters' in *The English Historical Review*, July 1947, Vol LXII, No. 244, pp. 355 *et seq*.
15 Erbenald is called Ermenhald in Domesday Book.

16 See *VCH Cornwall*, ii 66.
17 *Tavistock Abbey* (1959), p. 19. In *West Country Historical Studies* (1969), at p. 95, Finberg listed Antony, St John and *Rame*, rather than Sheviock, as the churches within the honour of Sheviock. This must have been a momentary lapse on his part.
18 R. Lennard, *Rural England* (1959), p. 213.
19 Pope Celestine III lived from 1106 to 1198. He was elected Pope in 1191, at the advanced age of 85. He was a pupil and friend of the scholar, Peter Abelard, and a friend of Thomas à Becket.
20 It is published in the original Latin version in G. Oliver's *Monasticon Diocesis Exoniensis* (1846), p. 95.
21 See generally on church dedications, N. Orme, *English Church Dedications: with a Survey of Cornwall and Devon* (1996).
22 See *The Registers of Walter Bronescombe (A.D. 1257-1280)*, ed. F.C. Hingeston-Randolph (1889), p. 180.
23 As to tithes, see Chapter 33, *Tithes*. The Easter offering survived until 1839, when it was brought within the legislation commuting tithes.
24 Kempthorne (*c*.1934), p.36.
25 Transcribed by Finberg. See note 14 above.
26 According to Finberg, the feast of St Rumon must be the one held on the anniversary of his death, namely 30 August. The feast of the Purification was also known as Candlemas. This was held on 2 February. In the Church of England, this day is kept as the feast of The Presentation of Christ in the Temple. The feast of the birth of St John the Baptist was held on 24 June.
27 Kempthorne (*c*.1934), p. 36.
28 *The Cornwall Register*, ed. J. Wallis (1847), p. 22.
29 His account is set out partly (for the glebe) in Chapter 10, *Sheviock Churchtown*, and partly (for the tithes) in Chapter 33, *Tithes*.
30 I am grateful to Professor N. Orme for the reading of 'Lananta', and for its identification with Lelant.
31 Transcribed by Finberg: see note 14 above. The dispute was ended symbolically by the folding and exchange of knives.
32 See further, Chapter 11, *The Borough of Crafthole*.
33 TNA: *De Banco*, No 155 m117d.
34 For the population growth in England at this time, see C. Dyer, *Making a Living in the Middle Ages* (2002), pp. 95, 101.
35 For William of Worcester's *Itinerary* (1478), see Lake's *Parochial History*, Vol. IV (1872), p. 93. For his description of Bronescombe, in relation to the foundation of Glasney College, Penryn, see ibid., p. 107. The bishop is buried between the Lady Chapel and the chapel of St Gabriel in Exeter Cathedral.
36 See *The Registers of Walter Bronescombe (A.D. 1257-1280)*, ed. the Revd F.C. Hingeston-Randolph (1889).
37 Work on the new cathedral started in about 1275.
38 The Latin hymn is still included in modern Hymnals as 'Christ is made the sure foundation'. It was sung also at the consecration of the new cathedral at Truro on 3 November 1887: see *The Cornish Church Guide*, p. 40.
39 See L.E. Elliott-Binns, *Medieval Cornwall* (1955), p. 265.
40 The problem of overcrowding was of course dramatically and tragically solved in 1348-9, when the Black Death wiped out between one third and one half of the population. When, a century later, the population again reached the pre-plague level, the north aisle was added to the church.
41 *Survey* (1602), p. 108v.
42 Some writers (e.g. A. Jewers in Heraldic Church Notes (after 1886), at p. 15) have assumed that the builders responsible for the church and the barn were Sir Edward Courtenay and Lady Emmeline sometime between 1346 and 1370. But this cannot be so, because the style is early 14th century, and Sir Edward Courtenay could hardly be described as 'one of these Dannyes ancestours'.
43 Calendars of Patent Rolls, 13 August 1309.
44 *Buildings of England, Cornwall* (1951), p. 193 (2nd ed. (1970), p. 212).
45 See *Cornish Church Guide*, p. 190, and Elliott-Binns, *Medieval Cornwall* (1955), p. 379.
46 See Lake's *Parochial History* (1872-3), Vol. IV, p. 146.

47 See N. Orme, *English Church Dedications* (1996), p. 6.
48 C.S.Gilbert's *Historical Survey of the County of Cornwall* (1820), Vol. II, p. 399.
49 See W.H.H. Rogers, *The Antient Sepulchral Effigies and Monumental and Memorial Sculpture of Devon* (1877).
50 *Historical Survey of the County of Cornwall*, Vol. II (1820), p. 399.
51 According to Kempthorne (*c*.1934), p. 34, a note made by Reginald Pole Carew in 1797 stated that, up until 15 years before, the arms of Dawney impaling Courtenay could still be seen over the back of the lady's head on the stone partition separating the two figures.
52 According to Polsue (in Lake's *Parochial History*, Vol. IV, at p. 146), following C.S.Gilbert's *Historical Survey*, Vol. II (1820), at p. 399, the tomb is that of an unnamed brother of Lady Emmeline. According to Pevsner, it is Sir Edward's father. Both attributions are incorrect.
53 *Survey* (1602), p. 108v.
54 See J. Barker, *Agincourt* (pb ed. 2006), p. 331.
55 See *The Antient Sepulchral Effigies and Monumental and memorial Sculpture of Devon* (1877).
56 The information on the dating of the dress and armour was very kindly supplied by Fergus Cannan, Assistant Curator of Sculpture at the Victoria and Albert Museum in London.
57 The stained-glass windows in St Neot's church, which include depictions of wealthy parishioners kneeling in pews, suggest that that church also introduced pews in the late 1400s or early 1500s. See Joanna Mattingly, 'Stories in the Glass – Reconstructing the St Neot Pre-Reformation Glazing Scheme', *JRIC* 2000, pp. 19, 20, 22, 43.
58 See Pevsner, *Cornwall* (revised ed., 1983), p. 212.
59 Opinion given to the author by Stephen Clare, founder of Holy Well Glass, Wells, Somerset.
60 All Souls' Day is 2 November. Interestingly enough, the tradition of ringing early in November survived (or was revived after) the Reformation. The 'Singing Feast' of 4 and 5 November (Guy Fawkes' night) was ushered in by the ringing of bells.
61 See Kempthorne (*c*.1934), p. 37, and TNA: KR, church goods 12/42, 1 and 2 Philip and Mary.

Chapter 27, *Church Life in the Middle Ages*

1 The main sources for this chapter are Eamon Duffy's three books, *The Stripping of the Altars* (1992), *The Voices of Morebath* (2001), and *Marking the Hours: English People and their Prayers, 1240-1570* (2006), and Nicholas Orme's three books, *Unity and Variety: A History of the Church in Devon and Cornwall* (1991), *Cornwall and the Cross: Christianity 500-1560* (2007), and *Cornish Wills 1342-1540* (2007).
2 See N. Orme (ed.), *Unity and Variety: A History of the Church in Devon and Cornwall* (1991), p. 60.
3 See N. Orme, 'Prayer and Education in 15th-Century Camborne', *JRIC* 2006, p. 95, which sets out the list in full.
4 Quoted in E. Duffy, *The Stripping of the Altars* (1992), p. 162.
5 E.g. Heckington, Lincs. See E. Duffy, *The Stripping of the Altars* (1992), p. 32 and plate 7.
6 E. Duffy, *The Stripping of the Altars* (1992), p. 30.
7 See further E. Duffy, *Marking the Hours: English People and their Prayers, 1240-1570* (2006).
8 See E. Duffy, *The Stripping of the Altars* (1992), pp. 281-2.
9 See E. Duffy, *The Stripping of the Altars* (1992), p. 16.
10 See E. Duffy, *The Stripping of the Altars* (1992), p. 23.
11 CM/B/101.
12 N. Orme, *Cornish Wills 1342-1540* (2007), p. 77.
13 For T. Pride's map, see CP/FX/11; for the Tithe Redemption Map, see CRO: P208/27/1.
14 The Latin original is published in *The Register of Edmund Lacy, Bishop of Exeter 1420-1455*, ed. G.R.Dunstan (1971) (Devon and Cornwall Record Society, New Series, Vol 16).
15 See E. Duffy, *The Voices of Morebath* (2001), p. 14.
16 Hugh's elder brother died before his father, and so Hugh became the fourth earl on the death of his father in 1419.
17 Plympton Priory was re-founded by Bishop Warelwast of Exeter (1107-37), as a house for canons regular of St Augustine. It was said to be the richest monastic house in Devon: see George Oliver, *Historic Collections relating to the Monasteries of Devon* (1841), p. 30. Walter de Valletort, Lord of Trematon was

among its many benefactors. Nicholas Selman was abbot at the time of John Walle's death. There was a parochial chapel dedicated to St Mary within the cemetery of the conventual church (now the parish church of Plympton St Mary).

18 J. Moorman, *Church Life in England in the Thirteenth Century* (1945), p. 300.

19 I am grateful to Professor N. Orme for allowing me to use his English translation from *Cornish Wills 1342-1540* (2007).

20 This reference to Peter and Paul has been the subject of much debate, and 580 years on, the meaning is still a matter of conjecture. If Walle had intended to be buried in his own parish, he should have said '*in cimiterio ecclesiae beatae Mariae de Sevioch*'. The matter was discussed in correspondence between the Revd F.C. Hingeston-Randolph, editor of *The Episcopal Registers of the Diocese of Exeter* (1886), and the rector of Sheviock, the Revd G. Pole Carew. In a letter dated 10 November 1902, Hingeston-Randolph wrote, 'I think the clerk who copied [the will] into the Bishop's Register did not do his work as carefully as he ought to have done … it looks as if the name of the church in the cemetery of which he desired to be buried was omitted by the copyist. In another will close by, the Cathedral is described in the exact words of this will – '*Ecclesia Petri et Pauli*'. The Mother Church of Plympton is commonly described in the exact words of this will '*Ecclesia Sanctorum Apostolorum Petri et Pauli*. To me, long accustomed to such documents, the language of Walle's will is *un*accustomed, as given in the Register.' Referring to the many clerical beneficiaries mentioned in the will, he goes on to say, 'I cannot understand there being so many clerics in Sheviock Church', and he added in a postscript, 'Walle's will … contains internal evidence that Sheviock & the *eiusdem ecclesie* were not identical. I do not doubt that [Walle] directed his *burial to be at Plympton* and that the copying clerk muddled the matter. Walle was evidently referring to two distinct churches.' A more recent authority, Professor Nicholas Orme, is of the view that Sheviock's church was probably dedicated to the Blessed Mary *and* to St Peter and St Paul, and that Walle intended to be *buried at Sheviock*. However, there is no evidence, apart from this will, that the church at Sheviock was dedicated to St Peter and St Paul as well as to the blessed Mary. All other medieval references to the church both before and after 1427 are to St Mary alone.

21 The distribution of money to the poor, called 'the dole', was common in wills at this time. Such works of mercy were thought to help the souls of the deceased on their passage to heaven. John Walle left three doles (20s. on the day of his burial; 13s. 4d. on the day of his obit; and 10s. as directed by the executors).

22 Walter Colle (or Cole) was instituted to the rectory of Milton Damerel on 16 October 1413, and on the same day received licence of non-residence to study at Oxford for three years. Colle resigned his rectory in 1415 and may then have moved to Tiverton, the home town of the earls of Devon. He was not instituted to the rectory of Tiverton (Pitt Portion) until 18 July 1426. Colle and his brother, William, were nephews of Walter Robert, LLB, Rector of Northill, Cornwall and of Tiverton, Devon, and Canon of Ottery. John Walle was a friend of the family, and had acted as proxy for Walter Robert. Both Walle and Colle were protegés of the earl of Devon. Sir Adam Cole was steward to the earl's household in 1381-2 and his son, John Cole, was a liveried familiar of the earl in 1384-5: see Martin Cherry, 'The Courtenay Earls of Devon: The Formation and Disintegration of a Late Medieval Aristocratic Affinity' in *Southern History*, Vol. 1 (1979), pp. 71 *et seq*. Oxford University had been founded in 1167. Walter Stapledon, Bishop of Exeter (1308-26), founded Exeter College for West Country students in 1314.

23 Joce Trevysa (also spelled Trevyda) was illegitimate, and received the necessary *dispensacio super defectu natalium*, to become a priest on 7 March 1415-16. Like Walle, he was a non-graduate priest.

24 Ladycourth, also a non-graduate priest, seems to have been a few years older than his friends. He was ordained at Crediton on 9 June 1408. He was instituted to Clare Portion in Tiverton Church on 30 March 1432.

25 The 'clerk of the town' is more likely to refer to Plympton, an important town in the medieval period, than to Sheviock.

26 The wording shows that there were at least two holy-water clerks. For further discussion, see N. Orme, *Cornish Wills 1342-1540*.

27 An obit is a commemorative service held on the anniversary of a person's death.

28 The usual cost of paying a priest to say a *dirige* at this time was 4d.; so a total sum of £1 13s. 4d. would have been payable from the estate for the 100 masses.

29 The site of 'Hellemar' can no longer be identified. The horse bequeathed to Richard was probably worth between 10s. and £1 6s. 8d. In 1468, Henry Bodrugan, an important Cornish landowner and a tenant of the earls of Devon, ordered a horse valued at the latter sum to be given to a local rector: see J. Whetter, *The Bodrugans* (1995).

30 The context suggests that the intended recipients of the dole of 10s. were inhabitants of the parish of Sheviock.

31 Sir Hugh Courtenay of Boconnoc was the great-grandson of Lady Emmeline Dawney.

32 See J. Whetter, *The Bodrugans* (1995), p. 98.

Chapter 28, *Church Administration in the Middle Ages. Medieval Rectors*

1 Assistant priests were supposed to receive 50s. per annum and clerks 40s.: see J. Moorman, *Church Life in England in the Thirteenth Century* (1945), pp. 56, 58.

2 In 1287, Bishop Quinil of Exeter ordered each incumbent to provide himself with a written *summula*, or primer of Christian faith, which he was to learn by heart: see Moorman (1945), p. 91. Few individual priests possessed copies of the Vulgate (the Latin Bible).

3 See N. Orme, *Cornish Wills 1342-1540* (2007), pp. 42, 43.

4 CM/B/98.

5 See N. Orme, *Cornish Wills 1342-1540* (2007), p. 166.

6 The pre-Reformation accounts of the parish of Morebath in Devon have survived. They show that the parish had five stores: the store of St George (the patronal saint), managed by the churchwardens; St Anthony's store; the store of Jesus and St Sidwell; the maiden light (kept by the maidens of the parish); and the young men's light. See E. Duffy, *The Stripping of the Altars* (1992), p. 498.

7 See Lawrence Blair, *English Church Ales* (1940), which contains verbatim extracts from the surviving churchwardens' accounts relating to church ales held in the 15th and 16th centuries.

8 J. Charles Cox, *Notes on the Churches of Derbyshire*, 4 vols. (1875-9).

9 As to Sheviock's church-house, see Chapter 10, *Sheviock Churchtown*.

10 CM/B/98.

11 Hallowmas was the feast of All Hallows (1 November). Hocktide was the Monday and Tuesday following Easter. On the Monday the men, and on the Tuesday the women, 'hooked' members of the opposite sex and only released them when they had paid a 'fine' to the church. Hence the expression 'in hock'.

12 See L. Blair, *English Church Ales* (1940), p. 13.

13 *The Survey of Cornwall* (1602), p. 68v.

14 *The Anatomy of Abuses* (1585), quoted in L. Blair, *English Church Ales* (1940), p. 1.

15 The list is taken from Kempthorne (*c.*1934), pp. 45 et seq.

16 i.e. invested with the spiritual part of his benefice by the Bishop.

17 Kempthorne (c.1934), p. 10.

18 See further Chapter 27, *Church Life in the Middle Ages*, note 20, and 'The renaming of the church' in Chapter 31, *St Mary's after the Reformation*.

19 Founded by Bishop Bronescombe in 1265.

Chapter 29, *The Reformation in the West Country*

1 In 1541, St Germans' Priory was sold to the Champernowne family. John Eliot purchased it from them in 1565.

2 Plympton Priory and Tavistock Abbey were both dissolved in 1539. The lands of Tavistock Abbey passed to the Russell family.

3 *An Answer unto Sir Thomas More's Dialogue* (1531), quoted in D. Daniell, *The Bible in English* (2003), p. 223.

4 See D. Daniell, *The Bible in English* (2003), p. 223.

5 See Henderson MS, *Materials for a Parochial History of East Cornwall* (begun 1924) in the RIC library, Truro (Ref. H79 (Sheviock)).

6 See A.L.Rowse, *Tudor Cornwall* (1941), p. 257.

7 David Daniell's *The Bible in English* (2003) is the source from which, with the permission of the author, much of the material in this Chapter has been taken.

8 The disparaging name 'Lollard' derives from the Middle Dutch *lollaert*, meaning a mumbler.
9 See N. Orme, *Unity and Variety: A History of the Church in Devon and Cornwall* (1991), p. 75.
10 See Joyce Youings, 'The South-Western Rebellion of 1549', *Southern History*, Vol 1, p. 106.
11 He was shown in the 1544 Subsidy roll as being the second wealthiest man in the parish. He somehow managed to survive both the rebellion and its bloody aftermath, dying peacefully on 28 April 1569.
12 See F. Rose-Troup, *The Western Rebellion of 1549* (1913), pp. 220, 221.
13 Joyce Youings, op. cit., poses the question whether he was the real leader of the rebels.
14 From the indictment against the captured rebels. See Rose-Troup, *The Western Rebellion of 1549* (1913), p. 128.
15 Russell was rewarded for his pains with the Earldom of Bedford and the lands of Thorney Abbey at Woburn: Rose-Troup, *The Western Rebellion of 1549* (1913), p. 290.
16 See Rose-Troup (1913), p. 408.
17 E. Cleaveland, *A Genealogical History of the Noble and Illustrious Family of Courtenay, etc.* (1735), p. 251.
18 See further as to Sir Walter, Chapter 5, *Lords of the Manor.*
19 See D. MacCulloch, *Reformation: Europe's House Divided* (2003), p. 284.
20 For the text, see Chapter 11, *The School in Sheviock and other Local Schools.* See also Henderson MS, *Materials for a Parochial History of East Cornwall* (begun 1924, RIC, Truro).
21 *Survey* (1602), p. 124v.
22 However, there may also have been personal grievances against him: see Chapter 15, *The Landing Place and Quay at Portwrinkle.*
23 An interesting contrast with the situation at Sheviock is provided by that at Lanreath, where the lord of the manor, Sir John Grylls, who was Royalist and High Church in sympathy, erected a large and prominent 'Letter of Thanks' board and was able to preserve the rood screen from destruction during the Civil War.
24 See Joanna Mattingly, 'Stories in the Glass – Reconstructing the St Neot Pre-Reformation Glazing Scheme', *JRIC* 2000, p. 9.
25 According to the witness, Abraham Chubb, in the tithe case of *Rolle* v *Blake* (1669-70), John Gey had previously been in receipt of the tithes of the parish. He received some consolation for his loss of office: in John Rawling's Account of Sheviocke Manor between 1656 and 1660, Gey is shown as a conventionary tenant of the manor (CM/B/98). A survey of the manor made in June 1691 shows that Gey's holding consisted of 25 acres in Trewrickle. He was no longer the tenant by then, and had presumably expired (CM/F2/158).

Chapter 30, *Church Administration after 1534. Post-Reformation Rectors*

1 27 Hen.VIII, cap. 25 (1536) forbade the medieval practice of establishing or bequeathing common and open doles and distributing ready money in alms to the poor.
2 H.R. Trevor-Roper, *Archbishop Laud* (1940), p. 157.
3 Many of the payments on repairs and maintenance are mentioned in Chapter 39, *Trades and Crafts.*
4 CM/B/98.
5 See N. Orme, *Unity and Variety: A History of the Church in Devon and Cornwall* (1991), p. 78.
6 See Chapter 12, *Courts and Officials of the Borough of Crafthole.*
7 CM/B/98.
8 For the overseers' accounts, see CRO: P 208/12/1.
9 See Sir William Dale, *The Law of the Parish Church* (7th edn., 1998).
10 CRO: TER/573.
11 See also 'Davey' in Appendix 1, *Families.*
12 Tilland Quarry is a mile or two north of Tideford.
13 The list, up to 1919, was originally compiled by Kempthorne (*c.*1934), at pp. 45 *et seq.*
14 CE/G/19/1.
15 CE/G/19/4.
16 See Chapter 15, *The Landing Place and Quay at Portwrinkle.*
17 See Chapter 33, *Tithes.*

18 A. Jewers, *Heraldic Church Notes from Cornwall* (after 1886), p. 28.
19 See 'Rectories' in Chapter 10, *Sheviock Churchtown.*
20 CE/G/19/6.
21 See A. Jewers, *Heraldic Church Notes from Cornwall* (after 1886), p. 156.
22 Quoted in G. and F. L. Harris, *The Making of a Cornish Town; Torpoint and Neighbourhood through Two Hundred Years* (1976), p. 100.
23 See further, Chapter 32, *Church Music in Sheviock.*
24 See also Chapter 37, *The Parish in the Two World Wars.*
25 See further 'The Renaming of the Church' in Chapter 31, *St Mary's after the Reformation.*
26 The list of curates to 1811 is taken from Kempthorne (*c.*1934), p. 51.

Chapter 31, *St Mary's after the Reformation. The Tractarian Movement and afterwards*

1 Under Edward VI (1547-53) sermons also became compulsory, making pews a virtual necessity.
2 The bench ends at Altarnun, probably carved between 1523 and 1554, straddle the transitional period between late Catholic worship and the early Reformation. They include both instruments of the passion and Renaissance motifs: see Joanna Mattingly, 'The Dating of Bench-Ends in Cornish Churches', *JRIC* 1991, p. 58. The best Cornish example of Renaissance decorative art at this time is Prior Vyvyan's tomb at St Petroc's church, Bodmin (1533).
3 See e.g. the illustrations in E. Duffy, *Marking the Hours: English People and their Prayers 1240-1570* (2006), pp. 120, 153.
4 A guinea was a gold coin introduced in 1663. Its value fluctuated between £1 and 30s. until 1717, when it was fixed at £1 1s.
5 The population in 1801 was 409, consisting of 89 families and 78 houses; in 1836 it was 453 (Kempthorne (*c.*1934), p. 56). The censuses show that in 1841, the population was 567; in 1921, it was 529; and in 2001, it was 683.
6 C.S. Gilbert, *Historical Survey of the County of Cornwall* (1820), Vol. II, opposite p. 399.
7 Pole was writing to his uncle, the Rt. Hon. Reginald Pole Carew of Antony. Charles Dickens used the name 'Sowerby' for the undertaker in his novel, *Oliver Twist* (1837-39). For the correspondence concerning the dispute, see CE/G/23.
8 A patch of light-coloured stone in the pillar, immediately facing the south door, probably shows where one end of the 'boulk' – the horizontal beam for the gallery – was inserted.
9 *West of England Conservative and Plymouth, Devonport and Stonehouse Advertiser* for 3 July 1850.
10 Ibid.
11 The initials are no doubt those of the churchwardens responsible for raising the money to purchase the bells. The two men most likely to be 'P.B.' are Philip Bloy or Philip Blake. Philip Bloy was a co-tenant with Philip Palmer of Bayliffe's Meadow in Sheviock churchtown in 1691. As John Bloy was named on the tenor bell, Philip Bloy has a strong claim. Philip Blake (1604-89) was a prominent local gentleman farmer who, in 1655, became tenant of the farmhouse now known as Orchard Cottage next to the church. The identity of 'F.P.' has not been ascertained.
12 RIC, Truro: H.11/378.
13 This stricture seems too harsh. See the section on Georgian church music in Chapter 32, below.
14 *West of England Conservative and Plymouth, Devonport and Stonehouse Advertiser* for 3 July 1850.
15 G. Oliver, *Monasticon Diocesis Exoniensis* (1846), p. 442.
16 This is translated in Chapter 27, *Church Life in the Middle Ages.*
17 The architect, George Edmund Street of London, directed the work. The builders were William and Thomas May of Devonport.
18 The firm had commenced making stained glass in 1841. It later made the glass for the Revd John Keble's parish church, All Saints, Hursley, Hampshire, to a scheme prepared by William Butterfield, architect of Keble College, Oxford. The west window of that church is dated 1858.
19 Oliphant also designed the windows in the ante-chapel at King's College, Cambridge, and the choristers' window at Ely Cathedral.

20 *West of England Conservative and Plymouth, Devonport and Stonehouse Advertiser* for 3 July 1850.
21 The 'sedilia' are the three canopied stone seats for the use of the clergy. The 'piscina' is the perforated stone basin used for carrying away the ablutions of the priest during the celebration of communion.
22 A small shelf to hold the Eucharistic elements before the consecration.
23 The tile works of Minton Ltd were located in Stoke-on-Trent. The firm was founded by Herbert Minton (1793-1858) in 1835. In 1844, he acquired patent rights to a method of making encaustic tiles. Minton tiles were laid in Osborne House, built for Queen Victoria and Prince Albert on the Isle of Wight in 1844, and in the Houses of Parliament in 1845. The tiles won the top award at the Great Exhibition of 1851. See further D.S. Skinner and Hans van Lemmen, *Minton Tiles 1835-1935* (1984).
24 The Revd S.W. Wallis of Trethill, in particular, may not have been as enthusiastic about the service as the reporter. His brother, a churchwarden, was among those who wrote to the bishop with objections.
25 Tatham was married to Jemima Glanville. She was the daughter of Amabel (née Pole Carew), who lived at Sconner Villa.
26 A 'seraphine' is a kind of primitive harmonium. See further Chapter 32, CHURCH MUSUC IN SHEVIOCK.
27 This was about a third of the number attending the Wesleyan Methodist chapel at Crafthole.
28 The newspaper report was dated 3 July 1850.
29 This whole episode is recounted in H. Miles Brown, *The Catholic Revival in Cornish Anglicanism* (1980).
30 See the Revd H.C. Glanville's prefatory note in the rebound Churchwardens' Account Book in the CRO.
31 C.S. Gilbert, *Historical Survey of the County of Cornwall* (1820).
32 Third edition 1902, ed. Revd J. Birkbeck.
33 CRO: DDP 208/2/2.
34 At p. 33. Pevsner quite correctly followed this usage in his volume on *Cornwall* (1951) in the Buildings of England series. A correction should have been made in the 2nd edition, published in 1970.
35 PCC Minute Book 1920-1955, CRO: DDP 208/7/1.

Chapter 32, *Church Music in Sheviock*

1 Information supplied by the Rt. Revd and the Rt. Hon. Richard Chartres, Lord Bishop of London.
2 See *Grove's Dictionary of Music and Musicians* (5th ed., 1954), Vol. 4, p. 429, Vol. 13, p. 787; *Everyman's Encyclopaedia* (3rd ed. 1949-50), Vol. 7, p. 365.
3 T. Tatton-Brown and R. Mortimer, *Westminster Abbey: The Lady Chapel of Henry VII* (2004).
4 Chaucer lived *c.*1340-1400. The *Canterbury Tales* were written *c.*1386-7. The quotation is taken with permission from Nevill Coghill's translation in the Penguin Classics (1951; reprinted 1962).
5 See further 'The Rood Screen and Rood Loft' in Chapter 26, *The Early Church. the Medieval Fabric of St Mary's.*
6 An orpharyon is similar to a lute, but less costly and more robust. A cittern is an instrument of the guitar family. A base-viol is a stringed instrument held downwards resting on or between the knees. One of these was in use in Sheviock.
7 See *The Diary of Samuel Pepys* (ed. Latham and Matthews) (1974), Vol. VIII, p. 150, and note 2.
8 See N. Orme (ed.), *Unity and Variety: A History of the Church in Devon and Cornwall* (1991), p. 90.
9 These accounts are preserved in the Cornish Record Office in Truro.
10 The bass-viol was restored and passed on to an orchestra in Plymouth. Later it was exported to the United States. The first musicians' gallery would appear to have been erected in 1782-3 (see 'The Gallery' in Chapter 31, *St Mary's after the Reformation. the Tractarian Movement and Afterwards*).
11 See further Chapter 41, *Inns and Innkeepers.* The rating lists for the church rate in both 1833-4 and 1845-6 show John Martin as the occupier of 'Martin's Tenement and Inn'. Francis Martin had been the tenant of Dewstowe's tenement (8 acres) in 1737: see Chapter 8, *Holdings on Sheviock Manor.*
12 In 1877, Thomas Moon of Liskeard, 'music seller', took a 30-year lease of a dwelling house and garden in Portwrinkle at an annual rental of £1 10s.: CD/AJ/57A &B.
13 The name of the choirmaster is also spelled 'Coombs'.
14 A 'William Coombe' was renting Bag Mill and Denabole Mill in 1834. It is not certain that the choirmaster was the same person.

15 George II reigned from 1727 to 1760. Britain changed from the Julian to the Gregorian calendar in September 1752; 2 September being followed immediately by 14 September in that year: see D.E. Duncan, *The Calendar* (1998), pp. 310, 311.

16 In years when the fortunes of war went against Britain, there were no celebrations. Instead, fasts were declared, and books of prayers were purchased 'for the fast' – e.g. in each year from 1776-7 until 1781-2. In 1784-5, at last, 1s. was spent on 'a book of thanksgiving' and the ringing re-commenced.

17 As to Mrs Mullis, whose house was used as the first licensed Methodist meeting place, see Appendix 1, *Families*.

18 A 'seraphine' is a kind of primitive harmonium, a reed instrument played with a keyboard. It remained in the church until it decomposed in the 1970s. Three manuscript music books for, respectively, treble, tenor and base parts for the choir have survived. They may be the ones used at the service on St Peter's Day 1850. See CR0: DDP 208/2/39, 1-3.

19 Note in the Sheviock School Minute Book, Sept. 1923, CRO: DDP208/2/23/3.

20 Information supplied by David Mashford, organist of St Mary's Church, Sheviock, at the time of writing.

21 Kempthorne (*c.*1934), p. 57.

22 This was the boat in which Goss competed in the 1996-7 Vendée Globe Single-handed Non-Stop Round-the-World Race. On Christmas Day 1996, he had to abandon the race to return and save the life of the Frenchman, Raphael Dinelli. The episode is described in Goss's book, *Close to the Wind* (1998; pb. ed. 1999).

23 Information supplied by the organist of St Mary's Church, Sheviock, David Mashford.

24 The first performance was given in Dublin on 13 April 1742.

25 Others are in St Martin's in the Fields, London, and St Patrick's Cathedral, Dublin.

Chapter 33, *Tithes*

1 S. M. Pearce, *The Kingdom of Dumnonia* (1978), p. 96.

2 See G. Oliver, *Monasticon Diocesis Exoniensis* (1846), p. 95.

3 *Cornwall in the Thirteenth Century* (1998), p. 163.

4 Kempthorne (*c.*1934), pp. 35, 36. It is headed '*Computus Iohannis Penhale procuratoris Rectorie ibidem a festo S. Michaelis anno regni Henrici Quarti duodecimo usque idem festum extume proxime sequens anno Domini Regis [xiij]*' (Account of John Penhale, steward of the rector of [Sheviock] from the feast of St Michael in the 12th year of the reign of Henry IV until the same festival at the end of the next year following, the [13th] year of the reign of our Lord King.).

5 Kempthorne (*c.*1934), p. 36. See also for Penhale's account for the glebe land, Chapter 10, *Sheviock Churchtown*.

6 Sir Alexander was executed by order of Parliament in December 1644 for an intention (which he denied) to surrender St Nicholas (or Drake) Island outside Plymouth to the King. It was for this reason that Sir John Carew inherited the baronetcy in his minority.

7 The reference number is E178/6177. There should also be another document relating to the case, ref. No. E134/25 Chas 2/Trin 3, but this was missing at the time of writing.

8 The manorial rolls are in the CRO: WH 5074.

9 The house at Liscawn was one of the largest in the parish, with five hearths (Cornwall hearth tax roll 1664). The roll has been transcribed and published by T. L. Stoate, from the original at TNA). Philip Blake's house also had five hearths (ibid.).

10 In 1636, the conventionary tenants were the rector, Gregory Arundell, Robert Williams and George Grilles.

11 CM/B/97 & 98.

12 See the Cornwall hearth tax roll.

13 C.S. Gilbert, *Historical Survey of the County of* Cornwall, Vol. II (1820), p. 339; Lake, Vol. III (1870), pp. 35, 37. The arms of Dandy, shown on William's tomb in Lanreath church, are the same as those of Dawney, except that cinquefoils have been substituted for annulets on the bend cotised. A William 'Dawnay' was rector of Lanreath before 1307.

14 Hannibal was born in Lanreath in 1622 and died there in 1694: information from family tree in Richard G. Grylls, *Grylls and Grills: The History of a Cornish Clan* (1999), Vol. II, p. 144.

15 Abraham Chubb is shown as living in a house with one hearth in the Hearth Tax Roll of 1664.

16 In 1544, Thomas Grylles, perhaps the grandfather of the witness, paid 8s. in Henry VIII's assessment. This was the fourth highest band in the parish, the highest being 15s.
17 *Grylls and Grills*, Vol. II (1999), p. 124.
18 A John Blake was shown living in a house with one hearth in the 1664 Hearth Tax Roll.
19 In 1695, John Dodridge, probably the son of the witness, paid the first instalment of a 'fyne' or premium of £550 for a lease of 'Sconner in Sheviock', which is next to Trewin.
20 A William Dewstowe is shown as living in a house with one hearth in the 1664 Hearth Tax Roll.
21 See E. J. Evans, *The Contentious Tithe: The Tithe Problem and English Agriculture 1750-1850* (1976).
22 Philip Blake, Antony's father, had purchased a tenement in St John from William Upton *c.*1649.
23 See further Chapter 24, *Fruit and Orchards*.
24 The existence of apple orchards is implied in this passage: 'Not long sithence, there came a flocke of Birds into Cornwall, about Harvest season, in bignesse not much exceeding a Sparrow, which made a foule spoyle of the Apples'. Richard Carew, *Survey of Cornwall* (1602), p. 25v.
25 A claim made in his manuscript book in the Antony archives: CZ/EE/32.
26 Dodridge lived at Trewin but he also had a small orchard situated in what are now the grounds of Trethill House.
27 Gregory Arundell had become rector of Ladock in 1613, when the living was in the gift of his kinsman, Sir John Arundell of Trerice. Gregory continued to hold this living in plurality when he became rector of Sheviock in 1622. He could thus afford to be 'negligent' in the collection of his tithes.
28 E. J. Evans, *The Contentious Tithe: The Tithe Problem and English Agriculture 1750-1850* (1976), p. 44.
29 Evans (1976), p. 30.
30 Evans (1976), p. 125.
31 Evans (1976), pp. 163-6.

Chapter 34, *Crafthole Methodist Chapel*

1 CD/AJ/44.
2 CM/A/73; CM/A/57.
3 CM/A/68. In 1818, the Mullis children, John and Elizabeth, surrendered their interests in the leases of the two tenements in Antony to Melchisedec Rogers: CM/A/71.
4 CM/A/72.
5 See Chapter 32, *Church Music in Sheviock*. For the site of her house, see the map in Chapter 13.
6 The dissenting groups included the Wesleyan Methodist Association (1843), which joined with other reforming groups as the United Methodist Free Churches in 1857, the Bible Christians, founded by William Bryant (later O'Bryan) in 1815, the Primitive Methodists, which came to Cornwall in 1825, and the Methodist New Connexion, which came to Cornwall in 1834. In 1907, all these groups, except the Primitive Methodists, united to form United Methodism. United Methodism joined with Primitive Methodism and the original Wesleyan Methodism to form the Methodist Church in 1932.
7 William Moon had taught singing in Sheviock parish church from 1790 to 1794. Thomas Moon, a music seller, was renting a house and garden in Portwrinkle in 1877: CD/AJ/57A & B.
8 The Sone family had lived in Crafthole for many generations. According to a Parliamentary Survey, in 1649 a Phillipp Sone occupied in Crafthole 'one tenement in two burgages of land by the yearly rent of one shilling six pence and for a relief': TNA: E317 Corn 10. For a copy made in 1798, see CM/A/75.
9 The school, now called the Sunday Club, still meets in the schoolroom under the 1867 chapel on Sunday evenings.
10 Richard Parsons of Antony may have been the son of Lewis Parsons, miller at Wacker: see CD/AJ/16A&B.
11 TNA: C54/15797.
12 Nicholas Roseveare, a relative of Samuel, was farming at Tredrossel.

Chapter 35, *The Norman Conquest to the Reign of Charles I*

1 But on his death in 1082, a Norman, Abbot Geoffrey (1082-8), replaced him.
2 See H.P.R. Finberg, *Tavistock Abbey* (1951), pp. 8, 9.

3 See generally on the Norman knights of the Abbey, H.P.R Finberg's *Tavistock Abbey* (1951), pp. 8 *et seq.* Under the classical system of knight service (1066-1166), a knight was bound to serve forty days and never outside the kingdom.
4 See H.P.R. Finberg, *Tavistock Abbey* (1951), p. 9.
5 A lord such as Erbenald, who was obliged to provide more than one knight, could either keep the necessary number of knights in his own household, or settle them on pieces of land, which they would thus hold as a knight's fee from the grantor: see T.F.T. Plucknett, *A Concise History of the Common Law*, (5th edn, 1956), pp. 531, 532.
6 The licence was issued on 2 February 1397: see Lake's *Parochial History*, Vol IV (1872), p. 110. Although Polsue says that it was licensed to the Dawneys, this cannot be so. The Cornish male line had come to an end in 1346, when their inheritance passed to the Courtenays.
7 The holding in question was probably coterminous with the present parish of Rame, consisting of about 1,250 acres. See also Kempthorne (*c.*1934), p. 11.
8 Cornwall Archaeological Unit, Truro.
9 J. Whetter, *Cornwall in the Thirteenth Century. A Study in Social and Economic History* (1998), p. 92.
10 See N. Denholm-Young, *Richard of Cornwall* (1947), p. 164.
11 See M. Kowaleski, *The Haveners' Accounts of the Earldom and Duchy of Cornwall 1287-1356* (2001), p. 307.
12 See Kempthorne (*c.*1934), pp. 12, 13.
13 The last assembly of the traditional feudal host was in 1385 in the reign of Richard II.
14 See Kempthorne (*c.*1934), pp. 16, 17. The list is in the National Archives in Kew.
15 Kempthorne suggests that they gave their name to Pool Farm.
16 Kempthorne (*c.*1934), writes at p. 17, 'The name Casset, spelt Casslake in the 15th century, suggests Carslake [i.e. Kerslake].' The Christian name, Baldewin, is an anglicisation of the Norman-French, Baudwin.
17 Perhaps the son of Roger Pole.
18 According to Kempthorne (*c.*1934), at p. 17, 'Tusket must be a form of Truscot, a name found in the early registers.'
19 Kempthorne (*c.*1934), at p. 17, says, 'Roger Skaner, we cannot doubt, came from Sconner Farm'.
20 Perhaps the same as the later Harry.
21 Perhaps the same as the later Toke. There is a Toke's Park at Tredrossel. In Cornish, *tiek* means a farmer.
22 See A. L. Rowse, *Tudor Cornwall* (1941), p. 226.
23 See T.L.Stoate, *Cornwall Subsidies in the Reign of Henry VIII 1524 & 1543 & the Benevolence of 1545* (1985).
24 No doubt Robert Smith from Liscawn.
25 i.e., full armour.
26 A brigandine was a piece of body armour composed of iron plates sewed upon, and covered with, canvas, linen or leather: see H.L. Douch (ed.), *The Cornwall Muster Roll for 1569* (1984).
27 See T.L. Stoate, *Cornwall Subsidies in the Reign of Henry VIII 1524 & 1543 & the Benevolence of 1545* (1985).
28 See generally on this subject: Lindsay Boynton, *The Elizabethan Militia 1558-1638* (pb. ed. 1971).
29 These were the Assize of Arms 1181 and the Statute of Winchester 1285.
30 See H.L.Douch (ed.), *The Cornwall Muster Roll for 1569* (1984), quoting Terence Wise, *Medieval Warfare* (1976).
31 See H.L.Douch (ed.), *The Cornwall Muster Roll for 1569* (1984).
32 See A.L. Rowse, *Tudor Cornwall* (1941), pp. 387-96.
33 Quoted in A. L. Rowse (1941), p. 393. Following the 1982 excavation, the Cornwall Archaeological Unit reported that the pottery sherds unearthed at Beacon Hill 'are probably associated with the use of the barrow as a beacon from at least 1564'.
34 L. Boynton, *The Elizabethan Militia 1558-1638* (London, 1967; pb. ed., 1971), p. 133.
35 L. Boynton (1971), p. 134.
36 John Bruce MP , *Report on the Arrangements which were Made for the Internal Defence of these Kingdoms when Spain by its Armada Projected the Invasion and Conquest of England etc.* (London 1798).
37 Quoted in A. L. Rowse, *Tudor Cornwall* (1941), p. 393.

38 John Bruce's *Report* (1798), p. 24.
39 'A plott of all the coast of Cornwall and Devonshire, as they were to be fortyfied in 1588, against the landing of an enemy'. BL Cotton MS. Augustus l.i.6.
40 Lord Howard of Effingham, Commander of the English fleet.
41 A.L. Rowse (1941), p. 397. Reproduced with permission.
42 The Armada was composed of ships from Andalusia, Barcelona, the Bay of Biscay, Castile, and Guipuzcoa in Spain; Genoa, Tuscany, Naples, and Venice in Italy; and Sicily and Portugal (recently conquered by Spain).
43 A.L. Rowse (1941), *Tudor Cornwall*, p. 397. Reproduced with permission.
44 i.e. closest.
45 *Survey* (1602), p. 84v.
46 *Survey* (1602), p. 99r.
47 See further as this ship, Chapter 16, *The* Dayestarr *and her Crew.*
48 Anne Duffin, *Faction and Faith: Politics and Religion of the Cornish Gentry before the Civil War* (1996), pp. 127, 128.
49 C.K.C.Andrew, 'Grievances from St Cleer 1628-9': DCNQ, Vol. XIX (1937), p. 160.
50 Giles Milton, *White Gold* (2004), p. 11.
51 Anne Duffin, *Faction and Faith: Politics and Religion of the Cornish Gentry before the Civil War* (1996), p. 134.

Chapter 36, *The Civil War to the Reign of Queen Victoria*

1 For John Hunkyn, see M. Coate, *Cornwall in the Great Civil War and Interregnum 1642-1660* (1933; 2nd edn, 1963), p. 370.
2 For Walter Langdon, see Coate (2nd edn, 1963), pp. 31, 216, 356, 371.
3 For the pre-war court rolls, see CM/B/77-87. See also A. Duffin, *Faction and Faith: Politics and Religion of the Cornish Gentry before the Civil War* (1996).
4 See A. Duffin (1996), p. 202.
5 See further Chapter 15, *The Landing Place and Quay at Portwrinkle.*
6 *Bellum Civile: Hopton's Narrative of his Campaign in the West (1642-1644)* (Ed. C.E.H.Chadwyck Healey, 1902), p. 20. 'Able men' meant the fit men of military age.
7 Ibid.
8 *Bellum Civile*, p. 21. 'Very well affected' meant very loyal to the king. Sir John Grylls's Cornish motto was *Rag y mattern ha y pobel* (for our king and our people). His Latin motto, *Vires agminis unus habet* (One man has the strength of a column), may be a reference to the posse that he recruited.
9 *Bellum Civile*, p. 22.
10 Ibid.
11 *Bellum Civile*, p. 23.
12 Ibid. A cannon ball embedded in the floor of a cellar at Trethill House may be a relict of these Civil War skirmishes. Sir Alexander Carew was later appointed Governor of the fort on St Nicholas Island (Drake Island), which defended the seaward approaches to Plymouth. In August 1644, when the Royalists' fortunes were riding high, Carew was accused of plotting to betray the fort to the Royalists, but he was discovered, sent to the Tower of London and executed in December of that year. After the Restoration in 1660, his brother, John, was executed as a regicide.
13 *Bellum Civile*, pp. 23, 24.
14 *Bellum Civile*, p. 24.
15 The site of the battle is now thought to have been one mile to the north-east of Braddock Church, near to Middle Taphouse: see R. Wilton, 'Some Notes on the Battle of Braddock Down' in DCNQ, Vol. XXXV, Pt. VII (Spring 1985), pp. 246-53. Wilton's conclusions have been accepted by the Ordnance Survey (Pathfinder 1347. SX 06/16) and by English Heritage, whose views have been published on the Internet.
16 Sir John Grylls had been knighted by the king at Liskeard on 3 August 1644. He and his son, Charles, joined one of the regular Royalist regiments after the disbanding of the Posse.
17 See M Coate, *Cornwall in the Great Civil War and Interregnum 1642-1660* (1933; 2nd edn, 1963), p. 188.

18 See 'A note of ye Arrears to 1656': CM/B/98.

19 For a useful summary of the Dutch Wars, see R. Latham, *The Diary of Samuel Pepys*, Vol. X, Companion (1983), p. 110.

20 Quoted in G. and F.L. Harris, *The Making of a Cornish Town, Torpoint and Neighbourhood through Two Hundred Years* (1976), at p. 34. The original is at Wesley Cottage, Trewint, Altarnun.

21 About 1763, John Couch, a poor old man 'employed in hoisting the signals', was murdered in Maker tower by one Maunder, a labourer, in order to steal his silver watch and buckles. Maunder was convicted and executed: see *The Cornwall Register* (1847).

22 Semaphore was developed in France in 1794 by Claude Chappe. It was quickly taken up by the British Admiralty. The development of radio telegraphy by Marconi *c.*1900, made the semaphore stations redundant. In 1906, the Beacon Hill mound was topped with a marker cross and used as a landmark for shipping. The post was reduced to a stump by 1934: information from the Cornwall Archaeological Unit.

23 Anthony Pike, a local farmer.

24 Erasmus Roberts of Trevol in Antony (d.1816). His brother, the Revd Brian Roberts, was married to Ann Wallis, who had inherited the Trethill estate in 1795.

25 John Jeffery (not Jeffries) and William Lyne were members respectively of the Antony and Sheviock parish vestries. Samuel Lyne (1772-1863), who farmed at Liscawn until he retired to Crafthole, was perhaps William's son.

26 Quoted in G. and F.L. Harris, *The Making of a Cornish Town, Torpoint and Neighbourhood through Two Hundred Years* (1976), p. 72.

27 Kempthorne (*c.*1934), p. 55. See also Chapter 32, *Church Music in Sheviock.*

28 The general in charge, Sir Hugh (later Viscount) Gough (1779-1869), believed in direct frontal assaults, and sustained heavy losses as a result. The British and their native infantry sustained more than 2,300 casualties. In the next and final battle of the campaign, Gujrat (February 1849), the British were victorious and the Punjab was annexed to British India, thus completing the conquest of the whole of the sub-continent. Gough's tactics, which cost so many casualties, were criticised and he was later replaced as commander-in-chief in India by Sir Charles Napier. See L. James, *Raj: The Making and Unmaking of British India* (1997), p. 117.

Chapter 37, *The Parish in the Two World Wars*

1 The 'precautionary telegram' was the warning telegram authorised by the Prime Minister, Herbert Asquith, to be sent by the War Office and the Admiralty as the arranged signal to initiate a 'precautionary period' before hostilities with Germany and Austro-Hungary actually commenced at 11 p.m. on 4 August 1914.

2 Information provided by the late Bert Pengelly.

3 For a picture of the battalion disembarking from the Torpoint ferry, see p.and F. Manning, *Torpoint* (Archive Photographs series, Stroud), 1997, p. 15.

4 Alfred Callaghan, a Chief Petty Officer in the Royal Naval Division, was killed at Gallipoli. He was the husband of Ethel and brother of Eddy, the golf professional at the Whitsand Bay Golf Club. Joseph Giddy RN, a Petty Officer Stoker on HMS *Cassandra,* died in December 1918. Reginald George Ough RN, a Leading Stoker, went down with his ship, HMS *Defence* in May 1916. He was the son of Harry and Annie Ough. C.H. Ward RN, a Leading Seaman on HMS *Laverock*, was killed in August 1918. He is buried in the churchyard at Sheviock. Harry Davey was killed at the battle of the Somme in March 1918. He was serving with the Duke of Cornwall's Light Infantry (DCLI). Charles Hoskin, a gunner in the Royal Garrison Artillery, was killed in France in 1918. Charles Pearn of the DCLI was killed in the Middle East in 1917 and is buried in Jerusalem.

5 The First World War also left its mark on Sheviock in the shape of a number of army huts, which were removed from Tregantle after the war and re-erected in Sheviock. One became an extension to the Andrews' cottage next to the chapel in Crafthole. William Andrew bought the hut in 1922 for £300 and erected it himself. It was only removed in 2001-2. Another army hut became the recreation hall in Polbathic. Three huts were erected and inhabited in Sheviock churchtown: the Retreat, Ednaville, and a

dwelling near the church (1 the Orchard) inhabited by the Lawson family. All three have now disappeared.

6 Information from Valerie Milford.

7 Information from Fred Paul.

8 Letter passed to the author by his son, Ian Whittaker.

9 See Phyllis Rowe and Ivan Rabey, *When Bombs Fell: the Air Raids on Cornwall During the Second World War* (1987).

10 The field was farmed by Arnold Hoskin as part of Crafthole Farm. He called it 'Jorris Park', but on the 1840 Tithe Map and on Antony Estate maps it is called 'Tory's Park'. The correct name is 'Jory's Park'.

11 Named after Lady Cynthia Carew Pole, née Burns (d.1977), first wife of Sir John Carew Pole (1902-93).

12 See further Chapter 13, *Houses, Shops and Farms in Crafthole.*

13 John's mother was the sister of Mrs Crispin.

14 In a letter to the author.

15 Harold was Albert Bersey's brother.

16 Information given to the author by John Biles.

17 The golf professional. He was the senior local Air Raid Precautions (ARP) warden and lived at the Cottage, Crafthole.

18 Daughter of Mr and Mrs Hearn, who was then living at the *New Inn* with her husband, Wilfred Lee.

19 Vera Leather, Terry's six-year-old sister.

20 Mrs Hylda Hearn.

21 For 17 August 1940, the day following the raid.

22 Information passed to the author by John Kentisbeer.

23 Information from Hal Whittaker.

24 For the proceedings of the committee, see Appendix 3.

25 Now Mrs Milford.

26 As to Sheviock's Armada beacon, see Chapter 35, *The Norman Conquest to the Reign of Charles I.*

27 Including Pauline Davey's grandfather.

28 See Chapter 25, *Farming after 1800.*

29 See Jill Thomas, *Some Aspects of the History of the Town of St Germans from 1850* (1988). The name DUKW comes from the terminology used for military vehicles in the Second World War; the *D* indicates a vehicle designed in 1942, the *U* means 'utility (amphibious)', the *K* indicates all-wheel drive and the *W* indicates two powered rear axles: *Wikipedia.*

30 See further 'Sheviock Parish Recreation Club' in Chapter 43, *Leisure, Sport and Tourism.* The late Mrs Theodora Colwill often played the piano for these dances. Black and white troops attended on alternate Saturdays.

31 See Crispin Gill, *Plymouth: A New History* (single volume edition, 1993), p. 262.

32 For example, Margaret Foster, aged eight in 1940, was placed with Richard and Gladys Pryn at No. 1 Kowloon, and her brother, Ernest, aged ten, resided with Harold and Beatrice Dawe and Tom and Phyllis Ough next door at No. 2. Irene Marsh, aged ten, and her sister Jean, aged six, lived at the Cottage, Crafthole, with Eddy Callaghan and his wife, Frances (Doll), but their brother, Donald, aged seven, boarded with the Worthingtons and their three children at 1 Council Cottages in West Lane. Mrs Ethel Bridle and her two youngest children, Jean, aged six, and Brenda, aged two, boarded with Mrs Gregory at 1 Coastguards Cottages, Portwrinkle, but another daughter, Evelyn, aged nine, lived with Nicholas and Winifred Dawe at 1 the Terrace, Portwrinkle. Another child, Sylvia, aged eight, was staying with John and Kathleen Triscott at Coombe Villa, and yet another, Audrey, lived with John and Jessie Rowe at Riversdale in Portwrinkle.

33 For example, Edward Whiting, aged seven, and his sister Beryl, aged five, both lived with the Andrew family at the Bungalow, Crafthole, together with another evacuee, Sydney Terry, aged nine. Doreen Payne, aged ten, and her brother Peter, aged seven, both lived together with Harry and Hilda Lawson at 1 the Orchard. Harry Gawan, aged eight, and his sister, Ellen, aged nine, lived with the Berseys at Sheviock Barton, along with two other evacuees, Fred and Jean Brown. Hilda Waller, aged eight in 1940, and her sister, Doreen, aged six, also lived together with farmer Hevan Higman and his wife, Mabel, at Trewrickle Farm.

34 For Terry's experiences on Lantic farm, run by Mr and Mrs Herbert Bean, see Chapter 25, *Farming after 1800*. For his adventures going fishing, see Chapter 17, *The Fishing Industry at Portwrinkle*. For his schooldays, see Chapter 38, *The School in Sheviock and other Local Schools*.

35 The old Recreation Club is now Coombe Barn Cottage. The billeting officer was Miss Laura Hooper, who lived at Cobblestones in Crafthole.

36 Miss Hearn became Mrs Lowton. Mrs Lee recollects, 'On the appointed day of arrival my sister, Loveday, and I went to the village hall to await the arrival of the buses from St Germans Railway Station. It was a heart-rending sight to see all these little children coming off the buses with their labels attached to their coats, their gas-masks around their shoulders and their little packages of belongings. Our mother had told us to bring two little boys. We found one, who was holding tight to his little sister. He said, "My mother told me to stay with Vera. We must keep together." Little did we know that they would be with us for seven years.'

37 Now the *Finnygook Inn*.

38 A Devon recipe, using the same filling as for a Cornish pasty, but made in a flat dish.

39 The original name of Sheviock, *siviek*, is Cornish for strawberry place.

40 She was the Liberty ship, *James Eagan Layne*, torpedoed near the Eddystone on 2 March 1945. She had been built in New Orleans in just 40 days. Today the wreck is a favourite haunt of divers.

41 The roll of honour is set out in Appendix 4.

42 Those who died were Leslie Baker of Sydenham House, Desmond Bean of Fernleigh, Donald Bean of Portwrinkle, Anthony Garland of Portwrinkle, William Hitt of the US Army, who had married Susan Channings, and George Paul, of 3 the Terrace, Sheviock churchtown.

Chapter 38, *The School in Sheviock and other Local Schools*

1 See generally on medieval education, N. Orme, *Education in the West of England 1066-1548* (1976), from which, with permission, parts of this section are drawn.

2 *Education in the West of England 1066-1548* (1976).

3 *Medieval Schools* (2006), p. 349.

4 DCNQ, Vol. XIX (1937), p. 82.

5 He also founded the Gilbertine Order of nuns, and was canonised in 1202.

6 John Hooker was the author of a description of Devon and Cornwall called *Synopsis Corographicall*: British Museum, MS Harley 5827, fol. 45d. He is quoted in F. Rose-Troup, *The Western Rebellion of 1549* (1913), p. 108.

7 The bishop of Exeter at the time was William Cotton.

8 See Henderson MS, *Materials for a Parochial History of East Cornwall* (begun 1924, RIC, Truro).

9 Gregory and Emanuel went to Oxford to study, and Gregory in due course became rector of Sheviock. George and Alexander stayed and farmed in Sheviock.

10 See N. Orme, *Education in the West of England 1066-1548* (1976), pp. 103, 106.

11 Ibid., p. 169.

12 See *Survey of Cornwall* (1602), p. 119v. Dame Thomasine's school survived the suppression of chantries in 1548, but it was relocated to Launceston, where it merged with the local grammar school.

13 CRO: N 223/2.

14 CM/B/18.

15 See S. and D. Lysons, *Magna Britannia*, Vol. III, Cornwall (1814), p. 117.

16 On leaving the Revd Eare's school in July 1695, Sir Richard presented him with a silver tankard, costing £6 10s.: CA/HI/2.

17 CA/HI/3. The cost of his schooling and board and lodging for himself and his manservant came to £6 5s. per quarter.

18 Lake, Vol. III (1870), p. 157.

19 Cornwall Federation of Women's Institutes, *The Cornwall Village Book*, new ed. (2000), p. 11.

20 For the school at Antony, see G. and F. L. Harris, *The Making of a Cornish Town; Torpoint and Neighbourhood through Two Hundred Years* (1976), p. 102.

21 Thomas Shaw, *A History of Cornish Methodism* (1967).
22 CRO: DDP 208/2/15.
23 A fashion for antiquarian spellings led to an extra 'e' being added to Sheviock at this time.
24 The Minute Books of the Foundation Managers are preserved at the County Record Office, Truro CRO: SRM/Sheviock/2.
25 The council in question was the Saltash and Callington District Council, which had certain statutory responsibilities for education in south-east Cornwall.
26 Kelly's Directory 1910.
27 CRO: CC/ED/6/91.
28 Information from Tom Bersey.
29 See further, Chapter 37, *The Parish in the Two World Wars*.
30 As a result of the influx of evacuees, the school doubled in size. An additional teacher, also an evacuee, was added to the staff. Fred Paul, then a pupil at the school, writes of the evacuees: 'They were a great bunch of kids. Before they arrived there were only a handful of children of school age in Sheviock village. We soon all played games together. I remember in our gang Harry Gowan, who lived at Barton Farm, Peter Payne, who lived with Mr and Mrs Lawson, and Norman Foster, who was at Haye Farm. The one word we locals had never heard of before was "twerp" – all the Cockney kids called each other this!'
31 This was run by Mrs Kate Carpenter from her house at 4 the Terrace, Sheviock village.
32 This was Tredrossel, the largest cider-making farm in the parish. It is shown on the 1840 tithe map as having eight orchards, though there were probably fewer in 1940.
33 Information from Hal Whitaker. Dorothy married John Hoskin at the end of the war.

Chapter 39, *Trades and Crafts*

1 CD/AH/4.
2 TNA: E178/6177.
3 CA/HI/8.
4 TNA: SC/2/158/39, 40. See further Chapter 12, *Courts and Officials of the Borough of Crafthole*.
5 CD/AG/55.
6 J. Manco, *The History of Trewin House, Sheviock, Cornwall* (2008).
7 CRO: AD587/9/3.
8 CD/AJ/16A&B.
9 CD/AH/15.
10 CD/AH/18.
11 CD/AH/26.
12 CD/AH/39A&B and CD/AH/40A &B.
13 CD/AH/59. For the location of the premises, see 'The Blacksmiths' Cottages and Shops' in Chapter 13, *Houses, Shops and Farms in Crafthole*.
14 CRO: P208/21/1.
15 Catherine Davey was rated five pence halfpenny for a tenement in Sheviock in 1754.
16 For location, see note 13 above.
17 Harrison, Harrod & Co. *Postal Directory* (1862).
18 CD/AH/65 & 65C.
19 William Bickford Jnr. was rated for Sconner Farm in 1809-10 and Richard Bickford was rated for it in 1820-1.
20 CRO: EM 20/4. For the location of these premises, see 'The Blacksmiths' Cottages and Shops' in Chapter 13, *Houses, Shops and Farms in Crafthole*.
21 CD/AH/19A and B.
22 See also for Blake, Chapter 33, *Tithes*.
23 CD/AH/59.
24 CD/AH/43.
25 See further Chapter 13, *Houses, Shops and Farms in Crafthole*.

26 CD/AH/10.
27 CD/AH/28A.
28 CD/AH/37.
29 CD/AH/20.
30 He had vacated the premises by 1764, when they were let to Thomas Bews: CD/AI/32. See further Appendix 1, *Families*. Dorcas Prin was one of the signatories of 'an account of money laid out at interest for the use of the poor of the parish of Sheviock' in about 1750. The account has been copied into the churchwardens' account book.
31 Censuses; Harrison, Harrod & Co., *Postal Directory* (1862).
32 In 1877, Thomas Moon of Liskeard, 'music seller', took a 30-year lease of a dwelling house and garden in Portwrinkle at an annual rental of £1 10s.: CD/AJ/57A &B.
33 A map of Crafthole made in 1825 shows a small house and garden called 'Warrens', then belonging to Lord Clinton, on the road to Polscoe. This may have been the house occupied by William Warren in 1767.
34 Charles Peake was another carrier mentioned in 1821-2 and 1825-6 in connection with the carriage of lathes, rafters and nails.
35 See Chapter 17, *The Fishing Industry at Portwrinkle.*
36 CD/AH/1.
37 CD/AH/11A.
38 CD/AH/35A.
39 CD/AH/2A&B.
40 CD/AH/35.
41 CD/AJ/35B.
42 CD/AG/28.
43 See 'Receipts from Fishing Operations' in Chapter 7, *Manorial Revenues.*
44 CD/AG/26.
45 CD/AF/27.
46 CD/AJ/20.
47 CD/AJ/21.
48 Kempthorne (*c.*1934), p. 67; BL: Sloan MS xxxiii, 86.
49 CD/AH/21.
50 CD/AH/30.
51 CD/AI/7.
52 CD/AI/11D&E.
53 H. Fox, *The Evolution of the Fishing Village: Landscape and Society along the South Devon Coast, 1086-1550* (2001), p. 33.
54 See K. Isham, *Lime Kilns and Limeburners in Cornwall: an Introduction* (2000).
55 Richard Polgreen was the registrar of St Germans parish in 1862. This may have been his house.
56 CM/B/98.
57 CD/AF/42.
58 Henry Short of Sheviock donated £2 to parish funds 'for the use of the poor' on 13 May 1738. See the churchwardens' accounts.
59 CM/B/98.
60 CD/AI/45-49.
61 CD/AH/30.
62 CD/AH/41.
63 After this big expenditure, only small sums were paid each year to the new mason, John Brown, for such work as 'repairing wall' and 'slating church' between 1824 and 1827.
64 H24/161.
65 See *Kelly's Post Office Directory 1856.*
66 CD/AE/11.
67 CD/AJ/8.

68 CD/AH/25.
69 CD/AH/35A.
70 See CD/AH/1 &2 (1603) and CM/B/86 (1640).
71 See further Chapter 19, *Smuggling, Coastguard and Wrecks.*
72 CD/AJ/17A &B.
73 CM/F2/158.
74 CRO: EM 20/4.
75 A John Landry is shown in a Parliamentary Survey of West Antony made in 1649 to have lived at Combe Park in that manor. The John Landry who married Ann Clinnick was baptised at St Cleer, but his ancestors seem to have lived at St Neot for many generations.
76 According to family tradition, Richard Landrey (1815-81) would take the bee-skeps out of their recesses in the wall and put them into the garden along the west side of the house (now part of the graveyard). When Richard died, his niece, Polly Weihtner (1841-1925) put crepe on his skeps. Information from T.G.Gregory-Smith.
77 Arthur Peter was rated 2s. 3d. for part of Poole and 7d. for Finnegook in 1754.
78 Information from David Dunn.
79 See further Chapter 38, *The School in Sheviock.*
80 See K. Isham, *Lime Kilns and Limeburners in Cornwall: an Introduction* (2000), pp. 44, 46.
81 CD/AI/50,51A.
82 CD/AI/52A&B.
83 CD/AI/53A&B.
84 CD/AI/54A&B.
85 CD/AG/45.
86 CD/AG/47.
87 CD/AH/56.
88 See John Smedley, 'A History of the Cornish Wool Industry and its People', *JRIC* (1994), pp. 96-7.
89 CD/AH/4. See also 'Bonne's Parks' in Chapter 8, *Holdings on Sheviock Manor.*
90 CD/AH/4.
91 CA/HI/2.
92 CM/B/98 and CM/F2/158.
93 CD/AH/29.
94 See the survey of 1775 (CM/B/101) which shows William Bray as the tenant of the Net Park in Portwrinkle 'by virtue of his office being Reeve of the Manor'.

Chapter 40, *Markets, Highways and Turnpikes*

1 The landing place was changed to the present one at Cremyll about 1730 by order of the Earl of Mount Edgcumbe: C.W.Bracken, *A History of Plymouth and her Neighbours* (1931), p. 192.
2 *The Illustrated Journeys of Celia Fiennes, 1685-c.1712*, ed. C. Morris (Stroud: Alan Sutton, 1995).
3 Domesday Book, f. 120v.
4 Daniel Defoe, *A Tour thro' the Whole Island of Great Britain* (1724-7), Vol. I, Letter III: 'From London to Land's End'.
5 Carew, *Survey*, p. 53v.
6 Recollections given to the author.
7 J. Whetter, *Cornwall in the 17th Century. An Economic Survey of Kernow* (1974), p. 124. See also Daniel Defoe, *A Tour thro' the Whole Island of Great Britain* (1724-7), Vol. I, Letter III: 'From London to Land's End'.
8 Lake, Vol. III (1870), p. 156.
9 N. Orme, *Cornish Wills 1342-1540* (2007), p. 245.
10 Carew, *Survey*, p. 53v.
11 Cal. Pat. Rolls 8 Ed. II; Kempthorne (*c.*1934), pp. 11, 24.
12 Lake. Vol. IV (1872), p. 148.
13 Lake, Vol II (1868), p. 206. The Pope's given name was Nicholas Breakspear.

14 In 1390, an Act of Parliament provided that pilgrims might only sail from Dover or Plymouth: C.W.Bracken, *A History of Plymouth and her Neighbours* (1931), p. 39. The intention may have been to initiate a convoy system for the protection of the pilgrims. The legislation was later modified. Penzance ships were licensed to carry pilgrims to Compostela in 1425, 1432 and 1440: P.A.S.Pool, *The History of the Town and Borough of Penzance* (1974), p. 19.

15 Carew, *Survey* (1602), p. 53v.

16 See Chapter 16, *The* Dayestarr *and her Crew*.

17 Carew, *Survey* (1602), p. 32v.

18 TNA: SC/2/158/39.

19 A charter of King Athelstan, dated 936, removed all impositions from the bishopric of Cornwall except for 'expedition against enemies and sea-watches'. It is assumed that the Abbot of Tavistock had similar obligations in respect of his seaside parishes.

20 H.P.R. Finberg, *Tavistock Abbey* (1951), p. 209. One of his duties was to garrison Rougemont Castle at Exeter for so many days in the year.

21 'There [at Trematon] the count has a castle, and a market rendering 3s': Domesday Book, f. 122.

22 Finberg, *West-Country Historical Studies* (1969), p. 107.

23 Finberg, *Tavistock Abbey* (1951), p. 199.

24 CA/HI/8.

25 Carew, *Survey* (1602), p. 54r.

26 Carew, *Survey* (1602), p. 53v.

27 J. Whetter, *Cornwall in the 17th Century. An Economic Survey of Kernow* (1974), p. 107.

28 J. Whetter, *Cornwall in the 17th Century. An Economic Survey of Kernow* (1974), p. 109.

29 A. Jewers, *Heraldic Church Notes from Cornwall* (after 1886), p. 203.

30 CE/D/10. Quoted in G. and F. L Harris, *The Making of a Cornish Town: Torpoint and Neighbourhood through Two Hundred Years* (1976), p. 38, n.17.

31 *A Journey into Cornwall* (1799), p. 149. The 'crook' was the wooden frame to which the loads were tied.

32 The whole subject of highway administration is covered in Sidney & Beatrice Webb's textbook, *The Story of the King's Highway* (1913; reprinted 1963), from which the background for this section is derived.

33 CM/B/85. Ralph may have been a member of the family that farmed a tenement in Trewrickle called Holman's. It was one of the largest tenements in Trewrickle, consisting of some 45 acres.

34 He also paid the surveyors £1 3s. 4d. as composition for not working for the other four days that he was bound to work under the statute: CRO: P208/21/1.

35 CRO: P208/21/1.

36 As to the medieval crosses, see 'Processions' in Chapter 27, *Churchlife in the Middle Ages*. For T. Pride's map, see CP/FX/11.

37 Increased to 4d. in 1770.

38 Increased to 5d. in 1770.

39 'Neat' cattle are any cattle of the ox kind (OED).

40 10 Geo. III.

41 G. and F. L. Harris, *The Making of a Cornish Town: Torpoint and Neighbourhood through Two Hundred Years* (1976), p. 59.

42 Ibid., p. 60.

43 Ibid., p. 61.

44 Ibid., p. 156.

45 7 Geo. IV, *c.*84.

46 Quoted in Webb, *The Story of the King's Highway*, p. 138.

47 CD/AH/46.

48 CD/AH/45. There was a tenement in Trewrickle known as 'Blight's tenement' consisting of 30 acres in 1653: CM/B/97.

49 CD/AH/53.

50 CM/B/156.

51 CE/F/158.
52 CD/AG/53.
53 CE/F/10.
54 John Allen, *History of Liskeard* (1856), p. 341n; quoted in G. and F. L. Harris, *The Making of a Cornish Town: Torpoint and Neighbourhood through Two Hundred Years* (1976), p. 156.
55 See also 'The Manor Pound' in Chapter 4.
56 5 & 6 Wm. IV, *c*.50.
57 *West of England Conservative, and Plymouth, Devonport and Stonehouse Advertiser*, 17 July 1850.
58 Information given to the author.

Chapter 41, *Inns and Innkeepers*

1 Richard Carew makes it clear that by his time ale was no longer made from oats, but only from barley: *Survey*, 20r.
2 *Register of the Bishop of Exeter*, edited by F C Hingeston-Randolph (1889).
3 See J. Whetter, *Cornwall in the Thirteenth Century* (1998), p. 80.
4 George Grills was a conventionary tenant of Kerslake manor in 1636.
5 TNA: SP 16/234. The justices were Sir Richard Edgcumb, Sir Richard Buller and John Moyle of Bake.
6 See J. Whetter, *Cornwall in the Thirteenth Century* (1998), p. 90.
7 Poor taverns continued to display the sign of the bush until at least the 1600s. See *The Remains of Thomas Hearne*, pp. 105, 106 (London 1966): 'Five Taverns in Oxford in the year 1636 … the signs were the Mermayd, the Swan, the other three were only bushes' (diary for 7 December 1710).
8 See M.K. James (ed. E.M. Veale), *Studies in the Medieval Wine Trade* (1971).
9 Examples of St Germans pottery may be seen in the Royal Cornwall Museum in Truro.
10 TNA: E178/6177.
11 Former Church Houses were in fact often converted into taverns, and several such inns still survive in Devon. See further, S. and B. Webb, *English Poor Law History. Part I: The Old Poor Law*, p. 13.
12 CM/F2/158.
13 CM/B/98.
14 As to church ales, see Chapter 28, *Church Administration in the Middle Ages*.
15 *Survey*, pp. 68v–69v.
16 Information about the *Carew Arms* and the Landrey and Clinnick families supplied by T.G. Gregory-Smith.
17 CD/AE/40. In 1838, John Landry also rented Barn Cottage across the road.
18 Mill hill is in Antony parish.
19 CD/AG/57.
20 CD/AG/55.
21 The former inn was then divided into cottages, now nos. 1 and 2 Church Row. The rector's coachman occupied no. 1 and his gardener no. 2. A cobbler's shop had been attached to no. 3 as a lean-to. This was demolished and replaced by a new cottage which became no. 4. Behind was a skittle alley, still in existence, but now divided up among the occupants of the cottages. The front door of no. 2 opens into what was the main room of the inn. It contains the old large open fireplace, its arch supported by part of the wrought-iron tyre of a cart wheel.
22 TNA: E315/414 (Misc. Bks. Augmentation Office).
23 See further Chapter 42, *Mills and Millers*.
24 CRO: S129/1. A 'keeve' is defined as 'a vat for holding liquid in brewing' (OED).
25 The unusual name may be a compound of a Cornish word, *bron* (meaning a hill), and an English word, haye (meaning enclosure) – thus: *Bron[t] Hayes* – but this is mere conjecture.
26 CD/AH/39B.
27 CD/AH/40B.
28 CD/AH/38.
29 CD/AH/1.

30 CD/AH/35A&B.
31 CD/AH/35.
32 CM/B/79.
33 CM/B/94, 95.
34 CE/G/23.
35 See Chapter 19, *Smuggling, Coastguards and Wrecks.*
36 CD/AI/7.
37 *Historical Survey of the County of Cornwall*, Vol. II, p. 402.
38 CD/AH/3.
39 TNA: SC/2/158/39.
40 CD/AH/28.
41 CD/AG/44.
42 CA/HI/3.
43 CA/HI/7.
44 CD/AH/44.
45 In 1831, a descendant of Sampson Trevan, also called Sampson, was caught in a smuggling operation: see Chapter 19, *Smuggling, Coastguards and Wrecks.*
46 CD/AF/13.
47 CM/B/55.
48 CRO:EM/4.
49 CM/B/156.
50 See further Chapter 32, *Church Music in Sheviock.*
51 CD/AJ/22.
52 See further, Chapter 37, *The Parish in the Two World Wars.*
53 Information from Sir Richard Carew Pole, Bt.
54 See Lawrence Blair, *English Church Ales* (1940), p. 17: 'By the 13th century, the scotale, an entertainment given by the lord of the manor-house to his tenants and lower dependants, which their fealty bound them to attend, each with his "scot" or set contribution in hand, had become a universal custom on manorial tenures in England.'
55 CM/B/98.
56 An account has been preserved of another court dinner held at the Carew manor of Drewsteignton on 2 February 1794, when some 50 people were entertained. The provisions consumed were two pecks of wheat, one pound of butter, half a bushel of potatoes, ½d. worth of mustard, 3½d. worth of raisins, 2lbs 10oz of cheese (at 5¼d. per ounce), 36 quarts of beer, and ribs and a round of beef costing 14s. (49 lbs at 3½d. per lb). The cook was paid 5s. for cooking the dinner. The tenants sat around a fire that consumed a seam of wood. They smoked 4½d. worth of tobacco in pipes costing 1½d., and the room was illuminated by seven candles, costing ¼d. each, all of which were charged to the lord of the manor.
57 CM/B/156.
58 See further Chapter 9, *Outlying Houses and Farms.*

Chapter 42, *Mills and Millers*

1 For the licence, see CD/AE/3.
2 '*Scath* is thought to mean a particular type of boat, a large rowing boat': O.J. Padel, *A Popular Dictionary of Cornish Place-Names* (1988). A barge with sweeps would presumably fall within this category.
3 Eventually, Kerslake became a separate manor, with its own mill, manor-house and dovecote. See further 'Kerslake' in Chapter 9, *Outlying Farms and Houses.*
4 CD/AE/43b.
5 CM/F2/158.
6 CM/F2/160A.
7 CD/AE/4.

8 CA/HI/6.
9 CA/HI/2.
10 CA/HI/3.
11 CD/AF/38 and CM/F2/158.
12 CM/F2/160A.
13 CM/B/156; CM/F2/160A.
14 CD/AF/11.
15 CD/AE/8.
16 For the manorial rolls, see CRO: WH 5074.
17 CM/FX/11.
18 RIC, Truro: H.28/47.
19 CM/F2/158 and CM/B/18.
20 CD/AF/8.
21 CD/AF/10.
22 See also W. E. Minchinton and J.W. Perkins, 'Tidemills in Devon and Cornwall', Part II, *DCNQ* Vol. XXXII, pp. 1-7.
23 Margaret Parkinson, 'The Axe Estuary and its Marshes', *Rep. Trans. Devon Assoc. Advmt. Sci.* 117 (1985), p. 23.
24 See Kempthorne (*c.*1934), p. 14.
25 CE/C/18.
26 CM/F2/158 and CM/B/18.
27 CM/F2/160A.
28 See further Chapter 14, *The Quay at Porthroy and Fishing in the Lynher and Tamar Rivers.*
29 See H. Fox, *The Evolution of the Fishing Village: Landscape and Society along the South Devon Coast, 1086-1550* (2001), p. 22.
30 It is called Gilly Ball in a rental of 1663: CE/C/18.
31 The place called Mill Hill in St John's parish suggests that there were also other wind-driven mills on the Rame Peninsula in the Middle Ages.
32 A 'keeve' is defined as 'a vat for holding liquid in brewing' (OED).
33 See further Chapter 41, *Inns and Innkeepers* and 'Spiller' in Appendix 1, *Families.*
34 CE/C/18.

Chapter 43, *Leisure, Sport and Tourism*

1 Simon Usborne, *The Independent*, 16 September 2008.
2 Run by Tony and Carol Johnson.
3 *Survey of Cornwall* (1602), pp. 73v, 75v.
4 F.E. Halliday, *A History of Cornwall* (1959), p. 178.
5 *Survey of Cornwall* (1602), p. 73v-74r.
6 *Survey* (1602), p. 62v and 63r. A 'Butte length' is the length of the shooting butts for the practice of archery. The distance was probably 60 to 100 yards. The miller perched on top of the load may have been the miller from the manorial mill at Polscoe.
7 Nairn and Pevsner, *Buildings of England, Sussex* (1965), pp. 426, 438. The fashion for bathing in the sea began with Dr. Russell's *Dissertation concerning the Use of Sea Water in Diseases of the Glands.* This came out in Latin in 1750 and in English in 1753.
8 See Chapter 18, *The Village of Portwrinkle.*
9 On 4 September 1788: CE/C/24.
10 CE/C/24.
11 The extract is reproduced in K. Reilly and Jo Lanyon, *A Pictorial View of the East Cornwall Parish of St Germans* (1985), though without giving the source or its date. The hut in its heyday is illustrated on pp. 68 and 69 of their book.
12 The author is grateful to David and Rosalie Dunn for allowing him to see these particulars.

13 See generally on the Elmhurst's, Michael Young, *The Elmhurst's of Dartington: The Creation of an Utopian Community*(1982); and on Dartington Hall in its early days, Victor Bonham-Carter, *Dartington Hall: The History of an Experiment* (1958).
14 Letter dated 24 February from W.J.Pierre Hunt, chartered architect of Warren House, Polperro, to Leonard Elmhirst. The letter is in the Dartington Hall trust Archive.
15 Leonard wrote a number of times to the Press drawing attention to oil spillages and garbage dumped by the Royal Navy.
16 Quoted with permission of the Trustees, Dartington Hall Trust Archive.
17 Information supplied by Ian Whittaker.
18 The Crafthole mason, William Andrew, helped with the rebuilding and was responsible for the figures on top of the hotel.
19 For a picture of it on its old site, see p.and F. Manning, *Torpoint* (Archive Photographs series, Stroud, 1997), p. 34. For other inns in Sheviock, see Chapter 41, *Inns and Innkeepers*.
20 This section is based on information supplied by John Kentisbeer, who was at one time Hon. Sec. and Treasurer of the club.
21 The barn had previously been used as a workshop by Messrs. Davey and Sleep, Agricultural Machinery Makers.
22 British troops concerned with coastal defence had requisitioned the *Whitsand Bay Hotel*. The Royal Marines were encamped at Blerrick. American troops were stationed at Tregantle. They were also encamped at Bake in St Germans and manned an Anti Aircraft battery at Cross Park in Sheviock.

Appendices

1 CD/AH/20.
2 Kempthorne (*c.*1934), p. 30.
3 CE/G/19/4.
4 TNA: SC2/158/39.
5 CD/AE/12.
6 Kempthorne (*c.*1934), p. 47.
7 CD/AE/59.
8 The roll is in the CRO.
9 Kempthorne (*c.*1934), p. 65.
10 He witnessed a lease of ten yards of land in Portwrinkle to a William Odyorne on 20 July 1649: Antony archives, CD/AJ/15.
11 See A.J. Jewers, *Heraldic Church Notes from Cornwall* (after 1886), p. 26.
12 Kempthorne (*c.*1934), p. 48.
13 CM/B/96.
14 Revd G. Pole Carew's inventory of church goods, 1903.
15 CD/AH/14.
16 Kempthorne (*c.*1934), p. 68.
17 See Tithe Redemption map of 1840.
18 H. 28/46.
19 H. 28/44.
20 See Chapter 33, *Tithes*.
21 CM/F2/158.
22 See Chapter 33, *Tithes*.
23 See Whetter, *The Bodrugans* (1995), p. 98.
24 *The Survey of Cornwall* (1602), p. 62v and 63r.
25 CD/AJ/2.
26 CM/B/98 and CM/F2/158.
27 CM/B/98.
28 CD/AH/29. The premises are shown on Thomas Pride's map and survey of 1775.

29 CM/B/101.
30 CP/FX/11. The house and meadow are shown on a field map in the Antony archives.
31 See the survey of 1775 (CM/B/101).
32 For Sir Alexander Carew, see Chapter 5, *Lords of the Manor.*
33 Sir Nicholas is commemorated by a brass in the church at Haccombe.
34 See 'Thomas Carew' in Chapter 5, *Lords of the Manor.*
35 CM/B/97.
36 TNA: SC/2/158/39.
37 CM/B/97.
38 CD/AE/28.
39 CM/B/18.
40 CD/AE/30.
41 CD/AE/33.
42 CM/B/94.
43 See Thomas Pride's map (CP/FX/11) and survey (CM/B/101).
44 See Chapter 33, *Tithes.*
45 See Martin Cherry, 'The Courtenay Earls of Devon: The Formation and Disintegration of a Late Medieval Aristocratic Affinity' in *Southern History*, Vol 1 (1979), p. 72.
46 See Whetter, *The Bodrugans* (1995), p. 98. Members of the Bray family were earning their living from fishing in Sheviock in the early 1600s. For the Courtenay family, see Chapter 5, *Lords of the Manor.*
47 Kempthorne (*c.*1934), p. 33.
48 For the Courtenay family, see Chapter 5, *Lords of the Manor.*
49 CD/AE/7.
50 Catherine Davey was rated 5½d. for a tenement in Sheviock in 1754.
51 Harrison, Harrod & Co. *Postal Directory* (1862).
52 CA/HI/3.
53 See further, Chapter 43, *Leisure, Sport and Tourism.*
54 The story of the family has been told in Michael Young's *The Elmhirsts of Dartington: The Creation of an Utopian Community* (1982), and an earlier account of the Hall and the school is to be found in Victor Bonham-Carter's *Dartington Hall: The History of an Experiment* (1958). See also 'The Chalet in Portwrinkle' in Chapter 43, *Leisure, Sport and Tourism.*
55 Jean Manco, *The History of Trewin House, Sheviock, Cornwall* (2008).
56 CM/B/98.
57 George Grills was a conventionary tenant of Kerslake manor in 1636.
58 TNA: SP 16/234. The justices were Sir Richard Edgcumb, Sir Richard Buller and John Moyle of Bake.
59 CD/AE/59.
60 CM/B/98.
61 See Richard Grylls, *Grylls and Grills: the History of a Cornish Clan* (1999), Vol II, p. 127.
62 CA/HI/7.
63 Ibid. By then the cost of a barge-load of sand had risen from 10s. to 15s.
64 H.24/136.
65 Robert Sprye, possibly George's father had lived in Cutcrew in St Germans (Kneebone).
66 H. 28/44.
67 CD/AE/7.
68 CD/AE/7.
69 CD/AE/33B and 28A.
70 CM/B/80-3
71 CM/B/98.
72 CM/B/97.
73 See Kempthorne (*c.*1934), p. 70.
74 CM/B/98.

75 CM/F2/158.
76 See CD/AF/21.
77 CD/AF/21.
78 CM/B/97, 98.
79 CD/AE/43.
80 CD/AE/28.
81 CM/B/92.
82 See Kempthorne (*c.*1934), p. 70.
83 William left 40s. 'unto the childe that is nowe in the wombe of my wife'.
84 See further Chapter 16, *The* Dayestarr *and her Crew.*
85 CM/B/97.
86 CM/F2/158.
87 CA/HI/4.
88 CA/HI/4.
89 CD/AG/23.
90 CD/AH/21.
91 CM/B/98.
92 See further, Chapter 6, *Courts and Officials of the Manor.*
93 CM/B/98.
94 CD/AH/14.
95 CD/AJ/35A.
96 CD/AH/36.
97 CM/B/101.
98 Kempthorne (*c.*1934), p. 73.
99 See further 'Sheviock Barton' in Chapter 4, *The Manor of Sheviock.*
100 See further Chapter 8, *Holdings on Sheviock Manor.*
101 Kempthorne (*c.*1934), p. 63; J.L .Vivian, *The Visitations of Cornwall, comprising the Heralds' Visitations of 1530, 1573 and 1620* (1887).
102 CM/B/97.
103 CM/B/18.
104 CM/B/97.
105 CD/AJ/29.
106 See Lake, Vol. I (1867), p. 30.
107 CM/F2/158.
108 CRO: DDT 780/1 and 2.
109 CM/B/18.
110 CD/AH/56.
111 CD/AH/21.
112 CD/AH/1A.
113 CD/AH/2A.
114 CM/B/78 and 86.
115 Lake, Vol. II (1868), p. 58.
116 CD/AH/61A.
117 J. and J. A Venn, *Alumni Cantabrigienses 1752-1900* (1953).
118 CD/AE/7.
119 *History of the Parish of Sheviock*, at p. 33. A study of the Kingdon family (undated), entitled *The Kingdon Family* by F.B. Kingdon was published privately. There is a copy in the reference section of Liskeard Public Library.
120 For Walter Langdon, see Coate, (Oxford, 1933; 2 ed. Truro, 1963), pp. 31, 216, 356 and 371.
121 See Lake, Vol. III (1870), p. 268.
122 See also 'Bonne's Parks' in Chapter 8, *Holdings on Sheviock Manor.*

123 CD/AJ/3.
124 CM/B/98.
125 CD/AJ/20 and 21.
126 See A. J. Jewers, *Heraldic Church Notes from Cornwall* (after 1886), p. 26.
127 CD/AJ/20 and 21.
128 CD/AG/14.
129 See R. Carew, *Survey of Cornwall* (1602), p. 102r–v.
130 Jean Manco's *The History of Trewin House, Sheviock, Cornwall* (2008) is the source for much of the information on the Littleton family.
131 See C S Gilbert, *Historical Survey of Cornwall* (1820), Vol II, p. 401.
132 CRO: SF/35-6, SF/57.
133 A. Jewers, *Heraldic Church Notes from Cornwall* (after 1886), p. 21. There is a pedigree of Littleton up to the time of this Hugh (b.Lanlivery 1 May 1682) in J. L. Vivian's *The Visitations of Cornwall, comprising the Heralds' Visitations of 1530, 1573 and 1620* (1887).
134 There is a memorial to her in St Mary's Church, Sheviock.
135 CA/HI/8.
136 CRO: AP/L/1401. Transcript by J. Manco.
137 CRO: QS/1/6/598.
138 CD/AE/23.
139 Kempthorne (*c.*1934), p. 72.
140 CM/F2/160A.
141 Information from J. Manco.
142 J. and J. A. Venn, *Alumni Cantabrigienses 1752-1900*, part 2 (1953), p. 183.
143 See Lake, quoting Hals, Vol. I (1867), p. 303.
144 CRO: WH 5074.
145 CM/A/73.
146 CM/A/57.
147 CM/A/68.
148 CM/A/72.
149 CM/A/71.
150 I am most grateful to Ellan Odiorne Derow for her considerable help in relation to the Odiorne family.
151 See Kempthorne (*c.*1934), pp. 18, 35, 36. The roll was formerly in the muniment room of Exeter Corporation.
152 Kempthorne (*c.*1934), p. 62.
153 TNA: SC/2/158/38.
154 TNA: SC/2/158/39. See further 'Recovery of Debt' in Chapter 12, *Courts and Officials of the Borough of Crafthole.*
155 CM/B/97.
156 CM/B/98.
157 CM/B/98.
158 CD/AJ/6.
159 CD/AJ/15.
160 CM/B/98.
161 Will and inventory in the CRO.
162 Kempthorne (*c.*1934), p. 62.
163 CE/C/18.
164 CM/F2/158.
165 See further 'Lime Burners' in Chapter 39, *Trades and Crafts.*
166 CM/B/98.
167 CM/F2/158.
168 CM/F2/158.

169 The fisherman, William Pengelly, living in Portwrinkle in 1841, was probably his grandfather.
170 See Chapter 15, *The Landing Place and Quay at Portwrinkle.*
171 Will of Arthur Peters in National Archives.
172 CD/AF/25B.
173 CE/F/5.
174 Henry Short of Sheviock donated £2 to parish funds 'for the use of the poor' on 13 May 1738. See note in the Churchwardens' Book 1754-1843, CRO.
175 Letter dated 21 December 1831 in the DRO.
176 CD/AJ/8.
177 CD/AG/27.
178 CD/AI/32.
179 See *The Cornwall Register* (1847).
180 The Revd Reginald Pole's letter to the bishop, dated 26 Oct. 1837, is in the DRO, Basket D, D/7/178.
181 See further 'The Tractarian Movement and Religious Revival' in Chapter 31, *St Mary's after the Reformation.*
182 *JRIC* 1881. See further on the Beaker burial, Chapter 1, *From the Stone Age to the Roman Invasion.*
183 Oral testimony of Mrs Aldred, who knew Maisie and was a later owner of Trethill.
184 I am grateful to the Revd Dr J. E. Platt, formerly of Pembroke College, Oxford, for this information.
185 Article by C.T.Cooper in Cornwall FHS *Journal No.82,* December 1996, p. 3.
186 See Lake, Vol. I (1867), p. 2.
187 See Anne Duffin, *Faction and Faith. Politics and Religion of the Cornish Gentry before the Civil War* (1996), pp. 57,101,171.
188 A.J. Jewers, *Heraldic Church Notes from Cornwall* (after 1886), p. 203.
189 See *The Illustrated Journey of Celia Fiennes, 1685-c.1712,* ed. C. Morris (1982), at p. 197 'Exeter is a town very well built the streets are well pitch'd spacious noble streetes and a vast trade is carryd on; as Norwitch is for coapes callamanco and damaske soe this is for Serges – there is an increadible quantety of them made and sold in the town.' She describes 'the large Market house set on stone pillars which runs a great length on which they lay their packs of serges, just by it is another walke within pillars which is for the yarne.' The market house still stands.
190 A.J. Jewers, *Heraldic Church Notes from Cornwall* (after 1886), p. 203.
191 See further, Chapter 30, *Church Administration after 1534. Post-Reformation Rectors.*
192 CM/B/98.
193 CD/PP/34.
194 CD/AH/3.
195 TNA: SC/2/158/39.
196 TNA: E178/6177.
197 CD/PP/36.
198 See Chapter 12, *Courts and Officials of the Borough of Crafthole.*
199 Kempthorne (*c.*1934), p. 67.
200 See Col. Vivian's pedigree of the Smiths of Tregunnick in *The Visitations of Cornwall, comprising the Heralds' Visitations of 1530, 1573 and 1620* (1887).
201 Kempthorne (*c.*1934), p. 67; BL: Sloan MS, xxxiii, 71.
202 BL: Sloan MS, xxxiii, 75a.
203 BL: Sloan MS, xxxiii, 80.
204 See further Chapter 35, *The Norman Conquest to the Reign of Charles I.*
205 Kempthorne (*c.*1934), p. 67.
206 BL: Sloan MS xxxiii, 86.
207 CM/B/98. Ellan Odiorne Derow has traced the descent of many settlers in Maine and New Hampshire from 17th-century inhabitants of the parish of Sheviock. Settler families connected to inhabitants of the borough of Crafthole include those of Batten, Beard, Blighe, Bray, Earle, Geffery (Jeoffrey), Jenkyn (Genkin), Hancock, Harle (Hearle), Harris, Hicks, Langdon, Letheby, Lockwood, Mitchell, Naunter, Odiorne, Peperel, Peter, Rundle (Randall), Sargent, Searle, Symons, Toser, and Wallis. In addition, the

settler families of Giles, Lavers and Tinny were connected to fishing families at Portwrinkle. (Information from 'Living by the Sea: Fishing Families in Cornwall and America', presented to the London Cornish Association, Family History Day, April, 2009; forthcoming Odiorne Family Newsletter, Nov., 2009.)

208 CM/A/75.

209 Kempthorne (*c.*1934), p. 68.

210 CD/AJ/27.

211 Kempthorne (*c.*1934), p. 68.

212 CD/AJ/27.

213 TNA: E315/414 (Misc. Books Augmentation Office). See also Chapter 41, *Inns and Innkeepers.*

214 A 'keeve' is defined as 'a vat for holding liquid in brewing' (OED).

215 See further 'The Windmill at Gillball' in Chapter 42, *Mills and Millers.*

216 CD/AE/42.

217 CM/A/75.

218 See further, Kempthorne (*c.*1934), p. 71.

219 CD/AH/5A&B, 6. See also the survey of 1691: CM/F2/158. John Balsey and Emanuel Carkeet rented two of the cottages at an annual rent of 4s. each. Thomas Wayte rented the third at a rack rent of £1. The quarter of the house was not then tenanted, but was said to command a rent of 7s. a year.

220 Kempthorne (*c.*1934), p. 71.

221 1608 Survey of West Antony: CM/A/73.

222 *A Topographical and Historical Survey of Cornwall in 1650.* Edition of 1728 published by Frank Graham, Newcastle-upon-Tyne, 1966.

223 CM/F2/158.

224 CA/HI/2.

225 Jessica herself became a member of the Communist Party of America. See *Decca: The Letters of Jessica Mitford* (ed. Peter Y. Sussman) (2006), pp. 44, 67, 90-1.

226 J.A.C. Whetter, *Cornwall in the Thirteenth Century* (1998), p. 90.

227 Kempthorne (*c.*1934), p. 65.

228 H. 24/226.

229 CM/B/97.

230 Sheviock register of burials; Kempthorne (*c.*1934), p. 61.

231 CM/B/84.

232 TNA: E317/Corn.10; CM/A/75; Kempthorne (*c.*1934), pp. 25,26.

233 See CD/AH/17.

234 CD/AE/22.

235 See CD/AH/8A&B.

236 CD/AH/10.

237 CD/AH/13.

238 See further 'Blazor' in Chapter 4, *The Manor of Sheviock.*

239 CM/B/88.

240 CD/AJ/29.

241 Grace Popplestone, 'widdow', was one of the lives named on the 1694 lease of Sargent's tenement to Mary Wallis: see CD/AH/13. James Popplestone was one of the jurors of the borough of Crafthole in 1628 and 1630: see CM/B/ 77,78.

242 CM/F2/158.

243 CD/AH/15.

244 CD/AH/27.

245 See CD/AH/56 and the map CP/FX/11.

246 A tablet on the south wall of the church there commemorates a Digory Wallis, who died in 1560.

247 Sir John Maclean, *Parochial and Family History of the Deanery of Trigg Minor, in the County of Cornwall* (3 vols. London and Bodmin, 1872-79).

248 H. 28/44.

249 See the document, ref. DDT 780/1 and 2, in the CRO.
250 See CD/AG/48A.
251 See the entry for 1761 in the Sheviock Churchwardens' Book in the CRO.
252 CD/AG/48A.
253 For Wallis's log for the voyage of HMS *Dolphin*, see TNA: ADM 55/35; for his charts and maps, see BL: Addit. MS 21593. See also Hawkesworth, *Voyages of Discovery*, Vol. I (1773). See also entry in DNB.
254 C. Redding, *An Illustrated History of the County of Cornwall* (1842), p. 88.
255 Hearth Tax return.
256 Richard Sargent rented a property in 'Wrikell' for 6s. 8d.
257 CM/B/98.
258 CM/B/101; CD/AG/47.
259 CD/AH/60, 65A.
260 See CD/AH/65A.
261 CM/B/94.
262 CE/G/23.
263 See Thomas Pride's map (CP/FX/11) and survey (CM/B/101).
264 For map, see CRO: EM 20/4. For leases, see CD/AH/65 and 65C.
265 CD/AH/65B.
266 CD/AG/45.
267 CD/AF/27.
268 CM/B/98 – MAN 8/16.
269 CD/AJ/17.
270 Records of the Court Leet survive for 1576 and for ten of the last fourteen years of Queen Elizabeth's reign – that is, from 1590 to 1603, except for 1595, 1598, 1602 and 1603: TNA: SC/2/158/38. They also survive for most years of the reign of James I and for some years of the reign of Charles I: TNA: SC/2/158/39; SC/2/158/40. The court records for 1628 to 1644 (except 1642), and for 1663, 1712, 1713 and 1730 are preserved in the Antony archives: CM/B/77-91 and 93.
271 Michel lived beyond the age of 94 and in his younger days had been a servant of Sir Richard Carew. In his book, *Excellent Helps by a Warming-Stone* (1652; re-edited 1660), Carew told this story about him: 'Another of the age of ninetyfour years, by using the help of this stone hath been freed of a grief which continually pained him in his knees for two years before: and by sleeping on this stone hath so recovered his hearing, as he can understand anything that is spoken unto him, better now then he could do in above thirty years before, as myself know certainly: for he was a servant of this house then, and hath dwelt near to me ever since, and he likewise saith, that his decaying sight is much amended thereby.'
272 The slaughterhouse was attached to Mr Albert Bersey's butcher's shop.
273 Mrs W.A. Hearn was Hylda Hearn, wife of William Hearn. She kept the shop in Crafthole attached to the *New Inn*.
274 Mrs A. Carpenter was Kate Carpenter, wife of Arthur Carpenter. She kept the shop in Sheviock village at No 4 the Terrace.
275 Mrs S.Grills was Rita Grills, wife of farmer Steven Grills of Sydenham House, Crafthole.
276 Mrs H.A. Hoskin was Mollie Hoskin (Mrs Arnold Hoskin) of Crafthole Farm.
277 The survey made by Mrs Wilson now reposes in the CRO in Truro. It is a most valuable document, as it records not only the names of the local residents and their occupations, but also the names of the evacuees. It contains 591 names. A few of the houses listed were in St Germans parish.
278 John Triscott was a builder, who lived at Coombe Villa, Crafthole. On 10 August 1942, Mr William Andrew (mason), of the Bungalow, Crafthole, replaced him as the labour organiser.
279 Presumably the one at Polbathic.
280 William Holman, who farmed at the Glebe Farm in Sheviock village.
281 Edgar Bersey, who farmed at Sheviock Barton.
282 Their survey showed that there were 29 horses and 16 carts in the parish.
283 Air Raid Precautions.

284 A fire watch was kept every night.
285 Mrs Lee was named as deputy clerk in August.
286 The Sheviock WI had been started in 1941, with about 40 members.
287 This was still the case. It was not until the following month that Hitler abandoned the idea.
288 By the autumn of 1942, it was being recommended that 'everyone should have a supply of chloride of lime and a jar of chloride ointment, both these items may be purchased from any chemist'.
289 On 24 September 1941, Mr Crispin had written to J. Percival Heath, the Food Executive Officer at the RDC in Saltash to say that 'I have to-day interviewed the Rev. B.L.Lycett and he has agreed to place at my disposal the loft at the Rectory for the purpose of storing food stuff'.
290 Each ration was to last for five days and would cost six shillings. Ration books would have to be produced before any rations would be issued.
291 The street captains were Edgar Richards of Keyham Cottage, Crafthole, W.J.Dawe of Sheviock village (James Dawe of 2 the Orchard), and John Green (carpenter) of Bay View, Portwrinkle.
292 He worked on the land and lived at No 2 Council Cottages, Crafthole.
293 She was one of the three daughters of the postmistress and lived at Marlborough House, Crafthole. She was only 13 years old, a fact that was not drawn to the attention of the committee until 10 August.
294 The Joyce twins had been evacuated from London with their mother, who was the cook at Trethill House. They were 15 years old at the time. Peter Lumsden (agricultural labourer), who lived at the Bungalow, Sheviock churchtown, replaced them as messenger in September 1942.
295 See W.S.Churchill, *The Second World War*, Vol. II, p. 276 (1949).
296 Miss Roberts of Trethill House was in charge of the local WVS organisation.
297 She was not on Mrs Wilson's original list of residents of the parish made following the committee meeting of 20 August 1941.
298 This was Reginald Hoskin, son of George Hoskin (mason), and brother of Charles Hoskin, who had been killed in France in 1918.
299 The son of William and Mabel Baker, he was killed at El Alamein in 1942 and is buried at the El Alamein war cemetery in Egypt.
300 Although on Mr Crispin's original roll, his name does not appear on the war memorial, because Kerslake is in Antony parish. His name is inscribed on the tablet attached to Antony Memorial Hall.
301 Desmond Bean was lost on the aircraft carrier HMS *Courageous* when she was sunk by a U-boat in the Bristol Channel on 17 September 1939. Out of the crew of 1,260 more than 500 were drowned. Desmond Bean was not on Mr Crispin's original roll, because he had been living in Plymouth prior to the action in which he lost his life.
302 William Hitt was a soldier in the US Army. He married Sue Channings, daughter of the postmistress, Adèle Channings. He was killed in Normandy shortly after D-Day.
303 William George Paul was a Petty Officer (Sick Berth) on HMS *Dorsetshire*. He went down with his ship, sunk by the Japanese in the Indian Ocean on 5 April 1942.

Bibliography

Barber, Richard, *Edward, Prince of Wales and Aquitaine: A biography of the Black Prince* (Woodbridge, 1978)
Bates, David, *William the Conqueror* (London, 1989; pb. ed. 2004)
Beresford, M.W., *New Towns of the Middle Ages* (New York, 1967)
Beresford, M.W., and Finberg, H.P.R., *English Medieval Boroughs: a Hand-List* (Newton Abbot, 1973)
Beresford Ellis, P., *The Cornish Language and its Literature* (London, 1974)
Blair, Lawrence, *English Church Ales As Seen in English Churchwardens' Accounts and other Archival Sources of the 15th and 16th Centuries* (Ann Arbor, Michigan, 1940)
Bond, Francis, *Screens and Galleries in English Churches* (Oxford, 1908)
Bond, Thomas, *Topographical Sketches of the Boroughs of East and West Looe* (London, 1823)
Borlase, William, *Antiquities, Historical and Monumental, of the County of Cornwall* (Oxford, 1769)
Borlase, William, *The Natural History of Cornwall* (Oxford, 1758)
Boynton, Lindsay, *The Elizabethan Militia 1558-1638* (London, 1967; pb. ed., 1971)
Branigan, Keith and Fowler, P.J. (eds.), *The Roman West Country: Classical Culture and Celtic Society* (Newton Abbot, 1976)
Brown, H. Miles, *The Catholic Revival in Cornish Anglicanism: a study of the Tractarians of Cornwall 1833-1906* (1980)

Carew, Richard, *The Survey of Cornwall* (London, 1602/3; 2 ed. London, 1769; reprint of 1st ed., Exeter, 2004)
Carew, Richard, *Excellent Helps by a Warming-Stone* (London, 1640)
Carne, Tony, *Cornwall's Forgotten Corner* (Cawsand, 1985; 2 ed. 1990)
Cherry, Martin, 'The Courtenay Earls of Devon: The Formation and Disintegration of a Late Medieval Aristocratic Affinity', *Southern History*, vol. I (1979)
Cleaveland, Ezra, *A Genealogical History of the Noble and Illustrious Family of Courtenay, etc.* (Exeter, 1735)
Coate, Mary, *Cornwall in the Great Civil War and Interregnum 1642-1660* (Oxford, 1933; 2 ed. Truro, 1963)
Collins, Wilkie, *Rambles beyond Railways* (London, 1851)
Daniell, David, *The Bible in English* (New Haven & London, 2003).
Duffin, Anne, *Faction and Faith: Politics and Religion of the Cornish Gentry before the Civil War* (Exeter, 1996)
Duffy, Eamon, *Marking the Hours: English People and their Prayers, 1240-1570* (New Haven and London, 2006)
Duffy, Eamon, *The Stripping of the Altars* (New Haven & London, 1992)
Duffy, Eamon, *The Voices of Morebath* (New Haven & London, 2001)
Dyer, Christopher, *Making a Living in the Middle Ages: The People of Britain 850-1520* (New Haven & London, 2002)
Elliott-Binns, L. E., *Medieval Cornwall* (London, 1955)
Emden, A. B., A Biographical Register of the University of Oxford to A.D. 1500 (Oxford, 1957-59)
Evans, Eric J., *The Contentious Tithe. The Tithe Problem and English Agriculture 1750-1850* (London, 1976)

Field, John, *A History of English Field Names* (London, 1993)
Finberg, H.P.R., *The Formation of England 550-1042* (London, 1974; St Albans, 1976)
Finberg, H.P.R., *Tavistock Abbey* (Cambridge, 1951; 2 ed. 1969)
Finberg, H.P.R., *West-Country Historical Studies* (Newton Abbot, 1969)
Fox, Aileen, *South-West England 3,500 BC-A.D. 600* (London, 1964; revised ed., Newton Abbot, 1973)
Fox, Harold, *The Evolution of the Fishing Village: Landscape and Society along the South Devon Coast, 1086-1550* (Oxford, 2001)

Gilbert, C. S., *Historical Survey of the County of Cornwall* (Plymouth, vol. 1, 1817; vol. 2, 1820)
Gilbert, Davies, *The Parochial History of Cornwall* (4 vols., London, 1838)
Gover, J.B., *Place Names of Cornwall* (collected between 1922 and 1927; July 1948; typescript in Royal Institution of Cornwall Library, Truro)

Gray, Todd (ed.), *Early-Stuart Mariners and Shipping: the Maritime Surveys of Devon and Cornwall 1619-35* (Exeter, 1990)
Grylls, Richard G, *Grylls and Grills: The History of a Cornish Clan* (2 vols., London, 1999)

Halliday, F. E., *A Cornish Chronicle* (Newton Abbot, 1967)
Halliday, F. E. (ed.), *Richard Carew of Antony – The Survey of Cornwall* (Andrew Melrose, 1953)
Hanson, Neil, *The Confident Hope of a Miracle: the Real Story of the Spanish Armada* (London, 2003; pb. ed., 2004)
Harris, G. and F. L., *The Making of a Cornish Town, Torpoint and Neighbourhood through Two Hundred Years* (Exeter & Torpoint, 1976)
Harrison, Frank Ll., *Music in Medieval Britain* (London, 1958; 2nd edn. 1963)
Hatcher, John, *Rural Economy and Society in the Duchy of Cornwall 1300-1500* (London, 1970)
Henderson, Charles (ed. A.L.Rowse and M.I.Henderson), *Essays in Cornish History* (Oxford, 1935)
Hull, P.L. (ed.), *The Caption of Seisin of the Duchy of Cornwall, 1337* (Torquay, 1971)

Isham, Ken, *Lime Kilns and Limeburners in Cornwall: an Introduction* (St Austell, 2000)

Jackson, K, *Language and History in Early Britain: A Chronological Survey of the Brittonic Languages 1st to 12th c. A.D.* (Edinburgh, 1953)
Jaggard, Edwin, *An Exceptional Man: Reginald Pole Carew of Antony* (Bognor Regis), 2008
Jaggard, Edwin, *Cornwall Politics in the Age of Reform 1790-1885* (London, 1999)
Jewers, Arthur J., *Heraldic Church Notes from Cornwall* (London, after 1886)

Keats-Rohan, K.S.B, *Domesday People* (Woodbridge, 1999)
Keats-Rohan, K.S.B, *Domesday Descendants* (Woodbridge, 2002)
Kempthorne, G. A., *A History of the Parish of Sheviock* (Glasgow, *c.*1934)
Kneebone, Edward, *Description of East Hundred, co. Cornwall* (1684), BM Add. MS 33420 f.126
Kowaleski, Maryanne, *The Havener's Accounts of the Earldom and Duchy of Cornwall 1287-1356* (Exeter, 2001)
Kowaleski, Maryanne, *Local Markets and Regional Trade in Medieval Exeter* (Cambridge, 1994)

Lake, William. He was the publisher of Joseph Polsue's *Parochial History of the County of Cornwall* (Truro: vol.1, 1867; vol.2, 1868; vol.3, 1870; vol.4, 1872)
Lennard, R., *Rural England 1086-1135: A Study of Social and Agrarian Conditions* (Oxford, 1959)
Luck, Liz, *Green Lane Walks in South-east Cornwall*
Luck, Liz, *South Cornish Harbours* (revised ed. Fowey, 1995)
Lysons, The Revd Daniel and Samuel, *Magna Britannia, Vol. III, Cornwall* (London, 1814)

Maclean, Sir John, *Parochial and Family History of the Deanery of Trigg Minor, in the County of Cornwall* (3 vols. London and Bodmin, 1872-79)
Manco, Jean, *The History of Trewin House, Sheviock, Cornwall* (2008), commissioned by D. and A. Leighton- Squires.
Marshall, William, *Rural Economy of the West of England* (2 vols. London, 1796)
Mattingly, Joanna, *Cornwall and the Coast*, (Chichester, 2009)
McKisack, May, *The 14th Century* (Oxford, 1959)
Miles, David, *The Tribes of Britain* (London, 2005)
Miles Brown, H. See Brown, H. Miles
Milton, Giles, *White Gold* (London, 2004)
Moorman, John R.H., *Church Life in England in the Thirteenth Century* (Cambridge, 1945)
Morris, Chrisopher, *The Illustrated Journeys of Celia Fiennes* (pb.ed., Stroud, 1995)

Noall, Cyril, *Cornish Seines and Seiners* (Truro, 1972)
Noall, Cyril, *Smuggling in Cornwall* (Truro, 1971)

Oliver, The Revd G., *Monasticon Diocesis Exoniensis* (1846)
Olson, Lynette, *Early Monasteries in Cornwall* (Woodbridge, 1989)

Oppenheimer, Stephen, *The Origins of the British: A Genetic Detective Story* (London, 2006)
Orme, Nicholas, *Cornwall and the Cross: Christianity 500-1560* (Chichester, 2007)
Orme, Nicholas, *Cornish Wills 1342-1540* (Exeter, 2007)
Orme, Nicholas, *Education in the West of England 1066-1548* (Exeter, 1976)
Orme, Nicholas, *English Church Dedications: with a Survey of Cornwall and Devon* (Exeter, 1996)
Orme, Nicholas, *Medieval Children* (New Haven & London, 2001)
Orme, Nicholas (ed.), *Unity and Variety: A History of the Church in Devon and Cornwall* (Exeter, 1991)

Padel, O. J., *Cornish Place-Name Elements* (Nottingham, 1985)
Padel, O. J., *A Popular Dictionary of Cornish Place-Names* (Penzance, 1988)
Payton, Philip, *Cornwall* (Fowey, 1996)
Pearce, Susan M., *The Kingdom of Dumnonia* (Padstow, 1978)
Penhallurick, R.D., *The Birds of Cornwall and the Isles of Scilly* (Penzance, 1978)
Polsue, Joseph, *Parochial History of the County of Cornwall* (pub. Wm. Lake, Truro; vol.1, 1867; vol.2, 1868; vol.3, 1870; vol.4, 1872)

Rogers, W.H.H., *The Antient Sepulchral Effigies and Monumental and Memorial Sculpture of Devon* (Exeter, 1877)
Rose-Troup, Frances, *The Western Rebellion of 1549* (1913)
Rowse, A.L., *Tudor Cornwall: Portrait of a Society* (London, 1941)
Soulsby, I.N., *A History of Cornwall* (Chichester, 1986)
Soulsby, I.N., *The Cornwall Domesday* (London, 1988)
Spence, Jack, *The Smugglers of Cawsand Bay* (Cawsand, 2007)
Stanes, Robin, *The Old Farm* (Exeter, 1990)

Tate, W. E., *The Parish Chest. A Study of the Records of Parochial Administration in England* (Cambridge, 1946; 3rd edn., Chichester, 1983)
Thomas, Charles, *Archaeological Survey of the Rame Peninsula* (Redruth, 1974)
Thomas, Charles, *Celtic Britain* (London, 1st pb. edn. 1997)
Thomas, Charles, *Britain and Ireland in Early Christian Times A.D. 400-800* (1971)
Thomson, J.A.F., 'The Courtenay Family in the Yorkist Period', *Southern History*, Vol I (1979)
Thorold Rogers, James E., *Six Centuries of Work and Wages* (London, 1884)

Vallance, Aymer, *English Church Screens: being Great Roods, Screenwork & Rood-Lofts of Parish Churches in England & Wales* (London, 1936)
Venn, J. and J. A., *Alumni Cantabrigienses 1752-1900* (Cambridge, 1953)
Vivian, J.L., *The Visitations of Cornwall, comprising the Heralds' Visitations of 1530, 1573 and 1620* (Exeter, 1887)

Wallis, The Revd John, *The Cornwall Register* (Bodmin, 1847)
Webb, Sidney and Beatrice, selected volumes in the series, *English Local Government*, reprinted 1963: *The History of Liquor Licensing in England* (London, 1903); *The Parish and the County* (London, 1906); *The Manor and the Borough* (London, 1908); *The Story of the King's Highway* (London, 1913); *English Poor Law Policy* (London, 1910); *English Poor Law History, Part I: The Old Poor Law* (London, 1927); *Part II: The Last 100 Years* (London, 1929);
Whetter, James A.C., 'The Black Death in Cornwall', *An baner Kernewek*, No. 29, p. 14
Whetter, James A.C., *The Bodrugans. A Study of a Cornish Medieval Knightly Family* (Gorran, St Austell, 1995)
Whetter, James A.C., *Cornwall in the Thirteenth Century. A Study in Social and Economic History* (Gorran, St Austell, 1998)
Whetter, James A.C., *Cornwall in the 17th Century. An Economic Survey of Kernow* (Padstow, 1974)
White, Paul, *The Cornish Smuggling Industry* (Redruth, 1997)
Wrottesley, George, *Crécy and Calais* (London, 1898)

Young, Michael, *The Elmhirsts of Dartington. The Creation of an Utopian Community* (London, 1982)

Index

Illustration Acknowledgements

The author and publisher would like to thank the following for permission to reproduce copyright material. Any infringement of copyright is entirely inadvertent and accidental. Every care has been taken to contact or trace all copyright owners. We would be pleased to correct any errors or omissions brought to our attention in future editions. The references are to the illustration numbers listed at the front of the book.

* Indicates that the photograph was taken by Neville Cusworth with the permission of the owner of the original copyright material.

Aerial Photos, 91
Alecto Historical Editions, London, 160*
Bartlett, Margaret, 118, 128, 129, 130, 131, 133, 134, 138, 139, 142, 143, 144, 145, 148, 149, 153, 168, 169
Biles, Malcolm, 30, 31, 107, 198
The British Library Board, 120, 121 (both Refs. Maps 148.e.1); 202 (Ref. C.18.b.8); 203 (Ref. C.18.d.1); 219 (Ref Cotton Augustus I.i.6)
Carew Pole, Sir Richard, Front cover (map*), 15*, 17*, 26*, 44, 46, 48, 49, 50, 51, 52, 54*, 57*, 58*, 60*, 61*, 68*, 72*, 85*, 95*, 97*, 98*; 99*, 100*, 101*, 102*, 112*, 117*, 151*, 165*, 221, 226, 23*, 240*, 241*
Cole, Audrey, 256
Cornwall Record Office, 90*, 122* (both Refs. CRO: P208/27/1), 233 (Ref. AD587/9/3)
Cox, Mike, 207
Cusworth, Neville, Front cover (dovecote) and illustrations not otherwise credited
Cusworth, Dr Susan, 214
Devon and Cornwall Record Society, 45*
Devon Record Office, 123
Courtauld Institute (Private Collection), 41, 42
Dartington Hall Trust, 260
Downe, Diana, Viscountess, 35
English Heritage, 127
Finberg, J.N.P., 12
Kemp, Pauline, Mrs, 258
Kentisbeer, Joy, Mrs, 91, 105, 152
Knight Frank, 70
Leather, Terry, 109, 180, 227, 245, 246
Leighton Squires, Digby, 76
Martin, Mary, 174
Master and Fellows of Emmanuel College, 43
Mills, Jean, 82
National Maritime Museum, Greenwich, London, 75
Nethercott, Elizabeth, Mrs, 53, 229, 230
Ordnance Survey, 18
Paul, Frederick, 224
Pengelly, Peggy, Mrs, 125, 126, 136, 137, 154, 155, 156, 157, 223
Pryn, Henry and Constance, 78, 94, 104, 107, 164, 167, 172, 177, 178, 181, 231, 232, 237, 238, 244, 253, 257, 259
Royal Institution of Cornwall, 2*, 3*, 6*, 124, 243*
Truscott, James and Karen, 67, 73, 176, 179
Western Morning News, 225
Whittaker, Ian, 106, 255